THE LASTword

10th

CANADIAN EDITION

Macroeconomics

Campbell R. McConnell

Professor of Economics, Emeritus
University of Nebraska, Lincoln

Stanley L. Brue

Professor of Economics
Pacific Lutheran University

Thomas P. Barbiero

Professor of Economics
Ryerson University

McGraw-Hill Ryerson

Toronto Montréal Boston Burr Ridge, IL Dubuque, IA Madison, WI New York San Francisco
St. Louis Bangkok Bogotá Caracas Kuala Lumpur Lisbon London Madrid
Mexico City Milan New Delhi Santiago Seoul Singapore Sydney Taipei

Macroeconomics
10th Canadian Edition

Statistics Canada information is used with the permission of the Minister of Industry, as Minister responsible for Statistics Canada. Information on the availability of the wide range of data from Statistics Canada can be obtained from Statistics Canada's Regional Offices, its World Wide Web site at http://www.statcan.ca, and its toll-free access number 1-800-263-1136.

ISBN: 0-07-091656-X

1 2 3 4 5 6 7 8 9 10 TRI 0 9 8 7 6 5

Printed and bound in Canada

Care has been taken to trace ownership of copyright material contained in this text; however, the publisher will welcome any information that enables them to rectify any reference or credit for subsequent editions.

Vice President, Editorial and Media Technology: Patrick Ferrier
Executive Sponsoring Editor: Lynn Fisher
Economics Editor: Ron Doleman
Developmental Editor: Daphne Scriabin
Marketing Manager: Kelly Smyth
Supervising Editor: Joanne Murray
Copy Editor: Santo D'Agostino
Production Coordinator: Andrée Davis
Formatter: Michelle Losier, Finelines
Interior Design: Dianna Little
Cover Design: Dianna Little
Cover Image Credit: Background trees © Miles Ertman/Masterfile; Evergreen seedling © Corbis Corporation/Roy Morsch
Printer: Tri-Graphic Printing Limited

National Library of Canada Cataloguing in Publication

McConnell, Campbell R.
    Macroeconomics / Campbell R. McConnell, Stanley L. Brue, Thomas P. Barbiero. — 10th Canadian ed.

Includes bibliographical references and index.
ISBN 0-07-091656-X

1. Macroeconomics—Textbooks. I. Brue, Stanley L., 1945- II. Barbiero, Thomas Paul, 1952- III. Title.

HB172.M114 2004   339   C2003-905305-9

Dedication

This book is dedicated to Elsa, Marta, Emilia, and Robert.

About the Authors

Campbell R. McConnell earned his Ph.D. from the University of Iowa after receiving degrees from Cornell College and the University of Illinois. He taught at the University of Nebraska-Lincoln from 1953 until his retirement in 1990. He is also coauthor of *Contemporary Labor Economics*, 5th ed. (McGraw-Hill) and has edited readers for the principles and labour economics courses. He is a recipient of both the University of Nebraska Distinguished Teaching Award and the James A. Lake Academic Freedom Award, and is past-president of the Midwest Economics Association. Professor McConnell was awarded an honorary Doctor of Laws degree from Cornell College in 1973 and received its Distinguished Achievement Award in 1994. His primary areas of interest are labour economics and economic education. He has an extensive collection of jazz recordings and enjoys reading jazz history.

Stanley L. Brue did his undergraduate work at Augustana College (SD) and received his Ph.D. from the University of Nebraska-Lincoln. He teaches at Pacific Lutheran University, where he has been honoured as a recipient of the Burlington Northern Faculty Achievement Award. He has also received the national Leavey Award for excellence in economic education. Professor Brue is past president and a current member of the International Executive Board of Omicron Delta Epsilon International Economics Honorary. He is coauthor of *Economic Scenes*, 5th ed. (Prentice-Hall) and *Contemporary Labor Economics*, 5th ed. (McGraw-Hill) and author of *The Evolution of Economic Thought*, 5th ed. (HB/Dryden). For relaxation, he enjoys boating on Puget Sound and skiing trips with his family.

Thomas P. Barbiero received his Ph.D. from the University of Toronto after completing undergraduate studies at the same university. He has published papers on the role of the agricultural sector in the industrial development of northern Italy in the period 1861–1914. His research interest in the last few years has turned to economic methodology and the application of economic theory to explain social phenomena. Professor Barbiero spends part of his summer on the Amalfi Coast in Italy.

Brief Contents

Contents

Web Site Bonus Chapters (found at www.mcgrawhill.ca/college/mcconnell)

CHAPTER 3W:
Applications and Extensions of Supply and Demand Analysis

CHAPTER 18W:
Disputes over Macro Theory and Policy

CHAPTER 19W:
The Developing Economies

CHAPTER 20W:
Transitional Economies: Russia and China

Preface

Welcome to the Tenth Canadian Edition of *Macroeconomics*, the world's best-selling economics textbook. An estimated 13 million students worldwide have now used this book. *Macroeconomics* is available in American and Australian editions, and has been translated into Italian, Russian, Chinese, French, Spanish, Portuguese, and other languages.

Fundamental Objectives

Our three main goals for *Macroeconomics* are to:

- Help the beginning student master the principles essential for understanding economic problems, specific Canadian economic issues, and the policy alternatives.
- Help the student understand and apply the economic perspective and to reason accurately and objectively about economic matters.
- Promote a lasting student interest in economics and the economy.

What's New and Improved?

One of the benefits of writing a text that has met the market test is the opportunity to revise—to delete the outdated and install the new, to rewrite misleading or ambiguous statements, to introduce more relevant Canadian illustrations, to improve the organizational structure, and to enhance the learning aids. The more significant changes to the Tenth Canadian Edition include the following:

Two-Path Macro

We provide two alternative paths through the macro text. We know that some instructors like to cover the aggregate expenditures model and the basic relationships between income and consumption, real interest rate and investment, and changes in spending and changes in output. These topics are found in Chapter 7, "The Aggregate Expenditures Model." Instructors who choose not to cover the aggregate expenditures model can proceed directly to Chapter 8, "Aggregate Demand and Aggregate Supply." This organization allows instructors who prefer not to teach the equilibrium AE model to skip it without loss of continuity. As before, the remainder of the macro is AD-AS based.

Consider This Boxes

New to *Macroeconomics* are 17 analogies, examples, or stories that help drive home central economic ideas in a student-oriented, real-world manner. For instance, the analogy of a reservoir is used to help students to think about the distinction between a stock and a flow (page 110), and the idea of demand-pull inflation is described with the story of "clipping coins" (page 143). These brief vignettes drive home key points in a lively, colourful, and easy-to-remember way.

New Math Appendix

At the request of some of our users, we have included a new appendix to Chapter 7, which shows the math behind the aggregate expenditures model. To make it easier for students to understand the material the appendix includes graphs and a numerical example.

Contemporary Discussions and Examples

The Tenth Canadian Edition contains discussions of many new or extended topics. Here are a few:

- The dispute over the tariffs imposed on Canadian softwood lumber by the U.S.
- The federal budget of February 2003
- Provincial per capita net debt
- The Kyoto Accord and economic growth in Canada
- China's rapidly emerging economy
- Corporate financial and accounting misconduct
- Explosion of demand for DVD players, DVDs, and digital cameras
- Expansion of the European Union
- The economic slowdown of 2001 and the recovery of 2002
- The Bank of Canada engineered interest rate cuts
- The debate over artful monetary management versus inflation targeting
- The continuing productivity surge

Revised Demand and Supply Chapter

Instructors have told us they like to discuss price floors and price ceilings immediately after developing the idea of equilibrium price. So we have included a discussion of these government interventions in Chapter 3 on demand and supply. Previously, this discussion was found only in *Microeconomics*.

Four Bonus Web Chapters, Including a Second Supply and Demand Chapter

Four chapters are available for free use at our website, www.mcgrawhill.ca/college/. The first of these, 3W, "Applications and Extensions of Supply and Demand Analysis," is entirely new and provides real-world examples of changes in supply and demand, shortages and surpluses arising from pre-set prices, and overconsumption of non-priced goods (or factors of production). For instructors who want to extend the supply and demand analysis of Chapter 3, this chapter also explains consumer surplus, producer surplus, and efficiency losses. The other three Web chapters are 18W, "Disputes Over Macro Theory and Policy," 19W, "The Economics of Developing Economies," and 20W, "Transition Economies: Russia and China," are also available for instructors and students who have a special interest in those topics. The four Web chapters have the same design, colour, and features of regular book chapters, are readable in Adobe Acrobat format, and can be printed if desired.

New *Last Word* and *Global Perspective* Topics

New *Last Word* topics are efficiency gains from generic drugs (Chapter 3W); the production of Canadian currency (Chapter 11); the evolution of the monetary system in Canada prior to Confederation (Chapter 12); monetary policy and Taylor's rule (Chapter 13); the Kyoto Accord and economic growth in Canada (Chapter 15); and the Canadian-U.S. softwood lumber dispute (Chapter 16). In addition, a few Last Words have been relocated to match reorganized content.

New *Global Perspective* pieces include the top 12 globalized nations (Chapter 4), cyclically adjusted budget deficits or surpluses in selected nations (Chapter 9), and Canada's goods and services trade balance with selected nations (Chapter 16).

DISTINGUISHING FEATURES

- **Comprehensive Explanations at an Appropriate Level**   *Macroeconomics* is comprehensive, analytical, and challenging yet fully accessible to a wide range of students. Its thoroughness and accessibility enable instructors to select topics for special classroom emphasis with confidence that students can read and comprehend independently other assigned material in the book.

- **Fundamentals of the Market System**   Many economies throughout the world are making difficult transitions from planning to markets. Our detailed description of the institutions and operation of the *market system* in Chapter 4 is even more relevant than before. We pay particular attention to property rights, entrepreneurship, freedom of enterprise and choice, competition, and the role of profits because these concepts are often misunderstood by beginning students.

- **Early Integration of International Economics**   We give the principles and institutions of the global economy early treatment. Chapter 4 examines specialization and comparative advantage (without the more difficult graphs). This strong introduction to international economics permits "globalization" issues throughout the textbook.

- **Early and Extensive Treatment of Government**   Government is an integral component of modern capitalism. We introduce the economic functions of government early and accord them systematic treatment in Chapter 4. Government's role (including the role of the Bank of Canada) in promoting full employment, price-level stability, and economic growth is central to the macroeconomic policy chapters.

- **Building-Block Approach to Macro**   We believe that it is a mistake to yank the student back and forth between elaborate macro models. So we systematically present macroeconomics by

  - Examining the national income accounts and previewing economic growth, unemployment, and inflation.

  - Presenting the aggregate expenditures model (AE model) in a single chapter.

  - Developing the aggregate-demand–aggregate-supply model (AD-AS model).

  - Using the AD-AS model to discuss fiscal policy.

  - Introducing monetary considerations into the AD-AS model.

  - Using the AD-AS model to discuss monetary policy.

  - Extending the AD-AS model to include both short-run and long-run aggregate supply.

  - Applying the long-run AD-AS model to macroeconomic instability, economic growth, and disagreements on macro theory and policy.

- **Emphasis on Technological Change and Economic Growth**   This edition continues to emphasize economic growth. Chapter 2 uses the production possibilities curve to show the basic ingredients of growth. Chapter 6 explains how growth is measured and presents the facts of growth. Chapter 15 discusses the causes of growth, looks at productivity growth and the New Economy thesis, and addresses some of the controversies surrounding economic growth. Web Chapters 3W, 18W, 19W, and 20W are also available.

- **Integrated Text and Website**   *Macroeconomics* and its Web site are highly integrated through in-text Web buttons, Web-based end-of-chapter questions, bonus Web chapters, multiple-choice self-tests at the Web site, Web newspaper articles, Web math notes, and other features. Our Web site is part and parcel of our student learning package, and is customized to the book.

Organizational Alternatives

Although instructors generally agree as to the content of a principles of macroeconomics course, they often differ as to how to arrange the material. *Macroeconomics* includes five parts, and that provides considerable organizational flexibility. For example, the two-path macro enables covering the full aggregate expenditures model or advancing directly to the AD-AS model. Other options include covering the section of Chapter 14 that discusses the intricacies of the relationship between short-run and long-run aggregate immediately after Chapter 8 on AD and AS.

Pedagogical Aids for Students

Macroeconomics has always been student oriented. Economics is concerned with efficiency—accomplishing goals using the best methods. Therefore, we offer the student some brief introductory comments on how to improve efficiency and hence grades.

- ***In This Chapter You Will Learn***   We set out the learning objectives at the start of each chapter so the chapter's main concepts can be easily recognized. We have also tied the learning objectives to each of the numbered headings in each chapter. In addition, the chapter summaries are now organized by numbered headings.

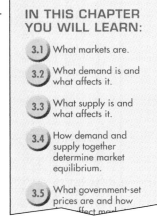

IN THIS CHAPTER YOU WILL LEARN:

3.1 What markets are.

3.2 What demand is and what affects it.

3.3 What supply is and what affects it.

3.4 How demand and supply together determine market equilibrium.

3.5 What government-set prices are and how they affect market...

According to an old joke, if you teach a parrot to say "demand and supply," you have an economist. There is much truth in this quip. The tools of demand and supply can take us far in understanding both specific economic issues and how the entire economy works.

With our circular flow model in Chapter 2, we identified the participants in the product market and factor market. We asserted that prices were determined by the "interaction" between buyers and sellers in those markets. In this chapter we examine that interaction in detail and explain how prices and output quantities are determined.

- ***Terminology***   A significant portion of any introductory course is terminology. In this edition key terms are highlighted in bold type the first time they appear in the text. Key terms are defined in the margin and a comprehensive list appears at the end of each chapter. A glossary of definitions can also be found at the end of the book and on the Web site.

- ***Ten Key Concepts***   Ten Key Concepts have been identified to help students organize the main principles. The Ten Key Concepts are introduced in Chapter 1 and each one is reinforced throughout the textbook by its individual icon.

Choosing a Little More or Less

The Influence of Incentives

CONCEPT 3 ("Choosing a Little More or Less"): Choices are usually made at the **margin**; we choose a "little" more or a "little" less of something.
CONCEPT 4 ("The Influence of Incentives"): The choices you make are influenced by **incentives**.

- **Data Updates**   Data updates for selected graphs and tables can be found on the McConnell-Brue-Barbiero Web site (www.mcgrawhill.ca/college/mcconnell).

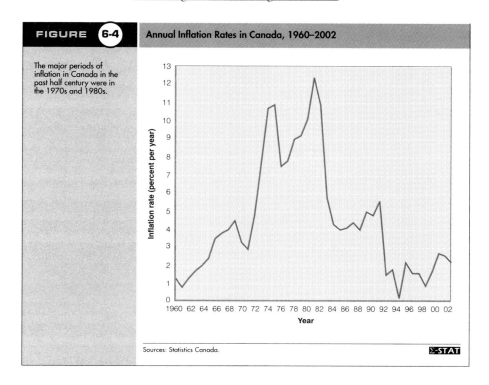

FIGURE 6-4   **Annual Inflation Rates in Canada, 1960–2002**

The major periods of inflation in Canada in the past half century were in the 1970s and 1980s.

Sources: Statistics Canada.

- **Graphics with Supporting Data**   Where possible we have provided data to support our graphs. In such cases a data table now appears in the same figure with the graph.

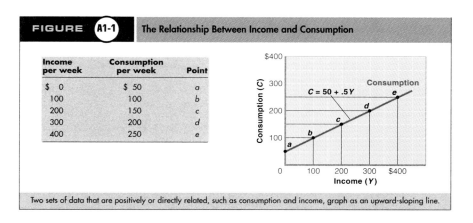

FIGURE A1-1   **The Relationship Between Income and Consumption**

Income per week	Consumption per week	Point
$ 0	$ 50	a
100	100	b
200	150	c
300	200	d
400	250	e

$C = 50 + .5Y$

Two sets of data that are positively or directly related, such as consumption and income, graph as an upward-sloping line.

- **Key Graphs**   We have labelled graphs that have special relevance as Key Graphs. Each Key Graph includes a quick quiz of four questions, with answers provided below.

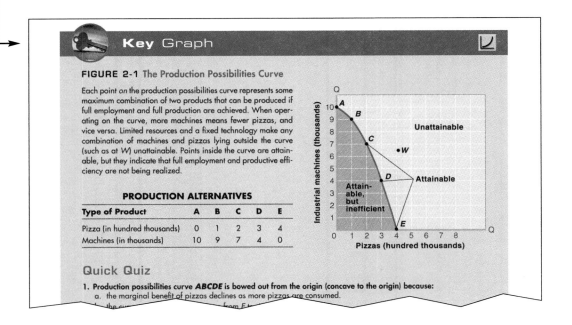

Key Graph

FIGURE 2-1 The Production Possibilities Curve

Each point *on* the production possibilities curve represents some maximum combination of two products that can be produced if full employment and full production are achieved. When operating on the curve, more machines means fewer pizzas, and vice versa. Limited resources and a fixed technology make any combination of machines and pizzas lying outside the curve (such as at *W*) unattainable. Points inside the curve are attainable, but they indicate that full employment and productive efficiency are not being realized.

PRODUCTION ALTERNATIVES

Type of Product	A	B	C	D	E
Pizza (in hundred thousands)	0	1	2	3	4
Machines (in thousands)	10	9	7	4	0

Quick Quiz

1. Production possibilities curve **ABCDE** is bowed out from the origin (concave to the origin) because:
   a. the marginal benefit of pizzas declines as more pizzas are consumed.

- **Interactive Graphs**   For selected Key Graphs, interactive graphs are available on the McConnell-Brue-Barbiero Web site (www.mcgrawhill.ca/college/mcconnell). Developed under the supervision of Norris Peterson of Pacific Lutheran University, this interactive feature depicts major graphs and instructs students to shift the curves, observe the outcomes, and derive relevant generalizations. New interactive graphs have been added in this edition.

- **Reviewing the Chapter**   Important things should be said more than once. You will find a Chapter Summary at the conclusion of every chapter, as well as two or three Quick Reviews within each chapter. The end-of-chapter summary is presented by numbered chapter section. These review statements will help students to focus on the essential ideas of each chapter and to study for exams.

QUICK REVIEW

- Economic growth can be measured as (a) an increase in real GDP over time or (b) an increase in real GDP per capita over time.

- Real GDP in Canada has grown at an average annual rate of almost 4 percent since 1950; real GDP per capita has grown at an annual rate of over 2 percent during that same period.

- The typical business cycle goes through four phases: peak, recession, trough, and recovery.

- During recession, industries that produce capital goods and consumer durables normally suffer greater output and employment declines than do service and non-durable consumer goods industries.

- *Global Perspective Boxes* Each nation functions increasingly in a global economy. To help the student gain appreciation of this wider economic environment, we provide Global Perspectives features, which compare Canada to other nations.

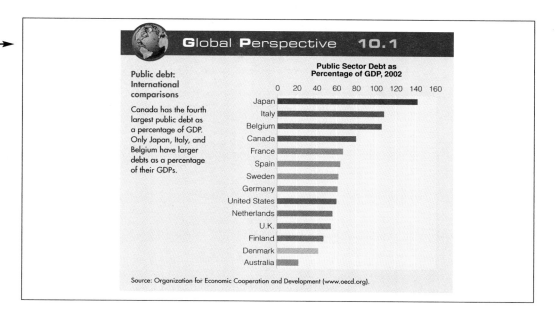

- *Consider This* This new feature highlights and emphasizes an important theoretical issue in each chapter, and makes it interesting to students through examples and analogies.

Paradox of Thrift

In Chapter 2 we said that a higher rate of saving is *good* for society because it frees resources from consumption uses and directs them toward investment goods. More machinery and equipment means a greater capacity for the economy to produce goods and services.

But implicit within this "saving is good" proposition is the assumption that increased saving will be borrowed and spent for investment goods. If investment does not increase along with saving, a curious irony called the *paradox of thrift* may arise. The attempt to save more may simply reduce GDP and leave actual saving unchanged.

Our analysis of the multiplier process helps explain this possibility. Suppose an economy that has an MPC of .75, an MPS of .25, and a multiplier of 4, decides to save an additional $20 billion. From the social viewpoint, a penny saved that is not invested is a penny not spent and therefore a decline in someone's income. Through the multiplier process, the $20 billion reduces consumption spending, and lowers real GDP by $80 billion (4 × $20 billion).

The $80 billion decline of real GDP, in turn, reduces saving by $20 billion (= MPS of .25 × $80 billion), which completely cancels the initial $20 billion increase of saving. Here, the attempt to increase saving is *bad* for the economy: It creates a recession and leaves saving unchanged.

For increased saving to be *good* for an economy, greater investment must accompany greater saving. If investment replaces consumption dollar-for-dollar, aggregate expenditures stay constant and the higher level of investment raises the economy's future growth rate.

Question: Your friend proudly tells you "I wear my brother's hand-me-down clothes and as a consequence I have doubled the size of my bank account." Is he a socially responsible person?

- **The Last Word**   *The Last Word* features, which reinforce chapter material with topics of interest, have been revised and updated.

THE LASTword — Lotteries: Facts and Controversies about a Way of Raising Government Revenues

Lotteries, which began in the 1970s, are a potentially important source of public revenue. What are the characteristics of lotteries? And what are the arguments for and against this means of increasing provincial government revenues?

In May of 2002 the Super 7 lottery jackpot prize reached over $34 million, the largest in Canadian history up to that point. Such a large jackpot drew much attention to government sponsored lotteries in Canada, which began in 1973 when the Olympic Corporation of Canada started selling tickets to help defray the costs of the 1976 Olympics in Montreal. It is estimated that over 80 percent of Canadian households now buy lottery tickets,

36 percent tax on ticket purchases. This tax is higher than the taxes on cigarettes and liquor. Furthermore, research indicates that the "lottery tax" is highly regressive in that there is little relationship between ticket purchases and household incomes. This means that low-income families spend a larger proportion of their incomes on lotteries than do high-income families. The 10 percent of the adults who patronize lotteries most heavily account for over half of total

ments about how people should spend their incomes. Individuals allegedly achieve the maximum satisfaction from their incomes by spending without interference. If some people derive satisfaction from participating in lotteries, they should be free to do so. Third, faced with tax revenue shortfalls and intense pressure not to raise taxes, lotteries are a relatively painless source of revenue to finance important services such as education and health care programs.

- **Appendix on Graphs**   Being comfortable with graphical analysis and a few related quantitative concepts will be a big advantage to students in understanding the principles of economics. The appendix to Chapter 1, which reviews graphing, slopes of lines, and linear equations, should not be skipped.

- **Study Questions**   A comprehensive list of questions is located at the end of each chapter. The old cliché that we learn by doing is very relevant to economics. Use of these questions will enhance students' understanding. For each chapter, we designate several as Key Questions and answer them in the Study Guide.

- **Internet Application Questions**   Students are presented with questions, relevant to the topic discussed in the chapter, to explore on the Internet. On the McConnell-Brue Barbiero Web site (www.mcgrawhill.ca/college/mcconnell), students will find direct links to the Web sites included in these questions.

INTERNET APPLICATION QUESTIONS

1. **How To Spot a Counterfeit Bank Note** Counterfeit bank notes have always been a concern for the Bank of Canada. Visit the Bank of Canada through the McConnell-Brue-Barbiero Web site (Chapter 12) to find out how to detect counterfeit Canadian bank notes.

2. **The Balance Sheet of Canadian Chartered Banks** Statistics Canada provides the balance sheet of chartered banks. Access their Web site through the McConnell-Brue-Barbiero homepage (Chapter 12). What has the trend been in the last five years for bank assets and liabilities?

   Σ-STAT

3. **Web-Based Question: The Canadian Payments Association (CPA) and Cheque Clearing** Visit the Canadian Payments Association Web site by going through the McConnell-Brue-Barbiero homepage (Chapter 12). How many transactions are cleared and settled through the CPA's systems each business day?

- *Origin of the Idea*   These brief histories, which can be found on the Web site, examine the origins of major ideas identified in the book. Students will find it interesting to learn about the person who first developed such ideas as opportunity cost, equilibrium price, the multiplier, comparative advantage, and elasticity.

- *Σ-STAT*   Σ-STAT is Statistics Canada's education resource that allows socioeconomic and demographic data to be viewed in charts, graphs, and maps. Access to Σ-STAT and the CAN-SIM II database is made available to purchasers of the book, via the McConnell-Brue-Barbiero Web site, by special agreement between McGraw-Hill Ryerson and Statistics Canada. The Online Learning Centre provides additional information.

Supplements for the Instructor

- *i-Learning Sales Specialist*   Your Integrated Learning Sales Specialist is a McGraw-Hill Ryerson representative who has the experience, product knowledge, training, and support to help you assess and integrate any of the below-noted products, technology, and services into your course for optimum teaching and learning performance. Whether it's using our test bank software, helping your students improve their grades, or putting your entire course online, your *i*-Learning Sales Specialist is there to help you do it. Contact your local *i*-Learning Sales Specialist today to learn how to maximize all of McGraw-Hill Ryerson's resources.

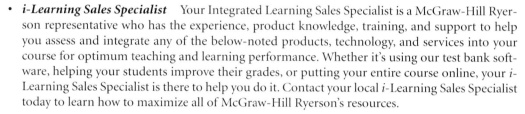

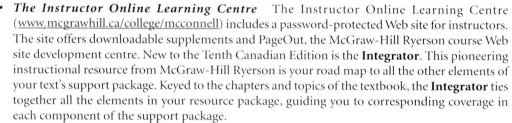

- *The Instructor Online Learning Centre*   The Instructor Online Learning Centre (www.mcgrawhill.ca/college/mcconnell) includes a password-protected Web site for instructors. The site offers downloadable supplements and PageOut, the McGraw-Hill Ryerson course Web site development centre. New to the Tenth Canadian Edition is the **Integrator**. This pioneering instructional resource from McGraw-Hill Ryerson is your road map to all the other elements of your text's support package. Keyed to the chapters and topics of the textbook, the **Integrator** ties together all the elements in your resource package, guiding you to corresponding coverage in each component of the support package.

- *Instructor's CD-ROM*   This CD-ROM contains all the necessary Instructor Supplements including:

  - *Instructor's Manual*   Thomas Barbiero, Ryerson University, has revised and updated the Instructor's Manual. It includes chapter summaries, listings of "what's new" in each chapter, teaching tips and suggestions, learning objectives, chapter outlines, and data and visual aid sources with suggestions for classroom use. It also provides answers to all end-of-chapter questions as well as an extra set of parallel end-of-chapter problems and solutions.

  - *Microsoft® PowerPoint® Slide Powernotes*   Prepared by Judith Skuce, Georgian College, this presentation system is found on the Instructor's CD-ROM and on the Instructor's Site of the Online Learning Centre. It offers visual presentations that may be edited and manipulated to fit a particular course format. They have been significantly revised for this edition and contain many animated graphs and figures that have been imported from Excel.

  - *Computerized Test Bank I*   Prepared by Nargess Kayhani, Mount St. Vincent University, the test bank includes more than 5400 mixed multiple-choice and true/false questions that are categorized by topic and learning objective. Each question has been checked for accuracy and content.

  - *New Test Bank II*   Prepared by Tom Fulton, Langara College. This test bank, available in Microsoft Word, contains for each chapter over 30 short-answer questions, with suggested answers.

- Also available, from the U.S. supplement list, is *U.S. Test Bank II*. This test bank contains more than 5200 multiple-choice and true/false questions. All *Test Bank II* questions are categorized according to level of difficulty.

- **CBC Videos and Video Cases**   These videos have been chosen to visually help students relate real-world economics issues to the text, and to illuminate key ideas and concepts presented in the text. A set of instructor notes accompanies the segments and is available at the Instructor Online Learning Centre. The video segments are available in VHS format for use in class and through video-streaming on the Online Learning Centre (where they are accessible by both instructors and students).

- **PageOut**   Visit **www.mhhe.com/pageout** to create a Web page for your course using our resources. PageOut is the McGraw-Hill Ryerson Web site development centre. This Web page generation software is free to adopters and is designed to help faculty create an online course, complete with assignments, quizzes, links to relevant Web sites, lecture notes, and more—all in a matter of minutes.

- In addition, content cartridges are available for course management systems such as WebCT and Blackboard. These platforms provide instructors with user-friendly, flexible teaching tools. Please contact your local McGraw-Hill Ryerson *i*-Learning Sales Specialist for additional information.

- **iLearning Services Program**   McGraw-Hill Ryerson offers a unique services package designed for Canadian faculty. It includes technical support, access to our educational technology conferences, and custom e-courses, to name just a few. Please speak to your *i*-Learning Sales Specialist for details.

Supplements for Students

- **Online Learning Centre**   The student Online Learning Centre is prepared by Beverly and Norman Cameron, University of Manitoba. This electronic learning aid, located at www.mcgrawhill.ca/college/mcconnell, offers a wealth of materials, including multiple-choice quizzes, interactive graphing exercises, Internet exercises, annotated Web links, CBC video cases, Econ GraphKit, access to ∑-STAT and the CANSIM II database, Want to See the Math, and much more!

- **Study Guide**   Torben Andersen, Chairperson of Humanities and Social Sciences at Red Deer College, has prepared the Tenth Edition of the Study Guide (ISBN 007-0922403), which many students find indispensable. Each chapter contains an overview of the major topics, a review of each numbered A-level head with a discussion of the learning objectives that apply to that section, a list of important terms, fill-in questions, true/false questions, multiple-choice tests, problems and projects identified by topic, discussion questions, and an answer section.

- **GradeSummit**   GradeSummit (**www.gradesummit.com**) is an Internet-based self-assessment service that offers a variety of ways for students to analyze what they know and don't know. By revealing subject strengths and weaknesses and by providing detailed feedback and direction, GradeSummit enables students to focus their study time on those areas where they are most in need of improvement. GradeSummit provides data about how much students know while they study for an exam—not after they have taken it. It helps the professor measure an individual student's progress and assess his or her progress relative to others in the class.

Acknowledgements

The Tenth Canadian Edition has benefited from a number of perceptive reviews, which were a rich source of suggestions for this revision. Reviewers include:

Ather Akbari, St. Mary's University

Morris Altman, University of Saskatchewan

Sal AmirKhalkhali, Saint Mary's University

Torben Andersen, Red Deer College

Michael Benarroch, University of Winnipeg

Bagala Biswal, Memorial University

Beverly Cameron, University of Manitoba

Doug Curtis, Trent University

Bruno Fullone, George Brown College

Ibrahim Hayani, Seneca College

James Hnatchuk, Concordia University

Geraldine Joosse, Lethbridge Community College

Nargess Kayhani, Mount St. Vincent University

Steve Rakoczy, Humber College

Duane Rockerbie, University of Lethbridge

Rob Scharff, Kwantlen University College

Judith Skuce, Georgian College

Lewis Soroka, Brock University

G. Voss, University of Victoria

Andrew Wong, Grant MacEwan College

Special thanks must be given to Morris Altman and to Torben Andersen, both of whom reviewed all stages of the manuscript in development and provided many suggestions for improvement. And special praise should go to David Cape, Ryerson University, for his vigilant efforts as the technical reviewer for the text. His keen eye and attention to detail has contributed greatly to the quality of the final product. Ben Miu, a student at Ryerson University, helped to compile the National Income Statistics found at the end of the book.

We are greatly indebted to the many professionals at McGraw-Hill Ryerson—in particular Lynn Fisher, Executive Sponsoring Editor; Ron Doleman, Economics Editor; Daphne Scriabin, Developmental Editor; Kelly Dickson, Manager, Editorial Services; Joanne Murray, Supervising Editor; and Kelly Smyth, Marketing Manager—for their publishing and marketing expertise. We thank Santo D'Agostino for his thorough and sensitive editing and Jacques Cournoyer for his vivid Last Word illustrations. Dianna Little developed the interior design and the colourful cover.

We also strongly acknowledge the McGraw-Hill Ryerson sales staff, who greeted this new Canadian edition with wholehearted enthusiasm.

Campbell R. McConnell
Stanley L. Brue
Thomas P. Barbiero

Online LearningCentre

www.mcgrawhill.ca/college/mcconnell

FOR THE STUDENT

- **Want to get higher grades?**

- **Want instant feedback on your comprehension *and* retention of the course material?**

- **Want to know how ready you *really* are to take your next exam?**

- **Want the extra help at *your* convenience?**

Of course you do!

Then check out your
Online Learning Centre!

- Online Quizzes
- Interactive Graphing Exercises
- CBC Videos and Cases
- Econ Graph Kit

Macroeconomics

10th CANADIAN EDITION

FOR THE INSTRUCTOR

- Want an easy way to test your students prior to an exam that *doesn't* create more work for you?

- Want to access your supplements *without* having to bring them all to class?

- Want to integrate current happenings into your lectures *without* all the searching and extra work?

- Want an *easy* way to get your course on-line?

- Want to *free up more time* in your day to get more done?

Of course you do!

Then check out your
Online Learning Centre!

- Downloadable Supplements
- PageOut
- Online Resources
- The Integrator!

Mc Graw Hill **McGraw-Hill Ryerson**

Higher Learning. Forward Thinking.™

Part 1

An Introduction to Economics and the Economy

1

Chapter

The Nature and Method of Economics

Want is a growing giant whom the coat of Have was never large enough to cover.

Ralph Waldo Emerson
The Conduct of Life, 1860

People's wants are many and diverse. Biologically, humans need only air, water, food, clothing, and shelter. But in contemporary Canada, as in many other nations, we also want the many goods and services associated with a comfortable standard of living. Fortunately, Canada is blessed with productive resources—labour and managerial talent, tools and machinery, land and mineral deposits—that are used to produce goods and services. This production satisfies many of our wants and takes place through the organizational mechanism called the *economic system* or, more simply, the *economy.*

economics
The social science concerned with the efficient use of scarce resources to obtain the maximum satisfaction of society's unlimited wants.

The blunt reality, however, is that our wants far exceed the productive capacity of our limited resources. So the complete satisfaction of society's wants is impossible. This fact provides our definition of **economics**: *it is the social science concerned with the efficient use of scarce resources to obtain the maximum satisfaction of society's unlimited wants.*

Numerous problems and issues arise from the challenge of using limited resources efficiently. Although it is tempting to plunge into them, that sort of analysis must wait. In this chapter, we need to discuss some important preliminaries.

1.1   Ten Key Concepts to Retain for a Lifetime

Economics is concerned with the efficient use of scarce resources to obtain the maximum satisfaction of society's unlimited wants.

Suppose you unexpectedly meet your introductory economics professor on the street five or ten years after you complete this course. What will you be able to tell her you retained from the course she taught? More than likely you will not be able to remember very much. To help you retain the main ideas that economics has to offer, we have come up with **Ten Key Concepts** we believe are essential to understand the world around you and help you in your chosen career. These key concepts will be reinforced throughout the textbook. When a key concept is about to be discussed you will be alerted with an icon and the concept description.

The 10 key concepts will simply be listed here; elaboration on each of the key concepts will be found as we progress through the textbook. At the end of the course you should review these 10 key concepts. They will help you organize and better understand the materials you have studied. We have divided the 10 key concepts into three categories: (a) those pertaining to the individual; (b) concepts that explain the interaction among individuals; and (c) concepts that deal with the economy as a whole and the standard of living.

The Individual

CONCEPT 1 ("Facing Tradeoffs"): Scarcity in relation to wants means you face **tradeoffs**; therefore you have to make choices.

CONCEPT 2 ("Opportunity Costs"): The cost of the choice you make is what you give up for it, or the **opportunity cost**.

CONCEPT 3 ("Choosing a Little More or Less"): Choices are usually made at the **margin**; we choose a "little" more or a "little" less of something.

CONCEPT 4 ("The Influence of Incentives"): The choices you make are influenced by **incentives**.

Interaction Among Individuals

CONCEPT 5 ("Specialization and Trade"): **Specialization** and **trade** will improve the well-being of all participants.

CONCEPT 6 ("The Effectiveness of Markets"): **Markets** usually do a good job of coordinating trade among individuals, groups, and nations.

CONCEPT 7 ("The Role of Governments"): **Governments** can occasionally improve the coordinating function of markets.

The Economy as a Whole and the Standard of Living

CONCEPT 8 ("Production and the Standard of Living"): The **standard of living** of the average person in a particular country is dependent on its production of goods and services. A rise in the standard of living requires a rise in the output of goods and services.

CONCEPT 9 ("Money and Inflation"): If the monetary authorities of a country annually print money in excess of the growth of output of goods and services it will eventually lead to **inflation**.

CONCEPT 10 ("Inflation-Unemployment Tradeoff"): In the short run, society faces a short-run **tradeoff** between **inflation** and its level of **unemployment**.

These concepts will be elaborated on throughout this textbook. Be sure to be on the lookout for the icon that alerts you that one of these concepts is being discussed. We now turn to our first topic, the economic way of thinking.

1.2   The Economic Perspective

economic perspective
A viewpoint that envisions individuals and institutions making rational decisions by comparing the marginal benefits and marginal costs associated with their actions.

Close your eyes for a minute and pretend you are in paradise, a place where you can have anything you want whenever you desire it. On a particular day you may decide you want a new pair of jeans, a new notebook computer, a cellular phone, tickets to see Avril Lavigne, and a new yellow Lamborghini sports car to cruise around in. Your friends may have a completely different list of wants, but all of their desires will also be satisfied. Indeed, everyone's desires are satisfied. The following day you can start all over and make any request you have, and they will all be fulfilled. And so it will continue forever. Your body will never get old or sick, you will have all the friends and love you want, etc., etc.

Of course, paradise may be waiting for us in the afterlife, but in this world our wants greatly outstrip our ability to satisfy them. Anytime there is a situation in which wants are greater than the resources to meet those desires, we have an economic problem. It is this reality that gives economists their unique perspective. This **economic perspective** or *economic way of thinking* has several critical and closely interrelated features.

Scarcity and Choice

From our definition of economics, it is easy to see why economists view the world through the lens of scarcity. Since resources are scarce (limited), it follows that the goods and services we produce must also be limited. Scarcity limits our options and means that we must make choices. Because we "can't have it all," we must decide what we will have, and what we must forgo.

Limited resources have given economics its core: the idea that "there is no free lunch." You may get treated to lunch, making it "free" to you, but there is a cost to someone or a group of people (see the Consider This box). Scarce inputs of land, equipment, farm labour, the labour of cooks and waiters, and managerial talent are required. Because these resources could be used in other production activities, they and the other goods and services they could have produced are sacrificed in making the lunch available. Economists call these sacrifices *opportunity costs*. To get more of one thing, you forgo the opportunity of getting something else. So, the cost of that which you get is the value of that which is sacrificed to obtain it. We will say much more about opportunity costs in Chapter 2.

Rational Behaviour

utility
The satisfaction a person gets from consuming a good or service.

The economic approach assumes that human behaviour reflects "rational self-interest." Individuals look for and pursue opportunities to increase their **utility**—that is, pleasure or satisfaction. They allocate their time, energy, and money to maximize their well-being. Because they weigh costs and benefits, their decisions are purposeful, not random.

Rational behaviour means that the same person may make different choices under different circumstances. For example, Gagnon may decide to buy Coca-Cola cans in bulk at a warehouse store rather than at a convenience store where they are much more expensive. That will leave him with extra money to buy something else that provides satisfaction. Yet, while on a Saturday drive, he may stop at a Mac's store to buy a single can of Coca-Cola. Both actions are rational.

Consider This

The Idea of a "Free Lunch"

If you have never been offered a free product, you must be living on a deserted island. Sellers from time to time offer free software (Corel Corp. of Ottawa), free cellphones (Telus and Rogers), and no-fee chequing accounts (all the major Canadian chartered banks). Dentists give out free toothbrushes. Advertisers tout that if you buy three tires, you get one free. At provincial visitors' centres, there are free brochures and maps. Publishers provide free CD-ROMs along with some of their textbooks.

You might think that the presence of so many free products contradicts the economist's assertion that "there is no free lunch." You would be wrong! Scarce resources are used to produce each of these products, and because those resources have alternative uses, society incurs an opportunity cost. Where there are opportunity costs, there are no free lunches.

So why are these goods offered for free? In a word: marketing. Firms sometimes offer free products to entice people to try them, hoping they will then purchase them (or upgraded versions of them) later. That free version of Word-Perfect software from Corel may eventually entice you to buy the next upgraded version. In other instances, the product contains advertising. Those free brochures contain advertising for shops and restaurants and free access to the Internet is filled with ads. In still other cases, the product is only "free" in conjunction with a purchase. To get the soft drink you must buy the large pizza. To get the free cellphone from Rogers or Telus you need to sign up for a year (or more) of cellphone service.

QUESTION: Is health care "free" in Canada?

Rational behaviour also means that choices will vary greatly among individuals. High school graduate Andrée, living in Montreal, may decide to attend college or university to major in business. Baker, in Saskatoon, may opt to take a job at a warehouse and buy a new car. Chin, from Kelowna, may accept a signing bonus and join the Armed Forces. All three choices reflect the pursuit of self-interest and are rational, but they are based on different preferences and circumstances.

Of course, rational decisions may change as costs and benefits change. Gagnon may switch to Pepsi when it is on sale. And, after taking a few business courses, Andrée may decide to change her major to social work.

Rational self-interest is not the same as selfishness. Many individuals make personal sacrifices to help family members or friends, and they contribute to charities because they derive pleasure from doing so. Parents help pay for their children's education for the same reason. These self-interested, but unselfish, acts help maximize the givers' satisfaction as much as any personal purchase of goods or services. Self-interested behaviour is simply behaviour that enables a person to achieve personal satisfaction, whatever the source of that satisfaction.

Marginal Analysis: Benefits and Costs

marginal analysis
The comparison of marginal ("extra" or "additional") benefits and marginal costs, usually for decision making.

Choosing a Little
More or Less

The economic perspective focuses on **marginal analysis**—comparisons of *marginal benefits* and *marginal costs*. (Used this way, "marginal" means "extra," "additional," or "a change in.") Most choices or decisions involve changes in the status quo (the existing state of affairs). Should you attend school for another year or not? Should you study an extra hour for an exam? Should you add fries to your fast-food order? Similarly, should a business expand or reduce its output? Should government increase or decrease health care funding?

Each option will have marginal benefits and marginal costs. In making choices, the decision maker will compare those two amounts. Example: You and your fiancé are shopping for an engagement ring. Should you buy a ¼-carat diamond, a ½-carat diamond, a ¾-carat diamond, or a larger one? The marginal cost of the larger diamond is the added expense beyond the smaller diamond. The marginal benefit is the greater lifetime pleasure (utility) from the larger stone. If the marginal benefit of the larger diamond exceeds its marginal cost, you buy the larger stone. But if the marginal cost is more than the marginal benefit, you purchase the smaller diamond instead.

In a world of scarcity, the marginal benefit associated with some specific option always includes the marginal cost of forgoing something else. For example, the money spent on the larger diamond may mean forgoing a honeymoon to an exotic location.

One surprising implication of decisions based on marginal analysis is that there can be too much of a good thing. Although certain goods and services such as education, health care, and a pristine environment are desirable, we can in fact produce too much of them. "Too much" occurs when we keep obtaining them beyond the point where their marginal cost (the value of the forgone options) equals their marginal benefit. Then we are sacrificing alternative products that are more valuable *at the margin*. Thus, society can have too much health care and you can buy too large a diamond. *(Key Question 4)*

This chapter's Last Word, on page 14, provides an everyday application of the economic perspective.

QUICK REVIEW

- Economics is concerned with obtaining maximum satisfaction through the efficient use of scarce resources.

- The economic perspective stresses (a) resource scarcity and the necessity of making choices, (b) the assumption of rational behaviour, and (c) comparisons of marginal benefit and marginal cost.

1.3   Economic Methodology

scientific method
The systematic pursuit of knowledge through the formulation of a problem, collection of data, and the formulation and testing of hypotheses.

Like the physical and life sciences, as well as other social sciences, economics relies on the **scientific method**. It consists of a number of elements:

- The observation of facts (real world data).

- Based on those facts, the formulation of possible explanations of cause and effect (hypotheses).

- The testing of these explanations by comparing the outcomes of specific events to the outcomes predicted by the hypotheses.

- The acceptance, rejection, or modification of the hypotheses, based on these comparisons.

- The continued testing of the hypotheses against the facts. As favourable results accumulate, the hypotheses evolve into a *theory*, sometimes referred to as a *model*. A very well-tested and widely accepted theory is referred to as a *law* or *principle*.

Laws, principles, and models enable the economist, like the natural scientist, to understand and explain economic phenomena and to predict the various outcomes of particular actions. But as we will soon see, economic laws and principles are usually less certain than the laws of physics or chemistry.

Deriving Theories

Economists develop models of the behaviour of individuals (consumers, workers) and institutions (business, government) engaged in the production, exchange, and consumption of goods and services. They start by gathering facts about economic activity and economic outcomes. Because the world is cluttered with innumerable interrelated facts, economists, like all scientists, must select what they consider useful information. They must determine which facts are relevant to the problem under consideration. But even when this sorting process is complete, the relevant information may at first seem random and unrelated.

The economist draws on the facts to establish cause-effect hypotheses about economic behaviour. Then the hypotheses are tested against real world observation and data. Through this process,

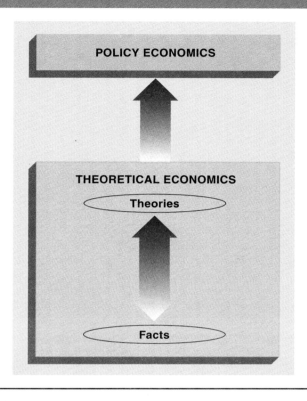

FIGURE 1-1

The Relationship Between Facts, Theories, and Policies in Economics

Theoretical economics involves establishing economic theories by gathering, systematically arranging, and generalizing from facts. Economic theories are tested for validity against facts. Economists use these theories—the most reliable of which are called *laws* or *principles*—to explain and analyze the economy. *Policy economics* entails using the economic laws and principles to formulate economic policies.

theoretical economics
The process of deriving and applying economic theories and principles.

principles
Statements about economic behaviour that enable prediction of the probable effects of certain actions.

the economist tries to discover hypotheses that can eventually rise to the level of theories and principles (or laws)—well-tested and widely accepted generalizations about how individuals and institutions behave. The process of deriving theories and principles is called **theoretical economics** (see the lower box in Figure 1-1). *The role of economic theorizing is to systematically arrange facts, interpret them, and generalize from them.* Theories and principles bring order and meaning to facts by arranging them in cause-and-effect order.

Observe that the arrow between "theories" and "facts" in Figure 1-1 moves in both directions. Some understanding of factual, real-world evidence is required to formulate meaningful hypotheses. And hypotheses are tested through gathering and organizing factual data to see if the hypotheses can be verified.

Economic theories and **principles** *are statements about economic behaviour that enable prediction of the probable effects of certain actions.* Good theories are those that explain and predict well. They are supported by facts of how individuals and institutions behave in producing, exchanging, and consuming goods and services. But these facts may change over time, so economists must continually check theories against the shifting economic environment.

Several other points relating to economic principles are important to know.

TERMINOLOGY

Economists speak of "hypotheses," "theories," "models," "laws," and "principles." These terms overlap but usually reflect the degree of confidence in the generalizations. A hypothesis needs initial testing; a theory has been tested but needs more testing; a law or principle is a theory that has proved highly reliable, over and over. The terms *economic laws* and *principles* are useful, even though they imply a degree of exactness and universal application that is rare in any social science. The word *theory* is often used in economics even though many people incorrectly believe theories have nothing to do with real-world applications.

In this book, custom and convenience will govern the use of "theory," "law," "principle," and "model." Thus, we will use the term *law of demand* to describe the relationship between the price of a product and the amount of it purchased, rather than the theory or principle of demand, simply because this is the custom. We will refer to the *circular flow model*, not the circular flow law, because it combines several ideas into a single representation.

GENERALIZATIONS

generalization
Statement of the nature of the relation between two or more sets of facts.

As we have already mentioned, economic theories, principles, and laws are **generalizations** relating to economic behaviour or to the economy itself. They are imprecise because economic facts are usually diverse; no two individuals or institutions act in exactly the same way. *Economic principles are expressed as the tendencies of typical or average consumers, workers, or business firms.* For example, when economists say that Canadian consumer spending rises when personal income increases, they are well aware that some Canadian households may save *all* of an increase in their incomes. But, on average, and for the entire economy, spending goes up when income increases. Similarly, economists claim that consumers buy more of a particular product when its price falls. Some consumers may increase their purchases by a large amount, others by a small amount, and a few not at all. This "price-quantity" principle, however, holds for the typical consumer and for consumers as a group.

OTHER-THINGS-EQUAL ASSUMPTION

other-things-equal assumption
The assumption that factors other than those being considered are held constant.

Like other scientists, economists use the *ceteris paribus* or **other-things-equal assumption** to arrive at their generalizations. They assume that all other variables except those under immediate consideration are held constant for a particular analysis. For example, consider the relationship between the price of Pepsi and the amount of it purchased. It helps to assume that, of all the factors that might influence the amount of Pepsi purchased (for example, the price of Pepsi, the price of Coca-Cola, and consumer incomes and preferences), only the price of Pepsi varies. We can then focus on the "price of Pepsi-purchases of Pepsi" relationship without being confused by changes in other variables.

Natural scientists such as chemists or physicists can usually conduct controlled experiments where "all other things" are in fact held constant (or virtually so). They can test with great precision the assumed relationship between two variables. For example, they might examine the height from which an object is dropped and the length of time it takes to hit the ground. But economics is not a laboratory science. Economists test their theories using real-world data, which are generated by the actual operation of the economy. In this complex environment, "other things" *do* change. Despite the development of sophisticated statistical techniques designed to hold other things equal, control is less than perfect. As a result, economic theories are less certain and less precise than those of laboratory sciences. That also means they generate more debate than many scientific theories (for example, the law of gravity.)

ABSTRACTIONS

Economic theories are *abstractions*—simplifications that omit irrelevant facts and circumstances. Economic models do *not* mirror the full complexity of the real world. The very process of sorting out and analyzing facts involves simplification and removal of clutter. Unfortunately, this "abstraction" leads some people to consider economic theory impractical and unrealistic. That is simply nonsense! Economic theories are practical precisely because they are abstractions. The full scope of economic reality itself is too complex to be understood as a whole. Economists abstract—that is, develop theories and build models—to give meaning to an otherwise overwhelming and confusing maze of facts. Theorizing for this purpose is highly practical.

GRAPHICAL EXPRESSION

Many of the economic models in this book are expressed graphically; the most important are labelled *Key Graphs*. Be sure to read the appendix to this chapter as a review of graphs.

Policy Economics

policy economics
The formulation of courses of action to bring about desired economic outcomes or to prevent undesired occurrences.

www.bankofcanada.ca
Bank of Canada

Applied economics, or **policy economics**, is the application of theories and data to formulate *policies* that aim to resolve a specific economic problem or bring about a desired economic outcome. Economic theories are the foundation of economic policy, as shown in the upper part of Figure 1-1. Economic policy normally is applied to problems after they arise. However, if economic analysis can predict some undesirable event, such as unemployment, inflation, or an increase in poverty, then it may be possible to avoid or moderate that event through economic policy. For example, you may read in the newspaper that the Bank of Canada has reduced interest rates to increase spending and prevent a recession.

FORMULATING ECONOMIC POLICY

Here are the basic steps in policy-making:

- *State the goal.* The first step is to make a clear statement of the economic goal. If we say that we want "full employment," do we mean that everyone between, say, 16 and 65 years of age should have a job? Or do we mean that everyone who *wants* to work should have a job? Should we allow for some unemployment caused by inevitable changes in the structure of industry and workers voluntarily changing jobs? The goal must be specific.

- *Determine the policy options.* The next step is to formulate alternative policies designed to achieve the goal, and determine the possible effects of each policy. This requires a detailed assessment of the economic impact, benefits, costs, and political feasibility of the alternative policies. For example, to achieve full employment in Canada, should the federal and provincial governments use fiscal policy (which involves changing government spending and taxes), monetary policy (which entails altering the supply of money), an education and training policy that enhances worker employability, or a policy of wage subsidies to firms that hire disadvantaged workers?

- *Implement and evaluate the policy that was selected.* After implementing the policy, we need to evaluate how well it worked. Only through unbiased evaluation can we improve on economic policy. Did a specific change in taxes or the money supply alter the level of employment to the extent predicted? Did deregulation of a particular industry (for example, banking) yield the predicted beneficial results? If not, why not? What were the harmful side effects, if any? How might the policy be altered to make it work better? *(Key Question 8)*

ECONOMIC GOALS

If economic policies are designed to achieve specific economic goals, then we need to recognize a number of goals that are widely accepted in Canada and many other countries. They include:

- *Economic growth*   Produce more and better goods and services, or, more simply, achieve a higher standard of living.

- *Full employment*   Provide suitable jobs for all citizens who are willing and able to work.

- *Economic efficiency*   Achieve the maximum output and satisfaction using the available productive resources.

- *Price-level stability*   Avoid large upswings and downswings in the general price level; that is, avoid inflation and deflation.

- *Economic freedom* Guarantee that businesses, workers, and consumers have a high degree of freedom of choice in their economic activities.

- *Equitable distribution of income* Ensure that no group of citizens faces poverty while most others enjoy abundance.

- *Economic security* Provide for those who are chronically ill, disabled, laid off, aged, or otherwise unable to earn minimal levels of income.

- *Balance of trade* Seek a reasonable overall balance with the rest of the world in international trade and financial transactions.

Although most of us might accept these goals as generally stated, we might also disagree substantially on their specific meanings. What are "large" changes in the price level? What is a "high degree" of economic freedom? What is an "equitable" distribution of income? How can we measure precisely such abstract goals as "economic freedom"? These objectives are often the subject of spirited public debate.

Also, some of these goals are complementary; when one is achieved, some other one will also be realized. For example, achieving full employment means eliminating unemployment, which is a basic cause of inequitable income distribution. But other goals may conflict or even be mutually exclusive. They may entail **tradeoffs**, meaning that to achieve one we must sacrifice another. For example, efforts to equalize the distribution of income may weaken incentives to work, invest, innovate, and take business risks, all of which promote economic growth. Taxing high-income people heavily and transferring the tax revenues to low-income people is one way to equalize the distribution of income. But then the incentives to high-income individuals may diminish because higher taxes reduce their rewards for working. Similarly, low-income individuals may be less motivated to work when government stands ready to subsidize them.

When goals conflict, society must develop a system to prioritize the objectives it seeks. If more economic freedom is accompanied by less economic security and more economic security allows less economic freedom, society must assess the tradeoffs and decide on the optimal (best) balance between them.

tradeoffs
The sacrifice of some or all of one economic goal, good, or service to achieve some other goal, good, or service.

Facing Tradeoffs

QUICK REVIEW

- Economists use the scientific method to establish theories, laws, and principles. Economic theories (laws, principles, or models) are generalizations relating to the economic behaviour of individuals and institutions; good theories are grounded in facts.

- Theoretical economics involves formulating theories (or laws and principles) and using them to understand and explain economic behaviour and the economy;

- policy economics involves using the theories to fix economic problems or promote economic goals.

- Policy-making requires a clear statement of goals, a thorough assessment of options, and an unbiased evaluation of results.

- Some of society's economic goals are complementary, while others conflict; where conflicts exist, tradeoffs arise.

1.4   Macroeconomics and Microeconomics

macroeconomics
The part of economics concerned with the economy as a whole.

aggregate
A collection of specific economic units treated as if they were one unit.

Economists derive and apply principles about economic behaviour at two levels.

Macroeconomics

Macroeconomics examines either the economy as a whole or its basic subdivisions or aggregates such as the government, household, and business sectors. An **aggregate** is a collection of specific economic units treated as if they were one unit. Therefore, we might lump together the millions of consumers in the Canadian economy and treat them as if they were one huge unit called "consumers."

In using aggregates, macroeconomics seeks to obtain an overview, or general outline, of the structure of the economy and the relationships of its major aggregates. Macroeconomics is concerned with such economic measures as *total* output, *total* employment, *total* income, *aggregate* expenditures, and the *general* level of prices in analyzing various economic problems. Very little attention is given to specific units making up the various aggregates. Macroeconomics examines the beach, not the sand, rocks, and shells.

Microeconomics

microeconomics
The part of economics concerned with such individual units as industries, firms, and households.

Microeconomics looks at specific economic units. At this level of analysis, we observe the details of an economic unit, or very small segment of the economy, under the microscope. In microeconomics we investigate an individual industry, firm, or household. We measure the price of a *specific* product, the number of workers employed by a *single* firm, the revenue or income of a *particular* firm or household, or the expenditures of a *specific* firm, government entity, or family. In microeconomics, we examine the sand, rocks, and shells, not the beach.

The macro-micro distinction does not mean that every topic can be readily labelled as either macro or micro; many topics and subdivisions of economics are rooted in both. Example: While the problem of unemployment is usually treated as a macroeconomic topic (because unemployment relates to *aggregate* spending), the decisions made by *individual* workers in searching for jobs and the way *specific* product and labour markets operate are also critical in determining the unemployment rate. *(Key Question 10)*

Positive and Normative Economics

positive economics
The analysis of facts or data to establish scientific generalizations about economic behaviour.

normative economics
The part of economics involving value judgments about what the economy should be like.

Both macroeconomics and microeconomics use facts, theories, and policies. Each contains elements of *positive* economics and *normative* economics. **Positive economics** focuses on facts and cause-and-effect relationships. Positive economics avoids value judgments, tries to establish scientific statements about economic behaviour, and deals with what the economy is actually like. Such factually based analysis is critical to good policy analysis.

In contrast **normative economics** incorporates a person's (or group of people's) value judgments about what the economy should be like. Normative economics looks at the subjective desirability of certain aspects of the economy, or the expressions of support for particular economic policies.

Positive economics concerns *what is,* while normative economics embodies subjective feelings about *what ought to be.* Here are some examples. Positive statement: "The unemployment rate in several European nations is higher than that in Canada." Normative statement: "European nations ought to undertake policies to reduce their unemployment rates." A second positive statement: "Other things equal, if tuition is substantially increased, college and university enrolment will fall." Normative statement: "College and university tuition should be lowered so that more students can obtain an education." Whenever words such as "ought" or "should" appear in a sentence, there is a strong chance you are encountering a normative statement.

Most of the disagreement among economists involves normative, value-based policy questions. Of course, there is often some disagreement about which theories or models best represent the economy and its parts. But economists agree on a full range of economic principles. Most economic controversy thus reflects differing opinions or value judgments about what society should be like. *(Key Question 11)*

There is one more thing to add to the normative-positive dichotomy, and that is to distinguish them from *prediction* about future factual issues. If I believe that Mary Smith will be elected the next prime minister of Canada, such a prediction of a future event should be distinguished from a value-based opinion, such as "Mary Smith should be elected the next prime minister of Canada."

> **QUICK REVIEW**
>
> - Macroeconomics examines the economy as a whole; microeconomics focuses on specific units of the economy.
> - Positive economics deals with factual statements ("what is"); normative economics involves value judgments ("what ought to be").

1.5   Pitfalls to Objective Thinking

Because they often affect us so personally, we often have difficulty thinking objectively about economic issues. Here are some common pitfalls to avoid in successfully applying the economic perspective.

Biases

Most people bring a bundle of biases and preconceptions when thinking about economic issues. For example, you might think that corporate profits are excessive or that borrowing money is never a good idea. Perhaps you believe that government is necessarily less efficient than businesses or that more government regulation is always better than less. Biases cloud thinking and interfere with objective analysis. The novice economics student must be willing to shed biases and preconceptions that are not supported by facts.

Loaded Terminology

The economic terminology used in newspapers and popular magazines is sometimes emotionally biased, or loaded. The writer or the interest group he or she represents may have a cause to promote or an axe to grind and may slant an article accordingly. High profits may be labelled "obscene," low wages may be called "exploitive," or self-interested behaviour may be "greed." Government workers may be referred to as "mindless bureaucrats," and those favouring stronger government regulations may be called "socialists." To objectively analyze economic issues, you must be prepared to reject or discount such terminology.

Definitions

Some of the terms used in economics have precise technical definitions that are quite different from those implied by their common usage. This is generally not a problem if everyone understands these definitions and uses them consistently. For example, *investment* to the average citizen means the purchase of stocks and bonds in security markets, as when someone "invests" in Royal Bank stock or government bonds. But to the economist, *investment* means the purchase of newly created real (physical) capital assets such as machinery and equipment or the construction of a new factory building.

Fallacy of Composition

fallacy of composition
Incorrectly reasoning that what is true for the individual (or part) is necessarily true for the group (or whole).

Another pitfall in economic thinking is the assumption that what is true for one individual is necessarily true for a group of individuals. This is a logical fallacy called the **fallacy of composition**; the assumption is *not* correct. A statement that is valid for an individual or part is *not* necessarily valid for the larger group.

Consider the following example from outside of economics. You are at a football game in Winnipeg and the home team makes an outstanding play. In the excitement, you leap to your feet to get a better view. A valid statement: "If you, *an individual*, stand, your view of the game is improved." But is this also true for the group—for everyone watching the play? Not necessarily. If *everyone* stands to watch the play, it is likely that nobody—including you—will have a better view than when all remain seated.

A second example comes from economics: An *individual* farmer who reaps a particularly large crop is likely to realize a sharp gain in income. But this statement cannot be generalized to farmers as a *group*. The individual farmer's large or "bumper" crop will not noticeably influence (reduce) crop prices because each farmer produces a negligible fraction of the total farm output. But for *all* farmers as a group, prices decline when total output increases. Thus, if all farmers reap bumper crops, the total output of farm products will rise, depressing crop prices. If the price declines are relatively large, total farm income might actually *fall*.

Recall our earlier distinction between macroeconomics and microeconomics: *The fallacy of composition reminds us that generalizations valid at one of these levels of analysis may or may not be valid at the other.*

Causation Fallacies

Causation is sometimes difficult to identify in economics. Two important fallacies often interfere with economic thinking.

POST HOC FALLACY

post hoc, ergo propter hoc fallacy
Incorrectly reasoning that when one event precedes another the first event must have caused the second event.

You must think very carefully before concluding that because event A precedes event B, A is the cause of B. This kind of faulty reasoning is known as the ***post hoc, ergo propter hoc*** or **"after this, therefore because of this" fallacy**.

Example: Suppose that early each spring the medicine man of a tribe performs a special dance. A week or so later the trees and grass turn green. Can we safely conclude that event A, the medicine man's dance, has caused event B, the landscape's turning green? Obviously not. The rooster crows before dawn, but that does not mean the rooster is responsible for the sunrise!

The Toronto Maple Leafs hire a new coach and the team's record improves. Is the new coach the cause? Maybe. But perhaps the presence of more experienced and talented players or an easier schedule is the true cause.

CORRELATION VERSUS CAUSATION

Do not confuse correlation, or connection, with causation. Correlation between two events indicates only that they are associated in some systematic and dependable way. For example, we may find that when variable X increases, Y also increases. But this correlation does not necessarily mean that there is causation—that an increase in X is the cause of an increase in Y. The relationship could be purely coincidental or dependent on some other factor, Z, not included in the analysis.

Here is an example: Economists have found a positive correlation between education and income. In general, people with more education earn higher incomes than those with less education. Common sense suggests education is the cause and higher incomes are the effect; more education implies a more knowledgeable and productive worker, and such workers receive larger salaries.

But causation could also partly run the other way. People with higher incomes could buy more education, just as they buy more furniture and organic foods. Or is part of the relationship explainable in still other ways? Are education and income correlated because the characteristics required to succeed in education—ability and motivation—are the same ones required to be a productive and highly paid worker? If so, then people with those traits will probably obtain more education *and* earn higher incomes. But greater education will not be the sole cause of the higher income. *(**Key Question 12**)*

A Look Ahead

The ideas in this chapter will come into much sharper focus as you advance through Part 1, where we develop specific economic principles and models. Specifically, in Chapter 2 we will build a model of the production choices facing an economy. In Chapter 3 we develop laws of demand and supply that will help you understand how prices and quantities of goods and services are established in markets. In Chapter 4 we combine all markets in the economy to see how the *market system* works and then proceed to look at international markets and the structure of the Canadian economy.

THE LASTword — Fast-Food Lines: An Economic Perspective

How can the economic perspective help us understand the behaviour of fast-food consumers?

You enter a fast-food restaurant on the outskirts of Halifax. Do you immediately look to see which line is the shortest? What do you do when you are in the middle of a long line and a new serving station opens? Have you ever gone to a fast-food restaurant, seen very long lines, and then left? Have you ever become annoyed when someone in front of you in line placed an order that took a long time to fill?

The economic perspective is useful in analyzing the behaviour of fast-food customers. These consumers are at the restaurant because they expect the marginal benefit from the food they buy to match or exceed its marginal cost. When customers enter the restaurant, they go to the shortest line, believing that it will minimize the time cost of obtaining their food. They are acting purposefully; time is limited and people prefer using it in some way other than standing in line.

If one fast-food line is temporarily shorter than other lines, some people will move toward that line. These movers apparently view the time saving associated with the shorter line to exceed the cost of moving from their present line. The line switching tends to equalize line lengths. No further movement of customers between lines occurs once all lines are about equal.

Fast-food customers face another cost-benefit decision when a clerk opens a new station at the counter.

Should they move to the new station or stay put? Those who shift to the new line decide that the time saving from the move exceeds the extra cost of physically moving. In so deciding, customers must also consider just how quickly they can get to the new station compared with others who may be contemplating the same move. (Those who hesitate in this situation are lost!)

Customers at the fast-food establishment do not have perfect information when they select lines. For example, they do not first survey those in the lines to determine what they are ordering before deciding which line to enter. There are two reasons for this. First, most customers would tell them "It's none of your business," and therefore no information would be forthcoming. Second, even if they could obtain the information, the amount of time necessary to get it (a cost) would most certainly exceed any time saving associated with finding the best line (the benefit). Because information is costly to obtain, fast-food patrons select lines without perfect information. Thus, not all decisions turn

out as expected. For example, you might enter a short line and find someone in front of you is ordering hamburgers and fries for 40 people in the Greyhound bus that just arrived from Moncton and is parked out back (and the employee is a trainee)! Nevertheless, at the time you made your decision, you thought it was optimal.

Imperfect information also explains why some people who arrive at a fast-food restaurant and observe long lines decide to leave. These people conclude that the marginal cost (monetary plus time costs) of obtaining the fast food is too large relative to the marginal benefit. They would not have come to the restaurant in the first place had they known the lines would be so long. But getting that information by, say, employing an advance scout with a cellphone would cost more than the perceived benefit.

Finally, customers must decide what food to order when they arrive at the counter. In making their choices they again compare marginal costs and marginal benefits in attempting to obtain the greatest personal satisfaction or well-being for their expenditure.

Economists believe that what is true for the behaviour of customers at fast-food restaurants is true for economic behaviour in general. Faced with an array of choices, consumers, workers, and businesses rationally compare marginal costs and marginal benefits in making decisions.

CHAPTER SUMMARY

1-1 TEN KEY CONCEPTS TO RETAIN FOR A LIFETIME

- There are ten key concepts to remember: four deal with the individual, three with interaction among individuals, and three with the economy as a whole.

1-2 THE ECONOMIC PERSPECTIVE

- Economics is the study of the efficient use of scarce resources in the production of goods and services to obtain the maximum satisfaction of society's unlimited wants.

- The economic perspective includes three elements: scarcity and choice, rational behaviour, and marginalism. It sees individuals and institutions making rational decisions based on comparisons of marginal costs and marginal benefits.

1-3 ECONOMIC METHODOLOGY

- Economists employ the scientific method to form and test hypotheses of cause-and-effect relationships, in order to generate theories, laws, and principles.

- Generalizations are called principles, theories, laws, or models. Good theories explain real-world relationships and predict real-world outcomes.

- Economic policy is designed to identify and solve problems to the greatest extent possible and at the least pos-

sible cost. This application of economics is called policy economics.

- Our society accepts certain shared economic goals, including economic growth, full employment, economic efficiency, price-level stability, economic freedom, equity in the distribution of income, economic security, and a reasonable balance in international trade and finance. Some of these goals are complementary; others entail tradeoffs.

1-4 MACROECONOMICS AND MICROECONOMICS

- Macroeconomics looks at the economy as a whole or its major aggregates; microeconomics examines specific economic units or institutions.

- Positive statements state facts ("what is"); normative statements express value judgments ("what ought to be").

1-5 PITFALLS TO OBJECTIVE THINKING

- In studying economics we encounter pitfalls to straight thinking such as biases and preconceptions, unfamiliar or confusing terminology, the fallacy of composition, and the difficulty of establishing clear cause–effect relationships.

TERMS AND CONCEPTS

economics, p. 3
economic perspective, p. 4
utility, p. 4
marginal analysis, p. 5
scientific method, p. 6
theoretical economics, p. 7
principles, p. 7

generalization, p. 8
"other-things-equal"
  assumption, p. 8
policy economics, p. 9
tradeoffs, p. 10
macroeconomics, p. 10
aggregate, p. 10

microeconomics, p. 11
positive economics, p. 11
normative economics, p. 11
fallacy of composition, p. 12
post hoc, ergo propter hoc
  fallacy, p. 13

STUDY QUESTIONS

1. "Buy two, get one free." Explain why the "one free" is free to the buyer, but not to society.

2. What is meant by the term "utility" and how does it relate to the economic perspective?

3. Cite three examples of recent decisions that you made in which, at least implicitly, you weighed marginal costs and marginal benefits.

4. **KEY QUESTION** Use the economic perspective to explain why someone who is normally a light eater at a standard restaurant may become a bit of a glutton at

a buffet-style restaurant that charges a single price for all you can eat.

5. What is the scientific method and how does it relate to theoretical economics? What is the difference between a hypothesis and an economic law or principle?

6. Why is it significant that economics is not a laboratory science? What problems may be involved in deriving and applying economic principles?

7. Explain the following statements:

   a. Good economic policy requires good economic theory.

b. Generalization and abstraction are nearly synonymous.

c. Facts serve to sort out good and bad hypotheses.

d. The *other-things-equal assumption* helps isolate key economic relationships.

8. **KEY QUESTION** Explain in detail the interrelationships between economic facts, theory, and policy. Critically evaluate this statement: "The trouble with economic theory is that it is not practical. It is detached from the real world."

9. To what extent do you accept the eight economic goals stated and described in this chapter? What priorities do you assign to them?

10. **KEY QUESTION** Indicate whether each of the following statements applies to microeconomics or macroeconomics:

   a. The unemployment rate in Canada was 7.4 percent in January 2003.

   b. The fish processing plant in Torbay, Newfoundland, laid off 15 workers last month.

   c. An unexpected freeze in central Florida reduced the citrus crop and caused the price of oranges to rise.

   d. Canadian output, adjusted for inflation, grew by 13.4 percent in 2002.

   e. Last week the Royal Bank lowered its interest rate on business loans by one-half of 1 percentage point.

f. The consumer price index rose by 2.7 percent in 2002.

11. **KEY QUESTION** Identify each of the following as either a positive or a normative statement:

   a. The high temperature today was 30 degrees.

   b. It was too hot today in Edmonton.

   c. Other things equal, higher interest rates reduce the total amount of borrowing.

   d. Interest rates are too high.

12. **KEY QUESTION** Explain and give an example of (a) the fallacy of composition, and (b) the "after this, therefore because of this" fallacy. Why are cause-and-effect relationships difficult to isolate in economics?

13. Suppose studies show that students who study more hours receive higher grades. Does this relationship guarantee that any particular student who studies longer will get higher grades?

14. Studies indicate that married men on average earn more income than unmarried men of the same age. Why must we be cautious in concluding that marriage is the *cause* and higher income is the *effect*?

15. **(The Last Word)** Use the economic perspective to explain the behaviour of the *workers* (rather than the customers) observed at a fast-food restaurant. Why are these workers there, rather than, say, cruising around in their cars? Why do they work so diligently? Why do so many of them quit these jobs once they have graduated high school?

INTERNET APPLICATION QUESTIONS

1. **Three Economic Goals—Are They Being Achieved?** Three primary economic goals are economic growth (an increase in real GDP), full employment (less than 7 percent unemployment), and price-level stability (less than 2 percent as measured by the Consumer Price Index—CPI). Use the links to Canadian economic data on the McConnell-Brue-Barbiero Web site (Chapter 1) to assess whether these three goals are being met in Canada.

Σ-STAT

2. **Normative Economics—Canadian Politics.** Many economic policy statements made by the Liberal Party, the Reform Party, the Progressive Conservative Party, and the NDP can be considered normative rather than positive economic statements. Use the links on the McConnell-Brue-Barbiero Web site (Chapter 1) and compare and contrast their views on how to achieve economic goals. How much of the disagreement is based on positive statements and how much on normative statements? Give an example of loaded terminology from each site.

Appendix to Chapter 1

A1.1   Graphs and Their Meaning

If you glance quickly through this text, you will find many graphs. Some seem simple, others more complicated. All are important. They are used to help you visualize and understand economic relationships. Physicists and chemists sometimes illustrate their theories by building arrangements of multicoloured wooden balls, representing protons, neutrons, and electrons, which are held in proper relation to one another by wires or sticks. Economists use graphs to illustrate their models. By understanding these "pictures," you can more readily make sense of economic relationships. Most of our principles or models explain relationships between just two sets of economic facts, which can be conveniently represented with two-dimensional graphs.

Construction of a Graph

A graph is a visual representation of the relationship between two variables. Figure A1-1 is a hypothetical illustration showing the relationship between income and consumption for the economy as a whole. Without having studied economics, we would intuitively expect that people would buy more goods and services when their incomes go up. Thus it is not surprising to find in Figure A1-1 that total consumption in the economy increases as total income increases.

The information in Figure A1-1 is expressed both graphically and in table form. Here is how it is done: We want to show visually or graphically how consumption changes as income changes. Since income is the determining factor, we represent it on the **horizontal axis** of the graph, as is customary. And because consumption depends on income, we represent it on the **vertical axis** of the graph, as is also customary. Actually, what we are doing is representing the *independent variable* on the horizontal axis and the *dependent variable* on the vertical axis.

Now we arrange the vertical and horizontal scales of the graph to reflect the ranges of values of consumption and income, and we mark the scales in convenient increments. As you can see in Figure A1-1, the values marked on the scales cover all the values in the table. The increments on both scales are $100 for approximately each 1.25 centimetres.

Because this type of *graph* has two dimensions, each point within it represents an income value and its associated consumption value. To find a point that represents one of the five income-consumption combinations in the table, we draw perpendiculars from the appropriate values on the vertical and horizontal axes. For example, to plot point *c* (the $200 income-$150 consumption point), perpendiculars are drawn up from the horizontal (income) axis at $200 and across from the vertical (consumption) axis at $150. These perpendiculars intersect at point *c*, which represents this particular income-consumption combination. You should verify that the other income-consumption combinations shown in the table are properly located in the graph. Finally, by assuming that the same general relationship between income and consumption prevails for all other incomes, we draw a line or smooth curve to connect these points. That line or curve represents the income-consumption relationship.

horizontal axis
The "left-right" or "west-east" axis on a graph or grid.

vertical axis
The "up-down" or "north-south" axis on a graph or grid.

FIGURE A1-1   **The Relationship Between Income and Consumption**

Income per week	Consumption per week	Point
$ 0	$ 50	a
100	100	b
200	150	c
300	200	d
400	250	e

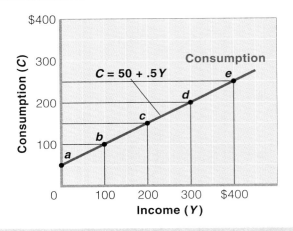

Two sets of data that are positively or directly related, such as consumption and income, graph as an upward-sloping line.

If the graph is a straight line, as in Figure A1-1, we say the relationship is *linear*.

Direct and Inverse Relationships

direct relationship
The (positive) relationship between two variables that change in the same direction, for example, product price and quantity supplied.

The line in Figure A1-1 slopes upward to the right, depicting a direct relationship between income and consumption. By a **direct relationship** (or positive relationship) we mean that two variables—in this case, consumption and income—change in the *same* direction. An increase in consumption is associated with an increase in income; a decrease in consumption accompanies a decrease in income. When two sets of data are positively or directly related, they always graph as an *upward-sloping* line, as in Figure A1-1.

inverse relationship
The (negative) relationship between two variables that change in opposite directions, for example, product price and quantity demanded.

In contrast, two sets of data may be inversely related. Consider Figure A1-2, which shows the relationship between the price of basketball tickets and game attendance at Informed University (IU). Here we have an **inverse relationship** (or negative relationship) because the two variables change in *opposite* directions. When ticket prices decrease, attendance increases. When ticket prices increase, attendance decreases. The six data points in the table are plotted in the graph. Observe that an inverse relationship always graphs as a *downward-sloping* line.

Dependent and Independent Variables

independent variable
The variable causing a change in some other (dependent) variable.

dependent variable
A variable that changes as a consequence of a change in some other (independent) variable; the "effect" or outcome.

Although it is not always easy, economists seek to determine which variable is the "cause" and which is the "effect." Or, more formally, they seek the independent variable and the dependent variable. The **independent variable** is the cause or source; it is the variable that changes first. The **dependent variable** is the effect or outcome; it is the variable that changes because of the change in the independent variable. As noted in our income–consumption example, income generally is the independent variable and consumption the dependent variable. Income causes consumption to be what it is rather than the other way around. Similarly, ticket prices (set in advance of the season) determine attendance at IU basketball games; attendance at games does not determine the ticket prices for those games. Ticket price is the independent variable, and the quantity of tickets purchased is the dependent variable.

You may recall from your high school courses that mathematicians always put the independent variable (cause) on the horizontal axis and the dependent variable (effect) on the vertical axis.

Economists are less tidy; their graphing of independent and dependent variables is more arbitrary. Their conventional graphing of the income-consumption relationship is consistent with mathematical presentation, but economists put price and cost data on the vertical axis.

Other Things Equal

Our simple two-variable graphs purposely ignore many other factors that might affect the amount of consumption occurring at each income level or the number of people who attend IU basketball games at each possible ticket price. When economists plot the relationship between any two variables, they employ the *ceteris paribus* (other-things-equal) assumption. Thus, in Figure A1-1 all factors other than income that might affect the amount of consumption are held constant. Similarly, in Figure A1-2 all factors other than ticket price that might influence attendance at IU basketball games are held constant. In reality, "other things" are not equal; they often change, and when they do, the relationship represented in our two tables and graphs will change. Specifically, the lines we have plotted will shift to new locations.

Consider a stock market "crash." The dramatic drop in the value of stocks might cause people to feel less wealthy and therefore less willing to consume at each level of income. The result might be a downward shift of the consumption line. To see this, you should plot a new consumption line in Figure A1-1, assuming that consumption is, say, $20 less at each income level. Note that the relationship remains direct; the line merely shifts downward to reflect less consumption spending at each income level.

Similarly, factors other than ticket prices might affect IU game attendance. If IU loses most of its games, attendance at IU games might fall at each ticket price. To see this, redraw the graph in Figure A1-2, assuming that 2000 fewer fans attend IU games at each ticket price. *(Key Appendix Question 2)*

FIGURE A1-2 **The Relationship Between Ticket Prices and Attendance**

Ticket price	Attendance, thousands	Point
$50	0	a
40	4	b
30	8	c
20	12	d
10	16	e
0	20	f

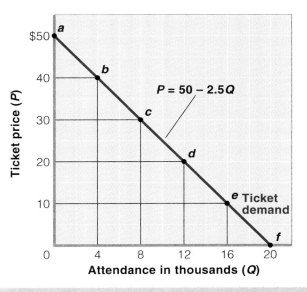

$P = 50 - 2.5Q$

Two sets of data that are negatively or inversely related, such as ticket price and the attendance at basketball games, graph as a downward-sloping line.

Slope of a Line

slope of a line
The ratio of the vertical change (the rise or fall) to the horizontal change (the run) between any two points on a line. The slope of an upward sloping line is positive, reflecting a direct relationship between two variables; the slope of a downward sloping line is negative, reflecting an inverse relationship between two variables.

Lines can be described in terms of their slopes and their intercepts. The **slope of a straight line** is the ratio of the vertical change (the rise or drop) to the horizontal change (the run) between any two points of the line, or "rise" over "run."

POSITIVE SLOPE

Between point b and point c in Figure A1-1 the rise or vertical change (the change in consumption) is +$50 and the run or horizontal change (the change in income) is +$100. Therefore:

$$\text{Slope} = \frac{\text{vertical change}}{\text{horizontal change}} = \frac{+50}{+100} = \frac{1}{2} = .5$$

Note that our slope of ½ or .5 is positive because consumption and income change in the same direction; that is, consumption and income are directly or positively related.

The slope of .5 tells us there will be a $1 increase in consumption for every $2 increase in income. Similarly, it indicates that for every $2 decrease in income there will be a $1 decrease in consumption.

NEGATIVE SLOPE

Between any two of the identified points in Figure A1-2, say, point c and point d, the vertical change is −10 (the drop) and the horizontal change is +4 (the run). Therefore:

$$\text{Slope} = \frac{\text{vertical change}}{\text{horizontal change}} = \frac{-10}{+4} = -2\frac{1}{2} = -2.5$$

This slope is negative because ticket price and attendance have an inverse or negative relationship.

Note that on the horizontal axis attendance is stated in thousands of people. So the slope of −10/+4 or −2.5 means that lowering the price by $10 will increase attendance by 4000 people. This is the same as saying that a $2.50 price reduction will increase attendance by 1000 people.

SLOPES AND MEASUREMENT UNITS

The slope of a line will be affected by the choice of units for either variable. If, in our ticket price illustration, we had chosen to measure attendance in individual people, our horizontal change would have been 4000 and the slope would have been

$$\text{Slope} = \frac{-10}{+4000} = \frac{-1}{+400} = -.0025$$

The slope depends on the units by which variables are measured.

SLOPES AND MARGINAL ANALYSIS

Recall that economics largely deals with changes from the status quo. The concept of slope is important in economics because it reflects marginal changes—those involving one more (or one less) unit. For example, in Figure A1-1 the .5 slope shows that $.50 of extra or marginal consumption is associated with each $1 change in income. In this example, people collectively will consume $.50 of any $1 increase in their incomes and reduce their consumption by $.50 for each $1 decline in income.

INFINITE AND ZERO SLOPES

Many variables are unrelated or independent of one another. For example, the quantity of digital cameras purchased is not related to the price of bananas. In Figure A1-3(a) we represent the price of bananas on the vertical axis and the quantity of digital cameras demanded on the

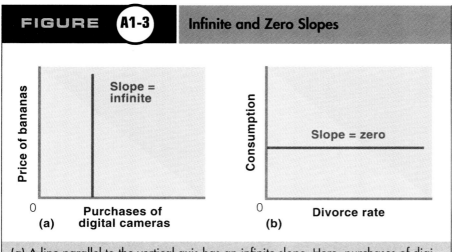

FIGURE A1-3   Infinite and Zero Slopes

(a) A line parallel to the vertical axis has an infinite slope. Here, purchases of digital cameras remain the same no matter what happens to the price of bananas.
(b) A line parallel to the horizontal axis has a slope of zero. Here, consumption remains the same no matter what happens to the divorce rate. In both (a) and (b), the two variables are totally unrelated to one another.

horizontal axis. The graph of their relationship is the line parallel to the vertical axis, indicating that the same quantity of cameras is purchased no matter what the price of bananas. The slope of such a line is *infinite*.

Similarly, aggregate consumption is completely unrelated to the nation's divorce rate. In Figure A1-3(b) we put consumption on the vertical axis and the divorce rate on the horizontal axis. The line parallel to the horizontal axis represents this lack of relatedness. This line has a slope of *zero*.

Vertical Intercept

A line can be located on a graph (without plotting points) if we know its slope and its vertical intercept. The **vertical intercept** of a line is the point where the line meets the vertical axis.

vertical intercept
The point at which a line meets the vertical axis of a graph.

In Figure A1-1 the intercept is $50. This intercept means that if current income were zero, consumers would still spend $50. They might do this through borrowing or by selling some of their assets. Similarly, the $50 vertical intercept in Figure A1-2 shows that at a $50 ticket price, IU's basketball team would be playing in an empty arena.

Equation of a Linear Relationship

If we know the vertical intercept and slope, we can describe a line succinctly in equation form. In its general form, the equation of a straight line is

$$y = a + bx$$

where y = dependent variable

a = vertical intercept

b = slope of line

x = independent variable

For our income-consumption example, if C represents consumption (the dependent variable) and Y represents income (the independent variable), we can write $C = a + bY$. By substituting the known values of the intercept and the slope, we get

$$C = 50 + .5Y$$

This equation also allows us to determine the amount of consumption C at any specific level of income. You should use it to confirm that at the $250 income level, consumption is $175.

When economists reverse mathematical convention by putting the independent variable on the vertical axis and the dependent variable on the horizontal axis, then y stands for the independent variable, rather than the dependent variable in the general form. We noted previously that this case is relevant for our IU ticket price-attendance data. If P represents the ticket price (independent variable) and Q represents attendance (dependent variable), their relationship is given by

$$P = 50 - 2.5Q$$

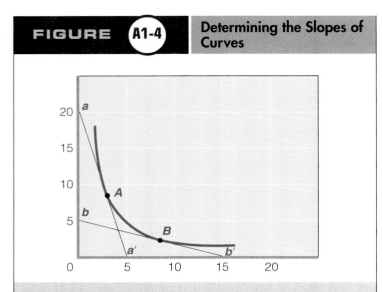

FIGURE A1-4 **Determining the Slopes of Curves**

The slope of a non-linear curve changes from point to point on the curve. The slope at any point (say, B) can be determined by drawing a straight line that is tangent to that point (line bb) and calculating the slope of that line.

where the vertical intercept is 50 and the negative slope is –2½ or –2.5. Knowing the value of *P* lets us solve for *Q*, our dependent variable. You should use this equation to predict IU ticket sales when the ticket price is $15. *(Key Appendix Question 3)*

Slope of a Non-Linear Curve

We now move from the simple world of linear relationships (straight lines) to the more complex world of non-linear relationships. The slope of a straight line is the same at all its points. The slope of a line representing a non-linear relationship changes from one point to another. Such lines are referred to as *curves*. (It is also permissible to refer to a straight line as a "curve.")

Consider the downward-sloping curve in Figure A1-4. Its slope is negative throughout, but the curve flattens as we move down along it. Thus, its slope constantly changes; the curve has a different slope at each point.

To measure the slope at a specific point, we draw a straight line tangent to the curve at that point. A line is *tangent* at a point if it touches, but does not intersect, the curve at that point. Thus line *aa'* is tangent to the curve in Figure A1-4 at point A. The slope of the curve at that point is equal to the slope of the tangent line. Specifically, the total vertical change (drop) in the tangent line *aa'* is –20 and the total horizontal change (run) is +5. Because the slope of the tangent line *aa'* is –20/+5, or –4, the slope of the curve at point A is also –4.

Line *bb'* in Figure A1-4 is tangent to the curve at point B. Following the same procedure, we find the slope at B to be –5/+15, or –¹⁄₃. Thus, in this flatter part of the curve, the slope is less negative. *(Key Appendix Question 7)*

APPENDIX SUMMARY

A1.1 GRAPHS AND THEIR MEANING

- Graphs are a convenient and revealing way to represent economic relationships.

- Two variables are positively or directly related when their values change in the same direction. The line (curve) representing two directly related variables slopes upward.

- Two variables are negatively or inversely related when their values change in opposite directions. The curve representing two inversely related variables slopes downward.

- The value of the dependent variable (the "effect") is determined by the value of the independent variable (the "cause").

- When the "other factors" that might affect a two-variable relationship are allowed to change, the graph of the relationship will likely shift to a new location.

- The slope of a straight line is the ratio of the vertical change to the horizontal change between any two points. The slope of an upward-sloping line is positive; the slope of a downward-sloping line is negative.

- The slope of a line or curve depends on the units used in measuring the variables. It is especially relevant for economics because it measures marginal changes.

- The slope of a horizontal line is zero; the slope of a vertical line is infinite.

- The vertical intercept and slope of a line determine its location; they are used in expressing the line—and the relationship between the two variables—as an equation.

- The slope of a curve at any point is determined by calculating the slope of a straight-line tangent to the curve at that point.

APPENDIX TERMS AND CONCEPTS

horizontal axis, p. 17
vertical axis, p. 17
direct relationship, p. 18

inverse relationship, p. 18
independent variable, p. 18
dependent variable, p. 18

slope of a line, p. 20
vertical intercept, p. 21

APPENDIX STUDY QUESTIONS

1. Briefly explain the use of graphs as a way to represent economic relationships. What is an inverse relationship? How does it graph? What is a direct relationship? How does it graph? Graph and explain the relationships you would expect to find between (a) the number of centimetres of rainfall per month and the sale of umbrellas, (b) the amount of tuition and the level of enrolment at a college or university, and (c) the popularity of a music artist and the price of her concert tickets.

   In each case cite and explain how variables other than those specifically mentioned might upset the expected relationship. Is your graph in part (b), above, consistent with the fact that, historically, enrolments and tuition have both increased? If not, explain any difference.

2. **KEY APPENDIX QUESTION**   Indicate how each of the following might affect the data shown in Figure A1-2 of this appendix:

   a. IU's athletic director schedules higher-quality opponents.

   b. A National Basketball Association (NBA) team locates in the city where IU also plays.

   c. IU contracts to have all its home games televised.

3. **KEY APPENDIX QUESTION**   The following table contains data on the relationship between saving and income. Rearrange these data into a meaningful order and graph them on the accompanying grid. What is the slope of the line? The vertical intercept? Interpret the meaning of both the slope and the intercept. Write the equation that represents this line. What would you predict saving to be at the $12,500 level of income?

Income (per year)	Saving (per year)
$15,000	$1,000
0	−500
10,000	500
5,000	0
20,000	1,500

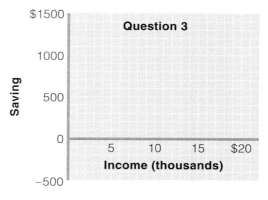

4. Construct a table from the data shown on the graph below. Which is the dependent variable and which the independent variable? Summarize the data in equation form.

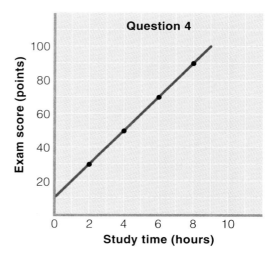

5. Suppose that when the interest rate on loans is 16 percent, businesses find it unprofitable to invest in machinery and equipment. However, when the interest rate is 14 percent, $5 billion worth of investment is profitable. At 12 percent interest, a total of $10 billion of investment is profitable. Similarly, total investment increases by $5 billion for each successive 2-percentage-point decline in the interest rate. Describe the relevant relationship between the interest rate and investment in

words, in a table, graphically, and as an equation. Put the interest rate on the vertical axis and investment on the horizontal axis. In your equation use the form $i = a - bI$, where i is the interest rate, a is the vertical intercept, $-b$ is the slope of the line (which is negative), and I is the level of investment. Comment on the advantages and disadvantages of the verbal, tabular, graphical, and equation forms of description.

6. Suppose that $C = a + bY$, where C = consumption, a = consumption at zero income, b = slope, and Y = income.

   a. Are C and Y positively related or are they negatively related?

   b. If graphed, would the curve for this equation slope upward or slope downward?

   c. Are the variables C and Y inversely related or directly related?

   d. What is the value of C if $a = 10$, $b = .50$, and $Y = 200$?

   e. What is the value of Y if $C = 100$, $a = 10$, and $b = .25$?

7. **KEY APPENDIX QUESTION**   The accompanying graph shows curve XX' and tangents at points A, B, and C. Calculate the slope of the curve at these three points.

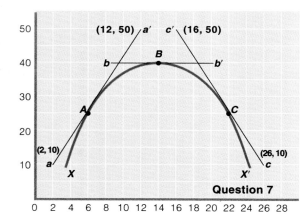

Question 7

8. In the accompanying graph, is the slope of curve AA' positive or negative? Does the slope increase or decrease as we move along the curve from A to A'? Answer the same two questions for curve BB'.

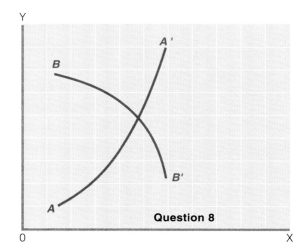

Question 8

2 Chapter

The Economic Problem
Scarcity, Wants, and Choices

You make decisions every day that capture the essence of economics. Suppose you have $40 and are deciding how to spend it. Should you buy a new pair of jeans? Two or three compact discs? A ticket for a concert?

Should you forgo work while you are attending college or university and concentrate solely on your coursework and grades? Is that an option for you, given the rising cost of post-secondary education? If you decide to work, should it be full-time or part-time? Should you work on campus at lower pay or off campus at higher pay? What are the implications for your course grades if you decide to take a job?

Money and time are both scarce, and making decisions in the context of scarcity always means there are costs. If you choose the jeans, the cost is the forgone CDs or concert. If you work full-time, the cost might be greater stress, poorer performance in your classes, or an extra year or two in school.

This chapter examines the fundamentals of economics—scarcity, wants and choices. We first examine the *economic problem,* focusing closely on *wants* and *resources.* Next, we develop two economic models: (1) a *production possibilities* model that incorporates and illustrates several key ideas, and (2) a simple *circular flow model* that identifies the major decision makers and markets in the economy.

2.1   The Foundation of Economics

economic problem
Choices are necessary because society's material wants for goods and services are unlimited but the resources available to satisfy these wants are limited (scarce).

Two fundamental facts together create the **economic problem** and provide a foundation for economics:

- Society's wants are virtually unlimited.
- The resources for producing the goods and services to satisfy society's wants are limited (or scarce).

All that follows depends directly on these two facts.

Unlimited Wants

By "wants" we mean the desires of consumers to obtain and use various goods and services that provide utility—that is, pleasure or satisfaction. These wants extend over a wide range of products, from *necessities* (food, shelter, and clothing) to *luxuries* (perfumes, yachts, race cars). Some wants—basic food, clothing, and shelter—have biological roots. Other wants—for example, the specific kinds of food, clothing, and shelter we seek—are rooted in the conventions and customs of society.

Over time, wants change and tend to multiply, fuelled by new products. Not long ago, we did not want personal computers, Internet service, digital cameras, or cellphones because they simply did not exist. Also, the satisfaction of certain wants tends to trigger others: The acquisition of a Focus or Civic has been known to whet the appetite for a Ferrari or a BMW.

Services, as well as products, satisfy our wants. Car repair work, the removal of an inflamed appendix, legal and accounting advice, and haircuts all satisfy human wants. Actually, we buy many goods, such as automobiles and washing machines, for the services they render. The differences between goods and services are often smaller than they appear to be.

Businesses and units of government add to the wants of consumers. Businesses want factories, machinery, trucks, warehouses, and phone systems to help them achieve their production goals. Government, reflecting the collective wants of its citizens or goals of its own, seeks highways, schools, and hospitals.

All these wants are *insatiable,* or *unlimited,* meaning that our desires for goods and services cannot be completely satisfied. Our desires for a *particular* good or service can be satisfied; over a short period of time we can surely get enough toothpaste or pasta. And one appendectomy is plenty. But goods and services *in general* are another story. We do not, and presumably cannot, get enough. Suppose all members of society were asked to list the goods and services they would buy if they had unlimited income. That list would probably never end.

In short, individuals and institutions have innumerable unfilled wants. *The objective of all economic activity is to fulfill wants.*

Scarce Resources

economic resources
The land, labour, capital, and entrepreneurial ability that are used in the production of goods and services.

The second fundamental fact is that *resources needed to produce the goods and services people want are limited or scarce.* By **economic resources** we mean all natural, human, and manufactured resources that go into the production of goods and services. That includes all the factory and farm buildings and all the equipment, tools, and machinery used to produce manufactured goods and agricultural products; all transportation and communication facilities; all types of labour; and land and mineral resources. Economists classify all these resources as either *property* resources—land and raw materials and capital—or *human* resources—labour and entrepreneurial ability.

RESOURCE CATEGORIES

Resources used in the production of goods and services can be divided into four categories.

land
Natural resources ("free gifts of nature") used to produce goods and services.

Land   **Land** means much more to the economist than it does to most people. Land includes all natural resources—all "gifts of nature"—used in the production process, such as arable land, forests, mineral and oil deposits, and water resources.

capital
Human-made resources (buildings, machinery, and equipment) used to produce goods and services.

Capital   **Capital** (or *capital goods* or *investment goods*) includes all manufactured aids used in producing consumer goods and services—that is, all tools, machinery, equipment, factory, storage, transportation, and distribution facilities. The process of producing and purchasing capital goods is known as **investment**.

investment
Spending for the production and accumulation of capital and additions to inventories.

Capital goods differ from consumer goods in that *consumer goods* satisfy wants directly, but capital goods do so indirectly by aiding the production of consumer goods. Note that the term "capital" as used by economists does *not* refer to money, but to *real capital*—tools, machinery, and other productive equipment. Money produces nothing; it is *not* an economic resource. So-called "money capital" or "financial capital" is simply a means for purchasing real capital.

labour
The physical and mental talents and efforts of people used to produce goods and services.

Labour   **Labour** is a broad term for all the physical and mental talents of individuals usable in producing goods and services that individuals want. The services of a logger, retail clerk, machinist, professor, professional football player, and nuclear physicist all fall under the general heading "labour."

entrepreneurial ability
The human talents that combine the other resources to produce a product, make non-routine decisions, innovate, and bear risks.

Entrepreneurial Ability   Finally, there is the special human resource, distinct from labour, that we label **entrepreneurial ability**. The entrepreneur performs several functions:

- The entrepreneur *takes the initiative* in combining the resources of land, capital, and labour to produce a good or a service in what is hoped will be a successful business venture.

- The entrepreneur *makes the non-routine policy decisions* that set the course of a business enterprise.

- The entrepreneur is an *innovator*—the one who commercializes new products or new production techniques, or creates new forms of business organization.

- The entrepreneur is a *risk bearer*. The entrepreneur in a market system has no guarantee of profit. The reward for the entrepreneur's time, efforts, and abilities may be profits *or* losses.

Because these four productive resources—land, labour, capital, and entrepreneurial ability—are combined to *produce* goods and services, they are called the **factors of production**. *(Key Question 4)*

factors of production
Economic resources: land, capital, labour, and entrepreneurial ability.

RESOURCE PAYMENTS

The income received from supplying raw materials and capital equipment (the property resources) is called *rental income* and *interest income*, respectively. The income accruing to those who supply labour is called *wages*, which includes salaries and all wage and salary supplements such as bonuses, commissions, and royalties. Entrepreneurial income is called *profits*, which may be negative—that is, losses.

RELATIVE SCARCITY

The four factors of production, or *inputs*, have one significant characteristic in common: *They are limited in supply.* Our planet contains only finite amounts of arable land, mineral deposits, capital equipment, and labour. Their limited supply, or scarcity, puts a limit on the quantity of goods and services that a society can produce.

2.2 Efficiency: Getting the Most from Available Resources

The economic problem is at the heart of the definition of economics stated in Chapter 1: *Economics is the social science concerned with the efficient use of scarce resources to attain the maximum fulfillment of society's unlimited wants.* Economics is concerned with "doing the best with what we have." Society wants to use its limited resources efficiently; it desires to produce as many goods and services as possible from its available resources, thereby maximizing total satisfaction.

Full Employment: Using Available Resources

full employment
Use of all available resources to produce want-satisfying goods and services.

To get the most from its limited resources, a society must achieve both full employment and full production. By **full employment** we mean the use of all available resources. No workers should be out of work if they are willing and able to work. Nor should capital equipment or arable land sit idle. But note that we say all *available* resources should be employed. Each society has certain customs and practices that determine what resources are available for employment and what resources are not. For example, in most countries legislation and custom provide that children and the very aged should not be employed. And we should conserve some resources—the fishing stocks off the east and west coasts, and Canada's immense forests, for instance—for use by future generations.

Full Production: Using Resources Efficiently

full production
Employment of available resources so that the maximum amount of goods and services is produced.

productive efficiency
The production of a good in the least costly way.

allocative efficiency
The distribution of resources among firms and industries to produce the goods most wanted by society (consumers).

The employment of all available resources is not enough to achieve efficiency. We also need to achieve full production. **Full production** occurs when all employed resources are used so that they provide the maximum possible output so as to satisfy as many of our material wants as possible. If we fail to realize full production, our resources are *underemployed*.

Full production implies two kinds of efficiency—productive and allocative efficiency. **Productive efficiency** is the production of *goods and services in the least costly way*. When we produce, say, compact discs at the lowest achievable unit cost, we are using the smallest amount of resources to produce CDs, meaning more resources are available to produce other desired products. Suppose society has only $100 worth of resources available. If we can produce a CD for only $5 of those resources, then $95 will be available to produce other goods. This is preferable to producing the CD for $10 and having only $90 of resources available for alternative uses.

In contrast, **allocative efficiency** is the production of *goods and services most wanted by society*. For example, society wants resources allocated to compact discs and MP3 players, not to 45 rpm records. We want personal computers (PCs), not manual typewriters. Furthermore, we do not want to devote *all* our resources to producing CDs and PCs; we want to assign some of them to producing other goods that individuals and businesses desire, such as automobiles and office buildings. Allocative efficiency is achieved when an economy produces the "right" mix of goods and services, meaning the combination of goods and services it wants the most. *(Key Question 5)*

Production Possibilities Table

Because resources are scarce, a full-employment, full-production economy cannot have an unlimited output of goods and services. Consequently, society must choose which goods and services to produce and which to forgo. The necessity and consequences of those choices can best be understood through a *production possibilities model*. We examine the model first as a table, then as a graph.

ASSUMPTIONS

We begin our discussion of the production possibilities model with simplifying assumptions:

- *Full employment and productive efficiency*   The economy is employing all its available resources (full employment) and is producing goods and services at least cost (productive efficiency).

- *Fixed resources*   The available supplies of the factors of production are fixed in both quantity and quality, although they can be reallocated, within limits, among different uses; for example, land can be used either for factory sites or for food production.

- *Fixed technology*   The state of technology does not change during our analysis. We are looking at an economy at a particular point in time or over a very short period of time.

- *Two goods*   The economy produces only two goods: pizzas and industrial machines. Pizzas symbolize **consumer goods**, products that satisfy our wants *directly*; industrial machines symbolize **capital goods**, products that satisfy our wants *indirectly* by making possible more efficient production of consumer goods.

THE NEED FOR CHOICE

Given our assumptions, we see that society must choose among alternatives. Fixed resources mean limited outputs of pizza and machines. And since all available factors of production are fully employed, to increase the production of machines we must shift resources away from the production of pizzas. The reverse is also true: To increase the production of pizzas, we must shift resources away from the production of machines. There is no such thing as a free pizza. This, recall, is the essence of the economic problem.

A **production possibilities table** lists the different combinations of two products that can be produced with a specific set of resources (and with full employment *and* productive efficiency). Table 2-1 is such a table for a pizza-machine economy; the data are, of course, hypothetical. At alternative A, this economy devotes all its available resources to the production of machines (capital goods); at alternative E, all resources are used in pizza production (consumer goods). More typically, an economy produces both capital goods and consumer goods, as in B, C, and D. As we move from alternative A to E, we increase the production of pizza at the expense of machine production.

In producing more pizzas, society increases the current satisfaction of its wants. But there is a cost: more pizzas mean fewer machines. This shift of resources to consumer goods catches up with

consumer goods
Products and services that satisfy human wants directly.

capital goods
Goods that do not directly satisfy human wants.

production possibilities table
A table showing the different combinations of two products that can be produced with a specific set of resources in a full-employment, full-production economy.

society over time as the stock of capital goods dwindles, reducing the potential for greater future production. By moving toward alternative E, society chooses "more now" at the expense of "much more later."

By moving toward A, society chooses to forgo current consumption, freeing up resources that can be used to increase the production of capital goods. By building up its stock of capital, society will have greater future production and, therefore, greater future consumption. By moving toward A, society is choosing "more later" at the cost of "less now."

Generalization: *At any point in time, an economy achieving full employment and productive efficiency must sacrifice some of one good to obtain more of another good.*

TABLE 2-1 — Production Possibilities of Pizzas and Machines with Full Employment and Productive Efficiency					
PRODUCTION ALTERNATIVES					
Type of Product	**A**	**B**	**C**	**D**	**E**
Pizzas (in hundred thousands)	0	1	2	3	4
Machines (in thousands)	10	9	7	4	0

Production Possibilities Curve

The data presented in a production possibilities table can also be shown graphically. We use a simple two-dimensional graph, representing the output of capital goods (here, machines) on the vertical axis and the output of consumer goods (here, pizzas) on the horizontal axis, as shown in **Figure 2-1 (Key Graph)**. Following the procedure given in the appendix to Chapter 1, we can graph a **production possibilities curve**.

production possibilities curve
A curve showing the different combinations of goods and services that can be produced in a full-employment, full-production economy where the available supplies of resources and technology are fixed.

Each point on the production possibilities curve represents some maximum output of the two products. The curve is a production *frontier* because it shows the limit of attainable outputs. To obtain the various combinations of pizza and machines *on* the production possibilities curve, society must achieve both full employment and productive efficiency. Points lying *inside* the curve are also attainable, but they are inefficient and therefore are not as desirable as points on the curve. Points inside the curve imply that the economy could have more of both machines and pizzas if it achieved full employment and productive efficiency. Points lying *outside* the production possibilities curve, like point *W*, represent a greater output than the output at any point on the curve. Points outside the production possibility curve, however, are unattainable with current supplies of resources and technology.

Law of Increasing Opportunity Cost

Because resources are scarce relative to the virtually unlimited wants they can be used to satisfy, people must choose among alternatives. More pizzas mean fewer machines. The amount of other products that must be sacrificed to obtain one unit of a specific good is called the **opportunity cost** of that good (see the Consider This box on page 32). In our case, the number of machines that must be given up to get another unit of pizza is the *opportunity cost*, or simply the *cost*, of that unit of pizza.

opportunity cost
The amount of other products that must be forgone or sacrificed to produce a unit of a product.

In moving from alternative A to alternative B in Table 2-1, the cost of 1 additional unit of pizzas is 1 less unit of machines. But as we pursue the concept of cost through the additional production possibilities—B to C, C to D, and D to E—an important economic principle is revealed: The opportunity cost of each additional unit of pizza increases. When we move from A to B, just 1 unit of machines is sacrificed for 1 more unit of pizza; but in going from B to C we sacrifice 2 additional units of machines for 1 more unit of pizza; then 3 more of machines for 1 more of pizza; and finally 4 for 1. Conversely, confirm that as we move from E to A, the cost of an additional machine is ¼, ⅓, ½, and 1 unit of pizza, respectively, for the four successive moves.

Note two points about these opportunity costs:

• Here opportunity costs are being measured in *real* terms, that is, in actual goods rather than in money terms.

Key Graph

FIGURE 2-1 The Production Possibilities Curve

Each point *on* the production possibilities curve represents some maximum combination of two products that can be produced if full employment and full production are achieved. When operating on the curve, more machines means fewer pizzas, and vice versa. Limited resources and a fixed technology make any combination of machines and pizzas lying outside the curve (such as at *W*) unattainable. Points inside the curve are attainable, but they indicate that full employment and productive efficiency are not being realized.

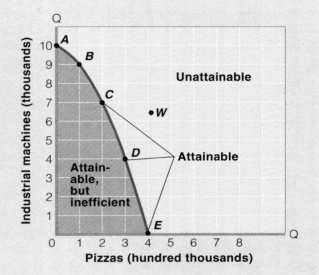

PRODUCTION ALTERNATIVES

Type of Product	A	B	C	D	E
Pizzas (in hundred thousands)	0	1	2	3	4
Machines (in thousands)	10	9	7	4	0

Quick Quiz

1. Production possibilities curve *ABCDE* is bowed out from the origin (concave to the origin) because:
   a. the marginal benefit of pizzas declines as more pizzas are consumed.
   b. the curve gets steeper as we move from *E* to *A*.
   c. it reflects the law of increasing opportunity costs.
   d. resources are scarce.

2. The marginal opportunity cost of the second unit of pizzas is:
   a. 2 units of machines.
   b. 3 units of machines.
   c. 7 units of machines.
   d. 9 units of machines.

3. The total opportunity cost of 7 units of machines is:
   a. 1 unit of pizzas.
   b. 2 units of pizzas.
   c. 3 units of pizzas.
   d. 4 units of pizzas.

4. All points on this production possibilities curve necessarily represent:
   a. allocative efficiency.
   b. less than full use of resources.
   c. unattainable levels of output.
   d. productive efficiency.

ANSWERS: 1. c; 2. a; 3. b; 4. d

Consider This

Opportunity Cost

The concept of opportunity cost can be illustrated through the eyes of a small child. Suppose that a young girl named Amber receives a $30 gift certificate from her grandparents to be used at the Hudson's Bay Company. The grandparents take the girl to the store, where she spots several toys she would like—all priced above $30. After gaining a sense of what is affordable, Amber narrows her focus to small stuffed animals ($10 each) and picture books ($5 each).

The grandparents tell Amber that she can buy three stuffed animals, six books, or some limited combinations of the two items. She initially settles on one stuffed animal at $10 and four picture books at $5 each. The grandparents assure her that this selection works; it will exactly use up the $30 certificate. Amber takes the goods to the checkout counter.

But while waiting to pay, she changes her mind. She decides she wants another stuffed animal because they are so cute. What should she do? The grandparents tell her to go pick out a second stuffed animal and then return two of her four books to the shelf. She makes the exchange, ending up with two stuffed animals at $10 each and two picture books at $5 each.

From an adult's perspective, the second stuffed animal cost $10. But in the eyes of the child, *it cost two picture books*. To get the second stuffed animal, Amber had to give up two books. That sacrifice was the *opportunity cost* of her last-minute decision. Amber's way of looking at cost is one of the fundamental ideas in economics.

Question: List some of the opportunity costs of going to a party on a Friday night.

- We are discussing *marginal* (meaning "extra") opportunity costs, rather than cumulative or total opportunity costs. For example, the marginal opportunity cost of the third unit of pizza in Table 2-1 is 3 units of machines (= 7 − 4). But the *total* opportunity cost of 3 units of pizza is 6 units of machines (= 1 unit of machines for the first unit of pizza *plus* 2 units of machines for the second unit of pizza *plus* 3 units of machines for the third unit of pizza).

law of increasing opportunity costs
As the production of a good increases, the opportunity cost of producing an additional unit rises.

Our example illustrates the **law of increasing opportunity costs**: The more of a product that is produced, the greater is its opportunity cost.

SHAPE OF THE CURVE

The law of increasing opportunity costs is reflected in the shape of the production possibilities curve: The curve is bowed out from the origin of the graph. Figure 2-1 shows that when the economy moves from *A* to *E*, successively larger numbers of machines (1, 2, 3, and 4) are given up to acquire equal increments of pizza (1, 1, 1, and 1). This is shown in the slope of the production possibilities curve, which becomes steeper as we move from *A* to *E*. A curve that gets steeper as we move down it is "concave to the origin."

ECONOMIC RATIONALE

The economic rationale for the law of increasing opportunity costs is that *resources are not completely adaptable to alternative uses*. Many resources are better at producing one good than at producing others. Fertile farmland is highly suited to producing the ingredients needed to make pizzas, and land rich in mineral deposits is highly suited to producing the materials needed to make machines. As we step up pizza production, resources that are less and less adaptable to making pizzas must be "pushed" into pizza production. Thus, it will take more and more of such resources, and thus greater sacrifices of machines, to achieve each increase of 1 unit in the production of pizzas. This lack of perfect flexibility, or interchangeability, on the part of resources is the cause of increasing opportunity costs. *(Key Question 6)*

Allocative Efficiency Revisited

So far, we have assumed full employment and productive efficiency, both of which are necessary to realize *any point* on an economy's production possibilities curve. We now turn to allocative efficiency, which requires that the economy produce at the most valued, or *optimal*, point on the production possibilities curve. What specific quantities of resources should be allocated to pizzas and what specific quantities to machines in order to maximize satisfaction?

Our discussion of the *economic perspective* in Chapter 1 helps us answer this question. Recall that economic decisions compare marginal benefits and marginal costs. Any economic activity—for example, production or consumption—should be expanded as long as marginal benefit exceeds marginal cost and should be reduced if marginal cost exceeds marginal benefit. The optimal amount of the activity occurs where MB = MC.

Consider pizzas. We already know from the law of increasing opportunity costs that the marginal cost (MC) of additional units of pizzas will rise as more units are produced. This can be shown by an upward-sloping MC curve, as in Figure 2-2. We also know that we get marginal benefits (MB) from additional units of pizzas. However, although material wants in the aggregate are insatiable, studies reveal that the consumption of the second unit of a particular product or service yields less additional benefit to a person than the first. And a third provides even less MB than the second. The same is true for society as a whole. We therefore can portray the marginal benefits from pizzas with a downward-sloping MB curve, as in Figure 2-2. Although total benefits rise when society consumes more pizzas, marginal benefits decline.

The optimal quantity of pizza production is indicated by the intersection of the MB and MC curves: 200,000 units in Figure 2-2. Why is this the optimal quantity? If only 100,000 pizzas were produced, the marginal benefit of pizzas would exceed its marginal cost. In money terms, MB might be $15, while MC is only $5. This means that society is *underallocating* resources to pizza production and that more of it should be produced.

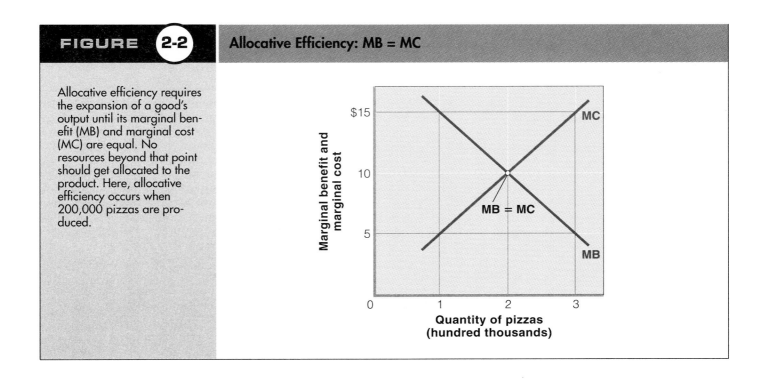

FIGURE 2-2

Allocative Efficiency: MB = MC

Allocative efficiency requires the expansion of a good's output until its marginal benefit (MB) and marginal cost (MC) are equal. No resources beyond that point should get allocated to the product. Here, allocative efficiency occurs when 200,000 pizzas are produced.

How do we know? Because society values an additional pizza as being worth $15, but the alternative products that those resources could produce are worth only $5. Society benefits whenever it can gain something valued $15 by forgoing something valued only $5. Each additional pizza up to 200,000 would provide such a gain, indicating that allocative efficiency would be improved by that production. Allocative efficiency is achieved where MB = MC.

The production of 300,000 pizzas would represent an *overallocation* of resources to pizza production. Here the MC of pizzas is $15 and its MB is only $5. This means that 1 unit of pizza is worth only $5 to society, but the alternative products that those resources could otherwise produce are valued at $15. By producing 1 less unit, society loses a pizza worth $5. But by reallocating the freed resources, it gains other products worth $15. In Figure 2-2, net gains can be realized until pizza production has been reduced to 200,000.

Generalization: *Resources are being efficiently allocated to any product when the marginal benefit and marginal cost of its output are equal (MB = MC).* Suppose that by applying the above analysis to machines, we find their optimal (MB = MC) output is 7000. This would mean that alternative C on our production possibilities curve—200,000 pizzas and 7000 machines—would result in allocative efficiency for our hypothetical economy. *(Key Question 9)*

QUICK REVIEW

- The production possibilities curve illustrates four concepts: (a) *scarcity* of resources is implied by the area of unattainable combinations of output lying outside the production possibilities curve; (b) *choice* among outputs is reflected in the variety of attainable combinations of goods lying along the curve; (c) *opportunity cost* is illustrated by the downward slope of the curve; (d) the law of *increasing opportunity costs* is implied by the concavity of the curve.

- Full employment and productive efficiency must be realized in order for the economy to operate on its production possibilities curve.

- A comparison of marginal benefits and marginal costs is needed to determine allocative efficiency—the best or optimal output mix on the curve.

2.3   Unemployment, Growth, and The Future

Let's now discard the first three assumptions underlying the production possibilities curve and see what happens.

Unemployment and Productive Inefficiency

The first assumption was that our economy was achieving full employment and productive efficiency. Our analysis and conclusions change if some resources are idle (unemployment) or if least-cost production is not realized.

Graphically, we represent situations of unemployment or productive inefficiency by points *inside* the original production possibilities curve (reproduced in Figure 2-3). Point *U* is one such point. Here the economy is falling short of the various maximum combinations of pizzas and machines that could be produced. The arrows in Figure 2-3 indicate three possible paths back to full employment and least-cost production. A move toward full employment and productive efficiency would yield a greater output of one or both products.

A Growing Economy

Production and the Standard of Living

When we drop the assumptions that the quantity and quality of resources and technology are fixed, the production possibilities curve shifts positions—that is, the potential maximum output of the economy changes.

FIGURE 2-3 — Unemployment, Productive Inefficiency, and the Production Possibilities Curve

Any point inside the production possibilities curve, such as *U*, represents unemployment or a failure to achieve productive efficiency. The arrows indicate that, by realizing full employment and productive efficiency, the economy could operate on the curve. This means it could produce more of one or both products than it is producing at point *U*.

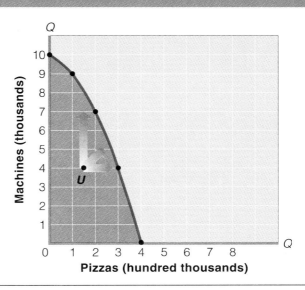

INCREASES IN FACTOR SUPPLIES

Although factor supplies are fixed at any specific moment, they can and do change over time. For example, a nation's growing population will increase the supplies of labour and entrepreneurial ability. Also, labour quality usually improves over time through education and training. Historically, the economy's stock of capital has increased at a significant, though unsteady, rate. And although we are depleting some of our energy and mineral resources, new sources are being discovered. The development of irrigation programs, for example, adds to the supply of arable land.

The net result of these increased supplies of the factors of production is the potential to produce more of both pizzas and machines. Thus, 20 years from now, the production possibilities curve in Figure 2-4 may supersede the one shown in Figure 2-3. The greater abundance of factors of production will result in a greater potential output of one or both products at each alternative. Society will have achieved economic growth in the form of an expanded potential output.

ADVANCES IN TECHNOLOGY

Our second assumption is that we have constant, unchanging technology. In reality, technology has progressed dramatically over time. An advancing technology brings both new and better goods *and* improved ways of producing them. For now, let's think of technological advance as being only improvements in the methods of production, for example, the introduction of computerized systems to manage inventories and schedule production. These advances alter our previous discussion of the economic problem by improving productive efficiency, thereby allowing society to produce more goods with fixed resources. As with increases in resource supplies, technological advances make possible the production of more machines *and* more pizzas.

Thus, when either supplies of factors of production increase or an improvement in technology occurs, the production possibilities curve in Figure 2-3 shifts outward and to the right, as illustrated by curve A′, B′, C′, D′, E′ in Figure 2-4. Such an outward shift of the production possibilities curve represents **economic growth**: *the ability to produce a larger total output.* This growth is the result of (1) increases in supplies of factors of production, (2) improvements in factor quality, and (3) technological advances.

Advancing technology brings both new and better goods and improved ways of producing them.

economic growth
An outward shift in the production possibilities curve that results from an increase in factor supplies or quality or an improvement in technology.

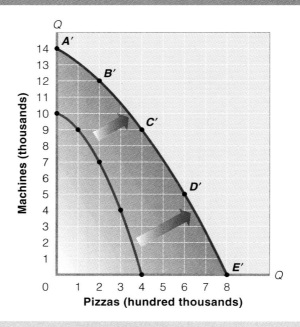

FIGURE 2-4	Economic Growth and the Production Possibilities Curve

PRODUCTION ALTERNATIVES

Type of product	A'	B'	C'	D'	E'
Pizzas (in hundred thousands)	0	2	4	6	8
Machines (in thousands)	14	12	9	5	0

The increase in supplies of resources, the improvements in resource quality, and the technological advances that occur in a dynamic economy move the production possibilities curve outward and to the right, allowing the economy to have larger quantities of both types of goods.

The consequence of growth is that our full-employment economy can enjoy a greater output of both machines and pizzas. *While a static, no-growth economy must sacrifice some of one product in order to get more of another, a dynamic, growing economy can have larger quantities of both products.*

Economic growth does not ordinarily mean proportionate increases in a nation's capacity to produce all its products. Note in Figure 2-4 that, at the maximums, the economy can produce twice as many pizzas as before but only 40 percent more machines. To reinforce your understanding of this concept, sketch in two new production possibilities curves: one showing the situation where a better technique for producing machines has been developed while the technology for producing pizzas is unchanged, and the other illustrating an improved technology for pizzas while the technology for producing machines remains constant.

PRESENT CHOICES AND FUTURE POSSIBILITIES

An economy's current position on its production possibilities curve is a basic determinant of the future location of that curve. Let's designate the two axes of the production possibilities curve as *goods for the future* and *goods for the present,* as in Figure 2-5. Goods for the future are such things as capital goods, research and education, and preventive medicine. (Global Perspective 2.1 shows expenditure on research and development in selected countries.) Goods for the future increase the quantity and quality of property resources, enlarge the stock of technological information, and improve the quality of human resources. As we have already seen, goods for the future, like industrial machines, are the ingredients of economic growth. Goods for the present are pure consumer goods, such as pizza, clothing, and soft drinks.

Now suppose there are two economies, Alta and Zorn, which are initially identical in every respect except one: Alta's current choice of positions on its production possibilities curve strongly favours

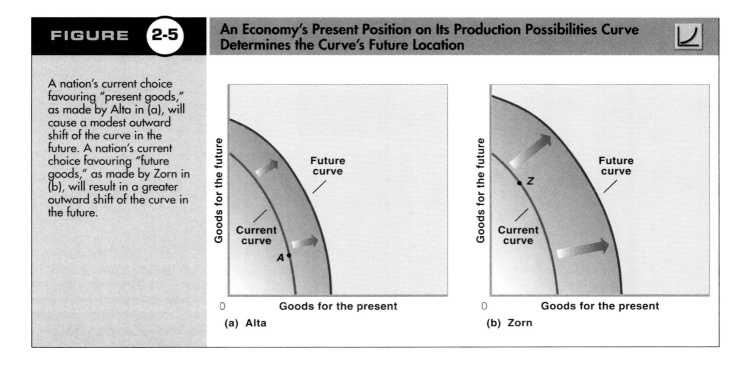

FIGURE 2-5

An Economy's Present Position on Its Production Possibilities Curve Determines the Curve's Future Location

A nation's current choice favouring "present goods," as made by Alta in (a), will cause a modest outward shift of the curve in the future. A nation's current choice favouring "future goods," as made by Zorn in (b), will result in a greater outward shift of the curve in the future.

present goods over future goods. Point *A* in Figure 2-5(a) indicates that choice. It is located quite far down the curve to the right, indicating a high priority for goods for the present, at the expense of fewer goods for the future. Zorn, in contrast, makes a current choice that stresses larger amounts of future goods and smaller amounts of present goods, as shown by point *Z* in Figure 2-5(b).

Other things equal, we can expect the future production possibilities curve of Zorn to be farther to the right than Alta's curve. By currently choosing an output more favourable to technological advances and to increases in the quantity and quality of resources, Zorn will achieve greater economic growth than Alta. In terms of capital goods, Zorn is choosing to make larger current additions to its "national factory"—to invest more of its current output—than Alta. The payoff from this choice for Zorn is more rapid growth—greater future production capacity. The opportunity cost is fewer consumer goods in the present for Zorn to enjoy.

Is Zorn's choice thus "better" than Alta's? It is impossible to say. The different outcomes reflect different preferences and priorities in the two countries. *(Key Questions 10 and 11)*

A Qualification: International Trade

Production possibilities analysis implies that a nation is limited to the combinations of output indicated by its production possibilities curve. *But we must modify this principle when international specialization and trade exist.*

You will see in later chapters that an economy can avoid, through international specialization and trade, the output limits imposed by its domestic production possibilities curve. *International specialization* means directing domestic resources to output that a nation is highly efficient at producing. *International trade* involves the exchange of these goods for goods produced abroad. Specialization and trade enable a nation to get more of a desired good at less sacrifice of some other good. For example, rather than sacrifice three machines to get a third unit of pizzas, as in Table 2-1, a nation might be able to obtain the third unit of pizzas by trading only two units of machines for it. Specialization and trade have the same effect as having more and better resources or discovering improved production techniques; both increase the quantities of capital and consumer goods available to society.

Global Perspective 2.1

Research and Development Spending, Selected Countries

Sweden leads the world on R&D expenditure. Canada spent just under 2 percent of GDP on R&D.

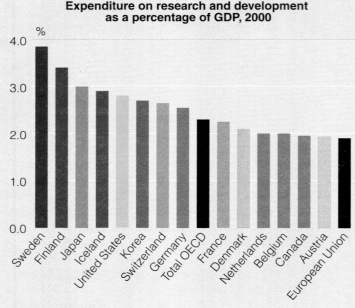

Expenditure on research and development as a percentage of GDP, 2000

Source: Organization for Economic Co-operation and Development (OECD)

QUICK REVIEW

- Unemployment and the failure to achieve productive efficiency cause an economy to operate at a point inside its production possibilities curve.

- Increases in resource supplies, improvements in resource quality, and technological advance cause economic growth, which is depicted as an outward shift of the production possibilities curve.

- Society's present choice of capital and consumer goods helps determine the future location of its production possibilities curve.

- International specialization and trade enable a nation to obtain more goods than its production possibilities curve indicates.

Examples and Applications

There are many possible applications and examples relating to the production possibilities model. We will discuss just a few of them.

UNEMPLOYMENT AND PRODUCTIVE INEFFICIENCY

In the depths of the Great Depression of the 1930s, Canada's economy operated well inside its production possibilities curve. At one point, 20 percent of Canadian workers were unemployed and almost one-third of Canadian production capacity was idle. Canada has suffered a number of much milder downturns since then, the latest occurring in 2001. In that year, unemployment increased, and the economy operated inside its production possibility curve.

Almost all nations have experienced widespread unemployment and unused production capacity at one time or another. Since 1995, for example, several nations including Argentina, Japan, Mexico, Germany, and South Korea have had economic downturns that placed them inside their production possibilities curves, at least temporarily.

Economies that experience substantial discrimination based on race, ethnicity, and gender do not achieve productive efficiency and thus operate inside their production possibilities curves. Because discrimination prevents those discriminated against from obtaining jobs that best use their skills, society has less output than otherwise. Eliminating discrimination would move such an economy from a point inside its production possibilities curve toward a point on its curve. Similarly, economies in which labour usage and production methods are based on custom, heredity, and caste, rather than on efficiency, operate well inside their production possibilities curves.

TRADEOFFS AND OPPORTUNITY COSTS

Many current controversies illustrate the tradeoffs and opportunity costs indicated in movements along a particular production possibilities curve. (Any two categories of "output" can be placed on the axes of production possibilities curves.) Should old-growth forests in British Columbia be used for logging or preserved as wilderness? If the land is used for logging, the opportunity cost is the forgone benefits of wilderness. If the land is used for wilderness, the opportunity cost is the lost value of the lumber that Canadian society forgoes.

Should Canadian society devote more resources to the health care system (doctors, medical equipment, and hospitals) or to education (teachers, books, and schools)? If Canada decides to devote more resources to the health care system, other things equal, the opportunity cost is forgone improvements in education. If more resources are allocated to education, the opportunity cost is the forgone benefits from an improved health care system.

SHIFTS IN PRODUCTION POSSIBILITIES CURVES

Canada has recently experienced a spurt of new technologies relating to computers, communications, and biotechnology. Technological advances have dropped the prices of computers and greatly enhanced their speed. Cellular phones and the Internet have increased communications capacity, enhancing production and improving the efficiency of markets. Advances in biotechnology, specifically genetic engineering, have resulted in important agricultural and medical discoveries. Many economists believe that these new technologies are so significant that they are contributing to faster-than-normal economic growth (faster rightward shifts of the production possibilities curve).

In some circumstances a nation's production possibilities curve can collapse inward. For example, in the late 1990s Yugoslavian forces began to "ethnically cleanse" Kosovo by driving out its Muslim residents. A decisive military response participated in by Canada and its allies eventually pushed the Yugoslavians out of Kosovo. The military action also devastated Yugoslavia's economy. Allied bombing inflicted great physical damage on Yugoslavia's production facilities and its system of roads, bridges, and communication. Consequently, Yugoslavia's production possibilities curve shifted inward.

2.4   Economic Systems

economic system
A particular set of institutional arrangements and a coordinating mechanism for producing goods and services.

Every society needs to develop an **economic system**—*a particular set of institutional arrangements and a coordinating mechanism*—to produce the goods and services its members desire. Economic systems differ as to (1) who owns the factors of production and (2) the method used to coordinate and direct economic activity. There are two general types of economic systems: the market system and the command system.

The Market System

market system
An economic system in which property resources are privately owned and markets and prices are used to direct and coordinate economic activities.

The private ownership of resources and the use of markets and prices to coordinate and direct economic activity characterize the **market system**, or *capitalism*. In that system each participant acts in his or her own self-interest; each individual or business seeks to maximize its satisfaction or profit through its own decisions regarding consumption or production. The system allows for the private ownership of capital, communicates through prices, and coordinates economic activity through *markets*—places where buyers and sellers come together. Goods and services are produced and resources are supplied by whoever is willing and able to do so. The result is competition among independently acting buyers and sellers of each product and resource. Thus, economic decision making is widely dispersed.

In *pure* capitalism—or *laissez-faire* capitalism—government's role is limited to protecting private property and establishing an environment appropriate to the operation of the market system. The term *laissez-faire* means "let it be," that is, keep government from interfering with the economy. The idea is that such interference will disturb the efficient working of the market system.

But in the capitalism practised in Canada and most other countries, government plays a substantial role in the economy. It not only provides the rules for economic activity but also promotes economic stability and growth, provides certain goods and services that would otherwise be underproduced or not produced at all, and modifies the distribution of income. The government, however, is not the dominant player in deciding what to produce, how to produce it, and who will get it. These decisions are determined by market forces.

The Command System

command system
An economic system in which most property resources are owned by the government and economic decisions are made by a central government body.

The alternative to the market system is the **command system**, also known as *socialism* or *communism*. In that system, government owns most property resources and economic decision making occurs through a central economic plan. A government central planning board determines nearly all the major decisions concerning the use of resources, the composition and distribution of output, and the organization of production. The government owns most of the business firms, which produce according to government directives. A central planning board determines production goals for each enterprise and specifies the amount of resources to be allocated to each enterprise so that it can reach its production goals. The division of output among the population is centrally decided, and capital goods are allocated among industries on the basis of the central planning board's long-term priorities.

A pure command economy would rely exclusively on a central plan to allocate the government-owned property resources. But, in reality, even the pre-eminent command economy—the Soviet Union—tolerated some private ownership and incorporated some markets before its demise in 1991. Recent reforms in Russia and most of the eastern European nations have to one degree or another transformed their command economies to market-oriented systems. China's reforms have not gone as far, but have reduced the reliance on central planning. Although there is still extensive government ownership of resources and capital in China, it has increasingly relied on free markets to organize and coordinate its economy. North Korea and Cuba are the last remaining examples of largely centrally planned economies.

2.5   The Circular Flow Model

Because nearly all of the major nations now use the market system, we need to gain a good understanding of how this system operates. Our goal in the remainder of this chapter is to identify the market economy's decision makers and major markets. In Chapter 3 we will explain how prices are established in individual markets. Then in Chapter 4 we will detail the characteristics of the market system and explain how it addresses the economic problem.

As shown in **Figure 2-6 (Key Graph)**, the market economy has two groups of decision makers: *households* and *businesses*. It also has two broad markets: the *factor market* and the *product market*.

Key Graph

FIGURE 2-6
The Circular Flow Diagram

Factors of production flow from households to businesses through the factor market and products flow from businesses to households through the product market. Opposite these real flows are monetary flows. Households receive income from businesses (their costs) through the factor market and businesses receive revenue from households (their expenditures) through the product market.

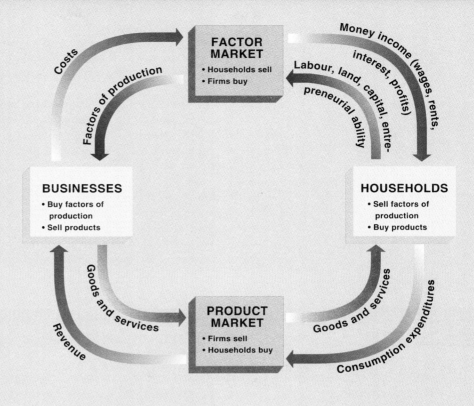

Quick Quiz

1. The factor market is where:
   a. households sell products and businesses buy products.
   b. businesses sell factors of production and households sell products.
   c. households sell factors of production and businesses buy factors of production (or the services of factors).
   d. businesses sell factors of production and households buy factors of production (or the services of factors).

2. Which of the following would be determined in the product market?
   a. a manager's salary
   b. the price of equipment used in a bottling plant
   c. the price of 80 hectares of farmland
   d. the price of a new pair of athletic shoes

3. In this circular flow diagram:
   a. money flows counterclockwise.
   b. resources flow counterclockwise.
   c. goods and services flow clockwise.
   d. households are on the selling side of the product market.

4. In this circular flow diagram:
   a. households spend income in the product market.
   b. firms sell resources to households.
   c. households receive income through the product market.
   d. households produce goods.

ANSWERS: 1. c; 2. d; 3. b; 4. a

factor market
A market in which households sell and firms buy factors of production.

The upper half of the diagram represents the **factor market**: *the place where factors of production are bought and sold.* In the factor market, households sell factors of production and businesses purchase them. Households (that is, people) own all factors of production, either directly as workers or entrepreneurs or indirectly through their ownership (through stocks) of business corporations. They sell their resources to businesses, which buy them because they are necessary for producing goods and services. The money that businesses pay for factors of production are costs to businesses but are flows of wage, rent, interest, and profit income to the households. Resources therefore flow from households to businesses, and money flows from businesses to households.

product market
A market in which products are sold by firms and bought by households.

Next consider the lower part of the diagram that represents the **product market**: *the place where goods and services produced by businesses are bought and sold.* In the product market, businesses combine the resources they have obtained to produce and sell goods and services. Households use the income they have received from the sale of resources to buy goods and services. The monetary flow of consumer spending on goods and services yields sales revenues for businesses.

circular flow model
The flow of resources from households to firms and of products from firms to households.

The **circular flow model** shows the interrelated web of decision making and economic activity involving businesses and households. Businesses and households are both buyers and sellers. Businesses buy resources and sell products. Households buy products and sell resources. As shown in Figure 2-6, there is a counterclockwise *real flow* of factors of production and finished goods and services, and a clockwise *money flow* of income and consumption expenditures.

THE LASTword   Women and Expanded Production Possibilities

A large increase in the number of employed women has shifted the Canadian production possibilities curve outward.

One of the more remarkable trends of the past half-century in Canada has been the substantial rise in the number of women working in the paid workforce. Today, nearly 70 percent of women in Canada work full-time or part-time in paid jobs, compared to only 31 percent in 1965. There are many reasons for this increase.

Women's Rising Wage Rates
Over recent years, women have greatly increased their productivity in the workplace, mostly by becoming better educated and professionally trained. As a result, they can earn higher wages. Because those higher wages have increased the opportunity

costs—the forgone wage earnings—of staying at home, women have substituted employment in the labour market for more "expensive" traditional home activities. This substitution has been particularly pronounced among married women.

Women's higher wages and longer hours away from home have produced creative reallocations of

time and purchasing patterns. Daycare services have partly replaced personal child care. Restaurants, take-home meals, and pizza delivery often substitute for traditional home cooking. Convenience stores and catalogue and Internet sales have proliferated, as have lawn-care and in-home cleaning services. Microwave ovens, dishwashers, automatic washers and dryers, and other household "capital goods" enhance domestic productivity.

Expanded Job Access Greater access to jobs is a second factor increasing the employment of women. Service industries—teaching, nursing, and clerical work, for instance—that traditionally have employed mainly women have expanded in the past several decades. Also, population in general has shifted from farms and rural regions to urban areas, where jobs for women are more abundant and more geographically accessible. The decline in the average length of the workweek and the increased availability of part-time jobs have also made it easier for women to combine labour market employment with child-rearing and household activities.

Changing Preferences and Attitudes Women collectively have changed their preferences from household activities to employment in the labour market. Many find personal fulfillment in jobs, careers, and earnings, as evidenced by the huge influx of women into law, medicine, business, and other professions. More broadly, most industrial societies now widely accept and encourage labour force participation by women, including those with very young children. Today about 60 percent of Canadian mothers with preschool children participate in the labour force, compared to only 30 percent in 1970. More than half return to work before their youngest child has reached the age of two.

Declining Birthrates There were 3.8 lifetime births per woman in 1957 at the peak of the baby boom. Today the number is less than 2. This marked decline in the size of the typical family, the result of changing lifestyles and the widespread availability of birth control, has freed up time for greater labour-force participation by women. Not only do women now have fewer children, their children are spaced closer together in age. Thus women who leave their jobs during their children's early years can return to the labour force sooner. Higher wage rates have also been a factor. On average, women with relatively high wage earnings have fewer children than women with lower earnings. The opportunity cost of children—the income sacrificed by not being employed—rises as wage earnings rise. In the language of economics, the higher "price" associated with children has reduced the "quantity" of children demanded.

Rising Divorce Rates Marital instability, as evidenced by high divorce rates, may have motivated many women to enter and remain in the labour market. Because alimony and child support payments are often erratic or non-existent, the economic impact of divorce on non-working women may be disastrous. Most nonworking women enter the labour force for the first time following divorce. And many married women— perhaps even women contemplating marriage—may have joined the labour force to protect themselves against the financial difficulties of potential divorce.

Slower Growth of Male Wages The earnings of many low-wage and middle-wage male workers grew slowly or even fell in Canada over the past three decades. Many wives may have entered the labour force to ensure the rise of household living standards. The median income of couples with children grew 28 percent between 1969 and 2002. Without the mothers' income, that growth would have been only 2 percent. Couples of all income levels may be concerned about their family income compared to other families. So, the entry of some women into the labour force may have encouraged still other women to enter in order to maintain their families' *relative* standard of living.

Taken together, these factors have produced a rapid rise in the presence of women workers in Canada. This increase in the *quantity of resources* has helped push the Canadian production possibilities curve outward. In other words, it has contributed greatly to Canada's economic growth, and thus per capita income.

CHAPTER SUMMARY

2.1 THE FOUNDATION OF ECONOMICS

- Economics is grounded on two basic facts: (a) wants are virtually unlimited; (b) resources are scarce.

- Resources may be classified as property resources—raw materials and capital—or as human resources—labour and entrepreneurial ability. These resources constitute the factors of production.

- Economics is concerned with the problem of using scarce resources to produce the goods and services that satisfy the material wants of society. Both full employment and the efficient use of available resources are essential to maximize want satisfaction.

2.2 EFFICIENCY: GETTING THE MOST FROM AVAILABLE RESOURCES

- Efficient use of resources consists of productive efficiency (producing all output combinations in the least costly way) and allocative efficiency (producing the specific output mix most desired by society).

- An economy that is achieving full employment and productive efficiency—that is operating on its production possibilities curve—must sacrifice the output of some types of goods and services in order to increase the production of others. Because resources are not equally productive in all possible uses, shifting resources from one use to another brings the law of increasing opportunity costs into play. The production of additional units of one product requires the sacrifice of *increasing* amounts of the other product.

- Allocative efficiency means operating at the optimal point on the production possibilities curve. That point represents the highest-valued mix of goods and is determined by expanding the production of each good until its marginal benefit (MB) equals its marginal cost (MC).

2.3 UNEMPLOYMENT, GROWTH, AND THE FUTURE

- Over time, technological advances and increases in the quantity and quality of resources enable the economy to produce more of all goods and services—that is, to experience economic growth. Society's choice as to the mix of consumer goods and capital goods in current output is a major determinant of the future location of the production possibilities curve and thus of economic growth.

2.4 ECONOMIC SYSTEMS

- The market system and the command system are the two broad types of economic systems used to address the economic problem. In the market system (or capitalism) private individuals own most resources and markets coordinate most economic activity. In the command system (or socialism or communism), government owns most resources and central planners coordinate most economic activity.

2.5 THE CIRCULAR FLOW MODEL

- The circular flow model locates the product and factor markets and shows the major real and money flows between businesses and households. Businesses are on the buying side of the factor market and the selling side of the product market. Households are on the selling side of the factor market and the buying side of the product market.

TERMS AND CONCEPTS

economic problem, p. 26
economic resources, p. 27
land, p. 27
capital, p. 27
investment, p. 27
labour, p. 27
entrepreneurial ability, p. 27
factors of production, p. 27
full employment, p. 28

full production, p. 28
productive efficiency, p. 28
allocative efficiency, p. 28
consumer goods, p. 29
capital goods, p. 29
production possibilities table, p. 29
production possibilities curve, p. 30
opportunity cost, p. 30

law of increasing opportunity costs,
    p. 32
economic growth, p. 35
economic system, p. 39
market system, p. 40
command system, p. 40
factor market, p. 42
product market, p. 42
circular flow model, p. 42

STUDY QUESTIONS

1. Critically analyze: "Wants aren't unlimited. I can prove it. I get all the coffee I want to drink every morning at breakfast." Explain: "Wants change as we move from childhood to adulthood, but do not diminish."

2. What are economic resources? What categories do economists use to classify them? Why are resources also called "factors of production?" Explain: "If resources were unlimited and freely available, there would be no subject called *economics*."

3. Why isn't money considered to be a capital resource in economics? Why is entrepreneurial ability considered to be a category of economic resource, distinct from "labour?" What are the major functions of the entrepreneur?

4. **KEY QUESTION** Classify the following Microsoft factors of production as labour, land, capital, or entrepreneurial ability: code writers for software; Bill Gates; production facility for Windows CD-ROMs; "campus" on which Microsoft buildings sit; grounds crew at Microsoft campus; Microsoft corporate jet.

5. **KEY QUESTION** Distinguish between "full employment" and "full production" as it relates to production possibilities analysis. Distinguish between "productive efficiency" and "allocative efficiency." Give an illustration of achieving productive efficiency but not achieving allocative efficiency.

6. **KEY QUESTION** Here is a production possibilities table for war goods and civilian goods:

PRODUCTION ALTERNATIVES

Type of production	A	B	C	D	E
Automobiles	0	2	4	6	8
Missiles	30	27	21	12	0

a. Show these data graphically. Upon what specific assumptions is this production possibilities curve based?

b. If the economy is at point C, what is the cost of one more automobile? One more rocket? Explain how the production possibilities curve reflects the law of increasing opportunity costs.

c. What must the economy do to operate at some point on the production possibilities curve?

7. What is the opportunity cost of attending college or university? In 2001 nearly 80 percent of Canadians with post-secondary education held jobs, whereas only about 40 percent of those who did not finish high school held jobs. How might this difference relate to opportunity costs?

8. Suppose you arrive at a store expecting to pay $100 for an item but learn that a store 2 kilometres away is charging $50 for it. Would you drive there and buy it? How does your decision benefit you? What is the opportunity cost of your decision? Now suppose you arrive at a store expecting to pay $6000 for an item but discover that it costs $5950 at the other store. Do you make the same decision as before? Perhaps surprisingly, you should! Explain why.

9. **KEY QUESTION** Specify and explain the shapes of the marginal-benefit and marginal-cost curves. How are these curves used to determine the optimal allocation of resources to a particular product? If current output is such that marginal cost exceeds marginal benefit, should more or fewer resources be allocated to this product? Explain.

10. **KEY QUESTION** Label point *G inside* the production possibilities curve you drew in question 6. What does it indicate? Label point *H outside* the curve. What does that point indicate? What must occur before the economy can attain the level of production shown by point *H*?

11. **KEY QUESTION** Referring again to question 6, suppose improvement occurs in the technology of producing missiles but not in the technology of producing automobiles. Draw the new production possibilities curve. Now assume that a technological advance occurs in producing automobiles but not in producing missiles. Draw the new production possibilities curve. Now draw a production possibilities curve that reflects technological improvement in the production of both products.

12. Explain how, if at all, each of the following events affects the location of the production possibilities curve:

a. Standardized examination scores of high school, university, and college students decline.

b. The unemployment rate falls from 9 to 6 percent of the labour force.

c. Defence spending is reduced to allow government to spend more on health care.

d. A new technique improves the efficiency of extracting copper from ore.

13. Explain: "Affluence tomorrow requires sacrifice today."

14. Suppose that, based on a nation's production possibilities curve, an economy must sacrifice 10,000 pizzas domestically to get the one additional industrial machine it desires, but that it can get the machine from another country in exchange for 9000 pizzas. Relate this information to the following statement: "Through international specialization and trade, a nation can reduce its opportunity cost of obtaining goods and thus 'move outside its production possibilities curve.' "

15. Contrast how a market system and a command economy respond to the economic problem.

16. Distinguish between the factor market and product market in the circular flow model. In what way are businesses and households both *sellers and buyers* in this model? What are the flows in the circular flow model?

17. **(The Last Word)** Which two of the six reasons listed in the Last Word do you think are the *most important* in explaining the rise in participation of women in the workplace? Explain your reasoning.

INTERNET APPLICATION QUESTIONS

1. **More Labour Resources—What is the Evidence for Canada and France?** Use the link in the McConnell-Brue-Barbiero Web site (Chapter 2) to find Canadian civilian employment data for the last 10 years. How many more workers were there at the end of the 10-year period than at the beginning? Next, find total employment growth in France over the last 10 years. In which of the two countries did "more labour resources" have the greatest impact in shifting the nation's production possibilities curve outward over the 10-year period?

2. **Relative Size of the Military—Who's Incurring the Largest Opportunity Cost?** To obtain military goods, a nation must sacrifice civilian goods. Of course, that sacrifice may be worthwhile in terms of national defence and protection of national interests. Use the link in the McConnell-Brue-Barbiero Web site (Chapter 2) to determine the amount of military expenditures, and military expenditures as a percentage of GDP, for each of the following five nations: Canada, Japan, North Korea, Russia, and the United States. Who is bearing the greatest opportunity costs?

3

Chapter

Individual Markets
Demand and Supply

According to an old joke, if you teach a parrot to say "demand and supply," you have an economist. There is much truth in this quip. The tools of demand and supply can take us far in understanding both specific economic issues and how the entire economy works.

With our circular flow model in Chapter 2, we identified the participants in the product market and factor market. We asserted that prices were determined by the "interaction" between buyers and sellers in those markets. In this chapter we examine that interaction in detail and explain how prices and output quantities are determined.

3.1 Markets

market
Any institution or mechanism that brings together buyers and sellers of particular goods, services, or resources for the purpose of exchange.

www.tse.com
Toronto Stock Exchange

Recall from Chapter 2 that a **market** is *an institution or mechanism that brings together buyers ("demanders") and sellers ("suppliers") of particular goods, services, or factors for the purpose of exchange.* Markets exist in many forms. The corner gas station, e-commerce sites, the local music store, a farmer's roadside stand—all are familiar markets. The Toronto Stock Exchange and the Chicago Board of Trade are markets where buyers and sellers of stocks and bonds and farm commodities from all over the world communicate with one another to buy and sell. Auctioneers bring together potential buyers and sellers of art, livestock, used farm equipment, and, sometimes, real estate. In labour markets, the professional hockey player and his agent bargain with the owner of an NHL team. A graduating finance major interviews with the Royal Bank or the Bank of Montreal at the university placement office.

All situations that link potential buyers with potential sellers are markets. Some markets are local, whereas others are national or international. Some are highly personal, involving face-to-face contact between demander and supplier; others are impersonal, with buyer and seller never seeing or knowing each other.

To keep things simple, we will focus in this chapter on markets consisting of large numbers of buyers and sellers of standardized products. These are the highly competitive markets such as a central grain exchange, a stock market, or a market for foreign currencies in which the price is "discovered" through the interacting decisions of buyers and sellers. They are *not* the markets in which one or a handful of producers "set" prices, such as the markets for commercial airplanes or operating software for personal computers.

3.2 Demand

Recall from Chapter 2 that the economic problem consists of unlimited wants and limited resources to produce the goods and services to satisfy those wants. We begin now to take a closer look at the nature of wants, or demand. Later in the chapter we will investigate the nature of supply.

Demand is *a schedule or a curve that shows the various amounts of a product that consumers are willing and able to purchase at each of a series of possible prices during a specified period of time.*[1] Demand shows the quantities of a product that will be purchased at various possible prices, *other things equal.* Demand can easily be shown in table form. Figure 3-1 shows a hypothetical demand schedule for a *single consumer* purchasing bushels of corn.

demand
A schedule or curve that shows the various amounts of a product that consumers are willing and able to purchase at each of a series of possible prices during a specified period of time.

Figure 3-1 reveals the relationship between the various prices of corn and the quantity of corn a particular consumer would be willing *and able* to purchase at each of these prices. We say willing *and able* because willingness alone is not effective in the market. You may be willing to buy a Porsche, but if that willingness is not backed by the necessary dollars, it will not be effective and, therefore, will not be reflected in the market. If the price of corn were $5 per bushel, our consumer would be willing and able to buy 10 bushels per week; if it were $4, the consumer would be willing and able to buy 20 bushels per week; and so forth.

Figure 3-1 does not tell us which of the five possible prices will actually exist in the corn market. That depends on demand and supply. Demand is simply a statement of a buyer's plans, or intentions, with respect to the purchase of a product.

To be meaningful, the quantities demanded at each price must relate to a specific period—a day, a week, a month. Saying "A consumer will buy 10 bushels of corn at $5 per bushel" is meaningless. Unless a specific time period is stated, we do not know whether the demand for a product is large or small.

---

[1]This definition obviously is worded to apply to product markets. To adjust it to apply to factor markets, substitute the word "factor" for "product" and the word "businesses" for "consumers."

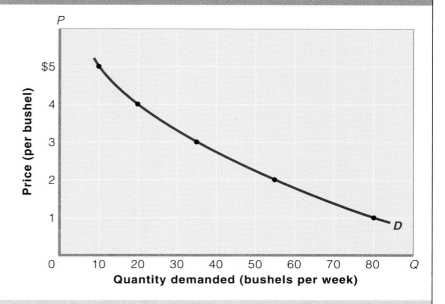

FIGURE 3-1 An Individual Buyer's Demand for Corn

Price per bushel	Quantity demanded (bushels per week)
$5	10
4	20
3	35
2	55
1	80

Because price and quantity demanded are inversely related, an individual's demand schedule graphs as a downward-sloping curve such as D. Specifically, the law of demand says that, other things equal, consumers will buy more of a product as its price declines. Here and in later figures, P stands for price, and Q stands for quantity (either demanded or supplied).

As price falls, the quantity demanded rises, and as price rises, the quantity demanded falls.

law of demand
All else equal, as price falls, the quantity demanded rises, and vice versa.

marginal utility
The extra utility a consumer obtains from the consumption of one additional unit of a good or service.

Law of Demand

A fundamental characteristic of demand is this: *All else equal, as price falls, the quantity demanded rises, and as price rises, the quantity demanded falls.* There is a negative or *inverse* relationship between price and quantity demanded. This inverse relationship is called the **law of demand**.

The "other-things-equal" assumption is critical here. Many factors other than the price of the product being considered affect the amount purchased. The quantity of Nikes purchased will depend not only on the price of Nikes but also on the prices of such substitutes as Reeboks, Adidas, and Filas. The law of demand in this case says that fewer Nikes will be purchased if the price of Nikes rises *and if the prices of Reeboks, Adidas, and Filas all remain constant*. Another way of stating it is that if the *relative price* of Nikes rises, fewer Nikes will be bought. However, if the price of Nikes and all other competing shoes increase by some amount—say, $5—consumers might buy more, fewer, or the same amount of Nikes.

Why the inverse relationship between price and quantity demanded? Let's look at two explanations:

- In any specific time period, each buyer of a product will derive less satisfaction (or benefit, or utility) from each successive unit of the product consumed. The second Big Mac will yield less satisfaction to the consumer than the first, and the third still less than the second. That is, consumption is subject to diminishing **marginal utility**. And because successive units of a particular product yield less and less marginal utility, consumers will buy additional units only if the price of those units is progressively reduced.

income effect
A change in the price of a product changes a consumer's real income (purchasing power) and thus the quantity of the product purchased.

substitution effect
A change in the price of a consumer good changes the relative expensiveness of that good and hence changes the willingness to buy it rather than other goods.

• We can also explain the law of demand in terms of income and substitution effects. The **income effect** indicates that a lower price increases the purchasing power of a buyer's money income, enabling the buyer to purchase more of the product than she or he could buy before. A higher price has the opposite effect. The **substitution effect** suggests that at a lower price, buyers have the incentive to substitute what is now a less expensive product for similar products that are now *relatively* more expensive. The product whose price has fallen is now "a better deal" relative to the other products.

For example, a decline in the price of chicken will increase the purchasing power of consumer incomes, enabling them to buy more chicken (the income effect). At a lower price, chicken is relatively more attractive and consumers tend to substitute it for pork, beef, and fish (the substitution effect). The income and substitution effects combine to make consumers able and willing to buy more of a product at a low price than at a high price.

The Demand Curve

The inverse relationship between price and quantity demanded for any product can be represented on a simple graph, in which, by convention, we measure *quantity demanded* on the horizontal axis and *price* on the vertical axis. In Figure 3-1 we have plotted the five price-quantity data points listed in the table and connected the points with a smooth curve, labelled D. Such a curve is called a **demand curve**. Its downward slope reflects the law of demand—more people buy more of a product or service as its price falls. The relationship between price and quantity demanded is inverse.

demand curve
A curve illustrating the inverse (negative) relationship between the quantity demanded of a good or service and its price, other things equal.

The table and graph in Figure 3-1 contain exactly the same data and reflect the same relationship between price and quantity demanded. But the graph shows that relationship more simply and clearly than a table or a description in words.

Market Demand

So far, we have concentrated on just one consumer. By adding the quantities demanded by all consumers at each of the various possible prices, we can get from *individual* demand to *market* demand. If there are just three buyers in the market, as represented in Figure 3-2, it is relatively easy to determine the total quantity demanded at each price. Figure 3-2 shows the graphical summing procedure: At each price we add the individual quantities demanded to obtain the total quantity demanded at that price; we then plot the price and the total quantity demanded as one point of the market demand curve.

Of course, there are usually many more than three buyers of a product. To avoid hundreds or thousands or millions of additions, we suppose that all the buyers in a market are willing and able to buy the same amounts at each of the possible prices. Then we just multiply those amounts by the number of buyers to obtain the market demand. This is the way we arrived at curve D_1, in Figure 3-3 on page 52, for a market with 200 corn buyers. The table in Figure 3-3 shows the calculations for 200 corn buyers.

In constructing a demand curve such as D_1 in Figure 3-3, we assume that price is the most important influence on the amount of any product purchased, even though other factors can and do affect purchases. These factors, called **determinants of demand**, are assumed to be constant when a demand curve like D_1 is drawn. They are the "other things equal" in the relationship between price and quantity demanded. When any of these determinants changes, the demand curve will shift to the right or left.

determinants of demand
Factors other than its price that determine the quantities demanded of a good or service.

The basic determinants of demand are (1) consumers' tastes (preferences), (2) the number of consumers in the market, (3) consumers' incomes, (4) the prices of related goods, and (5) consumer expectations about future prices and incomes.

FIGURE 3-2 | Market Demand for Corn, Three Buyers

| Price per bushel | Quantity demanded | | | Total quantity demanded per week |
	First buyer	Second buyer	Third buyer	
$5	10 +	12 +	8 =	30
4	20 +	23 +	17 =	60
3	35 +	39 +	26 =	100
2	55 +	60 +	39 =	154
1	80 +	87 +	54 =	221

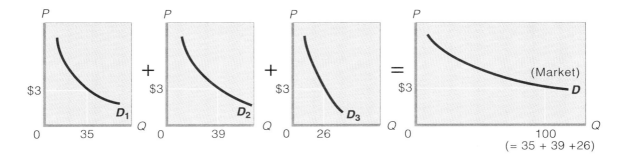

We establish the market demand curve D by adding horizontally the individual demand curves (D_1, D_2, and D_3) of all the consumers in the market. At the price of $3, for example, the three individual curves yield a total quantity demanded of 100 bushels.

Change in Demand

A change in one or more of the determinants of demand will change the demand data (the demand schedule) and therefore the location of the demand curve in Figure 3-3. A change in the demand schedule or, graphically, a shift in the demand curve, is called a *change in demand.*

If consumers desire to buy more corn at each possible price than is reflected in column 4 of the table in Figure 3-3, that *increase in demand* is shown as a shift of the demand curve to the right, say, from D_1 to D_2. Conversely, a *decrease in demand* occurs when consumers buy less corn at each possible price than is indicated in column 4 of the table in Figure 3-3. The leftward shift of the demand curve from D_1 to D_3 in Figure 3-3 shows that situation.

Now let's see how changes in each determinant affect demand.

TASTES

A favourable change in consumer tastes (preferences) for a product—a change that makes the product more desirable—means that more of it will be demanded at each price. Demand will increase; the demand curve will shift rightward. An unfavourable change in consumer preferences will decrease demand, shifting the demand curve to the left.

FIGURE **3-3** **Changes in the Demand for Corn**

A change in one or more of the determinants of demand causes a change in demand. An increase in demand is shown as a shift of the demand curve to the right, as from D_1 to D_2. A decrease in demand is shown as a shift of the demand curve to the left, as from D_1 to D_3. These changes in demand are to be distinguished from a change in quantity demanded, which is caused by a change in the price of the product, as shown by a movement from, say, point a to point b on fixed demand curve D_1.

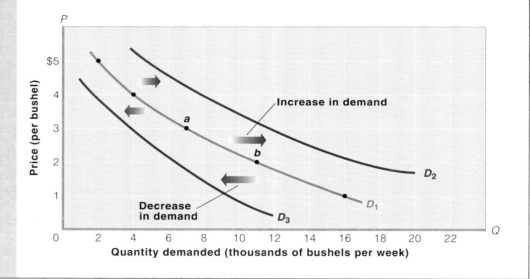

MARKET DEMAND FOR CORN, 200 BUYERS					
(1) Price per bushel	**(2)** Quantity demanded per week, single buyer		**(3)** Number of buyers in the market		**(4)** Total quantity demanded per week
$5	10	×	200	=	2,000
4	20	×	200	=	4,000
3	35	×	200	=	7,000
2	55	×	200	=	11,000
1	80	×	200	=	16,000

New products may affect consumer tastes; for example, the introduction of compact discs greatly decreased the demand for cassette tapes. Consumers' concern over the health hazards of cholesterol and obesity have increased the demand for broccoli, low-calorie sweeteners, and fresh fruit, while decreasing the demand for beef, veal, eggs, and whole milk.

NUMBER OF BUYERS

An increase in the number of buyers in a market increases demand. A decrease in the number of buyers in a market decreases demand. For example, the baby boom after World War II increased demand for diapers, baby lotion, and the services of obstetricians. When the baby boomers reached their 20s in the 1970s, the demand for housing increased. Also, an increase in life expectancy has increased the demand for medical care, retirement communities, and nursing homes.

INCOME

How changes in income affect demand is more complex. For most products, a rise in income causes an increase in demand. Consumers typically buy more steaks, furniture, and computers as their incomes increase. Conversely, the demand for such products declines as income falls. Products for which demand *varies* directly with money income are called **normal goods**.

Although most products are normal goods, there are some exceptions. As incomes increase beyond some point, the demand for used clothing, retread tires, and third-hand automobiles may decrease, because the higher incomes enable consumers to buy new versions of those products. Similarly, rising incomes may cause the demand for charcoal grills to decline as wealthier consumers switch to gas grills. Goods for which demand varies *inversely* with money income are called **inferior goods**.

PRICES OF RELATED GOODS

A change in the price of a related good may either increase or decrease the demand for a product, depending on whether the related good is a substitute or a complement.

- A **substitute good** is one that can be used in place of another good.
- A **complementary good** is one that is used together with another good.

Substitutes   Beef and chicken are examples of substitute goods, or simply *substitutes*. When the price of beef rises, consumers buy less beef, increasing the demand for chicken. Conversely, as the price of beef falls, consumers buy more beef, decreasing the demand for chicken. *When two products are substitutes, the price of one and the demand for the other move in the same direction.* So it is with pairs such as Nikes and Reeboks, Colgate and Crest, Toyotas and Hondas, and Coke and Pepsi. So-called *substitution in consumption* occurs when the price of one good rises relative to the price of a similar good. One can also buy services that are close substitutes. Examples include obstetricians and midwives, and, increasingly, physicians and nurse practitioners. Although in Canada government insurance pays for these services, if waiting times to see an obstetrician or a physician increase, consumers may turn to their close substitutes, for example, nurse practitioners.

Complements   Complementary goods (or simply *complements*) are goods that are used together and are usually demanded together. If the price of gasoline falls and, as a result, you drive your car more often, the extra driving increases your demand for motor oil. Thus, gas and motor oil are jointly demanded; they are complements. So it is with ham and eggs, tuition and textbooks, movies and popcorn, cameras and film. *When two products are complements, the price of one good and the demand for the other good move in opposite directions.*

Unrelated Goods   The vast majority of goods that are not related to one another are called *independent goods.* Examples are butter and golf balls, potatoes and automobiles, and bananas and wristwatches. A change in the price of one does not affect the demand for the other.

Expectations   Changes in consumer expectations may shift demand. A newly formed expectation of higher future prices may cause consumers to buy now in order to "beat" the anticipated price rises, thus increasing current demand. For example, when freezing weather destroys much of Florida's citrus crop, consumers may reason that the price of orange juice will rise. They may stock up on orange juice by purchasing large quantities now. In contrast, a newly formed expectation of falling prices or falling income may decrease current demand for products.

Finally, a change in expectations concerning future income may prompt consumers to change their current spending. For example, first-round NHL draft choices may splurge on new luxury cars in anticipation of a lucrative professional hockey contract. Or workers who become fearful of losing their jobs may reduce their demand for, say, vacation travel.

---

normal good
A good or service whose consumption rises when income increases and falls when income decreases, price remaining constant.

inferior good
A good or service whose consumption declines as income rises (and conversely), price remaining constant.

substitute goods
Products or services that can be used in place of each other.

complementary goods
Products and services that are used together.

In summary, an *increase* in demand—the decision by consumers to buy larger quantities of a product at each possible price—may be caused by:

· A favourable change in consumer tastes

· An increase in the number of buyers

· Rising incomes if the product is a normal good

· Falling incomes if the product is an inferior good

· An increase in the price of a substitute good

· A decrease in the price of a complementary good

· A new consumer expectation that prices and income will be higher in the future

You should "reverse" these generalizations to explain a *decrease* in demand. Table 3-1 provides additional illustrations of the determinants of demand. *(Key Question 2)*

Changes in Quantity Demanded

change in demand
A change in the quantity demanded of a good or service at every price.

A *change in demand* must not be confused with a *change in quantity demanded*. A **change in demand** is a shift of the entire demand curve to the right (an increase in demand) or to the left (a decrease in demand). It occurs because the consumer's state of mind about purchasing the product has been altered in response to a change in one or more of the determinants of demand. Recall that *demand* is a schedule or a curve; therefore, a *change in demand* means a change in the entire schedule and a shift of the entire curve.

change in quantity demanded
A movement from one point to another on a demand curve.

In contrast, a **change in quantity demanded** is a movement from one point to another point—from one price-quantity combination to another—on a fixed demand schedule or demand curve. The cause of such a change is an increase or decrease in the price of the product under consideration. In Figure 3-3, for example, a decline in the price of corn from $5 to $4 will increase the quantity of corn demanded from 2000 to 4000 bushels.

TABLE 3-1	Determinants of Demand Curve Shifts	

Determinant	Examples
Change in buyer tastes	Physical fitness rises in popularity, increasing the demand for jogging shoes and bicycles; Latin American music becomes more popular, increasing the demand for Latin CDs.
Change in number of buyers	A decline in the birthrate reduces the demand for children's toys.
Change in income	A rise in incomes increases the demand for such normal goods as butter, lobster, and filet mignon while reducing the demand for such inferior goods as cabbage, turnips, and cheap wine.
Change in the prices of related goods	A reduction in airfares reduces the demand for bus transportation (substitute goods); a decline in the price of compact disc players increases the demand for compact discs (complementary goods).
Change in expectations	Inclement weather in South America creates an expectation of higher future prices of coffee beans, thereby increasing today's demand for coffee beans.

In Figure 3-3 the shift of the demand curve D_1 to either D_2 or D_3 is a change in demand. But the movement from point *a* to point *b* on curve D_1 represents a change in quantity demanded: *demand has not changed; it is the entire curve, and it remains fixed in place.*

QUICK REVIEW

- A market is any arrangement that facilitates the purchase and sale of goods, services, or resources.

- Demand is a schedule or a curve showing the amount of a product that buyers are willing and able to purchase at each possible price in a series of prices, in a particular time period.

- The law of demand states that, other things equal, the quantity of a good purchased varies inversely with its price.

- The demand curve shifts because of changes in (a) consumer tastes, (b) the number of buyers in the market, (c) consumer income, (d) the prices of substitute or complementary goods, and (e) consumer expectations.

- A change in demand is a shift of the entire demand curve; a change in quantity demanded is a movement from one point to another on a demand curve.

3.3   Supply

Up to this point we have concentrated our attention on the nature of wants. In order for wants to be satisfied someone must produce the goods and services desired. We now turn to investigate the nature of supply.

supply
A schedule or curve that shows the amounts of a product that producers are willing and able to make available for sale at each of a series of possible prices during a specific period.

Supply is *a schedule or curve that shows the amounts of a product that producers are willing and able to make available for sale at each of a series of possible prices during a specific period.*[2] Figure 3-4 is a hypothetical supply schedule for a single producer of corn. It shows the quantities of corn that will be supplied at various prices, other things equal.

Law of Supply

law of supply
The principle that, other things equal, an increase in the price of a product will increase the quantity of it supplied; and conversely for a price decrease.

The table of Figure 3-4 shows a direct relationship between price and quantity supplied. *As price rises, the quantity supplied rises; as price falls, the quantity supplied falls.* This relationship is called the **law of supply**. A supply schedule tells us that firms will produce and offer for sale more of their product at a high price than at a low price. To a supplier, price represents *revenue,* which serves as an incentive to produce and sell a product. The higher the price, the greater the incentive and the greater the quantity supplied.

Consider a farmer in Manitoba who can shift resources among alternative farm products. As price moves up, as shown in Figure 3-4, the farmer finds it profitable to take land out of wheat, oats, and soybean production and put it into corn. And the higher corn prices enable the Manitoba farmer to cover the increased costs associated with more intensive cultivation and the use of more seed, fertilizer, and pesticides. The overall result is more corn.

Now consider a manufacturer. Beyond some quantity of production, manufacturers usually encounter increasing costs per added unit of output. The firm will not produce those more costly units unless it receives a higher price for them. Again, price and quantity supplied are directly related.

---

[2]This definition is worded to apply to product markets. To adjust it to apply to factor markets, substitute *factor* for *product* and *owner* for the word *producer.*

| FIGURE 3-4 | An Individual Producer's Supply of Corn |

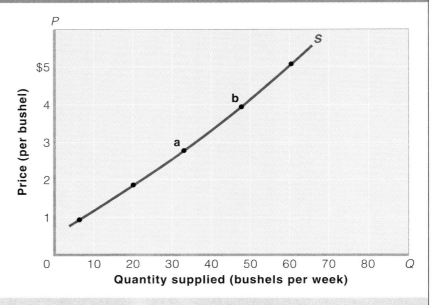

Price per bushel	Quantity supplied (bushels per week)
$5	60
4	50
3	35
2	20
1	5

Because price and quantity supplied are positively related, a firm's supply schedule is an upward-sloping curve such as *S*. Specifically, the law of supply says that, other things equal, firms will supply more of a product as its price rises.

The Market Supply Curve

In Figure 3-5, curve S_1 is a graph of the market supply data given in the table. Those data assume there are 200 suppliers in the market, each willing and able to supply corn according to the data in the table of Figure 3-4. The market **supply curve** is derived by horizontally adding the supply curves of the individual producers.

supply curve
A curve illustrating the positive (direct) relationship between the quantity supplied of a good or service and its price, other things equal.

Determinants of Supply

In constructing a supply curve, we assume that price is the most significant influence on the quantity supplied of any product. But other factors (the "other things equal") can and do affect supply. The supply curve is drawn on the assumption that these other things are fixed and do not change. If one of them does change, a *change in supply* will occur, meaning that the entire supply curve will shift.

determinants of supply
Causes other than its price that determine the quantities supplied of a good or service.

The basic **determinants of supply** are (1) factor prices, (2) technology, (3) taxes and subsidies, (4) prices of other goods, (5) price expectations, and (6) the number of sellers in the market. A change in any one or more of these determinants of supply will move the supply curve for a product either to the right or to the left. A shift to the *right*, as from S_1 to S_2 in Figure 3-5, signifies an *increase* in supply: Producers supply larger quantities of the product at each possible price. A shift to the *left*, as from S_1 to S_3, indicates a *decrease* in supply.

Changes in Supply

Let's consider how changes in each of the determinants affect supply. The key idea is that costs are a major factor underlying supply curves; anything that affects costs (other than changes in output itself) usually shifts the supply curve.

www.mcgrawhill.ca/college/mcconnell

FIGURE 3-5 — Changes in the Supply of Corn

A change in one or more of the determinants of supply causes a shift in supply. An increase in supply is shown as a rightward shift of the supply curve, as from S_1 to S_2. A decrease in supply is depicted as a leftward shift of the curve, as from S_1 to S_3. In contrast, a change in the *quantity supplied* is caused by a change in the product's price and is shown by a movement from one point to another, as from *a* to *b*, on a fixed supply curve.

MARKET SUPPLY OF CORN, 200 PRODUCERS						
(1) Price per bushel	(2) Quantity supplied per week, single producer		(3) Number of sellers in the market		(4) Total quantity supplied per week	
$5	60	×	200	=	12,000	
4	50	×	200	=	10,000	
3	35	×	200	=	7,000	
2	20	×	200	=	4,000	
1	5	×	200	=	1,000	

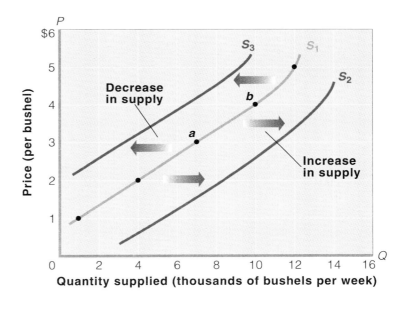

Quantity supplied (thousands of bushels per week)

FACTOR PRICES

The prices of the factors used as inputs in the production process determine the costs of production. Higher *factor* prices raise production costs and, assuming a particular *product* price, squeeze profits. That reduction in profits reduces the incentive for firms to supply output at each product price. For example, an increase in the prices of iron ore and coke will increase the cost of producing steel for Dofasco and reduce its supply.

In contrast, lower *factor* prices reduce production costs and increase profits. So, when input prices fall, firms supply greater output at each product price. For example, a decrease in the prices of seed and fertilizer will increase the supply of corn.

TECHNOLOGY

Improvements in technology (techniques of production) enable firms to produce units of output with fewer inputs. Because inputs are costly, using fewer of them lowers production costs and increases supply. Example: Recent improvements in the fuel efficiency of aircraft engines have reduced the cost of providing passenger air service. Thus, Air Canada and other airlines now offer more flights than previously at each ticket price; the supply of air service has increased. Similarly, technological improvement of medical diagnostic equipment can increase the number of patients that can have tests.

TAXES AND SUBSIDIES

Businesses treat most taxes as costs. An increase in sales or property taxes will increase production costs and reduce supply. In contrast, subsidies are "taxes in reverse." If the government subsidizes the production of a good, it in effect lowers the producers' costs and increases supply. Government subsidies will, for example, help increase the number of rural medical practitioners.

PRICES OF OTHER GOODS

Firms that produce a particular product, say, soccer balls, can sometimes use their plant and equipment to produce alternative goods, say, basketballs and volleyballs. The higher prices of these "other goods" may entice soccer ball producers to switch production to those other goods in order to increase profits. This *substitution in production* results in a decline in the supply of soccer balls. Alternatively, when the prices of basketballs and volleyballs decline relative to the price of soccer balls, producers of those goods may decide to produce more soccer balls instead, increasing their supply.

PRICE EXPECTATIONS

Changes in expectations about the future price of a product may affect the producer's current willingness to supply that product. It is difficult, however, to generalize about how a new expectation of higher prices affects the present supply of a product. Ontario farmers anticipating a higher corn price in the future might withhold some of their current corn harvest from the market, thereby causing a decrease in the current supply of corn. In contrast, in many types of manufacturing industries, newly formed expectations that price will increase may induce firms to add another shift of workers or to expand their production facilities, causing current supply to increase.

NUMBER OF SELLERS

Other things equal, the larger the number of suppliers, the greater the market supply. As more firms enter an industry, the supply curve shifts to the right. Conversely, the smaller the number of firms in the industry, the less the market supply. This means that as firms leave an industry, the supply curve shifts to the left. Example: Canada and the United States have imposed restrictions on haddock fishing to replenish dwindling stocks. As part of that policy, the federal government has bought the boats of some of the haddock fishermen as a way of putting them out of business and decreasing the catch. The result has been a decline in the market supply of haddock.

Table 3-2 is a checklist of the determinants of supply, along with further illustrations. *(Key Question 5)*

CHANGES IN QUANTITY SUPPLIED

change in supply
A change in the quantity supplied of a good or service at every price; a shift of the supply curve to the left or right.

The distinction between a *change in supply* and a *change in quantity supplied* parallels the distinction between a change in demand and a change in quantity demanded. Because supply is a schedule or curve, a **change in supply** means a change in the entire schedule and a shift of the entire curve. An increase in supply shifts the curve to the right; a decrease in supply shifts it to the left. The cause of a change in supply is a change in one or more of the determinants of supply.

TABLE 3-2	Determinants of Supply Curve Shifts	
Determinant	**Examples**	
Change in factor prices	A decrease in the price of microchips increases the supply of computers; an increase in the price of crude oil reduces the supply of gasoline.	
Change in technology	The development of more effective wireless technology increases the supply of cell phones.	
Changes in taxes and subsidies	An increase in the excise tax on cigarettes reduces the supply of cigarettes; a decline in subsidies to universities reduces the supply of higher education.	
Change in prices of other goods	An increase in the price of cucumbers decreases the supply of watermelons.	
Change in expectations	An expectation of a substantial rise in future log prices decreases the supply of logs today.	
Change in number of suppliers	An increase in the number of Internet service providers increases the supply of such services; the formation of women's professional basketball leagues increases the supply of women's professional basketball games.	

change in quantity supplied
A movement from one point to another on a fixed supply curve.

In contrast, a **change in quantity supplied** is a movement from one point to another on a fixed supply curve. The cause of such a movement is a change in the price of the specific product being considered. In Figure 3-5, a decline in the price of corn from $5 to $4 decreases the quantity of corn supplied per week from 12,000 to 10,000 bushels. This is a change in quantity supplied, not a change in supply. *Supply is the full schedule of prices and quantities shown, and this schedule does not change when price changes.*

QUICK REVIEW

- A supply schedule or curve shows that, other things equal, the quantity of a good supplied varies directly with its price.

- The supply curve shifts because of changes in (a) factor prices, (b) technology, (c) taxes or subsidies, (d) prices of other goods, (e) expectations of future prices, and (f) the number of suppliers.

- A change in supply is a shift of the supply curve; a change in quantity supplied is a movement from one point to another on a fixed supply curve.

3.4 Supply and Demand: Market Equilibrium

We can now bring together supply and demand to see how the buying decisions of households and the selling decisions of businesses interact to determine the price of a product and the quantity actually bought and sold. In the table of **Figure 3-6 (Key Graph)**, columns 1 and 2 repeat the market supply of corn (from Figure 3-5), and columns 2 and 3 repeat the market demand for corn (from Figure 3-3). We assume that this is a competitive market—neither buyers nor sellers can set the price (see the Consider This box).

Key Graph

FIGURE 3-6 Equilibrium Price and Quantity

The intersection of the downward-sloping demand curve *D* and the upward-sloping supply curve *S* indicates the equilibrium price and quantity, here $3 and 7000 bushels of corn. The shortages of corn at below-equilibrium prices (for example, 7000 bushels at $2), drive up price. These higher prices increase the quantity supplied and reduce the quantity demanded until equilibrium is achieved. The surpluses caused by above-equilibrium prices (for example, 6000 bushels at $4), push price down. As price drops, the quantity demanded rises and the quantity supplied falls until equilibrium is established. At the equilibrium price and quantity, there are neither shortages nor surpluses of corn.

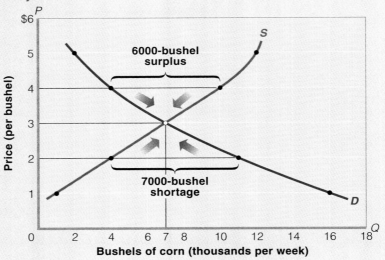

(1) Total quantity supplied per week	(2) Price per bushel	(3) Total quantity demanded per week	(4) Surplus (+) or shortage (−)
12,000	$5	2,000	+10,000↓
10,000	4	4,000	+ 6,000↓
7,000	3	7,000	0
4,000	2	11,000	− 7,000↑
1,000	1	16,000	−15,000↑

The arrows indicate the effect on price.

Quick Quiz

1. Demand curve *D* in Figure 3-6 is downward-sloping because:
   a. producers offer less product for sale as the price of the product falls.
   b. lower prices of a product create income and substitution effects, which lead consumers to purchase more of it.
   c. the larger the number of buyers in a market, the lower the product price.
   d. price and quantity demanded are directly (positively) related.

2. Supply curve *S*:
   a. reflects an inverse (negative) relationship between price and quantity supplied.
   b. reflects a direct (positive) relationship between price and quantity supplied.
   c. depicts the collective behaviour of buyers in this market.
   d. shows that producers will offer more of a product for sale at a low product price than at a high product price.

3. At the $3 price:
   a. quantity supplied exceeds quantity demanded.
   b. quantity demanded exceeds quantity supplied.
   c. the product is abundant and a surplus exists.
   d. there is no pressure on price to rise or fall.

4. At price $5 in this market:
   a. there will be a shortage of 10,000 units.
   b. there will be a surplus of 10,000 units.
   c. quantity demanded will be 12,000 units.
   d. quantity demanded will equal quantity supplied.

ANSWERS: 1. b; 2. b; 3. d; 4. b

Consider **T**his

Supply and Demand

In viewing demand and supply curves such as those shown in Figure 3-6, students taking introductory economics often wonder if demand is more important than supply in determining equilibrium price and quantity or if supply is more important than demand. The answer is that demand and supply are equally important.

Economist Alfred Marshall (1842–1924) used a vivid analogy to make this point. He likened demand and supply to the two blades of a pair of scissors. Which blade of the scissors cuts the paper? To be sure, if the lower blade is held in place and the upper blade is closed down upon it, one could argue that the upper blade has cut the paper. But would the paper have been cut without the lower blade? And if the upper blade is held in place and the lower blade is closed up against it, would the paper have been cut without the upper blade?

The answer to these questions is that it is the interaction of the two blades of the scissors that cuts the paper. Both are necessary and both are important. So it is with demand and supply in competitive markets. Demand (which reflects utility) and supply (which reflects costs) jointly determine equilibrium price and quantity. Without a demand curve, there is no equilibrium price and quantity. But the same is true for supply. Without it, no equilibrium price and quantity exist. Equilibrium price and quantity result from the *interaction* of demand and supply, and each is *equally* important.

Question: With the aid of demand and supply analysis, explain why prostitution exists.

Surpluses

We have limited our example to only five possible prices. Of these, which will actually prevail as the market price for corn? We can find an answer through trial and error. For no particular reason, let's start with $5. We see immediately that this cannot be the prevailing market price. At the $5 price, producers are willing to produce and offer for sale 12,000 bushels of corn, but buyers are willing to buy only 2000 bushels. The $5 price encourages farmers to produce lots of corn but discourages most consumers from buying it. The result is a 10,000-bushel **surplus** or *excess supply* of corn. This surplus, shown in column 4 of the table in Figure 3-6, is the excess of quantity supplied over quantity demanded at $5. Corn farmers would find themselves with 10,000 unsold bushels of output.

A price of $5, even if it existed temporarily in the corn market, could not persist over a period of time. The very large surplus of corn would drive competing sellers to lower the price to encourage buyers to take the surplus off their hands.

surplus
The amount by which the quantity supplied of a product exceeds the quantity demanded at a specific (above-equilibrium) price.

Shortages

Let's jump now to $1 as the possible market price of corn. Observe in column 4 of the table that at this price, quantity demanded exceeds quantity supplied by 15,000 units. The $1 price discourages farmers from devoting resources to corn production and encourages consumers to buy more than is available. The result is a 15,000-bushel **shortage** of, or *excess demand* for, corn. The $1 price cannot persist as the market price. Many consumers who want to buy at this price will not get corn. They will express a willingness to pay more than $1 to get some of the available output. Competition among these buyers will drive up the price to something greater than $1.

shortage
The amount by which the quantity demanded of a product exceeds the quantity supplied at a particular (below-equilibrium) price.

Equilibrium Price and Quantity

At $3, *and only at this price*, the quantity of corn that farmers are willing to produce and supply is identical with the quantity consumers are willing and able to buy. There is neither a shortage nor a surplus of corn at that price.

equilibrium price
The price in a competitive market at which the quantity demanded and the quantity supplied are equal.

equilibrium quantity
The quantity demanded and supplied at the equilibrium price in a competitive market.

With no shortage or surplus at $3, there is no reason for the price of corn to change. Economists call this price the *market-clearing* or **equilibrium price**, equilibrium meaning "in balance" or "at rest." At $3, quantity supplied and quantity demanded are in balance at the **equilibrium quantity** of 7000 bushels. So $3 is the only stable price of corn under the supply and demand conditions shown in Figure 3-6.

The price of corn, or of any other product bought and sold in competitive markets, will be established where the supply decisions of producers and the demand decisions of buyers are mutually consistent. Such decisions are consistent only at the equilibrium price (here, $3) and equilibrium quantity (here, 7000 bushels). At any higher price, suppliers want to sell more than consumers want to buy and a surplus results; at any lower price, consumers want to buy more than producers make available for sale and a shortage results. Such discrepancies between the supply and demand intentions of sellers and buyers then prompt price changes that bring the two sets of intentions into accord.

A graphical analysis of supply and demand yields these same conclusions. Figure 3-6 shows the market supply and demand curves for corn on the same graph. (The horizontal axis now measures both quantity demanded and quantity supplied.)

Graphically, the intersection of the supply curve and the demand curve for a product indicates the market equilibrium. Here, equilibrium price and quantity are $3 per bushel and 7000 bushels. At any above-equilibrium price, quantity supplied exceeds quantity demanded. This surplus of corn causes price reductions by sellers who are eager to rid themselves of their surplus. The falling price causes less corn to be offered and simultaneously encourages consumers to buy more. The market moves to its equilibrium.

Any price below the equilibrium price creates a shortage; quantity demanded then exceeds quantity supplied. Buyers try to obtain the product by offering to pay more for it; this drives the price upward toward its equilibrium level. The rising price simultaneously causes producers to increase the quantity supplied and prompts many buyers to leave the market, thus eliminating the shortage. Again the market moves to its equilibrium.

Rationing Function of Prices

rationing function of prices
The ability of market forces in a competitive market to equalize quantity demanded and quantity supplied and to eliminate shortages via changes in prices.

The ability of the competitive forces of supply and demand to establish a price at which selling and buying decisions are consistent is called the **rationing function of prices**. In our case, the equilibrium price of $3 clears the market, leaving no burdensome surplus for sellers and no inconvenient shortage for potential buyers. And it is the combination of freely made individual decisions that sets this market-clearing price. In effect, the market outcome says that all buyers who are willing and able to pay $3 for a bushel of corn will obtain it; all buyers who cannot or will not pay $3 will go without corn. Similarly, all producers who are willing and able to offer corn for sale at $3 a bushel will sell it; all producers who cannot or will not sell for $3 per bushel will not sell their product. (*Key Question 7*)

Changes in Supply, Demand, and Equilibrium

We know that demand might change because of fluctuations in consumer tastes or incomes, changes in consumer expectations, or variations in the prices of related goods. Supply might change in response to changes in resource prices, technology, or taxes. What effects will such changes in supply and demand have on equilibrium price and quantity?

CHANGES IN DEMAND

Suppose that supply is constant and demand increases, as shown in Figure 3-7(a). As a result, the new intersection of the supply and demand curves is at higher values on both the price and quantity axes. An increase in demand raises both equilibrium price and equilibrium quantity. Conversely, a decrease in demand, such as that shown in Figure 3-7(b), reduces both equilibrium price and equilibrium quantity. (The value of graphical analysis is now apparent: We need not fumble with columns of figures to determine the outcomes; we need only compare the new and the old points of intersection on the graph.)

CHANGES IN SUPPLY

Now suppose that demand is constant but supply increases, as in Figure 3-7(c). The new intersection of supply and demand is located at a lower equilibrium price but at a higher equilibrium quantity. An increase in supply reduces equilibrium price but increases equilibrium quantity. In contrast, if supply decreases, as in Figure 3-7(d), the equilibrium price rises while the equilibrium quantity declines.

FIGURE 3-7   Changes in Demand and Supply and the Effects on Price and Quantity

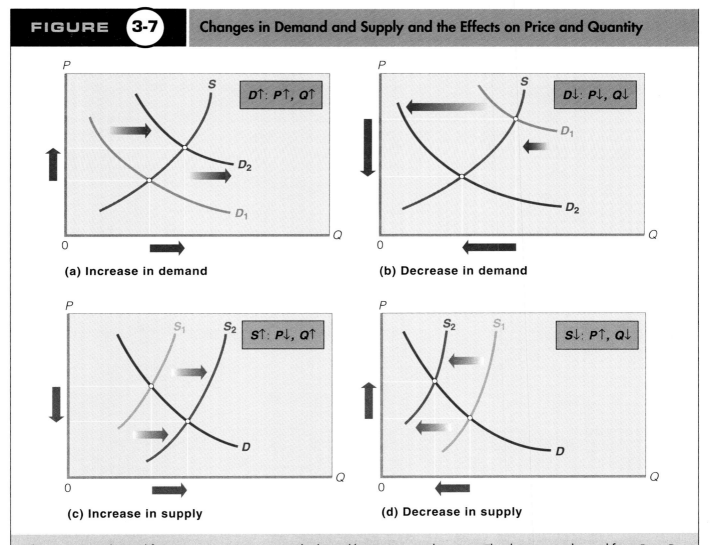

(a) Increase in demand

(b) Decrease in demand

(c) Increase in supply

(d) Decrease in supply

The increase in demand from D_1 to D_2 in (a) increases both equilibrium price and quantity. The decrease in demand from D_1 to D_2 in (b) decreases both equilibrium price and quantity. The increase in supply from S_1 to S_2 in (c) decreases equilibrium price and increases equilibrium quantity. The decline in supply from S_1 to S_2 in (d) increases equilibrium price and decreases equilibrium quantity. The boxes in the top right corners summarize the respective changes and outcomes. The upward arrows in those boxes signify increases in demand (D), supply (S), equilibrium price (P), and equilibrium quantity (Q); the downward arrows signify decreases in these items.

COMPLEX CASES

When both supply and demand change, the effect is a combination of the individual effects. As you study the following cases, keep in mind that each effect on the demand and supply curves has to be considered independently.

1. **Supply Increase; Demand Decrease**   What effect will a supply increase and a demand decrease have on equilibrium price? Both changes decrease price, so the net result is a price drop greater than that resulting from either change alone.

    What about equilibrium quantity? Here the effects of the changes in supply and demand are opposed: The increase in supply increases equilibrium quantity, but the decrease in demand reduces it. The direction of the change in quantity depends on the relative sizes of the changes in supply and demand. If the increase in supply is larger than the decrease in demand, the equilibrium quantity will increase. But if the decrease in demand is greater than the increase in supply, the equilibrium quantity will decrease.

2. **Supply Decrease; Demand Increase**   A decrease in supply and an increase in demand both increase price. Their combined effect is an increase in equilibrium price greater than that caused by either change separately. But their effect on equilibrium quantity is again indeterminate, depending on the relative sizes of the changes in supply and demand. If the decrease in supply is larger than the increase in demand, the equilibrium quantity will decrease. In contrast, if the increase in demand is greater than the decrease in supply, the equilibrium quantity will increase.

3. **Supply Increase; Demand Increase**   What if supply and demand both increase? A supply increase drops equilibrium price, while a demand increase boosts it. If the increase in supply is greater than the increase in demand, the equilibrium price will fall. If the opposite holds, the equilibrium price will rise.

    The effect on equilibrium quantity is certain: The increases in supply and in demand each raise equilibrium quantity. Therefore, the equilibrium quantity will increase by an amount greater than that caused by either change alone.

4. **Supply Decrease; Demand Decrease**   What about decreases in both supply and demand? If the decrease in supply is greater than the decrease in demand, equilibrium price will rise. If the reverse is true, equilibrium price will fall. Because decreases in supply and in demand each reduce equilibrium quantity, we can be sure that equilibrium quantity will fall.

Table 3-3 summarizes these four cases. To understand them fully you should draw supply and demand diagrams for each case to confirm the effects listed in Table 3-3.

Special cases arise when a decrease in demand and a decrease in supply, or an increase in demand and an increase in supply, exactly cancel out. In both cases, the net effect on equilibrium price will be zero; price will not change. *(Key Question 8)*

TABLE 3-3		Effects of Changes in Both Supply and Demand	
Change in supply	**Change in demand**	**Effect on equilibrium price**	**Effect on equilibrium quantity**
1 Increase	Decrease	Decrease	Indeterminate
2 Decrease	Increase	Increase	Indeterminate
3 Increase	Increase	Indeterminate	Increase
4 Decrease	Decrease	Indeterminate	Decrease

A Reminder: "Other Things Equal"

We must stress once again that specific demand and supply curves (such as those in Figure 3-7) show relationships between prices and quantities demanded and supplied, *other things equal.*

If you forget the other-things-equal assumption, you can encounter situations that *seem* to be in conflict with these basic principles. For example, suppose salsa manufacturers sell one million bottles of salsa at $4 a bottle in one year, two million bottles at $5 in the next year; and three million at $6 in the year thereafter. Price and quantity purchased vary directly, and these data seem to be at odds with the law of demand. But there is no conflict here; these data do not refute the law of demand. The catch is that the law of demand's other-things-equal assumption has been violated over the three years in the example. Specifically, because of changing tastes and rising incomes, the demand for salsa has increased sharply, as in Figure 3-7(a). The result is higher prices *and* larger quantities purchased.

Another example: The price of coffee occasionally has shot upward at the same time that the quantity of coffee produced has declined. These events seemingly contradict the direct relationship between price and quantity denoted by supply. The catch again is that the other-things-equal assumption underlying the upward-sloping supply curve was violated. Poor coffee harvests decreased supply, as in Figure 3-7(d), increasing the equilibrium price of coffee and reducing the equilibrium quantity.

These examples emphasize the importance of our earlier distinction between a change in quantity demanded (or supplied) and a change in demand (supply). In Figure 3-7(a) a change in demand causes a change in the quantity supplied. In Figure 3-7(d) a change in supply causes a change in quantity demanded.

3.5   Application: Government-set Prices

Prices in most markets are free to rise or fall to their equilibrium levels, no matter how high or low that might be. However, government sometimes concludes that supply and demand will produce prices that are unfairly high for buyers or unfairly low for sellers. So government may place legal limits on how high or low a price or prices may go. Is that a good idea?

price ceiling
A legally established maximum price for a good or service.

Price Ceilings and Shortages

A **price ceiling** is the maximum legal price a seller may charge for a product or service. A price at or below the ceiling is legal; a price above it is not. The rationale for establishing price ceilings (or ceiling prices) on specific products is that they purportedly enable consumers to obtain some essential good or service that they could not afford at the equilibrium price. Examples are rent controls and usury laws, which specify maximum prices in the forms of rent and interest that can be charged to borrowers. Also, the government has at times imposed price ceilings either on all products or on a very wide range of products—so-called price controls—to try to restrain inflation. Price controls were invoked in Canada during World War II and in the 1970s.

To be effective, a price ceiling on gasoline must be below the equilibrium price.

GRAPHICAL ANALYSIS

We can easily demonstrate the effects of price ceilings graphically. Let's suppose that rapidly rising world income boosts the purchase of automobiles and shifts the demand for gasoline to the right so that the equilibrium or market price reaches $1.25 per litre, shown as P_0 in Figure 3-8. The rapidly rising price of gasoline greatly burdens low-income and moderate-income households who pressure the federal government to "do something." To keep gasoline affordable for these households, the government imposes a ceiling price, P_c, of $.75 per litre. To be effective, a price ceiling must be below the equilibrium price. A ceiling price of $1.50, for example, would have no immediate effect on the gasoline market.

What are the effects of this $.75 ceiling price? The rationing ability of the free market is rendered ineffective. Because the ceiling price, P_c, is below the market-clearing price, P_0, there is a shortage of gasoline. The quantity of gasoline demanded at P_c is Q_d and the quantity supplied is only Q_s; an excess demand or shortage of amount $Q_d - Q_s$ occurs.

The important point is that the price ceiling, P_c, prevents the usual market adjustment in which competition among buyers bids up price, inducing more production and rationing some buyers out of the market. That process would continue until the shortage disappeared at the equilibrium price and quantity, P_0 and Q_0.

| FIGURE 3-8 | A Price Ceiling Results in a Shortage |

A price ceiling is a maximum legal price, such as P_c, that is below the equilibrium price. It results in a product shortage, here shown by the distance between Q_d and Q_s.

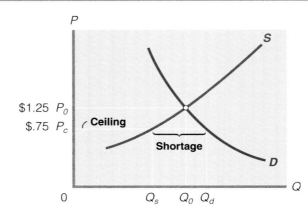

RATIONING PROBLEM

How will the government apportion the available supply, Q_s, among buyers who want the greater amount Q_d? Should gasoline be distributed on a first-come, first-served basis, that is, to those willing and able to get in line the soonest and to stay in line? Or should gas stations distribute it on the basis of favouritism? Since an unregulated shortage does not lead to an equitable distribution of gasoline, the federal government must establish some formal system for rationing it to consumers. One option is to issue ration coupons, which allow coupon-holders to purchase a fixed amount of gasoline per month. The rationing system would require the printing of coupons for Q_s litres of gasoline and then the equitable distribution of the coupons among consumers so that the wealthy family of four and the poor family of four both receive the same number of coupons.

BLACK MARKETS

Ration coupons would not prevent a second problem from arising. The demand curve in Figure 3-8 tells us that many buyers are willing to pay more than the ceiling price P_c, and, of course, it is more profitable for gasoline stations to sell at prices above the ceiling. Thus, despite the sizable enforcement bureaucracy that will accompany the price controls, *black markets* in which gasoline is illegally bought and sold at prices above the legal limits will flourish. Counterfeiting of ration coupons will also be a problem, and since the price of gasoline is now set by the federal government, there would be political pressure to set the price even lower.

CREDIT CARD INTEREST CEILINGS

Over the years there have been many calls in Canada for interest-rate ceilings on credit card accounts. The usual rationale for interest-rate ceilings is that the chartered banks and retail stores issuing such cards are presumably taking unfair advantage of users and, in particular, lower-income users by charging interest rates that average about 18 percent per year.

What might be the responses if the Canadian government imposed a below-equilibrium interest rate on credit cards? The lower interest income associated with a legal interest ceiling would require the issuers of cards to reduce their costs or enhance their revenues:

- Card issuers might tighten credit standards to reduce losses due to non-payment and collection costs. Then, low-income and young Canadians who have not yet established their creditworthiness would find it more difficult to obtain credit cards.

- The annual fee charged to cardholders might be increased, as might the fee charged to merchants for processing credit card sales. Similarly, card users might be charged a fee for every transaction.

- Card users now have a post-purchase grace period during which the credit provided is interest-free. That period might be shortened or eliminated.

- Certain "enhancements" that accompany some credit cards (for example, extended warranties on products bought with a card) might be eliminated.

- Retail stores, such as Hudson's Bay Company, that issue their own cards might increase their prices to help offset the decline of interest income; customers who pay cash would in effect be subsidizing customers who use credit cards.

Price Floors and Surpluses

price floors
Legally determined prices above equilibrium prices.

Price floors are minimum prices fixed by the government. A price at or above the price floor is legal; a price below it is not. Price floors above equilibrium prices are usually invoked when society believes that the free functioning of the market system has not provided a sufficient income for certain groups of resource suppliers or producers. Supported prices for some agricultural products and current minimum wages are two examples of price (or wage) floors. Let's look at the former.

Suppose the equilibrium price for wheat is $3 per bushel and, because of that low price, many Prairie farmers have extremely low incomes. The federal government decides to help by establishing a legal price floor or price support of $4 per bushel.

What will be the effects? At any price above the equilibrium price, quantity supplied will exceed quantity demanded—that is, there will be an excess supply or surplus of the product. Prairie farmers will be willing to produce and offer for sale more than private buyers are willing to purchase at the price floor. As we saw with a price ceiling, an imposed legal price disrupts the rationing ability of the free market.

Figure 3-9 illustrates the effect of a price floor. Suppose that S and D are the supply and demand curves for wheat. Equilibrium price and quantity are P_0 and Q_0, respectively. If the federal government imposes a price floor of P_f, farmers will produce Q_s, but private buyers will purchase only Q_d. The surplus is the excess of Q_s over Q_d.

Supported prices for some agricultural products are an example of price floors.

FIGURE 3-9	A Price Floor Results in a Surplus

A price floor is a minimum legal price, such as P_f, which results in a persistent product surplus, here shown by the horizontal distance between Q_s and Q_d.

The government can cope with the surplus resulting from a price floor in only two ways:

1. It can restrict supply (for example, by asking farmers in Alberta, Saskatchewan, and Manitoba to agree to take a certain amount of land out of production) or increase demand (for example, by researching new uses for the product involved). These actions may reduce the difference between the equilibrium price and the price floor and thereby reduce the size of the resulting surplus.

2. The federal government can purchase the surplus output at the $4 price (thereby subsidizing Prairie farmers) and store or otherwise dispose of it.

Controversial Tradeoffs

In a free market, the competitive forces match the supply decisions of producers and the demand decisions of buyers, but price ceilings and floors interfere with such an outcome. The government must provide a rationing system to handle product shortages stemming from price ceilings and devise ways to eliminate product surpluses arising from price floors. Legal maximum and minimum prices thus lead to controversial tradeoffs. The alleged benefits of price ceilings to consumers and price floors to producers must be balanced against the costs associated with shortages and surpluses.

Our discussion of price controls and interest-rate ceilings on credit cards shows that government interference with the market can have unintended, undesirable side effects. Price controls, for example, create illegal black markets. Rent controls may discourage housing construction and repair. Instead of protecting low-income families from higher interest charges, interest-rate ceilings may simply deny credit to those families. For all these reasons, economists generally oppose government-imposed prices.

ADDITIONAL CONSEQUENCES

Price floors such as P_f in Figure 3.9 not only disrupt the rationing ability of prices but also distort resource allocation. Without the price floor, the $3 equilibrium price of wheat would cause financial losses and force high-cost wheat producers to plant other crops or abandon farming altogether. But the $4 price floor allows them to continue to grow wheat and remain farmers. So society devotes too many of its scarce resources to wheat production and too little to producing other, more valuable, goods and services. It fails to achieve allocative efficiency.

That's not all. Consumers of wheat-based products pay higher prices because of the price floor. Taxpayers pay higher taxes to finance the government's purchase of the surplus. Also, the price floor causes potential environmental damage by encouraging wheat farmers to bring "marginal land" into production. The higher price also prompts imports of wheat. But, since such imports would increase the quantity of wheat supplied and thus undermine the price floor, the government needs to erect tariffs (taxes on imports) to keep the foreign wheat out. Such tariffs usually prompt other countries to retaliate with their own tariffs against Canadian agricultural or manufacturing exports.

It is easy to see why economists "raise the caution flag" when politicians advocate imposing price ceilings or price floors. In both cases, good intentions typically lead to bad economic outcomes. **(Key Question 12)**

QUICK REVIEW

- In competitive markets, prices adjust to the equilibrium level at which quantity demanded equals quantity supplied.

- The equilibrium price and quantity are those indicated by the intersection of the supply and demand curves for any product or resource.

- An increase in demand increases equilibrium price and quantity; a decrease in demand decreases equilibrium price and quantity.

- An increase in supply reduces equilibrium price but increases equilibrium quantity; a decrease in supply increases equilibrium price but reduces equilibrium quantity.

- Over time, equilibrium price and quantity may change in directions that seem at odds with the laws of demand and supply because the other-things-equal assumption is violated.

THE LASTword | Ticket Scalping: A Bum Rap?

Some market transactions get a bad name that is not warranted.

The Effectiveness of Markets

Tickets to athletic and artistic events are sometimes resold at higher-than-original prices—a market transaction known by the term "scalping." For example, the original buyer may resell a $50 ticket to an NHL game for $200, $250, or more. The media often denounce scalpers for "ripping off" buyers by charging "exorbitant" prices. Scalping and extortion are synonymous in some people's minds.

But is scalping really sinful? We must first recognize that such ticket resales are voluntary transactions. Both buyer and seller expect to gain from the exchange. Otherwise it would not occur! The seller must value the $200 more than seeing the event, and the buyer must value seeing the event more than the $200. So there are no losers or victims here: Both buyer and seller benefit from the transaction. The

"scalping" market simply redistributes assets (game or concert tickets) from those who value them less to those who value them more.

Does scalping impose losses or injury on other parties, in particular the sponsors of the event? If the sponsors are injured, it is because they initially priced tickets below the equilibrium level. In so doing they suffer an economic loss in the form of less revenue and profit than they might have otherwise received. But the loss is self-inflicted because of their pricing error.

That mistake is quite separate and distinct from the fact that some tickets were later sold at a higher price.

What about spectators? Does scalping deteriorate the enthusiasm of the audience? No! People who have the greatest interest in the event will pay the scalper's high prices. Ticket scalping also benefits the teams and performing artists, because they will appear before more dedicated audiences—ones that are more likely to buy souvenir items or CDs.

So, is ticket scalping undesirable? Not on economic grounds. Both seller and buyer of a "scalped" ticket benefit, and a more interested audience results. Event sponsors may sacrifice revenue and profits, but that stems from their own misjudgment of the equilibrium price.

CHAPTER SUMMARY

3.1 MARKETS

- A market is an institution or arrangement that brings together buyers and sellers of a product, service, or resource for the purpose of exchange.

3.2 DEMAND

- Demand is a schedule or curve representing the willingness of buyers in a specific period to purchase a particular product at each of various prices. The law of demand implies that consumers will buy more of a product at a low price than at a high price. Therefore, other things equal, the relationship between price and quantity demanded is negative or inverse and is graphed as a downward-sloping curve. Market demand curves are found by adding horizontally the demand curves of the many individual consumers in the market.

- Changes in one or more of the determinants of demand (consumer tastes, the number of buyers in the market, the money incomes of consumers, the prices of related goods, and price expectations) shift the market demand curve. A shift to the right is an increase in demand; a shift to the left is a decrease in demand. A change in demand is different from a change in the quantity demanded, the latter being a movement from one point to another point on a fixed demand curve because of a change in the product's price.

3.3 SUPPLY

- Supply is a schedule or curve showing the amounts of a product that producers are willing to offer in the market at each possible price during a specific period. The law of supply states that, other things equal, producers will offer more of a product at a high price than at a low price. Thus, the relationship between price and quantity supplied is positive or direct, and supply is graphed as an upward-sloping curve. The market supply curve is the horizontal summation of the supply curves of the individual producers of the product.

- Changes in one or more of the determinants of supply (resource prices, production techniques, taxes or subsidies, the prices of other goods, price expectations, or the number of sellers in the market) shift the supply curve of a product. A shift to the right is an increase in supply; a shift to the left is a decrease in supply. In contrast, a change in the price of the product being considered causes a change in the quantity supplied, which is shown as a movement from one point to another point on a fixed supply curve.

3.4 SUPPLY AND DEMAND: MARKET EQUILIBRIUM

- The equilibrium price and quantity are established at the intersection of the supply and demand curves. The interaction of market demand and market supply adjusts the price to the point at which the quantity demanded and supplied are equal. This is the equilibrium price. The corresponding quantity is the equilibrium quantity.

- The ability of market forces to synchronize selling and buying decisions to eliminate potential surpluses and shortages is known as the rationing function of prices.

- A change in either demand or supply changes the equilibrium price and quantity. Increases in demand raise both equilibrium price and equilibrium quantity; decreases in demand lower both equilibrium price and equilibrium quantity. Increases in supply lower equilibrium price and raise equilibrium quantity; decreases in supply raise equilibrium price and lower equilibrium quantity.

- Simultaneous changes in demand and supply affect equilibrium price and quantity in various ways, depending on their direction and relative magnitudes.

3.5 APPLICATION: GOVERNMENT-SET PRICES

- A price ceiling is a maximum price set by government and is designed to help consumers. A price floor is a minimum price set by government and is designed to aid producers.

- Legally fixed prices stifle the rationing function of prices and distort the allocation of resources. Effective price ceilings produce persistent product shortages, and if an equitable distribution of the product is sought, government must ration the product to consumers. Price floors lead to product surpluses; the government must either purchase the product or eliminate the surplus by imposing restrictions on production or increasing private demand.

TERMS AND CONCEPTS

market, p. 48
demand, p. 48
law of demand, p. 49
marginal utility, p. 49
income effect, p. 50

substitution effect, p. 50
demand curve, p. 50
determinants of demand, p. 50
normal good, p. 53
inferior good, p. 53

substitute goods, p. 53
complementary goods, p. 53
change in demand, p. 54
change in quantity demanded, p. 54
supply, p. 55

STUDY QUESTIONS

1. Explain the law of demand. Why does a demand curve slope downward? What are the determinants of demand? What happens to the demand curve when each of these determinants changes? Distinguish between a change in demand and a change in the quantity demanded, noting the cause(s) of each.

2. **KEY QUESTION**   What effect will each of the following have on the demand for product B?

   a. Product B becomes more fashionable.

   b. The price of substitute product C falls.

   c. Income declines and product B is an inferior good.

   d. Consumers anticipate the price of product B will be lower in the near future.

   e. The price of complementary product D falls.

3. Explain the following news dispatch from Hull, England: "The fish market here slumped today to what local commentators called 'a disastrous level'—all because of a shortage of potatoes. The potatoes are one of the main ingredients in a dish that figures on almost every café menu—fish and chips."

4. Explain the law of supply. Why does the supply curve slope upward? What are the determinants of supply? What happens to the supply curve when each of these determinants changes? Distinguish between a change in supply and a change in the quantity supplied, noting the cause(s) of each.

5. **KEY QUESTION**   What effect will each of the following have on the supply of product B?

   a. A technological advance in the methods of producing product B.

   b. A decline in the number of firms in industry B.

   c. An increase in the prices of resources required in the production of B.

   d. The expectation that the equilibrium price of B will be lower in the future than it is currently.

   e. A decline in the price of product A, a good whose production requires substantially the same techniques and resources as does the production of B.

   f. The levying of a specific sales tax on B.

   g. The granting of a 50-cent per-unit subsidy for each unit of B produced.

6. "In the corn market, demand often exceeds supply and supply sometimes exceeds demand." "The price of corn rises and falls in response to changes in supply and demand." In which of these two statements are the terms *supply* and *demand* used correctly? Explain.

7. **KEY QUESTION**   Suppose the total demand for wheat and the total supply of wheat per month in the Winnipeg grain market are as follows:

Thousands of bushels demanded	Price per bushel	Thousands of bushels supplied	Surplus (+) or shortage (−)
85	$3.40	72	_____
80	$3.70	73	_____
75	$4.00	75	_____
70	$4.30	77	_____
65	$4.60	79	_____
60	$4.90	81	_____

   a. What is the equilibrium price? What is the equilibrium quantity? Fill in the surplus-shortage column and use it to explain why your answers are correct.

   b. Graph the demand for wheat and the supply of wheat. Be sure to label the axes of your graph correctly. Label equilibrium price *P* and equilibrium quantity *Q*.

   c. Why will $3.40 not be the equilibrium price in this market? Why not $4.90? "Surpluses drive prices up; shortages drive them down." Do you agree?

8. **KEY QUESTION**   How will each of the following changes in demand and/or supply affect equilibrium price and equilibrium quantity in a competitive market; that is, do price and quantity rise, fall, or remain unchanged, or are the answers indeterminate because they depend on the magnitudes of the shifts? Use supply and demand diagrams to verify your answers.

   a. Supply decreases and demand is constant.

   b. Demand decreases and supply is constant.

   c. Supply increases and demand is constant.

   d. Demand increases and supply increases.

   e. Demand increases and supply is constant.

   f. Supply increases and demand decreases.

g. Demand increases and supply decreases.

h. Demand decreases and supply decreases.

9. In 2001, an outbreak of foot-and-mouth disease in Europe led to the burning of millions of cattle carcasses. What impact do you think this had on the supply of cattle hides, hide prices, the supply of leather goods, and the price of leather goods?

10. Explain: "Even though parking meters may yield little or no revenue, they should nevertheless be retained because of the rationing function they perform."

11. Refer to the table in Question 7. Suppose that the government establishes a price ceiling of $3.70 for wheat. What might prompt the government to establish this price ceiling? Explain carefully the main effects. Demonstrate your answer graphically. Next, suppose that the government establishes a price floor of $4.60 for wheat. What will be the main effects of this price floor? Demonstrate your answer graphically.

12. **KEY QUESTION**   What do economists mean when they say that "price floors and ceilings stifle the rationing function of prices and distort resource allocation?"

13. Critically evaluate: "In comparing the two equilibrium positions in Figure 13-7(a), I note that a larger amount is actually purchased at a higher price. This refutes the law of demand."

14. **Advanced analysis:** Assume that demand for a commodity is represented by the equation $P = 10 - .2Q_d$ and supply by the equation $P = 2 + .2Q_s$, where Q_d and Q_s are quantity demanded and quantity supplied, respectively, and P is price. Using the equilibrium condition $Q_s = Q_d$, solve the equations to determine equilibrium price. Now determine equilibrium quantity. Graph the two equations to substantiate your answers.

15. **(The Last Word)** Discuss the economic aspects of ticket scalping, specifying gainers and losers.

INTERNET APPLICATION QUESTION

1. **Changes in Demand—Baby Diapers and Retirement Villages** Other things equal, an increase in the number of buyers for a product or service will increase demand. Baby diapers and retirement villages are two products designed for different population groups. The McConnell-Brue-Barbiero Web site (Chapter 3) provides links to population pyramids (graphs that show the distribution of population by age and sex) for countries for the current year, 2025, and 2050. View the population pyramids for Mexico, Japan, and Canada. Which country would you expect to have the greatest percentage increase in demand for baby diapers in the year 2050? For retirement villages? Which country would you expect to have the greatest absolute increase in demand for baby diapers? For retirement villages?

Math Appendix to Chapter 3

A3.1   The Mathematics of Market Equilibrium

A market equilibrium is the price and the quantity, denoted as the pair $(Q^\star, P^\star)$, of a commodity bought or sold at price $P^\star$. The following mathematical note provides an introduction of how a market equilibrium $(Q^\star, P^\star)$ is derived.

The market equilibrium is found by using the market demand (buyers' behaviour), the market supply (sellers' behaviour), and the negotiating process (to find the agreed upon price and quantity, namely $P^\star$ and $Q^\star$, on which to transact). The market equilibrium is identified by the condition reached at the end of the negotiating process that at the price they negotiated, $P^\star$, the quantity of the commodity that buyers are willing to buy, denoted as Q_d, and the quantity sellers are willing to sell, denoted as Q_s, matches exactly.

The Demand Curve

The equation describing the downward-sloping demand when the demand curve is a straight line, in which Q_d represents the quantity demanded by buyers and P the price, is

$$P = a - bQ_d$$

The demand equation and curve below tell us that if the price is higher than a then the buyers will not buy; thus, for a transaction to occur the price must be lower. The demand equation and curve also tell us that at a price lower than a the quantity demanded by the buyers increases. Buyers' behaviour, as described by the demand equation, is that at lower prices buyers buy more quantity.

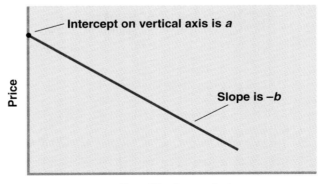

Intercept on vertical axis is *a*

Slope is *−b*

Price

Quantity demanded

The Supply Curve

The equation describing the upward sloping market supply function when the supply curve is a straight line, in which Q_s represents the quantity supplied by sellers and P the price, is

$$P = c + dQ_s$$

If the price is lower than c then the sellers will sell nothing, as the figure below shows. If the price is c or higher, then the supply equation states that sellers facing higher prices sell more quantity. Sellers' behaviour, as described by the supply curve and equation, is that at higher prices sellers make more quantity available.

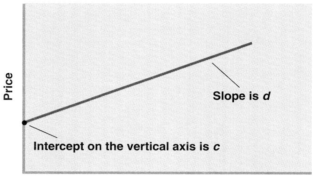

Quantity supplied

The Market Equilibrium

The negotiating process (in which price and quantity or both adjust) provides the mechanism by which, eventually, buyers and sellers agree upon a price, P^*, and a quantity, Q^*, at which they can buy and sell and thus complete the transaction. At the end of the negotiating process, the quantity demanded by the buyers, Q_d, is equal to the quantity supplied by the sellers, Q_s (at the agreed-upon price), and thus the market is in equilibrium. The mathematical representation of such a negotiating process is described as follows.

At the agreed price, P^*, the equilibrium condition of the negotiating process, the equality in the quantity demanded and supplied, is

$$Q_d = Q_s$$

Having denoted Q^* as the equilibrium quantity, then it must be that $Q^* = Q_d = Q_s$. To solve for the equilibrium quantity Q^* and the equilibrium price P^* the demand and supply functions are used. With Q^* the equilibrium quantity, for the buyers

$$P^* = a - bQ^*,$$

and for the sellers

$$P^* = c + dQ^*.$$

Now, since P^* is the same agreed-upon price by both buyer and seller, then

$$a - bQ^* = c + dQ^*,$$

giving the equilibrium quantity, Q^*, as

$$Q^* = \frac{(a - c)}{(b + d)}.$$

To find P^* substitute $\dfrac{(a-c)}{(b+d)}$ in the supply (or demand) function.

$$P^* = c + d\,\frac{(a-c)}{(b+d)}, \text{ thus}$$

$$P^* = \frac{(ad+bc)}{(b+d)}.$$

The equilibrium is $(Q^*, P^*) = \left[\dfrac{(a-c)}{(b+d)}, \dfrac{(ad+bc)}{(b+d)}\right].$

The market equilibrium may also be represented diagrammatically, as shown below.

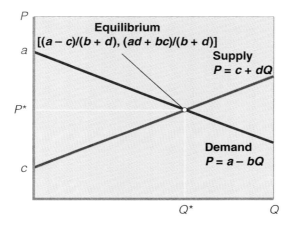

Example

Assume the demand for a pair of jeans is represented by the equation:

$$P = 100 - .2Q_d$$

Assume the supply of a pair of jeans is represented by the equation:

$$P = 20 + .2Q_s$$

Assume quantities are expressed in jeans per day, and the price in dollars.

To find the equilibrium price P^*, and equilibrium quantity Q^*, substitute Q^* for Q_d and Q_s and P^* for P in the demand and supply equations. To solve for Q^*:

$$100 - .2Q^* = 20 + .2Q^*$$

$$.4Q^* = 80$$

$$Q^* = 200$$

To solve for P^*:

$$P^* = 100 - .2(200)$$

$$= 60$$

The equilibrium quantity of jeans is 200 per day, and the equilibrium price is $60 per pair of jeans.

4

Chapter

The Market System and International Trade

Suppose that you were assigned to compile a list of all the individual goods and services available at a large shopping mall, including the different brands and variations of each type of product. We think you would agree that this task would be daunting and the list would be long! And, although a single shopping mall contains a remarkable quantity and variety of goods, it is only a minuscule part of the Canadian economy.

Who decided that the particular goods and services available at the mall and in the broader economy should be produced? How did the producers determine which technology and types of resources to use in producing these particular goods? Who will obtain these products? What accounts for the new and improved products among these goods?

In Chapter 3 we saw how equilibrium prices and quantities are established in *individual* product and factor markets. We now widen our focus to take in *all* product markets and factor markets, variously referred to as *capitalism, the private enterprise system,* or simply the *market system.* In this chapter we examine the characteristics of the market system and how it addresses the economic problem. We then look at international markets and Canada's trade with the rest of the world.

4.1   Characteristics of the Market System

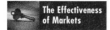

A market brings together buyers and sellers for the purpose of exchange. It can be a local market in which relatively few people participate, or it can be on an international scale where hundreds of millions of buyers and sellers from all over the globe participate. In order for the market system to function, several characteristics must be present: private property, freedom of enterprise and choice, self-interest as the dominant motive, competition, and a limited role for government.

Private Property

private property
The right of private persons and firms to obtain, own, control, employ, dispose of, and bequeath land, capital, and other property.

In a market system, individuals and firms, not the government, own most of the property resources (land and capital). In fact, it is the private ownership of capital that gives capitalism its name. This right of **private property**, coupled with the freedom to negotiate binding legal contracts, enables individuals and businesses to obtain, use, and dispose of property resources as they see fit. Also, with private property rights owners can designate who will receive their property when they die.

Property rights encourage investment, innovation, exchange, maintenance of property, and the expansion of the production of goods and services. Individuals stock stores, build factories, or clear land for farming because they can reap the rewards. Why would they do so if the government, or anyone else, could take that property from them?

Property rights also extend to intellectual property through patents, copyrights, and trademarks. Long-term protection encourages people to write books, music, and computer programs and to invent new products and production processes without fear that others will steal them and the rewards they may bring.

Property rights also facilitate exchange. The title to an automobile or the deed to a cattle ranch assures the buyer that the seller is the legitimate owner. Moreover, property rights encourage owners to maintain or improve their property so as to preserve or increase its value. Finally, property rights enable people to use their time and resources to produce more goods and services, rather than using them to protect and retain the property they have already produced or acquired.

If property rights did not exist, or were not enforced, it would make market exchange much more costly; it would also increase the price of goods and services exchanged on markets. Buyers would have to ascertain the origins of what they bought, and property would need to be protected from burglars.

Freedom of Enterprise and Choice

freedom of enterprise
The freedom of firms to obtain economic resources, to use these resources to produce products of the firm's own choosing, and to sell their products in markets of their choice.

Closely related to private ownership of property is freedom of enterprise and choice. The market system requires that various economic units make choices, which are expressed and implemented in the economy's markets.

- **Freedom of enterprise** ensures that entrepreneurs and private businesses are free to obtain and use resources to produce their choice of goods and services, and to sell them in the markets of their choice.

freedom of choice
The freedom of owners of property resources to employ or dispose of them as they see fit, and of consumers to spend their incomes in a manner that they think is appropriate.

- **Freedom of choice** allows owners to employ or dispose of their property and money as they see fit. It also allows workers to enter any line of work for which they are qualified. Finally, it ensures that consumers are free to buy the goods and services that best satisfy their wants.

These choices are free only within broad legal limitations, of course. Illegal choices such as selling human organs or buying illicit drugs are punished through fines and imprisonment. (Global Perspective 4.1 reveals that the degree of economic freedom varies greatly from nation to nation.)

Self-interest

self-interest
That which each firm, property owner, worker, and consumer believes is best for itself.

In the market system, **self-interest** is the motivating force of all the various economic units as they express their free choices. Self-interest means that each economic unit tries to do what is best for itself. Entrepreneurs try to maximize profit or minimize loss. Property owners try to get the highest price for the sale or rent of their resources. Workers try to maximize their utility (satisfaction) by finding jobs that offer the best combination of wages, hours, fringe benefits, and working conditions. Consumers try to obtain the products they want at the lowest possible price and apportion their expenditures to maximize their utility.

The pursuit of self-interest is not the same as selfishness. Self-interest simply means maximizing some benefit, and can include helping others. A stockholder in Halifax may invest to receive the best available corporate dividends and then donate a portion of them to the local United Way or give them to grandchildren. A worker in Winnipeg may take a second job to help pay college or university tuition for her or his children. An entrepreneur in Toronto may make a fortune and donate much of it to a charitable foundation.

Competition

competition
The presence in a market of a large number of independent buyers and sellers competing with one another and the freedom of buyers and sellers to enter and leave the market.

The market system fosters **competition** among economic units. The basis of this competition is freedom of choice exercised in pursuit of the best return. Very broadly defined, *competition* requires:

- Independently acting sellers and buyers operating in a particular product or factor market
- Freedom of sellers and buyers to enter or leave markets, based on their self-interest

Competition diffuses economic power within the businesses and households that make up the economy. When there are independently acting sellers and buyers in a market, no one buyer or seller is able to dictate the price of the product.

Consider the supply side of the product market. When a product becomes scarce, its price rises. An unseasonable frost in Southern Ontario may seriously reduce the supply of apple crops and sharply increase the price of apples. Similarly, if a single producer can restrict the total output of a product, the product's price will rise. By controlling market supply, a firm can "rig the market" to its own advantage. But that is not possible in markets in which suppliers compete. A firm that raises its price will lose part or all of its business to competitors.

The same reasoning applies to the demand side of the market. With multiple buyers, single buyers cannot manipulate the market to their own advantage by refusing to pay the market price.

Competition also implies that producers can enter or leave an industry; there are no insurmountable barriers to an industry expanding or contracting. This freedom of an industry to expand or contract provides the economy with the flexibility needed to remain efficient over time. Freedom of entry and exit enables the economy to adjust to changes in consumer tastes, technology, and resource availability.

The diffusion of economic power inherent in competition limits the potential abuse of that power. A producer who charges more than the competitive market price will lose sales to other producers. An employer who pays less than the competitive market wage will lose workers to other employers. A firm that fails to exploit new technology will lose profits to firms that do. Competition is the basic regulatory force in the market system.

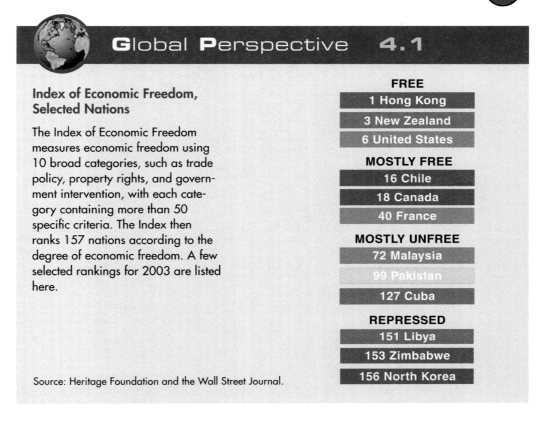

Global Perspective   4.1

Index of Economic Freedom, Selected Nations

The Index of Economic Freedom measures economic freedom using 10 broad categories, such as trade policy, property rights, and government intervention, with each category containing more than 50 specific criteria. The Index then ranks 157 nations according to the degree of economic freedom. A few selected rankings for 2003 are listed here.

Source: Heritage Foundation and the Wall Street Journal.

FREE
1 Hong Kong
3 New Zealand
6 United States

MOSTLY FREE
16 Chile
18 Canada
40 France

MOSTLY UNFREE
72 Malaysia
99 Pakistan
127 Cuba

REPRESSED
151 Libya
153 Zimbabwe
156 North Korea

Markets and Prices

Markets and prices are key characteristics of the market system. They give the market system its ability to coordinate millions of daily economic decisions. A market system is necessary to convey the decisions made by buyers and sellers of products and resources. The decisions made on each side of the market determine a set of product and resource prices that guide resource owners, entrepreneurs, and consumers as they make and revise their choices and pursue what is best for themselves.

The market system is an organizing mechanism. It serves as an elaborate communication network through which innumerable individual free choices are recorded, summarized, and balanced. Those who respond to market signals and obey market dictates are rewarded with greater profit and income; those who do not respond to these signals and choose to ignore market dictates are penalized. Through this mechanism millions of independent decisions by producers and consumers determine what the economy should produce, how production can be organized efficiently, and how the fruits of production are to be distributed among the various units that make up the economy.

Active but Limited Government

Another characteristic of the market system, as evidenced in modern economies, is an active but limited government. Although a market system promotes a high degree of efficiency in the use of its resources, it has certain shortcomings. We will discover later in this chapter that government can increase the overall effectiveness of the economic system in several ways.

Technology and Capital Goods

The market system facilitates the extensive use of capital goods. In the market system, competition, freedom of choice, self-interest, and personal reward provide the opportunity and motivation for technological advance. The monetary rewards for new products or production techniques accrue directly to the innovator. The market system therefore encourages extensive use and rapid development of complex capital goods: tools, machinery, large-scale factories, and facilities for storage, communication, transportation, and marketing.

roundabout production
The construction and use of capital to aid in the production of consumer goods.

Advanced technology and capital goods are important because the most direct methods of production are the least efficient. The only way to avoid that inefficiency is to rely on **roundabout production**. It would be ridiculous for a Prairie farmer to go at production with bare hands. There are huge benefits—in the form of more efficient production and, therefore, a more abundant output—to be derived from creating and using such tools of production (capital equipment) as plows, tractors, storage bins, and so on.

Specialization

specialization
The use of the resources of an individual, a firm, a region, or a nation to produce one or a few goods and services.

The extent to which market economies rely on **specialization** is extraordinary. The majority of consumers produce virtually none of the goods and services they consume, and they consume little or nothing of what they produce. The worker who devotes eight hours a day to installing windows in Fords may own a Honda. Many farmers sell their milk to the local dairy and then buy margarine at the local grocery store. Society learned long ago that self-sufficiency breeds inefficiency. The jack-of-all-trades may be a very colourful individual but is certainly not an efficient producer.

DIVISION OF LABOUR

division of labour
Dividing the work required to produce a product into a number of different tasks that are performed by different workers.

Human specialization—called the **division of labour**—contributes to a society's output in several ways.

- *Specialization makes use of differences in ability.* Specialization enables individuals to take advantage of existing differences in their abilities and skills. If caveman A is strong and swift, and good at tracking animals, and caveman B is weak and slow but patient, their distribution of talents can be most efficiently used if A hunts and B fishes.

- *Specialization fosters learning by doing.* Even if the abilities of A and B are identical, specialization may still be advantageous. By devoting all your time to a single task, you are more likely to develop the skills it requires and to devise improved techniques than you would by working at a number of different tasks. You learn to be a good hunter by going hunting every day.

- *Specialization saves time.* By devoting all your time to a single task you avoid the loss of time incurred in shifting from one job to another.

For all these reasons, specialization increases the total output society can get from limited resources.

GEOGRAPHIC SPECIALIZATION

Specialization also works on a regional and international basis. It is conceivable that apples could be grown in Saskatchewan, but because of the unsuitability of the land, rainfall, and temperature, the costs would be very high. And it is conceivable that wheat could be grown in British Columbia. But for similar reasons such production would be costly. So, Saskatchewan farmers produce products—wheat in particular—for which their resources are best suited, and British Columbians (in the Okanagan Valley) do the same, producing apples and other fruits. By specializing, both provinces' economies produce more than is needed locally. Then, very sensibly, they exchange some of their surpluses—wheat for apples, apples for wheat.

Similarly, on an international scale, Canada specializes in producing such items as telecommunication equipment (Nortel Networks) and small commercial aircraft (Bombardier), which it sells abroad in exchange for video recorders from Japan, bananas from Honduras, and woven baskets from Thailand. Both human specialization and geographical specialization are needed to achieve efficiency in the use of limited resources.

Use of Money

medium of exchange
Items sellers generally accept and buyers generally use to pay for a good or service.

barter
The exchange of one good or service for another good or service.

www.swp.com
Saskatchewan Wheat Pool

money
Any item that is generally acceptable to sellers in exchange for goods and services.

Specialization and trade require the use of money. Money performs several functions, but first and foremost it is a **medium of exchange**. It makes trade easier.

A convenient means of exchanging goods is required for specialization. Exchange can, and sometimes does, occur through **barter**—swapping goods for goods, say, wheat for apples. But barter poses serious problems for the economy because it requires a *coincidence of wants* between the buyer and seller. In our example, we assumed that Saskatchewan had excess wheat to trade and wanted apples. And we assumed that British Columbia had excess apples to trade and wanted wheat. So an exchange occurred. But if such a coincidence of wants is missing, trade cannot occur.

Suppose Saskatchewan has no interest in British Columbia's apples but wants potatoes from Prince Edward Island. And suppose that Prince Edward Island wants British Columbia's apples but not Saskatchewan's wheat. And, to complicate matters, suppose that British Columbia wants some of Saskatchewan's wheat but none of PEI's potatoes. We summarize the situation in Figure 4-1.

In none of these cases shown in the figure is there a coincidence of wants, thus trade by barter clearly would be difficult. Instead, people in each province use **money**, which is simply a convenient social invention to facilitate exchanges of goods and services. Historically, people have used cattle, cigarettes, shells, stones, pieces of metal, and many other commodities, with varying degrees of success, as a medium of exchange. But to serve as money, an item needs to pass only one test: *It must be generally acceptable to sellers in exchange for their goods and services.* Money is socially defined; whatever society accepts as a medium of exchange *is* money.

Most economies use pieces of paper as money. The use of paper dollars (currency) as a medium of exchange is what enables Saskatchewan, B.C., and P.E.I. to overcome their non-coincidence of wants.

On a global basis the fact that different nations have different currencies complicates specialization and exchange. However, markets in which currencies are bought and sold make it possible for residents of Canada, Japan, Germany, Britain, and Mexico, through the swapping of dollars, yen, euros, pounds, and pesos, one for another, to exchange goods and services.

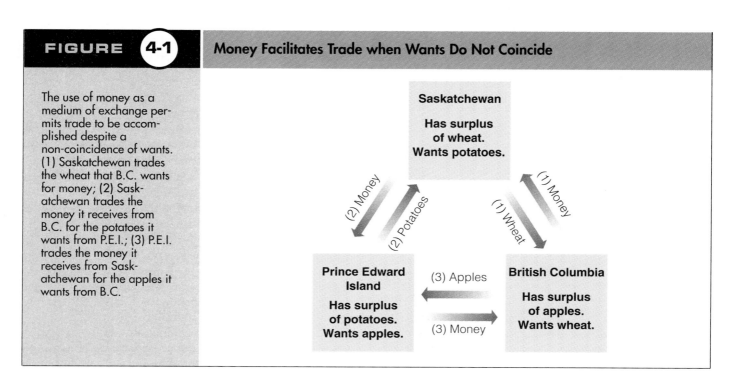

FIGURE 4-1   Money Facilitates Trade when Wants Do Not Coincide

The use of money as a medium of exchange permits trade to be accomplished despite a non-coincidence of wants. (1) Saskatchewan trades the wheat that B.C. wants for money; (2) Saskatchewan trades the money it receives from B.C. for the potatoes it wants from P.E.I.; (3) P.E.I. trades the money it receives from Saskatchewan for the apples it wants from B.C.

> ## QUICK REVIEW
>
> - The market system requires private ownership of property, freedom of enterprise, and freedom of choice.
>
> - The market system permits economic entities—business, resource suppliers, and consumers—to pursue and further their self-interest. It prevents any single economic entity from dictating the prices of products or resources.
>
> - The coordinating mechanism of the market system is a system of markets and prices.
>
> - The market systems of modern industrial economies are characterized by extensive use of technologically advanced capital goods. Such goods help these economies achieve greater efficiency in production.
>
> - Specialization is extensive in market systems; it enhances efficiency and output by enabling individuals, regions, and nations to produce those goods and services for which their resources are best suited.
>
> - The use of money in market systems facilitates specialization and the exchange of goods and services.

4.2 The Market System at Work

household
An economic unit (of one or more persons) that provides the economy with resources and uses the income received to purchase goods and services that satisfy material wants.

firm
An organization that employs resources to produce a good or service for profit.

There are two primary *decision makers* in a market economy: **households** (consumers) and **firms** (businesses). Households are the ultimate suppliers of economic resources (factors of production) and simultaneously the major spending group in the economy. Firms provide goods and services to the economy.

We have noted that a market system is characterized by competition, freedom of enterprise, and choice. Consumers are free to buy what they choose; entrepreneurs and firms are free to produce and sell what they choose; and resource suppliers are free to make their property and human resources available in whatever use or occupation they choose. We may wonder why such an economy does not collapse in chaos. If Canadian consumers want breakfast cereal but businesses choose to produce athletic shoes and resource suppliers decide to manufacture computer software, production would seem to be deadlocked by the apparent inconsistency of these free choices.

In reality, the millions of decisions made by Canadian households and businesses are highly consistent with one another. Firms *do* produce the goods and services that consumers want, and households *do* provide the kinds of labour that businesses want.

To understand the operation of the market system, you must first recognize that every economy must address **Four Fundamental Questions**:

Four Fundamental Questions
The four questions that every economy must answer.

- What goods and services will be produced?

- How will the goods and services be produced?

- Who will get the goods and services?

- How will the system accommodate change?

The Four Fundamental Questions highlight the economic choices underlying the production possibilities curve discussed in Chapter 2. Let's examine how the market system answers each of these questions and thus addresses the economic problem.

What Will Be Produced?

With product and resource prices in place, established through competition in both the product and factor markets, what will determine the specific types and quantities of goods that will be produced in the market system? *Because businesses seek profits and avoid losses, those goods and services produced at a continuing profit* will *be produced and those produced at a continuing loss will not.* Profits and losses depend on the difference between the total revenue a firm receives from selling its product and the total cost of producing the product.

Consumers register their preferences on the demand side of the product market; producers and suppliers of factors of production respond appropriately in seeking to further their own welfare. The market system communicates the wants of consumers to businesses and suppliers of factors of production and elicits appropriate responses.

CONSUMER SOVEREIGNTY AND "DOLLAR VOTES"

consumer sovereignty
Determination by consumers of the types and quantities of goods and services that will be produced with the scarce resources of the economy.

dollar votes
The "votes" that consumers and entrepreneurs cast for the production of consumer and capital goods, respectively, when they purchase them in product and factor markets.

In the market system, consumers are sovereign (in command). **Consumer sovereignty** works through consumer demand, and consumer demand is crucial in determining the types and quantities of goods produced. Consumers spend the income they earn from the sale of their resources on those goods they are most willing and able to buy. Through these **dollar votes** consumers register their wants via the demand side of the product market. If the dollar votes for a certain product are great enough to provide a normal profit, businesses will produce that product. If there is an increase in consumer demand, so that enough dollar votes are cast to provide above normal profit, the industry will expand, as will the output of the product.

Conversely, a decrease in consumer demand—meaning fewer dollar votes cast for the product—will result in losses, and, in time, the industry will contract. As firms leave the industry, the output of the product will decline. Indeed, the industry may even cease to exist. Again, the consumers are sovereign; they collectively direct resources away from industries that are not meeting consumer wants and toward those industries that do.

The dollar votes of consumers determine not only which industries will continue to exist but also which products will survive or fail. Example: In 1991, responding to doctors and nutritionists, McDonald's introduced its low-fat McLean burger. Good idea? Not really. Most consumers found the new product "too dry" and "not tasty," so sales were meagre. In 1996 McDonald's quietly dropped the McLean burger from its menu at the same time that it introduced its higher-fat Arch Deluxe burger. In effect, consumers had collectively "voted out" the McLean burger.

MARKET RESTRAINTS ON FREEDOM

Firms are not really free to produce whatever they wish. Consumers' buying decisions make the production of some products profitable and the production of other products unprofitable, thus restricting the choice of firms in deciding what to produce. Firms must match their production choices with consumer choices or else face losses and eventual bankruptcy.

derived demand
The demand for a factor of production that depends on the demand for the products it can be used to produce.

The same holds true for suppliers of factors of production. The demand for factors is a **derived demand**—derived, that is, from the demand for the goods and services that the factors help produce. There is a demand for autoworkers in Canada because there is a demand for automobiles. There is no demand for buggy-whip braiders because there is no demand for buggy whips. Suppliers of factors of production are not free to allocate their resources to the production of goods that consumers do not value highly. Consumers register their preferences on the demand side of the product market; producers and factor suppliers, prompted by their own self-interest, respond appropriately.

How Will the Goods and Services Be Produced?

The market system steers resources (factors of production) to those industries that have products consumers want—simply because those industries survive, are profitable, and pay for resources. Within each industry, the firms that survive are the ones that are profitable. Because competition weeds out high-cost producers, continued profitability requires that firms produce their output at minimum cost. Achieving least-cost production necessitates, among other things, that firms locate their production facilities optimally, taking into consideration such variables as factor prices, factor productivity, and transportation costs. Least-cost production also means that firms must employ the most economically efficient technique of production in producing their output.

Who Will Get the Goods and Services?

The market system enters the picture in two ways when solving the problem of distributing total output. Generally, any product will be distributed to consumers based on their ability and willingness to pay its existing market price. If the price of some product, say, a pocket calculator, is $15, then those buyers who are able and willing to pay that price will get a pocket calculator. This is the rationing function of equilibrium prices.

The ability to pay the equilibrium prices for pocket calculators and other products depends on the amount of income that consumers earn. If they earn sufficient income and want to spend their money on a particular good, they can have it. The amount of income they earn depends on (1) the quantities of the factors of production they supply and (2) the prices those factors of production command in the factor market. This in turn is dependent on the demand for the items produced with those factors. The prices of factors of production (wages and salaries in particular) are key in determining the size of each household's income and therefore each household's ability to buy part of the economy's output.

How Will the System Accommodate Change?

Consumer preferences, technology, and supplies of factors constantly change. A particular allocation of resources that is now the most efficient for a *specific* pattern of consumer tastes, range of technological alternatives, and supplies of resources may become obsolete and inefficient as consumer preferences change, new techniques of production are discovered, and factor supplies change over time. Can the market economy adjust to such changes and still use resources efficiently?

GUIDING FUNCTION OF PRICES

Suppose consumer tastes change. For instance, assume that consumers in Alberta decide they want more apple juice and less milk than the economy currently provides. Those changes in consumer tastes will be communicated to producers through an increase in demand for apples and a decline in demand for milk. Apple prices will rise and milk prices will fall.

Now, assuming that firms in both industries were enjoying profits before these changes in consumer demand set in, the higher apple prices will mean higher profit for the apple growing industry, and the lower milk prices will mean losses for the milk industry. Self-interest will induce new competitors to enter the prosperous apple growing industry and will in time force firms to leave the depressed milk industry.

The higher profit that initially follows the increase in demand for apples will not only induce that industry to expand but will also give it the revenue needed to obtain the resources essential to its growth. Higher apple prices will permit apple growers to pay higher prices for resources, thereby increasing resource demand and drawing resources from less urgent alternative employment. The reverse occurs in the milk industry, where resource demand declines and fewer workers and other factors of production are employed. These adjustments in the economy are appropriate responses to the changes in consumer tastes. This is consumer sovereignty at work.

The market system is a gigantic communications system. Through changes in prices it communicates changes in such basic matters as consumer tastes and elicits appropriate responses from businesses and the suppliers of factors of production. By affecting product prices and profits, changes in consumer tastes direct the expansion of some industries and the contraction of others. Those adjustments are conveyed to the factor market as expanding industries demand more resources and contracting industries demand fewer; the resulting changes in factor prices guide resources from the contracting industries to the expanding industries.

guiding function of prices
The ability of price changes to bring about changes in the quantities of products and factors of production demanded and supplied.

This *directing* or **guiding function of prices** is a core element of the market system. Without such a system, some administrative agency, such as a government planning board, would have to direct businesses and resources into the appropriate industries. A similar analysis shows that the system can and does adjust to other fundamental changes—for example, to changes in technology and in the availability of various resources.

ROLE IN PROMOTING PROGRESS

Adjusting to changes is one thing; initiating desirable changes is another. How does the market system promote technological improvements and capital accumulation—two changes that lead to greater productivity and a higher level of material well-being for society?

Technological Advance   The market system provides a strong incentive for technological advance and over time enables better products and processes to brush aside inferior ones. An entrepreneur or firm that introduces a popular new product will gain profit. Technological advance also includes new and improved methods that reduce production or distribution costs. By passing part of its cost reduction on to the consumer through a lower product price, the firm can increase sales and obtain above-normal profit at the expense of rival firms. Moreover, the market system is conducive to the *rapid spread* of technological advance throughout an industry. Rival firms must follow the lead of the most innovative firm or else suffer immediate losses and eventual failure. In some cases, the result is **creative destruction**: The creation of new products and production methods completely destroys the market positions of firms that are wedded to existing products and older ways of doing business. Example: The advent of personal computers and word processing software (for example, WordPerfect, produced by Corel Corp. of Ottawa) demolished the market for electric typewriters.

creative destruction
The hypothesis that the creation of new products and production methods simultaneously destroys the market power of existing monopolies.

Capital Accumulation   Most technological advances require additional capital goods. The market system provides the resources necessary to produce those goods by adjusting the product market and the factor market through increased dollar votes for capital goods.

But who will register votes for capital goods? Entrepreneurs and owners of businesses often use part of their profit income to purchase capital goods. Doing so yields even greater profit income in the future if the technological innovation is successful. Also, by paying interest or selling ownership shares, the entrepreneur and firm can attract some of the income of households to cast dollar votes for the production of more capital goods. *(Key Question 9)*

Competition and the "Invisible Hand"

In his 1776 book *The Wealth of Nations,* Adam Smith first noted that the operation of a market system creates a curious unity between private interests and public interests. Firms and suppliers of factors of production, seeking to further their own self-interest and operating within the framework of a highly competitive market system, will simultaneously, as though guided by an **"invisible hand,"** promote the public or social interest. In a competitive environment, businesses use the least-costly combination of resources to produce a specific output because it is in their self-interest to do so. To act otherwise would be to forgo profit or even to risk business failure. But, at the same time, to use scarce resources in the least-costly (most efficient) way is also in the public interest.

invisible hand
The tendency of firms and resource suppliers seeking to further their own self-interests in competitive markets to also promote the interests of society as a whole.

The Effectiveness of Markets

In our more-apple-juice-less-milk illustration, it is self-interest that induces responses appropriate to the change in society's wants. Canadian businesses seeking to make higher profits and to avoid losses, and suppliers of factors of production pursuing greater monetary rewards, negotiate changes in the allocation of resources and end up with the output that Canadians demand. Competition controls or guides self-interest in such a way that it automatically, and quite unintentionally, furthers the best interests of society. The "invisible hand" ensures us that when firms maximize their profits, they also maximize society's output and income.

Of the many virtues of the market system, three merit special emphasis:

- *Efficiency*   The basic economic argument for the market system is that it promotes the efficient use of resources, by guiding them into the production of those goods and services most wanted by society. It forces the use of the most efficient techniques in organizing resources for production, and it encourages the development and adoption of new and more efficient production techniques.

QUICK REVIEW

- The output mix of the market system is determined by profits, which in turn depend heavily on consumer preferences. Profits cause efficient industries to expand; losses cause inefficient industries to contract.

- Competition forces industries to use the least-costly (most efficient) production methods.

- In a market economy, consumer income and product prices determine how output will be distributed.

- Competitive markets reallocate resources in response to changes in consumer tastes, technological advances, and changes in supplies of factors of production.

- The "invisible hand" of the market system channels the pursuit of self-interest to the good of society.

- *Incentives* The market system encourages skill acquisition, hard work, and innovation. Greater work skills and effort mean greater production and higher incomes, which translate into a higher standard of living. Similarly, the assuming of risks by entrepreneurs can result in substantial profit incomes. Successful innovations generate economic rewards.

- *Freedom* The major non-economic argument for the market system is its emphasis on personal freedom. In contrast to central planning, the market system coordinates economic activity without coercion. The market system permits—indeed, it thrives on—freedom of enterprise and choice. Entrepreneurs and workers are free to further their own self-interest, subject to the rewards and penalties imposed by the market system itself.

4.3   Market Failure

market failure
The inability of markets to bring about the allocation of resources that best satisfies the wants of society.

The market system has many positive aspects in its favour. Unfortunately, there are instances when it doesn't work. **Market failure** occurs when the competitive market system (1) produces the "wrong" amounts of certain goods and services or (2) fails to allocate any resources whatsoever to the production of certain goods and services that are economically justified. The first type of failure results from what economists call *spillovers,* and the second type involves *public goods.* Both kinds of market failure can be corrected by government action.

Spillovers or Externalities

When we say that competitive markets automatically bring about the efficient use of resources, we assume that all the benefits and costs for each product are fully reflected in the market demand and supply curves. That is not always the case. In some markets certain benefits or costs may escape the buyer or seller.

A spillover occurs when some of the costs or the benefits of a good are passed on to or "spill over to" someone other than the immediate buyer or seller. Spillovers are also called *externalities* because they are benefits or costs that accrue to some third party that is external to the market transaction.

SPILLOVER COSTS

spillover costs
A cost imposed without compensation on third parties by the production or consumption of sellers or buyers.

Production or consumption costs inflicted on a third party without compensation are called **spillover costs**. Environmental pollution is an example. When a chemical manufacturer in southern Ontario or a meatpacking plant in Alberta dumps its wastes into a lake or river, swimmers, fishers, and boaters—and perhaps those who drink the water—suffer spillover costs. When a petroleum refinery in Sarnia, Ontario, pollutes the air with smoke or a paper mill in St-Félicien, Quebec, creates obnoxious odours, the local community experiences spillover costs for which it is not compensated. Cigarette smokers impose costs on those in close proximity by releasing second-hand smoke; in Canada, smokers also impose costs on others through increased use of the taxpayer-funded health care system.

What are the economic effects? Recall that costs determine the position of the firm's supply curve. When a firm avoids some costs by polluting, its supply curve lies farther to the right than it does when the firm bears the full costs of production. As a result, the price of the product is too low and the output of the product is too large to achieve allocative efficiency. A market failure occurs in the form of an overallocation of resources to the production of the good.

CORRECTING FOR SPILLOVER COSTS

Government can do two things to correct the overallocation of resources. Both solutions internalize external costs—that is, they make the offending firm pay the costs rather than shift them to others:

- *Legislation*   In cases of air and water pollution, the most direct action is legislation prohibiting or limiting the pollution. Such legislation forces potential polluters to pay for the proper disposal of industrial wastes—here, by installing smoke-abatement equipment or water-purification facilities. The idea is to force potential offenders, under the threat of legal action, to bear *all* the costs associated with production. For example, both Quebec and British Columbia have passed legislation to prevent pulp and paper mills from damaging the environment.

- *Specific taxes*   A less direct action is for government to levy a *specific tax*—that is, a tax confined to a particular product—on each unit of the polluting firm's output. The amount of this tax would roughly equal the estimated amount of the spillover cost arising from the production of each unit of output. Through this tax, government would pass back to the offending firm a cost equivalent to the spillover cost the firm is avoiding. This would shift the firm's supply curve to the left, reducing equilibrium output and eliminating the overallocation of resources. Governments in Canada levy high taxes on cigarettes to induce smokers to internalize the costs they impose on the rest of Canadians.

SPILLOVER BENEFITS

Sometimes spillovers appear as benefits. The production or consumption of certain goods and services may confer spillover or external benefits on third parties or on the community at large without compensating payment. Immunization against measles and polio results in direct benefits to the immediate consumer of those vaccines. But it also results in widespread substantial spillover benefits to the entire community.

spillover benefits
Benefit obtained without compensation by third parties from the production or consumption of sellers or buyers.

Education is another example of **spillover benefits**. Education benefits individual consumers: "Better-educated" people generally achieve higher incomes than "less-well-educated" people. But education also provides benefits to society, in the form of a more versatile and more productive labour force, on the one hand, and smaller outlays for crime prevention, law enforcement, and welfare programs, on the other.

Spillover benefits mean that the market demand curve, which reflects only private benefits, understates total benefits. The demand curve for the product lies farther to the left than it would if the market took all benefits into account. As a result, a smaller amount of the product will be produced or, alternatively, there will be an *underallocation* of resources to the product—again a market failure.

CORRECTING FOR SPILLOVER BENEFITS

How can the underallocation of resources associated with spillover benefits be corrected? The answer is either to subsidize consumers (to increase demand), to subsidize producers (to increase supply), or, in the extreme, to have government produce the product.

- *Subsidize consumers*   To correct the underallocation of resources to higher education, the federal and provincial governments provide low-interest loans to students so that they can afford more education. Those loans help increase the demand for higher education.

- *Subsidize suppliers*   In some cases governments find it more convenient and administratively simpler to correct an underallocation by subsidizing suppliers. For example, in Canada, provincial governments provide substantial portions of the budgets of public elementary and high schools, and colleges and universities. Such subsidies lower the costs of producing education and increase its supply. Publicly subsidized immunization programs, hospitals, and medical research are other examples.

- *Provide goods via government*   A third policy option may be appropriate where spillover benefits are extremely large: Government may finance or, in the extreme, own and operate the industry that is involved. In Canada, most hospitals are publicly owned and operated through provincial governments.

Public Goods and Services

Certain goods called *private goods* are produced through the competitive market system. Examples are the many items sold in stores. Private goods have two characteristics—*rivalry* and *excludability*. *Rivalry* means that when one person buys and consumes a product or service, it is not available for purchase and consumption by another person. What Joan purchases, Jane cannot have. *Excludability* means that buyers who are willing and able to pay the market price for the product obtain its benefits, but those unable or unwilling to pay that price do not. This characteristic makes it possible for private firms to profitably produce goods and services.

Certain other goods and services called **public goods** have the opposite characteristics—*non-rivalry* and *non-excludability*. Everyone can simultaneously obtain the benefit from a public good such as a global positioning system satellite, national defence, street lighting, and environmental protection. One person's benefit does not reduce the benefit available to others. More important, there is no effective way of excluding individuals from the benefit of the good once it comes into existence (see the Consider This box). The inability to exclude individuals from consumption of a good creates the **free-rider problem**, in which people can receive benefits from a public good without paying for it. The free-rider problem makes it unprofitable for a private firm to provide the product or service.

An example of a public good is the war on global terrorism. This expenditure on heightened security, for example at airports, is economically justified because the benefits to Canadians are thought to exceed the costs. Once these efforts are undertaken, however, the benefits accrue to all Canadians (non-rivalry). And, there is no practical way to exclude any Canadian from benefiting from these efforts (non-excludability).

No private firm will undertake the war on terrorism because the benefits cannot be profitably sold (due to the free-rider problem). So here we have a service that yields substantial benefits but to which the market system would not allocate resources. The war on terrorism is a public good. Society signals its desire for such goods by voting for particular political candidates who support their provision. Because of the free-rider problem, the public sector must provide these goods and finance them through compulsory charges in the form of taxes.

Quasi-public Goods

Government provides many goods that fit the economist's definition of a public good. However, it also provides other goods and services that could be produced and delivered in such a way that the exclusion principle would apply. Such goods, called **quasi-public goods**, include health care, education, streets and highways, police and fire protection, libraries and museums, preventive medicine, and sewage disposal. They could all be priced and provided by private firms through the

A public good can be simultaneously consumed by everyone. One person's benefit does not reduce the benefit available to others.

public good
A good or service that can be simultaneously consumed by everyone, and from which no one can be excluded, even if they don't pay for it.

free-rider problem
The inability of potential providers of an economically desirable but indivisible good or service to obtain payment from those who benefit.

quasi-public good
A good or service to which the exclusion principle could apply, but that has such a large spillover benefit that government sponsors its production to prevent an underallocation of resources.

Consider This

Public Goods

Street entertainers are often found in tourist areas of major cities, such as Vancouver and Quebec City. They can also be found in the subway stations of Toronto and Montreal. Some play violins, tubas, harmonicas, accordions, or other instruments, while others team up to sing songs or juggle various objects. Some street entertainers are highly creative and talented; others "need more practice." But, regardless of talent level, these entertainers illuminate the concepts of free riders and public goods.

Most street entertainers have a hard time earning a living from their activities (unless event organizers pay them). Their problem is that they have no way of excluding non-payers from the benefits of their entertainment. They essentially are providing public, not private, goods and must rely on voluntary payments.

The result is a significant free-rider problem. Only a few in the audience put money in the container or instrument case, and many who do contribute put in only token amounts. The rest are free riders. Because they did not ask the entertainers to perform, they rightfully feel no obligation to pay for the performances. Free riders obtain the benefits of the street entertainment and keep their money for purchases that *they* initiate.

Street entertainers are acutely aware of the free-rider problem and some have found creative ways to lessen it. For example, some entertainers involve the audience directly in the act. This usually creates a greater sense of audience willingness (or obligation) to contribute money at the end of the performance.

"Pay for performance" is another creative approach to lessening the free-rider problem. A good example is the street entertainer painted up to look like a statue. When people drop coins into the container, the "statue" makes a slight movement. The greater the contributions, the greater the movement. But these human "statues" still face the free-rider problem: Non-payers also get to enjoy the acts.

Some street entertainers supplement their earnings by selling CDs of their music to appreciative audience members. Unlike their public performances, the CDs are private goods. Only consumers who pay for the CDs obtain the benefits.

Finally, because talented street entertainers create a festive street environment, cities or retailers sometimes hire them to perform. The "free entertainment" attracts crowds of shoppers who buy goods from nearby retailers. In these instances the cities or retailers use tax revenue or commercial funds to pay the entertainers, in the former case validating them as public goods.

Question: If government is not providing street entertainment, why is it considered a public good?

market system. But, as we noted earlier, because they all have substantial spillover benefits, they would be underproduced by the market system. Therefore, government often provides them to avoid the underallocation of resources that would otherwise occur.

The Reallocation Process

How are resources reallocated from the production of private goods to the production of public and quasi-public goods? If the resources of the economy are fully employed, government must free up resources from the production of private goods and make them available for the production of public and quasi-public goods. It does so by reducing private demand for them. And it does that by levying taxes on households and businesses, taking some of their income out of the circular flow. With lower incomes, households and businesses are obliged to curtail their consumption and investment spending. As a result, the private demand for goods and services declines, as does the private demand for resources. So by diverting purchasing power from private spenders to government, taxes remove resources from private use. (Global Perspective 4.2 shows the extent to which various countries divert labour from the private sector to the public sector.)

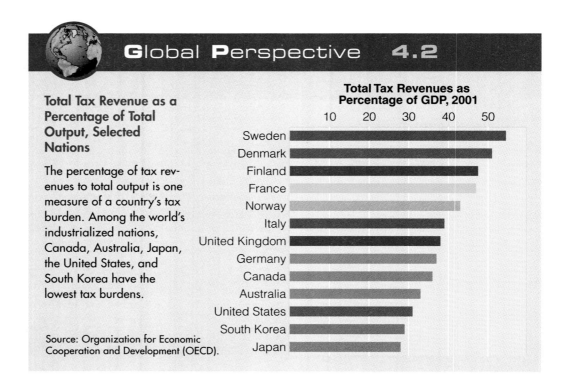

Global Perspective 4.2

Total Tax Revenue as a Percentage of Total Output, Selected Nations

The percentage of tax revenues to total output is one measure of a country's tax burden. Among the world's industrialized nations, Canada, Australia, Japan, the United States, and South Korea have the lowest tax burdens.

Source: Organization for Economic Cooperation and Development (OECD).

Total Tax Revenues as Percentage of GDP, 2001

Sweden	
Denmark	
Finland	
France	
Norway	
Italy	
United Kingdom	
Germany	
Canada	
Australia	
United States	
South Korea	
Japan	

Government then spends the tax proceeds to provide public and quasi-public goods and services. Taxation releases resources from the production of private consumer goods (food, clothing, television sets) and private investment goods (printing presses, boxcars, warehouses). Government shifts those resources to the production of public and quasi-public goods (post offices, health care, parks), changing the composition of the economy's total output. (Global Perspective 4.2 shows total tax revenues as a percentage of national output in several nations.) *(Key Questions 12 and 13)*

Limitations of the Market System

We end our discussion of the market system by re-emphasizing an important caution. Although the market system has remarkable virtues, its operation is not as smooth as some of its proponents imply. Both in its purest form and as practised in reality, the market system has well-known limitations. It fails to provide public goods. Unscrupulous people occasionally abuse it. Resource allocation does not always accurately reflect all costs and benefits, including those that spill over to society at large. It may generate more income inequality than many individuals feel is justified. It does not always produce full employment and price-level stability. And so on. In subsequent chapters, we discuss these limitations and how to address them.

The Circular Flow Revisited

Figure 4-2 integrates government into the circular flow model first shown in Figure 2-6. Here flows (1) through (4) are the same as the corresponding flows in that figure. Flows (1) and (2) show business expenditures for the factors of production provided by households. These expenditures are costs to businesses but represent wage, rent, interest, and profit income to households. Flows (3) and (4) show household expenditures for the goods and services produced by businesses.

Now consider what happens when we add government. Flows (5) through (8) illustrate that government makes purchases in both product and factor markets. Flows (5) and (6) represent government purchases of such products as paper, computers, and military hardware from private businesses. Flows (7) and (8) represent government purchases of resources. The federal government employs and pays salaries to members of Parliament, the armed forces, lawyers, meat inspectors, and so on. Provincial and municipal governments hire and pay teachers, bus drivers, police, and firefighters. The federal government might also lease or purchase land to expand an airport and a city might buy land on which to build a new elementary school.

Government then provides public goods and services to both households and businesses as shown by flows (9) and (10). To finance those public goods and services, businesses and households are required to pay taxes, as shown by flows (11) and (12). These flows are labelled as *net* taxes to indicate that they also include "taxes in reverse" in the form of transfer payments to households and subsidies to businesses. Thus, flow (11) includes various subsidies to farmers, shipbuilders, and airlines as well as income, sales, and excise taxes paid by businesses to government. Most subsidies to business are "concealed" in the form of low-interest loans, loan guarantees, tax concessions, or public facilities provided at prices below their cost. Similarly, flow (12) includes both taxes collected by government directly from households and transfer payments such as child-care benefits paid by the government.

We can use Figure 4-2 to review how government alters the distribution of income, reallocates resources, and changes the level of economic activity. The structure of taxes and transfer payments significantly affects income distribution. In flow (12), a tax structure that draws tax revenues primarily from well-to-do households, combined with a system of transfer payments to low-income households, reduces income inequality.

Flows (5) through (8) show that government diverts goods and resources away from private sector consumption and directs them to the public sector. This resource reallocation is required to provide public goods and services.

FIGURE 4-2

The Circular Flow and the Public Sector

Government buys products from the product market and employs factors of production from the factor market to provide public goods and services to households and businesses. Government finances its expenditures through the net tax revenues (taxes minus transfer payments) it receives from households and businesses.

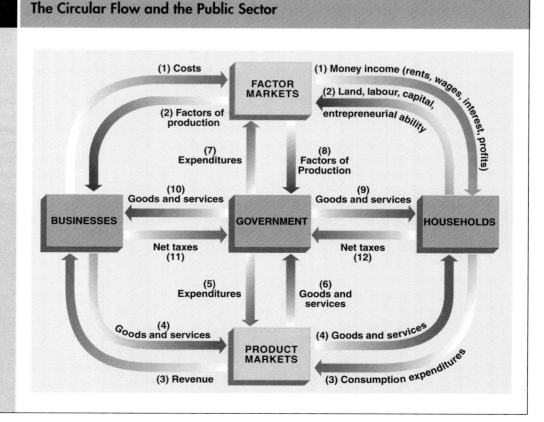

QUICK REVIEW

- Government can correct for the overallocation of resources associated with spillover costs through legislation or taxes; it can offset the underallocation of resources associated with spillover benefits by granting government subsidies.

- Government provides certain public goods for which there is non-rivalry in consumption and non-excludability of

benefits; government also provides many quasi-public goods because of their large spillover benefits.

- The circular flow model with foreign trade includes flows of exports from our domestic product market, imports to our domestic product market, and the corresponding flows of spending.

4.4   Canada and International Trade

Canadians consume many goods that are produced abroad.

As we noted earlier in the chapter, markets are made up of buyers and sellers that want to exchange goods. Up to this point we have implicitly assumed that markets are national in scope: Canadians buying and selling from each other. But a visit to any retail outlet will reveal that Canadians consume many goods produced abroad. And if you were to go abroad—say, to Europe—you would probably not have great difficulty finding beer, telecommunication equipment, or software produced in Canada.

Canadian backpackers in the wilderness of Banff National Park may like to think they are "leaving the world behind" but, like Atlas, they carry the world on their shoulders. Much of their equipment is likely imported—knives from Switzerland, rain gear from South Korea, cameras from Japan, aluminum pots from England, miniature stoves from Sweden, sleeping bags from China, and compasses from Finland. Moreover, they may have driven to the trailheads in Japanese-made Toyotas or Swedish-made Volvos, sipping coffee from Brazil or snacking on bananas from Honduras. Equally, Swiss backpackers may be carrying tents, prepackaged dehydrated meals, and hiking boots made in Canada.

Canada, with a limited domestic market, cannot efficiently produce the variety of goods its citizens want. Therefore, we must import goods from other nations. That, in turn, means that we must export, or sell abroad, some of our own products. For Canada, exports make up about 40 percent of our gross domestic product (GDP)—the market value of all goods and services produced in an economy. Other countries, such as the United States, have a large internal market. Although the total volume of trade in the United States is huge, it constitutes a much smaller percentage of GDP than in a number of other nations.

Global Trade and Competition

Globalization—the integration of industry, commerce, communication, travel, and culture among the world's nations—is one of the major trends of our time. (See Global Perspective 4.3 for a list of the top 12 globalized nations, according to one set of criteria.). There is a lively debate internationally as to whether globalization is a positive or negative force. Those who support globalization focus on the improvements to general standards of living that it brings. Those who oppose it express concerns about its impacts on the environment, unskilled and semi-skilled workers, and the poor.

One thing about globalization is certain and relevant to our present discussion: It has brought intense competition both within Canada and across the globe. In Canada, imports have gained major shares of many markets, including those for cars, tires, steel, clothing, sporting goods, electronics, and toys. Nevertheless, hundreds of Canadian firms have prospered in the global marketplace. Such firms as Bombardier, Nortel, Alcan, JDS Uniphase, ATI Technologies, and Cognos have continued to hold high market shares at home while greatly expanding their sales abroad. Of course, not all firms have been successful. Some have not been able to compete, because their

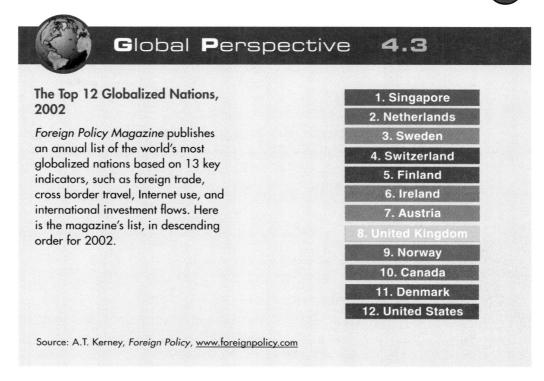

Global Perspective   4.3

The Top 12 Globalized Nations, 2002

Foreign Policy Magazine publishes an annual list of the world's most globalized nations based on 13 key indicators, such as foreign trade, cross border travel, Internet use, and international investment flows. Here is the magazine's list, in descending order for 2002.

1. Singapore
2. Netherlands
3. Sweden
4. Switzerland
5. Finland
6. Ireland
7. Austria
8. United Kingdom
9. Norway
10. Canada
11. Denmark
12. United States

Source: A.T. Kerney, *Foreign Policy*, www.foreignpolicy.com

international competitors either make higher-quality products, have lower production costs, or both.

International trade and the global economy affect all Canadians daily, whether we are hiking in the wilderness, driving our cars, listening to music, or working at our jobs. We cannot "leave the world behind." We are enmeshed in a global web of economic relationships—trading of goods and services, multinational corporations, cooperative ventures among the world's firms, and ties among the world's financial markets. That web is so complex that sometimes it is difficult to determine just what is a Canadian product. A Finnish company owns Wilson sporting goods; a Swiss company owns Gerber baby food; and a British corporation owns Burger King. The Toyota Corolla sedan is manufactured in Canada. Some Volvo models are assembled in Nova Scotia. Many "Canadian" products are made with components from abroad, and, conversely, many "foreign" products contain numerous Canadian-produced parts.

International Linkages

Several economic flows link the Canadian economy and the economies of other nations:

- *Goods and services flows*   Canada exports goods and services to other nations and imports goods and services from them.

- *Capital and labour flows*   Canadian firms establish production facilities in foreign countries and foreign firms establish production facilities in Canada. Labour also moves between nations. Each year between 200,000 and 400,000 people immigrate to Canada and some Canadians move to other nations.

- *Information and technology flows*   Canada transmits information to other nations about Canadian products, prices, interest rates, and investment opportunities and receives such information from abroad. Firms in other countries use technology created in Canada and Canadian businesses incorporate technology developed abroad.

- *Financial flows*   Money is transferred between Canada and other countries for several purposes, for example, paying for imports, buying foreign assets, paying interest on debt, and providing foreign aid.

We will soon see that international trade provides significant benefits to each participating nation. We now turn to investigating how the gains from international trade come about.

Specialization and Comparative Advantage

Recall from Chapter 2 that the economic problem consists of limited resources, unlimited wants, and thus the need for choice. If a nation can get more output from its limited resources, the constraint it faces is less severe. In Chapter 2 we also pointed out that specialization and international trade provide one way to get more output from limited resources. *Specialization and international trade increase the productivity of a nation's resources and allow for greater total output than would otherwise be possible.* This idea is not new. Adam Smith pointed it out over 200 years ago. Nations specialize and trade for the same reasons as individuals do: Specialization and exchange result in greater overall output and income.

Basic Principle

In the early 1800s British economist David Ricardo expanded Smith's idea, observing that it pays for a person or a country to specialize and exchange even if that person or nation is more productive than a potential trading partner in *all* economic activities.

Consider an example of a chartered accountant (CA) who is also a skilled house painter. Suppose the CA can paint her house in less time than the professional painter she is thinking of hiring. Also suppose the CA can earn $50 per hour doing her accounting and must pay the painter $15 per hour. Let's say that it will take the accountant 30 hours to paint her house; the painter, 40 hours.

Should the CA take time from her accounting to paint her own house or should she hire the painter? The CA's opportunity cost of painting her house is $1500 (= 30 hours × $50 per hour of sacrificed income). The cost of hiring the painter is only $600 (40 hours × $15 per hour paid to the painter). The CA is better at both accounting and painting—she has an **absolute advantage** in both accounting and painting. But her relative advantage (about which more below) is in accounting. She *will get her house painted at a lower cost by specializing in accounting and using some of the earnings from accounting to hire a house painter.*

Similarly, the house painter can reduce his cost of obtaining accounting services by specializing in painting and using some of his income to hire the CA to prepare his income tax forms. Suppose that it would take the painter ten hours to prepare his tax return, while the CA could handle this task in two hours. The house painter would sacrifice $150 of income (= 10 hours × $15 per hour of sacrificed time) to accomplish a task that he could hire the CA to do for $100 (= 2 hours × $50 per hour of the CA's time). By using the CA to prepare his tax return, the painter lowers *his cost of getting the tax return prepared.*

What is true for our CA and house painter is also true for nations. Specializing enables nations to reduce the cost of obtaining the goods and services they desire.

absolute advantage
When a region or nation can produce more of good Z and good Y with less resources compared to other regions or nations.

Comparative Costs

Our simple example shows that specialization is economically desirable because it results in more efficient production. Let's now put specialization in the context of trading nations, using the familiar concept of the production possibilities table for our analysis. Suppose production possibilities for two products in Mexico and Canada are as shown in Tables 4-1 and 4-2. In these tables we assume constant costs. Each country must give up a constant amount of one product to secure a particular increment of the other product. (This assumption simplifies our discussion without impairing the validity of our conclusions.)

TABLE 4-1	Mexico's Production Possibilities Table (in Tonnes)

PRODUCTION ALTERNATIVES

Product	A	B	C	D	E
Corn	0	20	24	40	60
Soybeans	15	10	9	5	0

TABLE 4-2	Canada's Production Possibilities Table (in Tonnes)

PRODUCTION ALTERNATIVES

Product	R	S	T	U	V
Corn	0	30	33	60	90
Soybeans	30	20	19	10	0

comparative advantage
When a region or nation can produce a good at a lower domestic opportunity cost compared to a potential trading partner.

Specialization and trade are mutually beneficial or "profitable" to the two nations if the comparative costs of the two products within the two nations differ. What are the comparative costs of corn and soybeans in Mexico? By comparing production alternatives A and B in Table 4-1, we see that 5 tonnes of soybeans (= 15 − 10) must be sacrificed to produce 20 tonnes of corn (= 20 − 0). Or more simply, in Mexico it costs one tonne of soybeans (S) to produce four tonnes of corn (C); that is, 1S ≡ 4C. Because we assumed constant costs, this domestic *comparative-cost ratio* will not change as Mexico expands the output of either product. This is evident from looking at production possibilities B and C, where we see that four more tonnes of corn (= 24 − 20) cost one tonne of soybeans (= 10 − 9).

Similarly, in Table 4-2, comparing Canadian production alternatives R and S reveals that in Canada it costs 10 tonnes of soybeans (= 30 − 20) to obtain 30 tonnes of corn (= 30 − 0). That is, the domestic comparative-cost ratio for the two products in Canada is 1S ≡ 3C. Comparing production alternatives S and T reinforces this; an extra three tonnes of corn (= 33 − 30) comes at the direct sacrifice of one tonne of soybeans (= 20 − 19).

The comparative costs, or internal terms of trade, of the two products within the two nations are clearly different. Economists say that Canada has a **comparative advantage** over Mexico in soybeans. Canada must forgo only three tonnes of corn to get one tonne of soybeans, but Mexico must forgo four tonnes of corn to get one tonne of soybeans. In terms of domestic opportunity costs, soybeans are relatively cheaper in Canada. *A nation has a comparative advantage in some product when it can produce that product at a lower domestic opportunity cost than can a potential trading partner.* Mexico, in contrast, has a comparative advantage in corn. While one tonne of corn costs one-third tonne of soybeans in Canada, it costs only one-quarter tonne of soybeans in Mexico. Comparatively speaking, corn is cheaper in Mexico. We summarize the situation in Table 4-3.

Because of these differences in domestic comparative costs, if both nations specialize, each according to its comparative advantage, each can achieve a larger total output with the same total input of resources. Together they will be using their scarce resources more efficiently.

terms of trade
The amount of one good or service that must be given up to obtain one unit of another good or service.

Terms of Trade

Canada can shift production between soybeans and corn at the rate of 1S for 3C. Thus, Canadians would specialize in soybeans only if they could obtain *more than* three tonnes of corn for one tonne of soybeans by trading with Mexico. Similarly, Mexico can shift production at the rate of 4C for 1S. So it would be advantageous to Mexico to specialize in corn if it could get one tonne of soybeans for *less than* four tonnes of corn.

Suppose that through negotiation the two nations agree on an exchange rate of one tonne of soybeans for three-and-a-half tonnes of corn. These **terms of trade** are mutually beneficial to both countries since each can "do better" through such trade than via domestic production alone. Canadians can get three-and-a-half tonnes of corn by sending one tonne of soybeans to Mexico, while they can get only three tonnes of corn by shifting resources domestically from soybeans to corn. Mexicans can obtain one tonne of soybeans at a lower cost of three-and-a-half tonnes of corn through trade with Canada, compared to the cost of four tonnes if Mexicans produce one tonne of corn themselves.

TABLE 4-3	Comparative Advantage Example: A Summary

Soybeans	Corn
Mexico: Must give up 4 tonnes of corn to get 1 tonne of soybeans	*Mexico:* Must give up ¼ tonne of soybeans to get 1 tonne of corn
Canada: Must give up 3 tonnes of corn to get 1 tonne of soybeans	*Canada:* Must give up ⅓ tonne of soybeans to get 1 tonne of corn
Comparative advantage: Canada	Comparative advantage: Mexico

Gains from Specialization and Trade

Let's pinpoint the size of the gains in total output from specialization and trade. Suppose that before specialization and trade, production alternative C in Table 4-1 and alternative T in Table 4-2 are the optimal product mixes for the two countries. These outputs are shown in column 1 of Table 4-4. That is, Mexicans prefer 24 tonnes of corn and 9 tonnes of soybeans (Table 4-1) and Canadians prefer 33 tonnes of corn and 19 tonnes of soybeans (Table 4-2) to all other alternatives.

Now assume both nations specialize according to comparative advantage, Mexico producing 60 tonnes of corn and no soybeans (alternative E) and Canada producing no corn and 30 tonnes of soybeans (alternative R). These outputs are reflected in column 2 of Table 4-4. Using our 1S = 3½C terms of trade, assume Mexico exchanges 35 tonnes of corn for 10 tonnes of Canadian soybeans. Column 3 of Table 4-4 shows the quantities exchanged in this trade. As indicated in Column 4, after trade Mexicans have 25 tonnes of corn and 10 tonnes of soybeans, while Canadians have 35 tonnes of corn and 20 tonnes of soybeans. Compared with their optimum product mixes before specialization and trade (column 1), *both* nations now enjoy more corn and more soybeans! Specifically, Mexico has gained one tonne of corn and one tonne of soybeans. Canada has gained two tonnes of corn and one tonne of soybeans. These gains are shown in column 5.

Specialization based on comparative advantage improves resource allocation. The same total inputs of world resources result in a larger global output. If Mexico and Canada allocate all their resources to corn and soybeans respectively, the same total inputs of resources can produce more output between them, indicating that resources are being used or allocated more efficiently.

We noted in Chapter 2 that through specialization and international trade a nation can overcome the production constraints imposed by its domestic production possibilities table and curve. Table 4-4 and its discussion show just how this is done. The domestic production possibilities data of the two countries have not changed, meaning that neither nation's production possibilities curve has shifted. But specialization and trade mean that citizens of both countries enjoy increased consumption. Thus, specialization and trade have the same effect as an increase in resources or technological progress: they make more goods available to an economy. *(Key Question 16)*

Back to the Circular Flow Model

We can easily add "the rest of the world" to the circular flow model. We do so in Figure 4-3 via two adjustments.

1. Our previous "Factor Markets" and "Product Markets" now become "Canadian Factor Markets" and "Canadian Product Markets." Similarly, we add the modifier "Canadian" to the "Businesses," "Government," and "Households" sectors.

TABLE 4-4	Specialization According to Comparative Advantage and the Gains from Trade (in Tonnes)				
Country	(1) Outputs before specialization	(2) Outputs after specialization	(3) Amounts traded	(4) Outputs available after trade	(5) Gains from specialization and trade (4) − (1)
Mexico	24 corn	60 corn	−35 corn	25 corn	1 corn
	9 soybeans	0 soybeans	+10 soybeans	10 soybeans	1 soybeans
Canada	33 corn	0 corn	+35 corn	35 corn	2 corn
	19 soybeans	30 soybeans	−10 soybeans	20 soybeans	1 soybeans

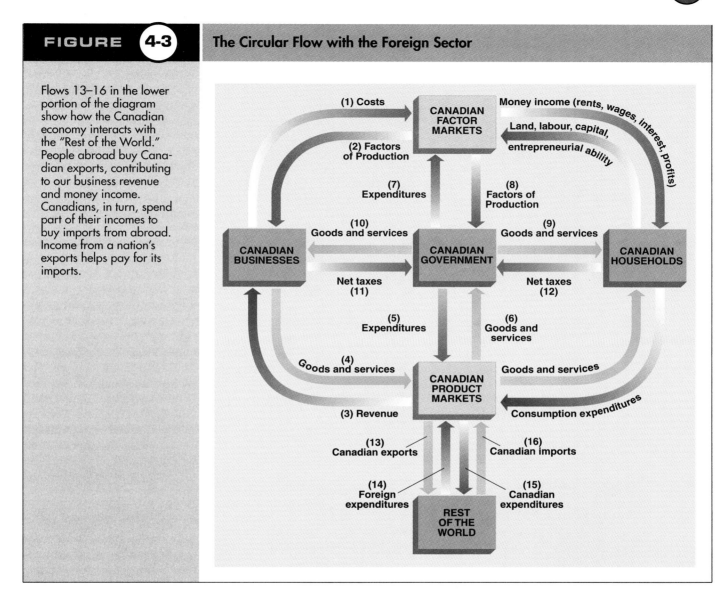

FIGURE 4-3 The Circular Flow with the Foreign Sector

Flows 13–16 in the lower portion of the diagram show how the Canadian economy interacts with the "Rest of the World." People abroad buy Canadian exports, contributing to our business revenue and money income. Canadians, in turn, spend part of their incomes to buy imports from abroad. Income from a nation's exports helps pay for its imports.

2. We place the foreign sector—the "Rest of the World"—so that it interacts with Canadian Product Markets. This sector designates all foreign nations that we deal with and the individuals, businesses, and governments that make them up.

Flow (13) in Figure 4-3 shows that people, businesses, and governments abroad buy Canadian products—our exports—from our product market. This goods and services flow of Canadian exports to foreign nations is accompanied by an opposite monetary revenue flow (14) from the rest of the world to us. In response to these revenues from abroad, Canadian businesses demand more domestic factors of production (flow 2) to produce the goods for export; they pay for these inputs with revenues from abroad. Thus, the domestic flow (1) of money income (rents, wages, interest, and profits) to Canadian households rises.

But our exports are only half the picture. Flow (15) shows that Canadian households, businesses, and government spend some of their income on foreign products. These products, of course, are our imports (flow 16). Purchases of imports, say, autos from Japan and electronic equipment from South Korea, contribute to foreign output and income, which in turn provides the means for foreign households to buy Canadian exports.

Canada imports and exports not only products, but also factors of production. For example, we import some crude oil and export raw logs. Moreover, some Canadian firms choose to engage in production abroad, which diverts spending on capital from our domestic market to markets in other nations. For instance, Nortel has an assembly plant in the U.S. Or flowing in the other direction, Sony might construct a plant for manufacturing CD players in Canada.

There are also international flows of labour. Hundreds of thousands of immigrants enter Canada each year. These immigrants expand the availability of labour resources in Canada, raising our total output and income.

The expanded circular flow model also demonstrates that a nation engaged in world trade faces potential sources of economic fluctuations that would not affect a "closed" nation. Recessions and inflation can be highly contagious among nations. Suppose the United States experiences a severe recession. As its income declines, its purchases of Canadian exports fall. As a result, flows (13) and (14) in Figure 4-3 decline and inventories of unsold Canadian goods rise. Canadian firms would respond by limiting their production and employment, reducing the flow of money income to Canadian households (flow 1). Recession in the United States in this case contributes to a recession in Canada.

Figure 4-3 also helps us to see that the foreign sector alters resource allocation and incomes in the Canadian economy. With a foreign sector, we produce more of some goods (our exports) and fewer of others (our imports) than we would otherwise. Thus, Canadian labour and other factors are shifted toward export industries and away from import industries. We use more of our own factors of production to manufacture autos and telecommunication equipment. So we ask: "Do these shifts of resources make economic sense? Do they enhance our total output and thus our standard of living?" We look at some answers next.

QUICK REVIEW

- There are four main categories of economic flows linking nations: goods and services flows, capital and labour flows, information and technology flows, and financial flows.

- A country has a comparative advantage when it can produce a product at a lower domestic opportunity cost than can a potential trading partner.

- Specialization based on comparative advantage increases the total output available for nations that trade with one another.

- The circular flow model with foreign trade includes flows of exports from our domestic product market, imports to our domestic product market, and the corresponding flows of spending.

THE LASTword   Market Failure and the Need for Government

Private markets fulfill individual desires very well, but where there is a need for collective action, they often fail.

Suppose a municipality, say, Brandon, Manitoba, requires a new road. In the absence of a government request that a private firm build it, it is unlikely that a private firm will build the required road on its own initiative. Or, to express it in another way, private markets will not make available public goods. The citizens of Brandon have to elect a government to either direct a private firm to build the road, or hire the people and buy the capital equipment needed to construct the road on its own.

Why would a private firm not undertake to build a road on its own? The obstacle is common property rights. The land on which the road is to be built must be owned by the firm before it would consider building the road. Lands used by all citizens are most often held publicly. The firm would thus need to get the consent of all the citizens affected. Such unanimity would be difficult to achieve. Indeed, it is the difficulty of making collective decisions that makes government action essential in the creation of an infrastructure—such as roads and airports—necessary to facilitate the functioning of markets. Not only must

a decision be made to build the road, but then the decision must be made as to who should bear the cost. The free-rider problem arises here. Every individual hopes someone will pay for the needed road. This way he or she can have the benefits without contributing to its cost. The free-rider problem can potentially arise in all situations where collective action must be taken. Unless we have a central authority—government—with the monopoly power to impose costs on all members of a society, many socially useful projects will not be undertaken.

In a pathbreaking book, *The Logic of Collective Action*,[1] Mancur Olson pointed out almost 40 years ago that contrary to popular belief, groups of individuals with common interest do not necessarily attempt to further those common interests. In many instances group members attempt to further their own personal interests. A few years later, the political scientist Garrett Hardin popularized the term "the tragedy of the commons"[2] to describe the problems that arise when there are common property rights. For example, where there are common property rights to a natural resource, it is typi-

cally overexploited. The cod stocks on Canada's east coast have suffered just that fate.

Where collective action is required, or where there are common property rights, governments are needed because markets fail to bring together the interests of the individual and those of society. The federal government has had to impose mandatory fishing restrictions to save the cod stocks from dwindling further. Similarly, governments must make decisions to construct a road, otherwise the road might never get built. Clearly, markets work best where there are private property rights.

But we do not want to leave the impression that all government interventions to rectify market failure succeed. Some individuals point to the failure of the Canadian federal government to properly manage the cod stocks off the eastern seaboard as a case in point.

[1] Mancur Olson, *The Logic of Collective Action* (Cambridge: Cambridge University Press, 1965).

[2] Garrett Hardin, "The Tragedy of the Commons," *Science* 162 (1968): 1243–48.

CHAPTER SUMMARY

4.1 CHARACTERISTICS OF THE MARKET SYSTEM

- The market system—known also as the private-enterprise system or capitalism—is characterized by the private ownership of resources, including capital, and the freedom of individuals to engage in economic activities of their choice to advance their material well-being. Self interest is the driving force of such an economy, and competition functions as a regulatory or control mechanism.

- In the market system, markets and prices organize and make effective the many millions of individual decisions that determine what is produced, the methods of production, and the sharing of output.

- Specialization, use of advanced technology, and the extensive use of capital goods are facilitated by the market system.

- Functioning as a medium of exchange, money eliminates the problems of bartering and permits easy trade and greater specialization, both domestically and internationally.

4.2 THE MARKET SYSTEM AT WORK

- Every economy faces Four Fundamental Questions: (a) What goods and services will be produced? (b) How will the goods and services be produced? (c) Who will get the goods and services? (d) How will the system accommodate changes in consumer tastes, factor supplies, and technology?

- The market system produces those products of which production and sale yield total revenue sufficient to cover all costs, including a profit (a cost). It does not produce those products that do not yield a profit.

- Profit indicates that an industry is prosperous and promotes its expansion. Losses signify that an industry is not prosperous and hasten its contraction.

- Consumer sovereignty means that both businesses and suppliers of factors of production are subject to the wants of consumers. Through their dollar votes, consumers decide on the composition of output.

- Competition forces firms to use the lowest-cost and therefore the most economically efficient production techniques.

- The prices that a household receives for the resources it supplies to the economy determine that household's income. This income determines the household's claim on the economy's output. Those who have income to spend get the products produced in the market system.

- By communicating changes in consumer tastes to suppliers of factors of production and entrepreneurs, the market system prompts appropriate adjustments in the allocation of the economy's resources. The market system also encourages technological advance and capital accumulation.

- Competition, the primary mechanism of control in the market economy, promotes a unity of self-interest and public interests; as though directed by an "invisible hand," competition harnesses the self-interest motives of businesses and suppliers of factors of production to further the public interest.

4.3 MARKET FAILURE

- Spillovers, or externalities, cause the equilibrium output of certain goods to vary from the socially efficient output. Spillover costs result in an overallocation of resources, which can be corrected by legislation or by specific taxes. Spillover benefits are accompanied by an underallocation of resources, which can be corrected by government subsidies to consumers or producers.

- Only government can provide public goods, which are indivisible and entail benefits from which non-paying consumers (free riders) cannot be excluded. Private firms will not produce public goods. Quasi-public goods have some of the characteristics of public goods and some of the characteristics of private goods; government provides them because the private sector would underallocate resources to their production.

4.4 CANADA AND INTERNATIONAL TRADE

- Specialization based on comparative advantage enables nations to achieve higher standards of living through trade with other countries. A trading partner should specialize in products and services for which its domestic opportunity costs are lowest. The terms of trade must be such that both nations can obtain more of some products via trade than they could obtain by producing them at home.

TERMS AND CONCEPTS

private property, p. 77
freedom of enterprise, p. 77
freedom of choice, p. 78
self-interest, p. 78
competition, p. 78
roundabout production, p. 80
specialization, p. 80
division of labour, p. 80
medium of exchange, p. 81
barter, p. 81

money, p. 81
household, p. 82
firm, p. 82
Four Fundamental Questions, p. 82
consumer sovereignty, p. 83
dollar votes, p. 83
derived demand, p. 83
guiding function of prices, p. 84
creative destruction, p. 85
"invisible hand," p. 85

market failure, p. 86
spillover costs, p. 86
spillover benefits, p. 87
public good, p. 88
free-rider problem, p. 88
quasi-public good, p. 88
absolute advantage, p.94
comparative advantage, p.95
terms of trade, p.95

STUDY QUESTIONS

1. Explain each of the following statements:

   a. The market system not only accepts self-interest as a fact of human existence, it relies on self-interest to achieve society's material goals.

   b. The market system provides such a variety of desired goods and services precisely because no single individual or small group is deciding what the economy will produce.

   c. Entrepreneurs and business are at the helm of the economy, but their commanders are consumers.

2. Why is private property, and the protection of property rights, so critical to the success of the market system?

3. What are the advantages of "roundabout" production? What is meant by the term "division of labour"? What are the advantages of specialization in the use of human and material resources? Explain: "Exchange is the necessary consequence of specialization."

4. What problem does barter entail? Indicate the economic significance of money as a medium of exchange. What is meant by the statement "We want money only to part with it"?

5. Evaluate and explain the following statements:

   a. The market system is a profit-and-loss system.

   b. Competition is the indispensable disciplinarian of the market economy.

   c. Production methods that are inferior in the engineering sense may be the most efficient methods in the economic sense, once resource prices are considered.

6. In the 1990s, thousands of "dot-com" companies emerged with great fanfare to take advantage of the Internet and new information technologies. A few, like Yahoo, eBay, and Amazon, thrived and prospered but many others struggled and eventually failed. Relate these outcomes to how the market system answers the question, "What goods and services will be produced?"

7. Explain the meaning and implications of the following quotation.

   > The beautiful consequence of the market is that it is its own guardian. If output or prices or certain kinds of remuneration stray away from their socially ordained levels, forces are set into motion to bring them back to the fold. A curious paradox thus ensues: the market, which is the acme of individual economic freedom, is the strictest taskmaster of all. One may appeal the ruling of a planning board or win the dispensation of a [government] minister; but there is no appeal, no dispensation, from the anonymous pressures of the market mechanism. Economic freedom is thus more illusory than at first appears. One can do as one pleases in the market. But if one pleases to do what the market disapproves, the price of individual freedom is economic ruination.[1]

8. Suppose the demand for bagels rises dramatically while the demand for breakfast cereal falls. Briefly explain how the competitive market economy will make the needed adjustments to re-establish an efficient allocation of society's scarce resources.

9. **KEY QUESTION** Some large hardware stores, such as Canadian Tire, boast of carrying as many as 20,000 different products in each store. What motivated the producers of those products—everything from screwdrivers to ladders to water heaters—to make them and offer them for sale? How did the producers decide on the best combinations of factors of production to use? Who made those factors available, and why? Who decides whether these particular hardware products should continue to get produced and offered for sale?

10. In a single sentence, describe the meaning of the phrase "invisible hand."

11. What divergences arise between equilibrium output and efficient output when (a) spillover costs and (b) spillover benefits are present? How might government correct for these divergences? "The presence of spillover costs suggests the underallocation of resources to a particular product and the need for governmental subsidies." Do you agree? Why or why not? Explain how zoning and seat-belt laws might be used to deal with a problem of spillover costs.

12. **KEY QUESTION** What are the two characteristics of public goods? Explain the significance of each for public provision as opposed to private provision. What is the free-rider problem, as it relates to public goods? Is Canada's border patrol a public good or a private good? Why or why not? How about satellite TV? Explain.

13. **KEY QUESTION** Draw a production possibilities curve with public goods on the vertical axis and private goods on the horizontal axis. Assuming the economy is initially operating *on the curve,* indicate how the production of public goods might be increased. How might the output of public goods be increased if the economy is initially operating at a point *inside the curve?*

14. Use your understanding of the characteristics of private and public goods to determine whether the following should be produced through the market system or provided by government: (a) French fries; (b) airport screening; (c) court systems; (d) mail delivery; and (e) medical care. State why you answered as you did in each case.

15. Use the circular flow diagram to show how each of the following government actions simultaneously affect the allocation of resources and the distribution of income:

   a. The construction of a new high school.

   b. A 2 percentage-point reduction of the corporate income tax.

   c. An expansion of preschool programs for disadvantaged children.

   d. The levying of an excise tax on polluters.

---

[1]Robert L. Heilbroner, *The Worldly Philosophers,* 7th ed. (New York: Simon & Schuster, 1999), pp. 57–58.

16. **KEY QUESTION** The following are production possibilities tables for South Korea and Canada. Assume that before specialization and trade the optimal product mix for South Korea is alternative B and for Canada alternative D.

PRODUCT	SOUTH KOREA'S PRODUCTION ALTERNATIVES					
	A	**B**	**C**	**D**	**E**	**F**
Radios (in thousands)	30	24	18	12	6	0
Chemicals (in tonnes)	0	6	12	18	24	30

PRODUCT	CANADA'S PRODUCTION ALTERNATIVES					
	A	**B**	**C**	**D**	**E**	**F**
Radios (in thousands)	10	8	6	4	2	0
Chemicals (in tonnes)	0	4	8	12	16	20

a. Are comparative-cost conditions such that the two areas should specialize? If so, what product should each produce?

b. What is the total gain in radio and chemical output that results from this specialization?

c. What are the limits of the terms of trade? Suppose actual terms of trade are 1 unit of radios for 1½ units of chemicals and that 4 units of radios are exchanged for 6 units of chemicals. What are the gains from specialization and trade for each area?

d. Can you conclude from this illustration that specialization according to comparative advantage results in more efficient use of world resources? Explain.

17. Suppose that the comparative-cost ratios of two products—baby formula and tuna fish—are as follows in the hypothetical nations of Canswicki and Tunata.

Canswicki: 1 can baby formula ≡ 2 cans tuna fish

Tunata: 1 can baby formula ≡ 4 cans tuna fish

In what product should each nation specialize? Explain why terms of trade of 1 can baby formula = 2½ cans tuna fish would be acceptable to both nations.

18. (**The Last Word**) Why do private markets fail? In your answer, refer to the dwindling cod stocks on Canada's east coast.

INTERNET APPLICATION QUESTIONS

1. **Sparkly Things—Interested in Buying One?** Use the link in the McConnell-Brue-Barbiero Web site (Chapter 4) to connect to the eBay auction site. How many diamonds are for sale at the moment? How many rubies, sapphires, and opals? Note the wide array of sizes and prices of the gemstones. In what sense is there competition among the sellers in these markets? How does that competition influence prices? In what sense is there competition among buyers? How does that competition influence prices? See something interesting, there or elsewhere on eBay? Go ahead and buy it!

2. **Barter and the Canada Customs and Revenue Agency** Bartering occurs when goods or services are exchanged without the exchange of money. For some, barter's popularity is that it enables them to avoid paying taxes to the government. How might such avoidance occur? Use the link in the McConnell-Brue-Barbiero Web site (Chapter 4) to access the Canada Customs and Revenue Agency's interpretation of barter transactions. Does CCRA treat barter as taxable or non-taxable income? How is the value of a barter transaction determined?

Part 2

Macroeconomic Measurements, National Income Determination, and Fiscal Policy

Chapter 5

Measuring the Economy's Output

"Disposable Income Flat." "Personal Consumption Surges." "Investment Spending Stagnates." "GDP Up 4 Percent."

These headlines, typical of those in the *Globe and Mail* or *National Post*, give economists valuable information on the state of the economy. To novice economics students, however, they may be gibberish. This chapter will help you learn the language of macroeconomics and national income accounting and will provide you with a basic understanding that you can build on in the next several chapters.

5.1   Measuring the Economy's Performance: GDP

National income accounting measures the economy's overall performance. It does for the economy as a whole what private accounting does for the individual firm or for the individual household.

A firm measures its flows of income and expenditures regularly—usually every three months or once a year. With that information in hand, the firm can gauge its economic health. If things are going well and profits are good, the accounting data can be used to explain that success. Were costs down? Was output up? Have market prices risen? If things are going badly and profits are poor, the firm may be able to identify the reason by studying the record over several accounting periods. All this information helps the firm's managers to plot their future strategy.

National income accounting operates in much the same way for the economy as a whole. Statistics Canada compiles the national income accounts for the Canadian economy. This accounting allows economists and policy-makers to:

national income accounting
The techniques used to measure the overall production of the economy and other related variables for the nation as a whole.

- Assess the health of the economy by comparing levels of production at regular intervals.

- Track the long-run course of the economy to see whether it has grown, been constant, or declined.

- Formulate policies that will maintain and improve the economy's health.

Gross Domestic Product

The main measure of the economy's performance is its annual total output of goods and services or, as it is called, *aggregate output*. Aggregate output is labelled **gross domestic product (GDP)**: *the total market value of all final goods and services produced in a given year in a country.* GDP includes all goods and services produced by either citizen-supplied or foreign-supplied resources employed within the country. The Canadian GDP includes the market value of the telephone switches produced by a Canadian-owned factory in Quebec and the market value of a Honda produced by a Japanese-owned factory in Ontario.

gross domestic product (GDP)
The total market value of all final goods and services produced annually within the boundaries of Canada.

A Monetary Measure

If the economy produces three sofas and two computers in year 1 and two sofas and three computers in year 2, in which year is output greater? We can't answer that question until we attach a price tag to each of the two products to indicate how society evaluates their relative worth.

That's what GDP does. It is a *monetary measure of the output of a nation.* Without such a measure we would have no way of comparing the relative values of the vast number of goods and services produced in different years. In Table 5-1 the price of sofas is $500 and the price of computers is $2000. GDP would gauge the output of year 2 ($7000) as greater than the output of year 1 ($5500), because society places a higher monetary value on the output of year 2. Society is willing to pay $1500 more for the combination of goods produced in year 2 than for the combination of goods produced in year 1.

TABLE 5-1	Comparing Heterogeneous Outputs by Using Money Prices

Year	Annual output	Market value
1	3 sofas and 2 computers	3 at $500 + 2 at $2,000 = $5,500
2	2 sofas and 3 computers	2 at $500 + 3 at $2,000 = $7,000

Avoiding Multiple Counting

To measure aggregate output accurately, all goods and services produced in a particular year must be counted only once. Because most products go through a series of production stages before they reach the market, some of their components are bought and sold many times. To avoid counting those components more than once, GDP includes only the market value of *final goods* and ignores *intermediate goods* altogether.

intermediate goods
Products that are purchased for resale or further processing or manufacturing.

final goods
Goods and services that have been purchased for final use and not for resale or further processing or manufacturing.

multiple counting
Wrongly including the value of intermediate goods in the gross domestic product.

value added
The value of the product sold by a firm, less the value of the products purchased and used by the firm to produce the product.

www.statcan.ca/english/
Pgdb/Economy/Economic/
econ05.htm
Statistics Canada

Intermediate goods are goods and services that are purchased for resale or for further processing or manufacturing. **Final goods** are goods and services that are acquired for final use by the purchaser, and not for resale or for further processing or manufacturing.

Why is the value of final goods included in GDP, but the value of intermediate goods excluded? Because the value of final goods already includes the value of all the intermediate goods that were used in producing them. To include the value of intermediate goods would amount to **multiple counting**, and that would distort the value of GDP.

To see why, suppose that there are five stages to manufacturing a wool suit and getting it to the consumer—the final user. Table 5-2 shows that firm A, a sheep ranch, sells $120 worth of wool to firm B, a wool processor. Firm A pays out the $120 in wages, rent, interest, and profit. Firm B processes the wool and sells it to firm C, a suit manufacturer, for $180. What does firm B do with the $180 it receives? It pays $120 to firm A for the wool and uses the remaining $60 to pay wages, rent, interest, and profit for the resources used in processing the wool. Firm C, the manufacturer, sells the suit to firm D, a wholesaler, who sells it to firm E, a retailer. Then at last a consumer, the final user, comes in and buys the suit for $350.

How much of these amounts should we include in GDP to account for the production of the suit? Just $350, the value of the final product. The $350 includes all the intermediate transactions leading up to the product's final sale. To include the sum of all the intermediate sales, $1140, in GDP would amount to multiple counting. The production and sale of the final suit generated just $350, not $1140.

Alternatively, we could avoid multiple counting by measuring and cumulating only the *value added* at each stage. **Value added** is the market value of a firm's output *less* the value of the inputs the firm bought from others. At each stage, the difference between what a firm pays for a product and what it receives from selling the product is paid out as wages, rent, interest, and profit. Column 3 of Table 5-2 shows that the value added by firm B is $60, the difference between the $180 value of its output and the $120 it paid for the input from firm A. We find the total of the suit by adding together all the values added by the five firms. Similarly, by calculating and summing the values added to all the goods and services produced by all firms in the economy, we can find the market value of the economy's total output—its GDP.

GDP Excludes Non-Production Transactions

Although many monetary transactions in the economy involve final goods and services, many others do not. Those non-production transactions must be excluded from GDP because they have nothing to do with the production of final goods. *Non-production transactions* are of two types: purely financial transactions and second-hand sales.

TABLE 5-2	**Value Added in a Five-stage Production Process**	
(1) Stage of production	**(2)** Sales value of materials or product	**(3)** Value added
	0	
Firm A, sheep ranch	$ 120	$120 (= $120 – $ 0)
Firm B, wool processor	180	60 (= 180 – 120)
Firm C, suit manufacturer	220	40 (= 220 – 180)
Firm D, clothing wholesaler	270	50 (= 270 – 220)
Firm E, retail clothier	**350**	80 (= 350 – 270)
Total sales values	$1,140	
Value added (total income)		**$350**

FINANCIAL TRANSACTIONS

Purely financial transactions include the following:

- *Public transfer payments* These are the social insurance payments, such as welfare payments, and employment insurance payments that the government makes directly to households. Since the recipients contribute nothing to *current production* in return, inclusion of such payments in GDP would overstate the year's output.

- *Private transfer payments* Such payments include, for example, the money that parents give children or the cash gifts given at Christmas time. They produce no output. They simply transfer funds from one individual to another and consequently do not enter into GDP.

- *Stock-market transactions*   The buying and selling of stocks (and bonds) is just a matter of swapping bits of paper. Stock-market transactions do not directly contribute to current production and are not included in GDP. Payments for the services of a security broker *are* included, however, because those services do contribute to current output.

SECOND-HAND SALES

Second-hand sales contribute nothing to current production and for that reason are excluded from GDP. Suppose you sell your 2000 Ford Mustang to a friend; that transaction would not be included in calculating this year's GDP because it generates no current production. The same would be true if you sold a brand-new Mustang to a neighbour a week after you purchased it. *(Key Question 3)*

Two Ways of Calculating GDP: Spending and Income

Let's look again at how the market value of total output is measured. Given the data listed in Table 5-2, how can we measure the market value of a suit?

The final-product approach and the value-added approach are two ways of looking at the same thing. (See The Last Word in this chapter for more details on how Statistics Canada uses the value added approach to compute GDP.) *What is spent on making a product is income to those who helped to make it.* If $350 is spent on manufacturing a suit, then $350 is the total income derived from its production.

We can look at GDP in the same two ways. We can view GDP as the sum of all the money spent in buying final goods and services, called the **expenditures approach**. Or we can view GDP in terms of the income derived or created from producing final goods and services, or the **income approach**. Buying (spending money) and selling (receiving income) are two aspects of the same transaction. On the expenditures side of GDP, all final goods produced by the economy are bought either by three domestic sectors (households, businesses, and government) or by buyers abroad. On the income side (once certain statistical adjustments are made), the total receipts from the sale of that total output go to the suppliers as wage, rent, interest, and profit income.

The Expenditures Approach

To determine GDP using the expenditures approach, we add up all the spending on final goods and services that has taken place throughout the year. There are precise terms for the types of spending listed in Table 5-3.

Personal Consumption Expenditures (C)

What we have called "consumption expenditures by households," the national income accountants call **personal consumption expenditures**. That term covers all expenditures by households on *durable consumer goods* (automobiles, refrigerators, DVD players), *non-durable consumer goods* (bread, milk, vitamins, pencils, toothpaste), and *consumer expenditures for services* (of lawyers, doctors, mechanics, barbers). The symbol *C* is used to designate this component of GDP.

expenditures approach
The method that adds all expenditures made for final goods and services to measure the gross domestic product.

income approach
The method that adds up all the income generated by the production of final goods and services to measure the gross domestic product.

personal consumption expenditures
The expenditures of households for durable and non-durable consumer goods and services.

TABLE 5-3	Calculating GDP: The Expenditure Approach (Billions of dollars)
Personal consumption expenditure (C)	656.2
Gross investment (I_g)	196.8
Government current purchases of goods and services (G)	251.6
Net exports (X_n)	50.3
Gross domestic product at market prices	$1,154.9

Source: Statistics Canada. Data updates may be retrieved from www.mcgrawhill.ca/college/mcconnell. **Σ-STAT**

Gross Investment (I_g)

gross investment
Expenditures for newly produced capital goods (such as machinery, equipment, tools, and buildings) and for additions to inventories.

Under the heading **gross investment** (I_g), the following items are included:

- All final purchases of machinery, equipment, and tools by businesses

- All construction

- Changes in inventories

Notice that this list, except for the first item, includes more than we have meant by "investment" so far, particularly in our discussion of the production possibility curve in Chapter 2. The second item includes residential construction as well as the construction of new factories, warehouses, and stores. Why is residential construction regarded as investment rather than consumption? Because apartment buildings and houses, like factories and stores, earn income when they are rented or leased. Owner-occupied houses are treated as investment goods because they *could be* rented to bring in an income return. So, the national income accountants treat all residential construction as investment. Finally, increases in inventories (unsold goods) are considered to be investment because they represent, in effect, "unconsumed output."

Increases in inventories (unsold goods) are considered to be investment because they are unconsumed output.

POSITIVE AND NEGATIVE CHANGES IN INVENTORIES

Let's look at changes in inventories more closely. Inventories can either increase or decrease over some period. Suppose they increased by $10 billion between December 31, 2002, and December 31, 2003. That means the economy produced $10 billion more output than was purchased in 2003. We need to count all output produced in 2003 as part of that year's GDP, even though some of it remained unsold at the end of the year. This is accomplished by including the $10 billion increase in inventories as investment in 2003. That way the expenditures in 2003 will correctly measure the output produced that year.

Alternatively, suppose that inventories decreased by $10 billion in 2003. This "drawing down of inventories" means that the economy sold $10 billion more of output in 2003 than it produced that year. It did this by selling goods produced in prior years—goods already counted as GDP in those years. Unless corrected, expenditures in 2003 will overstate GDP for 2003. So, in 2003 we consider the $10 billion decline in inventories as "negative investment" and subtract it from total investment that year. Thus, expenditures in 2003 will correctly measure the output produced in 2003.

NON-INVESTMENT TRANSACTIONS

So much for what investment is. You need to know what it isn't. Investment does *not* include the transfer of paper assets (stocks, bonds) or the resale of tangible assets (houses, jewellery, boats). Such transactions merely transfer the ownership of existing assets. Investment has to do with the creation of *new,* physical capital assets—assets that create jobs and income. The transfer (sale) of claims to existing capital goods does not create new capital.

GROSS INVESTMENT VERSUS NET INVESTMENT

As we have seen, the category gross investment, or *gross capital formation,* includes (1) all final purchases of machinery, equipment, and tools; (2) all construction; and (3) changes in inventories. The word *gross* means that we are referring to all investment goods—both those that replace machinery, equipment, and buildings that were used up (worn out or made obsolete) in producing the current year's output and any net additions to the economy's stock of capital. Gross investment includes investment in replacement capital *and* in added capital.

net investment
Gross investment less consumption of fixed capital.

capital consumption allowance
Estimate of the amount of capital worn out or used up (consumed) in producing the gross domestic product; depreciation.

In contrast, **net investment** includes *only* investment of added capital. The amount of capital that is used up over the course of a year is called **capital consumption allowance**, or simply *depreciation.* So:

Net investment = gross investment – depreciation

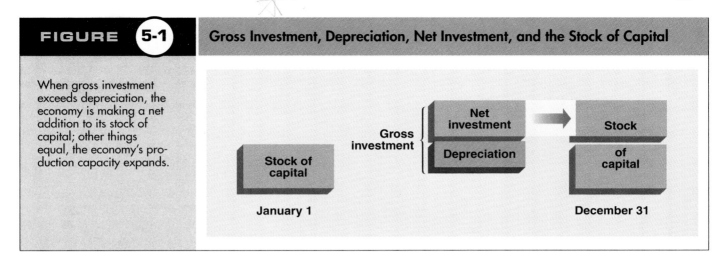

FIGURE 5-1 Gross Investment, Depreciation, Net Investment, and the Stock of Capital

When gross investment exceeds depreciation, the economy is making a net addition to its stock of capital; other things equal, the economy's production capacity expands.

In most years, gross investment exceeds depreciation. Thus net investment is positive and the nation's stock of capital rises, as illustrated in Figure 5-1. Such increases in capital shift the Canadian production possibilities curve outward and thus expand the nation's production capacity. In 2002 gross investment in Canada amounted to $196.8 million.

Gross investment need not always exceed depreciation, however. When gross investment and depreciation *are equal*, net investment is zero and there is no change in the size of the capital stock. When gross investment *is less than* depreciation, net investment is negative. The economy then is *disinvesting*—using up more capital than it is producing—and the nation's stock of capital shrinks. That happened in the Great Depression of the 1930s.

National income accountants use the symbol I for investment spending, along with the subscript g to signify gross investment. They use the subscript n to signify net investment. But it is gross investment, I_g, that they use in determining GDP.

Government Purchases (G)

government purchases
The expenditures of all governments in the economy for final goods and services.

The third category of expenditures in the national income accounts is **government purchases**, expenditures for goods and services that government consumes in providing public services. Government purchases (federal, provincial, and municipal) include all government expenditures on final goods, investment goods, and all direct purchases of resources, including labour. It does *not* include government transfer payments, because, as we have seen, they merely transfer government receipts to certain households and generate no production of any sort. Examples of government transfer payments are employment insurance benefits, welfare payments, and Canada Pension benefits. National income accountants use the symbol G to signify government purchases.

Net Exports (X_n)

International trade transactions are a significant item in national income accounting. We know that GDP records all spending on goods and services produced in Canada, including spending on Canadian output by people abroad. So we must include the value of exports when we are using the expenditures approach to determine GDP.

At the same time, we know that Canadians spend a great deal of money on imports—goods and services produced abroad. That spending shows up in some other nation's GDP. We must subtract the value of imports from GDP to avoid overstating total production in Canada.

net exports
Exports minus imports.

Rather than add exports and then subtract imports, we use "exports less imports," or **net exports**. We designate exports as X, imports as M, and net exports as X_n.

Net exports (X_n) = exports (X) – imports (M)

Consider This

Stocks and Flows

An analogy of a reservoir may be helpful in thinking about a nation's capital stock, investment, and depreciation. Picture a reservoir that has water flowing in from a river and flowing out from an outlet after it passes through turbines. The volume of water in the reservoir *at any particular time* is a "stock." In contrast, the inflow from the river and outflow from the outlet are "flows." Such flows are always measured over *some period of time*. Suppose that we measure these inflows and outflows at the end of each week and compare them with our measurements at the beginning of the week.

The volume or "stock" of water in the reservoir will rise if the weekly inflow exceeds the weekly outflow. It will fall if the inflow is less than the outflow. And, it will remain constant if the two flows are equal.

We could simplify further by thinking in terms of the *net inflow* (inflow *minus* outflow) into the reservoir, where the net inflow can be positive or negative. The volume of water in the reservoir will rise if the net inflow is positive, decline if it is negative, and remain constant if it is zero.

Now let's apply this analogy to the stock of capital, gross investment, and depreciation. The stock of capital is the total capital in place at any time. Changes in this stock over some period of time, for example, one year, depend on *gross investment* and *depreciation* (capital consumption allowance). Gross investment (the addition of capital goods) adds to the stock of capital and depreciation (the using up of capital goods) subtracts from it. The capital stock increases when gross investment exceeds depreciation, declines when gross investment is less than depreciation, and remains the same when gross investment and depreciation are equal.

Alternatively, the stock of capital increases when *net investment* (gross investment *minus* depreciation) is positive. When net investment is negative, the stock of capital declines, and when net investment is zero, the stock of capital remains constant.

Question: In 2001 gross investment in Canada totalled $216.5 billion and capital consumption allowance amounted to $144.3 billion. How much was added to the Canadian capital stock in 2001?

Table 5-3 shows that in 2002 people from other countries spent $50.3 billion more on Canadian exports than Canadians spent on imports. That is, net exports in 2002 were a *positive* $50.3 billion. In another year net exports could be *negative:* imports would be greater than exports in that case.

Putting It All Together: GDP = $C + I_g + G + X_n$

Taken together, these four categories of expenditures provide a measure of the market value of a certain year's total output—its GDP.

For Canada in 2002 (Table 5-3):

GDP = $656.2 + 196.8 + 251.6 + 50.3 = 1154.9

Global Perspective 5.1 lists the GDPs of several countries.

The Income Approach

Table 5-4 shows how 2002's $1154.9 billion of expenditures were allocated as income to those producing the output. It would be simple if we could say that it all flowed back to them in the form of wages, rent, interest, and profit, but the Canadian national accounts do not record each of these four factor incomes. Moreover, we have to make a few adjustments to balance the expenditures and income sides of the account. We look first at the items that make up the income approach in Table 5-4. Then we turn to the adjustments.

TABLE 5-4	Calculating GDP: The Income Approach (Billions of dollars)	
Wages, salaries, and supplementary labour income		$597.3
Profits of corporations and government enterprises before taxes*		140.3
Interest and investment income		49.4
Net income of farm and unincorporated businesses		74.7
Taxes less subsidies on factors of production		53.8
Indirect taxes less subsidies		84.4
Capital consumption allowances		155.0
Gross domestic product at market prices		$1,154.9

Source: Statistics Canada. Data updates may be retrieved from www.mcgrawhill.ca/college/mcconnell.
*Includes adjustments and statistical discrepancy.

Wages, Salaries, and Supplementary Labour Income

The largest income category is made up primarily of the wages and salaries paid by businesses and government to suppliers of labour. It also includes wage and salary supplements, in particular payments by employers of employment insurance premiums, workers' compensation premiums, and employer contributions to a variety of private and public pension funds for workers. Economists abbreviate all these as "wages."

Profits of Corporations and Government Enterprises before Taxes

Corporate profits are the earnings of government enterprises and owners of corporations. Profits of private corporations are divided into three categories:

- **Corporate income taxes** These taxes are levied on the corporations' net earnings and flow to the government.

- **Dividends** These are the part of corporate profits that are paid to the corporate stockholders and thus flow to households—the ultimate owners of all corporations.

- **Undistributed corporate profits** This is money saved by the corporations to be invested later in new plants and equipment. They are also called *retained earnings*.

Interest and Investment Income

Interest income consists of money paid by private businesses to the suppliers of money capital. This income includes interest on bonds and loans of money capital. Investment income includes rental income received by households and imputed rent; that is, the estimated rent on housing that households use for their own purpose.

Net Income from Farms and Unincorporated Businesses

This is the earnings of farmers and proprietors from their own businesses. These earnings represent a mixture of labour income and investment income that is impossible to segregate. Farm and non-farm proprietors supplying their own capital earn profits (or losses), interest, and rents mixed in with their labour income.

Adding Up Domestic Income

When we add up wages, salaries and supplementary labour income, corporate and government enterprise profits, interest and investment income, income of farm and non-farm unincorporated

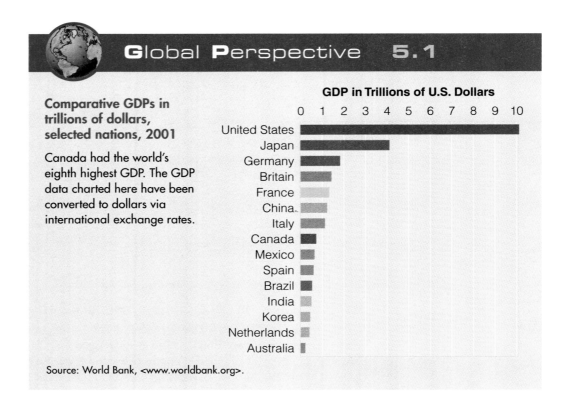

Global Perspective 5.1

Comparative GDPs in trillions of dollars, selected nations, 2001

Canada had the world's eighth highest GDP. The GDP data charted here have been converted to dollars via international exchange rates.

GDP in Trillions of U.S. Dollars

Source: World Bank, <www.worldbank.org>.

business, and make the appropriate inventory valuation adjustment, we get the *net domestic income at factor cost,* which is all the income earned by Canadian-supplied factors of production as wages, interest, rent and profit. But to arrive at GDP we have to make two adjustments.

INDIRECT TAXES

The first adjustment is to add to net domestic product **indirect taxes**, less subsidies, which include general sales taxes, including the GST, business property taxes, and custom duties.

To see why we must add indirect business taxes to net domestic income in balancing expenditures and income, assume that a firm produces a good selling at $1. Production of this item creates $1 of wage, rent, interest, and profit income. But now government imposes a 5 percent sales tax on all products sold at retail. The retailer adds the tax to the price of the product, raising its price from $1 to $1.05. But the $.05 is *not* earned income because government contributes nothing directly to the production of the good in return for the tax receipt. Only $1 of what consumers pay goes out as wage, rent, interest, and profit income. So national income accountants need to add the $.05 to the $1 of net domestic income in calculating GDP and make this adjustment for the entire economy.

DEPRECIATION: CAPITAL CONSUMPTION ALLOWANCE

The useful life of capital equipment extends far beyond the year in which it was produced. To avoid understatement of profit and income in the year of purchase, and to avoid overstating profit and income in succeeding years, the cost of such goods must be allocated over their lives. The amount allocated is an estimate of the capital being used up each year in production, called *depreciation.*

The depreciation charge against gross investment is the capital consumption allowance—the allowance for capital goods "consumed" in producing this year's GDP. It is the portion of GDP that must be set aside to pay for the replacement of the capital goods used up in production. That part of this charge is the difference between gross investment, I_g, and net investment, I_n.

The money allocated to consumption of fixed capital (the depreciation allowance) is a cost of production and thus included in the gross value of output. Unlike other costs of production, it does not add to anyone's income, so it is not included in national income. We must therefore add consumption of fixed capital to net domestic income to achieve balance with the economy's expenditures, as in Table 5-4. *(Key Question 8)*

QUICK REVIEW

- Gross domestic product (GDP) measures the total market value of all final goods and services produced within a nation in a specific year.

- When net investment is positive, the economy's production capacity increases; when net investment is negative, the economy's production capacity decreases.

- The expenditures approach to GDP sums total spending on final goods and services: $GDP = C + I_g + G + X_n$.

- The income approach to GDP sums the total income earned by a nation's resource suppliers, then adds in indirect taxes and capital consumption allowance.

5.2   Other National Accounts

Several other national accounts provide additional useful information about the economy's performance. We can derive these accounts by making various adjustments to GDP.

Gross National Product (GNP)

Until 1986, *gross national product (GNP)* was the main aggregate in the national accounts published by Statistics Canada. GNP is the total income that residents of a country earn within the year. The change was made because in Canada foreign investment is significant, and GDP would give us a better indication of output *produced* in Canada and the total income derived from that output. GNP measures output by Canadians here and abroad, but excludes the contribution to Canadian output from investments of non-residents. For example, the production of cars in the Honda factory in Alliston, Ontario is included in both Canadian GDP and GNP. But GNP excludes profit (referred to as net-investments from non-residents) sent to foreign shareholders of Honda, but this profit is included in Canadian GDP. Because there are many foreign-owned firms in Canada (compared to Canadian-owned firms abroad), GNP is less than GDP. As Table 5-5 shows, Canadian GNP for 2002 totalled $1070.0 billion, whereas GDP was $1154.9 billion.

Net Domestic Product (NDP)   *GNP − Depre*

As a measure of total output, GNP does not make allowances for replacing the capital goods used up in each year's production. As a result, it does not tell us how much new output was available for consumption and for additions to the stock of capital. To determine that, we must subtract from GNP the capital that was consumed in producing the GNP and that had to be replaced. That is, we need to subtract consumption of fixed capital (depreciation) from GNP. The result is a measure of **net domestic product (NDP)**. NDP measures the total annual output that the entire economy—households, businesses, government, and foreigners—can consume without impairing its capacity to produce in ensuing years. For 2002, NDP totalled $915.0 billion.

Net National Income at Basic Prices (NNI)

net domestic product (NDP)
GNP less the part of the year's output needed to replace the capital goods worn out in producing the output.

net national income (NNI)
Total income earned by resource suppliers for their contribution to GDP.

Sometimes it is useful to know how much Canadians earned for their contributions of land, labour, capital, and entrepreneurial talent. Canadian **net national income (NNI)** includes all income earned through the use of Canadian-owned resources, whether they are located at home or abroad. To derive

TABLE 5-5	The Relationships between GNP, GDP, NDP, NNI, PI, and DI in Canada, 2002	
Gross domestic product (GDP)		$1,154.9
Net investments from non-residents		−84.9
Gross national product (GNP)		1,070.0
Capital consumption allowance (depreciation)		−155.0
Net domestic product (NDP)		915.0
Indirect business taxes less subsidies		−138.2
Net National income (NNI)		$776.8
Undistributed corporate profits		−49.0
Government transfer payments		+71.3
Personal income (PI)		848.1
Personal taxes		−152.2
Disposable income (DI)		$695.9

NNI from NDP, we must *subtract indirect business taxes.* Because government is not an economic resource, the indirect business taxes it collects do not qualify as payments to productive resources and thus are not included in national income. In 2002, NNI at basic prices amounted to $776.8 billion.

Personal Income (PI)

personal income
The earned and unearned income available to resource suppliers and others before the payment of personal income taxes.

Personal income (PI) includes all income *received* by households, earned or unearned. It is likely to differ from NNI because some income that is earned—corporate income taxes, undistributed corporate profits, government investment income, and social insurance contributions—is not actually received by households, and conversely, some income that is received—transfer payments—is not currently earned. Transfer payments are made up of such items as (1) Canada and Quebec Pension Plan payments, old age security pension payments, and employment insurance benefits; (2) welfare payments; and (3) a variety of veterans' payments. To arrive at personal income, we must subtract from NNI income that is earned but not received and add in income received but not currently earned. For 2002, PI totalled $848.1 billion.

Disposable Income (DI)

disposable income
Personal income less personal taxes.

Disposable income is personal income less personal taxes and other personal transfers to government. *Personal taxes* are made up of personal income taxes and personal property taxes. In 2002, DI amounted to $695.9 billion.

Households use their disposable income in two ways: consumption (C) and savings (S):

DI = C + S

Table 5-5 summarizes the relationships among GNP, GDP, NDP, NNI, PI, and DI. *(Key Question 9)*

QUICK REVIEW

- GNP is derived by subtracting net investments from non-residents from GDP.
- Net domestic product (NDP) is equal to GNP minus capital consumption allowances (depreciation).
- Net national income (NNI) is all income earned through the use of Canadian-owned resources, whether located at home or abroad.
- Personal income (PI) is all income received by households, whether earned or not.
- Disposable income (DI) is all income received by households minus personal taxes.

FIGURE 5-2   Canadian Domestic Output and the Flows of Expenditure and Income

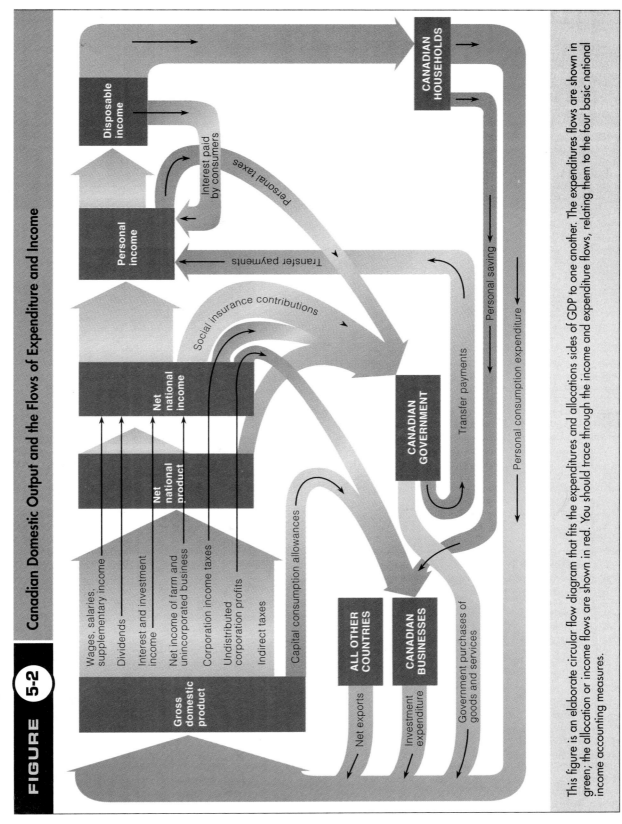

This figure is an elaborate circular flow diagram that fits the expenditures and allocations sides of GDP to one another. The expenditures flows are shown in green; the allocation or income flows are shown in red. You should trace through the income and expenditure flows, relating them to the four basic national income accounting measures.

The Circular Flow Revisited

Figure 5-2 is an elaborate flow diagram that shows the economy's four main sectors along with the flows of expenditures and allocations that determine GDP, NDP, NNI, PI, and DI. The green arrows represent the spending flows—$C + I_g + G + X_n$—that together measure gross domestic product (GDP). To the right of the GDP rectangle are red arrows that show first the allocations of GDP and then the adjustments needed to derive NDP, NNI, PI, and DI.

The diagram illustrates the adjustments necessary to determine each of the national income accounts. For example, net domestic income is smaller than GDP because consumption of fixed capital flows away from GDP in determining NDP.

Note the three domestic sectors of the economy: households, government, and businesses. The household sector has an inflow of disposable income and outflows of consumption spending and saving. Some of the consumption spending is for foreign goods and services. The government sector has an inflow of revenue in the form of types of taxes and outflow of government disbursements in the form of purchases and transfers. The business sector has inflows of three major sources of funds for business investment and an outflow of investment expenditures.

Finally, note the foreign sector (all other countries) in the flow diagram. Spending by foreigners on Canadian exports adds to Canadian GDP, but some of Canadian consumption, government, and investment expenditures buy imported products. The flow from foreign markets shows that we handle this complication by calculating net exports (Canadian exports minus Canadian imports). The net export flow may be a positive or negative amount, adding to or subtracting from Canadian GDP.

Figure 5-2 shows that flows of expenditures and income are part of a continuous, repetitive process. Cause and effect are intermingled: Expenditures create income, and from this income arise expenditures, which again flow to resource owners as income.

5.3   Nominal GDP Versus Real GDP

Recall that GDP is a measure of the market or money value of all final goods and services produced by the economy in a given year. We use money or nominal values to sum that heterogeneous output into a meaningful total. But that creates a problem: How can we compare the market values of GDP from year to year if the value of money itself changes because of inflation or deflation? After all, we determine the value of GDP by multiplying total output (Q) by market prices (P).

Whether there is a 5 percent increase in output (Q) with no change in prices (P) or a 5 percent increase in prices (P) with no change in output (Q), the change in the value of GDP will be the same. And yet it is the *quantity* (Q) of goods that gets produced and distributed to households that affects our standard of living, not the price (P) of the goods. The hamburger that sold for $2.00 in 2003 yields the same satisfaction as an identical hamburger that sold for 50 cents in 1970.

The way around this problem is to *deflate* GDP when prices rise and to *inflate* GDP when prices fall. These adjustments give us a measure of GDP for various years as if the value of the dollar had always been the same as it was in some reference (base) year. A GDP based on prices when the output was produced is called unadjusted GDP, or **nominal GDP**. A GDP that has been deflated or inflated to reflect changes in the price level is called adjusted GDP, or **real GDP**.

nominal GDP
The gross domestic product measured in terms of the price level at the time of measurement (unadjusted for inflation).

real GDP
Nominal gross domestic product adjusted for inflation.

Adjustment Process in a One-Product Economy

There are two ways we can adjust nominal GDP to reflect price changes. For simplicity, let's assume that the economy produces only one good, pizza, in the amount indicated in Table 5-6 for years 1, 2, and 3. Suppose that we gather revenue data directly from the financial reports of the pizza business to measure nominal GDP in various years. After completing our effort we would have calculated nominal GDP for each year, as shown in column 4 of Table 5-6. But we would have no way of knowing to what extent changes in price and/or changes in quantity of output have accounted for the increases or decreases in nominal GDP that we observe.

TABLE 5-6			Calculating Real GDP		
Year	(1) Units of output (Q)	(2) Price of pizza per unit (P)	(3) Price index (year 1 = 100)	(4) Unadjusted, or nominal, GDP (Q) × (P)	(5) Adjusted, or real, GDP
1	5	$10	100	$ 50	$50
2	7	20	200	140	70
3	8	25	250	200	80
4	10	30	_300_	_300_	_100_
5	11	28	_280_	_308_	_148_

PRICE INDEX

How can we calculate real GDP in our pizza-economy? One way is to assemble data on the price changes that occurred over various years (column 2) and use them to establish an overall price index for the entire period. Then we can use the index in each year to adjust nominal GDP to real GDP for that year.

price index
An index number that shows how the weighted average price of a "market basket" of goods and services changes through time.

A **price index** *is a measure of the price of a specified collection of goods and services, called a "market basket," in a specific year as compared to the price of an identical (or highly similar) collection of goods and services in a reference year.* That point of reference, or benchmark, is known as the base period or base year. More formally,

$$\text{Price index in specific year} = \frac{\text{price of market basket in specific year}}{\text{price of same market basket in base year}} \times 100 \qquad (1)$$

By convention, the price ratio between a given year and the base year is multiplied by 100 to facilitate computation. For example, a price ratio of 2/1 (= 2) is expressed as a price index of 200. A price ratio of 1/3 (= .33) is expressed as a price index of 33.

In our pizza-only example, of course, our market basket consists of only one product. Column 2 of Table 5-6 reveals that the price of pizza was $10 in year 1, $20 in year 2, $25 in year 3, and so on. Let's select year 1 as our base year. Now we can express the successive prices of the contents of our market basket in, say, years 2 and 3 as compared to the price of the market basket in year 1:

$$\text{Price index, year 2} = \frac{\$20}{\$10} \times 100 = 200$$

$$\text{Price index, year 3} = \frac{\$25}{\$10} \times 100 = 250$$

For year 1, the base year, the price index is 100.

The index numbers tell us that the price of pizza rose from year 1 to year 2 by 100 percent [= (200 − 100)/100 × 100] and from year 1 to year 3 by 150 percent [= (250 − 100)/100 × 100].

DIVIDING NOMINAL GDP BY THE PRICE INDEX

We can now use the index numbers shown in column 3 to deflate or inflate the nominal GDP figures in column 4. The simplest and most direct method of deflating (or inflating) is to divide the price index into the corresponding nominal GDP. That gives us real GDP:

$$\text{Real GDP} = \frac{\text{nominal GDP}}{\text{price index}} \times 100 \qquad (2)$$

Column 5 of Table 5-6 shows the results. These figures for real GDP measure the market value of the output of pizza in years 1, 2, and 3 as if the price of pizza had been a constant $10 throughout the three-year period.

To test your understanding, extend Table 5-6 to years 4 and 5, using equation (2). Then run through the entire deflating procedure, using year 3 as the base period. This time you will have to inflate some of the nominal GDP data, using the same procedure as we used in the examples.

An Alternative Method

Another way to calculate real GDP is to gather separate data on physical outputs (Q) (as in column 1) and their prices (P) (as in column 2) of Table 5-6. We could then determine the market value of outputs in successive years *if the base-year price ($10) had prevailed.* In year 2, the 7 units of pizza would have a value of $70 (= 7 units × $10). As column 5 confirms, that $70 worth of output is year 2's real GDP. Similarly, we could determine the real GDP for year 3 by multiplying the 8 units of output that year by the $10 price in the base year.

Once we have determined real GDP through this method, we can identify the *implicit price index,* or **GDP deflator**, for a given year simply by dividing the nominal GDP by the real GDP for that year.

GDP deflator
An implicit price index calculated by dividing nominal GDP by real GDP and multiplying by 100.

$$\text{GDP deflator} = \frac{\text{nominal GDP}}{\text{real GDP}} \times 100 \qquad (3)$$

Example: In year 2 we get a GDP deflator of 200, which equals the nominal GDP of $140 divided by the real GDP of $70 (× 100). Note that equation (3) is simply a rearrangement of equation (2). Table 5-7 summarizes the two methods of determining real GDP in our single-good economy. *(Key Question 11)*

Real-World Considerations and Data

In the real world of many goods and services, of course, determining GDP and constructing a reliable price index are far more complex matters than in our pizza-only economy. The national income accountants must assign a "weight" to each of the 380 categories of goods and services based on the relative proportion of each category in total output. They update the weights as expenditure patterns change.

Table 5-8 shows some of the real-world relationships between nominal GDP, real GDP, and the GDP price index. Here the reference year is 1997, the base year Statistics Canada currently uses, and the index is set at 100. Because the price level has been rising over the long run, the pre-1997 val-

TABLE 5-7	Steps for Deriving Real GDP from Nominal GDP

Method 1

1. Find nominal GDP for each year.
2. Compute a price index.
3. Divide each year's nominal GDP by that year's price index, then multiply by 100 to determine real GDP.

Method 2

1. Break down nominal GDP into physical quantities of output and prices for each year.
2. Find real GDP for each year by determining the dollar amount that each year's physical output would have sold for if base-year prices had prevailed. (The implicit price index, or GDP deflator, can then be found by dividing nominal GDP by real GDP, and then multiplying by 100.)

TABLE 5-8	Nominal GDP, Real GDP, and the GDP Deflator,* Selected Years		
(1) Year	(2) Nominal GDP	(3) Real GDP	(4) GDP deflator 1997 = 100
1965	58.1	303.0	19.2
1970	90.4	378.6	*23.9*
1975	173.9	480.3	36.2
1980	315.2	*576.2*	54.7
1985	485.7	660.3	73.6
1990	679.9	762.4	89.2
1992	700.5	754.8	92.8
1995	810.5	*832.1*	97.4
1997	882.7	882.7	100.0
2000	1,075.6	1,020.8	*105.4*
2002	1,154.9	1,074.5	107.5

*Chain-type annual-weights price index.

Source: Statistics Canada. For updates on nominal and real GDP visit www.mcgrawhill.ca/college/mcconnell.

Σ-STAT

ues of real GDP (column 3) are higher than the nominal values of GDP for those years (column 2). This upward adjustment means that prices were lower in the years before 1997, and thus nominal GDP understated the real output of those years and must be inflated.

Conversely, the rising price level on the post-1997 years caused nominal GDP figures for those years to overstate real output. So statisticians deflate those figures to determine what real GDP would have been in other years if 1997 prices had prevailed. Doing so reveals that real GDP has been less than nominal GDP since 1997.

By inflating the nominal pre-1997 GDP data and deflating the post-1997 data, government accountants determine annual real GDP, which can then be compared with the real GDP of any other year in the series of years. So the real GDP values in column 3 are directly comparable with one another.

Once we have determined nominal GDP and real GDP, we can calculate the GDP deflator. And once we have determined nominal GDP and the price index, we can calculate real GDP. Example: Nominal GDP in 2002 was $1154.9 billion and real GDP was $1074.5 billion. So the price level in 2002 was 107.5 (= $1154.9/$1074.5 × 100), or 7.5 percent higher than in 1997. To find real GDP for 2002 we divide the nominal GDP of $1154.9 by the 2002 GDP deflator, and multiply by 100.

To test your understanding of the relationships between nominal GDP, real GDP, and the GDP deflator, determine the values of the GDP deflator for 1970 and 2000 in Table 5-8 and determine real GDP for 1980 and 1995. We have left those figures out on purpose. *(Key Question 13)*

Chain Weighted Index

Up to 2001, Statistics Canada established weights, based on price, for a base year for the 380 categories it uses in calculating the implicit price index, and changed these weights approximately every ten years. Statistics Canada last used 1992 as the base year. This *fixed based price index* method, which we just studied, worked well as long as the weights remained relatively constant from year to year. But with the rapid expansion of the information technology sector, many prices for the outputs of this sector fell dramatically. Using 1992 prices as weights for the outputs of the information technology sector would result in "overweighting" of these goods and services. Since the output of the information technology sector grew rapidly in the 1990s, such overweighting in essence over-estimated GDP growth during that decade. Thus in May of 2001 Statistics Canada began to calculate a *chain weighted index,* or chain Fisher index, which is adjusted annually to better represent the weight of each category, particularly the information technology sector.

To better understand why Statistics Canada now calculates a chain weighted index, let's look at an example. Consider an economy that has only two sectors, computers and pears, and consumers spend half of their income on pears and the other half on computers. We assume that the output of computers is rising at a very rapid 10 percent per year, while pear production is stagnant, remaining the same from year to year. We further assume that the price of computers falls relative to the price of pears over time due to the rapid expansion of computer production. If we construct a fixed weighted index using prices (weights) prevailing in, say 2002, the rapid output growth of computers will also translate into a very rapid growth rate of GDP. But that very rapid GDP growth rate is actually overstated because the price (the weight) of computers is falling. Moreover, consumers have not changed the proportion of their income they spend on pears and computers. Thus in a situations where prices of some goods in the economy are falling, as has been the case in Canada in the information technology sector in the last 15 years or so, the traditional fixed weight index to calculate real GDP in inadequate.

Rather than using only a base year, the new method of calculating GDP by Statistics Canada considers both quantities and prices in the base year and the following year, and then averages the two. For example, If using 2002 prices as weights yields a real GDP increase of 4 percent in 2003 but using 2003 prices yields a GDP increase of 3 percent because some prices in the economy declined, the new chain weighted index would give an increase of real GDP in 2003 of 3.5 percent (= (4 + 3)/2). You can see in this simple example that falling prices for some output in 2003 has reduced the growth rate of GDP compared to the fixed weighted method of calculating GDP.

The new index used by Statistics Canada is referred to as a chain weighted index because it links each year to the previous year through the use of both the prior year prices and current year prices. For example, the calculation of the chain weighted index would use both 2003 and 2004 prices to calculate real GDP growth in 2004. Since the 2003 chain weighted index was arrived at by using both 2002 and 2003 prices, the year 2004 is "linked" back, as the links of a chain are, to 2003, 2002, and to previous years as well.

QUICK REVIEW

- Nominal GDP is output valued at current prices. Real GDP is output valued at constant base-year prices.

- A price index compares the price (market value) of a basket of goods and services in a given year to the price of the same market basket in a reference year.

- Nominal GDP can be transformed into real GDP by dividing the nominal GDP by the GDP deflator and then multiplying by 100.

5.4 Shortcomings of GDP

GDP is a reasonably accurate and highly useful measure of how well or how poorly the economy is performing. But it has several shortcomings as a measure of total output and of well-being (total utility).

Measurement Shortcomings

Although GDP is the best measure of overall output in an economy, it suffers from a number of omissions which tend to understate total output.

NON-MARKET TRANSACTIONS

Certain production transactions do not take place in any market—the services of homemakers, for example, and the labour of carpenters who repair their own homes. Such activities never show up in GDP, which measures only the *market value* of output. Consequently GDP understates a nation's total output.

THE UNDERGROUND ECONOMY

In the Canadian economy there is a flourishing, productive underground sector. Some of the people who conduct business there are gamblers, smugglers, prostitutes, "fences" of stolen goods, drug growers, and drug dealers. They have good reason to conceal their income.

Most participants in the underground economy, however, engage in perfectly legal activities but choose not to report their full income to the Canada Customs and Revenue Agency. A bell captain at a hotel may report just a portion of the tips received from customers. Storekeepers may report only a portion of their sales receipts. Workers who want to hold onto their employment insurance benefits may take an "off the books" or "cash only" job. A brick mason may agree to rebuild a neighbour's fireplace in exchange for the neighbour's repairing his boat engine. The value of such transactions does not show up in GDP.

That value of underground transactions is estimated to be about 15 percent of the recorded GDP in Canada. That would mean that GDP in 2002 was understated by over $170 billion. Global Perspective 5.2 shows estimates of the relative sizes of underground economies in selected nations.

LEISURE

The average workweek in Canada has declined since the turn of the century—from about 53 hours to about 35 hours. Moreover, the greater frequency of paid vacations, holidays, and leave time has shortened the work year itself. This increase in leisure time has had a positive effect on overall well-being. But our system of national income accounting understates well-being by ignoring leisure's value. Nor does the system measure the satisfaction—the "psychic income"—that many people derive from their work.

Improved Product Quality

Because GDP is a quantitative measure rather than a qualitative measure, it fails to take into account the value of improvements in product quality. There is a very real difference in quality between a $3000 personal computer purchased today and a computer that cost that same amount just five years ago. Today's computer has far more speed and storage capacity, a clearer monitor, and enhanced multimedia capabilities.

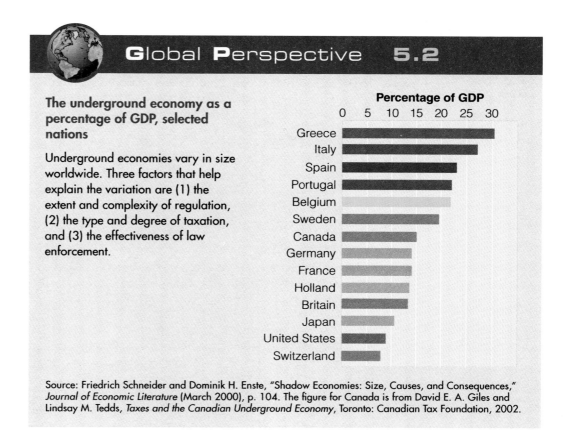

Global Perspective 5.2

The underground economy as a percentage of GDP, selected nations

Underground economies vary in size worldwide. Three factors that help explain the variation are (1) the extent and complexity of regulation, (2) the type and degree of taxation, and (3) the effectiveness of law enforcement.

Source: Friedrich Schneider and Dominik H. Enste, "Shadow Economies: Size, Causes, and Consequences," *Journal of Economic Literature* (March 2000), p. 104. The figure for Canada is from David E. A. Giles and Lindsay M. Tedds, *Taxes and the Canadian Underground Economy*, Toronto: Canadian Tax Foundation, 2002.

Obviously quality improvement has a great effect on economic well-being, as does the quantity of goods produced. But again, GDP does not measure quality improvements as well as we would like.

Well-Being Measure Shortcomings

Although the output of goods and services is an important aspect of the well-being of the citizens of a nation, it is not the only factor. We must also consider environmental degradation caused by the production of goods and services, the composition and distribution of that output, and the importance of non-material sources of well-being, which are not captured by GDP.

GDP AND THE ENVIRONMENT

The growth of GDP is inevitably accompanied by "gross domestic by-products," including dirty air and polluted water, toxic waste, congestion, and noise. The social costs of those negative by-products reduce our economic well-being. And since those costs are not deducted from total output, GDP overstates our national well-being. Ironically, when money is spent to clean up pollution and reduce congestion, those expenses are added to the GDP!

COMPOSITION AND DISTRIBUTION OF OUTPUT

The composition of output is undoubtedly important for well-being. But GDP does not tell us whether the mix of goods and services is enriching or potentially detrimental to society. GDP assigns equal weight to an assault rifle and a computer, so long as both sell for the same price. Moreover, GDP reveals nothing about the way the output is distributed. Does 90 percent of the output go to 10 percent of the households, for example, or is the output more evenly distributed? The distribution of output may make a big difference for society's overall well-being.

NON-MATERIAL SOURCES OF WELL-BEING

Finally, the connection between GDP and well-being is problematic for another reason. Just as a household's income does not measure its total happiness, a nation's GDP does not measure its total well-being. There are many things that could make a society better off without necessarily raising GDP: a reduction of crime and violence, peaceful relations with other countries, greater civility toward one another, better understanding between parents and children, and a reduction of drug and alcohol abuse.

THE LASTword | Value Added and GDP

The third method by which Statistics Canada arrives at GDP is through the value added approach. In this piece, Statistics Canada compares and contrasts the value added approach with the expenditure and income approach in computing GDP in Canada.

Gross Domestic Product (GDP) by industry is one of the three GDP series produced by the Canadian System of National Accounts (CSNA). It is also known as the output-based GDP, because it sums the value added (output less intermediate consumption of goods and services) of all industries in Canada. This GDP series is published on a monthly basis and thus delivers the earliest and most up-to-date information on current developments in the economy. The other two GDP series are the income-based GDP, which tallies earnings that are generated by productive activity, and the expenditure-based GDP, which is equal to final expenditure on goods and services produced. Both the income-based and expenditure-based GDP measures are published on a quarterly basis.

The meaning of the word "output" in the output-based GDP needs to be elaborated to avoid any confusion between its present definition in the international System of National Accounts 1993 (SNA1993) and its earlier use. The output of an economy was always meant to be equal to "net output" ("gross output" of goods and services less the intermediate use of

goods and services in its production). This "net output" is now called "value added" and the terms "gross output" and "net output" are no longer used in the SNA1993. The three alternative GDPs are designed to independently but equivalently portray the production activity of the country, seen from different perspectives. With information on the sources of goods, services, and incomes generated by processes of production, the output-based GDP and the income-based GDP provide a comprehensive and detailed description of the supply side of domestic production. Expenditure-based GDP, on the other hand, traces the disposition of the output produced among the various categories of demand, and thus offers a demand-side view of the Canadian economy. Changes in the level of production are key indicators of economic activity. Evaluating production therefore is fundamental in monitoring the behaviour of the economy. For this reason GDP is an indispensable tool for a broad range of analytical, modelling, and policy-formulation purposes. Governments, businesses, trade and labour organizations, academic researchers, journalists and the general public use GDP figures to evaluate the

performance of the economy, to appraise the success of monetary and industrial policies, to explore past trends in production, to forecast future prospects for economic growth, to carry out international comparisons, and so on. Since economic activity is one of the several major factors influencing welfare policy, movements in GDP may also play a role in the assessment of the general well-being of the country. Estimates of the three GDP series are produced within the highly integrated conceptual and statistical framework of the CSNA, sharing a consistent set of concepts, definitions, and classifications. On an annual basis, the growth rates of the income-based and expenditure-based GDP are identical, and the year-to-year movements of the output-based GDP deviate only slightly. The small discrepancies in growth rates (less than two-tenths of one percent in any of the years between 1990 and 1998) are caused primarily by differences in the treatment of taxes and subsidies.

Source: Statistics Canada, Gross Domestic Product by Industry: Sources and Methods, 2002, pg.7 (Available at http://www.statcan.ca/english/freepub/15-547-XIE/15-547-XIE02001.pdf.)

CHAPTER SUMMARY

5.1 MEASURING THE ECONOMY'S PERFORMANCE: GDP

- Gross domestic product (GDP), a basic measure of economic performance, is the market value of all final goods and services produced within the borders of a nation in a year.

- Intermediate goods, non-production transactions, and second-hand sales are purposely excluded in calculating GDP.

- GDP may be calculated by summing total expenditures on all final output or by summing the income derived from the production of that output.

- By the expenditures approach, GDP is determined by adding consumer purchases of goods and services, gross investment spending by businesses, government purchases, and net exports: $GDP = C + I_g + G + X_n$.

- Gross investment is divided into (a) replacement investment (required to maintain the nation's stock of capital at its existing level), and (b) net investment (the net increase in the stock of capital). Positive net investment is associated with an expanding production capacity; negative net investment, with a declining production capacity.

- By the income approach, GDP is calculated as the sum of wages and salaries, profits of corporations and government enterprises before taxes, interest and investment income, net income of farmers and unincorporated businesses, and the two non-income charges (indirect taxes less subsidies and capital consumption allowances).

5.2 OTHER NATIONAL ACCOUNTS

- Other national income accounting measures are derived from the GDP. Gross national product (GNP) is the total income that residents of a country earn each year. Net domestic product (NDP) is GDP less the consumption of fixed capital. Net national income (NNI) is total income earned by resource suppliers; it is found by subtracting indirect taxes and capital consumption allowances from GDP. Personal income (PI) is the total income paid to households prior to any allowance for personal taxes. Disposable income (DI) is personal income after personal taxes have been paid. DI measures the amount of income households have available to consume or save.

5.3 NOMINAL GDP VERSUS REAL GDP

- Price indexes are computed by dividing the price of a specific collection or market basket of output in a particular period by the price of the same market basket in a base period and multiplying the result (the quotient) by 100.

- The implicit price index, or GDP deflator, is used to adjust nominal GDP for inflation or deflation and thereby obtain real GDP.

- Nominal (current-dollar) GDP measures each year's output valued in terms of the prices prevailing in that year. Real (constant-dollar) GDP measures each year's output in terms of the prices that prevailed in a selected base year. Because real GDP is adjusted for price-level changes, differences in real GDP are due only to differences in production activity.

- A chain weighted index to compute real GDP is constructed using an average of current and past prices as weights. It is particularly useful in an economy in which the prices of some outputs are declining.

5.4 SHORTCOMINGS OF GDP

- GDP is a reasonably accurate and very useful indicator of a nation's economic performance, but it has its limitations. It fails to account for non-market and illegal transactions, changes in leisure and in product quality, the composition and distribution of output, and the environmental effects of production. The link between GDP and overall well-being is tenuous.

TERMS AND CONCEPTS

national income accounting, p. 105
gross domestic product (GDP), p. 105
intermediate goods, p. 106
final goods, p. 106
multiple counting, p. 106
value added, p. 106
expenditures approach, p. 107
income approach, p. 107

personal consumption expenditures, p. 107
gross investment, p. 108
net investment, p. 108
capital consumption allowance, p. 108
government purchases, p. 109
net exports, p. 109
indirect taxes, p. 112

net domestic product (NDP), p. 113
net national income (NNI), p. 113
personal income, p. 114
disposable income, p. 114
nominal GDP, p. 116
real GDP, p. 116
price index, p. 117
GDP deflator, p. 118

STUDY QUESTIONS

1. In what ways are national income statistics useful?

2. Explain why an economy's output, in essence, is also its income.

3. **KEY QUESTION**   Why do national income accountants include only final goods in measuring GDP for a particular year? Why don't they include the value of the stocks and bonds bought and sold? Why don't they include the value of the used furniture bought and sold?

4. What is the difference between gross investment and net investment?

5. Why are changes in inventories included as part of investment spending? Suppose inventories declined by $1 billion during 2001. How would this affect the size of gross investment and gross domestic product in 2001? Explain.

6. Use the concepts of gross and net investment to distinguish between an expanding, a static, and a declining economy. "In 1933 net investment was minus $324 million. This means in that particular year the economy produced no capital goods at all." Do you agree? Explain: "Though net investment can be positive, negative, or zero, it is quite impossible for gross investment to be less than zero."

7. Define net exports. Explain how Canadian exports and imports each affect domestic production. Suppose foreigners spend $7 billion on Canadian exports in a given year and Canadians spend $5 billion on imports from abroad in the same year. What is the amount of Canada's net exports? Explain how net exports might be a negative amount.

8. **KEY QUESTION**   Following is a list of national income figures for a certain year. All figures are in billions. Calculate GDP by both the expenditure and income methods. The answers derived by each approach should be the same.

Personal consumption expenditures	$120
Capital consumption allowances (depreciation)	20
Interest and investment income	10
Net income of farms and unincorporated businesses	17
Net exports	+5
Profits of corporations and government enterprises before taxes	42
Wages, salaries, and supplementary labour income	113
Indirect business taxes less subsidies	11
Government current purchases of goods and services	40
Net investment (net capital formation)	30
Taxes less subsidies on factors of production	10

9. **KEY QUESTION**   Using the following national income accounting data, compute (a) GDP, (b) GNP, (c) NDP, (d) NNI, (e) PI, (f) DI. All figures are in billions.

Wages, salaries, and supplementary labour income	$194.2
Canadian exports of goods and services	17.8
Capital consumption allowances (depreciation)	11.8
Government current purchases of goods and services	59.4
Indirect business taxes less subsidies	14.4
Net investment (net capital formation)	52.1
Government transfer payments	13.9
Canadian imports of goods and services	16.5
Personal taxes	40.5
Personal consumption expenditures	219.1
Net investments from non-residents	2.2
Undistributed corporate profits	10

10. Why do national income accountants compare the market value of the total outputs in various years rather than actual physical volumes of production? Explain. What problem is posed by any comparison, over time, of the market values of various total outputs? How is this problem resolved?

11. **KEY QUESTION**   Suppose that in 1984 the total output in a single-good economy was 7000 buckets of chicken. Also suppose that in 1984 each bucket of chicken was priced at $10. Finally, assume that in 1992 the price per bucket of chicken was $16 and that 22,000 buckets were purchased. Determine the GDP price index for 1984, using 1992 as the base year. By what percentage did the price level, as measured by this index, rise between 1984 and 1992? Use the two methods listed in Tables 5-3 and 5-4 to determine real GDP for 1984 and 1992.

12. Distinguish between a fixed based price index and a chain weighted index. Why can a fixed based price index exaggerate GDP growth?

13. **KEY QUESTION**   The following table shows nominal GDP and an appropriate price index group of selected years. Compute real GDP. Indicate in each calculation whether you are inflating or deflating the nominal GDP data.

Year	Nominal GDP (billions)	GDP deflator (1997 = 100)	Real GDP (billions)
1929	$ 6.1	8.6	$_____
1933	3.5	7.0	$_____
1962	44.8	17.6	$_____
1974	173.9	32.8	$_____
1984	449.6	71.8	$_____
1994	770.9	95.2	$_____
2002	1,154.9	107.5	$_____

14. Which of the following are actually included in deriving this year's GDP? Explain your answer in each case.

   a. Interest on a Bell Canada bond.

   b. Canada Pension payments received by a retired factory worker.

   c. The services of a painter in painting the family home.

   d. The income of a dentist.

   e. The money received by Smith when she resells her economics textbook to a book buyer.

   f. The monthly allowance a college student receives from home.

   g. Rent received on a two-bedroom apartment.

   h. The money received by Mac when he resells this year's Ford Mustang to Stan.

   i. Interest received on government bonds.

   j. A two-hour decline in the length of the workweek.

   k. The purchase of a Quebec Hydro bond.

   l. A $2-billion increase in business inventories.

   m. The purchase of 100 shares of Nortel Networks common stock.

   n. The purchase of an insurance policy.

15. **(The Last Word)** Distinguish between (a) the value added approach; (b) the expenditure approach; (c) the income approach to calculating GDP.

INTERNET APPLICATION QUESTIONS

1. **Nominal and Real GDP** Visit Statistics Canada through the McConnell-Brue-Barbiero home page (Chapter 5) and select *National Accounts*. Under *Gross Domestic Product, Expenditure Based,* identify the current-dollar GDP (nominal GDP) for the past four years. Return to the original site and choose *Gross Domestic Product at 1997 prices (expenditure based)* and identify real GDP data for the last four years. Why was current-dollar GDP higher than real GDP in each of those years? What were the percentage changes in current-dollar GDP and real GDP for the most recent year? How do those percentage changes compare to those for the prior three years?

Σ-STAT

2. **GDPs in the Americas—How do nations compare?** Visit the World Bank Web site through the McConnell-Brue-Barbiero homepage (Chapter 5) and type "GDP" in the search space. Find the latest values for Total GDP (not PPP GDP) for the North and South American countries listed. Arrange the countries by highest to lowest GDPs and express their GDPs as ratios of Canadian GDP.

6

Chapter

Introduction to Economic Growth, Unemployment, and Inflation

Between 1996 and 2000, real GDP in Canada expanded quickly and price level rose only slowly. The economy experienced neither significant unemployment nor inflation. Some observers felt that the Canadian economy, along with that of the U.S.A. to the south, had entered a "new era" in which the business cycle was dead. But that wishful thinking came to an end in 2001, when the economy slowed down, although it did not slip into recession as the American economy did. Within approximately the past five decades, real GDP has declined in Canada in four periods: 1945–1946, 1954, 1981–1982, and 1991–1992.

Although the Canadian economy has experienced remarkable economic growth over time, high unemployment or inflation has sometimes been a problem. For example, between January 2001 and January 2002, unemployment rose by over 100,000 workers, and the unemployment rate edged up to 7.7 percent from 7.2 percent of the labour force. The rate of inflation in Canada was 10.2 percent in 1980 and 4.8 percent in 1990. Further, other nations have suffered high unemployment rates or inflation rates in recent years. For example, the unemployment rate in Germany reached 8.7 percent in 2002. The inflation rate was 45 percent in Turkey in 2002.

In this chapter we provide an introductory look at the trend of real GDP growth in Canada and the macroeconomic fluctuations that have occasionally accompanied it. Our specific topics are economic growth, the business cycle, unemployment, and inflation.

6.1   Economic Growth

economic growth
An increase either in real output (gross domestic product) or in real output per capita.

Economists define and measure **economic growth** as either:

- An increase in real GDP occurring over some time period.
- An increase in real GDP per capita occurring over some time period.

With either definition, economic growth is calculated as a percentage rate of growth per quarter (3-month period) or per year. For the first definition, for example, if real GDP was $200 billion in the hypothetical country of Zorn last year (year 1) and $210 billion this year (year 2), the rate of economic growth in Zorn would be 5 percent per year, calculated as follows:

$$\% \text{ change in growth} = [(\text{Year 2 real GDP} - \text{Year 1 real GDP}) / \text{Year 1 GDP}] \times 100$$

$$= [(\$210 \text{ billion} - \$200 \text{ billion})/\$200 \text{ billion}] \times 100$$

$$= 5\%$$

Economic growth is calculated as a percentage rate of growth per quarter or per year.

The second definition takes into consideration the size of the population. **Real GDP per capita** (or per capita output) is found by dividing real GDP by population. The resulting number is then compared in percentage terms with that of the previous period. For example, if real GDP in Zorn was $200 billion last year and its population was 40 million, its real GDP per capita would be $5000. If real per capita GDP rose to $5100 this year, Zorn's rate of growth of real GDP per capita for the year would be 2 percent (= [($5100 − $5000)/$5000] × 100).

Unless specified otherwise, growth rates reported in the news and by international agencies use the growth of real GDP. For comparing living standards, however, the second definition is superior. While China's GDP in 2001 was U.S. $1.1 trillion compared with Denmark's $166 billion, Denmark's real GDP per capita was $31,090 compared with China's meagre $890. And in some cases, growth of real GDP can be misleading. Madagascar's real GDP grew at a rate of 2.4 percent per year from 1990 to 2001. But over the same period its annual population growth was 2.9 percent, resulting in a decline in real GDP per capita of approximately 0.5 percent per year. *(Key Question 2)*

real GDP per capita
The real GDP per person, found by dividing real GDP by a country's population.

Growth as a Goal

Growth is a widely held economic goal. The expansion of total output relative to population results in rising real wages and incomes and thus higher standards of living. An economy that is experiencing economic growth is better able to meet people's wants and resolve socioeconomic problems. Rising real wages and income provide richer opportunities to individuals and families—a vacation trip, a personal computer, a higher education—without sacrificing other opportunities and pleasures. A growing economy can undertake new programs to alleviate poverty and protect the environment without impairing existing levels of consumption, investment, and public goods production. In short, *growth lessens the burden of scarcity.*

Arithmetic of Growth

Why do economists pay so much attention to small changes in the rate of growth? Because such changes really matter! For Canada, with a current real GDP of over $1 trillion, the difference between a 3 percent and a 4 percent rate of growth is more than $10 billion of output each year. For a poor country, a difference of one-half percentage point in the rate of growth may mean the difference between hunger and starvation.

rule of 70
A method for determining the number of years it will take for some measure to double, given its annual percentage increase, by dividing that percentage increase into 70.

The mathematical approximation called the **rule of 70** provides a quantitative grasp of the effect of economic growth. It tells us that we can find the number of years it will take for some measure to double, given its annual percentage increase, by dividing that percentage increase into the number 70. So,

$$\frac{\text{Approximate number of years}}{\text{required to double real GDP}} = \frac{70}{\text{annual percentage rate of growth}}$$

Examples: A 3 percent annual rate of growth will double real GDP in about 23 years (= 70 ÷ 3). Growth of 8 percent per year will double real GDP in about 9 years (= 70 ÷ 8). The rule of 70 is generally applicable. For example, it works for estimating how long it will take the price level or a saving account to double at various percentage rates of inflation or interest.

When compounded over many years, an apparently small difference in the rate of growth thus becomes highly significant. Suppose Alta and Zorn have identical GDPs, but Alta grows at a 4 percent yearly rate, while Zorn grows at 2 percent. Alta's GDP would double in about 18 years but Zorn's GDP would double in 35 years.

Main Sources of Growth

There are two ways society can increase its real output and income: (1) by increasing its inputs of resources, and (2) by increasing the productivity of those inputs. Other things equal, increases in land, labour, capital, and entrepreneurial resources yield additional outputs. But economic growth also occurs through increases in **productivity**—measured broadly as real output per unit of input. Productivity rises when the health, training, education, and motivation of workers are improved; when workers have more and better machinery and natural resources with which to work; when production is better organized and managed; and when labour is reallocated from less efficient industries to more efficient industries. About two-thirds of Canada's growth comes from more inputs. The remaining one-third results from improved productivity.

productivity
A measure of average output or real output per unit of input.

TABLE 6-1	Real GDP and Per Capita GDP, 1926–2002		
(1) Year	(2) GDP (billions of 1997 dollars)	(3) Population (millions)	(4) Per capita GDP (1997 dollars) (2) ÷ (3)
1926	59.1	9.5	6,221
1929	71.4	10.0	7,114
1933	49.9	10.6	4,708
1939	74.9	11.0	6,809
1942	115.3	11.5	10,026
1946	118.8	12.3	9,659
1951	149.2	14.0	10,659
1956	205.6	16.1	12,770
1961	237.9	18.2	13,071
1966	322.9	20.0	16,145
1971	420.9	21.6	19,486
1976	506.7	23.0	22,030
1981	594.1	24.3	24,449
1986	667.8	25.4	26,291
1991	747.9	27.0	27,700
1996	845.2	29.9	28,268
2002	1,074.5	31.0	34,661

Sources: Statistics Canada. Data updates may be retrieved from www.mcgrawhill.ca/college/mcconnell. **Σ-STAT**

Growth in Canada

Table 6-1 gives an overview of economic growth in Canada over past years. Column 2 reveals strong growth as measured by increases in real GDP. Note that between 1946 and 2002 real GDP increased more than eightfold. But the Canadian population also increased. Nevertheless, in column 4 we find that real GDP per capita rose almost fourfold over these years.

What has been the *rate* of growth in Canada? Real GDP grew at an annual rate of almost 4 percent between 1950 and 2002. Real GDP per capita increased more than 2 percent per year over that time. But we must qualify these numbers in several ways:

- ***Improved products and services*** Since the numbers in Table 6-1 do not fully account for the improvements in products and services, they understate the growth of economic well-being. Such purely quantitative data do not fully compare an era of iceboxes and adding machines with an era of refrigerators and personal computers.

- *Added leisure*   The increases in real GDP and per capita GDP identified in Table 6-1 were accomplished despite large increases in leisure. The standard workweek, once 50 hours, is now about 35 hours. Again the raw growth numbers understate the gain in economic well-being.

- *Other impacts*   These measures of growth do not account for any effects growth may have had on the environment and the quality of life. If growth debases the physical environment and creates a stressful work environment, the bare growth numbers will overstate the gains in well-being that result from growth. On the other hand, if growth leads to stronger environmental protections and greater human security, these numbers will understate the gains in well-being.

Relative Growth Rates

Viewed from the perspective of the last half century, economic growth in Canada lagged behind Japan and Germany. Japan's annual growth rate, in fact, averaged a third more than that of Canada. But the 1990s were quite another matter. As shown in Global Perspective 6.1, Canada's growth rate surged ahead of the rates of many other industrial nations, surpassing even the U.S., between 2000 and 2002.

6.2   The Business Cycle

Long-run economic growth in Canada has been interrupted by periods of economic fluctuations. At various times, growth has given way to recession—that is, to declines in real GDP and significant increases in unemployment. At other times, rapid economic growth has been marred by rapid inflation. Both higher unemployment and higher inflation often are associated with *business cycles*.

Phases of the Business Cycle

business cycle
Recurring increase and decrease in the level of economic activity over periods of years.

The term **business cycle** refers to alternating rises and declines in the level of economic activity, sometimes extending over several years. Individual cycles (one "up" followed by one "down") vary substantially in duration and intensity. Yet all display certain phases, to which economists have assigned various labels. Figure 6-1 shows the four phases of a generalized business cycle.

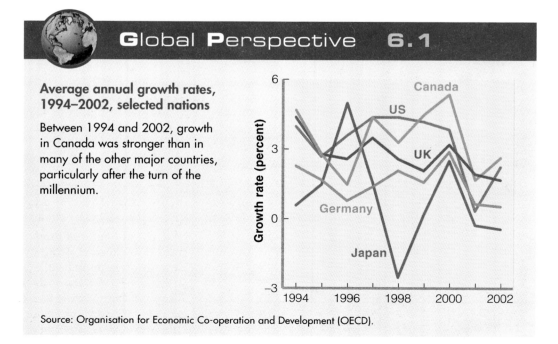

Global Perspective   6.1

Average annual growth rates, 1994–2002, selected nations

Between 1994 and 2002, growth in Canada was stronger than in many of the other major countries, particularly after the turn of the millennium.

Source: Organisation for Economic Co-operation and Development (OECD).

FIGURE 6-1   The Business Cycle

Economists distinguish four phases of the business cycle; the duration and strength of each phase may vary.

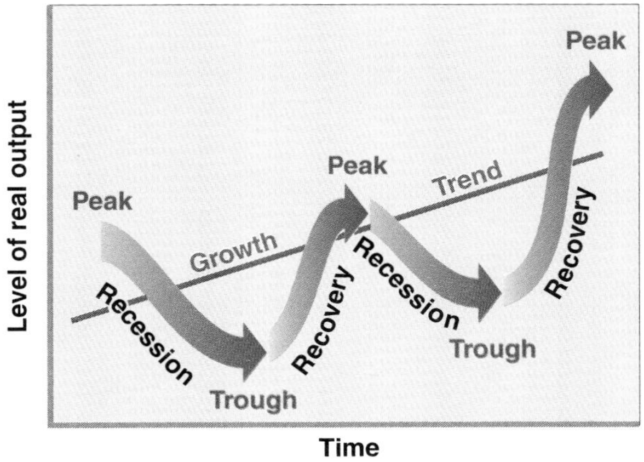

peak
A phase in the business cycle during which the economy is at full employment and the level of real output is at or very close to the economy's capacity.

recession
A period of declining real GDP, accompanied by lower real income and higher unemployment.

trough
A recession or depression, when output and employment reach their lowest levels.

recovery
The expansion phase of the business cycle, during which output and employment rise toward full employment.

• *Peak*   At a **peak**, such as the middle peak shown in Figure 6-1, business activity reaches a temporary maximum. Here the economy is at full employment and the level of real output is at or very close to the economy's capacity. The price level is likely to rise during this phase.

• *Recession*   A peak is followed by a **recession**—a period of decline in total output, income, and employment. This downturn, which lasts six months or more, is marked by the widespread contraction of business activity in many sectors of the economy. But because many prices and wages do not fall easily, the price level is likely to go down only if the recession is severe and prolonged.

• *Trough*   In the **trough** of the recession or depression, output and employment "bottom out" at their lowest levels. The trough phase may be either short-lived or quite long.

• *Recovery*   In the expansion or **recovery** phase, output and employment rise toward full employment. As recovery approaches full employment, the price level may begin to rise.

Although business cycles all pass through the same phases, they vary greatly in duration and intensity. That is why many economists prefer to talk of business *fluctuations* rather than cycles, because cycles imply regularity but fluctuations do not. The Great Depression of the 1930s resulted in a 27.5 percent decline in real GDP over a three-year period in Canada and seriously impaired business activity for a decade. By comparison, more recent Canadian recessions, detailed in Table 6-2, were relatively mild in both intensity and duration.

TABLE 6-2   Canadian Recessions Since 1930

Year	Depth (decline in real GDP)
1930–33	−27.5%
1945	− 2.4
1946	− 2.2
1954	− 1.1
1982	− 3.2
1991	− 1.7

Source: Statistics Canada.

Provincial Variations

National GDP data for Canada conceal significant differences in economic fluctuations among Canada's provinces and territories. Table 6-3 gives a breakdown of economic growth. In 2001, for example, GDP grew by 2.6 percent in Ontario, but Saskatchewan's economy actually shrank by 1.3 percent.

Recessions, of course, occur in other countries, too. At one time or another during the past 10 years, Argentina, Brazil, Columbia, Japan, Indonesia, Mexico, South Korea, and the United States also experienced recessions.

TABLE 6-3	Percentage Change in Real GDP for Provinces and Territories
	2002
CANADA	3.3
Newfoundland and Labrador	1.3
P.E.I.	5.6
Nova Scotia	3.8
New Brunswick	3.3
Quebec	4.3
Ontario	3.9
Manitoba	2.4
Saskatchewan	−1.4
Alberta	1.7
British Columbia	1.8
Yukon	0.1
Northwest Territories	3.3
Nunavut	3.1

Source: Statistics Canada

Causation: A First Glance

Economists have suggested many theories to explain fluctuations in business activity. Some say that momentous innovations, such as the railroad, the automobile, synthetic fibres, and microchips, have great impact on investment and consumption spending and therefore on output, employment, and the price level. Such major innovations occur irregularly and thus contribute to the variability of economic activity.

Some economists see major changes in productivity as causes of business cycles. When productivity expands, the economy booms; when productivity falls, the economy recedes. Still others view the business cycle as a purely monetary phenomenon. When government creates too much money, they say, an inflationary boom occurs. Too little money triggers a decline in output and employment, and eventually, the price level.

Most economists, however, believe that the immediate cause of cyclical changes in the levels of real output and employment is changes in the level of total spending. In a market economy, businesses produce goods or services only if they can sell them at a profit. If total spending sinks, many businesses find that it is no longer profitable to go on producing their current volume of goods and services. As a consequence, output, employment, and incomes all fall. When the level of spending rises, an increase in production becomes profitable, and output, employment, and incomes will rise accordingly. Once the economy nears full employment, however, further gains in real output become more difficult to achieve. Continued increases in spending may raise the price level as producers bid more for scarce supplies of labour and capital, and pass the higher costs on to customers in the form of higher prices.

We have seen that the long-run growth trend of the Canadian economy is one of expansion. Note that the stylized cycle of Figure 6-1 is drawn against a trend of economic growth.

Cyclical Impact: Durables and Non-Durables

Although the business cycle is felt everywhere in the economy, it affects different segments in different ways and to different degrees.

Firms and industries producing *capital goods* (for example, housing, commercial buildings, heavy equipment, and farm implements) and *consumer durables* (for example, automobiles and refrigerators) are affected most by the business cycle. Within limits, firms can postpone the purchase of capital goods. As the economy recedes, producers frequently delay the purchase of new equipment and the construction of new plants. The business outlook simply does not warrant increases in the stock of capital goods. In good times, capital goods are usually replaced before they depreciate completely. But when recession strikes, firms patch up their old equipment and make do. As a result, investment in capital goods declines sharply. Firms that have excess plant capacity may not even bother to replace all the capital that is depreciating. For them, net investment may be negative. The pattern is much the same for consumer durables such as automobiles and major appliances. When recession occurs and households must trim their budgets, purchases of these goods are often deferred. Families repair their old cars and appliances rather than buy new ones, and the firms producing these products suffer. (Of course, producers of capital goods and consumer durables also benefit most from expansions.)

In contrast, *service* industries and industries that produce *non-durable consumer goods* are somewhat insulated from the most severe effects of recession. People find it difficult to cut back on needed medical and legal services, for example. And a recession actually helps some service firms, such as pawnbrokers and law firms that specialize in bankruptcies. The service sector accounts for the great majority of GDP during recessions. Nor are the purchases of many non-durable goods such as food and clothing easy to postpone. The quantity and quality of purchases of non-durables will decline, but not so much as will purchases of capital goods and consumer durables. *(Key Question 4)*

QUICK REVIEW

- Economic growth can be measured as (a) an increase in real GDP over time or (b) an increase in real GDP per capita over time.

- Real GDP in Canada has grown at an average annual rate of almost 4 percent since 1950; real GDP per capita has grown at an annual rate of over 2 percent during that same period.

- The typical business cycle goes through four phases: peak, recession, trough, and recovery.

- During recession, industries that produce capital goods and consumer durables normally suffer greater output and employment declines than do service and non-durable consumer goods industries.

6.3 Unemployment

The twin problems that arise from economic fluctuations are unemployment and inflation. Let's look at unemployment first.

When there is brisk GDP growth in an economy it is usually accompanied by a fall in the unemployment rate. For example, the rapid growth of the Canadian economy between 1996 and 2000 saw the unemployment rate fall from 9.6 percent of the labour force in 1996, to 6.8 percent in 2000. But the GDP growth slowed in 2001 and 2002 and the unemployment rate went back up to 7.7 percent. Before we can understand the causes of these fluctuations we need to have a better grasp of the nature of unemployment.

Measurement of Unemployment

To measure the unemployment rate we must first determine who is eligible and available to work. Figure 6-2 provides a helpful starting point. It divides the total Canadian population into three groups. One group is made up of people under 15 years of age and people who are institutionalized, for example, in psychiatric hospitals or correctional institutions. Such people are not considered potential members of the labour force.

A second group, labelled "Not in labour force," is composed of adults who are potential workers but are not employed and are not seeking work. For example, they are homemakers, full-time students, or retired.

labour force
Persons 15 years of age and older who are not in institutions and who are employed or are unemployed and seeking work.

unemployment rate
The percentage of the labour force unemployed at any time.

The third group is the **labour force**, which constituted almost 50 percent of the total population in 2002. The labour force consists of people who are able and willing to work. Both those who are employed and those who are unemployed but actively seeking work are counted as being in the labour force. The labour force *participation rate* is defined as the percentage of the population 15 years and over (about 61.6% in 2002) that is currently in the labour force. The **unemployment rate** is the percentage of the labour force unemployed:

$$\text{Unemployment rate} = \frac{\text{unemployed}}{\text{labour force}} \times 100$$

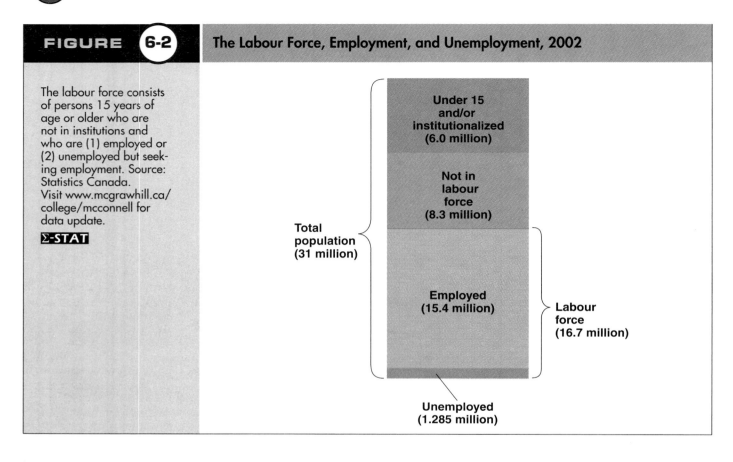

FIGURE 6-2

The Labour Force, Employment, and Unemployment, 2002

The labour force consists of persons 15 years of age or older who are not in institutions and who are (1) employed or (2) unemployed but seeking employment. Source: Statistics Canada. Visit www.mcgrawhill.ca/college/mcconnell for data update.

Σ-STAT

Under 15 and/or institutionalized (6.0 million)

Not in labour force (8.3 million)

Total population (31 million)

Employed (15.4 million)

Labour force (16.7 million)

Unemployed (1.285 million)

The statistics included in Figure 6-2 show that in 2002 the unemployment rate was

$$\frac{1,285,000}{16,700,000} \times 100 = 7.7\%$$

Unemployment rates for select years between 1926 and 2002 appear on the inside covers of this book.

Statistics Canada conducts a nationwide random survey of some 50,000 households each month to determine who is employed and who is not employed. In a series of questions, it asks which members of the household are working, unemployed and looking for work, not looking for work, and so on. From the answers it determines an unemployment rate for the entire nation. Despite the use of scientific sampling and interviewing techniques, the data collected in this survey are subject to criticism:

- **Part-time employment** Statistics Canada fails to distinguish between fully and partially employed workers. In 2002 about 2.9 million people worked part-time. By counting them as fully employed, say critics, the official Statistics Canada data understate the unemployment rate.

- **Discouraged workers** You must be actively seeking work in order to be counted as unemployed. An unemployed individual who is not actively seeking employment is classified as "not in the labour force." The problem is that many workers, after unsuccessfully seeking employment for a time, become discouraged and drop out of the labour force. The number of such **discouraged workers** is larger during recession than during prosperity. By not counting discouraged workers as unemployed, say critics, the official Statistics Canada data understate the unemployment rate. Moreover, an increase in discouraged workers will lead to a fall in the unemployment rate, which the uninitiated may take as a sign that the economy is recovering. *(Key Question 6)*

discouraged workers
People who have left the labour force because they have not been able to find employment.

Types of Unemployment

There are three *types* of unemployment: frictional, structural, and cyclical.

FRICTIONAL UNEMPLOYMENT

At any particular time some workers are "between jobs." Some of them will be moving voluntarily from one job to another. Others will have been fired and will be seeking re-employment. Still others will have been laid off temporarily because of seasonal demand. In addition to those between jobs, many young workers will be searching for their first job.

As these unemployed people find jobs or are called back from temporary layoffs, other job seekers and laid-off workers will replace them in the "unemployment pool." So, even though the workers who are unemployed for such reasons change from month to month, this type of unemployment persists.

Economists use the term **frictional unemployment** for workers who are either searching for jobs or waiting to take jobs in the near future. The word *frictional* implies that the labour market does not operate perfectly and instantaneously (without friction) in matching workers and jobs.

Frictional unemployment is inevitable and, at least in part, desirable. Many workers who are voluntarily between jobs are moving from low-paying, low-productivity jobs to higher-paying, higher-productivity positions. That means greater income for the workers, a better allocation of labour resources, and a larger real GDP for the economy.

frictional unemployment
A type of unemployment caused by workers voluntarily changing jobs and by temporary layoffs; unemployed workers between jobs.

STRUCTURAL UNEMPLOYMENT

Frictional unemployment blurs into a category called **structural unemployment**. Here, economists use *structural* in the sense of *compositional*. Changes over time in consumer demand and in technology alter the "structure" of the total demand for labour, both occupationally and geographically.

Occupationally, the demand for certain skills (for example, sewing clothes or working on farms) may decline or even vanish. The demand for other skills (for example, designing software or maintaining computer systems) will intensify. Unemployment results because the composition of the labour force does not respond immediately or completely to the new structure of job opportunities. Workers who find that their skills and experience have become obsolete thus find that they have no marketable talents. They are structurally unemployed until they adapt or develop skills that employers want.

Geographically, the demand for labour also changes over time. An example: Industry and thus employment opportunities have migrated from the Maritimes to Central Canada over the past few decades. There has also been migration of labour in Western Canada to Alberta.

The distinction between frictional and structural unemployment is hazy at best. The key difference is that *frictionally* unemployed workers have salable skills and either live in areas where jobs exist or are able to move to areas where they do. *Structurally* unemployed workers find it hard to find new jobs without retraining, gaining additional education, or relocating. Frictional unemployment is short-term; structural unemployment is more likely to be long-term and consequently more serious.

structural unemployment
Unemployment of workers whose skills are not demanded by employers, who lack sufficient skill to obtain employment, or who cannot easily move to locations where jobs are available.

CYCLICAL UNEMPLOYMENT

Cyclical unemployment is caused by a decline in total spending and is likely to arise in the recession phase of the business cycle. As the demand for goods and services decreases, employment falls and unemployment rises. For this reason, **cyclical unemployment** is sometimes called deficient-demand unemployment. The 20 percent unemployment rate in the depth of the Great Depression in 1933 reflected mainly cyclical unemployment, as did significant parts of the 11 percent unemployment rate during the recession year 1982 and the 11.3 percent rate in the recession year 1991.

Cyclical unemployment is a very serious problem when it occurs. We will say more about its high costs later, but first we need to define "full employment."

cyclical unemployment
Unemployment caused by a decline in total spending (or by insufficient aggregate demand).

Definition of Full Employment

Because frictional and structural unemployment is largely unavoidable in a dynamic economy, *full employment* is something less than 100-percent employment of the labour force. Economists say that the economy is "fully employed" when it is experiencing only frictional and structural unemployment. That is, full employment occurs when there is no cyclical unemployment.

Economists describe the unemployment rate that is consistent with full employment as the *full-employment rate of unemployment,* or the **natural rate of unemployment** (**NRU**). At the NRU, the economy is said to be producing its non-inflationary **potential GDP**. This is the real GDP that the economy would produce at full employment.

The NRU occurs when the number of *job seekers* equals the number of *job vacancies.* Even when labour markets are in balance, however, the NRU is some positive percentage because it takes time for frictionally unemployed job seekers to find open jobs they can fill. Also, it takes time for the structurally unemployed to achieve the skills and geographic relocation needed for re-employment.

"Natural" does not mean, however, that the economy will always operate at this rate and thus realize its potential output. When cyclical unemployment occurs, the economy has much more unemployment than that which would occur at the NRU. Moreover, the economy can operate for a while at an unemployment rate *below* the NRU. At times, the demand for labour may be so great that firms take a stronger initiative to hire and train the structurally unemployed. Also, some homemakers, teenagers, college and university students, and retirees who were casually looking for just the right part-time or full-time jobs may quickly find them. Thus the unemployment rate temporarily falls below the natural rate.

Also, the NRU can vary over time. In the 1980s, the NRU was about 7.5 percent. Today, it is estimated to be 6 to 7 percent. Why the decline?

- The growing proportion of younger workers in the labour force has declined as the baby boom generation has aged. The labour force now has a larger proportion of middle-aged workers, who traditionally have lower unemployment rates, perhaps because of less turnover.

- The growth of temporary-help agencies and the improved information resulting from the Internet have lowered the NRU by enabling workers to find jobs more quickly.

A decade ago, a 6 to 7 percent rate of unemployment would have reflected excessive spending, an unbalanced labour market, and rising inflation; today, that same rate is consistent with a balanced labour market and a stable, low rate of inflation.

Economic Cost of Unemployment

Unemployment that is above the natural rate involves great economic and social costs.

GDP GAP AND OKUN'S LAW

The basic economic cost of unemployment is forgone output. *When the economy fails to create enough jobs for all who are able and willing to work, potential production of goods and services is irretrievably lost.* In terms of the analysis in Chapter 2, unemployment above the natural rate means that society is operating at some point inside its production possibilities curve. Economists call this sacrifice of output a **GDP gap**—the difference between actual and potential GDP. That is:

GDP gap = actual GDP − potential GDP

The GDP gap can be either negative (actual GDP < potential GDP) or positive (actual GDP > potential GDP). In this case it is negative because actual GDP falls short of potential GDP.

Potential GDP is determined by assuming that the natural rate of unemployment prevails. The growth of potential GDP is simply projected forward on the basis of the economy's "normal" growth rate of real GDP. Figure 6-3 shows the GDP gap for recent years in Canada. It also indicates the close correlation between the actual unemployment rate (Figure 6-3b) and the GDP gap (Figure 6-3a). The higher the unemployment rate, the larger is the GDP gap.

natural rate of unemployment (NRU)
The unemployment rate occurring when there is no cyclical unemployment and the economy is achieving its potential output.

potential GDP
The real output an economy can produce when it fully employs its available resources.

GDP gap
The amount by which actual gross domestic product falls below potential gross domestic product.

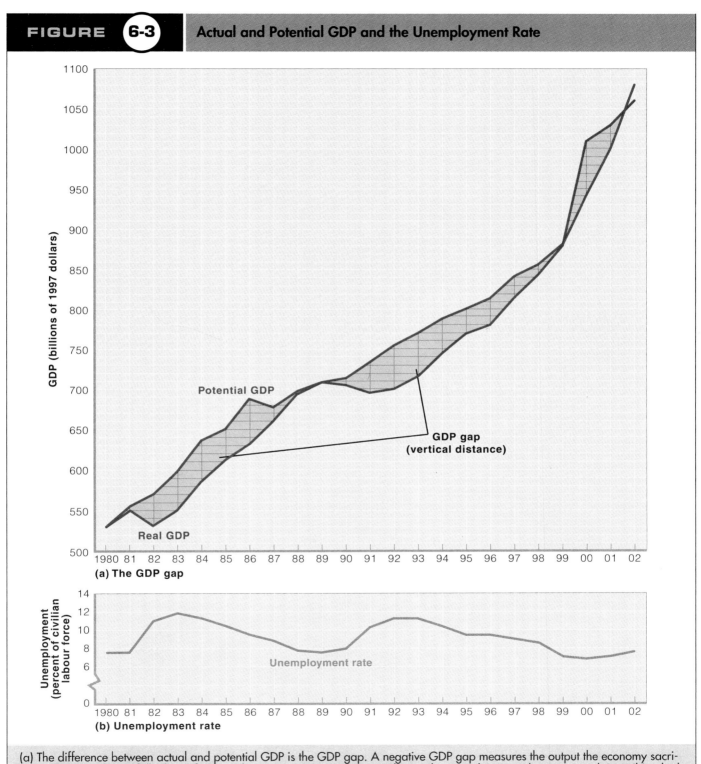

FIGURE 6-3   Actual and Potential GDP and the Unemployment Rate

(a) The GDP gap

(b) Unemployment rate

(a) The difference between actual and potential GDP is the GDP gap. A negative GDP gap measures the output the economy sacrifices when actual GDP falls short of potential GDP. A positive GDP gap indicates that actual GDP is above potential GDP. (b) A high unemployment rate means a large GDP gap (negative), and a low unemployment rate means a small or even positive GDP gap.

Source: Statistics Canada. Potential GDP is author's own assumptions and calculations.

Okun's law
The generalization that any one percentage point rise in the unemployment rate above the natural rate of unemployment will decrease the GDP by 2 percent of the potential output (GDP) of the economy.

Macroeconomist Arthur Okun was the first to quantify the relationship between the unemployment rate and the GDP gap. Based on recent estimates, **Okun's law** indicates that *for every one percentage point by which the actual unemployment rate exceeds the natural rate, a GDP gap (shortfall) of about 2 percent occurs.* With this information, we can calculate the absolute loss of output associated with any above-natural unemployment rate. For example, in 1992 the unemployment rate was 11.3 percent, or 3.8 percentage points above the then 7.5 percent natural rate of unemployment. Multiplying this 3.8 percent by Okun's 2 indicates that 1992's GDP gap was 7.6 percent of potential GDP (in real terms). By applying this 7.6 percent loss to 1992's potential GDP of $770 billion, we find that the economy sacrificed $59 billion of real output because the natural rate of unemployment was not achieved. *(Key Question 8)*

Sometimes the economy's actual output will exceed its potential GDP, or full-employment GDP, creating a "positive" GDP gap. Potential GDP can occasionally be exceeded, but the excess of actual over potential GDP eventually causes inflation and cannot be sustained indefinitely. Wartime is often a situation where real GDP is likely to exceed potential GDP.

UNEQUAL BURDENS

An increase in the unemployment rate from 8 to, say, 9 or 10 percent might be more tolerable to society if every worker's hours of work and wage income were reduced proportionally. But this is not the case. Part of the burden of unemployment is that its cost is unequally distributed.

Table 6-4 examines unemployment rates for various labour market groups for two years. The 1991–92 recession pushed the 1992 unemployment rate to 11.2 percent. In 2000, the Canadian economy was close to full employment, with a 6.8 percent unemployment rate. By observing the large variations in unemployment rates for the different groups within each year and comparing the rates between the two years, we can generalize as follows.

- *Occupation*   Workers in lower-skilled occupations have higher unemployment rates than workers in higher-skilled occupations. Lower-skilled workers have more and longer spells of structural unemployment than higher-skilled workers. Moreover, lower-skilled workers usually bear the brunt of recessions. Businesses usually retain most of their higher-skilled workers, in whom they have invested the expense of training.

- *Age*   Teenagers have much higher unemployment rates than adults. Teenagers have lower skill levels, quit their jobs more frequently, are more frequently "fired," and have less geographic mobility than adults. Many unemployed teenagers are new in the labour market, searching for their first job. Male aboriginal teenagers, in particular, have very high unemployment rates.

- *Gender*   The unemployment rates for men and women are very similar. (The lower unemployment rate for women in 1992 occurred because of the greater incidence of male workers in such cyclically vulnerable industries as automobiles, steel, and construction.)

- *Education*   Less-educated workers, on average, have higher unemployment rates than workers with more education. Less education is usually associated with lower-skilled, less permanent jobs, more time between jobs, and jobs that are more vulnerable to cyclical layoff.

TABLE 6-4	Unemployment by Demographic Group: Recession (1992) and Full employment (2000)	
Demographic group	**Unemployment rate, March 1992**	**Unemployment rate, March 2000**
Overall	11.2%	6.8%
Occupation		
Manufacturing	12.7	7.1
Services	9.2	6.2
Age		
15–24 years	19.1	12.6
25 years and over	11.1	5.7
Sex		
Male	13.9	6.9
Female	10.8	6.7

Source: Statistics Canada.

Σ-STAT

TABLE 6-5	Provincial Breakdown of the Unemployment Rate (Percentage)	
		2002
CANADA		7.7
Newfoundland and Labrador		16.9
Prince Edward Island		12.1
Nova Scotia		9.7
New Brunswick		10.4
Quebec		8.6
Ontario		7.1
Manitoba		5.2
Saskatchewan		5.7
Alberta		5.3
British Columbia		8.5

Source: Statistics Canada.
Visit www.mcgrawhill.ca/college/mcconnell for data updates.   **Σ-STAT**

Non-Economic Costs

Severe cyclical unemployment is more than an economic malady; it is a social catastrophe. Unemployment means idleness. And idleness means loss of skills, loss of self-respect, plummeting morale, family disintegration, and sociopolitical unrest. Widespread joblessness increases poverty, heightens racial and ethnic tensions, and reduces hope for material advancement. History demonstrates that severe unemployment can lead to rapid and sometimes violent social and political change. At the individual level, research links increases in suicide, homicide, fatal heart attacks and strokes, and mental illness to higher unemployment.

Regional Variations

The national unemployment rate in Canada does not reveal the significant diversity in regional unemployment. Table 6-5 gives both the national unemployment rate and a provincial breakdown. For 2002 the national rate was 7.7 percent but as high as 16.9 percent in Newfoundland and as low as 5.2 percent in Manitoba.

International Comparisons

Unemployment rates differ greatly among nations at any given time. One reason is that nations have different natural rates of unemployment. Another is that nations may be in different phases of their business cycles. Global Perspective 6.2 shows unemployment rates for five industrialized nations in recent years. Between 1993 and 2002, the Canadian unemployment rate came down steadily, and by the turn of the millennium Canada had an unemployment rate still above many other industrialized countries.

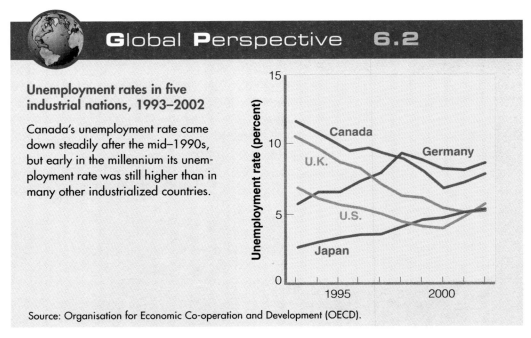

Global Perspective 6.2

Unemployment rates in five industrial nations, 1993–2002

Canada's unemployment rate came down steadily after the mid–1990s, but early in the millennium its unemployment rate was still higher than in many other industrialized countries.

Source: Organisation for Economic Co-operation and Development (OECD).

QUICK REVIEW

- Unemployment is of three general types: frictional, structural, and cyclical.

- The natural unemployment rate (frictional plus structural) is presently 6 to 7 percent.

- Society loses real GDP when cyclical unemployment occurs; according to Okun's law, for each one percentage point of unemployment above the natural rate, the Canadian economy suffers a 2-percent shortfall in real GDP below its potential GDP.

- Lower-skilled workers, teenagers, and less well-educated workers bear a disproportionate burden of unemployment.

6.4   Inflation

We now turn to inflation, another aspect of macroeconomic fluctuations. The problems inflation poses are subtler than those posed by unemployment.

Meaning of Inflation

inflation
A rise in the general level of prices in an economy.

Inflation is a continual rise in the *general level of prices.* This does not mean that *all* prices are rising. Even during periods of rapid inflation, some prices may be relatively constant while others are falling. For example, although Canada experienced high rates of inflation in the 1970s and early 1980s, the prices of video recorders, digital watches, and personal computers declined. As you will see, one troublesome aspect of inflation is that prices rise unevenly. Some shoot upward; others rise slowly; still others do not rise at all.

Measurement of Inflation

Consumer Price Index (CPI)
An index that measures the prices of a fixed "market basket" of goods and services that is bought by a "typical" consumer.

The main measure of inflation in Canada is the **Consumer Price Index (CPI)**, compiled by Statistics Canada. The government uses this index to report inflation rates each month and each year. It also uses the CPI to adjust social benefits and income tax brackets for inflation. The CPI reports the price of a "market basket" of over 600 consumer goods and services that are purchased by a typical Canadian consumer. (The GDP price index of Chapter 5 is a much broader measure of inflation since it includes not only consumer goods and services but also capital goods, goods and services purchased by government, and goods and services that enter world trade.)

The composition of the CPI market basket is based on spending patterns of Canadian consumers in a specific period, presently 1992. (See The Last Word for more detailed information about the eight main categories). Statistics Canada sets the CPI equal to 100 for 1992. So the CPI for any particular year is found as follows:

www.statcan.ca/english/
Subjects/Cpi/cpi-en.htm
Statistics Canada

$$\text{CPI} = \frac{\text{Price of the 1992 basket in the particular year } \small{1996}}{\text{Price of the same basket in the base year (1992) } \small{1997}} \times 100$$

The rate of inflation for a certain year (say, 2002) is found by comparing, in percentage terms, that year's index with the index in the previous year. For example, the CPI was 119.0 in 2002, up from 116.4 in 2001. So the rate of inflation for 2002 is calculated as follows:

$$\text{Rate of inflation} = \frac{119.0 - 116.4}{116.4} \times 100 = 2.2\%$$

Recall that the mathematical approximation called the *rule of 70* tells us that we can find the number of years it will take for some measure to double, given its annual percentage increase, by dividing that percentage increase into the number 70. So, with a 3 percent annual rate of inflation the price level will double in about 23 years (= 70 ÷ 3). Inflation of 8 percent per year will double the price level in about 9 years (= 70 ÷ 8). *(Key Question 11)*

Facts of Inflation

Figure 6-4 shows the annual rates of inflation in Canada between 1960 and 2002. Observe that inflation reached double-digit rates in the 1970s and early 1980s, but has since declined and has been relatively mild recently.

In recent years inflation in Canada has been unusually low relative to inflation in several other industrial countries (see Global Perspective 6.3). Some nations (not shown) have had double-digit, triple-digit, or even higher annual rates of inflation in recent years. In 2002, for example, the annual

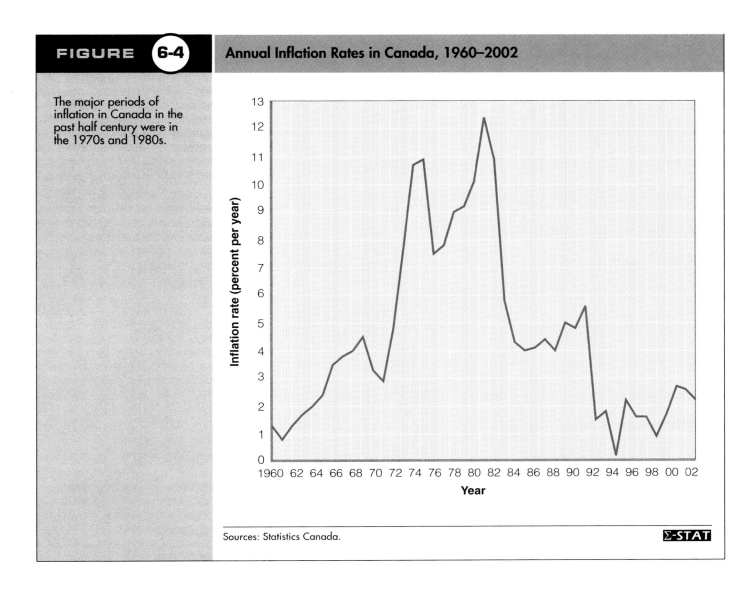

FIGURE 6-4

Annual Inflation Rates in Canada, 1960–2002

The major periods of inflation in Canada in the past half century were in the 1970s and 1980s.

Sources: Statistics Canada.

Σ-STAT

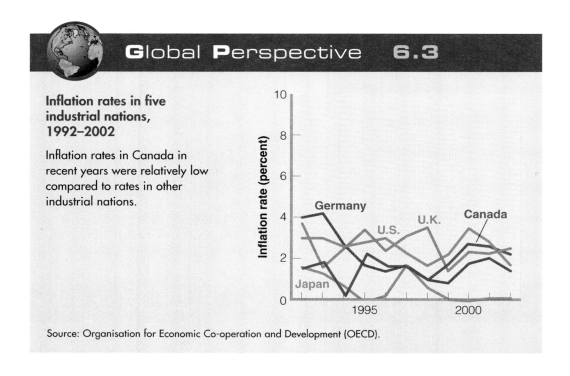

Global Perspective 6.3

Inflation rates in five industrial nations, 1992–2002

Inflation rates in Canada in recent years were relatively low compared to rates in other industrial nations.

Source: Organisation for Economic Co-operation and Development (OECD).

inflation rate in Romania was 23 percent; in Belarus, 43 percent; in Turkey, 45 percent; and in Myanmar, 57 percent.

Types of Inflation

Economists distinguish between two types of inflation: *demand-pull inflation* and *cost-push inflation*.

DEMAND-PULL INFLATION

Usually, changes in the price level are caused by an excess of total spending beyond the economy's capacity to produce. When resources are already fully employed, the business sector cannot respond to this excess demand by expanding output. So the excess demand bids up the prices of the limited real output, causing **demand-pull inflation**. The essence of this type of inflation is "too much spending chasing too few goods."

demand-pull inflation
Increases in the price level caused by an excess of total spending beyond the economy's capacity to produce.

COST-PUSH INFLATION

Inflation may also arise on the supply, or cost, side of the economy. During some periods in Canadian economic history, including the mid-1970s, the price level increased even though output and employment grew slowly (evidence that total demand was not excessive).

The theory of **cost-push inflation** explains rising prices in terms of factors that raise *per-unit production costs* at each level of spending. A per-unit production cost is the average cost of a particular level of output. This average cost is found by dividing the total cost of all resource inputs by the amount of output produced. That is,

cost-push inflation
Increases in the price level resulting from an increase in resource costs and hence in per-unit production costs.

$$\text{Per-unit production cost} = \frac{\text{total input cost}}{\text{units of output}}$$

Rising per-unit production costs reduce profits and reduce the amount of output firms are willing to supply at the existing price level. As a result, the economy's supply of goods and services declines

Consider This

Money and Inflation

Loosely defined, demand-pull inflation is "too much money chasing too few goods." Some interesting early episodes of demand-pull inflation occurred in Europe during the 9th to the 15th centuries under feudalism. In that economic system *lords* (or *princes*) ruled individual fiefdoms and their *vassals* (or *peasants*) worked the fields. The peasants initially paid parts of their harvest as taxes to the princes. Later, when the princes began issuing "coins of the realm," peasants began paying their taxes with gold coins.

Some princes soon discovered a way to transfer purchasing power from their vassals to themselves without explicitly increasing taxes. As coins came into the treasury, princes clipped off parts of the gold coins, making them slightly smaller. From the clippings they minted new coins and used them to buy more goods for themselves.

This practice of clipping coins was a subtle form of taxation. The quantity of goods being produced in the fiefdom remained the same, but the number of gold coins increased.

With "too much money chasing too few goods," inflation occurred. Each gold coin earned by the peasants therefore had less purchasing power than previously because prices were higher. The increase of the money supply shifted purchasing power away from the peasants and toward the princes just as surely as if the princes had increased taxation of the peasants.

In more recent eras some dictators have simply printed money to buy more goods for themselves, their relatives, and their key loyalists. These dictators, too, have levied hidden taxes on their populations by creating inflation.

The moral of the story is quite simple: A society that values price-level stability should not entrust the control of its money supply to people who benefit from inflation.

Question: What is the modern version of "clipping coins?" Briefly explain how it causes inflation.

and the price level rises. In this scenario, costs are *pushing* the price level upward, whereas in demand-pull inflation demand is *pulling* it upward.

The major sources of cost-push inflation have been so-called *supply shocks.* Specifically, abrupt increases in the costs of raw materials or energy inputs have on occasion driven up per-unit production costs and thus product prices. For example, the rocketing prices of imported oil in 1973–74 and again in 1979–80 increased the costs of producing and transporting virtually every product in the economy, and thus cost-push inflation ensued.

Complexities

It is often difficult to distinguish between demand-pull and cost-push inflation unless the original source of inflation is known. For example, suppose a significant increase in total spending occurs in a fully employed economy, causing demand-pull inflation. But as the demand-pull stimulus works its way through various product and resource markets, individual firms find their wage costs, material costs, and fuel prices rising. Firms must raise their prices because production costs (someone else's prices) have risen. Although this inflation is clearly demand-pull in origin, it may mistakenly appear to be cost-push inflation to business firms and to government. By misidentifying the source of the inflation, government may be slow to enact policies to reduce excessive total spending.

Another complexity is that cost-push inflation and demand-pull inflation differ in their persistence. Demand-pull inflation will continue as long as there is excess total spending. Cost-push inflation is automatically self-limiting; it will die out by itself. Increased per-unit costs will reduce supply, which means lower real output and employment. Those decreases will constrain further per-unit cost increases.

QUICK REVIEW

- Inflation is a rising general level of prices and is measured as percentage change in a price index such as the CPI.

- The consumer price index (CPI) measures changes in the prices of a fixed market basket of goods and services bought by the typical urban consumer.

- The inflation rate in Canada has been within the lower range of rates compared to other advanced industrial nations and far below the rates experienced by some nations.

- Demand-pull inflation occurs when total spending exceeds the economy's ability to provide goods and services at the existing price level; total spending *pulls* the price level upward.

- Cost-push inflation occurs when factors such as excessive wage increases and rapid increases in raw-material prices (supply shocks) drive up per-unit production costs at each level of output; higher costs *push* the price level upward.

6.5   Redistribution Effects of Inflation

Inflation hurts some people, leaves others unaffected, and actually helps still others. That is, inflation redistributes real income from some people to others. Who gets hurt? Who benefits? Before we can answer, we need to discuss some terminology.

Nominal and Real Income

nominal income
The number of current dollars received as wages, rent, interest, or profits.

real income
The amount of goods and services nominal income can buy.

There is a difference between money (or nominal) income and real income. **Nominal income** is the number of dollars received as wages, rent, interest, or profits. **Real income** is a measure of the amount of goods and services nominal income can buy; it is the purchasing power of nominal income, or income adjusted for inflation. That is,

$$\text{Real income} = \frac{\text{nominal income}}{\text{price index}} \times 100$$

Inflation need not alter an economy's overall real income. It is evident from the above equation that real income will remain the same when nominal income rises at the same rate as the price index.

But when inflation occurs, not everyone's nominal income rises at the same pace as the price level. Therein lies the potential for redistribution of real income from some to others. If the change in the price level differs from the change in a person's nominal income, his or her real income will be affected. The following rule of thumb tells us approximately by how much real income will change:

| Percentage change in real income | = | percentage change in nominal income | − | percentage change in price level |

For example, suppose that the price level rises by 6 percent in some period. If Bob's nominal income rises by 6 percent, his real income will *remain unchanged.* But if his nominal income instead rises by 10 percent, his real income will *increase* by about 4 percent. And, if Bob's nominal income rises by only 2 percent, his real income will *decline* by about 4 percent.[1]

---

[1] A more precise calculation uses our equation for real income. In our first illustration above, if nominal income rises by 10 percent from $100 to $110 and the price level (index) rises by 6 percent from 100 to 106, then real income has increased as follows:

$$\frac{\$110}{106} \times 100 = \$103.77$$

The 4 percent increase in real income shown by the simple formula in the text is a reasonable approximation of the 3.77 percent yielded by our more precise formula.

EXPECTATIONS

anticipated inflation
Increases in the price level that occur at the expected rate.

unanticipated inflation
Increases in the price level that occur at a rate greater than expected.

The redistribution effects of inflation depend on whether or not inflation is expected. With fully expected or **anticipated inflation**, an income receiver may be able to avoid or lessen the adverse effects of inflation on real income. The generalizations that follow assume **unanticipated inflation**—inflation for which the full extent was not expected.

Who Is Hurt by Inflation?

Unanticipated inflation hurts people on fixed incomes, savers, and creditors. It redistributes real income away from them and toward others.

FIXED-INCOME RECEIVERS

People whose income is fixed see their real income fall when inflation occurs. The classic case is the elderly couple living on a private pension or annuity that provides a fixed amount of nominal income each month. They may have retired in, say, 1992 on what appeared to be an adequate pension. However, by 1998 they would have discovered that inflation has cut the purchasing power of that pension—their real income—by twenty percent.

Similarly, landlords who receive lease payments of fixed dollar amounts will be hurt by inflation as they receive dollars of declining value over time. Public sector workers whose incomes are dictated by fixed pay schedules may also suffer from inflation. The fixed "steps" (the upward yearly increases) in their pay schedules may not keep up with inflation. Minimum-wage workers and families living on fixed welfare incomes will also be hurt by inflation.

SAVERS

Unanticipated inflation hurts savers. As prices rise, the real value, or purchasing power, of an accumulation of savings deteriorates. Paper assets such as savings accounts, insurance policies, and annuities that were once adequate to meet rainy-day contingencies or provide for a comfortable retirement decline in real value during inflationary periods.

Example: A household may save $1000 in a guaranteed investment certificate (GIC) in a chartered bank at 6 percent annual interest. But if inflation is 13 percent, the real value or purchasing power of that $1000 will be cut to about $938 by the end of the year. Although the saver will receive $1060 (equal to $1000 plus $60 of interest), deflating that $1060 for 13 percent inflation means that its real value is only about $938 (= $1060 ÷ 1.13).

CREDITORS

Unanticipated inflation harms creditors (lenders). Suppose Manitoba Bank lends Bob $1000, to be repaid in two years. If in that time the price level doubles, the $1000 that Bob repays will have only half the purchasing power of the $1000 he borrowed. Because of inflation, each of those dollars will buy only half as much as it did when the loan was negotiated. As prices go up, the value of the dollar goes down. Thus, the borrower is lent "dear" dollars but, because of inflation, pays back "cheap" dollars. The owners of Manitoba Bank suffer a loss of real income.

Who Is Unaffected or Helped by Inflation?

Some people are unaffected by inflation and others may actually be helped by it. For the second group, inflation redistributes real income toward them and away from others.

FLEXIBLE-INCOME RECEIVERS

Individuals who derive their income solely from social programs are largely unaffected by inflation, because payments are *indexed* to the CPI. Benefits automatically increase when the CPI increases, preventing erosion of benefits from inflation. Some union workers also get automatic

cost-of-living adjustment (COLA)
An automatic increase in the income (wages) of workers when inflation occurs.

cost-of-living adjustments (COLAs) in their pay when the CPI rises, although such increases rarely equal the full percentage rise in inflation.

All borrowers are helped by unanticipated inflation. Rapid inflation may cause some nominal incomes to spurt ahead of the price level, thereby enhancing their real incomes. For some, the 3 percent increase in nominal income that occurs when inflation is 2 percent may become a 6 percent increase when inflation is 5 percent. As an example, property owners faced with an inflation-induced real-estate boom may be able to raise rents more rapidly than the rate of inflation. Also, some business owners may benefit from inflation. If product prices rise faster than resource prices, business revenues will grow more rapidly than costs. In those cases, the growth rate of profit incomes will outpace the rate of inflation.

DEBTORS

Unanticipated inflation benefits debtors (borrowers). In our previous example, Manitoba Bank's loss of real income from inflation is Bob's gain of real income. Debtor Bob borrows "dear" dollars but, because of inflation, pays back the principle and interest with "cheap" dollars of which purchasing power has been eroded by inflation. Real income is redistributed away from the owners of Manitoba Bank toward borrowers such as Bob.

As a historical example, the inflation of the 1970s and 1980s created a windfall of capital gains for people who purchased homes in earlier periods with low, fixed-interest-rate mortgages. Inflation greatly reduced the real burden of their mortgage indebtedness. They also benefited because the nominal value of housing in that period increased much more rapidly than the overall price level.

Anticipated Inflation

The redistribution effects of inflation are less severe or are eliminated altogether if people anticipate inflation and can adjust their nominal incomes to reflect the expected price-level rises. The prolonged inflation that began in the late 1960s prompted many labour unions in the 1970s to insist on labour contracts with cost-of-living adjustment clauses.

Similarly, if inflation is anticipated, the redistribution of income from lender to borrower may be altered. Suppose a lender (perhaps a chartered bank or a credit union) and a borrower (a household) both agree that 5 percent is a fair rate of interest on a one-year loan provided the price level is stable. But assume that inflation has been occurring and is expected to be 6 percent over the next year. If the bank lends the household $100 at 5 percent interest, the bank will be paid back $105 at the end of the year. But if 6 percent inflation does occur during that year, the purchasing power of the $105 will have been reduced to about $99. The lender will in effect have paid the borrower $1 for the use of the lender's money for a year.

The lender can avoid this subsidy by charging an *inflation premium*—that is, by raising the interest rate by 6 percent, the amount of the anticipated inflation. By charging 11 percent, the lender will receive back $111 at the end of the year. Adjusted for the 6 percent inflation, that amount will have the purchasing power of today's $105. The result then will be a mutually agreeable transfer of purchasing power from borrower to lender of $5, or 5 percent, for the use of $100 for one year. Financial institutions have also developed variable-interest-rate mortgages to protect themselves from the adverse effects of inflation. (Incidentally, this example points out that, rather than being a *cause* of inflation, high nominal interest rates are a *consequence* of inflation.)

real interest rate
The interest rate expressed in dollars of constant value (adjusted for inflation).

nominal interest rate
The interest rate expressed in terms of annual amounts currently charged for interest and not adjusted for inflation.

Our example reveals the difference between the real rate of interest and the nominal rate of interest. The **real interest rate** is the percentage increase in *purchasing power* that the borrower pays the lender. In our example the real interest rate is 5 percent. The **nominal interest rate** is the percentage increase in *money* that the borrower pays the lender, including that resulting from the built-in expectation of inflation, if any. In equation form:

Nominal interest rate = real interest rate + inflation premium (the expected rate of inflation).

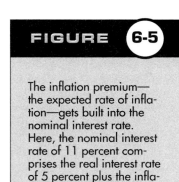

FIGURE 6-5

The Inflation Premium and Nominal and Real Interest Rates

The inflation premium—the expected rate of inflation—gets built into the nominal interest rate. Here, the nominal interest rate of 11 percent comprises the real interest rate of 5 percent plus the inflation premium of 6 percent.

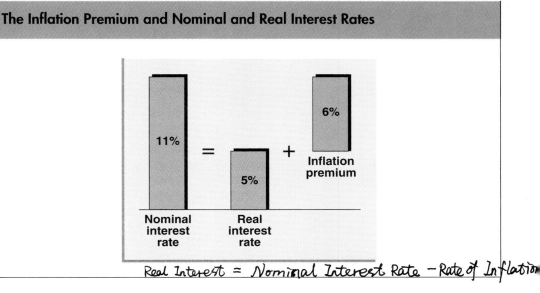

Real Interest = Nominal Interest Rate − Rate of Inflation

As illustrated in Figure 6-5, the nominal interest rate in our example is 11 percent.

Addenda

We end our discussion of the redistribution effects of inflation by making three final points.

deflation
A decline in the economy's price level.

- **Deflation**   The effects of unanticipated **deflation**—declines in the price level—are the reverse of those of inflation. People with fixed nominal income will find their real incomes enhanced. Creditors will benefit at the expense of debtors. As prices and wages fall, fixed debt obligations actually rise as a percentage of disposable income. And savers will discover that the purchasing power of their savings has grown because of the falling prices. Japan has been experiencing deflationary pressures in the last decade.

- **Mixed effects**   A person who is an income earner, a holder of financial assets, and an owner of real assets simultaneously will probably find that the redistribution impact of inflation is cushioned. If the person owns fixed-value monetary assets (savings accounts, bonds, and insurance policies), inflation will lessen their real value. But that same inflation may increase the real value of any property assets (a house, land) that the person owns. In short, many individuals are simultaneously hurt and benefited by inflation. All these effects must be considered before we can conclude that any particular person's net position is better or worse because of inflation.

- **Arbitrariness**   The redistribution effects of inflation occur regardless of society's goals and values. Inflation lacks a social conscience and takes from some and gives to others, whether they are rich, poor, young, old, healthy, or infirm.

QUICK REVIEW

- Inflation harms those who receive relatively fixed nominal incomes and either leaves unaffected or helps those who receive flexible nominal incomes.

- Unanticipated inflation hurts savers and creditors while benefiting debtors.

- The nominal interest rate equals the real interest rate plus the inflation premium (the expected rate of inflation).

6.6   Effects of Inflation on Output

Thus far, our discussion has focused on how inflation redistributes a given level of total real income. But inflation may also affect an economy's level of real output (and thus its level of real income). The direction and significance of this effect on output depends on the type of inflation and its severity.

Cost-Push Inflation and Real Output

Recall that abrupt and unexpected rises in key resource prices can drive up overall production costs sufficiently to cause cost-push inflation. As prices rise, the quantity of goods and services demanded falls. So, firms respond by producing less output, and unemployment goes up.

Economic events of the 1970s provide an example of how inflation can reduce real output. In late 1973 the Organization of Petroleum Exporting Countries (OPEC), by exerting its market power, managed to quadruple the price of oil. The cost-push inflationary effects generated rapid price-level increases in the 1973–75 period, particularly in oil-importing provinces of Central Canada. At the same time, the Canadian unemployment rate rose from slightly less than 6 percent in 1973 to 8.1 percent in 1976. Similar outcomes occurred in 1979–80 in response to a second OPEC oil supply shock.

In short, cost-push inflation reduces real output. It redistributes a decreased level of real income.

www.opec.org
OPEC

Demand-Pull Inflation and Real Output

Economists do not fully agree on the effects of mild inflation (less than 3 percent) on real output. One perspective is that even low levels of inflation reduce real output, because inflation diverts time and effort toward activities designed to hedge against inflation. Examples:

- Businesses must incur the cost of changing thousands of prices on their shelves and in their computers simply to reflect inflation.

- Households and businesses must spend considerable time and effort obtaining the information they need to distinguish between real and nominal values such as prices, wages, and interest rates.

- To limit the loss of purchasing power from inflation, people try to limit the amount of money they hold in their wallets and chequing accounts at any one time and instead put more money into interest-bearing accounts and stock and bond funds. But cash and cheques are needed in even greater amounts to buy the higher priced goods and services. So more frequent trips, phone calls, or Internet visits to financial institutions are required to transfer funds to chequing accounts and wallets, when needed.

Without inflation, these uses of resources, time, and effort would not be needed and they could be diverted toward producing more valuable goods and services. Proponents of "zero-inflation" bolster their case by pointing to cross-country studies that indicate that lower rates of inflation are associated with higher rates of economic growth.

In contrast, other economists point out that full employment and economic growth depend on strong levels of total spending. Such spending creates high profits, strong demand for labour, and a powerful incentive for firms to expand their plant and equipment. In this view, the mild inflation that is a by-product of this strong spending is a small price to pay for full employment and continued economic growth. Moreover, a little inflation may have positive effects because it makes it easier for firms to adjust real wages downward when the demands for their products fall. With mild inflation, firms can reduce real wages by holding nominal wages steady. With zero inflation, firms would need to cut nominal wages to reduce real wages. Such cuts in nominal wages are highly visible and may cause considerable worker resistance and labour strife.

Finally, defenders of mild inflation say that it is much better for an economy to err on the side of strong spending, full employment, economic growth, and mild inflation, than on the side of weak spending, unemployment, recession, and deflation.

Hyperinflation and Breakdown

hyperinflation
A very rapid rise in the general price level.

All economists agree that the nation's policy makers must carefully monitor mild inflation so that it does not snowball into higher rates of inflation, or even into **hyperinflation**. The latter is an extremely rapid inflation, which has an impact on real output and employment that usually is devastating. When inflation begins to escalate, consumers, workers, and businesses assume that it will rise even further. So, rather than let their idle savings and current incomes depreciate, consumers "spend now" to beat the anticipated price rises. Businesses do the same by buying capital goods. Workers demand and receiver higher nominal wages to recoup lost purchasing power and to maintain future purchasing power in the face of expected higher inflation. Actions based on these inflationary expectations then intensify the pressure on prices, and inflation feeds on itself.

Aside from its disruptive redistribution effects, hyperinflation may cause economic collapse. Severe inflation encourages speculative activity. Businesses, anticipating further price increases, may find it profitable to hoard both materials and finished products. But restricting the availability of materials and products intensifies the inflationary pressure. Also, rather than investing in capital equipment, businesses and individual savers may decide to purchase non-productive wealth—jewels, gold and other precious metals, real estate, and so forth—as a hedge against inflation.

In the extreme, as prices shoot up sharply and unevenly, normal economic relationships are disrupted. Business owners do not know what to charge for their products. Consumers do not know what to pay. Resource suppliers want to be paid with actual output, rather than with rapidly depreciating money. Creditors avoid debtors to keep them from repaying their debts with cheap money. Money eventually becomes almost worthless and ceases to do its job as a medium of exchange. The economy may be thrown into a state of barter, and production and exchange drop dramatically. The net result is economic, social, and possibly political chaos. Hyperinflation has precipitated monetary collapse, depression, and sociopolitical disorder.

History reveals a number of examples that fit this scenario. Consider the effects of World War II on price levels in Hungary and Japan.

> The inflation in Hungary exceeded all known records of the past. In August 1946, 828 octillion (1 followed by 27 zeros) depreciated pengös equaled the value of 1 prewar pengö. The price of the American dollar reached a value of 3×10^{22} (3 followed by 22 zeros) pengös. Fishermen and farmers in 1947 Japan used scales to weigh currency and change, rather than bothering to count it. Prices rose some 116 times in Japan, 1938 to 1948.[2]

The German inflation of the 1920s also was catastrophic. The German Weimar Republic printed so much money to pay its bills that,

> During 1922, the German price level went up 5,470 percent. In 1923, the situation worsened; the German price level rose 1,300,000,000,000 times. By October of 1923, the postage on the lightest letter sent from Germany to the United States was 200,000 marks.... Prices increased so rapidly that waiters changed the prices on the menu several times during the course of a lunch. Sometimes customers had to pay double the price listed on the menu when they ordered.[3]

---

[2]Theodore Morgan, *Income and Employment*, 2d ed. (Englewood Cliffs, NJ: Prentice-Hall, 1952), p. 361.

[3]Raburn M. Williams, *Inflation! Money, Jobs, and Politicians* (Arlington Heights, IL: AHM Publishing Corporation, 1980), p. 2.

There are also more recent examples of hyperinflation:[4]

- Between June 1986 and March 1991 the cumulative inflation in Nicaragua was 11,895,866,143 percent.
- From November 1993 to December 1994 the cumulative inflation rate in the Democratic Republic of Congo was 69,502 percent.
- From February 1993 to January 1994 the cumulative inflation in Serbia was 156,312,790 percent.

Such dramatic hyperinflations are almost invariably the consequence of highly imprudent expansions of the money supply by government. The rocketing money supply produces frenzied total spending and severe demand-pull inflation.

THE LASTword   The Stock Market and the Economy

How, if at all, do changes in stock prices relate to macroeconomic instability?

Every day, the individual stocks (ownership shares) of thousands of corporations are bought and sold in the stock market. The owners of the individual stocks receive dividends—a portion of that firm's profit. Supply and demand in the stock market determine the price of each firm's stock, with individual stock prices generally rising and falling in concert with the collective expectations for each firm's profits. Greater profits normally result in higher dividends to the stockowners, and in anticipation of higher dividends, people are willing to pay a higher price for the stock.

The media closely monitor and report stock market averages such as the weighted-average price of the stocks of 100 major Canadian firms, called the S&P/TSX composite index (TSX refers to the Toronto Stock Exchange). It is common for these price averages to change over time, or even to rise or fall sharply during a single day. On "Black Monday," October 19, 1987, the S&P/TSX composite fell by 20 percent. A sharp drop in stock prices also occurred in October 1997, mainly in response to rapid declines in stock prices in Hong Kong and other Southeast Asian stock markets. In contrast, the stock market averages rose in 1999 and 2000, with the S&P/TSX composite rising respecively, 31 percent and 6 percent in those two years.

The volatility of the stock market raises this question: Do changes in stock price averages and thus stock market wealth cause macroeconomic

instability? There are linkages between the stock market and the economy that might lead us to answer "yes." Consider a sharp increase in stock prices. Feeling wealthier, stockowners respond by increasing their spending (the *wealth effect*). Firms react by increasing their purchases of new capital goods, because they can finance such purchases through issuing new shares of high-valued stock (the *investment effect*). Of course, sharp declines in stock prices would produce the opposite results.

Studies find that changes in stock prices do affect consumption and investment, but that these consumption and investment impacts are relatively weak. For example, a 10 percent sustained increase in stock market values in one year is associated with a 4 percent increase in consumption spending over the next three years. The investment response is even weaker. So, typical day-to-day and year-to-year

---

[4]Stanley Fischer, Ratna Sahay, and Carlos Végh, "Modern Hyper- and High Inflations," *Journal of Economic Literature* (September 2002), p. 840.

changes in stock market values have little impact on the macroeconomy.

In contrast, *stock market bubbles* can be detrimental to an economy. Such bubbles are huge run ups of overall stock prices, caused by excessive optimism and frenzied buying. The rising stock values are unsupported by realistic prospects of the future strength of the economy and the firms operating in it. Rather than slowly decompress, such bubbles may burst and cause harm to the economy. The free fall of stock values, if long lasting, causes reverse wealth effects. The stock market crash may also create an overall pessimism about the economy that undermines consumption and investment spending even further.

A related question: Even though typical changes in stock prices do not cause recession or inflation, might they predict such maladies? That is, since stock market values are based on expected profits, wouldn't we expect rapid changes in stock price averages to forecast changes in future business conditions? Indeed, stock prices often do fall prior to recessions and rise prior to expansions. For this reason stock prices are among a group of 10 variables that constitute an index of leading indicators (The Last Word, Chapter 9). Such an index may provide a useful clue to the future direction of the economy. But taken alone, stock market prices are not a reliable predictor of changes in GDP. Stock prices have fallen rapidly in some instances with no recession following. Black Monday itself did not produce a recession during the following two years. In other instances, recessions have occurred with no prior decline in stock market prices.

CHAPTER SUMMARY

6.1 ECONOMIC GROWTH

- Economic growth may be defined as either (a) an increase in real GDP over time or (b) an increase in real GDP per capita over time. Growth lessens the burden of scarcity and provides increases in real GDP that can be used to resolve socioeconomic problems. Since World War II, real GDP growth in Canada has been slightly more than 4 percent annually; real GDP per capita has grown at about a 2 percent annual rate.

6.2 THE BUSINESS CYCLE

- Canada and other industrial economies have gone through periods of fluctuations in real GDP, employment, and price level. Although they have certain phases in common—peak, recession, trough, recovery—business cycles vary greatly in duration and intensity.

- Although economists explain the business cycle in terms of such causal factors as major innovations, political events, and money creation, they generally agree that the level of total spending is the immediate determinant of real output and employment.

- The business cycle affects all sectors of the economy, though in varying ways and degrees. The cycle has greater effects on output and employment in the capital goods and durable consumer goods industries than in the services and non-durable goods industries.

6.3 UNEMPLOYMENT

- Economists distinguish among frictional, structural, and cyclical unemployment. The full-employment or natural rate of unemployment, which is made up of frictional and structural unemployment, is currently between 6 and 7 percent. The presence of part-time and discouraged workers makes it difficult to measure unemployment accurately.

- The economic cost of unemployment, as measured by the GDP gap, consists of the goods and services forgone by society when its resources are involuntarily idle. Okun's law suggests that every increase in unemployment by 1 percent above the natural rate causes an additional 2 percent negative GDP gap.

- Unemployment rates vary widely globally. Unemployment rates differ because nations have different natural rates of unemployment and often are in different phases of their business cycles.

6.4 INFLATION

- Inflation is a rise in the general price level and is measured in Canada by the Consumer Price Index (CPI). When inflation occurs, each dollar of income will buy fewer goods and services than before. That is, inflation reduces the purchasing power of money.

- Economists discern both demand-pull and cost-push (supply-side) inflation. Demand-pull inflation results from an excess of total spending relative to the economy's capacity to produce. The main source of cost-push inflation is abrupt and rapid increases in the prices of key resources. These supply shocks push up per-unit production costs and ultimately the prices of consumer goods.

6.5 REDISTRIBUTION EFFECTS OF INFLATION

- Unanticipated inflation arbitrarily redistributes real income at the expense of fixed-income receivers, creditors, and savers. If inflation is anticipated, individuals and businesses may be able to take steps to lessen or eliminate adverse redistribution effects.

- When inflation is anticipated, lenders add an inflation premium to the interest rate charged on loans. The nominal interest rate thus reflects the real interest rate plus the inflation premium (the expected rate of inflation).

6.6 EFFECTS OF INFLATION ON OUTPUT

- Cost-push inflation reduces real output and employment. Proponents of zero inflation argue that even mild demand-pull inflation (1–3 percent) reduces the economy's real output. Other economists say that mild inflation may be a necessary by-product of the high and growing spending that produces high levels of output, full employment, and economic growth. Hyperinflation, usually associated with injudicious government policy, may undermine the monetary system and cause severe declines in real output.

TERMS AND CONCEPTS

real GDP per capita, p. 128
economic growth, p. 128
rule of 70, p. 129
productivity, p. 129
business cycle, p. 130
peak, p. 131
recession, p. 131
trough, p. 131
recovery, p. 131
labour force, p. 133
unemployment rate, p. 133
discouraged workers, p. 134

frictional unemployment, p. 135
structural unemployment, p. 135
cyclical unemployment, p. 135
natural rate of unemployment (NRU),
   p. 136
potential GDP, p. 136
GDP gap, p. 136
Okun's law, p. 138
inflation, p. 140
consumer price index (CPI), p. 140
demand-pull inflation, p. 142
cost-push inflation, p. 142

nominal income, p. 144
real income, p. 144
anticipated inflation, p. 145
unanticipated inflation, p. 145
cost-of-living adjustment (COLA),
   p. 146
real interest rate, p. 146
nominal interest rate, p. 146
deflation, p. 147
hyperinflation, p. 149

STUDY QUESTIONS

1. Why is economic growth important? Why could the difference between a 2.5 percent and a 3.0 percent annual growth rate be of great significance over several decades?

2. **KEY QUESTION**   Suppose an economy's real GDP is $30,000 in year 1 and $31,200 in year 2. What is the growth rate of its real GDP? Assume that the population is 100 in year 1 and 102 in year 2. What is the growth rate of GDP per capita?

3. Briefly describe the growth record of Canada. Compare the rates of growth of real GDP and real GDP per capita, explaining any differences. Compare the economic growth rate of Japan and Canada between 1992 and 2002. To what extent might growth rates understate or overstate economic well-being?

4. **KEY QUESTION**   What are the four phases of the business cycle? How long do business cycles last? How do seasonal variations and long-run trends complicate

measurement of the business cycle? Why does the business cycle affect output and employment in capital goods industries and consumer durable goods industries more severely than in industries producing consumer non-durables?

5. What factors make it difficult to determine the unemployment rate? Why is it difficult to distinguish among frictional, structural, and cyclical unemployment? Why is unemployment an economic problem? What are the consequences of a GDP gap? What are the non-economic effects of unemployment?

6. **KEY QUESTION**   Use the following data to calculate (a) the size of the labour force and (b) the official unemployment rate: total population, 500; population under 15 years of age or institutionalized, 120; not in labour force, 150; unemployed, 23; part-time workers looking for full-time jobs, 10.

7. Since Canada has an employment insurance program that provides income for those out of work, why should we worry about unemployment?

8. **KEY QUESTION** Assume that in a particular year the natural rate of unemployment is 5 percent and the actual rate of unemployment is 9 percent. Use Okun's law to determine the size of the GDP gap in percentage-point terms. If the nominal GDP is $500 billion in that year, how much output is being forgone because of cyclical unemployment?

9. Explain how an increase in your nominal income and a decrease in your real income might occur simultaneously. Who loses from inflation? Who loses from unemployment? If you had to choose between (a) full employment with a 6 percent annual rate of inflation and (b) price stability with an 8 percent unemployment rate, which would you choose? Why?

10. What is the Consumer Price Index (CPI) and how is it determined each month? How does Statistics Canada calculate the rate of inflation from one year to the next? What effect does inflation have on the purchasing power of a dollar? On the gap, if any, between nominal and real interest rates? How does deflation differ from inflation?

11. **KEY QUESTION** If the price index was 110 last year and is 121 this year, what is this year's rate of inflation? What is the "rule of 70"? How long would it take for the price level to double if inflation persisted at (a) 2 percent, (b) 5 percent, and (c) 10 percent per year?

12. Distinguish between demand-pull and cost-push inflation. Which of the two types is most likely to be associated with a (negative) GDP gap? Which with a positive GDP gap (in which actual GDP exceeds potential GDP)?

13. Explain how hyperinflation might lead to a severe decline in total output.

14. Evaluate as accurately as you can how each of the following individuals would be affected by unanticipated inflation of 10 percent per year:

   a. A pensioned railroad worker

   b. A department-store clerk

   c. A unionized automobile assembly-line worker

   d. A heavily indebted farmer

   e. A retired business executive whose current income comes entirely from interest on government bonds

   f. The owner of an independent small-town department store

15. **(The Last Word)** Suppose that stock prices were to fall by 10 percent in the stock market. All else equal, would these lower stock prices be likely to cause a decrease in real GDP? How might they predict a decline in real GDP?

INTERNET APPLICATION QUESTIONS

1. **The Employment Situation—Write the News Release** Visit the Statistics Canada Web site through the McConnell-Brue-Barbiero home page (Chapter 6) and look at the current national employment situation summary for the latest month. Then rewrite the following paragraph.

   Employment in Canada (rose/fell/remained unchanged), and the unemployment rate edged (up/down/stayed unchanged) to (?) percent in the latest month. The unemployment rate had (risen/fallen/stayed unchanged) from (?) percent in (previous month) to (?) percent in (latest month). The number of jobs (increased/decreased/was unchanged) by (? thousand) in the latest month.

   Σ-STAT

2. **Inflation and the "Official CPI"** Each month, Statistics Canada releases thousands of detailed CPI numbers to the press. However, the press generally focuses on the broadest, most comprehensive CPI, called the official CPI. Go to the McConnell-Brue-Barbiero Web site (Chapter 6) and find the figures for the official CPI: **a** index level for all items for the current month (for example, December 2002 = 120.4 for all items); **b** 12-month percentage change (for example, December 2001 to December 2002 = 3.9 percent for all items); **c** 1-month percentage change (for example, from March 2003 to April 2003 = – 0.7 for all items); and **d** the annual percentage rate of change so far this year for all items. Click on the "List of Tables" and look at the CPI for the provinces; which province had the highest/lowest change in the CPI for the last 12 months?

   Σ-STAT

7

Chapter

The Aggregate Expenditures Model

Two of the most critical questions in macroeconomics are: (1) What determines the level of GDP, given a nation's production capacity? (2) What causes real GDP to rise in one period and to fall in another? To answer these questions, we construct the aggregate expenditures (AE) model, which has its origins in the 1936 writings of the British economist John Maynard Keynes (pronounced "Caines"). Our strategy in this chapter is to analyze the consumption and investment components of aggregate expenditures and derive a simple, private (no-government), closed (no-international-trade) model of equilibrium GDP and employment. We then add net exports and the public sector to the model.

7.1 ## The Aggregate Expenditures Model: Consumption and Saving

The basic premise of the aggregate expenditures (AE) model—also known as the "Keynesian cross model"—is that the amount of goods and services produced (and therefore the level of employment in the short run) depends directly on the level of aggregate expenditures (total spending). We emphasize that this is a short-run model of employment and income determination. Businesses will produce only a level of output that they think they can profitably sell. They will lay off their workers when markets for their goods and services shrink. When aggregate expenditures fall, total output and employment decrease; when aggregate expenditures rise, total output and employment increase.

As we begin, we assume that the economy has both excess production capacity and unemployed labour (unless specified otherwise). Thus, an increase in aggregate expenditures will increase real output and employment but not raise the price level. *In fact, unless we state otherwise, we will assume that the price level is constant.*

Simplifications

We initially build a model of "a private closed economy," leaving to the second half of the chapter the complications arising from government expenditures, taxes, exports, and imports. Also, to keep things simple, we will assume that all saving consists of personal saving and depreciation is zero. That is, there is no business saving, and gross investment equals net investment.

These simplifying assumptions have two implications. First, aggregate spending initially consists of only *consumption* and *investment*. Second, gross domestic product (GDP), net domestic product (NDP), personal income (PI), and disposable income (DI) are equal. So, if $500 billion of output is produced as GDP, households will receive exactly $500 billion of disposable income (DI) to consume or to save.

The Income-Consumption and Income-Saving Relationships

In examining the relationship between income and consumption we are also exploring the relationship between income and saving. Economists define personal saving as "not spending" or "that part of disposable (after-tax) income not consumed." Saving (S) equals disposable income (DI) *minus* consumption (C).

Many factors determine the nation's levels of consumption and saving, but the most significant is disposable income. Consider some recent historical data for Canada. In Figure 7-1 each dot represents consumption and disposable income for one year since 1980. The line C fitted to these points shows that consumption is directly (positively) related to disposable income; moreover, households spend a large part of their income.

45° (degree) line
A reference line that bisects the 90° angle formed by the two axes, and along which consumption equals disposable income.

But we can say more. The **45° (degree) line** is a reference line. Because it bisects the 90° angle formed by the two axes of the graph, each point on it is equidistant from the two axes. At each point on the 45° line, consumption equals disposable income, or $C = DI$. Therefore the vertical distance between the 45° line and any point on the horizontal axis measures either consumption *or* disposable income. If we let it measure disposable income, the vertical distance between it and the line labeled C represents the amount of saving (S) in that year.

Saving is the amount by which actual consumption in any year falls short of the 45° line— ($S = DI - C$). For example, in 2002 disposable income was $696 billion and consumption was $651 billion; so, saving was $45 billion. Observe that the vertical distance between the 45° line and line C increases as we move rightward along the horizontal axis and decreases as we move leftward. Like consumption, saving varies directly with the level of disposable income: As DI rises, saving increases; as DI falls, saving decreases.

The Consumption Schedule

The dots in Figure 7-1 represent the actual amounts of DI, C, and S in Canada over a period of years. But, for analytical purposes, we need a schedule that shows the various amounts that households would plan to consume at each of the various levels of disposable income that might prevail at some time. Columns 1 and 2 of Table 7-1, represented in **Figure 7-2a (Key Graph)**, shows a hypothetical consumption schedule of the type that we require. This **consumption schedule** (or "consumption function") reflects the direct consumption-disposable income relationship. Note that, in the aggregate, households increase their spending as their disposable income rises and spend a larger proportion of a small disposable income than a larger disposable income.

consumption schedule
A schedule showing the amounts households plan to spend for consumer goods at different levels of disposable income.

The Saving Schedule

It is relatively simple to derive a **saving schedule** (or "saving function"). Because saving equals disposable income less consumption ($S = DI - C$), we need only subtract consumption (Table 7-1, column 2) from disposable income (column 1) to find the amount saved (column 3) at each DI. Thus, columns 1 and 3 in Table 7-1 are the saving schedule, represented in Figure 7-2b. The graph shows

saving schedule
A schedule that shows the amounts households plan to save at different levels of disposable income.

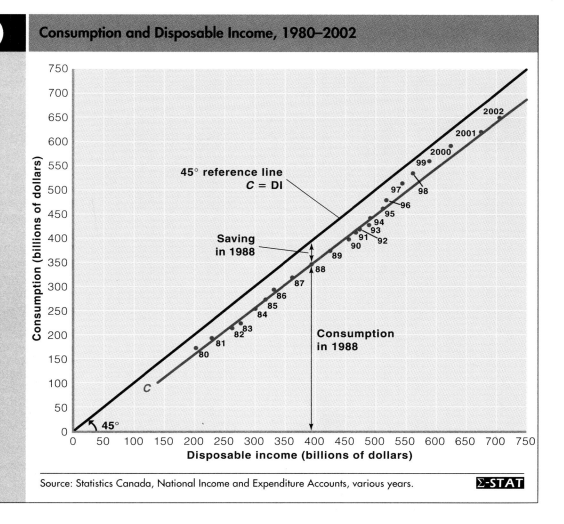

FIGURE 7-1

Consumption and Disposable Income, 1980–2002

Each dot in this figure shows consumption and disposable income in a specific year. The line C, which generalizes the relationship between consumption and disposable income, indicates a direct relationship and shows that households consume most of their income.

Source: Statistics Canada, National Income and Expenditure Accounts, various years.   Σ-STAT

there is a direct relationship between saving and DI but that saving is a smaller proportion of a small DI than of a large DI.

Since each point on the 45-degree line consumption equals DI, we see dissaving at relatively low DIs, such as $370 billion (row 1, Table 7-1), at which consumption is $375 billion. Households can consume more than their income by liquidating (selling for cash) accumulated wealth or by borrowing. Graphically, dissaving is shown as the vertical distance of the consumption schedule above the 45-degree line or as the vertical distance of the saving schedule below the horizontal axis. We have marked the dissaving at the $370 billion level of income in both Figures 7-2a and b. Both vertical distances measure the $5 billion of dissaving that occurs at $370 billion of income.

In our example, the **break-even income** is $390 billion (row 2). This is the income level at which households plan to consume their entire incomes (C = DI). Graphically, the consumption schedule cuts the 45-degree line, and the saving schedule cuts the horizontal axis (saving is zero) at the break-even income level.

At all higher incomes, households plan to save part of their income. Graphically, the vertical distance that the consumption schedule lies below the 45-degree line measures this saving, as does the vertical distance that the saving schedule lies above the horizontal axis. For example, at the $410 billion level of income (row 3), both these distances indicate $5 billion of saving (also see Figure 7-2a and b).

break-even income
The level of disposable income at which households plan to consume all their income and to save none of it.

Average and Marginal Propensities

Columns 4 to 7 in Table 7-1 show additional characteristics of the consumption and saving schedules.

TABLE 7-1	Consumption and Saving Schedules (in Billions) and Propensities to Consume and Save					
(1) Level of output and income (GDP = DI)	(2) Consumption (C)	(3) Saving (S) (1) – (2)	(4) Average propensity to consume (APC) (2)/(1)	(5) Average propensity to save (APS) (3)/(1)	(6) Marginal propensity to consume (MPC) Δ(2)/Δ(1)*	(7) Marginal propensity to save (MPS) Δ(3)/Δ(1)*
(1) $370	$375	$–5	1.01	–.01		
					.75	.25
(2) 390	390	0	1.00	.00		
					.75	.25
(3) 410	405	5	.99	.01		
					.75	.25
(4) 430	420	10	.98	.02		
					.75	.25
(5) 450	435	15	.97	.03		
					.75	.25
(6) 470	450	20	.96	.04		
					.75	.25
(7) 490	465	25	.95	.05		
					.75	.25
(8) 510	480	30	.94	.06		
					.75	.25
(9) 530	495	35	.93	.07		
					.75	.25
(10) 550	510	40	.93	.07		

*The Greek letter Δ, delta, means "the change in."

Σ-STAT

Key Graph

FIGURE 7-2 (A) Consumption and (B) Saving Schedules

The two parts of this figure show the income-consumption and income-saving relationships in Table 7-1 graphically. The saving schedule in (b) is found by sub-tracting the consumption schedule in (a) vertically from the 45-degree line. Consumption equals dispos-able income (and saving thus equals zero) at $390 billion for these hypothetical data.

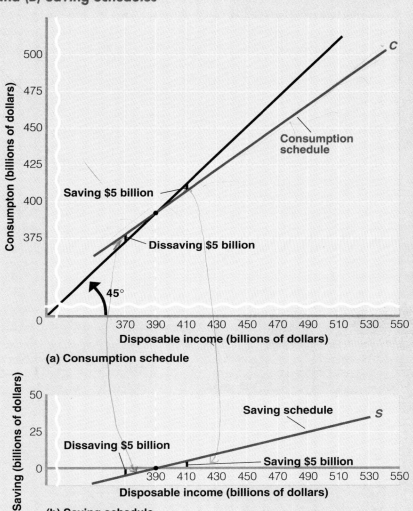

(a) Consumption schedule

(b) Saving schedule

Quick Quiz

1. **The slope of the consumption schedule in this figure is .75. Thus the**
   a. slope of the saving schedule is 1.33.
   b. marginal propensity to consume is .75.
   c. average propensity to consume is .25.
   d. slope of the saving schedule is also .75.

2. **In this figure, when consumption is a positive amount, saving**
   a. must be a negative amount.
   b. must also be a positive amount.
   c. can be either a positive or a negative amount.
   d. is zero.

3. In this figure,
   a.   the marginal propensity to consume is constant at all levels of income.
   b.   the marginal propensity to save rises as disposable income rises.
   c.   consumption is inversely (negatively) related to disposable income.
   d.   saving is inversely (negatively) related to disposable income.

4. When consumption equals disposable income,
   a.   the marginal propensity to consume is zero.
   b.   the average propensity to consume is zero.
   c.   consumption and saving must be equal.
   d.   saving must be zero.

ANSWERS: 1.b, 2.c, 3.a, 4.d.

APC AND APS

average propensity to consume
The fraction (or percentage) of disposable income that households plan to spend for consumer goods and services.

average propensity to save
The fraction (or percentage) of disposable income that households save.

The fraction, or percentage, of total income that is consumed is the **average propensity to consume (APC)**. The fraction of total income that is saved is the **average propensity to save (APS)**. That is,

$$APC = \frac{consumption}{income}$$

and

$$APS = \frac{saving}{income}$$

For example, at $470 billion of income (row 6) in Table 7-1, the APC is 450/470 = 45/47, or about 96 percent, and the APS is 20/470 = 2/47, or about 4 percent. Columns 4 and 5 in Table 7-1 show the APC and APS at each of the 10 levels of DI; note in the table that the APC falls and the APS rises as DI increases, as was implied in our previous comments.

Because disposable income is either consumed or saved, the fraction of any DI consumed plus the fraction saved (not consumed) must exhaust that income. Mathematically,

$$APC + APS = 1$$

at any level of disposable income, as columns 4 and 5 in Table 7-1 illustrate.

Global Perspective 7.1 shows APCs for several countries.

MPC AND MPS

marginal propensity to consume
The fraction (or percentage) of any change in disposable income spent for consumer goods.

marginal propensity to save
The fraction (or percentage) of any change in disposable income that households save.

The proportion, or fraction, of any change in income consumed is called the **marginal propensity to consume (MPC)**, *marginal* meaning "extra" or "a change in." The MPC is the ratio of a change in consumption to the change in the income that caused the consumption change:

$$MPC = \frac{change\ in\ consumption}{change\ in\ income}$$

Similarly, the fraction of any change in income saved is the **marginal propensity to save (MPS)**. The MPS is the ratio of a change in saving to the change in income that brought it about:

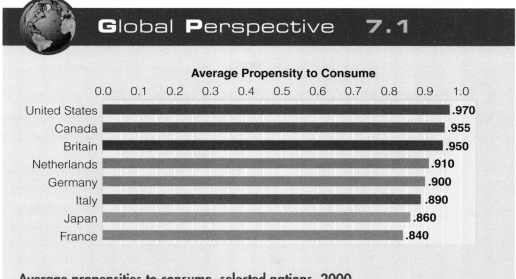

Average propensities to consume, selected nations, 2000.

There are surprisingly large differences in average propensities to consume (APCs) among nations. Canada and the United States in particular have substantially higher APCs, and thus lower APSs, than other advanced economies.

Source: *Statistical Abstract of the United States* 2002, p. 835 and author's calculations.

$$MPS = \frac{\text{change in saving}}{\text{change in income}}$$

If disposable income is \$470 billion (row 6 horizontally in Table 7-1) and household income rises by \$20 billion to \$490 billion (row 7), households will consume $^{15}/_{20}$, or $^{3}/_{4}$, and save $^{5}/_{20}$, or $^{1}/_{4}$, of that increase in income. In other words, the MPC is $^{3}/_{4}$ or .75, and the MPS is $^{1}/_{4}$ or .25, as shown in columns 6 and 7.

The sum of the MPC and the MPS for any change in disposable income must always be 1. Consuming or saving out of extra income is an either-or proposition; the fraction of any change in income not consumed is, by definition, saved. Therefore the fraction consumed (MPC) plus the fraction saved (MPS) must exhaust the whole change in income:

$$MPC + MPS = 1$$

In our example, .75 plus .25 equals 1.

MPC AND MPS AS SLOPES

The MPC is the numerical value of the slope of the consumption schedule, and the MPS is the numerical value of the slope of the saving schedule. We know from the appendix to Chapter 1 that the slope of any line is the ratio of the vertical change to the horizontal change.

Figure 7-3 shows how the slopes of the consumption and saving lines are calculated, using enlarged portions of Figures 7-2a and 7-2b. Observe that consumption changes by \$15 billion (vertical change) for each \$20 billion change in disposable income (horizontal change). The slope of the consumption line is thus .75 (= \$15/\$20)—the value of the MPC. Saving changes by \$5 billion (vertical change) for every \$20 billion change in disposable income (horizontal change). The slope of the saving line therefore is .25 (= \$5/\$20), which is the value of the MPS. *(Key Question 5)*

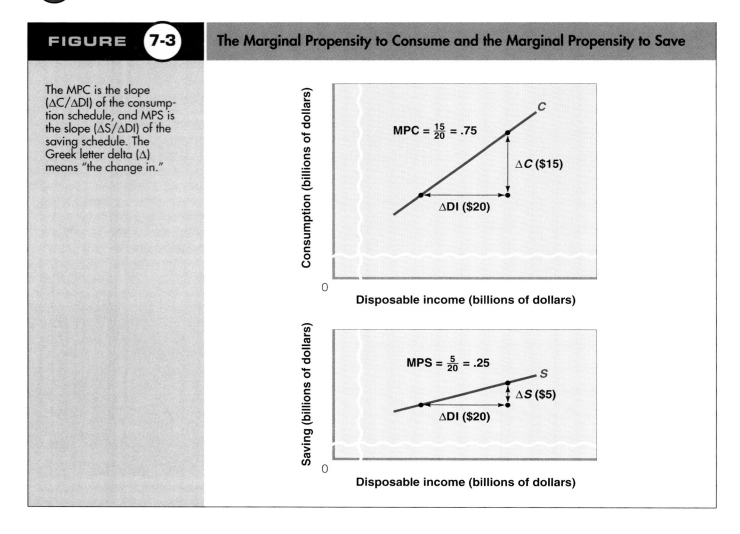

FIGURE 7-3 | **The Marginal Propensity to Consume and the Marginal Propensity to Save**

The MPC is the slope (ΔC/ΔDI) of the consumption schedule, and MPS is the slope (ΔS/ΔDI) of the saving schedule. The Greek letter delta (Δ) means "the change in."

Non-Income Determinants of Consumption and Saving

The amount of disposable income is the main determinant of the amounts households will consume and save. But certain determinants other than income will cause households to consume more or less at each possible level of income and thereby shift the consumption and saving schedules. Those other determinants are wealth, expectations, interest rates, indebtedness, and taxation.

WEALTH

wealth effect
A downward shift of the saving schedule and an upward shift of the consumption schedule due to higher asset wealth.

The amount that households spend and save from current income depends partly on the value of the existing wealth they have already accumulated. By "wealth" we mean the value of both real assets (for example, houses, land) and financial assets (for example, cash, savings accounts, stocks, bonds, pensions) that households own. Households save to accumulate wealth. When events increase the value of existing wealth, households increase their spending and reduce their saving. This so-called **wealth effect** shifts the *consumption schedule upward and the saving schedule downward*. Examples: In the late 1990s, rising stock values expanded the value of household wealth. Predictably, households spent more and saved less. In contrast, a "reverse wealth effect" occurred in 2000 and 2001 when stock prices fell sharply.

Expectations of rising prices tomorrow may trigger more spending and less saving today.

EXPECTATIONS

Household expectations about future prices and income affect current spending and saving. For example, expectations of rising prices tomorrow may trigger more spending and less saving today. Thus, the current consumption schedule shifts up and the current saving schedule shifts down. Or, expectations of lower income in the future may result in less consumption and more saving today. If so, the consumption schedule will shift down and saving schedule will shift up.

REAL INTEREST RATES

When real interest rates (those adjusted for inflation) fall, households tend to borrow more, consume more, and save less. A lower interest rate, for example, induces consumers to purchase automobiles and other goods bought on credit. A lower interest rate also diminishes the incentive to save because of the reduced interest "payment" to the saver. These effects on consumption and saving, however, are very modest. Lower interest rates shift the consumption schedule slightly upward and the saving schedule slightly downward. Higher interest rates do the opposite.

HOUSEHOLD DEBT

In drawing a particular consumption schedule, we hold household debt as a percentage of DI constant. But when consumers as a group initially increase their household debt, they can increase current consumption. Increased borrowing enables consumers to increase consumption at each level of DI; it shifts the consumption schedule upward. But when levels of household debt get abnormally high, households may decide to reduce their consumption to pay off some of their loans. At that time, the consumption schedule shifts downward.

TAXATION

Changes in taxes shift the consumption and saving schedules. Taxes are paid partly at the expense of consumption and partly at the expense of saving. So, an increase in taxes will shift both the consumption and saving schedules downward. Conversely, a tax reduction will be partly consumed and partly saved by households. A tax decrease will shift both the consumption and saving schedules upward.

Terminology, Shifts, and Stability

There are several additional points we need to make about the consumption and saving schedules:

- **Terminology**   The movement from one point to another on a consumption schedule (for example, from a to b on C_0 in Figure 7-4a)—a *change in the amount consumed*—is solely caused by a change in disposable income (or GDP). On the other hand, an upward or downward shift of the entire schedule—for example, a shift from C_0 to C_1 or C_2 in Figure 7-4a—is caused by changes in any one or more of the five *non-income* determinants of consumption just discussed.

   A similar distinction in terminology applies to the saving schedule in Figure 7-4b.

- **Schedule shifts**   Changes in wealth, expectations, real interest rates, and household debt will shift the consumption schedule in one direction and the saving schedule in the opposite direction. If households decide to consume more at each possible level of disposable income, they want to save less, and vice versa. (Even when they spend more by borrowing, they are, in effect, reducing their current saving by the amount borrowed.) Graphically, if the consumption schedule shifts from C_0 to C_1 in Figure 7-4a, the saving schedule will shift downward, from S_0 to S_1 in Figure 7-4b. Similarly, a downward shift of the consumption schedule from C_0 to C_2 means an upward shift of the saving schedule from S_0 to S_2.

   In contrast, a change in taxes will result in the consumption and saving schedules both moving in the same direction. A tax increase causes both schedules to shift downward and a tax decrease does just the opposite.

- **Stability**   Although changes in non-income determinants can shift the consumption and saving schedules, usually these schedules are relatively stable. Their stability may be because con-

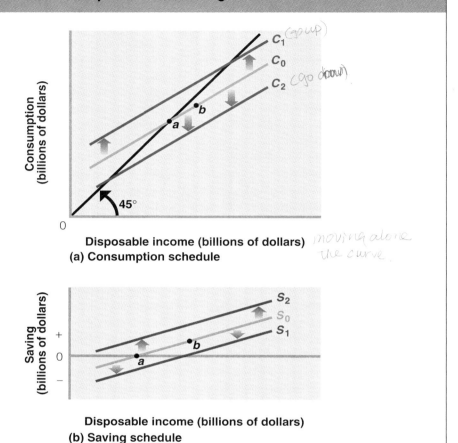

FIGURE 7-4 Shifts in the (A) Consumption and (B) Saving Schedules

Normally, if households consume more at each level of DI, they are necessarily saving less. Graphically this means that an upward shift of the consumption schedule (C_0 to C_1) entails a downward shift of the saving schedule (S_0 to S_1). If households consume less at each level of DI, they are saving more. A downward shift of the consumption schedule (C_0 to C_2) is reflected in an upward shift of the saving schedule (S_0 to S_2). (This pattern breaks down, however, when taxes change; then the consumption and saving schedules shift in the *same* direction—opposite to the direction of the tax change.)

sumption-saving decisions are strongly influenced by long-term considerations such as saving to meet emergencies or saving for retirement. It may also be because changes in the non-income determinants frequently work in opposite directions and therefore may cancel each other out.

QUICK REVIEW

- Both consumption spending and saving rise when disposable income increases; both fall when disposable income decreases.

- The average propensity to consume (APC) is the fraction of disposable income that is spent on consumer goods; the average propensity to save (APS) is the fraction of disposable income that is saved. The APC falls and the APS rises as disposable income increases.

- The marginal propensity to consume (MPC) is the fraction of a change in disposable income that is consumed and is the slope of the consumption schedule; the marginal propensity to save (MPS) is the fraction of a change in disposable income that is saved and is the slope of the saving schedule.

- Changes in consumer wealth, consumer expectations, interest rates, household debt, and taxes can shift the consumption and saving schedules.

7.2   Investment

Recall that investment consists of expenditures on new plants, capital equipment, machinery, inventories, and so on. The investment decision is a marginal-benefit–marginal-cost decision: The marginal benefit from investment is the expected rate of return businesses hope to realize. The marginal cost is the interest rate that must be paid for borrowing funds. We will see that businesses will invest in all projects for which the expected rate of return exceeds the interest rate. Expected returns (profits) and the interest rate therefore are the two basic determinants of investment spending.

Expected Rate of Return

Investment spending is guided by the profit motive; businesses buy capital goods only when such purchases will be profitable. Suppose the owner of a small cabinet-making shop is considering whether or not to invest in a new sanding machine that costs $1000 and has a useful life of only one year. The new machine will increase the firm's output and sales revenue. Suppose the net expected revenue from the machine (that is, after such operating costs as power, lumber, labour, and certain taxes have been subtracted) is $1100. Then, after operating costs have been accounted for, the remaining expected net revenue is sufficient to cover the $1000 cost of the machine and leave a profit of $100. Comparing this $100 profit with the $1000 cost of the machine, we find that the **expected rate of return**, r, on the machine is 10 percent (= $100/$1000). (The computation gets more complex when the return occurs over several years, but the concept remains the same.)

expected rate of return
The increase in profit a firm anticipates it will obtain by purchasing capital.

The Real Interest Rate

One important cost associated with investing that our example has ignored is interest—the financial cost of borrowing the *money* "capital" required to purchase the *real* capital (the sanding machine).

The interest cost is computed by applying the interest rate, i, to the amount borrowed—the cost of the machine. The cost of the machine is the same amount that we used to compute the rate of return, r. Thus, we can generalize as follows: If the expected rate of return (say, 10 percent) exceeds the interest rate (say, 7 percent), the investment will be profitable. But if the interest rate (say, 12 percent) exceeds the expected rate of return (10 percent), the investment will be unprofitable. The firm undertakes all profitable investment projects. That means it invests up to the point where $r = i$, because then it has undertaken all investment for which r exceeds i.

This guideline applies even if a firm finances the investment internally out of funds saved from past profit rather than borrowing the funds. The role of the interest rate in the investment decision does not change. When the firm uses money from savings to invest in the sander, it incurs an opportunity cost because it forgoes the interest income it could have earned by lending the funds to someone else. That interest cost, converted to percentage terms, needs to be weighed against the expected rate of return.

The *real* rate of interest, rather than the *nominal* rate, is crucial in making investment decisions. Recall from Chapter 6 that the nominal interest rate is expressed in dollars of current value, but the real interest rate is stated in dollars of constant or inflation-adjusted value. The *real interest rate* is the nominal rate less the rate of inflation. In our sanding machine illustration, our implicit assumption of a constant price level ensures that all our data, including the interest rate, are in real terms.

But what if inflation *is* occurring? Suppose a $1000 investment is expected to yield a real (inflation-adjusted) rate of return of 10 percent and the nominal interest rate is 15 percent. At first, we would say the investment would be unprofitable. But assume there is ongoing inflation of 10 percent per year. This means the investing firm will pay back dollars with approximately 10 percent less in purchasing power. While the nominal interest rate is 15 percent, the real rate is only 5 percent (= 15 percent – 10 percent). By comparing this 5 percent real interest rate with the 10 percent expected real rate of return, we find that the investment is profitable and should be undertaken. *(Key Question 7)*

TABLE 7-2	Rates of Expected Return and Investment
Expected rate of return (r)	**Cumulative amount of investment having this rate of return or higher, billions per year**
16%	$ 0
14	5
12	10
10	15
8	20
6	25
4	30
2	35
0	40

Investment Demand Curve

We now move from a single firm's investment decision to total demand for investment goods by the entire business sector. Assume that every firm has estimated the expected rates of return from all investment projects and has recorded those data. We can cumulate—successively sum—these data by asking: How many dollars' worth of investment projects have an expected rate of return of, say, 16 percent or more? Of 14 percent or more? Of 12 percent or more? And so on.

Suppose there are no prospective investments that yield an expected return of 16 percent or more. But suppose there are $5 billion of investment opportunities with expected rates of return between 14 and 16 percent; an additional $5 billion yielding between 12 and 14 percent; still an additional $5 billion yielding between 10 and 12 percent; and an additional $5 billion in each successive 2-percent range of yield down to and including the 0 to 2-percent range.

To cumulate these figures for each rate of return, r, we add the amounts of investment that will yield each particular rate of return r or higher. In this way we obtain the data in Table 7-2, shown graphically in **Figure 7-5 (Key Graph)**. In Table 7-2 the number opposite 12 percent, for example, tells us there are $10 billion of investment opportunities that will yield an expected rate of return of 12 percent or more. The $10 billion includes the $5 billion of investment expected to yield a return of 14 percent or more plus the $5 billion expected to yield between 12 and 14 percent.

We know from our example of the sanding machine that an investment project will be profitable, and will be undertaken, if its expected rate of return, r, exceeds the real interest rate, i. Let's first suppose i is 12 percent. Businesses will undertake all investments for which r is equal to or exceeds 12 percent. Figure 7-5 reveals that $10 billion of investment spending will be undertaken at a 12 percent interest rate; that means $10 billion of investment projects have an expected rate of return of 12 percent or more.

By applying the marginal-benefit–marginal-cost rule that investment projects should be undertaken up to the point where $r = i$, we see that we can add the real interest rate to the vertical axis in Figure 7-5. The curve in Figure 7-5 not only shows rates of return, it shows the quantity of investment demanded at each "price" i (interest rate) of investment. The vertical axis in Figure 7-5 shows the various possible real interest rates, and the horizontal axis shows the corresponding quantities of investment demanded. The inverse (downward-sloping) relationship between the interest rate (price) and dollar quantity of investment demanded conforms with the law of demand discussed in Chapter 3. The curve *ID* in Figure 7-5 is the economy's **investment demand curve**. It shows the amount of investment forthcoming at each real interest rate. *(Key Question 8)*

investment demand curve
A curve that shows the amount of investment demanded by an economy at a series of real interest rates.

Shifts in the Investment Demand Curve

Figure 7-5 shows the relationship between the interest rate and the amount of investment demanded, other things equal. When other things change, the investment demand curve shifts. In general, any factor that leads businesses collectively to expect greater rates of return on their investments increases investment demand; that factor shifts the investment demand curve to the right, as from ID_0 to ID_1 in Figure 7-6. Any factor that leads businesses collectively to expect lower rates of return on their investments shifts the curve to the left, as from ID_0 to ID_2. What are those non-interest-rate determinants of investment demand?

ACQUISITION, MAINTENANCE, AND OPERATING COSTS

The initial costs of capital goods, and the estimated costs of operating and maintaining those goods, affect the expected rate of return on investment. When costs fall, the expected rate of return from

Key Graph

FIGURE 7-5 The Investment Demand Curve

The investment demand curve is constructed by arraying all potential investment projects in descending order of their expected rates of return. The curve is downward-sloping, reflecting an inverse relationship between the real interest rate (the financial "price" of each dollar of investing) and the quantity of investment demanded.

Bank & Govt ?

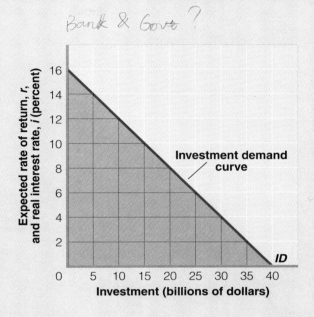

Quick Quiz

1. The investment demand curve:
   a. reflects a direct (positive) relationship between the real interest rate and investment.
   b. reflects an inverse (negative) relationship between the real interest rate and investment.
   c. shifts to the right when the real interest rate rises.
   d. shifts to the left when the real interest rate rises.

2. In this figure:
   a. greater cumulative amounts of investment are associated with lower expected rates of return on investment.
   b. lesser cumulative amounts of investment are associated with lower expected rates of return on investment.
   c. higher interest rates are associated with higher expected rates of return on investment, and therefore greater amounts of investment.
   d. interest rates and investment move in the same direction.

3. In this figure, if the real interest rate falls from 6 to 4 percent:
   a. investment will increase from 0 to $30 billion.
   b. investment will decrease by $5 billion.
   c. the expected rate of return will rise by $5 billion.
   d. investment will increase from $25 billion to $30 billion.

4. In this figure, investment will be:
   a. zero if the real interest rate is zero.
   b. $40 billion if the real interest rate is 16 percent.
   c. $30 billion if the real interest rate is 4 percent.
   d. $20 billion if the real interest rate is 12 percent.

ANSWERS: 1. b; 2. a; 3. d; 4. c

FIGURE 7-6	**Shifts in the Investment Demand Curve**

Increases in investment demand are shown as rightward shifts in the investment demand curve; decreases in investment demand are shown as leftward shifts in the investment demand curve.

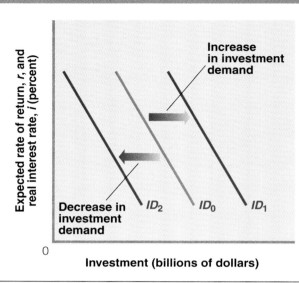

prospective investment projects rises, shifting the investment demand curve to the right. Example: Lower electricity costs associated with operating equipment shifts the investment demand curve to the right. Higher costs, in contrast, shift the curve to the left.

BUSINESS TAXES

When government is considered, firms look to expected returns *after taxes* in making their investment decisions. An increase in business taxes lowers the expected profitability of investments and shifts the investment demand curve to the left; a reduction of business taxes shifts it to the right.

TECHNOLOGICAL CHANGE

Technological progress—the development of new products, improvements in existing products, and the creation of new machinery and production processes—stimulates investment. The development of a more efficient machine, for example, lowers production costs or improves product quality and increases the expected rate of return from investing in the machine. Profitable new products (for example, cholesterol medications, Internet services, high-resolution televisions, cellular phones, and so on) induce a flurry of investment as firms tool up for expanded production. A rapid rate of technological progress shifts the investment demand curve to the right.

Technological progress stimulates investment.

STOCK OF CAPITAL GOODS ON HAND

The stock of capital goods on hand, relative to output and sales, influences investment decisions by firms. When the economy is overstocked with production facilities and when firms have excessive inventories of finished goods, the expected rate of return on new investment declines. Firms with excess production capacity have little incentive to invest in new capital. Therefore, less investment is forthcoming at each real interest rate; the investment demand curve shifts leftward.

When the economy is understocked with production facilities and when firms are selling their output as fast as they can produce it, the expected rate of return on new investment increases and the investment demand curve shifts rightward.

EXPECTATIONS

We noted that business investment is based on expected returns (expected additions to profit). Most capital goods are durable, with a life expectancy of 10 or 20 years. Thus, the expected rate of return on capital investment depends on the firm's expectations of future sales, future operating costs, and future profitability of the product that the capital helps to produce. These expectations are based on forecasts of future business conditions as well as on such elusive and difficult-to-predict factors as changes in the domestic political climate, the thrust of foreign affairs, population growth, and consumer tastes. If executives become more optimistic about future sales, costs, and profits, the investment demand curve will shift to the right; a pessimistic outlook will shift it to the left.

Global Perspective 7.2 compares investment spending relative to GDP for several nations in a recent year. Domestic real interest rates and investment demand determine the levels of investment relative to GDP.

QUICK REVIEW

- A specific investment will be undertaken if the expected rate of return, r, equals or exceeds the real interest rate, i.

- The investment demand curve shows the total monetary amounts that will be invested by an economy at various possible real interest rates.

- The investment demand curve shifts when changes occur in (a) the costs of acquiring, operating, and maintaining capital goods, (b) business taxes, (c) technology, (d) the stock of capital goods on hand, and (e) business expectations.

Investment Schedule

To add the investment decisions of businesses to the consumption plans of households, we must express investment plans in terms of the level of disposable income (DI) or gross domestic product (GDP). That is, we need to construct an investment schedule showing the amounts business

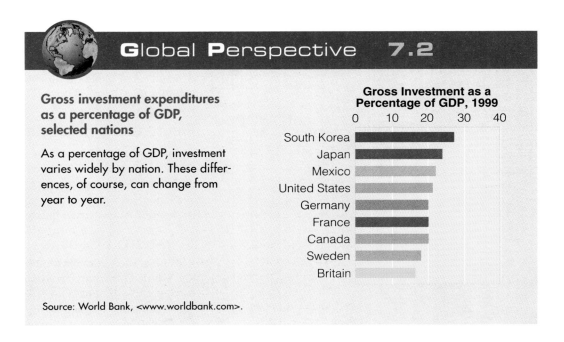

Global Perspective 7.2

Gross investment expenditures as a percentage of GDP, selected nations

As a percentage of GDP, investment varies widely by nation. These differences, of course, can change from year to year.

Gross Investment as a Percentage of GDP, 1999

South Korea	
Japan	
Mexico	
United States	
Germany	
France	
Canada	
Sweden	
Britain	

Source: World Bank, <www.worldbank.com>.

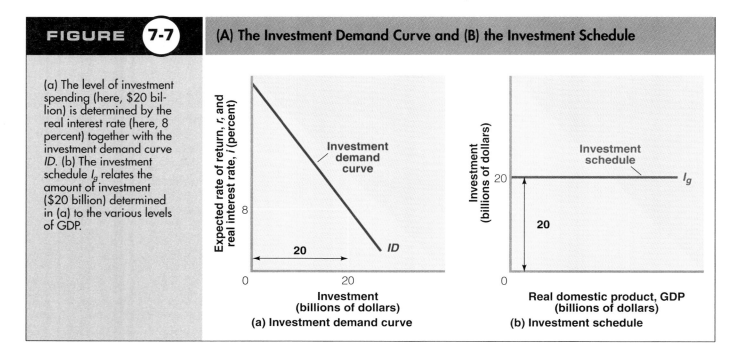

FIGURE 7-7 (A) The Investment Demand Curve and (B) the Investment Schedule

(a) The level of investment spending (here, $20 billion) is determined by the real interest rate (here, 8 percent) together with the investment demand curve ID. (b) The investment schedule I_g relates the amount of investment ($20 billion) determined in (a) to the various levels of GDP.

(a) Investment demand curve

(b) Investment schedule

firms collectively intend to invest at each possible level of GDP. Such a schedule represents the investment plans of businesses in the same way the consumption schedule represents the consumption plans of households. In developing the investment schedule, we will assume that this **planned investment** is independent of the level of current disposable income or real output.

Suppose the investment demand curve is as shown in Figure 7-7a and the current real interest rate is 8 percent. This means that firms will find it profitable to spend $20 billion on investment goods. The line I_g (*gross* investment) in Figure 7-7b shows the economy's **investment schedule**. You should not confuse this investment schedule I_g with the investment demand curve ID in Figure 7-7a. The investment schedule shows the amount of investment forthcoming at each level of GDP. As indicated in Figure 7-7, this amount ($20 billion) is determined by the interest rate together with the location of the investment demand curve. Table 7-3 shows the investment schedule in tabular form for the GDP levels in Table 7-1.

planned investment
The amount that firms plan or intend to invest.

investment schedule
A curve or schedule that shows the amounts firms plan to invest at various possible values of real GDP.

Fluctuations of Investment

In contrast to the consumption schedule, the investment schedule fluctuates quite a bit. Investment, in fact, is the most volatile component of total spending, as the Canadian investment data since 1965 in Figure 7.8 shows.

Several factors explain the variability of investment:

DURABILITY

Because of their durability, capital goods have an indefinite useful life. Within limits, purchases of capital goods are discretionary and therefore can be postponed. Firms can scrap or replace older equipment and buildings, or they can patch them up and use them for a few more years. Optimism about the future may prompt

TABLE 7-3 The Investment Schedule (in Billions)

(1) Level of real output and income	(2) Investment (I_g)
$370	$20
390	20
410	20
430	20
450	20
470	20
490	20
510	20
530	20
550	20

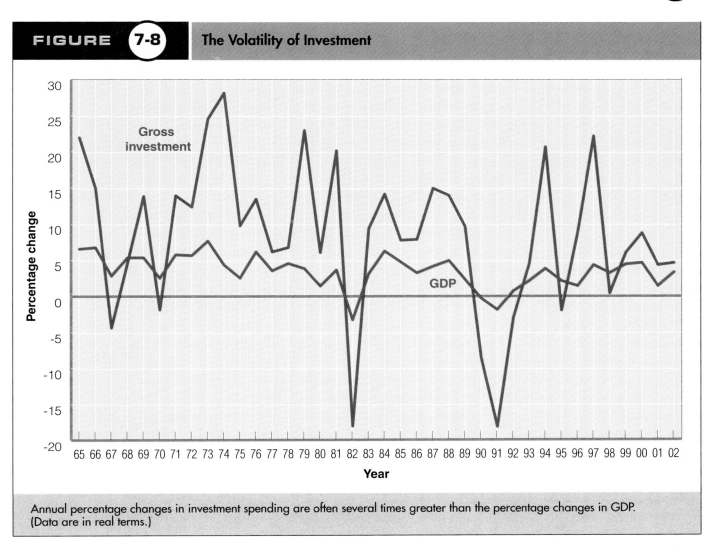

FIGURE 7-8   The Volatility of Investment

Annual percentage changes in investment spending are often several times greater than the percentage changes in GDP. (Data are in real terms.)

firms to replace their older facilities, and such modernizing will call for a high level of investment. A less optimistic view, however, may lead to smaller amounts of investment as firms repair older facilities and keep them in use.

IRREGULARITY OF INNOVATION

We know that technological progress is a major determinant of investment. New products and processes stimulate investment. But history suggests that major innovations such as railroads, electricity, automobiles, fibre optics, and computers occur quite irregularly. When they do happen, they induce a vast upsurge or "wave" of investment spending which in time recedes.

A contemporary example is the widespread acceptance of the personal computer and Internet, which has caused a wave of investment in those industries and in many related industries such as fibre optics, computer software and electronic commerce. Some time in the future, this surge of investment undoubtedly will level off. For example, the rapid expansion of fibre optics networks came to a virtual halt in 2001 and 2002 as overcapacity dogged the sector, with dire consequences for such well known Canadian firms as Nortel Networks and JDS Uniphase.

VARIABILITY OF PROFITS

The expectation of future profitability is influenced to some degree by the size of current profits. Current profits, however, are themselves highly variable. Thus, the variability of profits contributes to the volatile nature of the incentive to invest.

The fluctuations of profits may cause investment fluctuations in a second way. Profits are a major source of funds for business investment. Canadian businesses sometimes prefer this internal source of financing to increases in external debt or stock issue.

In short, expanding profits give firms both greater incentives and greater means to invest; declining profits have the reverse effects. The fact that actual profits are variable thus adds doubly to the fluctuation of investment.

VARIABILITY OF EXPECTATIONS

Firms tend to project current business conditions into the future. But their expectations can change quickly when some event suggests a significant possible change in future business conditions. Changes in exchange rates, changes in the outlook for international peace, court decisions in key labour or anti-combines cases, legislative actions, changes in trade barriers, changes in governmental economic policies, and a host of similar considerations may cause substantial shifts in business expectations.

The stock market can influence business expectations because firms look to it as one of several indicators of society's overall confidence in future business conditions. Rising stock prices tend to signify public confidence in the business future, whereas falling stock prices may imply a lack of confidence. The stock market, however, is quite speculative. Some participants buy when stock prices begin to rise and sell as soon as prices begin to fall. This behaviour can magnify what otherwise would be modest changes in stock prices. By creating swings in optimism and pessimism, the stock market may add to the instability of investment spending.

For all these reasons, changes in investment cause many of the fluctuations in output and employment. In terms of Figures 7.5 and 7.6, we would represent volatility of investment as occasional and substantial shifts in the investment demand curve.

7.3   Equilibrium GDP

Now let's combine the consumption and investment schedules to explain the equilibrium levels of output, income, and employment.

Tabular Analysis

Columns 2 through 5 in Table 7-4 repeat the consumption and saving schedules in Table 7-1 and the investment schedule in Table 7-3.

REAL DOMESTIC OUTPUT

Column 2 in Table 7-4 lists the various possible levels of total output—of real GDP—that the private sector might produce. Producers are willing to offer any of these 10 levels of output if they can expect to receive an identical level of income from the sale of that output. For example, firms will produce $370 billion of output, incurring $370 billion of costs (wages, rents, interest, and normal profit costs) only if they believe they can sell that output for $370 billion. Firms will offer $390 billion of output if they think they can sell that output for $390 billion. And so it is for all other possible levels of output.

AGGREGATE EXPENDITURES

In the private closed economy of Table 7-4, aggregate expenditures consist of consumption (column 3) plus investment (column 5). Their sum is shown in column 6, which with column 2 makes

TABLE 7-4	Determination of the Equilibrium Levels of Employment, Output, and Income: A Private Closed Economy						
(1) Possible levels of employment, millions	(2) Real domestic output (and income)(GDP = DI), billions	(3) Consumption (C), billions	(4) Saving (S), billions	(5) Investment (I_g), billions	(6) Aggregate expenditures (C + I_g), billions	(7) Unplanned changes in inventories (+) or (−)	(8) Tendency of employment, output, and income
(1) 2.5	$370	$375	$−5	$20	$395	$−25	Increase
(2) 5.0	390	390	0	20	410	−20	Increase
(3) 7.5	410	405	5	20	425	−15	Increase
(4) 10.0	430	420	10	20	440	−10	Increase
(5) 12.5	450	435	15	20	455	− 5	Increase
(6) 15.0	**470**	**450**	**20**	**20**	**470**	**0**	**Equilibrium**
(7) 17.5	490	465	25	20	485	+ 5	Decrease
(8) 20.0	510	480	30	20	500	+10	Decrease
(9) 22.5	530	495	35	20	515	+15	Decrease
(10) 25.0	550	510	40	20	530	+20	Decrease

aggregate expenditures schedule
A schedule or curve that shows the total amount spent for final goods and services at different levels of GDP.

up the **aggregate expenditures schedule** for the economy. This schedule shows the amount (C + I_g) that will be spent at each possible output or income level.

At this point we are working with *planned investment*—the data in column 5, Table 7-4. These data show the amounts firms intend to invest if there are unplanned changes in inventories. More about that shortly.

EQUILIBRIUM GDP

Of the 10 possible levels of GDP in Table 7-4, which is the equilibrium level? Which total output is the economy capable of sustaining?

The equilibrium output is that output which creates total spending just sufficient to produce that output. So the equilibrium level of GDP is the level at which the total quantity of goods produced (GDP) equals the total quantity of goods purchased (C + I_g). If you look at the domestic output levels in column 2 and the aggregate expenditures level in column 6, you will see that this equality exists only at $470 billion of GDP (row 6). There is no overproduction, which would result in a piling up of unsold goods and consequently cutbacks in the production rate. Nor is there an excess of total spending, which would draw down inventories of goods and prompt increases in the rate of production. In short, there is no reason for businesses to alter this rate of production; $470 billion is the **equilibrium GDP**.

equilibrium GDP
The level at which the total quantity of goods produced (GDP) equals the total quantity of goods purchased.

DISEQUILIBRIUM

No level of GDP other than the equilibrium level of GDP can be sustained. At levels of GDP *below* equilibrium, spending is higher than output. If, for example, firms produced $410 billion of GDP (row 3 in Table 7-4), they would find it would yield $405 billion in consumer spending. Supplemented by $20 billion of planned investment, aggregate expenditures (C + I_g) would be $425 billion, as shown in column 6. The economy would provide an annual rate of spending more than sufficient to purchase the $410 billion of annual production. Because buyers would be taking goods off the shelves faster than firms could produce them, an unintended decline in business inventories of $15 billion would occur (column 7). But businesses can adjust to such an imbalance between aggregate expenditures and real output by stepping up production. Greater output will increase employment and total income. This process will continue until the equilibrium level of GDP is reached ($470 billion).

The reverse is true at all levels of GDP above the $470 billion equilibrium level. Businesses will find that these total outputs fail to generate the spending needed to clear the shelves of goods.

Graphical Analysis

We can demonstrate the same analysis graphically in **Figure 7-9 (Key Graph)**. Recall that at any point on the 45° line, the value of what is being measured on the horizontal axis (here, GDP) is equal to the value of what is being measured on the vertical axis (here, aggregate expenditures, or $C + I_g$). Having discovered in our tabular analysis that the equilibrium level of domestic output is determined where $C + I_g$ equals GDP, we can say that the 45° line in Figure 7-9 is a graphical statement of that equilibrium condition.

Now we must graph the aggregate expenditures schedule onto Figure 7-9. To do this we duplicate the consumption schedule C in Figure 7-7a and add to it vertically the constant $20 billion amount of investment I_g from Figure 7-7b. This $20 billion is the amount we assumed firms plan to invest at all levels of GDP. Or, more directly, we can plot the $C + I_g$ data in column 6, Table 7-4.

Observe in Figure 7-9 that the aggregate expenditures line $C + I_g$ shows that total spending rises with income and output (GDP), but not as much as income rises. That is true because the marginal propensity to consume—the slope of line C—is less than 1. A part of any increase in income will be saved rather than spent. And because the aggregate expenditures line $C + I_g$ is parallel to the consumption line C, the slope of the aggregate expenditures line also equals the MPC for the economy and is less than 1. For our particular data, aggregate expenditures rise by $15 billion for every $20 billion increase in real output and income because $5 billion of each $20 billion increment is saved. Therefore, the slope of the aggregate expenditures line is .75 (= $\Delta\$15/\Delta\$20$).

The equilibrium level of GDP is determined by the intersection of the aggregate expenditures schedule and the 45° line. This intersection locates the only point at which aggregate expenditures (on the vertical axis) are equal to GDP (on the horizontal axis). Because Figure 7-9 is based on the data in Table 7-4, we once again find that equilibrium output is $470 billion. Observe that consumption at this output is $450 billion and investment is $20 billion.

It is evident from Figure 7-8 that no levels of GDP *above* the equilibrium level are sustainable because at those levels $C + I_g$ falls short of GDP. Underspending causes *inventories to rise*, prompting firms to readjust production downward in the direction of the $470 billion output level.

Conversely, at levels of GDP *below* $470 billion, $C + I_g$ exceeds total output. This overspending causes *inventories to decline*, prompting firms to raise production toward the $470 billion GDP.

Other Features of Equilibrium GDP

We have seen that $C + I_g$ = GDP at equilibrium in the private closed economy. A closer look at Table 7-4 reveals two more characteristics of equilibrium GDP:

• Saving and planned investment are equal.

• There are no unplanned changes in inventories.

Saving Equals Planned Investment

As shown by row 6 in Table 7-4, saving and planned investment are both $20 billion at the $470 billion equilibrium level of GDP.

leakage
A withdrawal of potential spending from the income-expenditures stream via saving, tax payments, or imports.

Savings is a **leakage** or withdrawal of spending from the income-expenditures stream. Saving is what causes consumption to be less than total output or GDP. As a result of saving, consumption is insufficient to take all domestic output off the shelves, setting the stage for a decline in total output.

However, firms do not intend to sell their entire output to consumers; some domestic output will consist of capital goods sold within the business sector. Investment can therefore be thought of as an **injection** of spending into the income-expenditures stream. Investment is thus a potential replacement for the leakage of saving.

injection
An addition of spending to the income-expenditure stream.

Key Graph

FIGURE 7-9 Equilibrium GDP

The aggregate expenditures schedule, $C + I_g$, is determined by adding the investment schedule I_g to the upward-sloping consumption schedule C. Since investment is assumed to be the same at each level of GDP, the vertical distances between C and $C + I_g$ do not change. Equilibrium GDP is determined where the aggregate expenditures schedule intersects the 45-degree line, in this case at $470 billion.

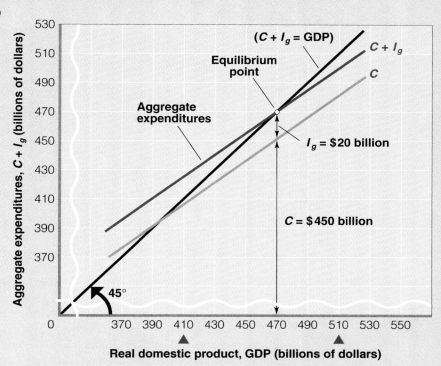

Quick Quiz

1. **In this figure, the slope of the aggregate expenditures schedule $C + I_g$:**
   a. increases as real GDP increases.
   b. decreases as real GDP increases.
   c. is constant and equals the MPC.
   d. is constant and equals the MPS.

2. **At all points on the 45-degree line:**
   a. equilibrium GDP is possible.
   b. aggregate expenditures exceed real GDP.
   c. consumption exceeds investment
   d. aggregate expenditures are less than real GDP.

3. **The $490 billion level of real GDP is not at equilibrium because:**
   a. investment exceeds consumption.
   b. consumption exceeds investment.
   c. planned $C + I_g$ exceeds real GDP.
   d. planned $C + I_g$ is less than real GDP.

4. **The $430 billion level of real GDP is not at equilibrium because:**
   a. investment exceeds consumption.
   b. consumption exceeds investment.
   c. planned $C + I_g$ exceeds real GDP.
   d. planned $C + I_g$ is less than real GDP.

ANSWERS: 1. c; 2. a; 3. d; 4. c

If the leakage of saving at a certain level of GDP exceeds the injection of investment, then $C + I_g$ will fall short of GDP and that level of GDP cannot be sustained. Any GDP for which saving exceeds investment is an above-equilibrium GDP. This spending deficiency will reduce real GDP.

Conversely, if the injection of investment exceeds the leakage of saving, then $C + I_g$ will be greater than GDP and drive GDP upward. Any GDP for which investment exceeds saving is a below-equilibrium GDP. Only where $S = I_g$—where the leakage of saving of $20 billion is exactly offset by the injection of investment of $20 billion—will aggregate expenditures equal real output. And that $C + I_g$ = GDP equality is what defines the equilibrium GDP. *(Key Question 10)*

No Unplanned Changes in Inventories

As part of their investment plans, firms may decide to increase or decrease their inventories. But, as confirmed in row 6 in Table 7-4, there are no **unplanned changes in inventories** at equilibrium GDP. This fact, along with $C + I_g$ = GDP, and $S = I$, is a characteristic of equilibrium GDP in the private closed economy.

unplanned changes in inventory
Changes in inventories that firms did not anticipate.

Unplanned changes in inventories play a major role in achieving equilibrium GDP. Consider, as an example, the $490 billion *above-equilibrium* GDP shown in row 7 of Table 7-4. What happens if firms produce that output, thinking they can sell it? Households save $25 billion of their $490 billion DI, so consumption is only $465 billion. Planned investment (column 5) is $20 billion. This means that aggregate expenditures $(C + I_g)$ are $485 billion and sales fall short of production by $5 billion. Firms retain that extra $5 billion of goods as an unplanned increase in inventories (column 7). It results from total spending being less than the amount needed to remove total output from the shelves.

actual investment
The amount that firms do invest; equal to planned investment plus unplanned investment.

Because changes in inventories are a part of investment, we note that **actual investment** is $25 billion. It consists of $20 billion of planned investment *plus* the $5 billion unplanned increase in inventories. Actual investment exactly equals the saving of $25 billion, even though saving exceeds planned investment by $5 billion. Because firms cannot earn profits by accumulating unwanted inventories, they will cut back production. GDP will fall to its equilibrium level of $470, at which changes in inventories are zero.

Now look at the *below-equilibrium* $450 billion output (row 5, Table 7-4). Because households save only $15 billion of their $450 billion DI, consumption is $435 billion. Planned investment by firms is $20 billion, so aggregate expenditures are $455 billion. Sales exceed production by $5 billion. This is so only because a $5 billion unplanned decrease in business inventories has occurred. Firms must *disinvest* $5 billion in inventories (column 7). Note again that actual investment is $15 billion ($20 billion planned *minus* the $5 billion decline in inventory investment) and is equal to saving of $15 billion, even though planned investment exceeds saving by $5 billion. The unplanned decline in inventories, resulting from the excess of sales over production, will encourage firms to expand production. GDP will rise to $470 billion, at which unplanned changes in inventories are zero.

When economists say differences between investment and saving can occur and bring about changes in equilibrium GDP, they are referring to planned investment and saving. Equilibrium occurs only when planned investment and saving are equal. *But when unplanned changes in inventories are considered, investment and saving are always equal, regardless of the level of GDP.* That is true because actual investment consists of planned investment and unplanned investment (unplanned changes in inventories). Unplanned changes in inventories act as a balancing item that equates the actual amounts saved and invested in any period. *(Key Question 10)*

QUICK REVIEW

- In a private closed economy, equilibrium GDP occurs where aggregate expenditures equal real domestic output ($C + I_g$ = GDP).

- At equilibrium GDP, saving equals planned investment ($S = I_g$).

- At equilibrium GDP, unplanned changes in inventories are zero.

- Actual investment consists of planned investment plus unplanned changes in inventories (+ or −) and is always equal to saving in a private closed economy.

7.4　Changes in Equilibrium GDP and the Multiplier

In the private closed economy, the equilibrium GDP will change in response to changes in either the investment schedule or the consumption schedule. Because changes in the investment schedule usually are the main source of fluctuations, we will direct our attention to them.

Figure 7-10 shows the effect of changes in investment spending on the equilibrium real GDP. Suppose that the expected rate of return on investment rises or that the real interest rate falls. In either case, investment spending will rise—let's say by $5 billion. We would show this increase as an upward shift of the I_g schedule depicted in Figure 7-7b. In Figure 7-10, the $5 billion increase of investment will shift the aggregate expenditures schedule upward from $(C + I_g)_0$ to $(C + I_g)_1$. Equilibrium real GDP will rise from $470 billion to $490 billion.

The Multiplier Effect

Other things equal, there is a direct relationship between changes in spending and changes in real GDP. That is, more spending results in a higher GDP; less spending results in a lower GDP. But there is more to this relationship. You may have noticed that in our example a $5 billion change in investment spending causes a $20 billion change in output and income. That surprising result is called the *multiplier effect*: a change in a component of total spending leads to a larger change in GDP. The **multiplier** determines how much larger that change will be; it is the ratio of a change in GDP to the initial change in spending (in this case, investment). Stated generally,

multiplier
The ratio of a change in the equilibrium GDP to the change in investment or in any other component of aggregate expenditures.

$$\text{Multiplier} = \frac{\text{change in real GDP}}{\text{initial change in spending}}$$

FIGURE　7-10

Changes in the Equilibrium GDP Caused by Shifts in the Aggregate Expenditures Schedule and the Investment Schedule

An upward shift of the aggregate expenditures schedule from $(C + I_g)_0$ to $(C + I_g)_1$ will increase the equilibrium GDP. A downward shift from $(C + I_g)_0$ to $(C + I_g)_2$ will lower the equilibrium GDP.

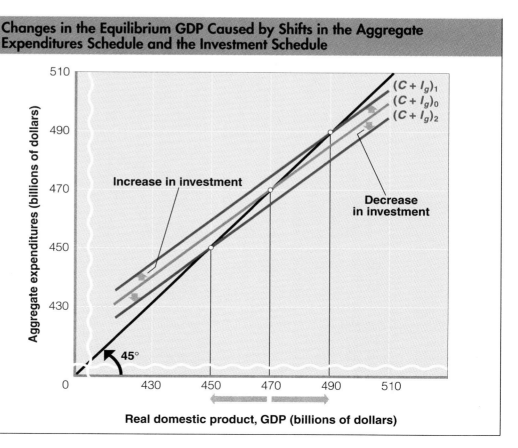

By rearranging this equation, we can also say that

Change in GDP = multiplier × initial change in spending

Note these three points about the multiplier:

- The "initial change in spending" is usually associated with investment spending because of investment's volatility. But changes in consumption (unrelated to changes in income), net exports, and government purchases also lead to the multiplier effect.
- The "initial change in spending" associated with investment spending results from either a change in the real interest rate and/or a shift of the investment demand curve.
- Implicit in the preceding point is that the multiplier works in both directions. An increase in initial spending may create a multiple increase in GDP, and a decrease in spending may be multiplied into a larger decrease in GDP.

RATIONALE

The multiplier effect follows from two facts. First, the economy supports repetitive, continuous flows of expenditures and income through which dollars spent by Smith are received as income by Chin and then spent by Chin and received as income by Dubois, and so on. Second, any change in income will vary both consumption and saving in the same direction as, and by a fraction of, the change in income.

It follows that an initial change in spending will set off a spending chain throughout the economy. That chain of spending, although of diminishing magnitude at each successive step, will cumulate to a multiple change in GDP. Initial changes in spending produce magnified changes in output and income.

Table 7-5 illustrates the rationale underlying the multiplier effect. Suppose that a $5 billion increase in investment spending occurs. We assume that the MPC is .75 and the MPS is .25.

The initial $5 billion increase in investment generates an equal amount of wage, rent, interest, and profit income, because spending income and receiving income are two sides of the same transaction. How much consumption will be induced by this $5 billion increase in the incomes of households? We find the answer by applying the marginal propensity to consume of .75 to this change in income. Thus, the $5 billion increase in income initially raises consumption by $3.75 (= .75 × $5) billion and saving by $1.25 (= .25 × $5) billion, as shown in columns 2 and 3 in Table 7-5.

Other households receive as income (second round) the $3.75 billion of consumption spending. Those households consume .75 of this $3.75 billion, or $2.81 billion, and save .25 of it, or $0.94 billion. The $2.81 billion that is consumed flows to still other households as income to be spent or saved (third round). And the process continues, with the added consumption and income becoming less in each round. The process ends when there is no more additional income to spend.

Figure 7-11 extends Table 7-5 and shows the cumulative effects of this full process. Each round adds an orange block to GDP. The accumulation of the additional income in each round—the sum of the orange blocks—is the total change in income or GDP. Although the spending and re-spending effects of the increase in investment diminish with each successive round of spending, the cumulative increase in output and income will be $20 billion. Thus, the multiplier is 4 (= $20 billion / $5 billion).

THE MULTIPLIER AND THE MARGINAL PROPENSITIES

You may have sensed from Table 7-5 that the fraction of an increase in income consumed (MPC) and saved (MPS)

TABLE 7-5	The Multiplier: A Tabular Illustration (in Billions)		
	(1) Change in income	(2) Change in consumption (MPC = .75)	(3) Change in saving (MPS = .25)
Increase in investment of $5.00	$ 5.00	$ 3.75	$1.25
Second round	3.75	2.81	0.94
Third round	2.81	2.11	0.70
Fourth round	2.11	1.58	0.53
Fifth round	1.58	1.19	0.39
All other rounds	4.75	3.56	1.19
Total	$20.00	$15.00	$5.00

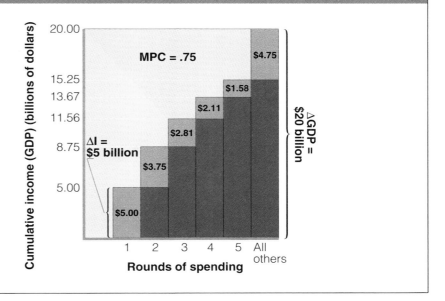

FIGURE 7-11

The Multiplier Process (MPC = .75)

An initial change in investment spending of $5 billion creates an equal $5 billion of new income in round 1. Households spend $3.75 (= .75 × $5) billion of this new income, creating $3.75 of added income in round 2. Of this $3.75 of new income, households spend $2.81 (= .75 × $3.75) billion, and income rises by that amount in round 3. The cumulation of such income increments over the entire process eventually results in a total change of income and GDP of $20 billion. The multiplier therefore is 4 (= $20 billion ÷ $5 billion).

determine the cumulative re-spending effects of any initial change in spending and therefore determines the size of the multiplier. *The MPC and the multiplier are directly related* and *the MPS and the multiplier are inversely related.* The precise formulas are as shown in the next two equations:

$$\text{Multiplier} = \frac{1}{1 - \text{MPC}}$$

Recall, too, that MPC + MPS = 1. Therefore MPS = 1 − MPC, which means we can also write the multiplier formula as

$$\text{Multiplier} = \frac{1}{\text{MPS}}$$

This latter formula is a quick way to determine the multiplier. All you need to know is the MPS.

The smaller the fraction of any change in income saved, the greater the respending at each round and, therefore, the greater the multiplier. When the MPS is .25, as in our example, the multiplier is 4. If the MPS were .2, the multiplier would be 5. If the MPS were .33, the multiplier would be 3. Let's see why.

Suppose the MPS is .2 and businesses increase investment by $5 billion. In the first round of Table 7-5, consumption will rise by $4.00 billion (= MPC of .8 × $5 billion) rather than by $3.75 billion because saving will increase by $1 billion (MPS of .2 × $5 billion) rather than $1.25 billion. The greater rise in consumption in round one will produce a greater increase in income in round two. The same will be true for all successive rounds. If we worked through all rounds of the multiplier, we would find that the process ends when income has cumulatively increased by $25 billion, not the $20 billion shown in the table. When the MPS is .2 rather than .25, the multiplier is 5 (= $25 billion/$5 billion) as opposed to 4 (= $20 billion/$5 billion.)

If the MPS were .33 rather than .25, the successive increases in consumption and income would be less than those in Table 7-5. We would discover that the process ended with a $15 billion increase in income rather than the $20 billion shown. When the MPS is .33, the multiplier is 3 (=$15 billion/$5 billion). The mathematics works such that the multiplier is equal to the reciprocal of the MPS. The reciprocal of any number is the quotient you obtain by dividing 1 by that number.

FIGURE 7-12   The MPC and the Multiplier

The larger the MPC (the smaller the MPS), the greater the size of the multiplier.

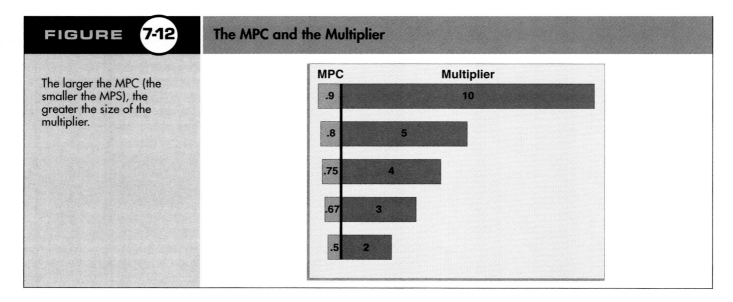

A large MPC (small MPS) means the succeeding rounds of consumption spending shown in Figure 7-3 diminish slowly and thereby cumulate to a large change in income. Conversely, a small MPC (a large MPS) causes the increases in consumption to decline quickly, so the cumulative change in income is small. The relationship between the MPC (and thus the MPS) and multiplier is summarized in Figure 7-12.

HOW LARGE IS THE ACTUAL MULTIPLIER EFFECT?

The multiplier we have just described is based on simplifying assumptions. Consumption of domestic output rises by the increases in income minus the increases in saving. But in reality, consumption of domestic output increases in each round by a lesser amount than implied by the MPS alone. In addition to saving, households use some of the extra income in each round to purchase additional goods from abroad (imports) and pay additional taxes. Because spending on imports and taxes do not directly create new income in the Canadian economy, the 1/MPS formula for the multiplier overstates the actual size of the multiplier effect. We can correct this problem by changing the multiplier equation to read: "1 divided by the fraction of the change in income that is not spent on domestic output." Also, we will find in later chapters that an increase in spending may be partly dissipated as inflation rather than realized fully as an increase in real GDP. That, too, reduces the size of the multiplier effect. (*Key Question 16*)

QUICK REVIEW

- The multiplier effect reveals that an initial change in spending can cause a larger change in domestic income and output. The multiplier is the factor by which the initial change is magnified: multiplier = change in real GDP/initial change in spending.

- The higher the marginal propensity to consume (the lower the marginal propensity to save), the larger the multiplier: multiplier = 1/MPS.

7.5   International Trade and Equilibrium Output

We next move from a "closed" economy to an "open" economy that incorporates exports (*X*) and imports (*M*). Our focus will be **net exports** (exports minus imports, or X_n), which may be positive or negative.

Net Exports and Aggregate Expenditures

Like consumption and investment, exports create domestic production, income, and employment for a nation. Foreign spending on Canadian goods and services increases production and creates jobs and incomes in Canada. We must therefore add exports as a component of each nation's aggregate expenditures.

Also, when an economy is open to international trade, part of its consumption and investment spending will be for imports—goods and services produced abroad rather than in domestic industries. To avoid overstating the value of domestic production, we must subtract expenditures on imports.

In short, for a closed economy, aggregate expenditures are $C + I_g$. But for an open economy with international trade, aggregate spending is $C + I_g + X_n$, where X_n represents $(X - M)$.

The Determinants of Imports and Exports and the Net Export Schedule

Note in Table 7-6 that exports are constant at all levels of GDP. This is because our exports are dependent on the GDPs of our trading partners. *If the GDP in other countries is growing, we can expect the demand for our exports to increase.* If GDP in the United States increases, we can expect that the U.S. will purchase more goods and services from Canada. For example, housing construction expands with the economy and, thus, if that sector were to expand in the United States, it would translate into higher sales of Canadian lumber. If the United States experiences a recession, our exports will decrease.

Our imports are dependent on our own GDP. When the Canadian economy expands, imports also rise. As the Canadian business sector expands and GDP rises, it will require machines and materials from abroad. Likewise, as consumer spending rises, some of it will go to imports.

Imports and exports are also affected by the exchange rate, the rate at which the Canadian dollar can be exchanged for other currencies.

marginal propensity to import
The fraction (or percentage) of any change in GDP spent for imported goods and services.

A *depreciation* of the Canadian dollar occurs when our currency buys fewer units of another currency or currencies. An *appreciation* of the Canadian dollar is the opposite: it occurs when the value of the Canadian dollar rises against other currencies.

Generally, an appreciation of the Canadian dollar will lead to a rise of imports and a decrease in exports, thus a decrease of net exports and aggregate expenditure. A depreciation of the Canadian dollar will increase net exports.

Imports and the Multiplier

A hypothetical *net export schedule* is shown in columns 1 to 4 of Table 7-6. Note that although exports are constant at all levels of GDP, imports, and therefore *net* exports $(X - M)$, change by $5 billion for every $20 billion change in GDP. The change in imports divided by a change in GDP is called the **marginal propensity to import** (MPM). In our example the marginal propensity to import is 0.25 (= $5 billion/$20 billion). Just as the marginal propensity to consume is the slope of the consumption schedule, so the marginal propensity to import is the slope of the net export schedule.

For convenience, let's call this new multiplier an "open-economy multiplier." Why

TABLE 7-6	**Net Export Schedule**			
(1) Domestic output (and income) (GDP = DI) (billions)	**(2)** Exports (billions) (X)	**(3)** Imports (billions) (M)	**(4)** Net exports (billions) (X_n) (2) – (3)	**(5)** Marginal propensity to import (MPM) Δ(3)/Δ(1)
$370	$40	$15	$25	0.25
390	40	20	20	0.25
410	40	25	15	0.25
430	40	30	10	0.25
450	40	35	5	0.25
470	40	40	0	0.25
490	40	45	– 5	0.25
510	40	50	–10	0.25
530	40	55	–15	0.25
550	40	60	–20	0.25

does it differ from the multiplier of 4 in the closed economy? Recall that for the closed economy the multiplier is 1/MPS or, for our data, 1/0.25 or 4. The multiplier is the reciprocal of the MPS, where the MPS is the fraction of any change in national income that "leaks" into saving. Moving to an open economy we add a second leakage—expenditures on imports. Since the marginal propensity to import (MPM) is the fraction of any change in disposable income spent on imports, we must add the MPM to the MPS in the denominator of the multiplier formula. The multiplier for an open economy (without a government sector) is therefore

$$\text{Open economy multiplier} = \frac{1}{\text{MPS} + \text{MPM}}$$

For the data of Table 7-5, the MPM is 5/20, or .25, and the open-economy multiplier is

$$\frac{1}{\text{MPS} + \text{MPM}} = \frac{1}{.25 + .25} = \frac{1}{.5} = 2$$

Net Exports and Equilibrium GDP

Let's now include exports and imports in our discussion of income determination. Columns 1 and 2 of Table 7-7 repeat columns 2 and 6 from Table 7-4, where the equilibrium GDP for a closed economy is $470 billion. Columns 3 to 5 of Table 7-7 repeat columns 2 to 4 of Table 7-6. In column 6, we have adjusted the domestic aggregate expenditures of column 2 for net exports, giving us aggregate expenditures for an open economy.

The export and import figures we have selected are such that foreign trade leaves the equilibrium GDP unchanged. Net exports are zero at the closed economy's equilibrium GDP of $470 billion, so aggregate expenditures for the open economy (column 6) equal domestic output (column 1) at $470 billion.

Figure 7-13 shows these results. The $(C + I_g + X_n)_0$ schedule is aggregate expenditures for the open economy. In this case, aggregate expenditures for the open economy intersect domestic out-

TABLE 7-7	Determinants of the Equilibrium Levels of Output and Income in an Open Economy (Without Government)				
(1) Domestic output (and income) (GDP = DI) (billions)	**(2)** Aggregate expenditures for closed economy, without government $(C + I_g)$ (billions)	**(3)** Exports (billions) (X)	**(4)** Imports (billions) (M)	**(5)** Net exports (billions) (X_n) (3) – (4)	**(6)** Aggregate expenditures for open economy, without government $(C + I_g + X_n)$ (billions) (2) + (5)
$370	$395	$40	$15	$25	$420
390	410	40	20	20	430
410	425	40	25	15	440
430	440	40	30	10	450
450	455	40	35	5	460
470	470	40	40	0	470
490	485	40	45	– 5	480
510	500	40	50	–10	490
530	515	40	55	–15	500
550	530	40	60	–20	510

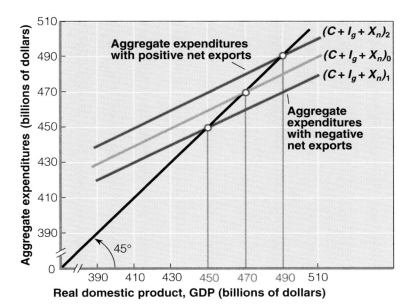

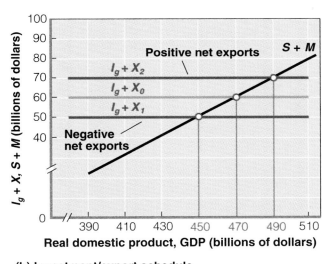

| FIGURE 7-13 | Net Exports and the Equilibrium GDP |

An increase in net exports raises the aggregate expenditures from $(C + I_g + X_n)_0$ to $(C + I_g + X_n)_2$ and increases the equilibrium GDP. Conversely, a decrease in net exports shifts the aggregate expenditures schedule downward from $(C + I_g + X_n)_0$ to $(C + I_g + X_n)_1$ and lowers the equilibrium GDP.

(a) Aggregate expenditures schedule

(b) Investment/export schedule

put at the same point as do aggregate expenditures for the closed economy, and therefore the $470 billion equilibrium GDP is unchanged by world trade.

POSITIVE NET EXPORTS

But there is no reason why net exports will have a neutral effect on equilibrium GDP. For example, by *either* increasing exports by $10 billion (from $40 to $50 billion) or decreasing imports by $10 billion at each GDP level, net exports become *plus* $10 billion at the original $470 billion GDP. With an open economy multiplier of 2, an increase in net exports of $10 billion results in a $20 billion increase in GDP. The recalculation of aggregate expenditures in column 6 of Table 7-7 reveals that the equilibrium GDP will shift from $470 to $490 billion.

In Figure 7-13a, the new open-economy aggregate expenditures line is $(C + I_g + X_n)_2$, which lies $10 billion above $(C + I_g + X_n)_0$ because of the $10 billion increase in net exports. This creates a $10 billion gap at the original $470 equilibrium GDP, and as a result the equilibrium GDP *increases* to $490 billion.

Figure 7-13b shows the same result. The new $I_g + X_2$ schedule (a $10 billion increase in exports: $I_g + X$ increases from $60 to $70 billion) intersects the $S + M$ schedule at the new equilibrium GDP of $490 billion.

NEGATIVE NET EXPORTS

By reducing net exports by $10 billion, GDP will fall by $20 billion, given an open economy multiplier of 2. Recalculating aggregate expenditures in column 6 of Table 7-7, the resulting net equilibrium GDP will be $450 billion.

Graphically, the new open-economy aggregate expenditures schedule is shown by $(C + I_g + X_n)_1$ in Figure 7-13a. This schedule lies $10 billion below $(C + I_g + X_n)_0$, reflecting the $10 billion decline in net exports. Thus, at the original $470 billion equilibrium GDP, a spending gap of $10 billion exists, which causes GDP to *decline* to $450 billion.

Figure 7-13b shows the same result. Note that the $I_g + X_0$ schedule intersects the "leakages," $S + M$, schedule at the equilibrium GDP of $470 billion. The new $I_g + X_1$ schedule intersects the $S + M$ schedule at the new equilibrium GDP of $450 billion.

The generalizations that follow from these examples are these: *Other things equal, a decline in net exports decreases aggregate expenditures and reduces a nation's GDP; conversely, a rise in net exports increases aggregate expenditures and raises a nation's GDP.*

Net exports vary greatly among the major industrial nations, as is shown in Global Perspective 7.3. (*Key Question 19*)

International Economic Linkages

Our analysis of net exports and real GDP reveals how circumstances or policies abroad can affect Canadian GDP.

PROSPERITY ABROAD

A rising level of real output and thus income among our trading partners enables Canada to sell more goods abroad, raising Canadian net exports and increasing our real GDP. We should be interested in the prosperity of our trading partners because if they do well they buy more of our exports, increasing our income and making it possible for us to buy more of their imports. Prosperity abroad transfers some of their prosperity to Canadians.

TARIFFS

Suppose our trading partners impose high tariffs on Canadian goods, such as softwood lumber, to reduce their imports and stimulate production in their economies. Their imports, however, are our exports. So when they restrict their imports to stimulate *their* economies, they are reducing Canadian exports and depressing *our* economy. We may retaliate by imposing trade barriers on their products. If so, their exports will decline and their net exports to us may fall. In the Great Depression of the 1930s various nations, including Canada, imposed trade barriers as a way to reduce domestic unemployment. But rounds of retaliation simply reduced world trade, worsened the depression, and increased unemployment.

EXCHANGE RATES

Depreciation of the Canadian dollar relative to other currencies means the price of Canadian goods in terms of these currencies will fall, stimulating purchases of our exports. Also, Canadian con-

Global Perspective 7.3

Net exports of goods, selected nations, 2001

Some nations, such as Canada, Japan, and Germany, have positive net exports; other countries, such as the United States and the United Kingdom, have negative net exports.

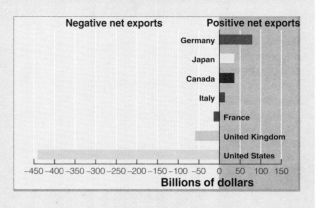

Source: World Trade Organization, <www.wto.org>.

sumers will find foreign goods more expensive and, consequently, will reduce their spending on imports. The increased Canadian exports and decreased imports will increase Canada's net exports and expand the nation's GDP.

Whether depreciation of the dollar will actually raise real GDP or produce inflation depends on the initial position of the economy relative to its full-employment output. If the economy is operating below its full employment level, depreciation of the Canadian dollar and the resulting rise in net exports will increase aggregate expenditures and thus expand real GDP. But if the economy already has full employment, the increase in net exports and aggregate expenditures will cause inflationary pressure.

This last example has been cast only in terms of *depreciation* of the dollar. Now think through the impact that *appreciation* of the dollar would have on net exports and equilibrium GDP.

QUICK REVIEW

- The main determinant of exports is the GDP in our trading partners. The main determinant of imports is our own GDP.

- Positive net exports increase aggregate expenditures on domestic output and increase equilibrium GDP.

- Negative net exports decrease aggregate expenditures on domestic output and reduce equilibrium GDP.

- The multiplier for an open economy is smaller than the multiplier for a closed economy. The higher the marginal propensity to import, the smaller is the open economy multiplier.

- In the open economy changes in (a) prosperity abroad, (b) tariffs, and (c) exchange rates can affect Canadian net exports and therefore Canadian aggregate expenditures and equilibrium GDP.

7.6   Adding the Public Sector

Our final step in constructing the aggregate expenditures model is to move the analysis from that of a private (no government) open economy to a mixed open economy that has a public sector. This means adding government spending and taxes to the model.

For simplicity, we assume that government purchases do not cause any upward or downward shifts in the consumption and investment schedules. Also, we assume that government's net tax revenues—total tax revenues less "negative taxes" in the form of transfer payments—are derived entirely from personal taxes. Finally, we assume that a fixed amount of taxes is collected regardless of the level of GDP.

Government Purchases and Equilibrium GDP

Suppose that government decides to purchase $40 billion of goods and services regardless of the level of GDP.

TABULAR EXAMPLE

Table 7-8 shows the impact of this purchase on the equilibrium GDP. Columns 1 to 7 are carried over from Tables 7-4 and 7-7 for the open economy in which the equilibrium GDP is $470 billion. The only new items are exports and imports in columns 5 and 6, and government purchases in column 8. By adding government purchases to private spending $(C + I_g + X_n)$, we get a new, higher level of aggregate expenditures, as shown in column 9. Comparing columns 1 and 9, we find that aggregate expenditures and real output are equal at a higher level of GDP. Without government spending, equilibrium GDP is $470 billion (row 6); with government spending, aggregate expenditures and real output are equal at $550 billion (row 10). *Increases in public spending, like increases in private spending, shift the aggregate expenditures schedule upward and result in a higher equilibrium GDP.*

Note, too, that government spending is subject to the open-economy multiplier. A $40 billion increase in government purchases has increased equilibrium GDP by $80 billion (from $470 billion to $550 billion). We have implicitly assumed the $40 billion in government expenditure has all gone to purchase domestic output.

This $40 billion increase in government spending is *not* financed by increased taxes. Soon we will find that increased taxes *reduce* equilibrium GDP.

TABLE 7-8	The Impact of Government Purchases on Equilibrium GDP							
(1) Domestic output (and income) (GDP = DI) (billions)	(2) Consumption (C) (billions)	(3) Saving (S) (billions)	(4) Investment (I_g) (billions)	(5) Exports (X) (billions)	(6) Imports (M) (billions)	(7) Net exports (X_n) (billions) (5) – (6)	(8) Government purchases (G) (billions)	(9) Aggregate expenditures $(C + I_g + X_n + G)$ (billions) (2) + (4) + (7) + (8)
(1) $370	$375	$–5	$20	$40	$15	$25	$40	$460
(2) 390	390	0	20	40	20	20	40	470
(3) 410	405	5	20	40	25	15	40	480
(4) 430	420	10	20	40	30	10	40	490
(5) 450	435	15	20	40	35	5	40	500
(6) 470	450	20	20	40	40	0	40	510
(7) 490	465	25	20	40	45	– 5	40	520
(8) 510	480	30	20	40	50	–10	40	530
(9) 530	495	35	20	40	55	–15	40	540
(10) 550	510	40	20	40	60	–20	40	550

GRAPHICAL ANALYSIS

In Figure 7-14 we add \$40 billion of government purchases, G, vertically to the level of private spending, $C + I_g + X_n$. That increases the aggregate expenditures schedule (private plus public) to $C + I_g + X_n + G$, resulting in the \$80 billion increase in equilibrium GDP shown from \$470 to \$550 billion.

A decline in government spending G will lower the aggregate expenditures schedule, and the result is a multiplied decline in the equilibrium GDP. Verify using Table 7-8 that if government spending were to decline from \$40 billion to \$20 billion, the equilibrium GDP would fall by \$40 billion.

Taxation and Equilibrium GDP

lump-sum tax
A tax that yields the same amount of tax revenue at all levels of GDP.

Government also collects taxes. Suppose it imposes a **lump-sum tax**, which is a *tax yielding the same amount of tax revenue at all levels of GDP*. For simplicity, we suppose this lump-sum tax is \$40 billion, so government obtains \$40 billion of tax revenue at each level of GDP. Generally, government revenues rise with GDP.

TABULAR EXAMPLE

In Table 7-9, which continues our example, we find taxes in column 2, and we see in column 3 that disposable (after-tax) income is lower than GDP (column 1) by the \$40 billion amount of the tax. Because disposable income is used for consumer spending and saving, the tax lowers both con-

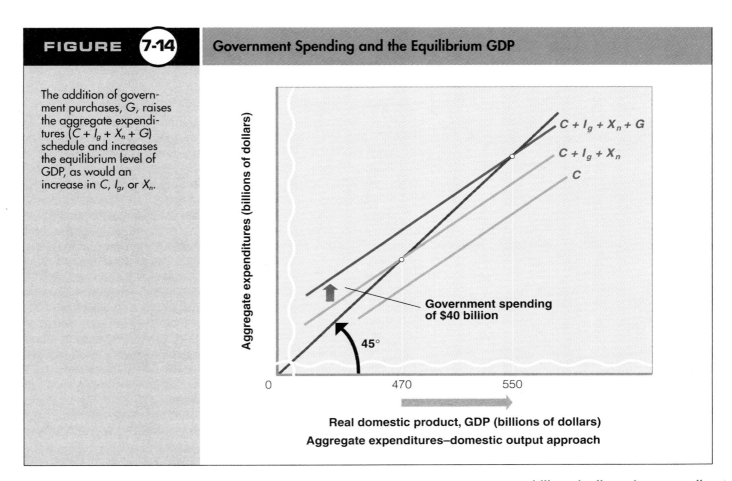

FIGURE 7-14   Government Spending and the Equilibrium GDP

The addition of government purchases, G, raises the aggregate expenditures ($C + I_g + X_n + G$) schedule and increases the equilibrium level of GDP, as would an increase in C, I_g, or X_n.

Aggregate expenditures (billions of dollars)

$C + I_g + X_n + G$

$C + I_g + X_n$

C

Government spending of \$40 billion

45°

0   470   550

Real domestic product, GDP (billions of dollars)
Aggregate expenditures–domestic output approach

TABLE 7-9			Determination of the Equilibrium Levels of Employment, Output, and Income (in Billions): Private and Public Sectors								
(1) Real domestic output (and income) (GDP = PI)	(2) Taxes (T)	(3) Disposable income (DI) (1) – (2)	(4) Con-sump-tion (C_a)	(5) Saving (S_a) (3) – (4)	(6) Invest-ment (I_g)	(7) Net exports (X_n) X	M_a	X_na	(8) Govern-ment purchases (G)	(9) Aggregate expenditures (C_a + I_g + X_na + G) (4) + (6) + (8) + (9)
---	---	---	---	---	---	---	---	---	---	---
(1) $370	$40	$330	$345	$–15	$20	$40	$ 5	$35	$40	$440
(2) 390	40	350	360	–10	20	40	10	30	40	450
(3) 410	40	370	375	– 5	20	40	15	25	40	460
(4) 430	40	390	390	0	20	40	20	20	40	470
(5) 450	40	410	405	5	20	40	25	15	40	480
(6) 470	40	430	420	10	20	40	30	10	40	490
(7) 490	40	450	435	15	20	40	35	5	40	500
(8) 510	40	470	450	20	20	40	40	0	40	510
(9) 530	40	490	465	25	20	40	45	– 5	40	520
(10) 550	40	510	480	30	20	40	50	–10	40	530

sumption and saving. But by how much will each decline as a result of the $40 billion in taxes? The MPC and MPS hold the answer: The MPC tells us what fraction of a decline in disposable income will come out of consumption, and the MPS indicates what fraction will come out of saving. Since the MPC is .75, if government collects $40 billion in taxes at each possible level of GDP, consumption will drop by $30 billion (= .75 × $40 billion). Since the MPS is .25, saving will fall by $10 billion (= .25 × $40 billion).

There is one more refinement we must make to the new lower consumption level brought about by the tax increase. In an open economy such as Canada's, consumption consists of both domestic and imported commodities. Of the $30 billion drop in total consumption, there will be a $10 billion decrease in M since the MPM equals ¼. The remaining $20 billion, therefore, comes out of domestic consumption.

Columns 4 and 5 of Table 7-9 list the amounts of consumption and saving *at each level of GDP*, which are $30 and $10 billion smaller, respectively, than those in Table 7-8. After taxes are imposed, DI is $410 billion, $40 billion short of the $450 billion GDP, with the result that consumption is only $405 billion, saving is $5 billion, and imports $25 billion (row 5 of Table 7-9).

Taxes reduce disposable income by the amount of the taxes. This decline in DI reduces consumption, saving, and imports at each level of GDP. The sizes of the declines in C, S, and M are determined by the MPC, the MPS, and the MPM, respectively.

To find out the effect of taxes on equilibrium GDP, we calculate aggregate expenditures once again, as shown in column 9 of Table 7-9. Aggregate spending is $20 billion less at each level of GDP than it was in Table 7-8. The reason is that after-tax consumption, C_a, is $30 billion less, and M_a is $10 billion less (therefore, X_{na} is $10 billion more) at each level of GDP. Comparing real output and aggregate expenditures, in columns 1 and 9, we see that the aggregate amounts produced and purchased are equal only at the $510 billion level of GDP (row 8). The $40 billion lump-sum tax has reduced equilibrium GDP from $550 billion (row 10 in Table 7-8) to $510 billion (row 8 in Table 7-6), not back to $470 billion.

GRAPHICAL ANALYSIS

In Figure 7-15 the $40 billion increase in taxes shows up as a $20 (not $40) billion decline in the aggregate expenditures ($C_a + I_g + X_{na} + G$) schedule. This decline in aggregate expenditures results solely from a decline in the consumption component C of the aggregate expenditures. The equilibrium GDP falls from $550 billion to $510 billion because of this tax-induced drop in consumption. *Increases in taxes lower the aggregate expenditures schedule relative to the 45-degree line and reduce the equilibrium GDP.*

In contrast to our previous case, a *decrease* in existing taxes will raise the aggregate expenditures schedule in Figure 7-15 as a result of an increase in the consumption at all GDP levels. You should confirm that a tax reduction of $20 billion (from the present $40 billion to $20 billion) will increase the equilibrium GDP from $510 billion to $530 billion. *(Key Question 22)*

DIFFERENTIAL IMPACTS

You may have noted that equal changes in G and T do not have equivalent impacts on GDP. The $40 billion increase in G in our illustration, subject to the multiplier of 2, produced an $80 billion increase in real GDP. But the $40 billion increase in taxes reduced GDP by only $40 billion. Given an MPC of .75, the tax increase of $40 billion reduced consumption by only $30 billion (not $40 billion) and domestic consumption by $20 billion because savings fell by $10 billion and imports fell by $10 billion. Subjecting the $20 billion decline in consumption to the multiplier of 2, we find the tax increase of $40 billion reduced GDP by $40 billion (not $80 billion).

Table 7-9 and Figure 7-15 constitute the complete aggregate expenditures model for an open economy with government. When total spending equals total production, the economy's output is in equilibrium. In the open mixed economy, equilibrium GDP occurs where:

$$C_a + I_g + X_n + G = \text{GDP}.$$

INJECTIONS, LEAKAGES, AND UNPLANNED CHANGES IN INVENTORIES

Moreover, the related characteristics of equilibrium that we noted for the private closed economy also apply to the complete model. Injections into the income-expenditures stream equal leakages

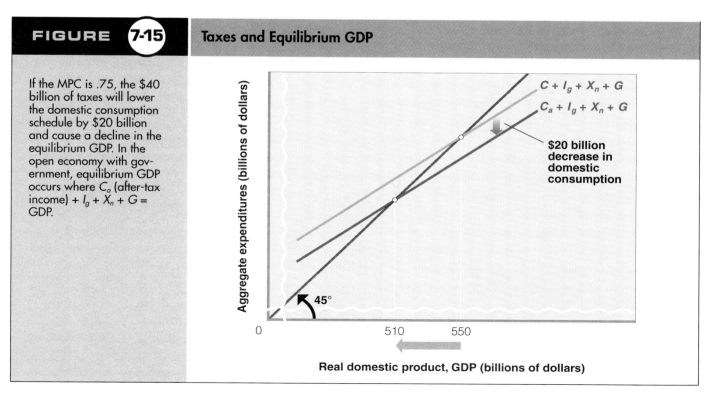

FIGURE 7-15

Taxes and Equilibrium GDP

If the MPC is .75, the $40 billion of taxes will lower the domestic consumption schedule by $20 billion and cause a decline in the equilibrium GDP. In the open economy with government, equilibrium GDP occurs where C_a (after-tax income) + I_g + X_n + G = GDP.

$C + I_g + X_n + G$

$C_a + I_g + X_n + G$

$20 billion decrease in domestic consumption

Aggregate expenditures (billions of dollars)

45°

0   510   550

Real domestic product, GDP (billions of dollars)

Consider This

Paradox of Thrift

In Chapter 2 we said that a higher rate of saving is *good* for society because it frees resources from consumption uses and directs them toward investment goods. More machinery and equipment means a greater capacity for the economy to produce goods and services.

But implicit within this "saving is good" proposition is the assumption that increased saving will be borrowed and spent for investment goods. If investment does not increase along with saving, a curious irony called the *paradox of thrift* may arise. The attempt to save more may simply reduce GDP and leave actual saving unchanged.

Our analysis of the multiplier process helps explain this possibility. Suppose an economy that has an MPC of .75, an MPS of .25, and a multiplier of 4, decides to save an additional $20 billion. From the social viewpoint, a penny saved that is not invested is a penny not spent and therefore a decline in someone's income. Through the multiplier process,

the $20 billion reduces consumption spending, and lowers real GDP by $80 billion (4 × $20 billion).

The $80 billion decline of real GDP, in turn, reduces saving by $20 billion (= MPS of .25 × $80 billion), which completely cancels the initial $20 billion increase of saving. Here, the attempt to increase saving is *bad* for the economy: It creates a recession and leaves saving unchanged.

For increased saving to be *good* for an economy, greater investment must accompany greater saving. If investment replaces consumption dollar-for-dollar, aggregate expenditures stay constant and the higher level of investment raises the economy's future growth rate.

Question: Your friend proudly tells you "I wear my brother's hand-me-down clothes and as a consequence I have doubled the size of my bank account." Is he a socially responsible person?

from the income stream. For the private closed economy, $S = I_g$. For the complete economy, imports and taxes are added leakages. Saving, importing, and paying taxes are all uses of income that subtract from potential consumption. Consumption will now be less than GDP—creating a potential spending gap—in the amount of after-tax saving (S_a), imports (M), and taxes (T). But exports (X) and government purchases (G), along with investment (I_g), are injections into the income-expenditures stream. At the equilibrium GDP, the sum of the leakages equals the sum of the injections. In symbols:

$$S_a + M + T = I_g + X + G$$

You should use the data in Table 7-8 to confirm this equality between leakages and injections at the equilibrium GDP of $490 billion. Also, verify that a lack of such an equality exists at all other possible levels of GDP.

Although not directly shown in Table 7-8, the equilibrium characteristic of "no unplanned changes in inventories" will also be fulfilled at the $490 billion GDP. Because aggregate expenditures equal GDP, all the goods and services produced will be purchased. There will be no unplanned increase or decrease in inventories

7.7 Equilibrium Versus Full-Employment GDP

Now let's use the full aggregate expenditures model to evaluate the equilibrium GDP. The $510 billion equilibrium GDP in our complete analysis (Table 7-9 and Figure 7-15) may or may not provide full employment. Indeed, our assumption thus far has been that the economy is operating at less than full employment.

Recessionary Gap

recessionary gap
The amount by which the equilibrium GDP falls short of full-employment GDP.

Assume in Figure **7-16a (Key Graph)** that the full-employment level of GDP is $530 billion and the aggregate expenditures schedule is AE_1. This schedule intersects the 45-degree line to the left of the full-employment output, so the economy's aggregate production is $20 billion short of its full employment output of $530 billion. According to column 1 in Table 7-4, employment at full-employment GDP is 22.5 million workers. But the economy depicted in Figure 7-16a is employing only 20 million workers; 2.5 million workers are unemployed. For that reason, the economy is sacrificing $20 billion of output.

The amount by which GDP falls short of the full-employment level of GDP (also called potential GDP) is called the **recessionary gap**. In Table 7-9, assuming the full-employment GDP to be $530 billion, the corresponding recessionary gap is $20 billion. The aggregate expenditures schedule would have to shift upward to realize the full-employment GDP. Because the multiplier is 2, there is a $20 billion differential ($10 billion times the multiplier of 2) between the equilibrium GDP and the full-employment GDP. This $20 billion difference is a negative *GDP gap*—an idea you first encountered when discussing cyclical unemployment (Chapter 6).

Inflationary Gap

inflationary gap
The amount by which the equilibrium GDP exceeds full-employment GDP.

The **inflationary gap** is the amount by which GDP exceeds *full-employment* GDP. In Figure 7-16b, there is a $20 billion inflationary gap at the $530 billion full-employment GDP. The actual aggregate expenditures schedule AE_2 is higher than the schedule AE_0 that would be just sufficient to achieve the $510 billion full-employment GDP. Thus, the aggregate expenditures schedule would have to shift downward to realize equilibrium at the full-employment GDP.

The effect of this inflationary gap—this excessive spending—is that it will pull up output prices. Since businesses cannot fully respond to the $20 billion in excessive spending, demand-pull inflation will occur. Nominal GDP will rise because of a higher price level, but real GDP will rise by less than nominal GDP. *(Key Question 23)*

Application: The Slowdown of the Canadian Economy in 2001

The Canadian economy grew at a healthy pace in the last half of the 1990s, with real GDP expanding at about 3.5 percent annually and the unemployment rate droping from 9.6 percent of the labour force in 1996 to 6.8 percent in 2000. The economic expansion and falling rates of unemployment, however, did not spark inflation, as had been the case in prior business cycles. By increasing the economy's production capacity, exceptionally strong productivity growth in the late 1990s accommodated the growing aggregate expenditures. In terms of Figure 7-16b, it was as if the full employment level of real GDP expanded from $530 billion to $550 billion at the same time as the aggregate expenditure curve rose from AE_0 to AE_2. So the inflationary gap of $20 billion never materialized. Inflation averaged less than 2.0 percent annually between 1995 and 2000.

But the booming economy of the second half of the 1990s produced notable excesses. A large number of ill-conceived Internet-related firms were born, attracting billions of investment dollars. Investment spending surged throughout the economy and added too much production capacity. A stock market "bubble" developed as stock market investing became a national pastime. Consumers increased their household debt to expand their consumption.

The boom ended in the early 2000s. Hundreds of Internet-related start-up firms folded. Many firms, particularly those in telecommunications, such as Nortel Networks and aircraft manufacturing, such as Bombardier, began to experience severe overcapacity. The stock market bubble burst, erasing billions of dollars of "paper" wealth. Firms significantly reduced their investment spending because of lower estimates of rates of return. The unemployment rate rose from 6.8 percent in February 2001 to 8.0 percent in December 2001. In terms of Figure 7-16a, a recessionary gap

Key Graph

FIGURE 7-16 **Recessionary and Inflationary Gaps**

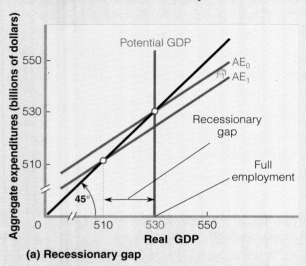

(a) Recessionary gap

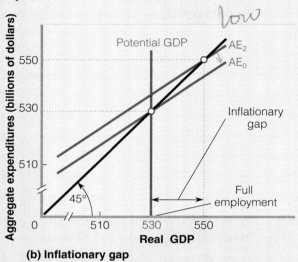

(b) Inflationary gap

The equilibrium and full-employment GDPs may not coincide. (a) A recessionary gap is the amount by which equilibrium GDP falls short of full-employment GDP. Here, the recessionary gap is $20 billion, caused by a $10 billion shortfall of aggregate expenditures. (b) An inflationary gap is the amount by which equilibrium GDP exceeds full-employment GDP. Here, the inflationary gap is $20 billion; this overspending brings about demand-pull inflation.

Quick Quiz

1. In the economy depicted,
   a. the MPS is .20.
   b. the multiplier is 2.
   c. the potential GDP level of real GDP is $510 billion.
   d. nominal GDP always equals real GDP.

2. The inflationary gap depicted will cause
   a. demand-pull inflation.
   b. cost-push inflation.
   c. cyclical unemployment.
   d. frictional unemployment.

3. The recessionary gap depicted will cause
   a. demand-pull inflation.
   b. cost-push inflation.
   c. cyclical unemployment.
   d. frictional unemployment.

4. In the economy depicted, the $20 billion inflationary gap
   a. expands full-employment real GDP to $550 billion.
   b. leaves full-employment real GDP at $530 billion, but causes inflation.
   c. could be remedied by equal $20 billion increases in taxes and government spending.
   d. implies that real GDP exceeds nominal GDP.

ANSWERS: 1. b; 2. a; 3. c; 4. b

emerged, although not a full fledged recession. In 2002 the economy resumed economic growth, but the unemployment rate still averaged 7.7 percent of the labour force in 2002.

QUICK REVIEW

- Government purchases shift the aggregate expenditures schedule upward and raise the equilibrium GDP.

- Taxes reduce disposable income, lower consumption spending on domestically produced goods and saving, shift the imported and aggregate expenditures schedules downward, and reduce the equilibrium GDP.

- A recessionary gap is the amount by which GDP falls short of potential GDP; the inflationary gap is the amount by which GDP exceeds potential GDP.

Limitations of the Model

This chapter's analysis demonstrates the power of the aggregate expenditures model to explain the economy, how recessions or depressions can occur, and how demand-pull inflation can arise. But this model has three well-known limitations:

- *It does not show price-level changes.* The model can account for demand-pull inflation, as in Figure 7-16b, but it does not indicate how much the price level will rise when aggregate expenditures are excessive relative to the economy's capacity. The aggregate expenditures model has no way of measuring the rate of inflation.

- *It does not deal with cost-push inflation.* We know from Chapter 6 that there are two general types of inflation: demand-pull inflation and cost-push inflation. The aggregate expenditures model does not address cost-push inflation.

- *It does not allow for "self-correction."* In reality, the economy contains some internal features that, given enough time, may correct a recessionary gap or an inflationary gap. The aggregate expenditures model does not contain those features.

In subsequent chapters we remedy these limitations, while preserving the many valuable insights of the aggregate expenditures model.

THE LASTword   Say's Law, the Great Depression, and Keynes

The aggregate expenditures theory emerged as a critique of classical economics and as a response to the Great Depression

Until the Great Depression of the 1930s, many prominent economists, including David Ricardo (1772–1823) and John Stuart Mill (1806–1873), believed that the market system would ensure full employment of an economy's resources. These so-called *classical economists* acknowledged that now and then abnormal circumstance such as wars, political upheavals, droughts, speculative crises, and gold rushes would occur, deflecting the economy from full-employment status. But when such deviations occurred, the economy would automatically adjust and soon restore the economy to full-employment output. For example, a slump in output and employment would result in lower prices, wages, and interest rates, which in turn would increase consumer spending, employment, and investment spending. Any excess supply of goods and workers would soon be eliminated.

Classical macroeconomists denied that the level of spending in an economy could be too low to bring about the purchase of the entire full-employment output. They based their denial of inadequate spending in part on *Say's law,* attributed to the nineteenth-century French economist J.B. Say (1767–1832). This law is the disarmingly simple idea that the very act of producing goods generates income equal to the value of the goods produced. The production of any output automatically provides the income needed to buy that output. More succinctly stated, *supply creates its own demand.*

Say's law can best be understood in terms of a barter economy. A woodworker, for example, produces or supplies furniture as a means of buying or demanding the food and clothing produced by other workers. The woodworker's supply of furniture is the income that he will "spend" to satisfy his demand for the other goods. The goods he buys (demands) will have a total value exactly equal to the goods he produces (supplies). And so it is for other producers and for the entire economy. Demand must be the same as supply!

Assuming that the composition of output is in accord with consumer preferences, all markets would be cleared of their outputs. It would seem that all firms need to do to sell a full-employment output is to produce that level of output. Say's law guarantees there will be sufficient spending to purchase it all.

The Great Depression of the 1930s called into question the theory that supply creates its own demand (Say's law). In Canada, real GDP declined by almost 30 percent and the unemployment rate rocketed to nearly 20 percent. Other nations experienced similar impacts. And cyclical unemployment lingered for a decade. An obvious inconsistency exists between a theory that says that unemployment is virtually impossible and the actual occurrence of a 10-year siege of substantial unemployment.

In 1936 British economist John Maynard Keynes (1883–1946) explained why cyclical employment could occur in a market economy. In his *General Theory of Employment, Interest, and Money,* Keynes attacked the foundations of classical theory and developed the ideas underlying the aggregate expenditures model. Keynes disputed Say's law, pointing out that not all income need be spent in the same period that it is produced. Investment spending, in particular, is volatile, said Keynes. A substantial decline in investment will lead to insufficient total spending. Unsold goods will accumulate in producers' warehouses and producers will respond by reducing their output and discharging workers. A recession or depression will result, and widespread cyclical unemployment will occur. Moreover, said Keynes, recessions or depressions are not likely to correct themselves. In contrast to the more laissez faire view of the classical economists, Keynes argued that government should play an active role in stabilizing the economy.

CHAPTER SUMMARY

7.1 THE AGGREGATE EXPENDITURES MODEL: CONSUMPTION AND SAVING

- Other things equal, there is a direct (positive) relationship between income and consumption and income and saving. The consumption and saving schedules show the various amounts that households intend to consume and save at the various income and output levels, assuming a fixed price level.

- The *average* propensities to consume and save show the fractions of any total income that are consumed and saved; APC + APS = 1. The *marginal* propensities to consume and save show the fractions of any change in total income that is consumed and saved; MPC + MPS = 1.

- The locations of the consumption and saving schedules are determined by (a) the amount of wealth owned by households; (b) expectations of future income, future prices, and product availability; (c) the relative size of household debt; and (d) taxation. The consumption and saving schedules are relatively stable.

7.2 INVESTMENT

- The immediate determinants of investment are (a) the expected rate of return and (b) the real rate of interest. The economy's investment demand curve is found by cumulating investment projects, arraying them in descending order according to their expected rates of return, graphing the result, and applying the rule that investment will be profitable up to the point at which the real interest rate, i, equals the expected rate of return, r. The investment demand curve reveals an inverse relationship between the interest rate and the level of aggregated investment.

- Shifts in the investment demand curve can occur as the result of changes in (a) the acquisition, maintenance, and operating costs of capital goods; (b) business taxes; (c) technology; (d) the stocks of capital goods on hand; and (e) expectations.

- Either changes in interest rates or shifts in the investment demand curve can shift the investment schedule.

- The durability of capital goods, the variability of expectations, and the irregular occurrence of major innovations all contribute to the high fluctuations of investment spending.

7.3 EQUILIBRIUM GDP

- For a private closed economy the equilibrium level of GDP occurs when aggregate expenditures and real output are equal or, graphically, where the $C + I_g$ line intersects the 45-degree line. At any GDP greater than equilibrium GDP, real output will exceed aggregate spending, resulting in unintended investment in inventories and eventual declines in output and income (GDP). At any below-equilibrium GDP, aggregate expenditures will exceed real output, resulting in unintended declines in inventories and eventual increases in GDP.

- At equilibrium GDP, the amount households save (leakages) and the amount businesses plan to invest (injections) are equal. Any excess of saving over planned investment will cause a shortage of total spending, forcing GDP to fall. Any excess of planned investment over saving will cause an excess of total spending, inducing GDP to rise. The change in GDP will in both cases correct the discrepancy between saving and planned investment.

- At equilibrium GDP, there are no unplanned changes in inventories. When aggregate expenditures diverge from GDP, an unplanned change in inventories occurs. Unplanned increases in inventories are followed by a cutback in production and a decline of real GDP. Unplanned decreases in inventories result in an increase in production and a rise of GDP.

- Actual investment consists of planned investment plus unplanned changes in inventories and is always equal to saving.

7.4 CHANGES IN EQUILIBRIUM GDP AND THE MULTIPLIER

- The multiplier is equal to the reciprocal of the marginal propensity to save: The greater is the marginal propensity to save, the smaller is the multiplier. Also, the greater is the marginal propensity to consume, the larger is the multiplier.

- A shift in the investment schedule (caused by changes in expected rates of return or changes in interest rates) shifts the aggregate expenditures curve and causes a new equilibrium level of real GDP. Real GDP changes by more than the amount of the initial change in investment. This multiplier effect ($\Delta GDP/\Delta I_g$) accompanies both increases and decreases in aggregate expenditures and also applies to changes in net exports (X_n) and government purchases (G).

7.5 INTERNATIONAL TRADE AND EQUILIBRIUM OUTPUT

- The net export schedule equates net exports (exports minus imports) to levels of real GDP. For simplicity, we assume that the level of net exports is the same at all levels of real GDP.

- Positive net exports increase aggregate expenditures to a higher level than they would be if the economy were "closed" to international trade. They raise equilibrium real GDP by a multiple of the net exports. Negative net exports decrease aggregate expenditures relative to those in a closed economy, decreasing equilibrium real GDP by a multiple of their amount. Increases in exports or decreases in imports have an expansionary effect on real GDP, but decreases in exports or increases in imports have a contractionary effect.

7.6 ADDING THE PUBLIC SECTOR

- Government purchases shift the aggregate expenditures schedule upward and raise GDP.

- Taxation reduces disposable income, lowers consumption spending *and* saving, shifts the aggregate expenditures curve downward, and reduces equilibrium GDP.

- In the complete aggregate expenditures model, equilibrium GDP occurs where $C_a + I_g + X_n + G = $ GDP. At the equilibrium GDP, *leakages* of after-tax saving (S_a), imports (M), and taxes (T) equal *injections* of investment (I_g), exports (X), and government purchases (G). Also, there are no unplanned changes in inventories.

7.7 EQUILIBRIUM VERSUS FULL EMPLOY- MENT GDP

- The equilibrium GDP and the full-employment GDP may differ. The recessionary gap is the amount by which GDP falls short of full-employment GDP. This gap produces a negative GDP gap (actual GDP minus potential GDP). The inflationary gap is the amount by which GDP exceeds full-employment GDP. This gap causes demand-pull inflation.

- The aggregate expenditures model provides many insights into the macroeconomy, but it does not (a) show price-level changes, (b) account for cost-push inflation, or allow for "self-correction" from a recessionary or inflationary gap.

TERMS AND CONCEPTS

STUDY QUESTIONS

1. Very briefly summarize what relationships are shown by (a) the consumption schedule, (b) the saving schedule, (c) the investment demand curve, and (d) the investment schedule. Which of these relationships are direct relationships and which are inverse (negative) relationships? Why are consumption and saving in Canada greater today than they were a decade ago?

2. Precisely how are the APC and the MPC different? Why must the sum of the MPC and the MPS equal 1? What are the basic determinants of the consumption and saving schedules? Of your own level of consumption?

3. Explain how each of the following will affect the consumption and saving schedules or the investment schedule, other things being equal.

   a. A large increase in the value of real estate, including private houses.

   b. The threat of limited, non-nuclear war, leading the public to expect future shortages of consumer durables.

   c. A decline in the real interest rate.

   d. A sharp, sustained decline in stock prices.

   e. An increase in the rate of population growth.

   f. The development of a cheaper method of manufacturing computer chips.

   g. A sizable increase in the age for collecting retirement benefits.

   h. The expectation that mild inflation will persist in the next decade.

   i. An increase in the federal personal income tax.

4. Explain why an upward shift of the consumption schedule typically involves an equal downward shift of the saving schedule. What is the exception to this relationship?

5. **KEY QUESTION**   Complete the following table:

Level of output and income (GDP = DI)	Consumption	Saving	APC	APS	MPC	MPS
$240	$_____	$–4	___	___		
260	_____	0	___	___	___	___
280	_____	4	___	___	___	___
300	_____	8	___	___	___	___
320	_____	12	___	___	___	___
340	_____	16	___	___	___	___
360	_____	20	___	___	___	___
380	_____	24	___	___	___	___
400	_____	28	___	___	___	___

a. Show the consumption and saving schedules graphically.

b. Find the break-even level of income. Explain how it is possible for households to dissave at very low income levels.

c. If the proportion of total income consumed (APC) decreases and the proportion saved (APS) increases as income rises, explain both verbally and graphically how the MPC and MPS can be constant at various levels of income.

6. What are the basic determinants of investment? Explain the relationship between the real interest rate and the level of investment. Why is investment spending less stable than consumption spending and saving?

7. **KEY QUESTION**   Suppose a hand-bill publisher can buy a new duplicating machine for $500 and the duplicator has a one-year life. The machine is expected to contribute $50 to the year's net revenue. What is the expected rate of return? If the real interest rate at which funds can be borrowed to purchase the machine is 8 percent, should the publisher choose to invest in the machine? Explain.

8. **KEY QUESTION**   Assume there are no investment projects in the economy that yield an expected rate of return of 25 percent or more. But suppose there are $10 billion of investment projects yielding expected returns of between 20 and 25 percent; another $10 billion yielding between 15 and 20 percent; another $10 billion between 10 and 15 percent; and so forth. Cumulate these data and present them graphically,

putting the expected rate of return on the vertical axis and the amount of investment on the horizontal axis. What will be the equilibrium level of aggregate investment if the real interest rate is (a) 15 percent, (b) 10 percent, and (c) 5 percent? Explain why this curve is the investment demand curve.

9. Explain graphically the determination of the equilibrium GDP for a private closed economy. Explain why the intersection of the aggregate expenditures schedule and the 45-degree line determines the equilibrium GDP.

10. **KEY QUESTION**   Assuming the level of investment is $16 billion and independent of the level of total output, complete the following table and determine the equilibrium levels of output and employment that this private closed economy would provide. What are the sizes of the MPC and MPS?

Possible levels of employment (millions)	Real domestic output (GDP = DI) (billions)	Consumption (billions)	Saving (billions)
40	$240	$244	$_____
45	260	260	_____
50	280	276	_____
55	300	292	_____
60	320	308	_____
65	340	324	_____
70	360	340	_____
75	380	356	_____
80	400	372	_____

11. **KEY QUESTION**   Using the consumption and saving data in question 10 and assuming investment is $16 billion, what are saving and planned investment at the $380 billion level of domestic output? What are saving and actual investment at that level? What are saving and planned investment at the $300 billion level of domestic output? What are the levels of saving and actual investment? Use the concept of unplanned investment to explain adjustments toward equilibrium from both the $380 and $300 billion levels of domestic output.

12. Why is saving called a *leakage*? Why is planned investment called an *injection*? Why must saving equal planned investment at equilibrium GDP? Are unplanned changes in inventories rising, falling, or constant at equilibrium GDP? Explain.

13. **Advanced analysis:** Linear equations for the consumption and saving schedules take the general form $C = a + bY$ and $S = -a + (1 - b)Y$, where C, S, and Y are

consumption, saving, and national income, respectively. The constant a represents the vertical intercept, and b the slope of the consumption schedule.

a. Use the following data to determine numerical values for a and b in the consumption and saving equations:

National Income (Y)	Consumption (C)
$ 0	$ 80
100	140
200	200
300	260
400	320

b. What is the economic meaning of b? Of $(1 - b)$?

c. Suppose the amount of saving that occurs at each level of national income falls by $20, but that the values of b and $(1 - b)$ remain unchanged. Restate the saving and consumption equations for the new numerical values, and cite a factor that might have caused the change.

14. **Advanced analysis:** Suppose that the linear equation for consumption in a hypothetical economy is $C = 40 + .8Y$. Also suppose that income (Y) is $400. Determine (a) the marginal propensity to consume, (b) the marginal propensity to save, (c) the level of consumption, (d) the average propensity to consume, (e) the level of saving, and (f) the average propensity to save.

15. What effect will each of the changes listed in Study Question 3 have on the equilibrium level of GDP? Explain your answers.

16. **KEY QUESTION** What is the multiplier effect? What relationship does the MPC bear to the size of the

multiplier? The MPS? What will the multiplier be when the MPS is 0, .4, .6, and 1? What will it be when the MPC is 1, .90, .67, .50, and 0? How much of a change in GDP will result if firms increase their level of investment by $8 billion and the MPC is .80? If the MPC is .67?

17. Depict graphically the aggregate expenditures model for a private closed economy. Now show a decrease in the aggregate expenditures schedule and explain why the decline in real GDP in your diagram is greater than the initial decline in aggregated expenditures. What would be the ratio of a decline in real GDP to the initial drop in aggregate expenditures if the slope of your aggregate expenditures schedule was .8?

18. Suppose that a certain country has an MPC of .9 and a real GDP of $400 billion. If its investment spending decreases by $4 billion, what will be its new level of real GDP in the aggregate expenditures model?

19. **KEY QUESTION** The data in columns 1 and 2 in the table below are for a private closed economy:

a. Use columns 1 and 2 to determine the equilibrium GDP for this hypothetical economy.

b. Now open up this economy to international trade by including the export and import figures of columns 3 and 4. Fill in columns 5 and 6 and determine the equilibrium GDP for the open economy. Explain why this equilibrium GDP differs from that of the closed economy.

c. Given the original $20 billion level of exports, what would be the equilibrium GDP if imports were $10 billion greater at each level of GDP?

d. What is the open-economy multiplier in these examples?

(1) Real domestic output (GDP = DI) (billions)	(2) Aggregate expenditures, private closed economy (billions)	(3) Exports (billions)	(4) Imports (billions)	(5) Net exports (billions)	(6) Aggregate expenditures, private open economy (billions)
$200	$240	$20	$30	$____	$_____
250	280	20	30	____	_____
300	320	20	30	____	_____
350	360	20	30	____	_____
400	400	20	30	____	_____
450	440	20	30	____	_____
500	480	20	30	____	_____
550	520	20	30	____	_____

20. Assume that, without taxes, the consumption schedule of an economy is as follows:

GDP, billions	Consumption, billions
$100	$120
200	200
300	280
400	360
500	440
600	520
700	600

   a. Graph this consumption schedule and determine the MPC.

   b. Assume now that a lump-sum tax is imposed such that the government collects $10 billion in taxes at all levels of GDP. Graph the resulting consumption schedule, and compare the MPC and the multiplier with those of the pretax consumption schedule.

21. Explain graphically the determination of equilibrium GDP for a private economy through the aggregate expenditures model. Now add government spending (any amount you choose) to your graph, showing its impact on equilibrium GDP. Finally, add taxation (any amount of lump-sum tax that you choose) to your graph and show its effect on equilibrium GDP. Looking at your graph, determine whether equilibrium GDP has increased, decreased, or stayed the same given the sizes of the government spending and taxes that you selected.

22. **KEY QUESTION**   Refer to columns 1 and 6 in the table for question 20. Incorporate government into the table by assuming that it plans to tax and spend $20 billion at each possible level of GDP. Also assume that the tax is a personal tax and that government spending does not induce a shift in the private aggregate expenditures schedule. Compute and explain the change in equilibrium GDP caused by the addition of government.

23. **KEY QUESTION**   Refer to the table below in answering the questions that follow:

(1) Possible levels of employment (millions)	(2) Real domestic output (billions)	(3) Aggregate expenditures $(C_a + I_g + X_n + G)$ (billions)
9	$500	$520
10	550	560
11	600	600
12	650	640
13	700	680

   a. If full employment in this economy is 13 million, will there be an inflationary or a recessionary gap? What will be the consequence of this gap? By how much would aggregate expenditures in column 3 have to change at each level of GDP to eliminate the inflationary or the recessionary gap? Explain. What is the multiplier in this example?

   b. Will there be an inflationary or a recessionary gap if the full-employment level of output is $500 billion? Explain the consequences. By how much would aggregate expenditures in column 3 have to change at each level of GDP to eliminate the inflationary or the recessionary gap? What is the multiplier in this example?

   c. Assuming that investment, net exports, and government expenditures do not change with changes in real GDP, what are the sizes of the MPC, the MPS, and the multiplier?

24. Answer the following questions that relate to the aggregate expenditures model:

   a. If C_a is $100, I_g is $50, X_n is $-10, and G is $30, what is the economy's equilibrium GDP?

   b. If real GDP in an economy is currently $200, C_a is $100, I_g is $50, X_n is $-10, and G is $30, will its real GDP rise, fall, or stay the same?

   c. Suppose that full-employment (and full-capacity) output in an economy is $200. If C_a is $150, I_g is $50, X_n is $-10, and G is $30, what will be the macroeconomic result?

25. **Advanced analysis:** Assume that the consumption schedule for a private open economy is such that consumption $C = 50 + 0.8Y$. Assume further that planned investment I_g and net exports X_n are independent of the level of real GDP and constant at $I_g = 30$ and $X_n = 10$. Recall also that, in equilibrium, the real output produced (Y) is equal to aggregate expenditures: $Y = C + I_g + X_n$.

   a. Calculate the equilibrium level of income or real GDP for this economy. Check your work by expressing the consumption, investment, and net export schedules in tabular form and determining the equilibrium GDP.

   b. What happens to equilibrium Y if I_g changes to 10? What does this outcome reveal about the size of the multiplier?

26. **(The Last Word)** What is Say's Law? How does it relate to the view held by classical economists that the economy generally will operate at a position on its production possibilities curve (Chapter 2). Use production possibility analysis to demonstrate Keynes's view on this matter.

INTERNET APPLICATION QUESTIONS

1. **The Multiplier—Calculate a Change in GDP** Statistics Canada has current data on national income and product accounts that can be accessed through the McConnell-Brue-Barbiero (Chapter 7) Web site. Find the most current values for GDP = $C + I + G + (X - M)$. Assume an MPC of .75, and that for each of the following, the values of the initial variables are those you just discovered. What would be the new value of GDP if (a) investment increased by 5 percent? (b) imports increased by 5 percent and exports increased by 5 percent? (c) consumption increased by 5 percent? (d) government spending increased by 5 percent? Which 5 percent increase caused GDP to change the most in absolute dollars?

Σ-STAT

2. **Net Exports—What Is the Current Economic Impact?** Positive net exports have an expansionary effect on domestic GDP; negative net exports have a contractionary effect. Check Statistics Canada's latest figures for exports and imports of goods and services at the McConnell-Brue-Barbiero (Chapter 7) Web site . Assume a multiplier of 2. Compared to the previous period, how much is GDP increased or decreased by a change in (a) net exports of goods, (b) net exports of services, and (c) net exports of goods and services? Which has the greatest impact? Should services be included or excluded from net exports?

Σ-STAT

Math Appendix to Chapter 7

The Math behind the Aggregate Expenditures Model

We begin with an explanation of the symbols we use:

- Aggregate expenditures, AE
- Real GDP, Y
- Consumption expenditure, C
- Autonomous consumption expenditure, a
- Investment expenditure, I_a
- Government Expenditure, G_a
- Exports, X_a
- Imports, M
- Autonomous taxes, T_a
- Marginal tax rate, t
- Marginal propensity to consume, b
- Marginal propensity to import, m
- Autonomous expenditure, A
- Marginal Propensity to Withdraw, W

AGGREGATE EXPENDITURES

We know that $AE = C + I + (X - M) + G$. Let's look at each of the components of aggregate expenditures in more detail.

CONSUMPTION EXPENDITURES

The consumption function is given by the linear equation $C = a + bY_d$. This means that consumption consists of an "autonomous" amount, a, plus a portion of disposable income Y_d, the portion being the product of Y_d and the marginal propensity to consume, b. To arrive at disposable income Y_d we must deduct net taxes. So far we have assumed that taxes are a lump sum, an assumption that made the exposition easier. We now assume that taxes consist of an autonomous amount T_a, plus an induced portion of Y, which is the marginal tax rate, t. So the consumption function becomes:

$$C = a + b(Y - T_a - tY)$$
$$= a - bT_a + b(1 - t)Y$$

INVESTMENT

We assume investment spending (I_a) to be autonomous, or a constant amount.

NET EXPORTS

Recall that in our expenditure model, exports (X_a) are determined abroad, so they are autonomous. Imports are determined by the level of our own GDP multiplied by the marginal propensity to import (m):

$$M = mY$$

GOVERNMENT EXPENDITURES

Our expenditure model assumes that government expenditures (G_a) are autonomous, or independent of GDP.

We can now put all the terms together to get:

$$AE = a - bT_a + b(1 - t)Y + I_a + G_a + X_a - mY \qquad (1)$$

AGGREGATE EXPENDITURES AND EQUILIBRIUM GDP

Equilibrium expenditures occurs when planned aggregate expenditures (AE) equals real GDP (Y):

$$Y = AE \qquad (2)$$

Substituting (2) into (1), we get

$$Y = a - bT_a + b(1 - t)Y + I_a + G_a + X_a - mY$$

We now solve for the value of Y that satisfies both equations (1) and (2). To do so we group the Y terms that are on the right side of the previous equation:

$$Y = Y[b(1 - t) - m] + a - bT_a + I_a + G_a + X_a$$

Bringing the Y terms to the left side of the equation leads us to the equilibrium condition:

$$Y = \frac{a - bT_a + I_a + G_a + X_a}{1 - [b(1 - t) - m]} \qquad (3)$$

Note that in the denominator, $[b(1 - t) - m]$ is the equivalent of the marginal propensity to consume, but that this term refers to the marginal propensity to spend out of national income, rather than just consumption. Note that the denominator $1 - [b(1 - t) - m]$ is a leakage, or a withdrawal from domestic expenditures, which apart from savings, also includes taxes and imports. We can simplify equation (3) by denoting the numerator, which consists of autonomous expenditures, by the letter A, and using the letter W for the marginal propensity to withdraw from domestic expenditures, to give us:

$$Y = A / W$$

GRAPHICAL ILLUSTRATION

In Figure A7-1 below we portray important features of the aggregate expenditures model graphically. In Figure A7-1a the slope of the aggregate expenditure curve, equal to the term $b(1 - t) - m$, is the marginal propensity to spend. Autonomous expenditure, A, is equal to the sum of $a - bT_a + I_a + G_a + X_a$.

Figure A7-1b shows that equilibrium in the aggregate expenditure model occurs where planned expenditure is equal to actual output.

NUMERICAL EXAMPLE

Let's look at a concrete example to calculate equilibrium income. Suppose you are given the following information:

$C = 60 + .6Y_d$	$G_a = 70$
$T = 40 + 0.25Y$	$X_a = 44$
$I_a = 60$	$M = 0.15Y$

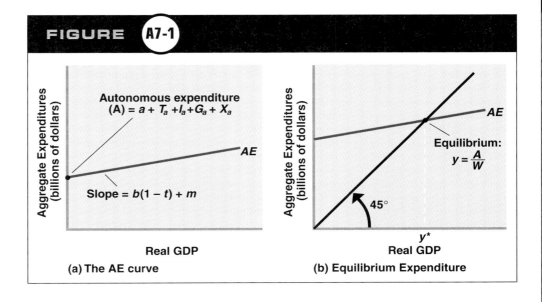

FIGURE A7-1

(a) The AE curve

Autonomous expenditure
$(A) = a + T_a + I_a + G_a + X_a$

Slope $= b(1 - t) + m$

AE

Aggregate Expenditures (billions of dollars)

Real GDP

(b) Equilibrium Expenditure

AE

Equilibrium:
$y = \dfrac{A}{W}$

45°

Aggregate Expenditures (billions of dollars)

Real GDP

y^*

There are two ways you can arrive at the result. The first as to substitute the numbers into equation (1):

At equilibrium $Y = AE$, or
$$Y = C + I + (X - M) + G$$

Substituting each of the components into the equation, we get:

$$Y = 60 + .6(Y - 40 - 0.25Y) + 60 + (44 - 0.15Y) + 70$$

Collecting the terms gives us:

$$Y = 210 + .3Y$$

Subtracting $.3Y$ from each side yields:

$$.7Y = 210$$

Dividing both sides of the equation by .7 gives us the equilibrium real GDP:

$$Y = 300$$

The second way is to substitute the numbers into equation (3):

$$Y = \frac{a - bT_a + I_a + G_a + X_a}{1 - [b(1 - t) - m]}$$

$$Y = \frac{60 - .6(40) + 60 + 70 + 44}{1 - [.6(1 - .25) - .15]}$$

$$Y = \frac{210}{1 - .3}$$

$$Y = \frac{210}{.7}$$

$$Y = 300$$

8

Chapter

Aggregate Demand and Aggregate Supply

In an update of its *Monetary Policy Report* in August 2000, the Bank of Canada reported:

> In terms of the risks to this outlook, developments since the last *Report* reinforce the uncertainties that the Bank has been highlighting for some time: the spillover of U.S. demand at a time of growing spending by Canadian consumers and businesses; the possibility of rising inflation pressures in the United States and the implications for Canada; and the uncertain balance between demand and supply in the Canadian economy, given some signs that the pressure on capacity have not been as intense as expected earlier.[1]

[1]Bank of Canada, *Monetary Policy Report,* Update, August, 2000, pg. 2.

aggregate demand-aggregate supply model
The macroeconomic model that uses aggregate demand and aggregate supply to explain price level and real domestic output.

This is precisely the language of the **aggregate demand-aggregate supply model** (AD-AS model), which we will develop in this chapter. The AD-AS model—the subject of this chapter—enables us to analyze changes in both real GDP and the price level simultaneously. The AD-AS model therefore provides insights on inflation, unemployment, and economic growth. In later chapters, we will see that it also explains the logic of macroeconomic stabilization policies.

8.1 Aggregate Demand

aggregate demand
A schedule or curve that shows the total quantity of goods and services demanded (purchased) at different price levels.

Aggregate demand is a schedule or curve that shows the amounts of real output that buyers collectively desire to purchase at each possible price level. The relationship between the price level and the amount of real GDP demanded is inverse or negative: When the price level rises, the quantity of real GDP demanded decreases; when the price level falls, the quantity of real GDP demanded increases.

Aggregate Demand Curve

The inverse relationship between the price level and real GDP is shown in Figure 8-1, where the aggregate demand curve AD slopes downward, as does the demand curve for an individual product.

Why the downward slope? *The explanation is not the same as that for why the demand for a single product slopes downward.* That explanation centred on the income effect and the substitution effect. When the price of an *individual* product falls, the consumer's (constant) nominal income allows a larger purchase of the product (the income effect). And, as price falls, the consumer wants to buy more of the product because it becomes relatively less expensive than other goods (the substitution effect).

But these explanations do not work for aggregates. In Figure 8-1, when the economy moves down its aggregate demand curve, it moves to a lower general price level. But our circular flow model tells us that when consumers pay lower prices for goods and services, less nominal income flows to suppliers of factors of production in the forms of wages, rent, interest, and profits. As a

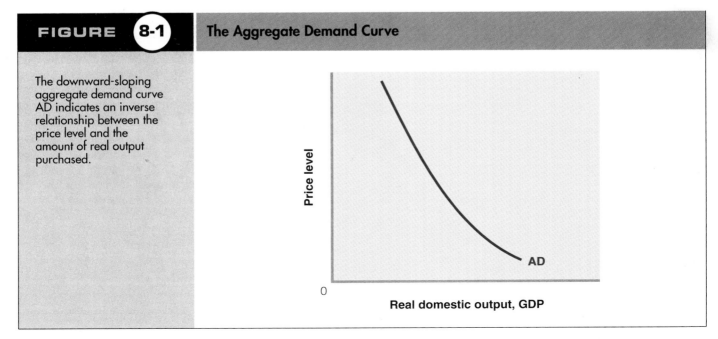

| FIGURE | 8-1 | The Aggregate Demand Curve |

The downward-sloping aggregate demand curve AD indicates an inverse relationship between the price level and the amount of real output purchased.

result, a decline in the price level does not necessarily mean an increase in the nominal income of the economy as a whole. Thus, a decline in the price level need not produce an income effect, where more output is purchased because lower prices leave buyers with greater real income.

Similarly, in Figure 8-1 prices in general are falling as we move down the aggregate demand curve, so the rationale for the substitution effect (where more of a product is purchased because it becomes cheaper relative to all other products) is not applicable. There is no *overall* substitution effect among domestically produced goods when the price level falls.

If the conventional substitution and income effects do not explain the downward slope of the aggregate demand curve, what does? That explanation rests on three effects of a price level change.

REAL-BALANCES EFFECT

real-balances effect
The inverse relationship between the price level and the real value (or purchasing power) of financial assets with fixed money value.

A change in the price level produces a **real-balances effect**. Here is how it works. A higher price level reduces the purchasing power of the public's accumulated saving balances. In particular, the real value of assets with fixed money values, such as savings accounts or bonds, diminishes. Because of the erosion of the purchasing power of such assets, the public is poorer in real terms and will reduce its spending. A household might buy a new car or a sailboat if the purchasing power of its financial asset balances is, say $50,000. But if inflation erodes the purchasing power of its asset balances to $30,000, the family may defer its purchase. So a higher price level means less consumption spending.

INTEREST-RATE EFFECT

interest-rate effect
The direct relationship between price level and the demand for money, which affects interest rates, and, as a result, total spending in the economy.

The aggregate demand curve also slopes downward because of the **interest-rate effect**. When we draw an aggregate demand curve, *we assume that the supply of money in the economy is fixed.* But when the price level rises, consumers need more money for purchases, and businesses need more money to meet their payrolls and to buy other resources. A $10 bill will do when the price of an item is $10, but a $10 bill plus a loonie is needed when the item costs $11. In short, a higher price level increases the demand for money. So, given a fixed supply of money, an increase in money demand will drive up the price paid for its use. The price of money is the interest rate.

Higher interest rates curtail investment spending and interest-sensitive consumption spending. Firms that expect a 6 percent rate of return on a potential purchase of capital will find that investment profitable when the interest rate is, say, 5 percent. But the investment will be unprofitable and will not be made when the interest rate has risen to 7 percent. Similarly, consumers may decide not to purchase a new house or new automobile when the interest rate on loans goes up. So, by increasing the demand for money and consequently the interest rate, a higher price level reduces the amount of real output demanded.

FOREIGN TRADE EFFECT

foreign trade effect
The inverse relationship between the net exports of an economy and its price level relative to price levels in the economies of trading partners.

The final reason why the aggregate demand curve slopes downward is the **foreign trade effect**. When the Canadian price level rises relative to foreign price levels, foreigners buy fewer Canadian goods and Canadians buy more foreign goods. Therefore, Canadian exports fall and Canadian imports rise. In short, the rise in the price level reduces the quantity of Canadian goods demanded as net exports.

These three effects, of course, work in the opposite directions for a decline in the price level. Then the quantity demanded of consumption goods, investment goods, and net exports rises.

Determinants of Aggregate Demand

determinants of aggregate demand
Factors (such as consumption spending, investment, government spending, and net exports) that shift the aggregate demand curve.

Other things equal, a change in the price level will change the amount of aggregate spending and therefore change the amount of real GDP demanded by the economy. Movements along a fixed aggregate demand curve represent these changes in real GDP. However, if one or more of those "other things" change, the entire aggregate demand curve will shift. We call these "other things" **determinants of aggregate demand**. They are listed in Figure 8-2.

In Figure 8-2, the rightward shift of the curve from AD_1 to AD_2 shows an increase in aggregate demand. At each price level, the amount of real goods and services demanded is larger than before. The leftward shift of the curve from AD_1 to AD_3 shows a decrease in aggregate demand, the lesser amount of real GDP demanded at each price level.

Let's examine each of the determinants of aggregate demand that are listed in Figure 8-2.

CONSUMER SPENDING

Even when the Canadian price level is constant, domestic consumers may change their purchases of Canadian-produced real output. If those consumers decide to buy more output at each price level, the aggregate demand curve will shift to the right, as from AD_1 to AD_2 in Figure 8-2. If they decide to buy less output, the aggregate demand curve will shift to the left, as from AD_1 to AD_3.

Several factors other than a change in the price level may change consumer spending and thus shift the aggregate demand curve. As Figure 8-2 shows, those factors are real consumer wealth, consumer expectations, household indebtedness, and taxes.

Consumer wealth   Consumer wealth includes both financial assets such as stocks and bonds and physical assets such as houses and land. A sharp increase in the real value of consumer wealth (for example, because of a rise in stock market values) prompts people to save less and buy more products. The resulting increase in consumer spending—called the *wealth effect*—will shift the aggregate demand curve to the right. In contrast, a major decrease in the real value of consumer wealth at each price level will reduce consumption spending and thus shift the aggregate demand curve to the left.

www.statcan.ca/Daily/English/
001212/d001212a.htm
Statistics Canada

FIGURE **8-2**	**Changes in Aggregate Demand**

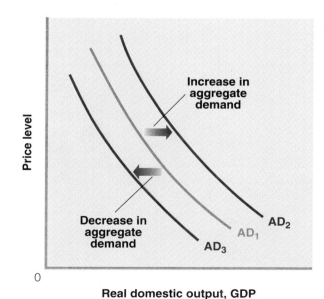

**Determinants of aggregate demand:
factors that shift the aggregate demand curve**

1. Change in consumer spending
   a. Consumer wealth
   b. Consumer expectations
   c. Household indebtedness
   d. Taxes
2. Change in investment spending
   a. Interest rates
   b. Expected returns
      • Expected future business conditions
      • Technology
      • Degree of excess capacity
      • Business taxes
3. Change in government spending
4. Change in net export spending
   a. National income abroad
   b. Exchange rates

A change in one or more of the listed determinants of aggregate demand will change aggregate demand. An increase in aggregate demand is shown as a rightward shift of the AD curve, here from AD_1 to AD_2; a decrease in aggregate demand is shown as a leftward shift, here from AD_1 to AD_3.

Consumer expectations   Changes in expectations about the future may change consumer spending. When people expect their future real income to rise, they spend more of their current income. Thus current consumption spending increases (current saving falls), and the aggregate demand curve shifts to the right. Similarly, a widely held expectation of surging inflation in the near future may increase aggregate demand today because consumers will want to buy products before their prices rise. Conversely, expectations of lower future income or lower future prices may reduce current consumption and shift the aggregate demand curve to the left.

Taxes   A reduction in personal income tax rates raises take-home income and increases consumer purchases at each possible price level. Tax cuts shift the aggregate demand curve to the right. Tax increases reduce consumption spending and shift the curve to the left.

Household indebtedness   Households finance some of their spending by borrowing. If household indebtedness from past spending rises beyond normal levels, consumers may be forced to cut current spending in order to pay the interest and principal on their debt. Consumption spending will then decline and the aggregate demand curve will shift to the left. Alternatively, when household indebtedness is unusually low, consumers have considerable leeway to borrow and spend today. Then the aggregate demand curve may shift to the right.

INVESTMENT SPENDING

Investment spending (the purchase of capital goods) is a second major determinant of aggregate demand. A decline in investment spending at each price level will shift the aggregate demand curve to the left. An increase in investment spending will shift it to the right.

Real Interest Rates   Other things equal, an increase in interest rates will lower investment spending and reduce aggregate demand. We are not referring here to the "interest-rate effect" resulting from a change in the price level. Instead, we are identifying a change in the interest rate resulting from, say, a change in the nation's money supply. An increase in the money supply lowers the interest rate, thereby increasing investment and aggregate demand. A decrease in the money supply raises the interest rate, reduces investment, and decreases aggregate demand.

Expected Returns   Higher expected returns on investment projects will increase the demand for capital goods and shift the aggregate demand curve to the right. Alternatively, declines in expected returns will decrease investment and shift the curve to the left. Expected returns, in turn, are influenced by several factors:

- *Expectations about future business conditions*   If firms are optimistic about future business conditions, they are more likely to invest more today. On the other hand, if they think the economy will deteriorate in the future, they will invest less today.

- *Technology*   New and improved technologies increase expected returns on investment and thus increase aggregate demand. For example, recent advances in microbiology have motivated pharmaceutical companies to establish new labs and production facilities.

- *Degree of excess capacity*   Other things equal, firms operating factories at well below capacity have little incentive to build new factories. But when firms discover that their excess capacity is dwindling or has completely disappeared, their expected returns on new investment in factories and capital equipment rises. Thus, they increase their investment spending and the aggregate demand curve shifts to the right.

- *Business Taxes*   An increase in business taxes will reduce after-tax profits from capital investment and lower expected returns. So investment and aggregate demand will decline. A decrease in business taxes will have the opposite effects.

GOVERNMENT SPENDING

Government purchases are the third determinant of aggregate demand. An increase in government purchases (for example, more computers for government agencies) will shift the aggregate demand curve to the right, so long as tax collections and interest rates do not change as a result. In contrast, a reduction in government spending (for example, a cutback in health care spending) will shift the curve to the left.

NET EXPORT SPENDING

The final determinant of aggregate demand is net export spending. A rise of Canadian *exports* means increased foreign demand for Canadian goods, whereas lower Canadian *imports* implies that Canadian consumers have decreased their demand for foreign-produced products. So, a rise in net exports (higher exports and/or lower imports) shifts the aggregate demand curve to the right. In contrast, a decrease in Canadian net exports shifts the aggregate demand curve leftward. (These changes in net exports are *not* those prompted by a change in the Canadian price level—those associated with the foreign-trade effect. The changes here explain shifts in the curve, not movements along the curve.)

What might cause net exports to change, other than the price level? Two possibilities are changes in national income abroad and changes in exchange rates.

National Income Abroad   Rising national income abroad encourages foreigners to buy more products, some of which are made in Canada. Canadian net exports thus rise and the Canadian aggregate demand curve shifts to the right. Declines in national income abroad, of course, do the opposite: They reduce Canadian net exports and shift the aggregate demand curve in Canada to the left.

www.europe.eu.int/euro/html
Euro

Exchange Rates   Changes in exchange rates may affect Canadian net exports and therefore aggregate demand. Suppose the Canadian dollar depreciates in terms of the euro (the euro appreciates in terms of the dollar). The new relative lower value of dollars and higher value of euros make Canadian goods less expensive, so European consumers buy more Canadian goods and Canadian exports rise. But Canadian consumers now find European goods more expensive, so reduce their imports from Europe. Canadian exports rise and Canadian imports fall. *Depreciation* of the dollar increases Canadian net exports, thereby shifting the Canadian aggregate demand curve to the right.

Think through the opposite scenario, in which the dollar *appreciates* and the euro depreciates.

QUICK REVIEW

- Aggregate demand reflects an inverse relationship between the price level and the amount of real output demanded.

- Changes in the price level create real-balances, interest-rate, and foreign-trade effects that explain the downward slope of the aggregate demand curve.

- Changes in one or more of the determinants of aggregate demand (Figure 8-2) alter the amounts of real GDP demanded at each price level; they shift the aggregate demand curve.

- An increase in aggregate demand is shown as a rightward shift of the aggregate demand curve; a decrease, as a leftward shift of the curve.

8.2   Aggregate Supply

Aggregate supply is a schedule or a curve showing the level of real domestic output that firms will produce at each price level. The production responses of firms to changes in the price level differ in the *long run*, which in macroeconomics is a period in which nominal wages (and other resource prices) have to fully adjust to changes in the price level—and the *short run*, a period in which nominal wages (and other resource prices) do not respond to price level changes. So the long and short runs vary by degree of wage adjustment, not by a set length of time such as one month, one year, or three years.

Aggregate Supply in the Long Run

In the long run, the aggregate supply curve is vertical at the economy's full-employment output (or its potential GDP), as represented by AS_{LR} in Figure 8-3. When changes in wages respond completely to changes in the price level, those price level changes do not alter the amount of real GDP produced and offered for sale.

Consider a one-firm economy in which the firm's owner must receive a real profit of $20 in order to produce the full-employment output of 100 units. The real reward the owner receives, not the level of prices, is what really counts. Assume the owner's only input (aside from entrepreneurial talent) is 10 units of hired labour at $8 per worker for a total wage cost of $80. Also, assume that the 100 units of output sell for $1 per unit, so that total revenue is $100. The firm's nominal profit is $20 (= $100 − $80), and using the base price index of 100, its real profit is also $20 (= [$20 ÷ 100] × 100). Well and good; the full-employment output is produced.

Next, suppose the price level doubles. Would the owner earn more than the $20 of real profit and therefore boost production beyond the 100-unit full-employment output? The answer is no, given the assumption that nominal wages and the price-level rise by the same amount. Once the product price has doubled to $2, total revenue will be $200 (= 100 × $2). But the cost of 10 units of labour will double from $80 to $160 because the wage rate rises from $8 to $16. Nominal profit thus increases to $40 (= $200 − $160). What about real profit? By dividing the nominal profit of $40 by the new price index of 200, we obtain real profit of $20 (= [$40 ÷ 200] × 100). Because real profit does not change, the firm will not alter its production. Real GDP will remain at its full-employment level.

In the long run, wages and other input prices rise or fall to match changes in the price level. Changes in the price level therefore do not change real profit and there is no change in real output. The **long-run aggregate supply curve** is vertical at the economy's potential output (or full-employment output), as in Figure 8-3.

long-run aggregate supply curve
The aggregate supply curve associated with a time period in which input prices (especially nominal wages) are fully responsive to changes in the price level.

Aggregate Supply in the Short Run

In reality, nominal wages adjust only slowly to changes in the price level and perfect adjustment may take several months or even a number of years. Reconsider our previous one-firm economy. If the $8 nominal wage for each of the 10 workers is unresponsive to the price level change, doubling of the price level will boost total revenue from $100 to $200 but leaves total cost unchanged at $80. Nominal profit will rise from $20 (= $100 − $80) to $120 (= $200 − $80). Dividing that $120 profit by the new price index of 200, we find that the real profit is now $60. The rise in the real profit from $20 to $60 prompts firms to produce more output. Conversely, price level declines reduce real prof-

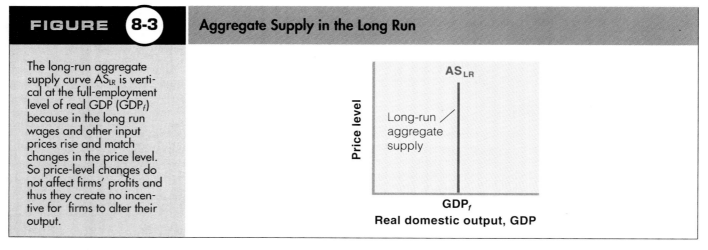

| FIGURE 8-3 | Aggregate Supply in the Long Run |

The long-run aggregate supply curve AS_{LR} is vertical at the full-employment level of real GDP (GDP_f) because in the long run wages and other input prices rise and match changes in the price level. So price-level changes do not affect firms' profits and thus they create no incentive for firms to alter their output.

its and cause firms collectively to reduce their output. So, in the short-run, there is a direct or positive relationship between the price level and real output, as in Figure 8-4.

The **short-run aggregate supply curve** is upward-sloping, as shown in Figure 8-4. A rise in the price level increases real output; a fall in the price level reduces it. Per-unit production costs underlie the aggregate supply curve. We calculate the per-unit production cost as follows:

$$\text{Per-unit production cost} = \frac{\text{total input cost}}{\text{units of output}}$$

The per-unit production cost of any specific level of output establishes that output's price level because the price level must cover all the costs of production, including profit "costs." As the economy expands in the short run, per-unit production costs generally rise because of reduced efficiency and rising input prices. But the extent of that rise depends on where the economy is operating relative to its capacity. The aggregate supply curve in Figure 8-4 is relatively flat at outputs below the full-employment output GDP_f and relatively steep at outputs above it. Why the difference?

When the economy is operating below its full-employment output, it has large amounts of unused machinery and equipment, and unemployed workers. Firms can put these idle human and property resources back to work with little upward pressure on per-unit production costs. Workers unemployed for 2 or 3 months will hardly expect a wage increase when recalled to their jobs. And, as output expands, no shortages of inputs or production bottlenecks will arise to raise per-unit production costs.

When the economy is operating beyond its full-employment output, the vast majority of its available resources are already employed. Adding more workers to a relatively fixed number of highly used capital resources such as machinery and equipment creates congestion in the workplace and reduces the efficiency (on average) of workers. Adding more capital, given the limited number of available workers, leaves equipment idle and reduces the efficiency of capital. Adding more land resources when capital and labour are highly constrained reduces the efficiency of land resources. Under these circumstances, total output rises less rapidly than total input cost. So per-unit production costs increase.

short-run aggregate supply
A schedule or curve that shows the level of real domestic output that will be produced at each price level.

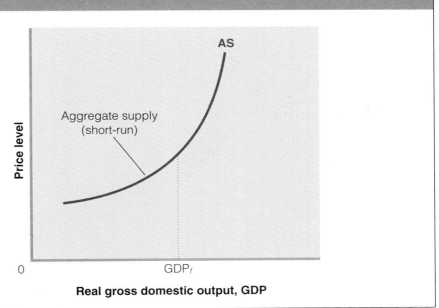

FIGURE 8-4

The Aggregate Supply Curve (Short-Run)

The upward-sloping aggregate supply curve AS indicates a direct (or positive) relationship between the price level and the amount of real output that firms will offer for sale. The AS curve is relatively flat below the full-employment output because unemployed resources and unused capacity allow firms to respond to price-level rises with large increases in real output. It is relatively steep beyond the full-employment output because resource shortages and capacity limitations make it difficult to expand real output as the price level rises.

Moreover, individual firms may try to expand their own production by bidding resources away from other firms. But the resources and additional production that one firm gains will be largely lost by other firms. The bidding will raise input prices, but real output will rise very little, if at all. That is a prescription for higher per-unit production costs.

Our focus in the first part of this chapter is on short-run aggregate supply, such as that shown in Figure 8-4. Unless stated otherwise, all references to "aggregate supply" are to aggregate supply in the short-run. We will bring long-run aggregate supply prominently back into the analysis in the second part of this chapter where we go into a little more detail about long-run wage adjustments.

An aggregate supply curve identifies the relationship between the price level and real output.

determinants of aggregate supply
Factors such as input prices, productivity, and the legal-institutional environment that shift the aggregate supply curve.

Determinants of Aggregate Supply

An existing aggregate supply curve identifies the relationship between the price level and real output, other things equal. But when one or more of these "other things" change, the curve itself shifts. The rightward shift of the curve from AS_1 to AS_3 in Figure 8-5 represents an increase in aggregate supply, indicating that firms are willing to produce and sell more real output at each price level. The leftward shift of the curve from AS_1 to AS_2 represents a decrease in aggregate supply. At each price level, firms will not produce as much output as before.

Figure 8-5 lists the "other things" that shift the aggregate supply curve. Called the **determinants of aggregate supply**, they collectively determine the location of the aggregate supply curve and shift the curve when they change. Changes in these determinants cause per-unit production costs to be either higher or lower than before *at each price level*. These changes in per-unit production cost affect profits, which leads firms to alter the amount of output they are willing to produce *at each price level*. For example, firms may collectively offer $1 trillion of real output at a price level of 1.0 (100 in index value), rather than $900 billion. Or, they may offer, $800 billion rather than $1 trillion. The point is that when one of the determinants listed in Figure 8-5 changes, the aggregate supply curve shifts to the right or left. Changes that reduce per-unit production cost shift the aggregate

---

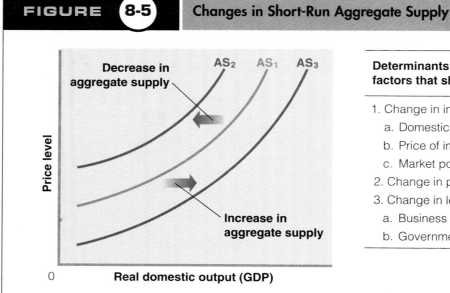

FIGURE 8-5 | **Changes in Short-Run Aggregate Supply**

Determinants of the short-run aggregate supply: factors that shift the aggregate supply curve

1. Change in input prices
   a. Domestic resource price
   b. Price of imported resources
   c. Market power
2. Change in productivity
3. Change in legal-institutional environment
   a. Business taxes and subsidies
   b. Government regulation

A change in one or more of the listed determinants of aggregate supply will shift the aggregate supply curve. The rightward shift of the aggregate supply curve from AS_1 to AS_3 represents an increase in aggregate supply; the leftward shift of the curve from AS_1 to AS_2 shows a decrease in aggregate supply.

supply curve to the right, as from AS$_1$ to AS$_2$; changes that increase per-unit production costs shift it to the left, as from AS$_1$ to AS$_3$. *When per-unit production costs change for reasons other than changes in real output, the aggregate supply curves shifts.*

The aggregate supply determinants listed in Figure 8-5 require more discussion.

INPUT PRICES

Input or resource prices—to be distinguished from the output prices that make up the price level—are a key determinant of aggregate supply. These resources can be either domestic or imported.

Domestic Resource Prices Wages and salaries make up about 75 percent of all business costs. Other things equal, decreases in wages and salaries reduce per-unit production costs. So the aggregate supply shifts to the right. Increases in wages and salaries shift the curve to the left. Examples:

- Labour supply increases because of substantial immigration. Wages and per-unit production costs fall, shifting the AS curve to the right.

- Labour supply decreases because of a rapid rise in pension income and early retirements. Wage rates and per-unit production costs rise, shifting the AS curve to the left.

Similarly, the aggregate supply curve shifts when the prices of land and capital inputs change. Examples:

- The price of capital (machinery and equipment) falls because of declines in the prices of steel and electronic components. Per-unit production costs decline and the AS shifts to the right.

- Land resources expand through discoveries of mineral deposits, irrigation of land, or technical innovations that transform "non-resources" (say, vast northern shrub lands) into valuable resources (productive lands). The price of land declines, per-unit production costs fall, and the AS curve shifts to the right.

Prices of Imported Resources   Just as foreign demand for Canadian goods contributes to Canadian aggregate demand, resources imported from abroad (such as oil, tin, and coffee beans) add to Canadian aggregate supply. Added resources—whether domestic or imported—boost production capacity. Generally, a decrease in the price of imported resources increases Canadian aggregate supply, and an increase in their price reduces Canadian aggregate supply.

Exchange-rate fluctuations are one factor that may change the price of imported resources. Suppose that the dollar appreciates. This means that domestic producers face a lower *dollar* price of imported resources. Canadian firms would respond by increasing their imports of foreign resources, thereby lowering their per-unit production costs at each level of output. Falling per-unit production costs would shift the Canadian aggregate supply curve to the right.

A depreciation of the dollar, in contrast, will have the opposite effects.

Market Power   A change in the degree of market power—the ability to set above-competitive prices—held by sellers of major inputs also can affect input prices and aggregate supply. An example is the fluctuating market power held by the Organization of Petroleum Exporting Countries (OPEC) over the past several decades. The tenfold increase in the price of oil that OPEC achieved during the 1970s drove up per-unit production costs and jolted the Canadian aggregate supply curve leftward. In 1999 OPEC reasserted its market power, creating higher oil prices that pushed up costs for some Canadian producers (for examples, airlines and truckers).

PRODUCTIVITY

The second major determinant of aggregate supply is *productivity,* which is a measure of the relationship between a nation's level of real output and the amount of resources used to produce it. Productivity is a measure of real output per unit of input:

$$\text{Productivity} = \frac{\text{total output}}{\text{total input}}$$

An increase in productivity enables the economy to obtain more real output from its limited resources. It does this by reducing the per-unit cost of output (per-unit production cost). Suppose, for example, that real output is 10 units, that 5 units of input are needed to produce that quantity, and that the price of each input unit is $2. Then

$$\text{Productivity} = \frac{\text{total output}}{\text{total input}} = \frac{10}{5} = 2$$

and

$$\text{Per-unit production cost} = \frac{\text{total input cost}}{\text{total output}} = \frac{(\$2 \times 5)}{10} = \$1$$

Note that we obtain the total input cost by multiplying the unit input cost by the number of inputs used.

Now suppose productivity increases so that real output doubles to 20 units, while the price and quantity of the input remain constant at $2 and 5 units. Using the above equations, we see that productivity rises from 2 to 4 and that the per-unit production cost of the output falls from $1 to $.50. The doubled productivity has reduced the per-unit production cost by half.

By reducing the per-unit production cost, an increase in productivity shifts the aggregate supply curve to the right. The main source of productivity advance is improved production technology, often embodied within new plant and equipment that replaces old plant and equipment. Other sources of productivity increases are a better-educated and trained workforce, improved forms of business enterprises, and the reallocation of labour resources from lower to higher productivity uses.

LEGAL-INSTITUTIONAL ENVIRONMENT

Changes in the legal-institutional setting in which businesses operate are the final determinant of aggregate supply. Such changes may alter the per-unit costs of output and, if so, shift the aggregate supply curve. Two changes of this type are (1) changes in business taxes and subsidies, and (2) changes in the extent of regulation.

Business Taxes and Subsidies   Higher business taxes, such as sales, excise, and payroll taxes, increase per-unit costs and reduce aggregate supply in much the same way as a wage increase does. An increase in such taxes paid by businesses will increase per-unit production costs and shift the aggregate supply curve to the left.

Similarly, a business subsidy—a payment or tax break by government to producers—lowers production costs and increases aggregate supply.

Government Regulation   It is usually costly for businesses to comply with government regulations. More regulation therefore tends to increase per-unit production costs and shift the aggregate supply curve to the left. "Supply-side" proponents of deregulation of the economy have argued forcefully that, by increasing efficiency and reducing the paperwork associated with complex regulations, deregulation will reduce per-unit costs and shift the aggregate supply curve to the right.

QUICK REVIEW

- The long-run aggregate supply curve is vertical because, given sufficient time, wages and other input prices rise and fall to match price-level changes; because price-level changes do not change real rewards, they do not change production decisions.

- The short-run aggregate supply curve (or simply the "aggregate supply curve") is upward sloping because the per-unit costs of production rise as output increases, even though wages and other input prices are constant. The underlying upward slope of the aggregate supply curve reflects rising per-unit production cost as output expands.

- By altering the per-unit production cost independent of changes in the level of output, changes in one or more of the determinants of aggregate supply (Figure 8-5) shift the short-run aggregate supply curve.

- An increase in short-run aggregate supply is shown as a rightward shift of the curve, a decrease is shown as a leftward shift of the curve.

8.3   Equilibrium GDP and Changes in Equilibrium

equilibrium price level
The price level at which the aggregate demand curve intersects the aggregate supply curve.

equilibrium real domestic output
The real domestic output at which the aggregate demand curve intersects the aggregate supply curve.

Out of all the possible combinations of price levels and levels of real GDP, which combination will the economy gravitate toward, at least in the short-run? **Figure 8-6 (Key Graph)** and its accompanying table provide the answer. Equilibrium occurs at the price level that equalizes the amount of real output demanded and supplied. The intersection of the aggregate demand curve AD and the aggregate supply curve AS establishes the economy's **equilibrium price level** and **equilibrium real output**. So, aggregate demand and aggregate supply jointly establish the price level and level of real GDP.

In Figure 8-6 the equilibrium price level and level of real output are 100 and $510 billion, respectively. To illustrate why, suppose the price level were 92 rather than 100. We see from the table that the lower price level would encourage businesses to produce real output of $502 billion. This is shown by point *a* on the AS curve in the graph. But, as revealed by the table and point *b* on the aggregate demand curve, buyers would want to purchase $514 billion of real output at price level 92. Competition among buyers to purchase the lesser available real output of $502 billion will eliminate the $12 billion (= $514 billion − $502 billion) shortage and pull up the price level to 100.

As the table and graph show, the excess demand for the output of the economy causes the price level to rise from 92 to 100, which encourages producers to increase their real output from $502 billion to $510 billion, thereby increasing GDP. In increasing their real output, producers hire more employees, reducing the unemployment level in the economy. When equality occurs between the amounts of real output produced and purchased, as it does at price level 100, the economy has achieved equilibrium (here at $510 billion of real GDP).

Now let's apply the AD-AS model to various situations that can confront the economy. For simplicity we will use *P* and GDP symbols, rather than actual numbers. Remember that these symbols represent price index values and real GDP amounts.

Increases in AD

Suppose households and businesses decide to increase their consumption and investment spending—actions that shift the aggregate demand curve to the right. Our list of determinants of aggregate demand (Figure 8-2) provides several reasons why this shift might occur. Perhaps consumers feel wealthier because of large gains in their stock holdings. As a result, consumers would consume more (save less) of their current income. Perhaps firms boost their investment spending because they anticipate higher future profits from investments in new capital. Those profits are based on having new equipment and facilities that incorporate a number of new technologies. And perhaps government increases spending in health care.

As shown in Figure 8-7, an increase in aggregate demand raises both real output (GDP$_1$ to GDP$_2$) and the price level (P_1 to P_2). Output expands but there is some inflation. Work out on your own the effects on the price level and equilibrium GDP if there is a fall in aggregate demand.

As shown by the rise in the price level from P_1 to P_2 in Figure 8-7, the increase in aggregate demand beyond the full-employment level of output causes inflation. This is *demand-pull inflation*, because the price level is being pulled up by the increase in aggregate demand. Also, observe that the increase in demand expands real output from GDP$_f$ to GDP$_1$. The distance between GDP$_1$ and GDP$_f$ is a positive *GDP gap*. Actual GDP exceeds potential GDP. *(Key Question 4)*

A careful examination of Figure 8-7 reveals an interesting point. The increase in aggregate demand from AD$_1$ to AD$_2$ increases real output only to GDP$_1$, not to GDP$_2$, because part of the increase in aggregate demand is absorbed as inflation as the price level rises from P_1 to P_2. Had the price level remained at P_1, the shift of aggregate demand from AD$_1$ to AD$_2$ would have increased real output to GDP$_2$. But in Figure 8-7 inflation reduced the increase in real output by about one-half. *For any initial increase in aggregate demand, the resulting increase in real output will be smaller the greater is the increase in the price level.*

Key Graph

FIGURE 8-6 The Equilibrium Price Level and Equilibrium Real GDP

The intersection of the aggregate demand curve and the aggregate supply curve determines the economy's equilibrium price level. At the equilibrium price level of 100 (in index-value terms) the $510 billion of real output demanded matches the $510 billion of real output supplied.

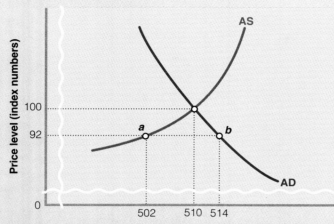

Real Output Demanded (Billions)	Price Level (Index Number)	Real Output Supplied (Billions)
$506	108	$513
508	104	512
510	**100**	**510**
512	96	505
514	92	502

Quick Quiz

1. The AD curve slopes downward because
   a. per-unit production costs fall as real GDP increases.
   b. the income and substitution effects are at work.
   c. changes in the determinants of AD alter the amounts of real GDP demanded at each price level.
   d. decreases in the price level give rise to wealth, interest-rate, and foreign-trade effects, which increase the amounts of real GDP demanded.

2. The AS curve slopes upward because
   a. per-unit production costs rise as real GDP expands towards and beyond its full-employment level.
   b. the income and substitution effects are at work.
   c. changes in the determinants of AS alter the amounts of real GDP supplied at each price level.
   d. increases in the price level give rise to wealth, interest-rate, and foreign-purchases effects, which increase the amounts of real GDP supplied.

3. At price level 92
   a. a GDP surplus of $12 billion occurs that drives the price level up to 100.
   b. a GDP shortage of $12 billion occurs that drives the price level up to 100.
   c. the aggregate amount of real GDP demanded is less than the aggregate amount of GDP supplied.
   d. the economy is operating beyond its capacity to produce.

4. Suppose real output demanded rises by $4 billion at each price level. The new equilibrium price level will be:
   a. 108.
   b. 104.
   c. 96.
   d. 92.

ANSWERS: 1. d; 2. a; 3. b; 4. d.

www.mcgrawhill.ca/college/mcconnell

FIGURE 8-7

Effects of AD Shifts, and Inflation

An increase in aggregate demand generally increases both the GDP and price level. The increase in aggregate demand from AD_1 to AD_2 is partly dissipated in inflation (P_1 to P_2) and real output increases only from GDP_f to GDP_2.

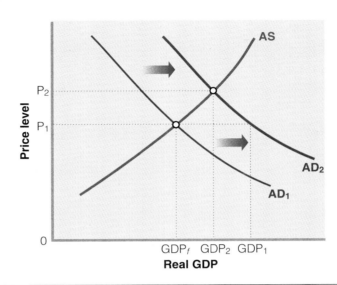

Decreases in AD: Recession and Cyclical Unemployment

Decreases in aggregate demand describe the opposite end of the business cycle: recession and cyclical unemployment (rather than above-full employment and demand-pull inflation). For example, in 2000 investment spending substantially declined because of an overexpansion of capital during the second half of the 1990s. In Figure 8-8 we show the resulting decline in aggregate demand as a leftward shift from AD_1 to AD_2.

But now we add an important twist to the analysis. What goes up—the price level—does not readily go down. *Deflation*—a decline in the price level—is a rarity in the Canadian economy. The economy represented by Figure 8-8 moves from *a* to *b*, rather than from *a* to *c*. The outcome is a decline of real output from GDP_f to GDP_1, with no change in the price level. It is as if the aggregate supply curve in Figure 8-8 is horizontal at P_1 leftward from GDP_f, as indicated by the dashed line. This decline of real output from GDP_f to GDP_1 constitutes a *recession*, and since fewer workers are needed to produce the lower output, *cyclical unemployment* arises. The distance between GDP_1 and GDP_f is a negative *GDP gap*—the amount by which actual output falls short of the full-employment output. Such a gap occurred during Canada in 2001 when unemployment rose to 7.7 percent of the labour force, from 6.8 percent in 2000. But unlike the American economy, Canada did not slip into recession in 2001, although economic growth slowed to 1.9 percent in 2001, from a strong 4.4 percent in 2000.

In this case, close inspection of Figure 8-8 reveals that, with the price level stuck at P_1, real GDP decreases by the full leftward shift of the AD curve. Real output takes the full brunt of the decline in aggregate demand in Figure 8-8 because product prices tend to be "sticky" or inflexible in a downward direction in the short run. There are numerous reasons for this.

- **Wage contracts**   In the short run wage rates often are inflexible downward and it usually is not profitable for firms to cut their product prices if they cannot also cut their wage rates. Wages tend to be inflexible downward because large parts of the labour force work under contracts prohibiting wage cuts for the duration of the contract. (It is not uncommon for collective bargaining agreements in major industries to run for three years.) Similarly, the wages and salaries of non-union workers are usually adjusted once a year, rather than quarterly or monthly.

FIGURE 8-8 | **A Decrease in Aggregate Demand that Causes a Recession**

If the price level is downwardly inflexible at P_1, a decline of aggregate demand from AD_1 to AD_2 will move the economy leftward along the horizontal broken-line segment and reduce real GDP from GDP_f to GDP_1. Idle production capacity, cyclical unemployment, and a negative GDP gap (of GDP_f minus GDP_1) will result.

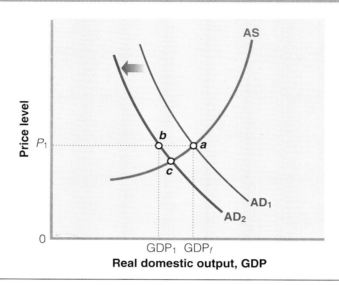

---

efficiency wages
Wages that elicit maximum work effort and thus minimize labour cost per unit of output.

- **Morale, effort, and productivity**   Wage inflexibility downward is reinforced by the reluctance of many employers to reduce wage rates. Current wages may be so-called **efficiency wages**— *wages that elicit maximum work effort and thus minimize labour cost per unit of output* (see the Consider This box). If worker productivity (output per hour of work) remains constant, lower wages *do* reduce labour costs per unit of output. But lower wages might impair worker morale and work effort, thereby reducing productivity. Considered alone, lower productivity raises labour costs per unit of output because less output is produced. If the higher labour costs resulting from reduced productivity exceed the cost savings from the lower wage, then wage cuts will increase rather than reduce labour costs per unit of output. In such situations, firms will therefore resist lowering wages when they are faced with a decline in aggregate demand.

- **Minimum wage**   A government-legislated minimum wage imposes a floor under the wages of the least-skilled workers. Firms cannot reduce that wage rate when aggregate demand declines.

menu costs
Costs associated with changing the prices of goods and services.

- **Menu costs**   Firms that think a recession will be relatively short-lived may be reluctant to cut their prices. One reason is so-called **menu costs**, named after their most obvious example: the cost of printing new menus when a restaurant changes its prices. But changes in prices create other costs of changing prices. There are the costs of (1) estimating the magnitude and duration of the shift in demand to determine whether prices should be lowered, (2) changing the price of items held in inventory, (3) printing and mailing new catalogues, and (4) communicating new prices to customers, perhaps through advertising. When menu costs are present, firms may choose to avoid them by retaining current prices. That is, they will wait to see if the decline in aggregate demand is permanent.

- **Fear of price wars**   Some firms may be concerned that if they reduce their prices, rivals not only will match their price cuts but may retaliate by making even deeper cuts. An initial price cut may touch off an unwanted *price war*: successively deeper and deeper rounds of price cuts. In such a situation, all the firms end up with far less profit than if they had simply maintained their prices. For this reason, each firm may resist making the initial price cut, choosing instead to reduce production and lay off workers.

Consider This

Efficiency Wages

The notion that higher wages promote greater productivity— *efficiency wages*—appears often in the history of economic thought. Although not credited with developing the term, Adam Smith (1723–1790) was one of the first to articulate the idea. Smith argued that there exists a positive relationship between wages and worker productivity. As Smith put it,

> The liberal reward for labour, as it encourages the propagation, so it increases the industry of the common people. The wages of labour are the encouragement of industry, which like every other human quality, improves in proportion to the encouragement it receives. A plentiful subsistence increases the bodily strength of the labourer, and the comfortable hope of bettering his position, and of ending his days in ease and plenty, animates him to exert that strength to the utmost. Where wages are high, accordingly, we shall always find the workmen more active, diligent, and expeditious, than where they are low.

Keep in mind that Smith was writing during the time of the industrial revolution in Great Britain. At that time it was common to have wages that barely provided for physical subsistence, and often fathers (the primary wage labourers), would forgo meals so that children could eat. Higher wages would allow workers, as Smith suggests, to increase bodily strength, an important dimension to productivity in late 18th century Britain. Modern efficiency wage theory focuses more on worker morale and labour turnover, and less on the physical needs of workers, a central issue in Smith's time.

Robert Owen (1771–1858), owner of the New Lanark spinning mills in Scotland, attempted to put the idea of efficiency wages into practice. Owen, who owned and ran the mills from 1800–1820, also established the model community of New Lanark. Operating during the industrial revolution, a period in which wages were pushed to subsistence, Owen paid his workers significantly more than the prevailing wages of the time, and his mills were both productive and profitable.

Several economists developed formal theories of efficiency wages. These theories are summarized by George Akerlof and Janet Yellen, eds., in their book, *Efficiency Wage Models of the Labor Market* (Cambridge: Cambridge University Press, 1986).

Question: If a company in a competitive sector pays a wage above the going equilibrium wage rate, or an efficiency wage, will it put that company at a competitive disadvantage?

But a "caution" is needed. Although most economists agree that wages and prices tend to be inflexible downward, many contend that wages and price are more flexible than in the past. The declining power of unions in Canada and intense foreign competition has undermined the ability of workers and firms to resist price and wage cuts when faced with falling aggregate demand. This increased flexibility may be one reason for the relatively mild recessions in recent times. In 2002 and 2003 Canadian auto manufacturers, for example, maintained output in the face of falling demand by offering zero-interest loans on auto purchases. This, in effect, was a disguised price cut. But, our description in Figure 8-8 remains valid. In 2001 the overall price level did not decline although unemployment rose by 80,000 workers.

Decreases in AS: Cost-Push Inflation

Suppose that a major terrorist attack on oil facilities severely disrupts world oil supplies and drives up oil prices by, say, 300 percent. Higher energy prices would spread through the economy, driving up production and distribution costs on a wide variety of goods. The Canadian aggregate supply curve would spring to the left, say, from AS_1 to AS_2 in Figure 8-9. The resulting increase in price-level would be *cost-push inflation*.

The effects of a leftward shift in aggregate supply are doubly bad. When aggregate supply shifts from AS_1 to AS_2, the economy moves from *a* to *b*. The price level rises from P_1 to P_2 and real output declines from GDP_f to GDP_2. Along with the cost-push inflation, a recession (and negative GDP gap) occurs. That is exactly what happened in Canada in the mid-1970s when the price of oil rock-

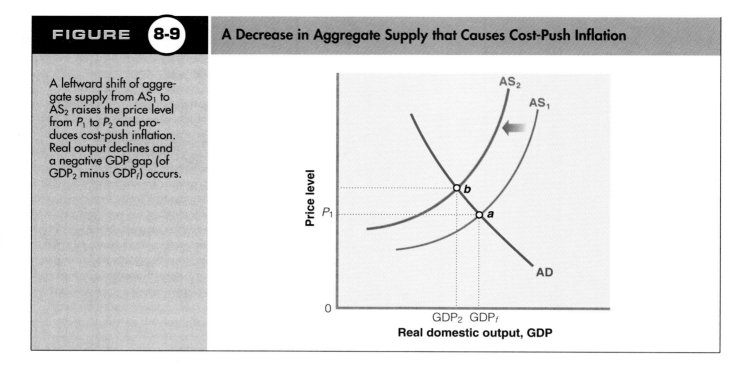

FIGURE 8-9

A Decrease in Aggregate Supply that Causes Cost-Push Inflation

A leftward shift of aggregate supply from AS_1 to AS_2 raises the price level from P_1 to P_2 and produces cost-push inflation. Real output declines and a negative GDP gap (of GDP_2 minus GDP_f) occurs.

eted upward. Then, oil expenditures were about 10 percent of Canadian GDP, compared to only 3 percent today. So the Canadian economy is now less vulnerable to cost-push inflation arising from such "aggregate supply shocks."

Increases in AS: Full Employment with Price-Level Stability

For the first time in more than a decade, in early 2000 Canada experienced full employment, strong economic growth, and very low inflation. Specifically, in 2000 the unemployment rate fell below 7 percent—a level not seen since 1975—and real GDP grew at 5.3 percent, *without igniting inflation.* At first thought, this "macroeconomic bliss" seems to be incompatible with the AD-AS model. An upward-sloping aggregate supply curve suggests that increases in aggregate demand that are sufficient for full employment (or overfull employment) will raise the price level. Higher inflation, so it would seem, is the inevitable price paid for expanding output to and beyond the full-employment level.

But inflation remained very mild in the late 1990s and early 2000s. Figure 8-10 helps explain why. Let's first suppose that aggregate demand increased from AD_1 to AD_2. Taken alone, that increase in aggregate demand would move the economy from *a* to *b*. Real output would rise from less than full-employment real output GDP_1 to full-capacity real output GDP_2. The economy would experience inflation as shown by the increase in the price level from P_1 to P_3. Such inflation had occurred at the end of previous vigorous expansions of aggregate demand.

In the more recent period, however, larger-than-usual increases in productivity occurred due to a burst of new technology relating to computers, the Internet, inventory management systems, electronic commerce, and so on. The quickened productivity growth reduced per-unit production cost and shifted the long-run aggregate supply curve to the right, as from AS_1 to AS_2 in Figure 8-10. The relevant aggregate demand and aggregate supply curves thus became AD_2 and AS_2, not AD_2 and AS_1. Instead of moving from *a* to *b*, the economy moved form *a* to *c*. Real output increased from GDP_1 to GDP_3 and the price level rose only modestly (from P_1 to P_2). The shift of the aggregate supply curve from AS_1 to AS_2 increased the economy's full-employment output and its full-capacity output. That accommodated the increase in aggregate demand without causing inflation.

A shift of the aggregate supply curve to the right shifts the economy's full employment and its full capacity output.

FIGURE 8-10   **Growth, Full Employment, and Relative Price Stability**

Normally, an increase in aggregate demand from AD_1 to AD_2 would move the economy from a to b along AS_1. Real output would expand to its full-capacity level (GDP_2), and inflation would result (P_1 to P_3). But in the late 1990s, significant increases in productivity shifted the aggregate supply curve, as from AS_1 to AS_2. The economy moved from a to c rather than from a to b. It experienced strong economic growth (GDP_1 to GDP_3), full employment, and only very mild inflation (P_1 to P_2).

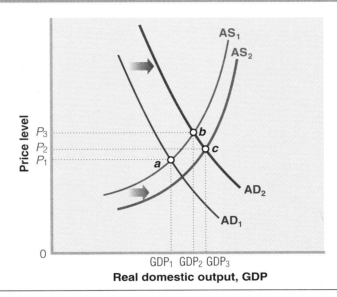

But in 2001 the macroeconomic bliss of the late 1990s came face to face with the old economic principles. Aggregate demand growth slowed because of a substantial fall in investment spending. The terrorist attacks of September 11, 2001 in the U.S. further dampened aggregate demand through lower exports to our largest trading partner. The unemployment rate inched up from 6.8 percent in January 2001 to 7.7 percent in mid-2002.

Throughout 2001 the Bank of Canada lowered interest rates to try to halt the slowdown and promote recovery. The lower interest rates spurred aggregate demand, particularly the demand for new housing, and helped spur recovery. The economy resumed its economic growth in 2002.

We will examine government stabilization policies, such as those carried out the by the Bank of Canada in the AD-AS context in chapters that follow. *(Key Questions 5, 6, and 7)*

QUICK REVIEW

- The equilibrium price level and amount of real output are determined at the intersection of the aggregate demand and aggregate supply curves.

- Increases in aggregate demand beyond the full employment level of real GDP causes demand-pull inflation.

- Decreases in aggregate demand cause recessions and cyclical unemployment, partly because the price level and wages tend to be "sticky" or inflexible in a downward direction.

- Decreases in aggregate supply cause cost-push inflation.

- Full employment, high economic growth, and price stability are compatible with one another if productivity-driven increases in aggregate supply are sufficient to balance growing aggregate demand.

8.4   From the Short Run to the Long Run

Until now we have assumed the aggregate supply curve remains stable when the aggregate demand curve shifts. For example, an increase in aggregate demand along the upward-sloping short-run aggregate supply curve raises both the price level and real output. That analysis accurate and realistic for the short run, which, you may recall, is a period in which nominal wages (and other input prices) do not respond to price-level changes.

We noted at the beginning of this chapter that there are at least two reasons why nominal wages and other input prices may remain constant in the short run even though the price level has changed:

1. Workers may not immediately be aware of the extent to which inflation (or deflation) has changed their real wages, and thus they may not adjust their labour supply decisions and wage demands accordingly.

2. Many employees are hired under fixed-wage contracts. For unionized employees, for example, nominal wages are spelled out in their collective bargaining agreements. Also, most managers and many professionals receive set salaries established in annual contracts. For them, wages remain constant for the life of the contracts, regardless of changes in the price level.

In such cases, price-level changes do not immediately give rise to changes in nominal wages. Instead, a considerable amount of time usually passes before such adjustments occur.

Once contracts have expired and nominal wage adjustments have been made, the economy enters the **long run**—*the period in which nominal wages are fully responsive to previous changes in the price level.* As time passes, workers gain full information about price-level changes and are able to determine how those changes have affected their real wages. For example, they may become aware that a rise in the price level has reduced their real wages. If your nominal wage was $10 an hour when the price index was 100, your real wage was also $10 (= $10 of nominal wage divided by 1.0). But when the price level rises to, say, 120, your $10 real wage declines to $8.33 (= $10/1.2). In such circumstance, you and other workers will demand and probably obtain increases in your nominal wage that will restore the purchasing power of an hour of work. In our example, your nominal wage is likely to rise from $10 to $12, returning your real wage to $10 (= $12/1.2).

long run
A period sufficiently long for nominal wages and other input prices to change in response to changes in the price level.

Short-Run Aggregate Supply

Our immediate objective is to demonstrate the relationship between short-run aggregate supply and long-run aggregate supplies. We begin by briefly reviewing short-run aggregate supply.

Consider the short-run aggregate supply curve AS_1 in Figure 8-11. This curve AS_1 is based on three assumptions: (1) the initial price level is P_1, (2) nominal wages have been established on the expectation that this price level will persist, and (3) the price level is flexible both upward and downward. Observe from point a_1 that at price level P_1 the economy is operating at its full-employment output GDP_f. This output is the real production forthcoming when the economy is operating at its natural rate of unemployment (or potential output).

Now let's determine the short-run consequences of changes in the price level. First we examine an increase in the price level from P_1 to P_2 in Figure 8-11a. The higher prices associated with P_2 increase revenues to firms, and because the nominal wages the firms are paying their workers are fixed, profits rise. Responding to the higher profits, firms collectively increase their output from GDP_f to GDP_2; the economy moves from a_1 to a_2 on curve AS_1. At GDP_2 the economy is operating beyond its full-employment output. The firms make this possible by extending the work hours of part-time and full-time workers, enticing new workers such as homemakers and retirees into the labour force, and hiring and training the structurally unemployed. Thus, the nation's unemployment rate declines below its natural rate.

How will firms respond when the price level *falls*, say, from P_1 to P_3 in Figure 8-11a? Firms then discover that their revenues and profits have diminished or disappeared. After all, the prices they receive for their products have dropped but the nominal wages they pay workers have not. Under these circumstances, firms reduce their employment and production, and, as shown by the movement from a_1 to a_3, real output falls to GDP_3. The decline in real output is accompanied by

| FIGURE 8-11 | Short-Run and Long-Run Aggregate Supply |

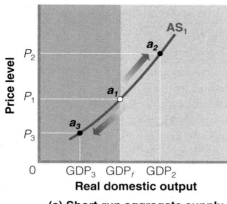

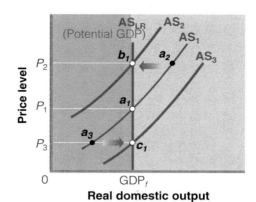

(a) Short-run aggregate supply

(b) Long-run aggregate supply

(a) In the short run, nominal wages are assumed to be fixed and based on price level P_1 and the expectation that it will continue. An increase in the price level from P_1 to P_2 increases profits and output, moving the economy from a_1 to a_2; a decrease in the price level from P_1 to P_3 reduces profits and real output, moving the economy from a_1 to a_3. The short-run aggregate supply curve therefore slopes upward. (b) In the long run, a price-level rise increases nominal wages and thus shifts the short-run aggregate supply curve leftward. Conversely, a decrease in the price level reduces nominal wages and shifts the short-run aggregate supply curve rightward. After such adjustments, the economy reaches equilibrium at points such as b_1 and c_1. Thus, the long-run aggregate supply curve is vertical.

increased unemployment; at output GDP_3 the unemployment rate is greater than the full employment associated with output GDP_f.

Long-Run Aggregate Supply

By definition, nominal wages in the long run are fully responsive to changes in the price level. What are the implications of that responsiveness for aggregate supply?

For the answer, look at Figure 8-11b, again assuming that the economy is initially at point a_1 (P_1 and GDP_f). As we just demonstrated, an increase in the price level from P_1 to P_2 will move the economy from point a_1 to a_2 along the short-run aggregate supply curve AS_1. In the long run, however, workers discover that their real wages have declined because of this increase in the price level. They demand and presumably obtain their previous level of real wages via hikes in their nominal wages. The short-run supply curve then shifts leftward from AS_1 to AS_2, which now reflects the higher price level P_2 and the new expectation that P_2, not P_1, will continue. The leftward shift in the short-run aggregate supply curve to AS_2 moves the economy from a_2 to b_1. Real output returns to its full-employment level GDP_f, and the unemployment rate returns to its natural rate.

What is the long-run outcome of a *decrease* in the price level? *Assuming downward wage flexibility*, a decline in the price level from P_1 to P_3 in Figure 8-11b works in the opposite way from a price-level increase. At first the economy moves from point a_1 to a_3 on AS_1. Profits are squeezed or eliminated because prices have fallen and nominal wages have not. But this movement along AS_1 is the short-run response. With enough time, the lower price level P_3—which has increased real wages—results in a decline in nominal wages such that the original real wage is restored. Sufficiently

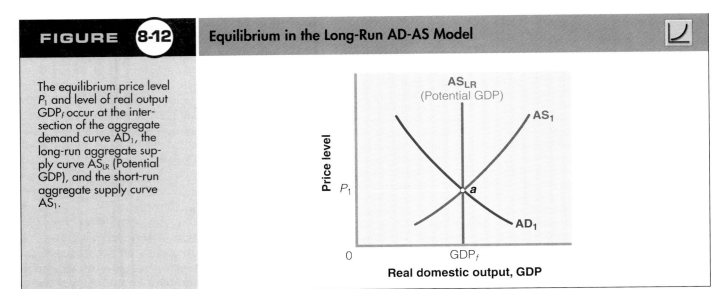

FIGURE 8-12

Equilibrium in the Long-Run AD-AS Model

The equilibrium price level P_1 and level of real output GDP_f occur at the intersection of the aggregate demand curve AD_1, the long-run aggregate supply curve AS_{LR} (Potential GDP), and the short-run aggregate supply curve AS_1.

lower nominal wages shift the short-run aggregate supply curve rightward from AS_1 to AS_3. Real output returns to its full-employment level of GDP_f at point c_1.

By tracing a line between the long-run equilibrium points b_1, a_1, and c_1, we obtain a long-run aggregate supply curve. Observe that it is vertical at the full-employment level of real GDP. After long-run adjustments in nominal wages, real output is GDP_f, regardless of the specific price level. *(Key Question 12)*

Equilibrium in the Long-Run AD-AS Model

Figure 8-12 shows the long-run equilibrium in the AD-AS model, now extended to include the distinction between short-run and long-run aggregate supply. Equilibrium in the figure occurs at point a, where the nation's aggregate demand curve AD_1 intersects the vertical long-run aggregate supply curve AS_{LR}. Observe at point a that the aggregate demand curve also intersects the short-run aggregate supply curve AS_1. In long-run equilibrium, the economy's price level and real output are P_1 and GDP_f.

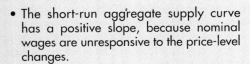

QUICK REVIEW

- The short-run aggregate supply curve has a positive slope, because nominal wages are unresponsive to the price-level changes.

- The long-run aggregate supply curve is vertical, because nominal wages eventu-

ally change by the same relative amount as changes in the price level.

- The equilibrium GDP and price level occur at the intersection of the aggregate demand curve, the long-run aggregate supply curve, and the short-run aggregate supply curve.

8.5   Equilibrium Versus Full-Employment GDP

Inflation-Unemployment Tradeoff

We now turn from explaining to evaluating equilibrium GDP. Previously we distinguished between the short-run and long-run aggregate supply curves. The long-run aggregate supply curve represents the economy's potential GDP, or full employment, a concept you first encountered in Chapter 6. In the long run, an economy will return to its natural rate of unemployment. But in the short run, the economy can come to rest at an equilibrium that is accompanied by a higher than desired rate of unemployment or inflation.

For example, in the early 1990s, the Canadian economy slowed down and actually contracted. The economy was in "equilibrium" in that at the lower rate of GDP aggregate demand equalled short-run aggregate supply. But the unemployment rate rose sharply from 7.5 percent in 1989 to over 11 percent in 1992. Clearly, the Canadian economy at that point was *below* potential GDP.

Conversely, the economy can settle at a short-run equilibrium above potential GDP and generate inflationary pressures. To measure the divergence of the economy from its full-employment potential, we use the notion of gaps, which you learned in Chapter 6.

Recessionary Gap

recessionary gap
The amount by which the equilibrium GDP falls short of full-employment GDP.

In **Figure 8-13a (Key Graph)** we have designated the full-employment non-inflationary level of output, or potential GDP, at $510 billion. Suppose aggregate demand falls from AD_0 to AD_1 because of a steep drop in net exports. AD_1 intersects the short-run aggregate supply AS at $490 billion, thus, the equilibrium level of GDP is $20 billion short of potential GDP. The **recessionary gap** is the amount by which equilibrium GDP falls short of full-employment GDP. A resolution of the recessionary gap requires a rightward shift of the aggregate demand curve, from AD_1 to AD_0, or a rightward shift of the short-run aggregate supply curve, from AS_0 to AS_1, or some combination of the two.

In Chapters 9 and 13 you will learn about policy tools at the disposal of governments that can shift aggregate demand to the right and close a recessionary gap. You will recall that a fall in the price level from P_0 to P_1 will shift the short-run aggregate supply curve from AS_0 to AS_1 so that in the long run the economy returns to full employment even without the help of a rightward shift of the aggregate demand curve. We want to stress that such a supply response could take an unacceptably long period of time.

Consider the length of time it took the Canadian economy to recover from the 1991–92 recession. The Canadian economy was at full employment in 1989 when the unemployment rate dropped to 7.5 percent. It took until 2000—a decade—before full employment was re-established, despite attempts by the Bank of Canada to stimulate the economy through lower interest rates. Such long adjustment periods mean that unless a nation is willing to suffer unacceptable levels of unemployment, recessions require stimulating aggregate demand through macroeconomic policy tools.

Inflationary Gap

inflationary gap
The amount by which the equilibrium GDP exceeds potential GDP.

Suppose the economy is at its full-employment long-run equilibrium and that there is a steep increase in net exports that shifts aggregate demand to the right. The amount by which equilibrium is above full employment GDP is an **inflationary gap**, created (Figure 8-13b) by the shift of the aggregate demand curve from AD_0 to AD_2. As noted earlier, an unemployment rate below the natural rate is made possible by extending the work hours of part-time and full-time workers, enticing new workers such as homemakers and retirees into the labour force, and hiring and training the structurally unemployed.

The government could undertake policies to quickly counteract the rise of aggregate demand and thereby close the inflationary gap. If the government chooses to do nothing about the inflationary gap, the higher price level P_2 would eventually lead to a shift of the short-run aggregate supply curve left to AS_2, which would push the price level higher still, to P_3. As with the elimination of a recessionary gap, an inflationary gap will take some time to close without specific government policies to hurry the process along.

Key Graph

FIGURE 8-13 Recessionary and Inflationary Gaps

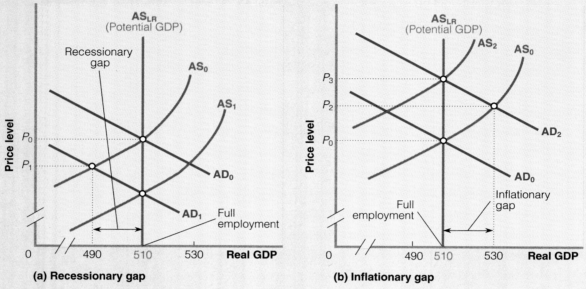

(a) Recessionary gap

(b) Inflationary gap

The equilibrium and full-employment GDPs may not coincide. A recessionary gap, shown in (a), is the amount by which equilibrium GDP falls short of full-employment GDP. The inflationary gap in (b) is the amount by which equilibrium GDP exceeds full-employment GDP. The elimination of a recessionary gap requires either an increase of aggregate demand from AD_1 to AD_0 or a rightward shift of the short-run aggregate supply curve. The elimination of an inflationary gap requires either a decrease in aggregate demand or a decrease in the short-run aggregate supply.

Quick Quiz

1. A recessionary gap can be eliminated by
  a. a contraction of consumption spending.
  b. a fall in government expenditures.
  c. an increase in investment spending.
  d. a fall in net exports.

2. At a GDP of $510 billion
  a. the economy is in recession.
  b. there is an inflationary gap.
  c. there is a recessionary gap.
  d. the economy is at full employment.

3. An inflationary gap will close if
  a. net exports rise sharply, other things equal.
  b. input prices fall, other things equal.
  c. productivity of the economy falls, other things equal.
  d. government spending rises sharply, other things equal.

4. A recessionary gap will close if
  a. input prices rise, other things equal.
  b. consumption spending rises sharply, other things equal.
  c. government regulation of business expands significantly, other things equal.
  d. government expenditures fall significantly, other things equal.

ANSWERS: 1. c; 2. d; 3. b; 4. b.

THE LASTword   Why is Unemployment in Europe So High?

Are the high unemployment rates in Europe the result of structural problems or of deficient aggregate demand?

Several European economies have had high unemployment rates in the past several years. For example, in 2000 France had an unemployment rate of 9.3 percent; Italy, 10.4 percent; Germany, 7.8 percent; and Spain, 11.3 percent. These rates compare to 6.8 percent for Canada and 4.5 percent in the United States.

Why are European unemployment rates so high? There are two views on this question.

1. High Natural Rates of Unemployment Many economists believe the high unemployment rates in Europe largely reflect high natural rates of unemployment. They envision a situation as in Figure 8-9a, where aggregate demand and aggregate supply have produced the full-employment level of real output GDP_f. But high levels of frictional and structural unemployment accompany such a level of output. In this view, the extensive unemployment in Europe has resulted from a high natural rate of unemployment, not from deficient aggregate demand. An increase in aggregate demand would push these economies beyond their full-employment levels of output, causing demand-pull inflation.

The sources of the high natural rates of unemployment are govern-ment policies and union contracts that have increased the costs of hiring workers and have reduced the cost of being unemployed. Examples: High minimum wages have discouraged employers from hiring low-skilled workers; generous welfare benefits have weakened incentives for people to take available jobs; restrictions against firings have discouraged firms from employing workers; 30 to 40 days per year of paid vacations and holidays have boosted the cost of hiring workers; high worker absenteeism has reduced productivity; and high employer costs of health, pension, disability, and other benefits have discouraged hiring.

2. Deficient Aggregate Demand Not all economists agree that government and union policies have pushed up Europe's natural rate of unemployment. Instead, they point to insufficient aggregate demand as the problem. They see the European

economies in terms of Figure 8-11a, where real output is less than it would be if aggregate demand were stronger. The argument is that the European governments have been so fearful of inflation that they have not undertaken appropriate fiscal and monetary policies (discussed in Chapters 9 and 13) to increase aggregate demand. In this view, increases in aggregate demand would not be inflationary, since these economies have considerable excess capacity. A rightward shift of their aggregate demand curves would expand output and employment without increasing inflation.

Conclusion: The debate over high unemployment in Europe reflects disagreement on where European aggregate demand curves lie relative to full-employment levels of output. If these curves are at the full-employment real GDP, then the high levels of unemployment are "natural." Public policies should focus on lowering minimum wages, reducing vacation time, reducing welfare benefits, easing restrictions on layoffs, and so on. But if the aggregate demand curves in the European nations lie to the left of their full-employment levels of output, as in Figure 8-11a, then expansionary government policies such as reduced interest rates or tax cuts may be in order.

CHAPTER SUMMARY

8.1 AGGREGATE DEMAND

- The aggregate demand-aggregate supply model (AD-AS model) is a variable-price model that enables analysis of simultaneous changes of real GDP and the price level.

- The aggregate demand curve shows the level of real output that the economy will purchase at each price level.

- The aggregate demand curve is downward sloping because of the wealth effect, the interest-rate effect, and the foreign trade effect. The wealth effect indicates that inflation reduces the real value or purchasing power of fixed-value financial assets held by households, causing them to retrench on their consumer spending. The interest-rate effect means that, with a specific supply of money, a higher price level increases the demand for money, raising the interest rate and reducing consumption and investment purchases. The foreign trade effect suggests that an increase in one country's price level relative to other countries' reduces the net exports component of that nation's aggregate demand.

- The determinants of aggregate demand are spending by domestic consumers, businesses, government, and foreign buyers. Changes in the factors listed in Figure 8-2 cause changes in spending by these groups and shift the aggregate demand curve.

8.2 AGGREGATE SUPPLY

- The aggregate supply curve shows the levels of real output that businesses will produce at various possible price levels. The long-run aggregate supply curve assumes that nominal wages and other input prices fully match any change in the price level. The curve is vertical at the full-employment output.

- The short-run aggregate supply curve (or simply "aggregate supply curve") assumes that nominal wages and other input prices do not respond to price level changes. The aggregate supply curve is generally upward sloping because per-unit production costs, and hence the prices that firms must receive, rise as real output expands. The aggregate supply curve is relatively steep to the right of the full-employment output and relatively flat to the left of it.

- Figure 8-5 lists the determinants of aggregate supply: input prices, productivity, and the legal-institutional environment. A change in any one of these factors will change per-unit production costs at each level of output and therefore alter the location of the aggregate supply curve.

8.3 EQUILIBRIUM GDP AND CHANGES IN EQUILIBRIUM

- The intersection of the aggregate demand and aggregate supply curves determines an economy's equilibrium price level and real GDP. At the intersection, the quantity of real GDP demanded equals the quantity of real GDP supplied.

- Increases in aggregate demand to the right of the full-employment output cause inflation and positive GDP gaps (actual GDP exceeds potential GDP). An upward-sloping aggregate supply curve weakens the effect of an increase in aggregate demand because a portion of the increase in aggregate demand is dissipated in inflation.

- Shifts of the aggregate demand curve to the left of the full employment output cause recession, negative GDP gaps, and cyclical unemployment. The price level may not fall during recessions because of downwardly inflexible prices and wages. This inflexibility results from wage contracts, efficiency wages, menu costs, minimum wages, and fears of price wars. When the price level is fixed, in essence there is a horizontal portion of the aggregate supply curve.

- Leftward shifts of the aggregate supply curve reflect increases in per-unit production costs and cause cost-push inflation, with accompanying negative GDP gaps.

- Rightward shifts of the aggregate supply curve, caused by large improvements in productivity, help explain the simultaneous achievement of full employment, economic growth, and price stability that Canada achieved between 1996 and 2000.

8.4 FROM THE SHORT RUN TO THE LONG RUN

- The short-run aggregate supply curve is upward-sloping. Because nominal wages are fixed, increases in the price level (prices received by firms) increase profits and real output. Conversely, decreases in the price level reduce profits and real output. However, the long-run aggregate supply curve is vertical. With sufficient time for adjustment, nominal wages rise and fall with the price level, moving the economy along a vertical aggregate supply curve at the economy's full-employment output.

8.5 EQUILIBRIUM VERSUS FULL-EMPLOYMENT GDP

- A recessionary gap is the amount by which equilibrium GDP falls short of full-employment GDP. An inflationary gap is the amount by which equilibrium GDP is above full-employment GDP.

TERMS AND CONCEPTS

aggregate demand-aggregate supply model, p. 205
aggregate demand, p. 205
real-balances effect, p. 206
interest-rate effect, p. 206
foreign trade effect, p. 206
determinants of aggregate demand, p. 206

long-run aggregate supply curve, p. 210
short-run aggregate supply, p. 211
determinants of aggregate supply, p. 212
equilibrium price level, p. 215

equilibrium real domestic output, p. 215
efficiency wages, p. 218
menu costs, p. 219
long run, p. 221
recessionary gap, p. 225
inflationary gap, p. 225

STUDY QUESTIONS

1. Why is the aggregate demand curve downward sloping? Specify how your explanation differs from that for the downward sloping demand curve for a single product.

2. Distinguish between the "real-balances effect" and the "wealth effect," as the terms are used in this chapter. How does each relate to the aggregate demand curve?

3. Why is the long-run aggregate supply curve vertical? Explain the shape of the short-run aggregate supply curve. Why is the short-run curve relatively flat to the left of the full-employment output and relatively steep to its right?

4. **KEY QUESTION** Suppose that the aggregate demand and the short-run supply schedules for a hypothetical economy are as shown below:

Amount of real domestic output demanded (billions)	Price level (price index)	Amount of real domestic output supplied (billions)
$100	300	$400
200	250	400
300	200	300
400	150	200
500	150	100

a. Use these data to graph the aggregate demand and supply curves. Find the equilibrium price level and level of real output in this hypothetical economy. Is the equilibrium real output also the potential GDP? Explain.

b. Why will a price level of 150 not be an equilibrium price level in this economy? Why not 250?

c. Suppose that buyers desire to purchase $200 billion of extra real output at each price level. Sketch in the new aggregate demand curve as AD_1. What factors might cause this change in aggregate demand? What are the new equilibrium price level and level of real output?

5. **KEY QUESTION** Suppose that the hypothetical economy in question 4 has the following relationship between its real output and the input quantities necessary for producing that output:

Input quantity	Real domestic output
150.0	400
112.5	300
75.0	200

a. What is productivity in this economy?

b. What is the per-unit cost of production if the price of each input unit is $2?

c. Assume that the input price increases from $2 to $3 with no accompanying change in productivity. What is the new per-unit cost of production? In what direction would the $1 increase in input price push the aggregate supply curve? What effect would this shift in the short-run aggregate supply have on the price level and the level of real output?

d. Suppose that the increase in input price does not occur but instead that productivity increases by 100 percent. What would be the new per-unit cost of production? What effect would this change in per-unit production cost have on the short-run aggregate supply curve? What effect would this shift in the short-run aggregate supply have on the price level and the level of real output?

6. **KEY QUESTION** What effects would each of the following have on aggregate demand or short-run aggregate supply? In each case use a diagram to show the expected effects on the equilibrium price level and level of real output. Assume all other things remain constant.

a. A widespread fear of recession among consumers.

b. A $2 per pack increase in the excise tax on cigarettes.

c. A reduction in interest rates at each price level.

d. A major increase in federal spending for health care.

e. The expectation of rapid inflation.

f. The complete disintegration of OPEC, causing oil prices to fall by one-half.

g. A 10 percent reduction in personal income tax rates.

h. An increase in labour productivity (with no change in nominal wages).

i. A 12 percent increase in nominal wages (with no change in productivity).

j. Depreciation in the international value of the dollar.

7. **KEY QUESTION** Other things equal, what effect will each of the following have on the equilibrium price level and level of real output?

a. An increase in aggregate demand in the steep portion of the aggregate supply curve.

b. An increase in aggregate supply, with no change in aggregate demand (assume that prices and wages are flexible upward and downward).

c. Equal increases in aggregate demand and aggregate supply.

d. A reduction in aggregate demand in the flat portion of the aggregate supply curve.

e. An increase in aggregate demand and a decrease in aggregate supply.

8. Explain how an upward-sloping aggregate supply curve weakens the impact of a rightward shift of the aggregate demand curve.

9. Why does a reduction in aggregate demand reduce real output, rather than the price level?

10. Explain: "Unemployment can be caused by a decrease of aggregate demand or a decrease of aggregate supply." In each case, specify the price-level outcomes.

11. Use shifts in the AD and AS curves to explain (a) the Canadian experience of strong economic growth, full employment, and price stability in the late 1990s and early 2000s; and (b) how a strong negative wealth effect from say, a precipitous drop in the stock market, could cause a recession even though productivity is surging.

12. **KEY QUESTION** Suppose the full-employment level of real output (Q) for a hypothetical economy is $250 and the price level (P) initially is 100. Use the short-run

aggregate supply schedules below to answer the questions that follow:

AS (P_{100})		AS (P_{125})		AS (P_{75})	
P	**Q**	**P**	**Q**	**P**	**Q**
125	280	125	250	125	310
100	250	100	220	100	280
75	220	75	190	75	250

a. What will be the level of real output in the *short run* if the price level unexpectedly rises from 100 to 125 because of an increase in aggregate demand? What if the price level falls unexpectedly from 100 to 75 because of a decrease in aggregate demand? Explain each situation, using numbers from the table.

b. What will be the level of real output in the *long run* when the price level rises from 100 to 125? When it falls from 100 to 75? Explain each situation.

c. Show the circumstances described in parts a and b on graph paper, and derive the long-run aggregate supply curve.

13. **KEY QUESTION** Use graphical analysis to show how each of the following would affect the economy first in the short run and then in the long run. Assume that Canada is initially operating at its full-employment level of output, that prices and wages are eventually flexible both upward and downward, and that there is no counteracting fiscal or monetary policy.

a. Because of a war abroad, the oil supply to Canada is disrupted, sending oil prices rocketing upward.

b. Construction spending on new homes rises dramatically, greatly increasing total Canadian investment spending.

c. Economic recession occurs abroad, significantly reducing foreign purchases of Canadian exports.

14. **(The Last Word)** State the alternative views on why unemployment in Europe has recently been so high. What are the policy implications of each view?

INTERNET APPLICATION QUESTIONS

1. **The Interest-Rate Effect—Price Levels and Interest Rates** The interest-rate effect suggests that as the price level rises, so do interest rates, and rising interest rates reduce certain kinds of consumption and investment spending. Visit the McConnell-Brue-Barbiero Web site (Chapter 8) and compare price levels (all items) and interest rates (prime business loan rate) over the past five years. Do the data support the link between the price level and interest rates?

Σ-STAT

2. **Aggregate Demand and Supply—Equilibrium Prices and GDPs** Go to the statistical section of the OECD through the McConnell-Brue-Barbiero Web site

(Chapter 8) to retrieve data on inflation (see CPI under Short-Term Indicators) and GDP (adjusted for inflation) for Canada, the United States, Germany, and Japan. Assume that the CPI and GDP numbers represent the equilibrium price levels and real GDPs for their respective years. Plot the price/GDP levels for the past three years for each country using a graph with the price level on the vertical axis and real GDP on the horizontal axis. Are there any similarities in the patterns among these countries? Speculate on changes in aggregate demand and aggregate supply that most likely produced the succession of equilibrium points. (Note: AS usually moves rightward at a slow, steady annual pace.)

Appendix to Chapter 8

The Relationship of the Aggregate Expenditures Model to the AD-AS Model[1]

Derivation of the Aggregate Demand Curve from the Aggregate Expenditures Model

We can derive the downward-sloping aggregate demand curve of Figure 8-1 directly from the aggregate expenditures model discussed in Chapter 7. We simply need to relate the various possible price levels to corresponding equilibrium GDPs. Note that in Figure A8-1 we have stacked the aggregate expenditures model (Figure A8-1a) and the aggregate demand curve (Figure A8-1b) vertically. We can do this because the horizontal axes of both models measure real GDP. Now let's derive the AD curve in three distinct steps. (Throughout this discussion, keep in mind that price level P_1 < price level P_2 < price level P_3):

- First suppose that the economy's price level is P_1 and its aggregate expenditures schedule is AE_1, the top schedule in Figure A8-1a. The equilibrium GDP is then GDP_1 at point 1. So in Figure A8-1b we can plot the equilibrium real output GDP_1 and the corresponding price level P_1. This gives us one point 1′ in Figure A8-1b.

- Now assume the price level rises from P_1 to P_2. Other things equal, this higher price level will (1) decrease the value of wealth, decreasing consumption expenditures; (2) increase the interest rate, reducing investment and interest-sensitive consumption expenditures; and (3) increase imports and decrease exports, reducing net export expenditures. The aggregate expenditures schedule will fall from AE_1 to, say, AE_2 in Figure A8-1a, giving us equilibrium GDP_2 at point 2. In Figure A8-1b we plot this new price-level–real-output combination, P_2 and GDP_2, as point 2′.

- Finally, suppose the price level rises from P_2 to P_3. The value of real wealth balances, the interest rate rises, exports fall, and imports rise. Consequently, the consumption, investment, and net export schedules fall, shifting the aggregate expenditures schedule downward from AE_2 to AE_3, which gives us equilibrium GDP_3 at point 3. In Figure A8-1b, this enables us to locate point 3′, where the price level is P_3 and real output is GDP_3.

In summary, increases in the economy's price level will successively shift its aggregate expenditures schedule downward and will reduce real GDP. The resulting price-

---

[1]This appendix presumes knowledge of the aggregate expenditures model discussed in Chapter 7.

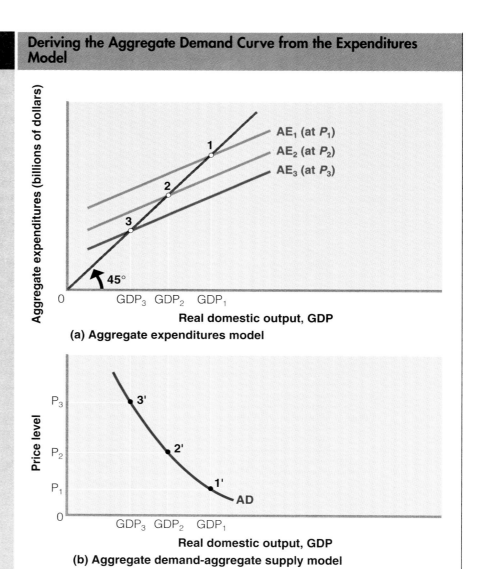

FIGURE A8-1

Deriving the Aggregate Demand Curve from the Expenditures Model

Through the real-balances, interest-rate, and foreign trade effects, the aggregate expenditures schedule will fall when the price level rises and will rise when the price level falls. If the aggregate expenditures schedule is AE_1 when the price level is P_1, the equilibrium output is GDP_1; then P_1 and GDP_1 determine one point (1′) on the aggregate demand curve. A higher price level such as P_2 reduces aggregate expenditures to AE_2, providing point 2′ on the aggregate demand curve. Similarly, an increase in the price level from P_2 to P_3 drops aggregate expenditures AE_3, so P_3 and GDP_3 yield another point on the aggregate demand curve at 3′.

(a) Aggregate expenditures model

(b) Aggregate demand-aggregate supply model

level–real-GDP combination will yield various points such as 1′, 2′, and 3′ in Figure A8-1b. Together, such points locate the downward-sloping aggregate demand curve for the economy.

Aggregate Demand Shifts and the Aggregate Expenditures Model

The determinants of aggregate demand listed in Figure 8-2 are the components of the aggregate expenditures model discussed in Chapter 7. When one of those determinants changes, the aggregate expenditures schedule shifts too. We can easily link such shifts in the aggregate expenditures schedule to shifts of the aggregate demand curve.

Let's suppose that the price level is constant. In Figure A8-2 we begin with the aggregate expenditures schedule at AE_1 in diagram (a), yielding real output of GDP_1. Assume

FIGURE A8-2	Shifts in the Aggregate Expenditures Schedule and in the Aggregate Demand Curve

(a) A change in some determinant of consumption, investment, or net exports (other than the price level) shifts the aggregate expenditures schedule upward from AE_1 to AE_2. The multiplier increases real output from GDP_1 to GDP_2. (b) The counterpart of this change is an initial rightward shift of the aggregate demand curve by the amount of initial new spending (from AD_1 to the broken curve). This leads to a multiplied rightward shift of the curve to AD_2, which is just sufficient to show the same increase in GDP as in the aggregate expenditures model.

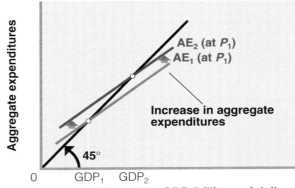

(a) Aggregate expenditures model

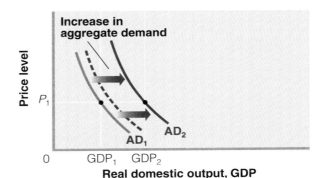

(b) Aggregate demand–aggregate supply model

now that investment spending increases in response to more optimistic business expectations, so that the aggregate expenditures schedule rises from AE_1 to AE_2. (The notation "at P_1" reminds us that the price level is assumed to be constant.) The result will be a multiplied increase in real output from GDP_1 to GDP_2.

In Figure A8-2b, the increase in investment spending is reflected in the horizontal distance between AD1 and the broken curve to its right. The immediate effect of the increase in investment is an increase in aggregate demand by the exact amount of the new spending. But then the multiplier process magnifies the initial increase in investment into successive rounds of consumption spending and an ultimate multiplied increase in aggregate demand from AD_1 to AD_2. Equilibrium real output rises from GDP_1 to GDP_2, the same multiplied increase in real GDP as that in Figure A8-2a. The initial increase in investment in (a) has shifted the AD curve in (b) by a horizontal distance equal to the change in investment times the multiplier. This particular change in real GDP is still associated with the constant price level P_1. To generalize,

Shift of AD curve = initial change in spending × multiplier

APPENDIX SUMMARY

1. A change in the price level alters the location of the aggregate expenditures schedule through the real balances, interest-rate, and foreign trade effects. The aggregate demand curve is derived from the aggregate expenditures model by allowing the price level to change and observing the effect on the aggregate expenditures schedule and thus on equilibrium GDP.

2. With the price level held constant, increases in consumption, investment, and net export expenditures shift the aggregate expenditures schedule upward and the aggregate demand curve to the right. Decreases in these spending components reduce the opposite effects.

APPENDIX STUDY QUESTIONS

1. Explain carefully: "A change in the price level shifts the aggregate expenditures curve but not the aggregate demand curve."

2. Suppose that the price level is constant and investment spending increases sharply. How would you show this increase in the aggregate expenditures model? What would be the outcome for real GDP? How would you show this rise in investment in the aggregate demand-aggregate supply model, assuming the economy is operating in what, in effect, is a horizontal range of the aggregate supply curve?

9

Chapter

Fiscal Policy

One of the major issues in macroeconomics is how to avoid or smooth out fluctuations in economic activity that cause recessions or inflation. In the previous chapter we saw that a significant decline in aggregate demand can cause recession and cyclical unemployment, whereas an excessive increase in aggregate demand can cause an inflationary gap. For those reasons, central governments sometimes use budgetary actions to try to "stimulate the economy" or "rein in inflation." Such so-called *fiscal policy* consists of deliberate changes in government spending and tax collections to achieve full employment, to control inflation, and to encourage economic growth.

The Canadian government has used fiscal policies in several circumstances with varying degrees of success. Other nations, too, have used fiscal policy to help cope with recession or inflation. For example, in recent years Japan launched a series of governmental spending programs designed to increase aggregate demand and pull its economy out of a major recession.

What is the legal mandate for fiscal policy in Canada? What is the logic behind such policy? Why do some economists question its effectiveness?

9.1   Fiscal Policy and the AD-AS Model

The Role of Governments

fiscal policy
Changes in government spending and tax collections designed to achieve a full-employment and non-inflationary domestic output.

Since 1945 one of the main tools used by government in stabilization policy has been **fiscal policy**, which includes changes in government spending and taxation designed to achieve full employment and a stable price level. In Canada, the idea that government fiscal actions can exert a stabilizing influence on the economy emerged from the Great Depression of the 1930s and the rise of Keynesian economics. Since then, macroeconomic theory has played a major role in the design of fiscal policy and the improved understanding of its limitations.

Fiscal policy is described as *discretionary* (or "active") if the changes in government spending and taxes are *at the option* of the government. They do not occur automatically, independent of parliamentary action. Such changes are *non-discretionary* (or "passive" or "automatic"), and we will examine them later in this chapter.

First, we'll examine fiscal policy in two situations: (1) a recessionary gap, and (2) an inflationary gap caused by demand-pull—a rightward shift of the aggregate demand curve beyond full employment GDP.

Expansionary Fiscal Policy

expansionary fiscal policy
An increase in government spending, a decrease in net taxes, or some combination of the two, for the purpose of increasing aggregate demand and expanding real output.

When recession occurs, an **expansionary fiscal policy** may be in order. Consider Figure 9-1, where we suppose a sharp decline in investment spending has shifted the economy's aggregate demand curve leftward from AD_1 to AD_0. Perhaps profit expectations on investment projects have dimmed, curtailing much investment spending and reducing aggregate demand. Consequently, real GDP has fallen to GDP_0 from its full-employment level of GDP_f. Accompanying this decline in real output is an increase in unemployment, since fewer workers are needed to produce the lower output. This economy is experiencing both recession and cyclical unemployment.

What fiscal policy should the federal government adopt to stimulate the economy? It has three main options: (1) increase government spending, (2) reduce taxes, or (3) some combination of the two. If the federal budget is balanced at the outset, expansionary fiscal policy will create a government **budget deficit**—government spending in excess of tax revenues.

budget deficit
The amount by which the expenditures of the federal government exceed its revenues in any year.

INCREASED GOVERNMENT SPENDING

Other things equal, a sufficient increase in government spending will shift an economy's aggregate demand curve to the right, from AD_0 to AD_1 in Figure 9-1. To see why, suppose that the recession prompts government to initiate new spending on highways, airports, education, and health care. At *each* price level the amount of real output demanded is greater than before the increase in government spending. Real output increases to GDP_f, closing the recessionary gap, therefore unemployment falls as firms increase their employment back to levels that existed before the recession.

If government initiates new spending on highways, airports, education, and health care, the amount of real output demanded rises.

TAX REDUCTIONS

Alternatively, the government could reduce taxes to shift the aggregate demand curve to the right, as from AD_0 to AD_1. Suppose the government cuts personal income taxes, which increases disposable income by the same amount. Consumption will rise by a fraction of the increase in disposable income—the other fraction goes to increased saving. The aggregate demand will shift to the right because of the increase in consumption produced by the tax cut. Real GDP rises and employment increases accordingly.

FIGURE **9-1**

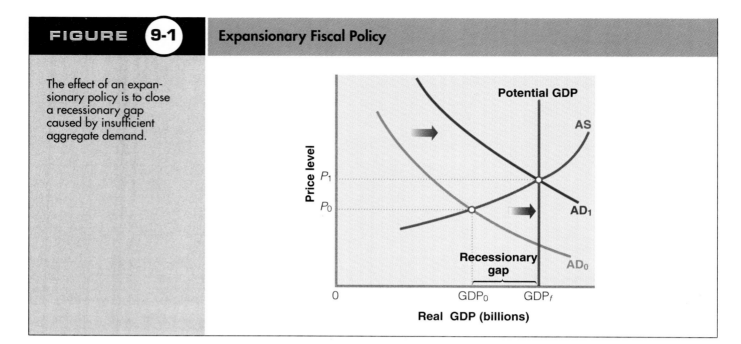

FIGURE **9-1**

Expansionary Fiscal Policy

The effect of an expansionary policy is to close a recessionary gap caused by insufficient aggregate demand.

COMBINED GOVERNMENT SPENDING INCREASES AND TAX REDUCTIONS

The government may combine spending increases and tax cuts to produce the desired initial increase in spending and eventual increase in aggregate demand and real GDP.

If the federal government chooses to do nothing about the recessionary gap, the lower price level P_0 will put downward pressure on input prices (particularly wages), that will eventually lead to a shift of the short-run aggregate supply curve to the right until it meets AD_0 at full employment at a lower price level. (You should pencil in the new short-run aggregate supply curve.) As already pointed out in Chapter 8, such a supply response would take a long time, and a nation would endure an unacceptably high rate of unemployment for a longer period than necessary.

(If you were assigned Chapter 7, you should think through these three fiscal policy options in terms of the aggregate expenditures model [Figure 7-16]. Recall from the Appendix to Chapter 9 that rightward shifts of the aggregate demand curve relate directly to upward shifts in the aggregate expenditures schedule.)

Contractionary Fiscal Policy

contractionary fiscal policy
A decrease in government spending, an increase in net taxes, or some combination of the two, for the purpose of decreasing aggregate demand and thus controlling inflation.

When the economy has an inflationary gap caused by excessive growth of aggregate demand, demand-pull inflation occurs, and a restrictive or **contractionary fiscal policy** may help control it. Look at Figure 9-2. Suppose that a shift of the aggregate demand curve from AD_2 to AD_3 above the full-employment level increases the price level from P_2 to P_3. This increase in aggregate demand might have resulted from a sharp increase in, say, investment or net export spending. If government looks to fiscal policy to control this inflation, its options are opposite those used to combat recession. It can (1) decrease government spending, (2) raise taxes, or (3) use some combination of these two policies. When the economy faces demand-pull inflation, fiscal policy should move towards a government **budget surplus**—tax revenues in excess of government spending.

budget surplus
The amount by which the revenues of the federal government exceed its expenditures in any year.

DECREASED GOVERNMENT SPENDING

Reduced government spending shifts the aggregate demand curve leftward from AD_3 to AD_2. Real output returns to its full-employment level of GDP_f.

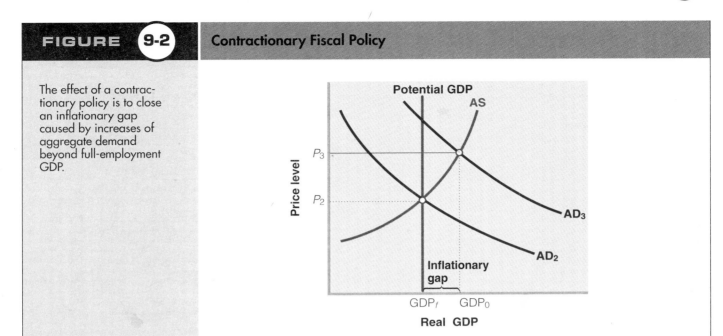

FIGURE 9-2

Contractionary Fiscal Policy

The effect of a contractionary policy is to close an inflationary gap caused by increases of aggregate demand beyond full-employment GDP.

INCREASED TAXES

Just as government can use tax cuts to increase consumption or investment spending, it can use tax *increases* to *reduce* consumption or investment spending. A tax increase reduces consumption (if it is borne by households), or investment spending, reducing aggregate demand from AD_3 to AD_2. The inflationary gap will have been closed and inflationary pressures alleviated.

COMBINED GOVERNMENT SPENDING DECREASES AND TAX INCREASES

The government can combine spending decreases and tax increases to reduce aggregate demand from AD_3 to AD_2 and check inflation.

If the government does not embark on a contractionary fiscal policy, the higher price level P_3 will eventually lead to a rise in input prices, thus to a shift of the short-run aggregate supply curve leftward until it meets AD_3 at potential GDP, closing the inflationary gap. (You should pencil in the new short-run aggregate supply curve.) Although such a supply response will be quicker than the case of a recessionary gap, the return to the economy's natural rate of unemployment will still require more time compared to pursuing an active anti-inflationary policy. *(Key Question 1)*

(If you were assigned Chapter 7, you should be able to explain the three fiscal policy options for fighting inflation in terms of the aggregate expenditures model [Figure 7-16]. Recall from the appendix to Chapter 8 that leftward shifts of the aggregate demand curve are associated with downward shifts of the aggregate expenditures schedule.)

Policy Options: *G* or *T*?

Which is preferable as a means of eliminating recession and inflation, the use of government spending or the use of taxes? The answer depends largely on one's view as to whether the government is too large or too small.

Economists who believe there are many unmet social and infrastructure needs usually recommend that government spending be increased during recessions. In times of demand-pull inflation, they usually recommend tax increases. Both actions either expand or preserve the size of government.

Economists who think that the government is too large and inefficient usually advocate tax cuts during recessions and cuts in government spending during times of demand-pull inflation. Both actions either restrain the growth of government or reduce its size.

The point is that discretionary fiscal policy designed to stabilize the economy can be associated with either an expanding government or with a contracting government.

QUICK REVIEW

- Discretionary fiscal policy is the purposeful change of government expenditures and tax collections by government to promote full employment, price stability, and economic growth.

- The government uses expansionary fiscal policy to shift the aggregate demand curve rightward in order to expand real output. This policy entails increases in

government spending, reductions in taxes, or some combination of the two.

- The government uses contractionary fiscal policy to shift the aggregate demand curve leftward in an effort to halt demand-pull inflation. This policy entails reductions in government spending, tax increases, or some combination of the two.

9.2 Built-In Stabilization

To some degree, government tax revenues change automatically over the course of the business cycle, in ways that stabilize the economy. This automatic response, or built-in stability, constitutes non-discretionary budgetary policy. We did not include this built-in stability in our discussion of fiscal policy because we implicitly assumed that the same amount of tax revenue was being collected at each level of GDP. But the actual Canadian tax system is such that *net tax revenues* vary directly with GDP. (Net taxes are tax revenues less transfers and subsidies. From here on, we will use the simpler "taxes" to mean "net taxes.")

Virtually any tax will yield more tax revenue as GDP rises. In particular, personal income taxes have progressive rates and thus generate more than proportionate increases in tax revenues as GDP expands. Furthermore, as GDP rises and more goods and services are purchased, revenues from corporate income taxes and from sales taxes also increase. And similarly, revenues from employment insurance and Canada pension (compulsory) contributions rise as economic expansion creates more jobs. Conversely, when GDP declines, tax revenues from all these sources also decline.

Transfer payments (or "negative taxes") behave in the opposite way from tax revenues. Unemployment compensation payments, welfare payments, and subsidies to farmers all decrease during economic expansion and increase during economic contraction.

Automatic or Built-In Stabilizers

built-in stabilizer
A mechanism that increases government's budget deficit (or reduces its surplus) during a recession and increases government's budget surplus (or reduces its deficit) during inflation without any action by policy-makers.

A **built-in stabilizer** is a structure of taxation and spending that increases the government's budget deficit (or reduces its budget surplus) during a recession and increases its budget surplus (or reduces its budget deficit) during inflation without requiring explicit action by policy-makers. As Figure 9-3 reveals, this is precisely what the Canadian tax system does.

Government expenditures G are fixed and assumed to be independent of the level of GDP. Parliament decides on a particular level of spending, but it does not determine the magnitude of tax revenues. Instead, it establishes tax rates, and then tax revenues vary directly with the level of GDP that the economy achieves. Line T represents that direct relationship between tax revenues and GDP.

ECONOMIC IMPORTANCE

The economic importance of this direct relationship between tax receipts and GDP becomes apparent when we consider that:

FIGURE 9-3 | **Built-in Stability**

Tax revenues *T* vary directly with GDP, and government spending *G* is assumed to be independent of GDP. As GDP falls in a recession, deficits occur automatically and help alleviate the recession. As GDP rises during expansion, surpluses occur automatically and help offset possible inflation.

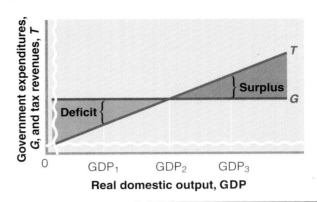

- Taxes reduce spending and aggregate demand.

- Reductions in spending are desirable when the economy is developing inflationary pressures, whereas increases in spending are desirable when the economy is slumping.

As shown in Figure 9-3, tax revenues automatically increase as GDP rises during prosperity, and, since taxes reduce household and business spending, they restrain the economic expansion. That is, as the economy moves toward a higher GDP, tax revenues automatically rise and move the budget from deficit toward surplus. In Figure 9-3, observe that the high and perhaps inflationary income level GDP_3 automatically generates a contractionary budget surplus.

Conversely, as GDP falls during recession, tax revenues automatically decline, reducing the fall in spending and cushioning the economic contraction. With a falling GDP, tax receipts decline and move the government's budget from surplus toward deficit. In Figure 9-3, the low level of income GDP_1 will automatically yield an expansionary budget deficit.

TAX PROGRESSIVITY

Figure 9-3 reveals that the size of the automatic budget deficits or surpluses—and therefore built-in stability—depends on the responsiveness of tax revenues to changes in GDP. If tax revenues change sharply as GDP changes, the slope of line *T* in the figure will be steep and the vertical distances between *T* and *G* (the deficits or surpluses) will be large. If tax revenues change very little when GDP changes, the slope will be gentle and built-in stability will be low.

The steepness of *T* in Figure 9-3 depends on the tax system itself. In a **progressive tax system**, the average tax rate (= tax revenue/GDP) rises with GDP. In a **proportional tax system**, the average tax rate remains constant as GDP rises. In a **regressive tax system**, the average tax rate falls as GDP rises. The progressive tax system has the steepest tax line *T* of the three. However, tax revenues will rise with GDP under both the progressive and proportional tax systems, and they may rise, fall, or stay the same under a regressive tax system. The main point is this: *The more progressive the tax system, the greater the economy's built-in stability.*

So, changes in public policies or laws that alter the progressivity of the tax system affect the degree of built-in stability. For example, during the 1960s and 1970s the marginal tax rates were raised. These increases in tax rates raised the overall progressivity of the tax system, bolstering the economy's built-in stability. As the economy expanded vigourously in the late 1990s, the federal budget swung from deficit to surplus. That swing helped dampen private spending and forestall inflation.

progressive tax
A tax with an average tax rate that increases as the taxpayer's income increases and decreases as the taxpayer's income decreases.

proportional tax
A tax with an average tax rate that remains constant as the taxpayer's income increases or decreases.

regressive tax
A tax with an average tax rate that decreases as the taxpayer's income increases and increases as the taxpayer's income decreases.

The built-in stability provided by the Canadian tax system has reduced the severity of business fluctuations. But built-in stabilizers can only diminish, not eliminate, swings in real GDP. Discretionary fiscal policy (changes in tax rates and expenditures) or monetary policy (central bank-caused changes in interest rates) may be needed to correct recession or inflation of any appreciable magnitude.

Evaluating Fiscal Policy

How can we determine whether discretionary fiscal policy is expansionary, neutral, or contractionary in a particular period? We cannot simply examine changes in the actual budget deficits or surpluses, because those changes may reflect automatic changes in tax revenues that accompany changes in GDP, not changes in discretionary fiscal policy. Moreover, the strength of any deliberate change in government spending or taxes depends on how large it is relative to the size of the economy. So, in evaluating the status of fiscal policy we must:

- Adjust deficits and surpluses to eliminate automatic changes in tax revenues.

- Compare the sizes of the adjusted budget deficits (or surpluses) to the levels of GDP.

Cyclically Adjusted Budget

cyclically adjusted budget
What the government budget balance would be if the economy were operating at full-employment.

Economists use the **cyclically adjusted budget** (also called the *full-employment budget*) to adjust the actual federal budget deficits and surpluses to eliminate the automatic changes in tax revenues. The cyclically adjusted budget measures what the federal budget deficit or surplus would be with existing tax rates and government spending levels if the economy had achieved its full-employment level of GDP (its potential output) in each year. The idea is to compare *actual* government expenditures for each year with the tax revenues *that would have occurred* in that year if the economy had achieved full-employment GDP. That procedure removes budget deficits or surpluses that arise simply because of changes in GDP, which then tell us only about changes in discretionary fiscal policy.

Consider Figure 9-4a, where line G represents government expenditures and line T represents tax revenues. In full-employment year 1, government expenditures of $500 billion equal tax revenues of $500 billion, as indicated by the intersection of lines G and T at point a. The cyclically adjusted budget deficit in year 1 is zero—government expenditures equal the tax revenues forthcoming at the full-employment output GDP_1. Obviously, the full-employment deficit *as a percentage of GDP* is also zero.

Now, suppose that a recession occurs and GDP falls from GDP_1 to GDP_2, as shown in Figure 9-4a. Let's also assume that the government takes no discretionary action, so that lines G and T remain as shown in the figure. Tax revenues automatically fall to $450 billion (point c) at GDP_2, while government spending remains unaltered at $500 billion (point b). A $50 billion budget deficit (represented by distance bc) arises. But this **cyclical deficit** is simply a by-product of the economy's slide into recession, not the result of discretionary fiscal actions by the government. We would be wrong to conclude from this deficit that the government is engaging in an expansionary fiscal policy.

cyclical deficit
A federal budget deficit that is caused by a recession and the consequent decline in tax revenues.

That fact is highlighted when we consider the cyclically adjusted budget deficit for year 2 in Figure 9-4a. The $500 billion of government expenditures in year 2 are shown by b on line G. And, as shown by a on line T, $500 billion of tax revenues would have occurred if the economy had achieved its full-employment GDP. Because both b and a represent $500 billion, the cyclically adjusted budget deficit in year 2 is zero, as is this deficit as a percentage of GDP. Since the cyclically adjusted budget deficits are zero in both years, we know that government did not change its discretionary fiscal policy, even though a recession occurred and an actual deficit of $50 billion resulted.

Next, consider Figure 9-4b. Suppose that real output declined from full-employment GDP_3 to GDP_4. But also suppose the federal government responded to the recession by reducing tax rates in

FIGURE 9-4 Cyclically Adjusted Deficits

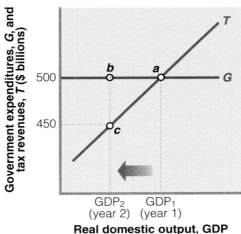

(a) Zero full-employment deficits, years 1 and 2

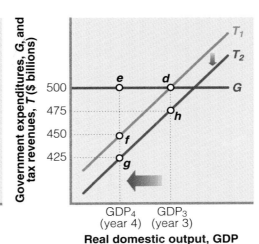

(b) Zero full-employment deficit, year 3; $25 billion full-employment deficit, year 4

(a) In the left-hand graph the cyclically adjusted deficit is zero at the full-employment output GDP_1. But it is also zero at the recessionary output GDP_2, because the $500 billion of government expenditures at GDP_2 equals the $500 of tax revenues that would be forthcoming at the full-employment GDP_1. There has been no change in fiscal policy. (b) In the right-hand graph, discretionary fiscal policy, as reflected in the downward shift of the tax line from T_1 to T_2, has increased the cyclically adjusted budget deficit from zero in year 3 to $25 billion in year 4. This is found by comparing the $500 billion of government spending in year 4 with the $475 billion of taxes that would accrue at the full-employment GDP_3. Such a rise in cyclically adjusted deficits (as a percentage of GDP) identifies an expansionary fiscal policy.

year 4, as represented by the downward shift of the tax line from T_1 to T_2. What has happened to the size of the cyclically adjusted deficit? Government expenditures in year 4 are $500 billion, as shown by e. We compare that amount with the $475 billion of tax revenues that would occur if the economy achieved its full-employment GDP. That is, we compare position e on line G with position h on line T_2. The $25 billion of tax revenues by which d exceeds h is the cyclically adjusted budget deficit for year 4. (It is equal to the actual deficit of eg in year 4 *minus* the cyclical deficit of ef.) As a percentage of GDP, the cyclically adjusted budget deficit has increased from zero in year 3 (before the tax rate cut) to some positive percentage [= ($25 billion/$GDP_4 \times 100$] in year 4. This increase in the relative size of the cyclically adjusted deficit between the two years reveals that fiscal policy is *expansionary*.

In contrast, if we observed a full-employment deficit (as a percentage of GDP) of zero in one year, followed by a cyclically adjusted budget surplus in the next, we could conclude that fiscal policy is contractionary. Because the cyclically adjusted budget adjusts for automatic changes in tax revenues, the increase in the cyclically adjusted budget surplus reveals that government either decreased its spending (G) or increased tax rates such that tax revenues (T) increased. These changes in G and T are precisely the discretionary actions that we have identified as elements of a *contractionary* fiscal policy.

TABLE 9-1	Federal Deficits (−) and Surpluses (+) as Percentage of GDP, 1991–2001	
(1) Year	**(2)** Actual deficit or surplus	**(3)** Cyclically Adjusted deficit or surplus
1991	−5.4	−4.6
1992	−5.1	−3.9
1993	−5.5	−4.4
1994	−4.6	−4.2
1995	−3.9	−3.6
1996	−2.0	−1.4
1997	+0.7	+1.1
1998	+0.8	+1.1
1999	+0.8	+0.7
2000	+1.7	+1.5
2001	+1.0	+1.3

Source: Minister of Public Works and Government Services Canada, Department of Finance, *Fiscal Reference Tables.*
Visit www.mcgrawhill.ca/college/mcconnell for data updates.

Recent Canadian Fiscal Policy

Table 9-1 lists the actual federal budget deficits and surpluses (column 2) and the cyclically adjusted deficits and surpluses (column 3), as percentages of GDP, for recent years. Observe that the cyclically adjusted (full-employment) deficits are generally smaller than the actual deficits. This is because the actual deficits include cyclical deficits, whereas the cyclically adjusted deficits do not. The latter deficits provide the information needed to assess discretionary fiscal policy.

Column 3 shows that fiscal policy was mildly expansionary in the early 1990s, but became contractionary in the later years shown. In this last regard, the cyclically adjusted budget moved from a deficit of 3.9 percent of GDP in 1995 to a surplus of 1.0 percent in 2001. This contractionary fiscal policy was appropriate in light of the rapidly growing Canadian economy over that period. This policy undoubtedly dampened the rapid growth of aggregate demand and contributed to price-level stability. Actual deficits have given way to actual surpluses, and cyclically adjusted (full-employment) deficits have given way to cyclically adjusted (full-employment) surpluses. Because of these surpluses, the federal government is better positioned to move toward an expansionary fiscal policy if the economy significantly weakens in the future, as it did in mid 2003 on account of the Severe Acute Respiratory Syndrome (SARS) outbreak, and the Mad Cow disease scare. *(Key Question 7)*

Global Perspective 9.1 shows the extent of the cyclically adjusted budget deficits or surpluses of a number of other countries in a recent year.

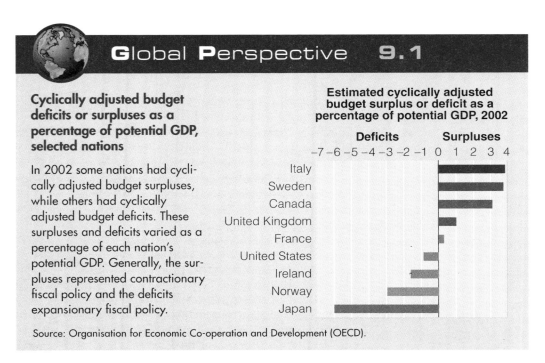

Global Perspective 9.1

Cyclically adjusted budget deficits or surpluses as a percentage of potential GDP, selected nations

In 2002 some nations had cyclically adjusted budget surpluses, while others had cyclically adjusted budget deficits. These surpluses and deficits varied as a percentage of each nation's potential GDP. Generally, the surpluses represented contractionary fiscal policy and the deficits expansionary fiscal policy.

Estimated cyclically adjusted budget surplus or deficit as a percentage of potential GDP, 2002

Deficits   Surpluses
−7 −6 −5 −4 −3 −2 −1 0 1 2 3 4

Italy
Sweden
Canada
United Kingdom
France
United States
Ireland
Norway
Japan

Source: Organisation for Economic Co-operation and Development (OECD).

QUICK REVIEW

- Tax revenues automatically increase during economic expansions and decrease during recessions; transfers automatically decrease during expansions and increase during recessions.

- Automatic changes in net taxes (taxes minus transfers) add a degree of built-in stability to the economy.

- The cyclically adjusted budget compares government spending to the tax revenues that would accrue if there were full employment; changes in cyclically adjusted budget deficits or surpluses (as percentages of GDP) reveal whether fiscal policy is expansionary, neutral, or contractionary.

- Cyclically adjusted budget deficits and surpluses are distinct from actual cyclical deficits, which simply reflect changes in tax revenues resulting from changes in GDP.

9.3   Problems, Criticisms, and Complications

Economists recognize that governments may encounter a number of significant problems in developing and applying fiscal policy.

Problems of Timing

Several problems of timing may arise in connection with fiscal policy:

- *Recognition lag*   The recognition lag is the time between the beginning of recession or inflation and the certain awareness that it is actually happening. This lag arises because of the difficulty in predicting the future course of economic activity. Although forecasting tools such as the index of leading indicators (see this chapter's Last Word) provide clues to the direction of the economy, the economy may be four or six months into a recession or inflation before that fact appears in relevant statistics. Meanwhile, the economic downslide or the inflation may become more serious than it would have if the situation had been identified and acted on sooner.

- *Administration lag*   The wheels of democratic government turn slowly. There will typically be a significant lag between the time the need for fiscal action is recognized and the time action is taken. The Canadian Parliament has on occasion taken so much time to adjust fiscal policy that the economic situation has changed in the interim, rendering the belated policy action inappropriate.

- *Operational lag*   A lag also occurs between the time fiscal action is taken and the time that action affects output, employment, or the price level. Although changes in tax rates can be put into effect relatively quickly, government spending on public works—the construction of dams, hospitals, and so on—requires long planning periods and even longer periods of construction. Such spending is of questionable use in offsetting short periods (for example, 6 to 18 months) of recession. Consequently, discretionary fiscal policy has increasingly relied on tax changes rather than on changes in spending as its main tool.

Political Considerations

Fiscal policy is conducted in a political arena. That reality may slow the enactment of fiscal policy, but it may also create the potential for political considerations swamping economic considerations in its formulation. It is a human trait to rationalize actions and policies that are in one's self-interest. Politicians are very human—they want to get re-elected. A strong economy at election time will certainly help them. So they may favour large tax cuts under the guise of expansionary fiscal policy even though that policy is economically inappropriate. Similarly, they may rationalize increased government spending on popular items such as farm subsidies, health care, and education.

At the extreme, elected officials and political parties might collectively "hijack" fiscal policy for political purposes, cause inappropriate changes in aggregate demand, and thereby cause (rather than avert) economic fluctuations. They may stimulate the economy using expansionary fiscal policy before elections and leave it to the Bank of Canada to raise interest rates to dampen excessive aggregate demand after the election. (Some may even criticize the Bank of Canada for the high interest rates!) In short, elected officials may cause so-called **political business cycles**. Such scenarios are difficult to document and prove, but there is little doubt that political considerations weigh heavily in the formulation of fiscal policy. The question is how often, if ever, those political considerations run counter to "sound economics" (see the Consider This box).

political business cycle
The alleged tendency of government to destabilize the economy by reducing taxes and increasing government expenditures before elections and to raise taxes and lower expenditures after elections.

Expectations of Reversals

Fiscal policy may fail to achieve its intended objectives if households expect future reversals of policy. Consider a tax cut, for example. If taxpayers believe the tax reduction is temporary, they may save a large portion of their tax saving, reasoning that rates will go up again in the future. The extra saving today will help them maintain their consumption at that time. But in the present, consumption spending and aggregate demand will not rise as much as our simple model (Figure 9-1) suggests.

The opposite may be true for a tax increase. If taxpayers think it is temporary, they may reduce their saving to pay the tax while maintaining their present consumption. They may reason that they can increase their saving when the tax rate again falls. So the tax increase will not reduce current consumption and aggregate demand by as much as the policymakers desired.

Consider This

The "Feel Good" Budget of 2003

In February 2003 the federal government brought down a "feel good" budget that some analysts at the time thought was more of a political budget than one made to order for the Canadian economy. The new budget increased spending by $14.3 billion, or 11 percent, from $124.3 billion in 2001-02, to $138.6 billion in 2002-03. Moreover, an additional $11 billion increase in spending was projected by 2005, bringing total federal government spending to almost $150 billion. The 2003 budget included more money for health care, the environment (to satisfy the Kyoto Protocol[1]), the country's infrastructure, and defence. The government noted that it had reduced the national debt by almost $47.6 billion by 2001-02 and that the Canadian economy had the best growth rate of any G7 country in 2002, so it could afford to increase spending.

The reactions by the media across Canada were on the whole somewhat negative. The conservative *National Post* proclaimed on its front page: "Social Spending Leads to Biggest Budget increase since Trudeau Era" (Trudeau was Prime Minister of Canada in the 1970s and early 1980s). Even the more moderate *Globe and Mail* proclaimed the budget "an old-style, big-spending blueprint." Surprisingly, the usually left-leaning *Toronto Star*, in its front page the day after the budget, referred to the Prime Minister and the Minister of

Finance at the time as "Big Spenders." The most vocal critics wanted the budget surplus at the time to have translated into a tax cut rather than a federal government spending increase.

But the media accusations of a spendthrift federal government may have been misplaced. Despite increased spending on social programs the federal government was still projected to end the 2002-03 fiscal year with a surplus. Moreover, to make sense of government spending and any resulting deficit or surplus, they must be expressed as a percentage of GDP and compared to historical values. If one looks at the federal government's annual budgets from the early 1990s to 2002, the reality is that it turned annual deficits to surpluses and the national debt as a percentage of GDP fell below 50 percent for the first time in decades.

---

[1]For details of the Kyoto Protocol see The Last Word in Chapter 15.

Question: Go to the Department of Finance home page, at http://www.fin.gc.ca/fin-eng.html, and click "Budget Info" to get information on the latest budget. Did this budget lead to a federal government deficit? Is this deficit or surplus large or small when expressed as a percentage of GDP?

To the extent that this so-called "consumption smoothing" occurs, fiscal policy will lose some of its strength. The lesson is that tax rate changes viewed by households as permanent are more likely to alter consumption and aggregate demand than tax changes viewed as temporary.

Offsetting Provincial and Municipal Finance

The fiscal policies of provincial and municipal governments are frequently *pro-cyclical*, meaning that they worsen rather than correct recession or inflation. Like households and private businesses, provincial and municipal governments increase their expenditures during prosperity and cut them during recession. During the recession of 1990–91, some provincial and municipal governments had to increase tax rates, impose new taxes, and reduce spending to offset falling tax revenues resulting from the reduced personal income and spending of their citizens. In 2002 and 2003 the Ontario government reduced provincial income tax rates even though the economy was doing well. These tax reductions were made affordable by increased federal government transfer payments. But it is worth noting that different regions of Canada can have simultaneously different fiscal policy needs; southern Ontario can be in a recession while the Alberta oil patch economy is booming.

Crowding-Out Effect

crowding-out effect
A rise in interest rates and a resulting decrease in planned investment caused by the federal government's increased borrowing in the money market.

We now move from the practical problems that arise in implementing fiscal policy to a criticism of fiscal policy itself. That criticism is based on the so-called **crowding-out effect**: An expansionary fiscal policy (deficit spending) will increase the interest rate and reduce private spending, thereby weakening or cancelling the stimulus of the expansionary policy. In this view, fiscal policy may be largely or totally ineffective!

Suppose the economy is in recession and government enacts a discretionary fiscal policy in the form of increased government spending. Also suppose that the monetary authorities hold the supply of money constant. To finance its budget deficit, the government borrows funds in the money market. The resulting increase in the demand for money (discussed in Chapter 13) raises the price paid for borrowing money: the interest rate. Because investment spending varies inversely with the interest rate, some investment will be choked off or crowded out. (Some interest-sensitive consumption spending, such as purchases of automobiles on credit, may also be crowded out.)

GRAPHICAL PRESENTATION

An upward-sloping aggregate supply curve causes a part of the increase in aggregate demand, as in Figure 9-5, to be dissipated in higher prices, with the result that the increase in real GDP is diminished. The price level rises from P_0 to P_1 and real domestic output increases to only GDP_1, rather than GDP_f.

CRITICISMS OF THE CROWDING-OUT EFFECT

Nearly all economists agree that a deficit is inappropriate when the economy has achieved full employment. Such a deficit will crowd out private investment. But there is disagreement on whether crowding out exists under all circumstances. Many economists believe that little crowding out will occur when fiscal policy is used during a severe recession. Both increased government spending and increased consumption spending resulting from tax cuts will likely improve the profit expectations of businesses. Those greater expected returns on private investment may encourage more of it. Thus, private investment need not fall, even though interest rates rise.

Critics also point out that policy-makers (specifically the Bank of Canada) can counteract the crowding-out effect by increasing the supply of money just enough to offset the deficit-caused increase in the demand for money. Then the equilibrium interest rate would not change, and the crowding-out effect would be zero. These issues will be discussed in Chapter 13.

Fiscal Policy in the Open Economy

An additional complication arises from the fact that each national economy is a component of the world economy.

another one P261

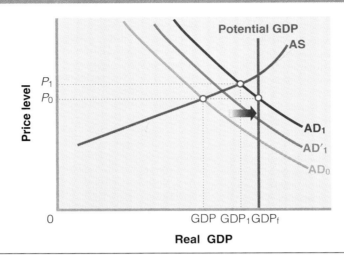

| FIGURE 9-5 | Fiscal Policy: The Effects of Crowding Out and the Net Export Effect |

With an upward sloping aggregate supply curve, a part of the impact of an expansionary policy will be reflected in a rise in the price level rather than an increase in real output and employment.

SHOCKS ORIGINATING FROM ABROAD

Events and policies abroad that affect a nation's net exports affect its own economy. Economies are open to unforeseen international *aggregate demand shocks* that can alter domestic GDP and make current domestic fiscal policy inappropriate.

Suppose Canada is in a recession and has enacted an expansionary fiscal policy to increase aggregate demand and GDP without igniting inflation. Now suppose the economies of Canada's major trading partners unexpectedly expand rapidly. Greater employment and rising incomes in those nations mean more purchases of Canadian goods. Canadian net exports rise, Canadian aggregate demand increases too rapidly; and Canada experiences demand-pull inflation. If Canadian policymakers had known in advance that net exports might rise significantly, Canada would have enacted a less expansionary fiscal policy. We see, then, that participation in the world economy brings with it the complications of mutual interdependence along with the gains from specialization and trade.

NET EXPORT EFFECT

net export effect
The idea that the impact of a change in monetary or fiscal policy will be strengthened or weakened by the consequent change in net exports.

The **net export effect** may also work through international trade to reduce the effectiveness of fiscal policy. We concluded in our discussion of the crowding-out effect that an expansionary fiscal policy might boost interest rates, reducing *investment* and weakening fiscal policy. Now we want to know what effect an interest-rate increase might have on a nation's *net exports* (exports minus imports).

Suppose Canada undertakes an expansionary fiscal policy that causes a higher Canadian interest rate. The higher interest rate will attract financial capital from abroad, where interest rates are unchanged. But foreign financial investors must acquire Canadian dollars to invest in Canadian securities. We know that an increase in the demand for a commodity—in this case, dollars—will raise its price. So the price of the Canadian dollar rises in terms of foreign currencies—that is, the dollar appreciates.

The impact of this dollar appreciation on Canadian net exports is that the rest of the world will see Canadian exports as being more expensive, and Canadian exports will decline. Canadians, who can now exchange their dollars for more units of foreign currencies, will buy more imports. Consequently, with Canadian exports falling and imports rising, net export expenditures in Canada will diminish; this is a contractionary change, so Canada's expansionary fiscal policy will be partially negated.[2]

---

[2]The appreciation of the dollar will also reduce the dollar price of foreign resources imported to Canada. As a result, aggregate supply will increase and part of the contractionary net export effect described here may be offset.

A return to our aggregate demand and supply analysis in Figure 9-5 will clarify this point. An expansionary fiscal policy aimed at increasing aggregate demand from AD_0 to AD_1 may hike the domestic interest rate and ultimately reduce net exports through the process just described. The decline in the net export component of aggregate demand will partially offset the expansionary fiscal policy. The aggregate demand curve will shift rightward from AD_0 to AD'_1, *not* to AD_1, and equilibrium GDP will not increase as much. Thus, the net export effect of fiscal policy joins the problems of timing, politics, and crowding out in complicating the "management" of aggregate demand.

 Table 9-2 summarizes the net export effect resulting from fiscal policy. Column 1 reviews the analysis just discussed. But note that the net export effect works in both directions. By reducing the domestic interest rate, a *contractionary* fiscal policy *increases* net exports. In this regard, you should follow through the analysis in column 2 in Table 9-2 and relate it to the aggregate demand-aggregate supply model. *(Key Question 7)*

QUICK REVIEW	
• Time lags and political problems complicate fiscal policy. • The crowding-out effect indicates that an expansionary fiscal policy may increase the interest rate and reduce investment spending.	• Fiscal policy may be weakened by the net export effect, which works through changes in (a) the interest rate, (b) exchange rates, and (c) exports and imports.

CURRENT THINKING ON FISCAL POLICY

Where do these complications leave us as to the advisability and effectiveness of discretionary fiscal policy? In view of the complications and uncertain outcomes of fiscal policy, some economists argue that it is better not to engage in it at all. Those holding this belief point to the superiority of monetary policy (changes in interest rates engineered by the Bank of Canada) as a stabilizing device or believe that most economic fluctuations tend to be mild and self-correcting. We will discuss monetary policy and the "self-correction" perspective in Chapter 13.

But most economists believe that fiscal policy remains an important, useful policy lever in the government's macroeconomic toolkit. The current popular view is that fiscal policy can help "push the economy" in a particular direction, but cannot "fine tune it" to a precise macroeconomic outcome. Mainstream economists generally agree that monetary policy is the best month-to-month stabilization tool for the Canadian economy. If monetary policy is doing its job, the government should maintain a relatively neutral fiscal policy, with a full-employment budget deficit or surplus of no more than 2 percent of potential GDP. It should hold major discretionary fiscal policy in reserve to help counter situations where recession threatens to be deep and long-lasting or inflation threatens to escalate rapidly despite the efforts of the Bank of Canada to stabilize the economy.

Finally, there is general agreement that proposed fiscal policy should be evaluated for its potential positive and negative impacts on long-run productivity growth. The short-run policy tools used for conducting discretionary fiscal policy often have long-run impacts. Fiscal policy designed to dampen economic fluctuations should be shaped to strengthen, or at least not impede, the growth of long-run aggregate supply. For example, a tax cut might be structured to enhance work effort, strengthen investment, and encourage innovation. Or an increase in government spending might centre on "public capital" (hospitals, highways, ports, airports) that are complementary to private investment and thus conducive to long-term economic growth.

TABLE 9-2	Fiscal Policy and the Net Export Effect
(1) Expansionary fiscal policy	**(2) Contractionary fiscal policy**
Problem: Recession, slow growth ↓	Problem: inflation ↓
Expansionary fiscal policy ↓	Contractionary fiscal policy ↓
Higher domestic interest rate ↓	Lower domestic interest rate ↓
Increased foreign demand for dollars ↓	Decreased foreign demand for dollars ↓
Dollar appreciates ↓	Dollar depreciates ↓
Net exports decline (aggregate demand decreases, partially offsetting the expansionary fiscal policy)	Net exports increase (aggregate demand increases, partially offsetting the contractionary fiscal policy)

THE LASTword | The Leading Indicators

One of the several tools policy-makers use to forecast the future direction of real GDP is a monthly index of a group of variables that in the past have provided advance notice of changes in GDP.

Statistics Canada's composite index of leading indicators has historically reached a peak or trough in advance of the corresponding turns in the business cycle. Thus, changes in the index of leading indicators provide a clue to the future direction of the economy and such advance warning helps policy-makers formulate appropriate macroeconomic policy.

Here is how each of the 10 components of the index would change if a decline in GDP were predicted, keeping in mind that the opposite changes forecast a rise in GDP.

1. Retail trade furniture and appliance sales A slump in these retail trade sales portends reduced future production—that is, a decline in GDP.

2. Other durable goods sales This part of retail trade is four times greater than the first. It includes sales of automobiles, which are more sensitive to interest rates than are purchases of other goods. A decline in sales here may be more a result of rising consumer loan rates than an impending downturn in the economy—though rising interest rates themselves often do precede a downturn.

3. Housing index This is a composite index of housing starts (units) and house sales. Decreases in the number of housing starts and in house sales forecast declines in investment and therefore the distinct possibility that GDP will decline or at least grow more slowly.

4. New orders for durable goods A decline in the number of orders received for durable goods indicates reduced future production—a decline in real GDP.

5. Shipment-to-inventory ratio of finished products A decline in the ratio—a decline in shipments and/or an increase in inventory—indicates that sales are declining and, probably, that undesired investment in inventories is occurring. In either case, a decline in production is probable.

6. Average workweek (hours) Decreases in the length of the average workweek in manufacturing foretell declines in future manufacturing output and a possible decline in GDP.

7. Business and personal service employment A decline in employment, especially in view of the continuing growth of our labour force of some 250,000 a year, indicates a serious slowdown in the economy and therefore GDP.

8. United States composite leading index Since 80 percent of our trade is with the United States—approximately 40 percent of our GDP—a slowdown in the United States is quickly transmitted to Canada. If the U.S. composite leading index is sharply down, Canada's GDP will almost certainly decline.

9. S&P/TSX composite index The Toronto Stock Exchange (TSX) is the country's largest, and the price movements of the 100 stocks that make up its index are a good indication of market sentiment in Canada. Declines in stock prices are often reflections of expected declines in cor-

porate sales and profits. Also, lower stock prices diminish consumer wealth, leading to possible cutbacks in consumer spending. Lower stock prices also make it less attractive for firms to issue new shares of stock as a way of raising funds for investment. Thus, declines in stock prices can bring forth declines in aggregate demand and real GDP.

10. Money supply Decreases in the nation's money supply are associated with falling real GDP.

None of these factors alone consistently predicts the future course of the economy. It is not unusual in any month, for example, for one or two of the indicators to be decreasing while the other indicators are increasing. Rather, changes in the composite of the 10 components are what in the past have provided advance notice of a change in the direction of GDP. The rule of thumb is that three successive monthly declines or increases in the index indicate the economy will soon turn in that same direction.

Although the composite index has correctly signaled business fluctuations on numerous occasions, it has not been infallible. At times the index has provided false warnings of recessions that never happened. In other instances, recessions have so closely followed the downturn in the index that policymakers have not had sufficient time to make use of the "early" warning. Moreover, changing structural features of the economy have, on occasion, rendered the existing index obsolete and necessitated its revision.

Given these caveats, the index of leading indicators can best be thought of as a useful but not totally reliable signaling device that authorities must employ with considerable caution in formulating macroeconomic policy.

CHAPTER SUMMARY

9.1 FISCAL POLICY AND THE AD-AS MODEL

- Other things equal, increases in government spending expand, and decreases contract, aggregate demand and equilibrium GDP. Increases in taxes reduce, and decreases expand, aggregate demand and equilibrium GDP. Fiscal policy therefore calls for increases in government spending and decreases in taxes—a budget deficit—to correct a recessionary gap. Decreases in government spending and increases in taxes—a budget surplus—are appropriate fiscal policy for correcting an inflationary gap.

9.2 BUILT-IN STABILIZATION

- Built-in stability arises from net tax revenues, which vary directly with the level of GDP. During recession, the federal budget automatically moves toward a stabilizing deficit; during expansion, the budget automatically moves toward an anti-inflationary surplus. Built-in stability lessens, but does not fully correct, undesired changes in the real GDP.

- The cyclically adjusted budget, or full-employment budget, measures the federal budget deficit or surplus that would occur if the economy operated at full employment throughout the year. Cyclical deficits or surpluses are those that result from changes in the real GDP.

- Changes in the cyclically adjusted deficit or surplus provide meaningful information as to whether the government's fiscal policy is expansionary, neutral, or contractionary. Changes in the actual budget deficit or surplus do not, since such deficits or surpluses can include cyclical deficits or surplus.

9.3 PROBLEMS, CRITICISMS, AND COMPLICATIONS

- Certain problems complicate the enactment and implementation of fiscal policy. They include: (a) timing problems associated with recognition, administrative, and operational lags; (b) the potential for misuse of fiscal policy for political rather than economic purposes; (c) provincial and municipal finances tend to be pro-cyclical; (d) potential ineffectiveness if households expect future policy reversals; (e) the possibility of fiscal policy crowding-out of private investment; and (f) complications relating to the effects of fiscal policy on exchange rates and net exports.

- The current mainstream view by economists is that fiscal policy can help "push" the economy in a desired direction, but cannot reliably be used to "fine tune" the economy. Nevertheless, fiscal policy is a valuable "reserve" tool for aiding monetary policy in fighting significant recession or inflation.

TERMS AND CONCEPTS

fiscal policy, p. 237
expansionary fiscal policy, p. 237
budget deficit, p. 237
contractionary fiscal policy, p. 238
budget surplus, p. 238

built-in stabilizer, p. 240
progressive tax, p. 241
proportional tax, p. 241
regressive tax, p. 241
cyclically adjusted budget, p. 242

cyclical deficit, p. 242
political business cycle, p. 246
crowding-out effect, p. 247
net export effect, p. 248

STUDY QUESTIONS

1. **KEY QUESTION** What are the government's fiscal policy options for an inflationary gap caused by demand-pull inflation? Use the aggregate demand-aggregate supply model to show the impact of these policies on the price level. Which of these fiscal options do you think a person who wants to preserve the size of government might favour? A person who thinks the public sector is too large?

2. (For students assigned Chapter 7) Use the aggregate expenditures model to show how government fiscal policy could eliminate either a recessionary gap or an inflationary gap (Figure 7-16). Use the concept of the balanced budget multiplier to explain how equal increases in *G* and *T* could eliminate a recessionary

gap and how equal decreases in *G* and *T* could eliminate an inflationary gap.

3. Indicate whether each statement is true or false and justify your answer.

   a. Expansionary fiscal policy during a recession will have a greater positive effect on real GDP if government borrows the money to finance the budget deficit than if it creates new money to finance the deficit.

   b. Contractionary fiscal policy will be more effective if government allows the budget surplus to remain idle rather than using the surplus to pay off some of its past debt.

4. Explain how the built-in (or automatic) stabilizers work. What are the differences between a proportional, progressive, and regressive tax system as they relate to an economy's built-in stability?

5. **KEY QUESTION** Define the cyclically adjusted budget, explain its significance, and state why it may differ from the actual budget. Suppose the full-employment, non-inflationary level of real output is GDP_3 (not GDP_2) in the economy depicted in Figure 9-3. If the economy is operating at GDP_2, instead of GDP_3, what is the status of its full-employment budget? Of its current fiscal policy? What change in fiscal policy would you recommend? How would you accomplish that in terms of the G and T lines in the figure?

6. Suppose the actual budget deficit (as a percentage of GDP) increased significantly, but the cyclically adjusted budget deficit remained relatively constant. What would explain this fact?

7. **KEY QUESTION** Briefly state and evaluate the problems in enacting and applying fiscal policy. Explain the notion of a political business cycle. What is the crowding-out effect and why is it relevant to fiscal policy? In what respect is the net export effect similar to the crowding-out effect?

8. In view of your answers to question 7, explain the following statement: "Although fiscal policy clearly is useful in combatting severe recession and demand-pull inflation, it is impossible to use fiscal policy to 'fine tune' the economy to the full-employment, non-inflationary level of real GDP and keep the economy there indefinitely."

9. Suppose that the government engages in deficit spending to push the economy from recession and that this spending is directed towards new "public capital" such as roads, bridges, dams, harbours, office parks, industrial sites, and the like. How might this spending increase the expected rate of return on some types of potential *private* investment projects? What are the implications for the crowding-out effect?

10. Use Figure 9-4b to explain why the deliberate increase of the cyclically adjusted budget (resulting from the tax cut) will reduce the size of the actual budget deficit if the fiscal policy

succeeds in pushing the economy to its full-employment output of GDP_3.

11. **Advanced Analysis** (For students assigned Chapter 7) Assume that, without taxes, the consumption schedule for an economy is as shown below:

GDP (billions)	Consumption (billions)
$100	$120
200	200
300	280
400	360
500	440
600	520
700	600

a. Graph this consumption schedule and determine the size of the MPC.

b. Assume a lump-sum (regressive) tax is imposed such that the government collects $10 billion in taxes at all levels of GDP. Calculate the tax rate at each level of GDP. Graph the resulting consumption schedule and compare the MPC and the multiplier with that of the pretax consumption schedule.

c. Now suppose a proportional tax with a 10 percent tax rate is imposed instead of the regressive tax. Calculate the new consumption schedule, graph it, and note the MPC and the multiplier.

d. Finally, impose a progressive tax such that the tax rate is zero percent when GDP is $100, 5 percent at $200, 10 percent at $300, 15 percent at $400, and so forth. Determine and graph the new consumption schedule, noting the effect of this tax on the MPC and the multiplier.

e. Explain why the proportional and progressive taxes contribute to greater economic stability, but the regressive tax does not. Demonstrate using a graph similar to Figure 9-3.

12. **(The Last Word)** What is the composite index of leading economic indicators and how does it relate to discretionary fiscal policy?

INTERNET APPLICATION QUESTIONS

1. **The Federal Budget Stance** Go to the Department of Finance home page through the McConnell-Brue-Barbiero Web site (Chapter 9) and click on the latest budget. Now, access the budget overview. What are the main targets of the federal government?

2. **Leading economic indicators—how goes the economy?** Statistics Canada tracks the leading economic indicators. Check the summary of the index of leading indicators and its individual components for the latest month at the McConnell-Brue-Barbiero Web site (Chapter 9). Is the index up or down? Which specific components are up, and which are down? What has been the trend of the composite index over the past three months?

10

Chapter

Deficits, Surpluses, and the Public Debt

Over the years, the government of Canada has accumulated about $641 billion of gross public debt, up enormously from a mere $46 billion in 1973. Since 1998 the Canadian government has been running surpluses for the first time in a generation. Still, should we be concerned about a public debt that is over half a *trillion* dollars?

In this chapter, we examine the public debt, budget deficits, and budget surpluses. What are the economic impacts of the public debt? Now that Canada is incurring budget surpluses, should we use them to reduce the public debt, cut personal taxes, or increase spending on existing and new social programs?

10.1   Defi cits, Surpluses, and Debt: Defi nitions and Philosophies

A *budget deficit* is the amount by which a government's expenditures exceed its revenues during a particular year. For example, during 1996–97 the federal government spent $166 billion and its receipts were only $152.5 billion, resulting in a $13.5 billion deficit. In contrast, a *budget surplus* is the amount by which government revenues exceed government expenditures in a given year. For example, federal government revenues of $192.3 billion in 2001–2002 exceeded expenditures of $183.9 billion, resulting in an $8.4 billion budget surplus.

public debt
The total amount owed by the federal government to the owners of government securities.

The national or **public debt** is the total accumulation of the federal government's total deficits and surpluses that have occurred through time. It represents the total amount of money owed by the federal government to holders of *Canadian government securities*. In 2002 the gross federal debt was $640 billion.

Budget Philosophies

Is it good or bad for a government to incur deficits or surpluses? Should the budget be balanced annually? We saw in Chapter 9 that fiscal policy should move the federal budget towards a deficit during recession and towards a surplus during expansion. This means discretionary fiscal policy is unlikely to result in a balanced budget in any particular year. Is this a matter for concern?

Let's approach this question by examining the economic implications of several contrasting budget philosophies.

Annually Balanced Budget

annually balanced budget
A budget in which government expenditures and tax collections are equal each year.

Until the Great Depression of the 1930s, the **annually balanced budget** was viewed as the desirable goal of public finance. However, an annually balanced budget is not compatible with government fiscal activity as a stabilizing force. Indeed, an annually balanced budget can intensify the business cycle.

Illustration: Suppose the Canadian economy experiences an onset of unemployment and falling incomes. In such circumstances tax receipts of both the federal and provincial governments automatically decline. To balance its budget, government must either (1) increase tax rates, (2) reduce government expenditures, or (3) do both. But all three policies are *contractionary;* each further dampens, rather than expands, aggregate demand.

Similarly, an annually balanced budget will intensify an inflationary gap. As nominal incomes rise in an over-heated economy, tax revenues automatically increase. To avoid the impending surplus, government must either (1) cut tax rates, (2) increase government expenditures, or (3) do both. But any of these policies adds to inflationary pressures.

An annually balanced budget is not neutral; the pursuit of such a policy can intensify the business cycle, not dampen it.

Some economists have advocated an annually balanced budget, not because of a fear of deficits and a mounting public debt, but because they believe an annually balanced budget constrains an undesirable expansion of the public sector. They believe government has a tendency to grow larger than it should because there is less popular opposition to this growth when it is financed by deficits rather than taxes. And when budget surpluses do occur, the tendency is for government to spend down the surpluses on new government programs, rather than cut taxes.

Cyclically Balanced Budget

cyclically balanced budget
The equality of government expenditures and net tax collections over the course of a business cycle.

The idea of a **cyclically balanced budget** is that government exerts a counter-cyclical influence and at the same time balances its budget. However, this budget would not be balanced annually, but rather over the course of the business cycle.

The rationale is simple and appealing. To offset recession, government should lower taxes and increase spending, purposely incurring a deficit. During the ensuing recovery, taxes would be raised and government spending slashed. Government would use the resulting surplus to pay down the federal debt incurred in offsetting the recession. Government fiscal operations would therefore exert a positive, counter-cyclical force, and the government could still balance its budget over a period of years.

The problem with this budget philosophy is that the upswings and downswings of the business cycle may not be of equal magnitude and duration. A long and severe slump followed by a modest and short period of prosperity could mean a large deficit during the slump, little or no surplus during prosperity, and a cyclical deficit in the budget.

Functional Finance

functional finance
The use of fiscal policy to achieve a non-inflationary full-employment GDP without regard to the effect on the public debt.

With **functional finance**, an annually or cyclically balanced budget is of secondary concern. The primary purpose of government finance is to provide non-inflationary full employment to balance the economy, not the budget. If this objective causes either persistent surpluses or a large and growing public debt, so be it. In this philosophy, the problems of government deficits or surpluses are minor compared with the undesirable alternatives of prolonged recession or persistent inflation. The federal budget is an instrument for achieving and maintaining macroeconomic stability. The best way to finance government spending—through taxation or borrowing—depends on current economic conditions. Government should not hesitate to incur any deficits and surpluses required to achieve macroeconomic stability and growth. *(Key Question 1)*

10.2   The Public Debt: Facts and Figures

Over the years, budget deficits have greatly exceeded budget surpluses, leading to a large public debt. As column 2 in Table 10-1 shows, in nominal terms the public debt was higher in 2002 than 50 years earlier. (Not shown, it is also higher in real terms.)

Causes

The main sources of large budget deficits in Canada and thus the public debt have been wars, recessions, and the lack of political will.

WARS

Some of the public debt in Canada has been incurred due to the deficit financing of wars. The public debt increased substantially during World War I and grew almost fourfold during World War II.

Consider World War II and the options it posed. The task was to reallocate a substantial portion of the economy's resources from civilian to war goods production. The federal government's expenditures for armaments and military personnel soared. There were three financing options for Ottawa: increase taxes, print the needed money, or use deficit financing. Government feared that tax financing would require tax rates so high that they would diminish incentives to work. The national interest required attracting more people into the labour force and encouraging those already participating to work longer hours. Very high tax rates would interfere with these goals. Printing and spending additional money would be inflationary. Thus, much of World War II was financed by selling bonds to the public, draining off spendable income and freeing resources from civilian production to make them available for defence industries.

Some of the public debt in Canada has been incurred due to the deficit financing of wars.

RECESSIONS

The public debt in Canada has also grown because of recessions, and, more specifically, the built-in stability characterizing Canada's fiscal system. In periods when income declines, tax collections

| TABLE 10-1 | The Government of Canada Public Debt and Interest Payments in Relation to GDP, Selected Years, 1926–2002* | | | | | |

(1) End of year	(2) Gross federal public debt (billions)	(3) Gross domestic product (billions)	(4) Interest payments (billions)	(5) Public debt as percentage of GDP (2)÷(3)	(6) Interest payments as percentage of GDP (4)÷(3)	(7) Per capita public debt
1926	$ 2.811	$ 5.354	$ 0.130	52.5%	2.4%	$ 298
1929	2.699	6.400	0.122	42.2	1.9	270
1940	4.029	6.987	0.137	57.7	2.0	354
1946	17.893	12.167	0.444	147.4	3.6	1,455
1954	17.558	26.531	0.482	66.2	1.8	1,149
1960	20.399	39.448	0.756	51.7	1.9	2,208
1966	27.738	64.943	1.151	42.7	2.4	1,385
1969	34.355	84.006	1.589	40.9	1.9	1,635
1973	46.211	129.196	2.518	35.8	1.9	2,096
1975	55.125	173.983	3.705	31.7	2.1	2,429
1979	100.492	280.309	8.080	35.8	2.9	4,232
1983	173.091	411.160	17.420	42.1	4.2	6,952
1988	349.894	611.785	31.882	57.2	5.2	13,510
1991	444.557	683.239	41.815	65.1	6.1	16,359
1997	651.124	877.921	44.916	74.1	5.1	21,560
2000	648.212	1,075.566	45.650	60.3	4.2	20,910
2002	640.526	1,154.949	40.487	55.4	3.5	20,232

*In current dollars.

Sources: Statistics Canada and Bank of Canada. Historical series from CANSIM D469409.
Visit www.mcgrawhill.ca/college/mcconnell for data update.

Σ-STAT

automatically fall and deficits arise. Thus the public debt rose during the recessions of 1981–82 and 1991–92. The gross federal public debt jumped more than 70 percent between 1979 and 1983, and increased 60 percent between 1988 and 1994.

LACK OF POLITICAL WILL

It can also be said that past deficits and the public debt are the result of lack of political will and determination to contain them. Spending; particularly on social programs, tends to gain votes; tax increases are dangerous politically. Although opposition to deficits is widely expressed both by politicians and by voters, *specific* proposals to raise taxes or cut programs encounter more opposition than support. University students may favour smaller deficits so long as funds for student loans are not eliminated in the process.

Quantitative Aspects

In 2002 the gross federal debt was approximately $640 billion, up from $46 billion in 1973. But these large, seemingly incomprehensible numbers are misleading.

Consider This

Federal and Provincial per Capita Net Debt, 2002

There is a significant variance in the per capita net debt among Canadian provinces. The federal government has a lower per capita debt than many provincial governments in Canada, at almost $8,000. Newfoundland, at over $17,000, has the highest provincial per capita net debt among the provinces. Not far behind are Quebec and Nova Scotia. The provinces with the least per capita debt are to be found in Western Canada. British Columbia's per capita debt, at $3,997, is about a quarter that of Nova Scotia's. Alberta has the distinction of being the only province with a per capita credit of $2,928! This distinction is attributable to the revenues the Alberta government gets from its oil and gas sector, which also gives it the luxury of not having to have a provincial sales tax.

Canada	$ 7,940
Newfoundland	17,084
Quebec	12,302
Nova Scotia	11,945
Saskatchewan	9,519
Manitoba	8,662
Ontario	8,570
New Brunswick	7,926
P.E.I.	7,734
British Columbia	3,997
Alberta	– 2,928

Source: Statistics Canada

Question: The absolute level of net debt in Ontario, with a population of over 12 million, was $103.5 billion and that of Nova Scotia, with a population of 945,000, was $11.3 billion in 2002. Why is the per capita debt more meaningful than the absolute debt level?

DEBT AND GDP

A simple statement of the absolute size of the debt ignores the fact that the wealth and productive ability of our economy have also increased tremendously. A wealthy, highly productive nation can more easily incur and carry a large public debt than can a poor nation. It is more meaningful to measure changes in the public debt *in relation* to the economy's GDP, as shown in column 5 in Table 10-1. Instead of the large increase in the debt between 1946 and 2002 shown in column 2, we now find that the *relative* size of the debt *declined* between 1946 and 1975. Still, our data do show that the relative size of the debt has increased significantly since 1975, from 32 percent of GDP to the present 56 percent of GDP, even if it began to decline from a peak of over 60 percent in the late 1990s.

INTERNATIONAL COMPARISONS

As shown in Global Perspective 10.1, Canada's public debt is the fourth highest as a percentage of GDP among the industrialized nations of the world.

INTEREST CHARGES

Many economists conclude that the primary burden of the debt is the annual interest charge accruing as a result. The absolute size of these interest payments is shown in column 4 of Table 10-1. Interest payments have increased sharply beginning in the mid-1970s. Interest charges as a percentage of the GDP are shown in column 6 of Table 10-1. Interest payments increased significantly as a proportion of GDP beginning in the early 1980s, but have recently started to decline. This ratio reflects the level of taxation (the average tax rate) required to service the public debt. In 2000 government had to collect taxes equal to 4 percent of GDP to pay interest on its debt.

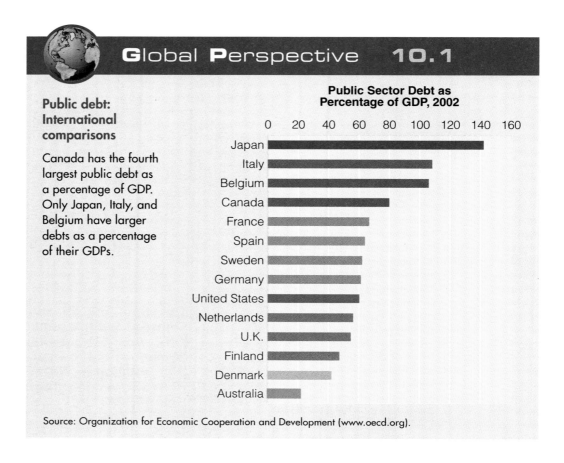

Global Perspective 10.1

Public debt: International comparisons

Canada has the fourth largest public debt as a percentage of GDP. Only Japan, Italy, and Belgium have larger debts as a percentage of their GDPs.

Public Sector Debt as Percentage of GDP, 2002

Japan, Italy, Belgium, Canada, France, Spain, Sweden, Germany, United States, Netherlands, U.K., Finland, Denmark, Australia

Source: Organization for Economic Cooperation and Development (www.oecd.org).

OWNERSHIP

www.bankofcanada.ca
Bank of Canada

Figure 10-1 shows that about 8 percent of the total public debt is held by the Bank of Canada, and the remaining 92 percent by private individuals, chartered banks, insurance companies, and corporations. About 17 percent of the total debt is held by foreigners. The vast majority of the gross federal debt is thus internally, not externally, held.

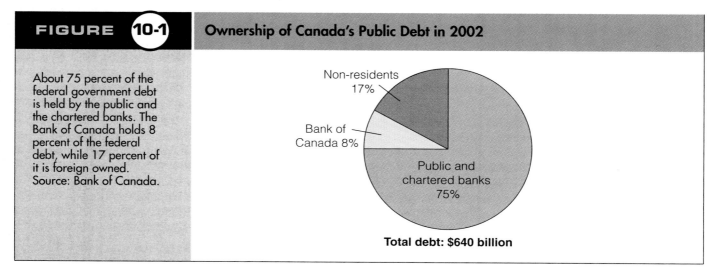

FIGURE 10-1   Ownership of Canada's Public Debt in 2002

About 75 percent of the federal government debt is held by the public and the chartered banks. The Bank of Canada holds 8 percent of the federal debt, while 17 percent of it is foreign owned.
Source: Bank of Canada.

Non-residents 17%

Bank of Canada 8%

Public and chartered banks 75%

Total debt: $640 billion

QUICK REVIEW

- A budget deficit is an excess of government expenditures over tax revenues in a particular year; a budget surplus is an excess of tax revenues over government expenditures in a given year; the public debt is the total accumulation of budget deficits minus surpluses through time.

- The three major budget philosophies are: (a) an annually balanced budget; (b) a budget balanced over the business cycle; and (c) functional finance.

- The $640 billion public debt of the federal government has resulted mainly from wartime financing, recessions, and lack of political will to contain it.

- Canada's public debt as a percentage of GDP grew rapidly between 1975 and 1995, but began to decline in the late 1990s.

10.3   False Concerns

You may wonder whether a large public debt might bankrupt Canada or at least place a burden on our children and grandchildren. Fortunately, these are false concerns.

Bankruptcy

The public debt does not threaten to bankrupt the federal government, leaving it unable to meet its financial obligations, for two main reasons.

- *Refinancing*   The public debt is easily refinanced. As portions of the debt come due each month, the government in Ottawa does not cut expenditures or raise taxes to provide the funds required for its operation. Rather, the federal government refinances the debt by selling new bonds and using the proceeds to pay off holders of the maturing bonds. The new bonds are in strong demand because lenders (purchasers of government bonds) can obtain a relatively good interest return with little risk of default by the federal government.

- *Taxation*   The federal government has the authority to levy and collect taxes. Parliament can impose a tax increase to pay interest and principal on the public debt. Financially distressed private households and corporations cannot resolve their financial difficulties by taxing the public. Private households and corporations can go bankrupt, but the federal government has the option to impose new taxes or increase existing tax rates if necessary to finance its debt.

Burdening Future Generations

In 2002, public debt per capita was $20,232. Was each child born in 2002 handed a $20,232 bill from Ottawa? Not really! The public debt does not impose as much of a debt on future generations as generally thought.

Canada owes a substantial portion of the public debt to itself. Over 80 percent of government of Canada bonds are held by citizens and institutions—banks, businesses, insurance companies, government agencies, and pensions and trust funds—within Canada. While the public debt is a liability to Canadians (as taxpayers), part of the same debt is simultaneously an asset to Canadians (as bondholders).

To eliminate the public debt would require a gigantic transfer payment from Canadians to Canadians. Taxpayers would pay higher taxes and the government, in turn, would pay out those tax revenues to those same taxpaying individuals. Only the repayment of the approximately 17 percent of the public debt owned by foreigners would have a negative impact on Canadian purchasing power.

We noted earlier that the public debt increased sharply during World War II. But the decision to finance military purchases through the sale of government bonds did not shift the economic burden to future generations. The burden of the war was borne almost entirely by the people who lived during the war. They were the ones who did without a multitude of consumer goods to permit Canada to arm itself and help arm its allies. The next generation inherited the debt from the war but also an equal amount of government bonds.

QUICK REVIEW

- There is no danger of the federal government going bankrupt because it need only refinance (not retire) the public debt and can raise revenues, if needed, through higher taxes.

- Usually, the public debt is not a means of shifting economic burdens to future generations.

10.4 Substantive Issues

Although the above issues are of no real concern, there are a number of substantive issues relating to the public debt. Economists, however, attach varying degrees of importance to them.

Income Distribution

The distribution of government securities ownership is uneven. Some people own much more than their $20,232 per-capita share of government securities; others own less or none at all. The ownership of the public debt is concentrated among wealthier groups. Because the federal tax system is only mildly progressive, payment of interest on the public debt probably increases income inequality. If greater income equality is one of our social goals, then this redistributive effect is undesirable.

Incentives

Table 10-1 indicates that the current federal public debt necessitated an annual interest payment of over $40 billion. This annual interest charge must be paid out of tax revenues. Higher taxes may dampen incentives to bear risk, to innovate, to invest, and to work. So, indirectly, the existence of a large debt may impair economic growth. As noted earlier, the ratio of interest payments to the GDP indicates the level of taxation needed to pay interest on the debt. Some economists are concerned that this percentage is double what it was in 1975 (column 6 of Table 10-1). But as you can see, the public debt has been shrinking as a percentage of GDP since 1997, as have interest payments as a percentage of GDP.

External Debt

external public debt
Public debt owed to foreign citizens, firms, and institutions.

The 17 percent of Canada's debt held by citizens and institutions of foreign countries is an economic burden to Canadians. Because we do not owe that portion of the debt "to ourselves," the payment of interest and principal on this **external public debt** enables foreigners to buy some of our output. In return for the benefits derived from the borrowed funds, Canada transfers goods and services to foreign lenders. Of course, Canadians also own debt issued by foreign governments, so payment on principal and interest by these governments transfers some of their goods and services to Canadians. *(Key Question 3)*

Crowding-Out and the Stock of Capital

There is a potentially more serious problem. The financing of the public debt can transfer a real economic burden to future generations by passing on a smaller stock of capital goods. This possibility involves the *crowding-out effect:* the idea that deficit financing will increase interest rates and thereby reduce private investment spending. When crowding-out is significant, future generations will inherit an economy with a smaller productive capacity and, other things equal, a lower standard of living.

Consider the investment demand curve I_{d1} in Figure 10-2. (Ignore curve Id_2 for now.) If government borrowing pushes up the interest rate from 6 percent to 10 percent, investment spending by firms will fall from $25 billion to $15 billion. That is, the deficit financing will crowd out $10 billion of private investment.

QUALIFICATIONS

But even if crowding-out occurs, there are two factors that could reduce the net economic burden shifted to future generations.

public investments
Government expenditures on public capital (such as roads and highways) and on human capital (such as education and health).

- **Public investment**   Part of government spending is for public investment outlays (for example, airports, highways, and mass transit systems) and "human capital" (for example, investments in education, job training, and health). Like private expenditures on machinery and equipment, those **public investments** increase the economy's future production capacity. That greater stock of public capital may offset the diminished stock of private capital resulting from the crowding-out effect.

- **Public-private complementarities**   Some public and private investments are complementary. Thus, the public investment financed through the debt could spur some private sector investment by increasing its expected rate of return. For example, a federal building in a city may encourage private investment in the form of nearby office buildings, shops, and restaurants. Through its complementary effect, the spending on public capital may shift the private investment demand curve to the right, as from I_{d1} to I_{d2} in Figure 10-2. Even though the government borrowing boosts the interest rate from 6 percent to 10 percent, total private investment need not fall. In the case shown in Figure 10-2, it remains at $25 billion. Of course, the increase in investment demand might be smaller than that shown. If it were smaller, the crowding-out effect would not be fully offset. But the point is that an increase in investment demand

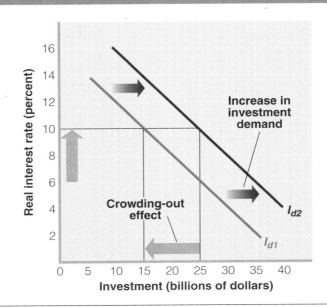

FIGURE 10-2   **The Investment Demand Curve and the Crowding-Out Effect**

If the investment demand curve (I_{d1}) is fixed, the increase in the interest rate from 6 percent to 10 percent caused by financing a large public debt will crowd out $10 billion of private investment and decrease the size of the capital stock inherited by future generations. However, if the government spending enabled by the debt improves the profit expectations of businesses, the private investment demand curve will shift rightward, as from I_{d1} to I_{d2}. That shift may offset the crowding-out effect wholly or in part.

may counter the decline in investment that would otherwise result from the higher interest rate. *(Key Question 7)*

10.5 Deficits and Surpluses: 1990 to the Present

Federal deficits and the growing public debt were the main focus of fiscal policy during the first half of the 1990s. As Figure 10-3 makes clear, the absolute sizes of annual federal deficits were large during that period. The budget deficit jumped from about $20 billion in 1990 to $40 billion in 1993, mainly because of the recession of 1990–91 and a weak recovery, which slowed the inflow of tax revenues.

Fiscal policy turned to reducing the deficits in order to promote a *reverse* crowding-out effect—that is, to lower interest rates and boost private investment spending. From a deficit of $40 billion in 1993, spending reductions and increases in tax revenues succeeded in turning a federal government budget surplus of over $6 billion in 2003.

www.statcan.ca/english/
Pgdb/State/Government/
govt02.htm
Statistics Canada

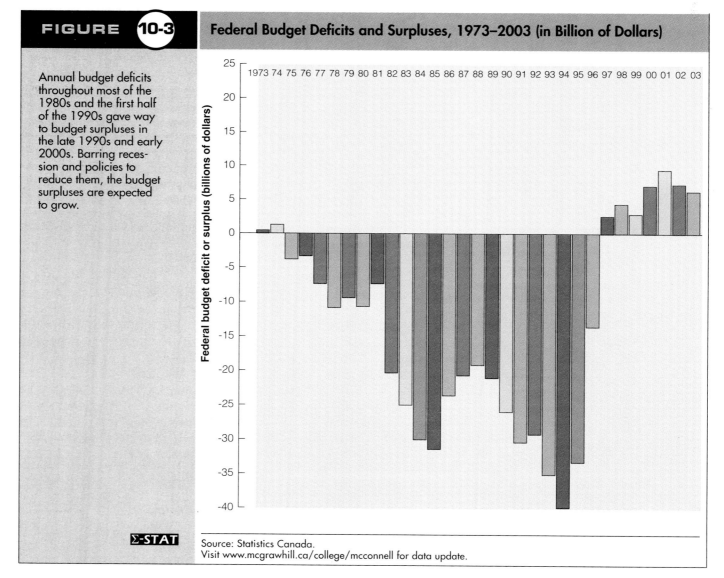

FIGURE 10-3

Federal Budget Deficits and Surpluses, 1973–2003 (in Billion of Dollars)

Annual budget deficits throughout most of the 1980s and the first half of the 1990s gave way to budget surpluses in the late 1990s and early 2000s. Barring recession and policies to reduce them, the budget surpluses are expected to grow.

Σ-STAT

Source: Statistics Canada.
Visit www.mcgrawhill.ca/college/mcconnell for data update.

What to do with the Surpluses?

The public debate over the federal budget has turned 180 degrees, from how to reduce large budget deficits to what should be done with budget surpluses. Without actions to reduce them, and assuming no recession, these surpluses could accumulate in the next decade. There are three main options for the surpluses, along with combinations of each: paying down the public debt, reducing taxes, and increasing government expenditures, particularly for social programs.

Pay Down the Public Debt   The federal government could use its surpluses to pay down the public debt. As government bonds come due, the federal government can pay them off and not reissue new bonds. Also, because Treasury bills (a short-term debt instrument issued by a government), notes, and bonds are bought and sold daily in financial markets, the federal government can reduce the public debt by simply purchasing government securities and retiring them.

Those who advocate using budget surpluses to pay down the public debt say that these actions will increase Canadian economic growth over the long run. The primary economic benefit from paying down the public debt is the reverse crowding-out effect, as previously mentioned. Less government borrowing in the money market would reduce the pressure on real interest rate, which in turn would promote private investment spending and thus potentially increase the stock of private capital in the economy. As we know, increases in capital per worker contribute to economic growth.

Many economists, however, are less enthusiastic about paying down the public debt. They doubt the alleged strength of the reverse crowding-out effect, arguing that government borrowing is just one of many determinants of interest rates. In this view, there is no particular urgency to pay down the public debt each year because with deficits in check, the debt and interest payments on it will both decline *as percentages of GDP* over time.

Critics of paying down the public debt also point out that the public debt plays a positive role in the economy. Government securities—Treasury bills, notes, and bonds, including Canada savings bonds—are important components of financial holdings of individuals, businesses, and provincial governments. When these securities are held to maturity (the date when the principal is paid back), they are virtually risk-free, and all but saving bonds can be bought and sold. Finally, the critics remind us that the main instrument of monetary policy (open-market operations) is based on buying and selling Canadian securities. Those operations require that the Bank of Canada, chartered banks, and the non-bank public have Canadian government securities to buy and sell. This topic will be taken up in depth in Chapters 11–13.

www.csb.gc.ca
Canada Savings Bonds

Reduce Taxes   A second option for dealing with budget surpluses is to cut tax rates. Proponents of this approach say that the surplus revenues came from taxpayers and should be returned to them. The most direct way to return this money is to reduce tax rates or eliminate certain taxes altogether. Some politicians, particularly those in the Canadian Alliance party, suggest cutting income tax rates. Others suggest increasing tax deductions and tax credits to reduce the expense of eldercare, attending college and university, childcare, and so on. Still others say that we should repeal the capital gains taxes.

Those who support tax cuts fear that without such cuts the federal government will spend the surpluses on new social programs. Tax cuts, they say, will ensure that federal government spending does not balloon along with the excess revenues. Also, tax reduction will increase disposable income, which will ensure that consumption spending remains strong through the coming years, even if the recent record gains in stock market valuations erode.

Critics of tax cuts believe that a permanent reduction of tax rates or elimination of certain taxes is an inappropriate response to a temporary increase in tax revenues. Moreover, say the critics, there are much better ways to use the surpluses, such as paying down the debt. They also point out that the timing of the tax cuts is wrong from a fiscal policy perspective. Budget surpluses are escalating precisely because the economy is growing so vigorously. Between 2000 and 2002 the Canadian economy outpaced that of the United States. While the American economy slipped into recession in 2001, the Canadian economy continued to grow. Those surpluses are therefore serving quite appropriately as an automatic stabilizer. Cutting taxes during a vigorous economic expansion is to invite demand-pull inflation.

Increase Public Expenditures   People who support using the surpluses to increase federal expenditures say there are a number of possible uses for the funds that would greatly benefit society and strengthen the economy over the long run. For example, one proposal is to spend part of the surpluses to finance a national childcare program. Another proposal is to undertake a massive effort to restore and upgrade a deteriorating infrastructure of such public capital as highways, bridges, air traffic control facilities, rail transit, school buildings, and textbooks.

Critics of using the surpluses to increase government spending say that, like tax cuts, they would be inflationary. Moreover, such increases would tilt the allocation of resources away from the high-tech, high-productivity private sector and toward the less productive public sector, blunting the very economic growth that generated the surpluses in the first place. And because higher program spending levels tend to get "institutionalized" into federal budgets, the enlarged government spending would continue even if tax revenues later declined as the economy slowed or receded.

Combinations of Policies

There are, of course, endless combinations of these options. For example, the federal government could use one-third of the budget surpluses for repayment of the debt, one-third to increase government expenditures, and one-third to reduce taxes. Or half could be used to cut taxes and half used to add to social programs. Different perspectives on what is best for society—or best for one's political constituents—will play a prominent role in the final decisions. In any event, deciding what to do with large budget surpluses is a more pleasant problem to have than dealing with large budget deficits.

LIKELY DIRECTIONS

The budget of February 2003 may have set the pattern for the spending of the surplus that appeared annually from 1997. The government indicated it planned to run a balanced budget for the next several years beginning with 2003, and that spending in a number of areas, particularly social services, would rise substantially. The biggest increase in spending was apportioned to health care, with a commitment of over $34 billion in new funds over five years to enhance the delivery of health care services. Increasing waiting times to see doctors, particularly specialists, has undermined confidence in the much admired Canadian health care system. The increased funding will certainly improve the delivery of health care across the country and restore confidence in a system most Canadians are very proud of. The budget of February 2003 also increased spending for the environment, to help pay for the Kyoto Accord, endorsed by Parliament in late 2002.

QUICK REVIEW

- The borrowing and interest payments associated with the public debt may (a) increase income inequality; (b) require higher taxes, which dampen incentives; and (c) impede the growth of the nation's capital stock through crowding-out of private investment.

- Over the past decade, the federal budget has moved from annual deficits to annual surpluses.

- The main options for using the budget surpluses are (a) to pay down the public debt, (b) to cut tax rates or eliminate certain taxes, and/or (c) to increase government expenditures on social programs.

THE LASTword

Lotteries: Facts and Controversies about a Way of Raising Government Revenues

Lotteries, which began in the 1970s, are a potentially important source of public revenue. What are the characteristics of lotteries? And what are the arguments for and against this means of increasing provincial government revenues?

In May of 2002 the Super 7 lottery jackpot prize reached over $34 million, the largest in Canadian history up to that point. Such a large jackpot drew much attention to government sponsored lotteries in Canada, which began in 1973 when the Olympic Corporation of Canada started selling tickets to help defray the costs of the 1976 Olympics in Montreal. It is estimated that over 80 percent of Canadian households now buy lottery tickets, each household spending about $250 per year.

The average government lottery returns about 50 percent of its gross revenues to ticket purchasers as prizes, and 36 percent goes to the provincial treasury. The remaining 14 percent is for designing and promoting the lottery and for commissions to retail outlets that sell tickets. Although provinces sponsoring lotteries currently obtain a small share of their total revenues in this way, per-capita sales of lottery tickets increased substantially in the 1975–2000 period. For example, the Ontario government generates over $500 million per year from lottery ticket sales, more that triple that if one includes the revenues from its gambling casinos.

Lotteries have been controversial. Critics make the following arguments. First, the 36 percent of gross revenues from lotteries that goes to the provincial governments is in effect a 36 percent tax on ticket purchases. This tax is higher than the taxes on cigarettes and liquor. Furthermore, research indicates that the "lottery tax" is highly regressive in that there is little relationship between ticket purchases and household incomes. This means that low-income families spend a larger proportion of their incomes on lotteries than do high-income families. The 10 percent of the adults who patronize lotteries most heavily account for one-half of total ticket sales. Second, critics argue that it is ethically wrong for the government to sponsor gambling. Gambling is generally regarded as immoral and, in other forms, is illegal in most provinces. It is also held that lotteries may whet the appetite for gambling and generate compulsive gamblers who will impoverish themselves and their families. Third, lotteries may be sending the message that luck and fate—rather than education, hard work, and saving and investing—are the route to success and wealth in Canada.

But there are counterarguments. It is contended, in the first place, that lottery revenue should not be regarded as a tax. Income tax collections are compulsory and involve coercion; the purchase of a lottery ticket is voluntary and a free consumer choice. A second and related argument is that within wide limits it is not appropriate to make moral judgments about how people should spend their incomes. Individuals allegedly achieve the maximum satisfaction from their incomes by spending without interference. If some people derive satisfaction from participating in lotteries, they should be free to do so. Third, faced with tax revenue shortfalls and intense pressure not to raise taxes, lotteries are a relatively painless source of revenue to finance important services such as education and health care programs. In Ontario for example, of the $521 million in lottery profits in 1999–2000, slightly over three quarters, or $395 million, went to running the province's hospitals. In Saskatchewan, almost a quarter of the government's lottery profits go to sport, culture, recreation, and community groups.

Two observations seem certain at the moment. One is that total lottery revenue will continue to increase. More provinces are establishing lotteries and people seem to enjoy gambling, particularly when they feel their losses are being used for "good causes." The other point is that this source of revenue will remain controversial.

Source: Adapted from Charles T. Clotfelter and Philip J. Cook, "On the Economics of State Lotteries," *Journal of Economic Perspectives*, Fall, 1990, pp. 105–119. Canadian statistics are from Linda Ward, "Lotteries," CBC News Online, www.cbc.ca.

CHAPTER SUMMARY

10.1 DEFICITS AND DEBTS: DEFINITIONS AND PHILOSOPHIES

- A budget deficit is the excess of government expenditures over its receipts. A budget surplus is an excess of government revenues over its expenditures. The public debt is the total accumulation of the government's deficits (minus surpluses) over time and consists of Treasury bills, Treasury notes, Treasury bonds, and Canada Savings Bonds.

- Among the various budget philosophies are the annually balanced budget, the cyclically balanced budget, and functional finance. The basic problem with an annually balanced budget is that it promotes swings in the business cycle rather than counters them. Similarly, it may be difficult to balance the budget over the course of the business cycle if upward and downward swings are not of roughly comparable magnitude. Functional finance is the view that the primary purpose of federal finance is to stabilize the economy, and that problems associated with consequent deficits or surpluses are of secondary importance.

10.2 THE PUBLIC DEBT: FACTS AND FIGURES

- Historically, the growth of the public debt has resulted from revenue declines during recessions, deficit financing of wars, and lack of political will to reduce government spending.

- In 2002 the Canadian public debt was $641 billion, or $20,232 per person. The public (here including chartered banks and provincial and municipal governments) holds 75 percent of that debt, the Bank of Canada holds 8 percent, and foreigners 17 percent. In the 1980s and early 1990s, the public debt increased sharply as a percentage of GDP. In more recent years, that percentage has substantially declined. Interest payments as a percentage of GDP were about 3.5 percent in 2002.

10.3 FALSE CONCERNS

- The concern that a large public debt may bankrupt the government is a misguided worry because (a) the debt need only be refinanced rather than refunded, and (b)

the federal government has the power to increase taxes if necessary to make interest payments on the debt.

- The crowding-out effect aside, the public debt is not a vehicle for shifting economic burdens to future generations. In general, Canadians inherit not only the public debt (a liability), but also the Canadian securities (an asset) that finance the debt and the infrastructure that the debt bought.

10.4 SUBSTANTIVE ISSUES

- More substantive problems associated with public debt include the following: (a) Payment of interest on the debt may increase income inequality. (b) Interest payments on the debt require higher taxes, which may impair incentives. (c) Paying interest or principal on the portion of the debt held by foreigners means a transfer of real output abroad. (d) Government borrowing to refinance or pay interest on the debt may increase interest rates and crowd out private investment spending, leaving future generations with a smaller stock of capital than they would have had otherwise.

- The increase in investment in public capital that may result from debt financing may partly or wholly offset the crowding-out effect of the public debt on private investment. Also, the added public investment may stimulate private investment, if the two are complements.

10.5 DEFICITS AND SURPLUSES: 1990 TO THE PRESENT

- The large federal budget deficits of the 1980s and early 1990s led the federal government to increase tax rates and limit government spending. As a result of these policies, along with a rapid economic expansion, the deficits dwindled. Budget surpluses occurred from 1998 to 2002.

- The actual and projected budget surpluses set off a policy debate over what to do with them. The main options are (a) paying down the public debt, (b) reducing tax rates or eliminating some taxes altogether, and (c) increasing government spending.

TERMS AND CONCEPTS

public debt, p. 254
annually balanced budget, p. 254

cyclically balanced budget, p. 254
functional finance, p. 255

external public debt, p. 260
public investments, p. 261

STUDY QUESTIONS

1. **KEY QUESTION**   Assess the leeway for using fiscal policy as a stabilization tool under (a) an annually balanced budget, (b) a cyclically balanced budget, and (c) functional finance.

2. What have been the three major sources of the public debt historically?

3. **KEY QUESTION**   What are the two main ways the size of the public debt is measured? Distinguish between refinancing the debt and retiring the debt. How does an internally held public debt differ from an externally held public debt? Contrast the effects of retiring an internally held debt and an externally held debt.

4. True or false? If the statement is false, explain why:

   a. An internally held public debt is like a debt of the left hand to the right hand.

   b. The Canadian public debt was smaller in percentage terms in 2000 than it was in 1946.

   c. The basic cause of the federal debt is a lack of political courage.

5. Why might economists be quite concerned if the annual interest payments on the debt sharply increased as a percentage of GDP?

6. Do you think that paying off the public debt would increase income inequality, or decrease it? Explain.

7. **KEY QUESTION**   Trace the cause-and-effect chain through which financing and refinancing of the public debt might affect real interest rates, private investment, the stock of capital, and economic growth. How might investment in public capital and complementarities between public and private capital alter the outcome of the cause-effect chain?

8. Why did budget deficits rise sharply in 1991 and 1992? What explains the budget surpluses of the late 1990s and early 2000s?

9. **(The Last Word)** What are the pros and cons of raising government revenues through lotteries?

INTERNET APPLICATION QUESTIONS

1. **The Debt** Go to the Statistics Canada home page through the McConnell-Brue-Barbiero Web site (Chapter 10) and find the amount of the gross federal debt in the most recent year. How does it compare to the gross federal debt five years earlier?

2. **Federal Government Deficits and Surpluses** Go to the Statistics Canada home page through the McConnell-Brue-Barbiero Web site (Chapter 10) and answer the following questions. What has the trend been in the federal government's deficit/surplus in the last five years? What is the largest expenditure category?

3. **Web-Based Question: What are the deficit/ surplus projections?** The Department of Finance periodically projects budget surpluses/deficits five years into the future. Go to its Web site through the McConnell-Brue-Barbiero homepage (Chapter 10), select "Budget Info" and then the 2002 budget. The projected deficits/ surpluses are under "Fiscal Situation and Outlook." What is the general direction of the projections? What might upset this generally positive outlook?

3

Part

Money, Banking, and Monetary Policy

Money and Banking

Friedrich A. Hayek, recipient of a Nobel Prize in economics, makes the following observation about money:

> Money, the very "coin" of ordinary interaction, is ... the object of the greatest unreasoning fantasy; and like sex it simultaneously fascinates, puzzles and repels. The literature treating it is probably greater than that devoted to any other single topic; and browsing through it inclines one to sympathise with the writer who long ago declared that no other subject, not even love, has driven more men to madness.[1]

---

[1] Hayek, F.A., *The Fatal Conceit* (Chicago: University of Chicago Press, 1988), pp. 101–102.

In this chapter and the two chapters that follow we explore the nature of money, and we investigate its critical role in the monetary system of the economy. When the monetary system is working properly, it provides the lifeblood of the circular flows of income and expenditure. A well-operating monetary system helps the economy achieve both full employment and the efficient use of resources. A malfunctioning monetary system creates severe fluctuations in the economy's levels of output, employment, and prices and distorts the allocation of resources.

11.1   The Definition and Functions of Money

medium of exchange
Items sellers generally accept and buyers generally use to pay for a good or service.

Money is a medium of exchange that is used to buy and sell goods and services.

unit of account
A standard unit in which prices can be stated and the value of goods and services can be compared.

store of value
An asset set aside for future use.

Just what is money? There is an old saying that "money *is* what money *does*." In a general sense, anything that performs the functions of money *is* money. Here are those functions.

- *Medium of exchange*   First and foremost, money is a **medium of exchange** that is used to buy and sell goods and services. A bakery worker in Montreal does not want to be paid 200 bagels per week. Nor does the bakery owner want to accept, say, halibut in exchange for bagels. Money, however, is readily acceptable as payment. As we saw in Chapter 4, money is a social invention with which resource suppliers and producers can be paid and that can be used to buy any of the full range of items available in the marketplace. As a medium of exchange, money allows society to escape the complications of barter. And, because it provides a convenient way of exchanging goods, money enables society to gain the advantages of geographic and human specialization.

- *Measure of value*   Money is also a measure of value, or more formally, a **unit of account**. A monetary unit—the dollar, in Canada—is a yardstick for measuring the relative worth of a wide variety of goods, services, and resources. Just as we measure distance in kilometres, we measure the value of goods and services in dollars.

  With money as an acceptable unit of account, the price of each item need be stated only in terms of the monetary unit. We need not state the price of cows in terms of corn, crayons, and cigars. Money allows buyers and sellers to easily compare the prices of various goods, services, and resources. It also permits us to define debt obligations, determine taxes owed, and calculate the nation's GDP.

- *Store of value*   Money also serves as a **store of value** that makes it possible to acquire goods and services at a future date. People normally do not spend all their income on the day they receive it. In order to buy things later, they store some of their wealth as money. The money you place in a safe or a chequing account will still be available to you a few weeks or months from now. Money is often the preferred store of value for short periods because it is the most liquid (spendable) of all assets. People can obtain their money nearly instantly and immediately use it to buy goods or take advantage of financial investment opportunities. When inflation is non-existent or mild, holding money is a relatively risk-free way to preserve your wealth for later use.

11.2   The Supply of Money

Societies have used many items as money, including whales' teeth, circular stones, elephant-tail bristles, gold coins, furs, cigarettes, playing cards and pieces of paper. Anything that is widely accepted as a medium of exchange can serve as money. In Canada, certain debts of government and of financial institutions are used as money, as you will see.

M1
Currency (coins and paper money) and demand deposits in chartered banks.

demand deposit
A deposit in a chartered bank against which cheques may be written.

Money Definition *M*1

The narrowest definition of the Canadian money supply is called **M1**. It consists of two items:

- Currency (coins and paper money) outside chartered banks
- All **demand deposits**, meaning chequing account deposits in chartered banks

Coins and paper money are issued by the Bank of Canada, and demand deposits—personal chequing accounts—are a debt of the chartered banks. Table 11-1 shows the amount of each in the M1 money supply.

CURRENCY: COINS + PAPER MONEY

From copper pennies to "toonies," coins are the "small change" of our money supply. Coins, however, constitute a small portion of M1.

token money
Coins having a face value greater than their intrinsic value.

All coins in circulation in Canada are **token money**. This means the *intrinsic value*, the value of the metal contained in the coin itself, is less than the face value of the coin. This is to prevent people from melting down the coins for sale as a "commodity," in this case, the metal. If our 25¢ pieces each contained 50¢ worth of silver bullion, it would be profitable to melt them and sell the metal. Although it is illegal to do so, 25¢ pieces would disappear from circulation. This happened with our *then* silver coins in the late 1960s and early 1970s. An 80-percent silver pre-1967 quarter is now worth several dollars.

Bank of Canada notes
Paper money issued by the Bank of Canada.

Paper money and coins constitute about 30 percent of the economy's narrowly defined (M1) money supply. Paper currency is in the form of **Bank of Canada notes**—the paper notes you carry in your wallet—issued by our government-owned central bank. Every bill has "Bank of Canada" printed at the top of the face of the bill.

Together coins and paper money amounted to $39.0 billion in December 2002, about 30 percent of M1.

DEMAND DEPOSITS

The safety and convenience of cheques and debit cards have made them the largest component of the M1 money supply. You would not think of stuffing $4,896 in bills in an envelope and dropping it in a mailbox to pay a debt. But to write and mail a cheque for a large sum is commonplace. A cheque must be endorsed (signed on the reverse) by the person cashing it. Similarly, because the writing of a cheque requires endorsement, the theft or loss of a cheque is not nearly as bad as los-

TABLE 11-1	Money in Canada[1], December 2002			
Money	Billions of dollars	Percentage of M1	Percentage of M2	Percentage of M2+
Currency held outside banks	$ 39.0	28.4	6.9	4.8
+ Demand deposits at chartered banks held by individuals and businesses	98.3	71.6	17.6	12.2
= M1	137.3	100.0	24.5	
+ Personal savings deposits and non-personal notice deposits at chartered banks	422.5		75.5	52.7
= M2	559.8		100.0	
+ Deposits at trust and mortgage companies, credit unions, *caisses populaires*, and government savings institutions	142.1			17.7
+ Money market mutual funds and life insurance annuities	99.9			12.6
= M2+	$801.8			100.0

[1]Seasonally adjusted average monthly data

Source: Bank of Canada, Weekly Financial Statistics, August 22, 2003. Visit www.mcgrawhill.ca/college/mcconnell for data update.

ing an identical amount of currency. Finally, it is more convenient to write a cheque than to transport and count out a large sum of currency. For all these reasons, chequebook money, or demand deposit, is a large component of the stock of money. About two-thirds of $M1$ is in the form of demand deposits, on which cheques can be drawn.

To summarize,

Money, $M1$ = currency in circulation + demand deposits

INSTITUTIONS THAT OFFER DEMAND DEPOSITS

In Canada, several types of financial institutions allow customers to write cheques on funds they have deposited. *Chartered banks* are the primary depository institutions. They accept the deposits of households and businesses, keep the money safe until it is demanded via cheques, and in the meantime use it to make available a wide variety of loans. Chartered bank loans provide short-term working capital to businesses, and finance consumer purchases of automobiles and other durable goods. There are six major chartered banks in Canada: the Royal Bank, the Canadian Imperial Bank of Commerce (CIBC), the Bank of Montreal, TD Canada Trust (TD), the Bank of Nova Scotia (Scotiabank), and the National Bank of Canada.

www.royalbank.com
Royal Bank

Money Definition *M2*

A second and broader definition of money includes $M1$ plus several near-monies. **Near-monies** are highly liquid financial assets that do not directly function as a medium of exchange but can be readily converted into currency or demand deposits. For example, you may withdraw currency from a *nonchequable savings account* at a chartered bank or trust and mortgage loan company, credit union, or *caisse populaire*. Or you may request that funds be transferred from a nonchequable savings account to a chequable account.

You cannot withdraw funds quickly from *term deposits*, which become available to a depositor only at maturity. The difference between a savings account and a term account is that there is a penalty if you withdraw money from your term account. For example, a 90-day or six-month term deposit is available when the designated period expires. Although term deposits are less liquid (spendable) than nonchequable savings accounts, they can be taken as currency or shifted into chequable accounts when they mature.

If these "near-monies" are added to $M1$, we arrive at a broader definition of money. This is also set out in Table 11-1. Adding personal savings deposits and non-personal (business) notice deposits (requiring notice before withdrawal) to $M1$ gives us **M2**. At the end of 2002, $M2$ in Canada was about $560 billion.

near-monies
Financial assets, such as saving and term deposits in banks and savings institutions, that are not a medium of exchange but can be readily converted into money.

Money Definition *M2+*

An even broader monetary aggregate is **M2+**, which is $M2$ plus deposits at trust and mortgage loan companies, and deposits at *caisses populaires* and credit unions, and other non-bank deposit-taking institutions, plus money market mutual funds. $M2+$ totalled about $808 billion in December 2002.

Note the following about non-chartered banks and other financial institutions. Trust companies, *caisses populaires*, and credit unions gather the savings of households and businesses that are then used to finance housing mortgages and provide other loans. *Credit unions* accept deposits from, and lend to, "members"—usually a group of individuals who work for the same company or live in the same area. Caisses populaires can be found in Manitoba, Ontario, Quebec, and New Brunswick. The largest in Canada are those associated with the Caisses Desjardin. Trust companies are rapidly dwindling in number in Canada, and particularly so when TD Bank merged with Canada Trust, to transform itself into TD Canada Trust. There are now some 646 credit unions of various sizes operating under the auspices of Credit Union Central of Canada.

Which definition of money shall we use? The simple $M1$ includes only items *directly* and *immediately* usable as a medium of exchange. For this reason it is an oft-cited statistic in discussions of

M2
A broad definition of money that includes M1 plus personal and business savings deposits requiring notice before withdrawal.

M2+
A very broad definition of money that includes M2, plus deposits at non-bank deposit-taking institutions, money market mutual funds, and individual annuities at life insurance companies.

Consider This

Are Credit Cards Money?

You may wonder if credit cards such as Visa and MasterCard are considered part of the money supply. After all, credit cards are a convenient way to make purchases. The answer is that a credit card is not really money but, rather, a means of obtaining a short-term loan from the chartered bank or other financial institution that issued the card.

What happens when you purchase an MP3 player with a credit card? The bank that issued the card will reimburse the store and later you will reimburse the bank. Credit cards are merely a means of deferring or postponing payment for a short period. You may have to pay an annual fee for the services provided and, if you repay the bank in instalments, you will pay a sizable interest charge on the loan that can amount to more than 20 percent per year.

However, credit cards and other forms of credit allow individuals and businesses to "economize" in the use of money. Credit cards enable you to hold less currency and fewer demand deposits for transactions. They help you coordinate your expenditures and your receipt of income, thereby reducing the cash and demand deposits you must keep available.

Credit cards have become a very popular way of paying for the goods and services we purchase. The table below provides some facts about credit card circulation and use in Canada. At the end of 2001 there were 44.1 million Visa and MasterCard credit cards in circulation, more than one for each man, woman and child in the country! The 44.1 mil-

lion figure for Visa and MasterCard does not include the many other credit cards, including ones for department stores, issued by various large firms. Visa and MasterCard are accepted at 663,000 outlets in Canada, and over 20 million locations around the world. Credit cards make it easy to spend money, as the growing outstanding balances show!

GENERAL STATISTICS

Visa & MasterCard	October 31, 2001	October 31, 2002
Number of cards in circulation (million)	44.1	49.4
Outstanding balances ($ billion)	$38.90	$43.99
Delinquency Ratios (90 days and over)	0.8%	0.7%
Retail Sales Volume ($ billion)	$121.82	$135.69
Sales Slips Processed (million)	1,226.6	1,390.50
Average Sale ($)	$99.16	$100.51
Sales and Cash Advance Volume ($ billion)	$138.63	$154.57

Source: Canadian Bankers Association

Question: Are credit cards money?

the money supply. However, for some purposes economists prefer the broader *M2* or *M2+* definition. The Bank of Canada now has an even broader measure of the money supply, *M2++*, which includes all types of mutual funds and Canadian savings bonds.

We will use the narrow *M1* definition of money in our discussion and analysis, unless stated otherwise. The important principles that apply to *M1* are also applicable to *M2* and *M2+* because *M1* is a base component in these broader measures. (*Key Question 3*)

QUICK REVIEW

- Money serves as a medium of exchange, a unit of account, and a store of value.

- The narrow *M1* definition of money includes currency held by the public and demand (chequable) deposits in chartered banks.

- The *M2* definition of money includes *M1* plus personal savings deposits and non-

personal notice deposits at chartered banks.

- *M2+* is made up of *M2* plus deposits at trust and mortgage loan companies, *caisses populaires*, and credit unions, plus money market mutual funds and deposits at other institutions.

11.3   What "Backs" the Money Supply?

The money supply in Canada essentially is "backed" (guaranteed) by government's ability to keep the value of money relatively stable. Nothing more!

Money as Debt

The major components of the money supply—paper money and demand deposits—are debts, or promises to pay. In Canada, paper money is the circulating debt of the Bank of Canada. Demand deposits are the debts of chartered banks.

Paper currency and demand deposits have no intrinsic value. A $5 bill is just an inscribed piece of paper. A demand deposit is merely a bookkeeping entry. And coins, we know, have less intrinsic value than their face value. Nor will government redeem the paper money you hold for anything tangible, such as gold. In effect, the government, through the Bank of Canada, has chosen to "manage" the nation's money supply. Its monetary authorities attempt to provide the amount of money needed for that particular volume of business activity that will promote full employment, price-level stability, and economic growth.

Once upon a time most paper currencies were convertible into gold or other precious metals. But managing the money supply is certainly more sensible than linking it to gold or to some other commodity whose supply might change arbitrarily and suddenly. A large increase in the nation's gold stock as the result of a new gold discovery might increase the money supply too rapidly and thereby trigger rapid inflation. Or a long-lasting decline in gold production might reduce the money supply to the point where recession and unemployment resulted.

In short, people cannot convert paper money into a fixed amount of gold or any other precious commodity. Money is exchangeable only for paper money. If you ask the Bank of Canada to redeem $5 of your paper money, it will swap one paper $5 bill for another bearing a different serial number. That is all you can get. Similarly, cheque money cannot be redeemed for gold but only for paper money, which, as we have just seen, the government will not redeem for anything tangible.

Value of Money

So why are currency and demand deposits money, whereas, say, Monopoly (the game) money is not? What gives a $20 bill or a $100 chequing account entry its value? The answer to these questions has three parts.

ACCEPTABILITY

Currency and demand deposits are money because people accept them as money. By virtue of long-standing business practice, currency and demand deposits perform the basic function of money: they are acceptable as a medium of exchange. We accept paper money in exchange because we are confident it will be exchangeable for real goods, services, and resources when we spend it.

LEGAL TENDER

Our confidence in the acceptability of paper money is strengthened because government has designated currency as **legal tender**. Specifically, each bill contains the statement "This note is legal tender." That means that paper currency must be accepted in payment of a debt. The paper money in our economy is *fiat money;* it is money because the government has declared it so, not because it can be redeemed for precious metal.

legal tender
Anything that government says must be accepted in payment of a debt.

RELATIVE SCARCITY

The value of money, like the economic value of anything else, depends on its supply and demand. Money derives its value from its scarcity relative to its utility (its want-satisfying power). The utility of money lies in its capacity to be exchanged for goods and services, now or in the future.

Money and Prices

The purchasing power of money is the amount of goods and services a unit of money will buy. When money rapidly loses its purchasing power, it loses its role as money.

THE PURCHASING POWER OF THE DOLLAR

The amount a dollar will buy varies inversely with the price level; that is, a reciprocal relationship exists between the general price level and the purchasing power of the dollar. When the consumer price index or "cost-of-living" index goes up, the purchasing power of the dollar goes down, and vice versa. Higher prices lower the purchasing power of the dollar, because more dollars are needed to buy a particular amount of goods, services, or resources. For example, if the price level doubles, the purchasing power of the dollar declines by one-half, or 50 percent.

Conversely, lower prices increase the purchasing power of the dollar, because fewer dollars are needed to obtain a specific quantity of goods and services. If the price level falls by, say, one-half, or 50 percent, the purchasing power of the dollar doubles.

In equation form, the relationship looks like this:

$$D = 1/P$$

To find the value of the dollar D, divide 1 by the price level P expressed as an index number (in hundredths). If the price level is 1.0, then the value of the dollar is 1. If the price level rises to, say, 1.20, D falls to .833; a 20 percent increase in the price level reduces the value of the dollar by 16.67 percent. Check your understanding of this reciprocal relationship by determining the value of D and its percentage rise when P falls by 20 percent to .80. *(Key Question 5)*

INFLATION AND ACCEPTABILITY

In Chapter 6 we noted situations in which a nation's currency became worthless and unacceptable in exchange. These were circumstances in which the government issued so many pieces of paper currency that the value of each of these units of money was almost totally undermined. The infamous post-World War I inflation in Germany is an example. In December 1919 there were about 50 billion marks in circulation. Four years later there were 496,585,345,900 billion marks in circulation! The result? The German mark in 1923 was worth a very small fraction of its 1919 value.

Runaway inflation will significantly depreciate the value of money between the time it is received and the time it is spent. Rapid declines in the value of a currency may cause it to cease being used as a medium of exchange. Businesses and households may refuse to accept paper money in exchange because they do not want to bear the loss in its value that will occur while it is in their possession. Without an acceptable domestic medium of exchange, individuals in an economy may try to substitute a more stable currency from another nation. Example: Many transactions in Russia now take place in U.S. dollars rather than in less-stable rubles. At the extreme, the economy may simply revert to barter.

Similarly, people will use money as a store of value only as long as there is no sizable deterioration in the value of that money because of inflation. And an economy can effectively employ money as a unit of account only when its purchasing power is relatively stable. When the value of the dollar is declining rapidly, sellers will not know what to charge, and buyers will not know what to pay, for goods and services.

QUICK REVIEW

- In Canada, all money consists essentially of the debts of government and chartered banks.

- These debts efficiently perform the functions of money so long as their value, or purchasing power, is relatively stable.

- The value of money is rooted not in specified quantities of precious metals but in the amount of goods, services, and resources that money will purchase.

11.4   The Demand for Money

Why does the public want to hold some of its wealth as *money*? There are two main reasons: to make purchases with it, and to hold it as an asset.

Transactions Demand, D_t

transactions demand for money
The amount of money people want to hold for use as a medium of exchange, and which varies directly with the nominal GDP.

People hold money because, as a medium of exchange, it is convenient for purchasing goods and services. Households must have enough money on hand to buy groceries and pay mortgage and utility bills. Businesses need money to pay for labour, materials, power, and other inputs. The demand for money for such uses is called the **transactions demand** for money.

The main determinant of the amount of money demanded for transactions is the level of nominal GDP. The larger the total money value of all goods and services exchanged in the economy, the larger the amount of money needed to negotiate those transactions. The transactions demand for money varies directly with nominal GDP. We specify nominal GDP because households and firms will want more money for transactions if prices rise or if real output increases. In both instances there will be a need for a larger dollar volume to accomplish the desired transactions.

In **Figure 11-1 (Key Graph)** we graph the quantity of money demand for transactions against the interest rate. For simplicity, we will assume that the amount demanded depends exclusively on the level of nominal GDP and is independent of the real interest rate. (In reality, higher interest rates are associated with slightly lower volumes of money demand for transactions.) Our simplifying assumption allows us to graph the transactions demand, D_t, as a vertical line. The transactions demand curve is positioned at $100 billion, on the assumption that each dollar held for transactions purposes is spent on an average of three times per year and that nominal GDP is $300 billion. Thus the public needs $100 billion (= $300 billion ÷ 3) to purchase that GDP.

Asset Demand, D_a

asset demand for money
The amount of money people want to hold as a store of value; this amount varies inversely with the rate of interest.

The second reason for holding money derives from money's function as a store of value. People may hold their financial assets in many forms, including corporate stocks, private or government bonds, or as money. Thus, there is an **asset demand** for money.

What determines the asset demand for money? First, we must recognize that each of the various ways of holding financial assets has advantages and disadvantages. To simplify, let's compare holding money as an asset with holding bonds. The advantages of holding money are its liquidity and lack of risk. Money is the most liquid of all assets; it is immediately usable in making purchases. Money is an attractive asset to be holding when the prices of goods, services, and other financial assets are expected to decline. But when the price of a bond falls, the bondholder who sells the bond before it matures will suffer a loss. There is no such risk in holding money.

The disadvantage of holding money as an asset is that, compared with holding bonds, it does not earn interest. Or, if it is in an interest-bearing chequing account, it does not earn as much interest as bonds or nonchequable deposits. Cash, of course, earns no interest at all.

Knowing this, the problem is deciding how much of your financial assets to hold as, say, bonds and how much as money. The answer depends primarily on the rate of interest. A household or a business incurs an opportunity cost when it holds money; in both cases, interest income is forgone or sacrificed. If a bond pays 6 percent interest, for example, it costs $6 per year of forgone income to hold $100 as cash or in a non-interest chequable account.

It is no surprise, then, that the asset demand for money varies inversely with the rate of interest. When the interest rate or opportunity cost of holding money as an asset is low, the public will choose to hold a large amount of money as assets because bond prices will be high. When the interest rate is high, it is costly to "be liquid" and the amount of assets held as money will be small. When it is expensive to hold money as an asset, people hold less of it; when money can be held cheaply, people hold more of it. This inverse relationship between the interest rate and the amount of money people want to hold as an asset is shown by D_a in Figure 11-1.

Key Graph

FIGURE 11-1 The Demand for Money and the Money Market

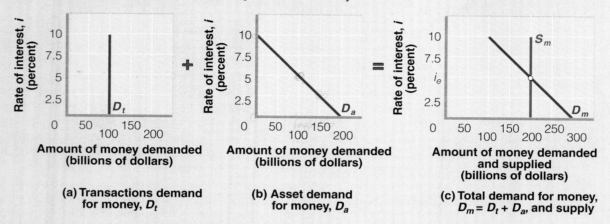

(a) Transactions demand for money, D_t

(b) Asset demand for money, D_a

(c) Total demand for money, $D_m = D_t + D_a$, and supply

The total demand for money D_m is determined by horizontally adding the asset demand for money D_a to the transactions demand D_t. The transactions demand is vertical because it is assumed to depend on nominal GDP rather than on the interest rate. The asset demand varies inversely with the interest rate because of the opportunity cost involved in holding currency and chequable deposits that pay no interest or very low interest. Combining the money supply (stock) S_m with total money demand D_m portrays the money market and determines the equilibrium interest rate i_e.

Quick Quiz

1. In this graph, at the interest rate i_e:
   a. the amount of money demanded as an asset is $50 billion.
   b. the amount of money demanded for transactions is $200 billion.
   c. bond prices will decline.
   d. $100 billion is demanded for transactions, $100 billion is demanded as an asset, and the money supply is $200 billion.

2. In this graph, at an interest rate of 10 percent:
   a. no money will be demanded as an asset.
   b. total money demanded will be $200 billion.
   c. the Bank of Canada will supply $100 billion of money.
   d. there will be a $100 billion shortage of money.

3. Curve D_a slopes downward because:
   a. lower interest rates increase the opportunity cost of holding money.
   b. lower interest rates reduce the opportunity cost of holding money.
   c. the asset demand for money varies directly (positively) with the interest rate.
   d. the transactions-demand-for-money curve is perfectly vertical.

4. Suppose the supply of money declines to $100 billion. The equilibrium interest rate would:
   a. fall, the amount of money demanded for transactions would rise, and the amount of money demanded as an asset would decline.
   b. rise, and the amounts of money demanded both for transactions and as an asset would fall.
   c. fall, and the amounts of money demanded both for transactions and as an asset would increase.
   d. rise, the amount of money demanded for transactions would be unchanged, and the amount of money demanded as an asset would decline.

ANSWERS: 1. d; 2. a; 3. b; 4. d

Total Money Demand, D_m

total demand for money
The sum of the transactions demand for money and the asset demand for money.

As shown in Figure 11-1, we find the **total demand for money**, D_m, by horizontally adding the asset demand to the transactions demand. The resulting downward-sloping line in Figure 11-1c represents the total amount of money the public wants to hold, both for transactions and as an asset, at each possible interest rate.

Recall that the transactions demand for money depends on the nominal GDP. A change in the nominal GDP—working through the transactions demand for money—will shift the total money demand curve. Specifically, an increase in nominal GDP means that the public wants to hold a larger amount of money for transactions, and that extra demand will shift the total money demand curve to the right. In contrast, a decline in the nominal GDP will shift the total money demand curve to the left. As an example, suppose nominal GDP increases from $300 to $450 billion and the average dollar held for transactions is still spent three times per year. Then the transactions demand curve will shift from $100 billion (= $300 billion ÷ 3) to $150 billion (= $450 billion ÷ 3). The total money demand curve will then lie $50 billion farther to the right at each possible interest rate.

11.5 Equilibrium in the Money Market

money market
The market in which the demand for and the supply of money determine the interest rate in the economy.

We can combine the demand for money with the supply of money to portray the **money market** and determine the equilibrium rate of interest. In Figure 11-2c the vertical line, S_m, represents the money supply. It is a vertical line because the monetary authorities and financial institutions have provided the economy with some particular stock of money, such as the M1 total shown in Table 11-1.

Just as in a product market or a resource market, the intersection of demand and supply determines equilibrium price. Here, the equilibrium "price" is the interest rate (i_e), which is the price paid for the use of money.

Adjustment to a Decline in the Money Supply

A decline in the supply of money will create a temporary shortage of money and increase the equilibrium interest rate. Consider Figure 11-2, which repeats Figure 11-1c and adds two alternative supply-of-money curves.

Suppose the monetary authorities reduce the supply of money from $200 billion, S_m, to $150 billion, S_{m1}. At the initial rate of 5 percent, the quantity of money demanded now exceeds the quantity supplied by $50 billion. People will attempt to make up for this shortage of money by selling some of the financial assets they own (we assume for simplicity that these assets are bonds). But one person's receipt of money through the sale of a bond is another person's loss of money through the purchase of that bond. *Overall, there is only $150 billion of money available.* The collective attempt to get more money by selling bonds will increase the supply of bonds relative to the demand for bonds in the bond market, but it will not increase the amount of money available as a whole. The outcome is that the price of bonds will fall and the interest rate will rise, here to 7.5 percent.

Generalization (a): *Lower bond prices are associated with higher interest rates.* To clarify, suppose a bond with no expiration date pays a fixed $50 annual interest and is selling for its face value of $1000. The interest yield on this bond is 5 percent:

$50/$1000 = 5%

Now suppose the price of this bond falls to $667 because of the increased supply of bonds. The $50 fixed annual interest payment will now yield 7.5 percent to whoever buys the bond:

$50/$667 = 7.5%

FIGURE 11-2   Changes in the Supply of Money, Bond Prices, and Interest Rates

When a decrease in the supply of money creates a temporary shortage of money in the money market, people and institutions try to gain more money by selling bonds. The supply of bonds therefore increases, which reduces bond prices and raises interest rates. At higher interest rates, people reduce the amount of money they want to hold. Thus, the amount of money supplied and demanded once again is equal at the higher interest rate. An increase in the supply of money creates a temporary surplus of money, resulting in an increase in the demand for bonds and higher bond prices. Interest rates fall and equilibrium is re-established in the money market.

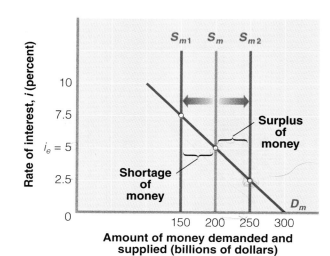

Because all borrowers must compete by offering to pay lenders interest yields similar to those available on bonds, a higher general interest rate emerges. In Figure 11-2 the interest rate rises from 5 percent with the money supply at $200 billion to 7.5 percent when the money supply is $150 billion. This higher interest rate raises the opportunity cost of holding money and consequently reduces the amount of money firms and households want to hold. Here, the amount of money demanded declines from $200 billion at the 5 percent interest rate to $150 billion at the 7.5 percent interest rate. The money market has achieved a new equilibrium, now with $150 billion of money demanded and supplied at the new 7.5 percent interest rate.

Adjustment to an Increase in the Money Supply

An increase in the supply of money from $200 billion, S_m, to $250 billion, S_{m2} in Figure 11-2 results in a surplus of $50 billion at the initial 5 percent interest rate. People will now try to get rid of money by purchasing more bonds. But one person's expenditure of money is another person's receipt of money. The collective attempt to buy more bonds will increase the demand for bonds, push bond prices upward, and lower interest rates.

Generalization (b): *Higher bond prices are associated with lower interest rates.* In our example, the $50 interest payment on a bond now priced at, say, $2000, will yield a bond buyer only 2.5 percent:

$$\$50/\$2000 = 2.5\%$$

The point is that interest rates in general will fall as people unsuccessfully attempt to reduce their money holdings below $250 billion by buying bonds. In this case, the interest rate will fall to a new equilibrium at 2.5 percent. Because the opportunity cost of holding money now is lower—that is, being liquid is less expensive—households and businesses will increase the amount of currency and chequable deposits they are willing to hold from $200 billion to $250 billion. Eventually, a new equilibrium in the money market will be achieved: The quantities of money demanded and supplied will each be $250 billion at an interest rate of 2.5 percent. **(Key Question 6)**

QUICK REVIEW

- People hold money for transaction and asset purposes.

- The total demand for money is the sum of the transactions and asset demands; it is graphed as an inverse relationship (downward-sloping line) between the interest rate and the quantity of money demanded.

- The equilibrium interest rate is determined by money demand and supply; it occurs when people are willing to hold the exact amount of money being supplied by the monetary authorities.

- Bond prices and interest rates are inversely related.

11.6　The Canadian Financial System

The main component of the money supply—demand deposits—is created by and comes into circulation through, the chartered banks. We now take a look at the framework of the Canadian banking system.

The Evolution of the Canadian Banking System

Money and banking are federal responsibilities. Under the Bank Act, each bank is incorporated under a separate Act of Parliament and granted a charter. This is the reason why Canadian commercial banks are called **chartered banks**.

At Confederation in 1867, there were 28 chartered banks; this number grew in the following years to 41, before failures and mergers brought the number to eight in the 1960s. The late 1960s and 1970s brought the formation of new banks, and after six more amalgamations and two failures, there were 16 domestically owned banks by 2003. With the 1980 Bank Act revisions, foreign banks were allowed to establish Canadian subsidiaries. By 2003, there were 33 foreign bank subsidiaries, as well as 20 foreign bank branches in Canada. In total these banks had $1.7 trillion in assets at the end of 2002.

Up to the mid-1950s the primary function of chartered banks in Canada was to accept deposits and grant commercial loans. In the last 25 years the Canadian financial industry has undergone considerable transformation and growth. As chartered banks faced increased competition from other financial institutions, revisions to Canada's Bank Act in 1954 and 1967 enabled chartered banks to offer new services such as mortgages and consumer loans that allowed them to compete. A major revision to the Bank Act in 1992 made it possible for chartered banks to own and operate trust companies and stock brokerage subsidiaries. During the course of the 1990s the main chartered banks purchased and operated stock brokerage services subsidiaries.

The largest of the current Canadian chartered banks control the lion's share of banking activity. About 90 percent of total banking assets and deposits and more than 75 percent of payments volume are accounted for by the big six chartered banks. One of the big chartered banks, TD Canada Trust, was created in 2000 after the Competition Bureau allowed a merger between the Toronto Dominion Bank and Canada Trust. The Canadian banking system is a more concentrated banking system compared to the one in the United States, where there are some 8600 commercial banks and 12,500 thrift institutions. The remaining smaller domestic chartered banks in Canada are Amicus Bank, Bank West, Canadian Western Bank, Citizens Bank of Canada, CS Alterna Bank, First Nations Bank of Canada, Laurentian Bank of Canada, Manulife Bank of Canada, Pacific & Western Bank of Canada, and President's Choice Bank.

In early 1998, the Royal Bank and the Bank of Montreal, and the Canadian Imperial Bank of Commerce and the Toronto-Dominion Bank, announced plans to merge. The federal government vetoed these two mergers on the grounds that they would hinder competition. If the proposed mergers had materialized, only four chartered banks would have been left, leading to an even more

chartered bank
One of the multi-branched, privately owned, commercial, financial intermediaries that have received charter by Act of Parliament and that may call themselves banks.

www.nbc.ca
National Bank of Canada

concentrated banking system. In early 2000 the federal government set out the rules under which Canadian chartered banks can merge. It remains to be seen whether any of the chartered banks will try to merge again under the new rules.

Global Perspective 11.1 lists the world's 10 largest commercial banks, along with all of Canada's largest chartered banks. The Royal Bank of Canada is the largest Canadian bank by assets, and ranks as the 48th largest bank in the world. If bank mergers materialize in the future, Canadian banks will certainly move up the ranks. It should be noted that the rankings change frequently.

Canada's Chartered Banks

Table 11-2 sets out the balance sheet of the Canadian chartered banks. Its cash reserves are only a small percentage of deposits. As will be discussed in the next chapter, our banking system is a *fractional reserve system*—chartered banks loan out most of their deposits, keeping only a small percentage to meet everyday cash withdrawals. If depositors in the chartered banks were to come all at once to withdraw their money, there would not be enough cash reserves to meet their requests. In such an unlikely event, chartered banks borrow from the Bank of Canada, the bankers' bank.

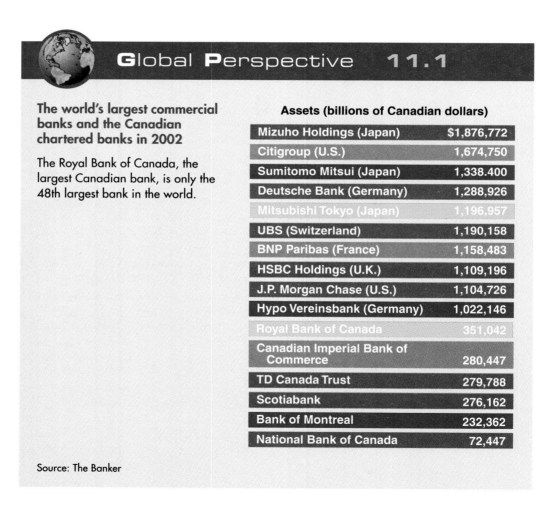

Global Perspective 11.1

The world's largest commercial banks and the Canadian chartered banks in 2002

The Royal Bank of Canada, the largest Canadian bank, is only the 48th largest bank in the world.

Assets (billions of Canadian dollars)	
Mizuho Holdings (Japan)	$1,876,772
Citigroup (U.S.)	1,674,750
Sumitomo Mitsui (Japan)	1,338.400
Deutsche Bank (Germany)	1,288,926
Mitsubishi Tokyo (Japan)	1,196,957
UBS (Switzerland)	1,190,158
BNP Paribas (France)	1,158,483
HSBC Holdings (U.K.)	1,109,196
J.P. Morgan Chase (U.S.)	1,104,726
Hypo Vereinsbank (Germany)	1,022,146
Royal Bank of Canada	351,042
Canadian Imperial Bank of Commerce	280,447
TD Canada Trust	279,788
Scotiabank	276,162
Bank of Montreal	232,362
National Bank of Canada	72,447

Source: The Banker

TABLE 11-2	The Balance Sheet of Canadian Chartered Banks, December 2002 (Billions of Dollars)		
Assets		**Liabilities**	
Reserves (currency and chartered banks' deposits with Bank of Canada)	0.5	Demand deposits	97.2
Loans (determined in Canadian dollars)	688.8	Savings deposits	131.1
Government of Canada securities	76.7	Term deposits	240.9
Foreign-currency assets	40.0	Foreign-currency liabilities	76.9
		Government of Canada deposit	2.0
Other assets	235.1	Other liabilities	493.0
Total	1,041.1	Total	1,041.1

Source: Bank of Canada, *Weekly Financial Statistics*, August 22, 2003.
Visit www.mcgrawhill.ca/college/mcconnell for data update.

Making Loans

Chartered banks are private companies owned by shareholders who seek a competitive return on their investments. Thus, the primary goal of chartered banks is to try to maximize profits. They loan out as much of their deposits as is prudently possible in order to increase profits. Those funds that cannot be safely loaned out are used to buy Government of Canada securities. The rate charged by banks on loans to their best corporate customers is referred to as the **prime rate**. Banks earn a profit on the spread between deposit interest rates and loan interest rates.

prime rate
The interest rate banks charge their most creditworthy borrowers.

Other Financial Intermediaries

Although the present analysis focuses on chartered banks, the banking system is supplemented by other **financial intermediaries**. These include trust companies, loan companies, credit unions, and *caisses populaires* that accept the funds of small savers and make them available to investors by extending mortgage loans or by purchasing marketable securities. Insurance companies accept large volumes of savings in the form of premiums on insurance policies and annuities and use these funds to buy a variety of private, corporate, and government securities.

financial intermediary
A chartered bank or other financial institution that uses the funds deposited with it to make loans.

The Canadian financial system has been undergoing restructuring to permit more competition among the former "Four Pillars:" the banking, insurance, trust, and securities industries.

Chartered banks and savings institutions have two basic functions: they hold the money deposits of businesses and households, and they make loans to the public in an effort to make profits. We will see in Chapter 12 that in doing so the intermediaries increase the economy's supply of money.

Cheque Clearing

A cheque is a written order that the drawer may use in making a purchase or paying a debt. A cheque is collected, or "cleared," when one or more banks or near-banks negotiates a transfer of part of the drawer's chequing account to the chequing account of the recipient of the cheque. If Jones and Smith have chequing accounts in the same bank and Jones gives Smith a $10 cheque, Smith can collect this cheque by taking it to the bank, where his account will be increased by $10 and Jones's reduced by $10. In many cases, however, the drawer and the receiver of a cheque will be located in different towns or provinces and therefore have their accounts in bank branches far from one another. Under federal law a *Canadian Payments Association* (CPA) was set up in 1982 to take over the inter-bank cheque clearing system, which had been run by the Canadian Bankers' Association. All the chartered banks are members of the CPA. The CPA makes provision for the clearing of near-bank cheques also.

11.7   Recent Developments in Money and Banking

The banking industry is undergoing a series of sweeping changes, spurred by competition from other financial institutions, globalization of banking, and advances in information technology.

Expansion of Services

Chartered banks, trust companies, credit unions, and other near-banks have begun offering a variety of new services. For example, chartered banks in Canada have increased their lending for commercial real estate projects such as housing developments, apartments, and office buildings. Banks and trust companies have developed new loan "products" such as home equity loans (loans based on the value of one's house) and low- or zero-down-payment mortgages. They also now offer a variety of interest-bearing accounts such as money market deposit accounts.

Banks have made banking more convenient by opening up full-service branch banks in suburbs and "minibanks" in shopping malls and grocery stores. Supplementing these branches has been an explosion in the number of bank-owned automated banking machines (ABMs) that allow customers to withdraw cash, deposit cheques, move money between accounts, and make other banking transactions. They have also introduced debit cards, "bank-by-telephone" and "bank-by-Internet" services. Table 11-3 sets out the transaction volumes of Canada's chartered banks. Note that the fastest growth area is Internet banking, which rose almost 150 percent between 2000 and 2001. Debit card use and telephone banking are also increasing rapidly.

TABLE 11-3	Number of Bank Transactions (in Millions)		
	2002	**2001**	**% Change 2001–02**
ABM	1,206.6	1,209.0	–0.2%
Deposits	249.2	249.9	–0.3
Withdrawals	848.6	846.2	0.3
Transfers	43.7	45.4	–3.7
Bill Payments	65.1	67.5	–3.4
Debit Cards	1,749.6	1,590.6	10.0%
Point of Sales Purchases	1,749.6	1,590.6	10.0
PC/Internet Banking	147.0	116.1	45.6%
Transfers	43.3	44.1	49.1
Bill Payments	103.7	72.0	44.2
Telephone Banking	92.1	94.6	–2.7%
Transfers	17.3	17.0	2.0
Bill Payments	74.8	77.6	–3.7

Source: Canadian Bankers Association

Globalization of Financial Markets

Another significant banking development is the increased integration of world financial markets. Major foreign financial institutions have operations in Canada, and Canadian financial institutions do business abroad. The six major Canadian chartered banks have a significant presence in areas such as the United States, Latin America, the Caribbean and Asia. The importance of the global market to Canadian banks is indicated by the fact that international operations accounted for approximately 33 per cent of their gross revenues in 2001.

Also, Visa and MasterCard credit cards issued in Canada offer worldwide services. Moreover, Canadian mutual fund companies now offer a variety of international stock and bond funds. Globally, financial capital increasingly flows in search of the highest risk-adjusted returns. As a result, Canadian chartered banks must increasingly compete with foreign banks for both deposits and loan customers.

Recent advances in computer and communications technology mean the trend toward international financial integration will accelerate. Nevertheless, we must not overstate the extent of this globalization. Studies indicate that the bulk of investment in the major economies of the world is still financed through domestic saving within each nation.

Electronic Transactions

Finally, the rapid advance of Internet commerce and "banking" (see Table 11-3) is of great significance to financial institutions and central banks. Consumers have increasingly used the Internet for

electronic transactions
Transactions that are made using an electronic medium.

such **electronic transactions** as buying goods (using credit cards), buying and selling stock and mutual fund shares, transferring bank funds between accounts, and paying bills.

Some experts believe the next step will be the widespread use of electronic money, which is simply an entry in an electronic file stored in a computer. Electronic money will be deposited, or "loaded," into an account through Internet payments such as a paycheque, retirement benefit, or stock dividend. The owner of the account will withdraw, or "unload," the money from his or her account through Internet payments to others for a wide variety of goods and services.

In the future, account holders may be able to insert so-called stored-value cards into slots in their computers and load electronic money onto the card. These plastic "smart cards" contain computer chips that store information, including the amount of electronic money the consumer has loaded. When purchases or payments are made, those amounts are automatically deducted from the balance in the card's memory. Consumers will be able to transfer traditional money to their smart cards through computers or cell phones or at automated teller machines. Thus, it will be possible for nearly all payments to be made through the Internet or a smart card.

Conceivably, any firm—a telephone company, a group of local merchants, or a hotel chain, for instance—could issue accounts and smart cards. Even computer-related firms such as software producers or Internet service providers might get into this form of "banking" by developing the software programs and Internet links. More likely, however, banks themselves will take the lead in establishing such systems of their own, since they know the banking business better than anyone else.

A few general-use smart cards that contain imbedded programmable computer chips are available in Canada, including ones issued by Visa, MasterCard, and American Express ("Blue Cards"). More common are stored value cards that facilitate specific purchases. Examples are prepaid phone cards, copy-machine cards, mass-transit cards, and single-store gift cards. Like the broader smart cards, these cards are "reloadable," meaning the amounts stored on them can be increased. A number of retailers have recently made stored-value cards available to their customers on a limited basis.

Although smart-card use in Canada has increased, it remains far below that in Europe. Credit cards are more widely issued and more heavily used in Canada. They are as convenient as stored-value cards and provide interest-free loans between the time of purchase and the due date on the credit card statement. Because smart cards involve "instant payments," they do not offer this *interest-free float*. It is simply too early to predict whether stored-value cards will catch on in Canada and challenge credit cards, debit cards, currency, and cheques as means of payment. In 2002 stored-value cards accounted for less than 2 percent of the dollar amount of purchases by Canadian consumers.

THE LASTword   The Production of Canadian Currency[2]

The Bank of Canada is the country's sole note-issuing authority and is responsible for designing, producing, and distributing Canada's bank notes.

The Bank of Canada must be prepared to supply financial institutions with enough bank notes to satisfy public demand. Financial institutions get bank notes through the country's Bank Note Distribution System and return bank notes that are considered unfit for further circulation to the Bank of Canada. These bank notes are verified on high-speed note processing equipment and then shredded. The resulting shred is then disposed of in landfill sites.

It can take a number of years to design a series of bank notes and once the design has been approved, the Bank contracts the printing of the bank notes to two security printing companies, Canadian Bank Note

Company, Limited and BA Banknote. The bank notes are printed 40 to a sheet, cut and delivered to the Bank.

Once a bank note design has been finalized, the process moves to production. Production standards and specifications established by the Bank of Canada ensure that available printing technology is fully exploited to produce bank notes of high and consistent quality.

First, a set of initial plates is made and tested for quality on small, hand-operated presses. When the Bank of Canada is satisfied with the print quality of a single note, large lithographic and intaglio plates are made to produce sheets of notes. The lithographic plates provide the smooth multi-

coloured portion of the design, while the intaglio plates provide the relief. Each plate carries a part of the total design of the bank note, with a total of eight plates required for a typical note.

Counterfeiting remains at relatively low levels in Canada—only a small fraction of one per cent of the total value of notes in circulation. It has, however, increased recently and the Bank of Canada has undertaken initiatives to strengthen the security and integrity of Canadian bank notes.

[2]Bank of Canada, http://www.bankofcanada.ca/en/banknotes/general/index.html.

CHAPTER SUMMARY

11.1 THE DEFINITION AND FUNCTIONS OF MONEY

- Anything that is accepted as (a) a medium of exchange, (b) a unit of monetary account, and (c) a store of value can be used as money.

11.2 THE SUPPLY OF MONEY

- Money is generally defined as demand deposits plus currency (coins and paper money) in circulation (M1). Demand deposits, the largest component of the money supply, are money because they can be spent by writing cheques against them. Savings, term, and notice deposits—some chequable and some not—are also money and are added to more broadly defined monetary aggregates (M2 and M2+). In our analysis we concentrate on M1 since its components are immediately spendable.

11.3 WHAT "BACKS" THE MONEY SUPPLY?

- Money is the debts of government and depository institutions (chartered banks, trust companies, and credit

unions) and has value because of goods, services, and resources it will command in the market. Maintaining the purchasing power of money depends largely on the government's effectiveness in managing the money supply.

11.4 THE DEMAND FOR MONEY

- The total demand for money is made up of the transactions and asset demands for money. The transactions demand varies directly with nominal GDP; the asset demand varies inversely with the interest rate. The money market combines the demand for money with the money supply to determine the equilibrium interest rate.

11.5 EQUILIBRIUM IN THE MONEY MARKET

- Other things equal, decreases in the supply of money raise interest rates, whereas increases in the supply of money decrease them. Interest rates and bond prices move in the opposite direction. At the equilibrium interest rate, bond prices tend to be stable and the amounts of money demanded and supplied are equal.

11.6 THE CANADIAN FINANCIAL SYSTEM

- The Canadian banking system is composed of (a) the Bank of Canada and (b) 16 Canadian-owned and 33 foreign-owned chartered banks. The chartered banks of the economy accept money deposits and make loans. The Canadian banking system is concentrated compared to other nations, particularly the United States.

11.7 RECENT DEVELOPMENTS IN MONEY AND BANKING

- Three recent developments in the Canadian banking system are the proposed bank mergers, the internationalization of banking, and the emergence of the Internet and electronic money, including smart cards.

TERMS AND CONCEPTS

medium of exchange, p. 271
unit of account, p. 271
store of value, p. 271
M1, p. 271
demand deposit, p. 271
token money, p. 272
Bank of Canada notes, p. 272

near-monies, p. 273
M2, p. 273
M2+, p. 273
legal tender, p. 275
transactions demand for money, p. 277
asset demand for money, p. 277

total demand for money, p. 279
money market, p. 279
chartered bank, p. 281
prime rate, p. 283
financial intermediary, p. 283
electronic transactions, p. 285

STUDY QUESTIONS

1. What are the three functions of money? Describe how rapid inflation can undermine money's ability to perform each of its three functions.

2. Explain and evaluate the following statements:

   a. The invention of money is one of the great achievements of humankind, for without it the enrichment that comes from broadening trade would have been impossible.

   b. Money is whatever society says it is.

   c. In most economies of the world, the debts of government and chartered banks are used as money.

   d. People often say they would like to have more money, but what they usually mean is that they would like to have more goods and services.

   e. When the prices of everything go up, it is not because everything is worth more but because the currency is worth less.

   f. Any central bank can create money; the trick is to create enough of it, but not too much of it.

3. **KEY QUESTION** What are the components of the M1 money supply? What is the largest component? Which of the components of M1 is *legal tender*? Why is the face value of a coin greater than its intrinsic value? Distinguish between M2 and M2+. What are near-monies?

4. What "backs" the money supply in Canada? What determines the value (domestic purchasing power) of money? How does the value of money relate to the price level? Who is responsible for maintaining the value of money?

5. **KEY QUESTION** Suppose the price level and the value of the dollar in year 1 are 1.0 and $1.00, respectively. If the price level rises to 1.25 in year 2, what is the new value of the dollar? If instead the price level had fallen to .50, what would have been the value of the dollar? What generalization can you draw from your answers?

6. **KEY QUESTION** What is the basic determinant of (a) the transactions demand and (b) the asset demand for money? Explain how these two demands might be combined graphically to determine total money demand. How is the equilibrium interest rate determined in the money market? How might (a) the expanded use of credit cards; (b) a shortening of worker pay periods; and (c) an increase in nominal GDP affect the transactions demand for money and the equilibrium interest rate?

7. Assume that the following data characterize a hypothetical economy: money supply = $200 billion; quantity of money demanded for transactions = $150 billion; quantity of money demanded as an asset = $10 billion at 12 percent interest, increasing by $10 billion for each 2-percentage-point fall in the interest rate.

   a. What is the equilibrium interest rate? Explain.

   b. At the equilibrium interest rate, what are the quantity of money supplied, the total quantity of money demanded, the amount of money demanded for transactions, and the amount of money demanded as an asset?

8. Suppose that a bond has a face value of $10,000 and annually pays a fixed amount of interest of $800. Com-

pute and enter in the space provided either the interest rate that a bond buyer could secure at each of the bond prices listed or the bond price at each of the interest rates shown. State the generalization that can be drawn from the completed table.

Bond price	Interest rate(s)
$ 8,000	_____
_____	8.9
$10,000	_____
$11,000	_____
_____	6.2

9. Assume the money market is initially in equilibrium and that the money supply is now increased. Explain the adjustments towards a new equilibrium interest rate. What effects would you expect this interest rate change to have on the levels of output, employment, and prices? Answer the same questions for a decrease in the money supply.

10. What are the two basic functions of our chartered banks? How do chartered banks differ from other financial intermediaries?

11. In what way are electronic money and smart cards potentially related? Do you think electronic money and smart cards will dominate transactions some time within the next 20 years? Why or why not?

12. **(The Last Word)** Why do you think the counterfeiting of paper money has increased?

INTERNET APPLICATION QUESTIONS

1. **Monetary Aggregates** Visit the Bank of Canada through the McConnell-Brue-Barbiero Web site (Chapter 11) and click on "Rates and Statistics," then click on "Weekly Financial Statistics." Find the seasonally adjusted data for M1, M2, and M2+ for the most recent month.

2. **Everything You Wanted to Know about Canadian Currency but Were Afraid to Ask** Visit the Bank of Canada through the McConnell-Brue-Barbiero Web site (Chapter 11) and click "Currency" then click "Currency Museum." Search for Canada's First Coinage and Canada's First Notes. What denomination were they?

12

Chapter

How Banks Create Money

We have seen that the $M1$ money supply consists of currency in the hands of the public (Bank of Canada notes and coins) and demand deposits. The Bank of Canada has the responsibility for printing Bank of Canada notes and minting coins. So who creates the demand deposits that make up more than half the nation's $M1$ money supply? Surprisingly, it is loan officers! Although that may sound like something a Parliamentary committee should investigate, the monetary authorities are well aware that banks create demand deposits. In fact, the Bank of Canada relies on these institutions to create this vital component of the nation's money supply.

This chapter explains how chartered banks can create *demand deposits*—chequing accounts—by issuing loans.

12.1   Chartered Banks and the Creation of Money

Have you ever considered how money is created? You may believe that it is simply printed by the Bank of Canada. Although this is true, the creation of money is slightly more complex, and it is actually done with the help of Canada's chartered banks. Let's take a closer look at them.

The Balance Sheet of a Chartered Bank

We will analyze the workings of the Canadian monetary system through certain items on a bank's balance sheet and the way that various transactions alter those items.

balance sheet
A statement of the assets, liabilities, and net worth of a firm or individual at a certain time.

The **balance sheet** of a chartered bank is a statement of assets and claims on assets that summarizes the financial position of the bank at a certain time. Every balance sheet must balance—that is, the value of *assets* must equal the amount of claims against those assets. The claims shown on a balance sheet are divided into two groups: the claims of non-owners against the firm's assets, called *liabilities*, and the claims of the owners of the firm against the firm's assets, called *net worth*. A balance sheet is balanced because

$$\text{Assets} = \text{liabilities} + \text{net worth}$$

Prologue: The Goldsmiths

fractional reserve
A reserve ratio that is less than 100 percent of the deposit liabilities of a chartered bank.

Canada, like most other countries today, has a **fractional reserve banking system** *in which only a fraction of the total money supply of deposit is held in reserve as currency.* Here is the history behind the idea.

When early traders began to use gold in making transactions, they soon realized that it was both unsafe and inconvenient to carry gold and to have it weighed and assayed (judged for purity) every time they negotiated a transaction. So, by the sixteenth century they had begun to deposit their gold with goldsmiths who would store it in vaults for a fee. On receiving a gold deposit, the goldsmith issued a receipt to the depositor. Soon people were paying for goods with goldsmiths' receipts, which served as the first kind of paper money.

But because of the public's acceptance of the goldsmiths' receipt as paper money, the goldsmiths soon realized that owners rarely redeemed the gold they had in storage.

At this point the goldsmiths—embryonic bankers—used a 100 percent reserve system; they backed their circulating paper money receipts fully with the gold that they held "in reserve" in their vaults. But because of the public's acceptance of the goldsmiths' receipts as paper money, the goldsmiths soon realized that owners rarely redeemed the gold they had in storage. In fact, the goldsmiths observed that the amount of gold being deposited with them in any week or month was likely to exceed the amount that was being withdrawn.

Then some clever goldsmith hit on the idea that paper "receipts" could be issued in excess of the amount of gold held. Goldsmiths would put these "receipts," which were redeemable in gold, into circulation by making interest-earning loans to merchants, producers, and consumers. Borrowers were willing to accept loans in the form of gold receipts because the receipts were accepted as a medium of exchange in the marketplace.

This was the beginning of the fractional reserve system of banking, in which reserves in bank vaults are a fraction of the total money supply. If, for example, the goldsmith issued $1 million in receipts for actual gold in storage and another $1 million receipts as loans, then the total value of paper money in circulation would be $2 million—twice the value of the gold. Gold reserves would be a fraction (in this case, one-half) of outstanding paper money.

Fractional reserve banking has two significant characteristics:

- *Money creation and reserves*   Banks can create money through lending. In fact, goldsmiths created money when they made loans by giving borrowers paper money that was not fully backed by gold reserves. The quantity of such money goldsmiths could create depended on the amount of reserves they deemed prudent to have available. The smaller the amount of reserves thought necessary, the larger the amount of paper money the goldsmiths could create. Today, gold is no longer used as bank reserves. Instead, the creation of demand deposit money by banks (via their lending) is limited by the amount of *currency reserves* that the banks believe they should keep.

• ***Bank panics and regulation*** Banks that operate on the basis of fractional reserves are vulnerable to "panics" or "runs." A goldsmith who issued paper money equal to twice the value of his gold reserves would be unable to convert all that paper money into gold if all the holders of that money appeared at his door at the same time demanding their gold. In fact, many European, U.S., and a few Canadian banks were once ruined by this unfortunate circumstance. However, a bank panic is highly unlikely if the banker's reserve and lending policies are prudent. Indeed, one reason why banking systems are highly regulated industries is to prevent runs on banks. This is also the reason why Canada has a system of deposit insurance.

A Single Chartered Bank

How can a chartered bank create money? If it can create money, can it destroy money too? What factors govern how a bank creates money?

Formation of a Chartered Bank

To answer these questions we must understand the items a bank carries on its balance sheet and how certain transactions affect the balance sheet. We begin with the organization of a local chartered bank.

TRANSACTION 1: CREATING A BANK

Suppose some citizens of Vancouver decide Canada in general, and their province in particular, needs a new chartered bank to provide the banking services for their growing city. Once they get the Parliament of Canada to pass an act granting a charter for their bank, they then sell, say, $250,000 worth of capital stock (equity shares) to buyers, both in and out of the province. The Bank of Vancouver now exists. What does the bank's balance statement look like at this stage?

The new owners of the bank have sold $250,000 worth of shares of stock in the bank—some to themselves and some to other people. As a result, the bank now has $250,000 in cash on hand and $250,000 worth of capital stock outstanding. The cash is an asset to the bank. Cash held by a bank is sometimes called **vault cash** or "till money." The bank's balance sheet reads:

vault cash
The currency a bank has in its vault and cash drawers.

CREATING A BANK

BALANCE SHEET 1: BANK OF VANCOUVER

Assets		Liabilities and net worth	
Cash	$250,000	Capital stock	$250,000

Each item listed in a balance sheet such as this is called an *account*.

TRANSACTION 2: ACQUIRING PROPERTY AND EQUIPMENT

The first step for the new bank will be to acquire property and equipment. The bank purchases buildings for $220,000 and buys $20,000 worth of office equipment. This transaction changes the composition of the bank's assets. The bank now has $240,000 less in cash and $240,000 of new property assets. Using blue type to denote those accounts affected by each transaction, we find that the bank's balance sheet at the conclusion of Transaction 2 appears as follows:

ACQUIRING PROPERTY AND EQUIPMENT

BALANCE SHEET 2: BANK OF VANCOUVER

Assets		Liabilities and net worth	
Cash	$10,000	Capital stock	$250,000
Property	240,000		

Note that the balance sheet still balances, as it must.

TRANSACTION 3: ACCEPTING DEPOSITS

Chartered banks have two basic functions: to accept deposits of money and to make loans. Now that our bank is in operation, suppose that the citizens and businesses of Vancouver decide to deposit $100,000 in the Bank of Vancouver. What happens to the bank's balance sheet?

The bank receives cash, an asset to the bank. Suppose this money is placed in the bank as demand deposits (chequing accounts), rather than savings accounts or term deposits. These newly created *demand deposits* are claims that depositors have against the assets of the Bank of Vancouver, thus creating a new liability account. The bank's balance sheet now looks like this:

ACCEPTING DEPOSITS

BALANCE SHEET 3: BANK OF VANCOUVER

Assets		Liabilities and net worth	
Cash	$110,000	Demand deposits	$100,000
Property	240,000	Capital stock	250,000

There has been no change in the economy's total supply of money, but a change has occurred in the composition of the money supply as a result of Transaction 3. Demand deposits have *increased* by $100,000 and currency in circulation has *decreased* by $100,000. Note that currency held by a bank is *not* part of the economy's money supply.

A withdrawal of cash will reduce the bank's demand-deposit liabilities and its holdings of cash by the amount of the withdrawal. This, too, changes the composition, but not the total supply, of money in the economy.

DEPOSITS IN THE BANK OF CANADA

The Bank of Vancouver has to have sufficient *cash reserves* to serve the daily cash needs of the chartered bank's customers. Some of these cash reserves are held at the Bank of Canada (see Table 12-1). Cash reserves are also called **desired reserves**. Generally, banks keep a minimum percentage of their holdings in cash reserves. We refer to the "specified percentage" of deposit liabilities the chartered bank chooses to keep as vault cash as the **desired reserve ratio**. Up to the mid 1990s the Bank of Canada actually required chartered banks to hold a specified percentage of demand, savings, and term deposits, and referred to this as *required reserves*. More will be said about this in Chapter 13. The desired reserve ratio is calculated as follows:

$$\text{Desired reserve ratio} = \frac{\text{chartered bank's desired reserves}}{\text{chartered bank's demand-deposit liabilities}}$$

If the desired reserve ratio is 20 percent, our bank, having accepted $100,000 in deposits from the public, would keep $20,000 as reserves to meet its daily cash needs.

There are two things to note about reserves:

1. **Excess Reserves**   A bank's **excess reserves** are found by subtracting *desired* reserves from its **actual reserves**.

   Excess reserves = actual reserves – desired reserves

   In this case,

Actual reserves	$110,000
Desired reserves	−20,000
Excess reserves	$ 90,000

desired reserves
The amount of vault cash each chartered bank chooses to keep on hand for daily transactions, plus its deposits at the Bank of Canada.

desired reserve ratio
The specified percentage of deposit liabilities a chartered bank chooses to keep as vault cash.

excess reserves
The amount by which a chartered bank's actual reserves exceed its desired reserves.

actual reserves
The funds that a bank has as vault cash plus any deposit it may have with the Bank of Canada.

The only reliable way of computing excess reserves is to multiply the bank's demand-deposit liabilities by the reserve ratio to obtain desired reserves ($100,000 × 20 percent = $20,000) and then to subtract desired reserves from the actual reserves listed on the asset side of the bank's balance sheet.

To test your understanding, compute the bank's excess reserves from balance sheet 3, assuming that the desired reserve ratio is (a) 5 percent, (b) 33.3 percent, and (c) 50 percent.

We will soon demonstrate that the ability of a chartered bank to make loans depends on the existence of excess reserves. So, understanding this concept is essential in seeing how the banking system creates money.

2. **Influence**   Excess reserves are a means by which the Bank of Canada can influence the lending ability of chartered banks. The next chapter will explain in detail how the Bank of Canada can implement certain policies that either increase or decrease chartered bank reserves and affect the ability of banks to make loans. To the degree that these policies are successful in influencing the volume of chartered bank credit, the Bank of Canada can help the economy smooth out business fluctuations. Another function of reserves is to facilitate the collection or "clearing" of cheques. *(Key Question 2)*

TRANSACTION 4: CLEARING A CHEQUE DRAWN AGAINST THE BANK

Assume that Clem Bradshaw, a Vancouver lumberyard owner, deposited a substantial portion of the $100,000 in demand deposits that the Bank of Vancouver received in Transaction 3. Suppose Bradshaw buys $50,000 worth of lumber from the Ajax Forest Products Company of Chilliwack. Bradshaw pays for this lumber by writing a $50,000 cheque against his deposit in the Bank of Vancouver. Ajax deposits the cheque in its account with the Bank of Manitoba, which has a branch in Chilliwack.

Note that the balance statements of the two banks will balance. The Bank of Vancouver will reduce both its assets and its liabilities by $50,000. The Bank of Manitoba will have $50,000 more in cash and in deposits.

Whenever a cheque is drawn against one bank and deposited in another bank, collection of that cheque will reduce both reserves and demand deposits by the bank on which the cheque is drawn. In our example, the Bank of Vancouver loses $50,000 in both reserves and deposits to the Bank of Manitoba. But there is no loss of reserves or deposits for the banking system as a whole. What one bank loses, another bank gains.

If we bring all the other assets and liabilities back into the picture, the Bank of Vancouver's balance sheet looks like this at the end of Transaction 4:

CLEARING A CHEQUE

BALANCE SHEET 4: BANK OF VANCOUVER

Assets		Liabilities and net worth	
Reserves	$ 60,000	Demand deposits	$ 50,000
Property	240,000	Capital stock	250,000

Verify that with a 20 percent desired reserve ratio, the bank's excess reserves now stand at $50,000.

QUICK REVIEW

- When a bank accepts deposits of cash, the composition of the money supply is changed, but the total supply of money is not directly altered.

- Chartered banks keep reserves (cash) equal to a desired percentage of their own deposit liabilities.

- The amount by which a bank's actual cash reserves exceeds its desired reserves is called excess reserves.

- A bank that has a cheque drawn and collected against it will lose to the recipient bank both cash and deposits equal to the value of the cheque.

Money-Creating Transactions of a Chartered Bank

The next two transactions are crucial because they explain (1) how a chartered bank can literally create money by making loans, (2) how money is destroyed when loans are repaid, and (3) how banks create money by purchasing government bonds from the public.

TRANSACTION 5: GRANTING A LOAN

Suppose the Grisley Meat Packing Company of Vancouver decides to expand. Suppose, too, that the company needs exactly $50,000—which just happens to be equal to the Bank of Vancouver's excess reserves—to finance this project.

Grisley requests a loan for this amount from the Bank of Vancouver. Convinced of Grisley's ability to repay, the bank grants the loan. Grisley hands a promissory note—a fancy IOU—to the bank. Grisley wants the convenience and safety of paying its obligations by cheque. So, instead of receiving cash from the bank, Grisley gets a $50,000 increase in its demand deposit account in the Bank of Vancouver.

The bank has acquired an interest-earning asset (the promissory note) and has created a deposit (a liability) to pay for this asset.

At the moment the loan is completed, the bank's position is shown by balance sheet 5A:

Consider This

Goldsmiths, Gold Reserves, and Deposit Insurance

Extending our previous story of the goldsmiths may help you better understand why the chartered banks' holdings of cash reserves to meet everyday customer transactions may be inadequate to stop bank runs and why deposit insurance is needed. Recall that goldsmiths created a fractional reserve system by issuing loans in the form of newly printed gold receipts—receipts that were not backed by gold held in storage. So the amount of gold receipts circulating in the economy was greater than the amount of gold "in reserve."

But even if the goldsmiths held, say, $1 of gold for every $10 of gold receipts in circulation, gold depositors would be subject to potential loss from a "run on the goldsmiths." If all the holders of gold receipts lost confidence in the goldsmiths and simultaneously demanded gold in exchange for their receipts, there would not be enough gold to go around. Anything less than 100 percent reserves ($1 of gold for $1 of gold receipts) would leave the goldsmiths short of gold.

So it is with the fractional reserve requirement in the modern Canadian banking system. The fact that chartered banks hold a percent of their total chequable (demand) deposits as currency reserves is inadequate to protect bank depositors from losses resulting from bank runs.

In the goldsmith economy, government could prevent panic retrieval of gold through deposit insurance that guaranteed gold payments (by government, if necessary) for gold receipts. The owners of the gold deposits therefore would view their receipts as "good as gold" and would be dissuaded from ever running *en masse* to exchange their receipts for gold.

The same logic applies to the modern economy. Because the Canada Deposit Insurance Corporation (CDIC) insures depositors' funds to a maximum of $60,000 per depositor, per institution, depositors view their demand deposits as "good as currency." So they have no incentive collectively to try to convert their chequable deposits to currency, even in circumstances in which chartered banks are experiencing financial difficulties. Note that financial institutions covered under the CDIC pay premia for this insurance.

But deposit insurance has a downside: it makes depositors less diligent about investigating the lending practices of the chartered banks. If depositors know that the $60,000 deposit in a chartered bank will not be lost, even if its reckless lending practices lead it to bankruptcy, they will not take the time and effort to verify that the bank's lending practices are sound.

Question: What would be the consequences if Canada's chartered banks decided to have fully backed reserves?

WHEN A LOAN IS NEGOTIATED

BALANCE SHEET 5A: BANK OF VANCOUVER

Assets		Liabilities and net worth	
Reserves	$60,000	Demand deposits	$100,000
Loans	50,000	Capital stock	250,000
Property	240,000		

A close examination of the bank's balance statement will reveal a startling fact: *When a bank makes loans, it creates money.* The president of Grisley went to the bank with something that is not money—her IOU—and walked out with something that *is* money—a demand deposit.

When banks lend, they create demand deposits (chequing accounts) that *are* money. By extending credit, the Bank of Vancouver has "monetized" an IOU. Grisley and the bank have created and then swapped claims. The claim created by the bank and given to the Grisley Company is money; cheques drawn against a deposit are acceptable as a medium of exchange. It is through the extension of credit by chartered banks that the bulk of the money used in our economy is created.

Assume that Grisley awards a $50,000 building contract to the Quickbuck Construction Company of Kamloops. Quickbuck completes the expansion job and is paid with a cheque for $50,000 drawn by Grisley against its demand deposit in the Bank of Vancouver. Quickbuck, with headquarters in Kamloops, does *not* deposit this cheque back in the Bank of Vancouver but instead deposits it in a Kamloops branch of the Bank of Manitoba. The Bank of Manitoba now has a $50,000 claim against the Bank of Vancouver. As a result, the Bank of Vancouver *loses* both reserves and deposits equal to the amount of the cheque; the Bank of Manitoba *acquires* $50,000 of reserves and deposits.

In summary, assuming a cheque is drawn by the borrower for the entire amount of the loan ($50,000) and given to a firm that deposits it in another bank, the Bank of Vancouver's balance sheet will read as follows *after the cheque has been cleared against it:*

AFTER A CHEQUE IS DRAWN ON THE LOAN

BALANCE SHEET 5B: BANK OF VANCOUVER

Assets		Liabilities and net worth	
Reserves	$10,000	Demand deposits	$50,000
Loans	50,000	Capital stock	250,000
Property	240,000		

After the cheque has been collected, the Bank of Vancouver is just barely meeting its desired reserve ratio of 20 percent. The bank has *no excess reserves*; it is "fully loaned up." The money supply has not decreased due to the cheque drawn on the Bank of Vancouver, the money is simply showing up in the Bank of Manitoba.

TRANSACTION 6: REPAYING A LOAN

If chartered banks create demand deposits—money—when they make loans, is money destroyed when the loans are repaid? Yes. Let's see what happens when the Grisley Company repays the $50,000 it borrowed by authorizing the bank to debit its current account.

The Bank of Vancouver's deposit liabilities decline by $50,000, and Grisley has given up $50,000 worth of its claim against the bank's assets. In turn, the bank will surrender Grisley's IOU. The bank and the company have re-swapped claims.

But the claim given up by Grisley is money; the claim it is repurchasing—its IOU—is not. The supply of money has therefore been reduced by $50,000; that amount of deposits has been destroyed, unaccompanied by any increase in the money supply elsewhere in the economy.

This fact is shown in Balance Sheet 6. The Bank of Vancouver's loans return to zero and its demand deposits have increased by $50,000.

REPAYING A LOAN

BALANCE SHEET 6: BANK OF VANCOUVER

Assets		Liabilities and net worth	
Reserves	$10,000	Demand deposits	$0
Loans	0	Capital stock	250,000
Property	240,000		

The decline in demand deposits increases the bank's holdings of excess reserves; this provides the basis for making new loans. *(Key Questions 4 and 8)*

TRANSACTION 7: BUYING GOVERNMENT SECURITIES

When a chartered bank buys government bonds from the public, the effect is substantially the same as lending. New money is created.

Assume that the Bank of Vancouver's balance sheet initially stands as it did at the end of Transaction 4. Now suppose that instead of making a $50,000 loan, the bank buys $50,000 of government securities from a securities dealer. The bank receives the interest-bearing bonds, which appear on its balance statement as the asset "Securities" and give the dealer an increase in its deposit account. The bank's balance sheet appears as follows:

BUYING GOVERNMENT SECURITIES

BALANCE SHEET 7: BANK OF VANCOUVER

Assets		Liabilities and net worth	
Reserves	$60,000	Demand deposits	$100,000
Securities	50,000	Capital stock	250,000
Property	240,000		

Demand deposits, that is, the supply of money, have increased by $50,000, as in Transaction 6. *Bond purchases from the public by chartered banks increase the supply of money in the same way as does lending to the public.*

Finally, the selling of government bonds to the public (including securities dealers) by a chartered bank—like the repayment of a loan—reduces the supply of money. The securities buyer pays by cheque and both "Securities" and "Demand deposits" (the latter being money) decline by the amount of the sale.

Profits, Liquidity, and the Overnight Loans Rate

The asset items on a chartered bank's balance sheet reflect the banker's pursuit of two conflicting goals:

1. **Profit**   One goal is profit. Chartered banks, like any other business, seek profits, which is why the bank makes loans and buys securities—the two major earning assets of chartered banks.

2. **Liquidity**   The other goal is safety. For a bank, safety lies in **liquidity**, specifically such liquid assets as cash and excess reserves. A bank must be on guard for depositors who want to transform their demand deposits into cash (see the Consider This box). Bankers thus seek a balance between prudence and profit. The compromise is between assets that earn high returns and highly liquid assets.

liquidity
The ease with which an asset can be converted into cash with little or no loss of purchasing power.

An interesting way in which banks can partly reconcile the goals of profit and liquidity is to lend temporary excess reserves to other chartered banks. Normal day-to-day flows of funds to banks rarely leave all banks with their exact levels of desired reserves. Banks therefore lend these excess reserves to other banks on an overnight basis as a way to earn additional interest without sacrificing long-term liquidity. Banks that borrow in this market do so because they are temporarily short of the level of reserves they wish to hold. The interest rate paid on these overnight loans is called the **overnight loans rate**.

overnight loans rate
The interest rate banks charge to borrow and lend one-day funds to each other.

QUICK REVIEW

- Banks create money when they make loans; money vanishes when bank loans are repaid.

- New money is created when banks buy government bonds from the public;

- money disappears when banks sell government bonds to the public.

- Banks balance profitability and safety in determining their mix of earning assets and highly liquid assets.

12.2   The Banking System: Multiple-Deposit Expansion

Thus far we have seen that a single bank in a banking system can lend one dollar for each dollar of its excess reserves. The situation is different for all chartered banks as a group. We will find that the chartered banking system can lend—that is, can create money—by a multiple of its excess reserves. This multiple lending is accomplished even though each bank in the system can only lend "dollar for dollar" with its excess reserves.

How do these seemingly paradoxical results come about? To answer this question we must keep our analysis uncluttered and rely on three simplifying assumptions:

- The desired reserve ratio for all chartered banks is 20 percent.

- Initially all banks are meeting this 20 percent desired reserve ratio. No excess reserves exist; or in the parlance of banking they are "loaned up" (or "loaned out").

- If any bank can increase its loans as a result of acquiring excess reserves, an amount equal to those excess reserves will be lent to one borrower, who will write a cheque for the entire amount of the loan and give it to someone else, who will deposit the cheque in another bank. This third assumption means that the worst thing possible happens to every lending bank—a cheque for the entire amount of the loan is drawn and cleared against it in favour of another bank.

The Banking System's Lending Potential

Suppose a junkyard owner in Saskatoon finds a $100 bill while dismantling a car that has been on the lot for years. He deposits the $100 in bank A, which adds the $100 to its reserves. We will record only changes in the balance sheets of the various chartered banks. The deposit changes bank A's balance sheet as shown by entries (a_1):

MULTIPLE-DEPOSIT EXPANSION PROCESS

BALANCE SHEET: CHARTERED BANK A

Assets		Liabilities and net worth	
Reserves	$+100 (a_1)	Demand deposits	$+100 (a_1)
	− 80 (a_3)		+ 80 (a_2)
Loans	+ 80 (a_2)		− 80 (a_3)

Recall from Transaction 3 that this $100 deposit of currency does not alter the money supply. Although $100 of demand-deposit money comes into being, it is offset by the $100 of currency no longer in the hands of the public (the junkyard owner). What has happened is that bank A has acquired excess reserves of $80. Of the newly acquired $100 in reserves, 20 percent, or $20, is earmarked for the desired reserves on the new $100 deposit, and the remaining $80 goes to excess reserves. Since a single chartered bank can lend only an amount equal to its excess reserves, we conclude that bank A can lend a maximum of $80. When a loan for this amount is made, bank A's loans increase by $80 and the borrower gets an $80 demand deposit. We add these figures—entries (a_2)—to bank A's balance sheet.

But now we make our third assumption: The borrower draws a cheque ($80) for the entire amount of the loan, and gives it to someone who deposits it in bank B, a different bank. As we saw in Transaction 6, bank A loses both reserves and deposits equal to the amount of the loan, as indicated in entries (a_3). The net result of these transactions is that bank A's reserves now stand at +$20 (= $100 – $80), loans at +$80, and demand deposits at +$100 (= $100 + $80 – $80). When the dust has settled, bank A is just meeting the 20 percent reserve ratio.

Recalling Transaction 5, we know that bank B acquires both the reserves and the deposits that bank A has lost. Bank B's balance sheet is changed as in entries (b_1):

MULTIPLE-DEPOSIT EXPANSION PROCESS

BALANCE SHEET: CHARTERED BANK B

Assets		Liabilities and net worth	
Reserves	$+80 (b_1)	Demand deposits	$+80 (b_1)
	–64 (b_3)		+64 (b_2)
Loans	+64 (b_2)		–64 (b_3)

When the borrower's cheque is drawn and cleared, bank A loses $80 in reserves and deposits and bank B gains $80 in reserves and deposits. But 20 percent, or $16, of bank B's new reserves are kept against the new $80 in demand deposits. This means that bank B has $64 (= $80 – $16) in excess reserves. It can therefore lend $64 [entries (b_2)]. When the new borrower draws a cheque for the entire amount and deposits it in bank C, the reserves and deposits of bank B both fall by the $64 [entries (b_3)]. As a result of these transactions, bank B's reserves now stand at +$16 (= $80 – $64), loans at +$64, and demand deposits at +$80 (= $80 + $64 – $64). After all this, bank B is just meeting the 20 percent desired reserve ratio.

We are off and running again. Bank C acquires the $64 in reserves and deposits lost by bank B. Its balance sheet changes as in entries (c_1):

MULTIPLE-DEPOSIT EXPANSION PROCESS

BALANCE SHEET: CHARTERED BANK C

Assets		Liabilities and net worth	
Reserves	$+64.00 (c_1)	Demand deposits	$+64.00 (c_1)
	–51.20 (c_3)		+51.20 (c_2)
Loans	+51.20 (c_2)		–51.20 (c_3)

Exactly 20 percent, or $12.80, of these new reserves will be kept as reserves, the remaining $51.20 being excess reserves. Hence, bank C can safely lend a maximum of $51.20. Suppose it does [entries (c_2)]. And suppose the borrower draws a cheque for the entire amount and gives it to someone who deposits it in another bank [entries (c_3)].

Bank D—the bank receiving the $51.20 in reserves and deposits—now notes these changes on its balance sheet [entries (d_1)]:

MULTIPLE-DEPOSIT EXPANSION PROCESS

BALANCE SHEET: CHARTERED BANK D

Assets		Liabilities and net worth	
Reserves	$+51.20 ($d_1$)	Demand deposits	$+51.20 ($d_1$)
	−40.96 (d_3)		+40.96 (d_2)
Loans	+40.96 (d_2)		−40.96 (d_3)

It can now lend $40.96 [entries ($d_2$)]. The newest borrower draws a cheque for the full amount and deposits it in still another bank [entries (d_3)].

We could go ahead with this procedure by bringing banks E, F, G, H, …, N into the picture. But we suggest that you work through the computations for banks E, F, and G to be sure you understand the procedure.

The entire analysis is summarized in Table 13-1. Data for banks E through N are supplied so that you can check your computations. Our conclusion is startling: On the basis of only $80 in excess reserves (acquired by the banking system when someone deposited $100 of currency in bank A), the entire chartered banking system is able to lend $400, the sum of the amounts in column 4. The banking system can lend excess reserves by a multiple of 5 when the reserve ratio is 20 percent. Yet each single bank in the banking system is lending only an amount equal to its own excess reserves. How do we explain this? How can the banking system lend by a multiple of its excess reserves, when each individual bank can only lend "dollar for dollar" with its excess reserves?

The answer is that reserves lost by a single bank are not lost to the banking system as a whole. The reserves lost by bank A are acquired by bank B. Those lost by B are gained by C. C loses to D,

	TABLE 12-1	Expansion of the Money Supply by the Chartered Banking System		
Bank	**(1)** Acquired reserves and deposits	**(2)** Desired reserves (reserve ratio = .2)	**(3)** Excess reserves, (1) − (2)	**(4)** Amount bank can lend; new money created = (3)
Bank A	$100.00 ($a_1$)	$20.00	$80.00	$ 80.00 (a_2)
Bank B	80.00 (a_3, b_1)	16.00	64.00	64.00 (b_2)
Bank C	64.00 (b_3, c_1)	12.80	51.20	51.20 (c_2)
Bank D	51.20 (c_3, d_1)	10.24	40.96	40.96 (d_2)
Bank E	40.96	8.19	32.77	32.77
Bank F	32.77	6.55	26.22	26.22
Bank G	26.22	5.24	20.98	20.98
Bank H	20.98	4.20	16.78	16.78
Bank I	16.78	3.36	13.42	13.42
Bank J	13.42	2.68	10.74	10.74
Bank K	10.74	2.15	8.59	8.59
Bank L	8.59	1.72	6.87	6.87
Bank M	6.87	1.37	5.50	5.50
Bank N	5.50	1.10	4.40	4.40
Other banks	21.97	4.40	17.57	17.57
Total amount of money created (sum of the amounts in column 4)				$400.00

greater the Currency drain   Lower the Potencil from the Banking $enclo

D to E, E to F, and so forth. Although reserves can be, and are, lost by individual banks in the banking system, there is no loss of reserves for the banking system as a whole.

An individual bank can safely lend only an amount equal to its excess reserves, but the chartered banking system can lend by a multiple of its excess reserves. This contrast, incidentally, is an illustration of why it is imperative that we keep the fallacy of composition (Chapter 1) firmly in mind. Chartered banks as a group can create money by lending in a manner much different from that of the individual banks in that group.

12.3   The Monetary Multiplier

monetary multiplier
The multiple of its excess reserves by which the banking system can expand demand deposits and thus the money supply by making new loans.

The banking system magnifies any original excess reserves into a larger amount of newly created demand-deposit money. The *demand-deposit multiplier*, or **monetary multiplier**, is similar in concept to the spending-income multiplier in Chapter 7. That multiplier exists because the expenditures of one household are received as income by another; it magnifies a change in initial spending into a larger change in GDP. The spending-income simple multiplier is the reciprocal of the MPS (the leakage into saving that occurs at each round of spending).

In contrast, the monetary multiplier exists because the reserves and deposits lost by one bank are received by another bank. It magnifies excess reserves into a larger creation of demand-deposit money. The monetary multiplier m is the reciprocal of the desired reserve ratio R (the leakage into cash reserves that occurs at each step in the lending process). In short,

Monetary multiplier = 1/desired reserve ratio

or, in symbols,

$$m = 1/R$$

In this formula, m represents the maximum amount of new demand-deposit that can be created by a single dollar of excess reserves, given the value of R. By multiplying the excess reserves E by m, we can find the maximum amount of new demand-deposit money, D, that can be created by the banking system. That is,

Maximum demand-deposit creation = excess reserves × monetary multiplier

or, more simply,

$$D = E \times m$$

In our example in Table 12-1, R is .20 so m is 5 (= 1/.20). Then

$$D = \$400 = \$80 \times 5$$

Higher desired reserve ratios mean lower monetary multipliers and therefore less creation of new deposit money via loans; smaller reserve ratios mean higher monetary multipliers and thus more creation of new deposit money via loans. With a high reserve ratio, say, 50 percent, the monetary multiplier would be 2 (= 1/.5), and in our example the banking system could create only $160 (= $80 of excess reserves × 2) of new deposit money. In the Consider This box we noted that if the reserve ratio is 100 percent, no new money can be created; the simple monetary multiplier in this case is zero. With a low desired reserve ratio, say, 5 percent, the monetary multiplier would be 20 (= 1/.05), and the banking system could create $1600 (= $80 of excess reserves × 20) of new deposit money. Again, note the similarities with the spending-income multiplier, in which higher MPS values mean lower multipliers and lower MPS values mean higher multipliers. Also, like the spending-income multiplier, the monetary multiplier works in both directions. The monetary multiplier applies to money destruction as well as to money creation.

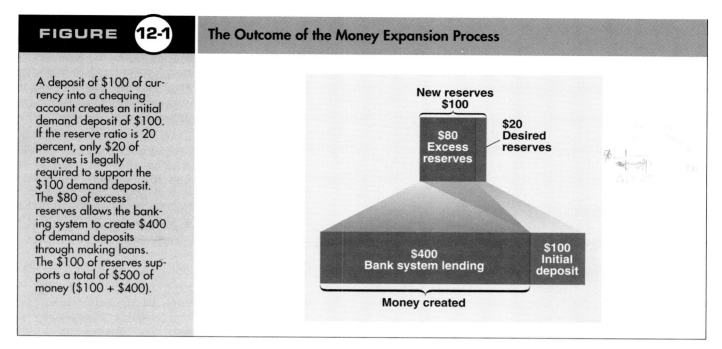

FIGURE 12-1

The Outcome of the Money Expansion Process

A deposit of $100 of currency into a chequing account creates an initial demand deposit of $100. If the reserve ratio is 20 percent, only $20 of reserves is legally required to support the $100 demand deposit. The $80 of excess reserves allows the banking system to create $400 of demand deposits through making loans. The $100 of reserves supports a total of $500 of money ($100 + $400).

Figure 12-1 depicts the final outcome of our example of a multiple-deposit expansion of the money supply. The initial deposit of $100 of currency into the bank (lower right-hand box) creates new reserves of an equal amount (upper box). With a 20 percent reserve ratio, however, only $20 of currency reserves is needed to "back up" this $100 demand deposit. The excess reserves of $80 permit the creation of $400 of new demand deposits via the making of loans, confirming a monetary multiplier of 5. The $100 of new reserves supports a total supply of money of $500, consisting of the $100 initial demand deposit plus $400 of demand deposits created through lending.

You might experiment with the following two situations to test your understanding of multiple credit expansion by the banking system:

1. Rework the analysis in Table 12-1 (at least three or four steps of it) assuming the reserve ratio is 10 percent. What is the maximum amount of money the banking system can create upon acquiring $100 in new reserves and deposits? (The answer is not $800!)

2. Suppose the banking system is "loaned up" and faces a 20 percent reserve ratio. Explain how it might have to reduce its outstanding loans by $400 when a $100 cash withdrawal from a demand-deposit account forces one bank to draw down its reserves by $100. *(Key Question 13)*

Some Modifications

There are certain complications that might modify the accuracy of our analysis, effectively reducing the monetary multiplier.

OTHER LEAKAGES

Aside from the leakage of desired reserves at each step of the lending process, two other leakages of money from chartered banks might dampen the money-creating potential of the banking system:

- *Currency drains* A borrower might request that part of his or her loan be paid in currency. If the person who borrowed the $80 from bank A in our illustration asked for $16 of it in cash and the remaining $64 as a demand deposit, bank B would later receive only $64 in new reserves (of which only $51.20 would be excess) rather than $80 (of which $64 was excess). This decline in excess reserves would reduce the lending potential of the banking system accordingly. In fact, if the first borrower had taken the entire $80 in cash and if this currency remained in circulation, the multiple expansion process would have stopped then and there. But the convenience and safety of demand deposits make this unlikely.

- ***Excess reserves*** Our analysis of the chartered banking system's ability to expand the money supply by lending is based on the assumption that chartered banks are willing to hold a specific desired reserve ratio. To the extent that bankers are forced to hold more than they desire—excess reserves—the overall credit expansion potential of the banking system will be reduced. For example, suppose bank A, upon receiving $100 in new cash, is forced to add $25, rather than $20, to its reserves because there are only very risky clients willing to borrow. Then it would lend only $75, rather than $80, and the monetary multiplier would be diminished accordingly.

QUICK REVIEW

- Although a single bank in a multibank system can safely lend (create money) by an amount equal to its excess reserves, the banking system can lend (create money) by a multiple of its excess reserves.

- The simple monetary multiplier is the reciprocal of the desired reserve ratio; it is the multiple by which the banking system can expand the money supply for each dollar of excess reserves.

- Currency drains and a desire by banks to hold excess reserves may reduce the size of the monetary multiplier.

Need for Monetary Control

Our illustration of the banking system's ability to create money rests on the assumption that chartered banks are willing to create money by lending and that households and businesses are willing to borrow. In reality, the willingness of banks to lend on the basis of excess reserves varies cyclically, and therein lies one of the main rationales for central bank control of the money supply to promote economic stability.

When prosperity reigns, chartered banks are likely to expand credit to the maximum of their ability. Loans are interest-earning assets, and in good economic times there is less fear of borrowers' defaulting. But, as you will find in Chapter 13, the money supply has an effect on aggregate demand. By lending and thereby creating money to the maximum of their ability during prosperity, chartered banks may contribute to excessive aggregate demand and therefore to inflation.

If recession appears on the economic horizon, bankers may hastily withdraw their invitations to borrow, seeking the safety of liquidity (excess reserves) even if it means sacrificing potential interest income. They may fear large-scale withdrawal of deposits by a panicky public and simultaneously doubt the ability of borrowers to repay.

We thus conclude that profit-motivated bankers can be expected to vary the money supply in a way that may reinforce cyclical fluctuations. For this reason the Bank of Canada has at its disposal certain monetary tools to alter the money supply in a *countercyclical*, rather than *procyclical*, fashion. We turn to an analysis of these tools in Chapter 13.

THE LASTword — Money in the Early History of Canada[1]

The story of the Canadian dollar begins in the currency chaos of the early French and British colonial period in North America. Through the 17th century and until well into the 19th, various coins from many countries circulated freely in the colonies. These included not only English and French coins, but also coins from Portugal, Spain, and the Spanish colonies in Latin America—notably Mexico, Peru, and Colombia. The hazards of sea travel and persistent trade imbalances with the home country left the colonies chronically short of coins.

The chronic coin shortage also encouraged the introduction of paper money. The most famous issue is undoubtedly the card money of New France. Introduced in 1685, card money initially consisted of playing cards cut to different sizes according to denomination and signed by colonial officials. Despite the protests of authorities in Paris, who objected to the loss of budgetary control, there were several issues of card money before it was withdrawn from circulation in 1719. Card money reappeared in 1729, however, and re-

mained readily accepted until rising inflation, associated with the financing of the Seven Years' War during the 1750s, undermined confidence in its value.

The first bank notes in Canada, issued by the Montreal Bank following its establishment in 1817, were also denominated in dollars. These notes could be redeemed in (gold) coin, upon demand. As new banks were incorporated in Upper and Lower Canada during the 1830s and 1840s, their bank notes were typically denominated in both dollars and pounds. These notes circulated freely through both Canadas and in the United States. Dollar-denominated bank notes issued by U.S. banks also circulated widely in Upper Canada during the early 1800s. This two-way movement of notes across the Canada-U.S. border strongly favoured the continued use of dollars and cents in Canada over pounds, shillings, and pence.

In contrast, bank notes circulating in New Brunswick, Nova Scotia, Prince Edward Island, and Newfoundland, before Confederation, were typically denominated in

pounds, shillings, and pence. This reflected both the stronger ties these provinces had with Great Britain and their weaker commercial links with the United States.

Confederation on 1 July 1867 brought sweeping changes to banking and currency legislation in the provinces of Canada, Nova Scotia, and New Brunswick. Under the British North America Act, the government of the new Dominion was given jurisdiction over currency and banking. The Dominion Notes Act came into effect the following year. Under this legislation, the Dominion took over the various provincial note issues. Provincial notes issued in the Province of Canada were renamed "dominion notes" and were made redeemable in Halifax and Saint John in addition to Montreal and Toronto. The Dominion Notes Act was subsequently extended to cover Prince Edward Island, Manitoba, and British Columbia in 1876 and the Northwest Territories in 1886.

---

[1] From Powell, James, *A History of the Canadian Dollar*, http://www.bankof canada.ca/en/dollar_book/index.htm.

CHAPTER SUMMARY

12.1 CHARTERED BANKS AND THE CREATION OF MONEY

- The operation of a chartered bank can be understood through its balance sheet, where assets equal liabilities plus net worth.

- Modern banking systems are fractional reserve systems: only a fraction of deposits are backed by currency.

- Chartered banks keep reserves as vault cash and a small amount in the Bank of Canada for cheque-clearing purposes. This reserve is equal to a desired per-

centage of the chartered bank's deposit liabilities. Excess reserves are equal to actual reserves minus desired reserves.

- Banks lose both reserves and deposits when cheques are drawn against them.

- Chartered banks create money—create demand deposits, or deposit money—when they make loans. The creation of demand deposits by bank lending is the most important source of money in the Canadian economy. Money is destroyed when bank loans are repaid.

- The ability of a single chartered bank to create money by lending depends on the size of its *excess reserves*. Generally speaking, a chartered bank lends only an amount equal to the amount of its excess reserves.

- Rather than making loans, chartered banks may decide to use excess reserves to buy bonds from the public. In doing so, banks merely credit the demand-deposit accounts of the bond sellers, thus creating demand-deposit money. Money vanishes when banks sell bonds to the public because bond buyers must draw down their demand-deposit balances to pay for the bonds.

- Banks earn interest by making loans and by purchasing bonds; they maintain liquidity by holding cash and excess reserves. Banks having temporary excess reserves often lend them overnight to banks that are short of desired cash reserves. The interest rate paid on loans in this market is called the overnight loans rate.

12.2 THE BANKING SYSTEM: MULTIPLE DEPOSIT EXPANSION

- The chartered banking system as a whole can lend by a multiple of its excess reserves because the banking system cannot lose reserves, although individual banks can lose reserves to other banks in the system.

12.3 THE MONETARY MULTIPLIER

- The multiple by which the banking system could lend on the basis of each dollar of excess reserves is the reciprocal of the desired reserve ratio. This multiple credit expansion process is reversible.

- The fact that profit-seeking banks would tend to alter the money supply in a pro-cyclical direction underlies the need for the Bank of Canada to control the money supply.

TERMS AND CONCEPTS

balance sheet, p. 290
fractional reserve, p. 290
vault cash, p. 291
desired reserves, p. 292

desired reserve ratio, p. 292
excess reserves, p. 292
actual reserves, p. 292
liquidity, p. 296

overnight loans rate, p. 297
monetary multiplier, p. 300

STUDY QUESTIONS

1. Why must a balance sheet always balance? What are the major assets and claims on a chartered bank's balance sheet?

2. **KEY QUESTION** Why do chartered banks hold reserves? Explain why reserves are an asset to chartered banks but a liability to the Bank of Canada. What are excess reserves? How do you calculate the amount of excess reserves held by a bank? What is the significance of excess reserves?

3. "Whenever currency is deposited in a chartered bank, cash goes out of circulation and, as a result, the supply of money is reduced." Do you agree? Explain why or why not.

4. **KEY QUESTION** "When a chartered bank makes loans, it creates money; when loans are repaid, money is destroyed." Explain.

5. Explain why a single chartered bank could lend an amount equal only to its excess reserves, but the chartered banking system could lend by a multiple of its excess reserves. What is the monetary multiplier and how does it relate to the desired reserve ratio?

6. Assume that Jones deposits $500 in currency in the Bank of Vancouver. A half-hour later, Smith obtains a loan for $750 at this bank. By how much and in what direction has the money supply changed? Explain.

7. Suppose the Bank of Newfoundland has excess reserves of $8000 and outstanding deposits of $150,000. If the desired reserve ratio is 10 percent, what is the size of the bank's actual reserves?

8. **KEY QUESTION** Suppose the Yukon Bank has the following simplified balance sheet and that the desired reserve ratio is 20 percent.

ASSETS

		(1)	(2)
Reserves	$22,000		
Securities	38,000		
Loans	40,000		

LIABILITIES AND NET WORTH

		(1)	(2)
Deposits	$100,000		

a. What is the maximum amount of new loans this bank can make? Show in column 1 how the bank's balance sheet will appear after the bank has loaned this additional amount.

b. By how much has the supply of money changed? Explain.

c. How will the bank's balance sheet appear after cheques drawn for the entire amount of the new loans have been cleared against this bank? Show this new balance sheet in column 2.

d. Answer questions a, b, and c on the assumption that the desired reserve ratio is 15 percent.

9. The Bank of Manitoba has reserves of $20,000 and deposits of $100,000. The desired reserve ratio is 20 percent. Households deposit $5000 in currency in the bank, which is added to reserves. How much excess reserves does the bank now have?

10. Suppose again that the Bank of Manitoba has reserves of $20,000 and deposits of $100,000. The desired reserve ratio is 20 percent. The bank now sells $5000 in securities to the Bank of Canada, receiving a $5000 increase in its deposit there in return. How much excess reserves does the bank now have? Why does your answer differ (yes, it does!) from the answer to question 9?

11. Suppose a chartered bank discovers its reserves will temporarily fall slightly short of those it desires to hold. How might it remedy this situation? Now, assume the bank finds that its reserves will be substantially and permanently deficient. What remedy is available to this bank? (Hint: Recall your answer to question 4.)

12. Suppose that Bob withdraws $100 of cash from his chequing account at Calgary Chartered Bank and uses it to buy a camera from Joe, who deposits the $100 in his chequing account in Annapolis Valley Chartered Bank. Assuming a desired reserve ratio of 10 percent and no initial excess reserves, determine the extent to which (a) Calgary Chartered Bank must reduce its loans and demand deposits because of the cash withdrawal and (b) Annapolis Valley Chartered Bank can safely increase its loans and demand deposits because of the cash deposit. Have the cash withdrawal and deposit changed the money supply?

13. **KEY QUESTION** Suppose the simplified consolidated balance sheet shown below is for the entire chartered banking system. All figures are in billions. The desired reserve ratio is 25 percent.

ASSETS

		(1)
Reserves	$ 52	_____
Securities	48	_____
Loans	100	_____

LIABILITIES AND NET WORTH

		(1)
Demand deposits	$200	_____

a. How much excess reserves does the chartered banking system have? What is the maximum amount the banking system might lend? Show in column 1 how the consolidated balance sheet would look after this amount has been lent. What is the monetary multiplier?

b. Answer the questions in 13a assuming that the desired reserve ratio is 20 percent. Explain the resulting difference in the lending ability of the chartered banking system.

14. What are banking "leakages"? How might they affect the money-creating potential of the banking system?

15. Explain why there is a need for the Bank of Canada to control the money supply.

16. **(The Last Word)** The first bank notes were issued by the Bank of Montreal in 1817. What backed up these notes? If it was a banking system with fully backed reserves, how could new money be created?

INTERNET APPLICATION QUESTIONS

1. **How To Spot a Counterfeit Bank Note** Counterfeit bank notes have always been a concern for the Bank of Canada. Visit the Bank of Canada through the McConnell-Brue-Barbiero Web site (Chapter 12) to find out how to detect counterfeit Canadian bank notes.

2. **The Balance Sheet of Canadian Chartered Banks** Statistics Canada provides the balance sheet of chartered banks. Access their Web site through the McConnell-Brue-Barbiero homepage (Chapter 12). What has the trend been in the last five years for bank assets and liabilities?

Σ-STAT

3. **Web-Based Question: The Canadian Payments Association (CPA) and Cheque Clearing** Visit the Canadian Payments Association Web site by going through the McConnell-Brue-Barbiero homepage (Chapter12). How many transactions are cleared and settled through the CPA's systems each business day?

The Bank of Canada and Monetary Policy

In the previous two chapters you have become acquainted with the function of money in a market economy and how money is created (and destroyed). But what is the connection between the total money supply and the output performance and price level in an economy?

Recall from Chapter 6 that market economies are subject to fluctuations, often experiencing substantial unemployment and sometimes inflationary pressures. In this chapter you will learn that a change in money supply affects interest rates, which influence the level of investment and real GDP. Thus the Bank of Canada, within limits, can help smooth out the fluctuations in the Canadian economy by influencing interest rates through its control of the money supply. The main goal of the Bank of Canada policies is to achieve and maintain price stability, but it would also like to see the economy achieve full employment. Price stability facilitates the ultimate aim of ensuring a nation is employing all its resources—particularly its labour force—to their fullest extent.

13.1   Functions of the Bank of Canada

The functions of the Bank of Canada, a crown corporation, can be divided into five categories. The most important will be discussed last.

1. **Acting as the "Bankers' Bank"**   You head for the nearest chartered bank if you want to deposit, withdraw, or borrow money; the chartered banks turn to the Bank of Canada as their "bank." There are times when the chartered banks need to borrow from the central bank. Chartered banks also keep minimal reserves with the Bank of Canada to settle bilateral payment balances among themselves.

2. **Issuing Currency**   The Bank of Canada supplies the economy with needed paper currency—Bank of Canada notes—and coins. This involves note and coin design, and ensuring the printing, stamping, and distribution of new bank notes and coins, and the replacement of worn currency.

3. **Acting as Fiscal Agent**   The Bank of Canada acts as the fiscal agent (provider of financial services, including banking) for the federal government. The federal government collects funds through taxation, spends these funds on a variety of goods and services, and sells and redeems bonds. The federal government uses the Bank of Canada's facilities to carry out these activities.

4. **Supervising the Chartered Banks**   The Department of Finance and the Bank of Canada supervise the operations of chartered banks and other non-bank financial institutions. The Bank of Canada makes periodic assessments of the banks' profitability, to check that the chartered banks perform in accordance with the many regulations to which they are subject and to uncover questionable practices or fraud.

5. **Regulating the Supply of Money**   Finally, and most importantly, the Bank of Canada has ultimate responsibility for regulating the supply of money, and this in turn enables it to influence interest rates. The major task of the central bank is to manage the money supply (and thus interest rates) according to the needs of the economy. This involves making an amount of money available that is consistent with high and steadily rising levels of output and employment and a relatively constant price level. All of the other functions of the Bank of Canada are more or less routine or of a service nature, but managing the money supply requires making policy decisions.

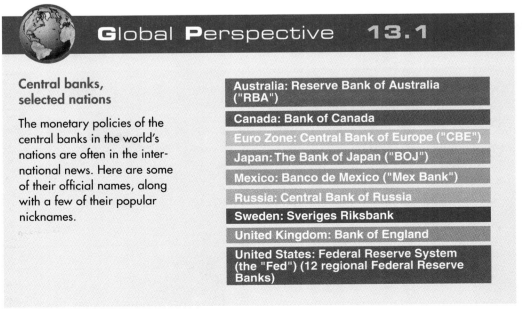

Global Perspective 13.1

Central banks, selected nations

The monetary policies of the central banks in the world's nations are often in the international news. Here are some of their official names, along with a few of their popular nicknames.

Australia: Reserve Bank of Australia ("RBA")

Canada: Bank of Canada

Euro Zone: Central Bank of Europe ("CBE")

Japan: The Bank of Japan ("BOJ")

Mexico: Banco de Mexico ("Mex Bank")

Russia: Central Bank of Russia

Sweden: Sveriges Riksbank

United Kingdom: Bank of England

United States: Federal Reserve System (the "Fed") (12 regional Federal Reserve Banks)

Bank of Canada Independence

The independence of the Bank of Canada is a matter of continuing controversy. Opponents of an independent central bank say that it is undemocratic to have a powerful economic agency with members who are not elected and thus not directly subject to the will of the people. Defenders of Bank of Canada independence, including most economists, contend that the Bank of Canada must be protected from political pressures so that it can effectively control the money supply and maintain price stability. They point out that countries with less central bank independence, on average, have higher rates of inflation than countries with more central bank independence.

Consolidated Balance Sheet of the Bank of Canada

The Bank of Canada balance sheet helps us consider how it conducts monetary policy. Table 13-1 consolidates the assets and liabilities of the Bank of Canada. You will see that some of the Bank of Canada's assets and liabilities differ from those found on the balance sheet of chartered banks.

Assets

The two main assets of the Bank of Canada are securities and (much smaller) advances to the chartered banks.

www.bankofcanada.ca/en/
wfsgen.htm
Bank of Canada

1. **Securities**   The securities shown in Table 13-1 are Government of Canada bonds (long-term securities) and Treasury bills (short-term securities) issued by the government of Canada to finance past and present budget deficits. These securities are part of the public debt—money borrowed by the federal government. Some were bought directly from the government, but most from the public (through investment dealers) and the chartered banks. Although they are an important source of interest income to the Bank of Canada, they are bought and sold primarily to influence the amount of chartered bank reserves, and therefore the banks' ability to create money by lending. Government of Canada securities make up over 90 percent of the Bank of Canada's assets, yet are important for monetary policy, as we shall see later.

2. **Advances to Chartered Banks**   For reasons that will soon become clear, chartered banks occasionally borrow from the Bank of Canada. The IOUs the chartered banks give to the Bank of Canada in negotiating advances are listed as advances to chartered banks. These IOUs are assets to the Bank of Canada because they are claims against the chartered banks. To the chartered banks, these IOUs are liabilities. Through borrowing, the chartered banks obtain increases in their reserves. Note that advances to the chartered banks are not large, making up less than 2 percent of its assets.

TABLE 13-1	Bank of Canada Statement of Assets and Liabilities, December 31, 2002 (in Millions)		
Assets		**Liabilities**	
Advances to chartered banks	$ 596	Notes in circulation	$39,782
Treasury bills of Canada	13,359	Government of Canada deposits	1,640
Other securities issued or		Chartered bank deposits	604
guaranteed by Canada	27,262	Other deposits	330
Foreign currency deposits	392	Other liabilities	623
Other assets	1,370	Total	$42,979
Total	$42,979		

Source: Bank of Canada Weekly Financial Statistics, Feb. 14, 2003.
Visit www.mcgrawhill.ca/college/mcconnell for data update.

Liabilities

On the liability side of the Bank of Canada's consolidated balance sheet, there are three main items: chartered bank deposits, Government of Canada deposits, and notes in circulation.

1. **Chartered Bank Deposits**   These deposits are assets of the chartered banks but a liability to the Bank of Canada. Up to the early 1990s chartered banks were required by law to keep a specified percentage of their reserves with the Bank of Canada. Since the abolition of required reserves, these deposits have been considerably reduced because their only function is to permit cheque-clearing to settle payment balances among the chartered banks.

2. **Government of Canada Deposits**   The federal government keeps deposits at the Bank of Canada and draws cheques on them to pay its obligations. To the government, all such deposits are assets, while to the banks, including the central bank, they are liabilities.

3. **Notes in Circulation**   The supply of paper money in Canada consists of bank notes issued by the Bank of Canada. When this paper money is circulating outside the Bank of Canada, it is treated as claims against the assets of the Bank of Canada and is thus a liability.

13.2   Goals and Tools of Monetary Policy

The Bank of Canada is responsible for supervising and controlling the operation of the Canadian financial system. (For the names of central banks in various nations, see Global Perspective 13.1.) The bank formulates the basic policies that the banking system follows. Because it is a public body, its decisions are made in what it perceives to be the public interest.

monetary policy
A central bank's changing of the money supply to influence interest rates and assist the economy in achieving a full-employment, non-inflationary level of total output.

The objective of the Bank of Canada's **monetary policy** is to keep inflation low, stable, and predictable so as to help to moderate the business cycle, and help the economy attain full employment and sustained economic growth. At the present time the Bank of Canada has an inflation target range of 1 to 3 percent annually. Monetary policy consists of altering the economy's money supply to influence interest rates, which indirectly affect the inflation rate, employment, and the level of economic activity in the Canadian economy. In a recession, or the anticipation of a slowdown, the Bank of Canada would increase the money supply, which decreases interest rates, to stimulate spending. If the Canadian economy were expanding too quickly and accompanied by inflation above 3 percent, the Bank of Canada would restrict the money supply to raise interest rates, which would help slow down the economy.

The Bank of Canada alters the amount of the nation's money supply by manipulating the amount of excess reserves held by chartered banks. Excess reserves, you will recall, are critical to the money-creating ability of the banking system. Once we see how the Bank of Canada controls excess reserves and the money supply, we will explain how changes in the stock of money affect interest rates, aggregate demand, and the economy.

Tools of Monetary Policy

The Bank of Canada implements monetary policy through its influence on short-term interest rates. We will see later in this chapter that monetary policy also affects the value of the Canadian dollar on foreign exchange markets. The Bank of Canada keeps a watchful eye on the Canadian dollar exchange rate, the output performance of the Canadian economy, and the behaviour of the consumer price index (CPI) and implements monetary policy accordingly. Monetary policy is implemented primarily by influencing chartered bank reserves.

The Bank of Canada can use three instruments to influence and change chartered bank reserves:

• Open-market operations

• Government deposit shifting

• Bank rate

Open-Market Operations

The Bank of Canada's **open-market operations** consist of buying bonds from and selling them to chartered banks and the general public through investment dealers. Bond markets are "open" to all buyers and sellers of corporate and government bonds (securities). Here is the way it works.

BUYING SECURITIES

Suppose the Bank of Canada decides to buy government bonds. It can purchase these bonds from chartered banks or the general public. In both cases, reserves of the chartered banks will increase.

FROM CHARTERED BANKS

When the Bank of Canada buys government bonds *from chartered banks,*

(a) The chartered banks give up a part of their holdings of securities (the government bonds) to the Bank of Canada.

(b) When the Bank of Canada pays for these securities, it increases the deposits of the chartered banks, i.e., their reserves, by the amount of the purchase.

We show these outcomes as (a) and (b) on the following consolidated balance sheet of the chartered banks and the Bank of Canada.

BANK OF CANADA BUYS BONDS FROM CHARTERED BANKS

BANK OF CANADA

Assets	Liabilities
+ Securities (a)	+ Deposits of chartered banks (b)
(a) Securities ↑	(b) Reserves ↓

CHARTERED BANKS

Assets	Liabilities
− Securities (a)	
+ Reserves (b)	

The upward arrow shows that securities have moved from the chartered banks to the Bank of Canada. Therefore, we write "−Securities" (minus securities) in the asset column of the balance sheet of the chartered banks. For the same reason, we write "+Securities" in the asset column of the balance sheet of the Bank of Canada.

The downward arrow indicates that the Bank of Canada has provided reserves to the chartered banks. Therefore we write "+Reserves" in the asset column of the balance sheet of the chartered banks. The plus sign in the liability column of the balance sheet of the Bank of Canada indicates that chartered bank deposits have increased; they are a liability to the Bank of Canada.

The result of this transaction is that when the Bank of Canada purchases securities from chartered banks, it increases the reserves in the banking system, which then increases the lending ability of the chartered banks.

FROM THE PUBLIC

The effect on chartered bank reserves is much the same when the Bank of Canada purchases securities from the public (through investment dealers). Suppose Mariposa Investments Limited (a large

Toronto dealer representing the public) has Government of Canada bonds that it sells in the open market to the Bank of Canada. The transaction goes like this:

(a) Mariposa Investments gives up securities to the Bank of Canada and gets in payment a cheque drawn by the Bank of Canada on itself.

(b) Mariposa Investments promptly deposits this cheque in its account with the Bank of York.

(c) The Bank of York collects from the Bank of Canada and thus increases its reserves.

The balance sheet changes labeled to correspond with the elements of the transaction are as follows:

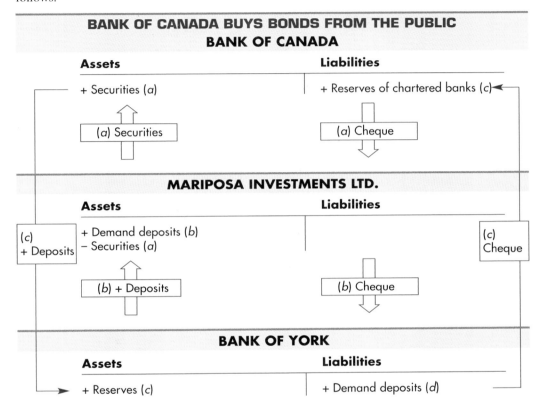

Two aspects of this transaction are particularly important. First, as with Bank of Canada purchases of securities directly from chartered banks, the purchases of securities increases the reserves and lending ability of the chartered banking system. Second, the supply of money is directly increased by the central bank's purchase of government bonds (aside from any expansion of the money supply that may occur from the increase in chartered bank reserves). This direct increase in the money supply has taken the form of an increased amount of chequing account money in the economy as a result of Mariposa's deposit. Because these demand deposits are an asset as viewed by Mariposa Investments, demand deposits have increased on Mariposa Investments' balance sheet.

There is a slight difference between the Bank of Canada's purchases of securities from the chartered banks and from the public. If we assume all chartered banks are "loaned up" initially, the Bank of Canada bond purchases *from chartered banks* increase actual reserves and excess reserves of chartered banks by the entire amount of the bond purchases. As shown in the left panel of Figure 13-1, a $1,000 bond purchase from a chartered bank would increase both the actual and excess reserves of the chartered bank by $1,000.

In contrast, Bank of Canada purchases of bonds *from the public* increase actual reserves but also increase demand deposits. Thus, a $1000 bond purchase from the public would increase demand

FIGURE 13-1　**The Bank of Canada's Purchase of Bonds and the Expansion of the Money Supply**

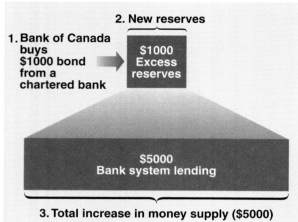

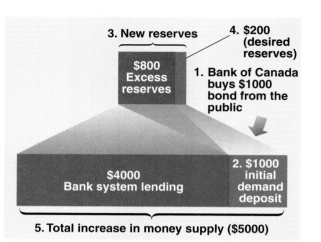

Assuming all chartered banks are "loaned up" initially, a Bank of Canada purchase of a $1000 bond from either a chartered bank or the public can increase the money supply by $5000 when the desired reserve ratio is 20 percent. In the left portion of the diagram, the purchase of a $1000 bond from a chartered bank creates $1000 of excess reserves that support an expansion of demand deposits of $5000 through making loans. In the right portion, the purchase of a $1000 bond from the public creates only $800 of excess reserves, because $100 of reserves are needed to "back up" the $1000 new demand deposit in the banking system. The chartered banks can therefore expand the money supply by $4000 by making loans. This $4000 of chequing account money plus the initial new demand deposit of $1000 together equal $5000 of new money.

deposits and hence actual reserves of the "loaned up" banking system by $1000. But with a 20 percent desired reserve ratio applied to demand deposits, the excess reserves of the banking system would be only $800.

However, although the initial change in the supply of money is different in the two transactions, the result is the same: *When the Bank of Canada buys securities (bonds) in the open market, chartered banks' reserves are increased.* When the chartered banks lend out their excess reserves, the nation's money supply will rise. Observe in Figure 13-1 that a $1000 purchase of bonds by the Bank of Canada results in $5000 of additional money, regardless of whether the purchase was made from the banks or the general public.

SELLING SECURITIES

As you may suspect, when the Bank of Canada sells government bonds chartered bank reserves are reduced. Let's see why.

To Chartered Banks　When the Bank of Canada sells government bonds, in the open market to chartered banks:

(a) The Bank of Canada gives up securities that the chartered banks acquire.

(b) Chartered banks pay for these securities by drawing cheques against their deposits—that is, against their reserves—in the Bank of Canada. The Bank of Canada collects these cheques by reducing the chartered banks' reserves accordingly.

The balance sheet changes, again identified by (a) and (b), appear as follows:

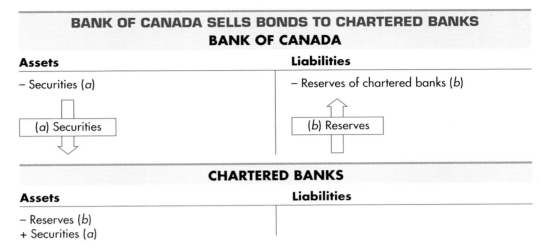

BANK OF CANADA SELLS BONDS TO CHARTERED BANKS

The reduction in chartered bank deposits in the Bank of Canada is indicated by the minus signs before these entries.

To the Public   When the Bank of Canada sells securities *to the public* the outcome is the same. Let's put Mariposa Investments Ltd. on the buying end of government bonds that the Bank of Canada is selling:

(a) The Bank of Canada sells Government of Canada bonds to Mariposa Investments, which pays for these securities by a cheque drawn on the Bank of York.

(b) The Bank of Canada clears this cheque against the Bank of York by reducing York's reserves.

(c) The Bank of York returns the cancelled cheque to Mariposa Investments, reducing the company's demand deposit accordingly.

The balance sheet changes will be as follows:

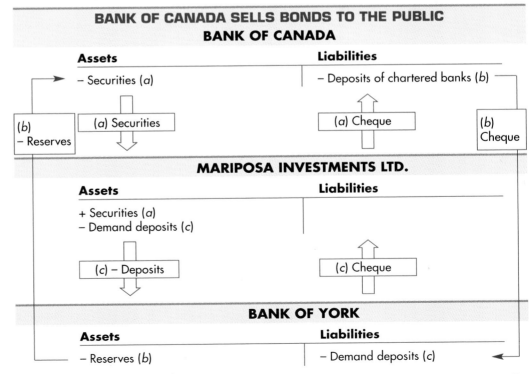

BANK OF CANADA SELLS BONDS TO THE PUBLIC

The Bank of Canada bond sales of $1000 to the chartered banking system reduce the system's actual and excess reserves by $1000. But a $1000 bond sale to the public reduces excess reserves by $800, because demand deposit money is also reduced by $1000 in the sale. Since the chartered banking system has reduced its outstanding deposits by $1000 it need only keep $200 less in reserves.

Whether the Bank of Canada sells securities to the public or to chartered banks, the conclusion is the same: *When the Bank of Canada sells securities in the open market, chartered bank reserves are reduced.*

If all excess reserves are already lent out, this decline in chartered bank reserves will translate into a decline in the nation's money supply. In our example, a $1000 sale of government securities will result in a $5000 decline in the money supply, whether the sale was made to chartered banks or the public. You can verify this by re-examining Figure 13-1 and tracing the effects of *a sale* of a $1000 bond by the Bank of Canada either to chartered banks or the public.

What makes chartered banks and the public willing to sell government securities to, or buy them from, the Bank of Canada? The answer lies in the price of bonds and their interest rates. We know from Chapter 11 that bond prices and interest rates are inversely related. When the Bank of Canada buys government bonds, the demand for them increases. Government bond prices rise and their interest rates decline. The higher bond prices and their lower interest rates prompt banks, securities firms, and individual holders of government bonds to sell them to the Bank of Canada.

When the Bank of Canada sells government bonds, the additional supply of bonds in the bond market lowers bond prices and raises their interest rates, making government bonds attractive purchases for banks and the public.

Switching Government of Canada Deposits

government deposit switching
Action of the Bank of Canada to increase (decrease) backing for money supply by switching government deposits from (to) itself to (from) the chartered banks.

The chartered banks' lending power (and thus money-creating power) is restricted by their demand deposits and reserves. The Bank of Canada can affect the chartered banks' demand deposits and reserves by either depositing or withdrawing funds from the banking system. The Bank of Canada is the federal government's bank, and thus has billions of dollars of government deposits in its possession at any given time. Table 13.1 shows that at the end of 2002, for example, the Bank of Canada had over $1.6 billion in Government of Canada deposits. By **government deposit switching** from chartered banks to itself, the Bank of Canada immediately *reduces* the deposits and the reserves of the chartered banks by the amount of the switched deposits. The effect on the money supply is similar to the open-market operation of selling government bonds.

Alternatively, by switching government deposits from itself to the chartered banks, the Bank of Canada *increases* the deposits and the reserves of the chartered banks, making it possible to increase the nation's money supply. The effect of switching government deposits to the chartered banks will be the same as the Bank of Canada buying bonds on the open market.

The Bank Rate and the Overnight Lending Rate

bank rate
The interest rate that the Bank of Canada charges on advances made to the chartered banks.

One of the functions of a central bank is to be a "lender of last resort," or, as we noted earlier, "the banker's bank." Occasionally, chartered banks have unexpected and immediate needs for additional funds. In such cases, the Bank of Canada will make short-term loans to chartered banks.

When a chartered bank borrows, it gives the Bank of Canada a promissory note (IOU) drawn against itself and secured by acceptable collateral—typically, Canadian government securities. Just as chartered banks charge interest on their loans, so too the Bank of Canada charges interest on loans it grants to chartered banks. The interest rate they charge is called the **bank rate**. The bank rate influences other interest rates in the economy, and thereby indirectly the amount of lending by chartered banks.

In providing the loan, the Bank of Canada increases the reserves of the borrowing chartered bank. All new reserves acquired by borrowing from the Bank of Canada are excess reserves. *In short, borrowing from the Bank of Canada by chartered banks increases the reserves of the chartered banks and enhances their ability to extend credit.*

operating band
The Bank of Canada's 50-basis-point range (one-half of one percentage point) for the overnight lending rate.

overnight lending rate
The interest rate at which major participants in the money market borrow and lend one-day funds to each other.

Since February 1996, the bank rate has been set at the upper end of the Bank of Canada's **operating band** for the **overnight lending rate**, the interest rate at which chartered banks, investment dealers, and other financial market participants borrow and lend funds for one day. The Bank of Canada has a publicized target on the overnight lending rate, and maintains it within a range of one-half of a percentage point (50 basis points) of the target range through its three main monetary policy tools. By lending and borrowing in the overnight market, the Bank of Canada affects the liquidity position of the chartered banks. *(Key Question 2)*

Easy Money and Tight Money

Suppose the Canadian economy faces recession and unemployment. The Bank of Canada decides that an increase in the supply of money is needed to increase aggregate demand and close the recessionary GDP gap. To increase the supply of money, the Bank of Canada must increase the reserves of the chartered banks. How can the Bank of Canada do that?

For recession

- *Buy securities* By purchasing securities on the open market, the Bank of Canada increases chartered bank reserves.
- *Switch government deposits to chartered banks* By switching government deposits to the chartered banks, those deposits instantly create more excess reserves.
- *Reduce the bank rate* By reducing the bank rate the Bank of Canada entices the chartered banks to borrow more reserves from the Bank of Canada.

easy money policy
Bank of Canada actions that increase the money supply to lower interest rates and expand real GDP.

These actions are called an **easy money policy** (or *expansionary monetary policy*). The purpose of an easy monetary policy is to make bank loans less expensive and more available, thereby increasing aggregate demand, output and employment.

Suppose, on the other hand, excessive spending is pushing the economy into an inflationary spiral. Then the Bank of Canada should try to reduce aggregate demand by contracting or reducing the growth of the supply of money. That means reducing the reserves of the chartered banks. How is that done?

inflation hi

- *Sell securities* By selling securities on the open market, the Bank of Canada decreases chartered bank reserves.
- *Switch government deposits from chartered banks* By switching government deposits from the chartered banks into the Bank of Canada, reserves of the chartered banks are immediately reduced.
- *Increase the bank rate* By increasing the bank rate the Bank of Canada discourages the chartered banks from borrowing reserves from the Bank of Canada.

tight money policy
Bank of Canada actions that contract, or restrict, the growth of the nation's money supply for the purpose of reducing or eliminating inflation.

These actions are called a **tight money policy** (or *contractionary monetary policy*). The objective is to restrict the supply of money in order to reduce spending and control inflation.

Relative Importance

Of the three policy instruments, buying and selling securities in the open market is by far the most important. We will see shortly that the Bank of Canada carries out open-market operations on the overnight loans market to achieve the desired interest rate. Open-market operations have the advantage of flexibility and the impact on chartered bank reserves is prompt. And compared to the other policy tools, open-market operations work subtly and less directly. Furthermore, there is virtually no question about the ability of the Bank of Canada to affect chartered bank reserves through the purchase and sale of securities. A glance at the consolidated balance sheet for the Bank of Canada (Table 13-1) reveals very large holdings of treasury bills and other government securities ($30.5 billion). The sale of those securities would reduce chartered bank reserves.

The other tools of monetary policy are of secondary importance to open-market operations. Switching government deposits is used now and then, but on a relatively small scale and only to reinforce what the Bank of Canada in doing on the open market in the overnight loans market. The bank rate is actually a signaling device of the Bank of Canada's stance on monetary policy, which it supports through open market operations.

QUICK REVIEW

- The main objective of monetary policy is to achieve price stability, and thereby help the economy achieve full-employment.

- The Bank of Canada has three instruments of monetary control, each of which works

by changing the amount of reserves in the banking system. They are (a) open-market operations, (b) switching Government of Canada deposits, and (c) the bank rate. Open-market operations are by far the most important of the policy instruments.

13.3   Monetary Policy, Real GDP, and Price Level

So far we have explained only how the Bank of Canada can change the money supply. Now we need to link up the money supply, the interest rate, investment spending, and aggregate demand to see how monetary policy affects the economy. How does monetary policy work?

Cause-Effect Chain: The Transmission Mechanism

The three diagrams in **Figure 13-2 (Key Graph)** will help you understand how monetary policy works toward the goal of achieving price stability, and, indirectly, full employment.

MONEY MARKET

Figure 13-2a represents the money market, in which the demand curve for money and the supply curve for money are brought together. Recall that the total demand for money is made up of transactions demand and asset demand. The transactions demand is directly related to the nominal GDP. The asset demand is inversely related to the interest rate. The interest rate is the opportunity cost of holding money as an asset; the higher the cost, the smaller the amount of money the public wants to hold. The total demand for money D_m is thus inversely related to the interest rate, as indicated in Figure 13-2a. Also, recall that an increase in nominal GDP will shift D_m to the right and a decline in nominal GDP will shift D_m to the left.

This figure also shows three potential money supply curves, S_{m0}, S_{m1}, and S_{m2}. In each case the money supply is shown as a vertical line representing some fixed amount of money determined by the Bank of Canada. While monetary policy helps determine the interest rate, the interest rate does *not* determine the location of the money supply curve.

The equilibrium interest rate is the interest rate at which the amount of money demanded and supplied are equal. With money demand D_m in Figure 13-2a, if the supply of money is $50 billion ($S_{m0}$), the equilibrium interest rate is 10 percent. With a money supply of $75 billion ($S_{m1}$), the interest rate is 8 percent; with a money supply of $100 billion ($S_{m2}$), it is 6 percent.

You know that the real, not the nominal, rate of interest is critical for investment decisions. So here we assume Figure 13-2a portrays real interest rates.

INVESTMENT

These 10 percent, 8 percent, and 6 percent real interest rates are carried rightward to the investment demand curve of Figure 13-2b. This curve shows the inverse relationship between the interest rate—the cost of borrowing to invest—and the amount of investment spending. At the 10 percent interest rate it will be profitable for the nation's businesses to invest $15 billion; at 8 percent, $20 billion; at 6 percent, $25 billion.

Key Graph

FIGURE 13-2 Monetary Policy and Equilibrium GDP

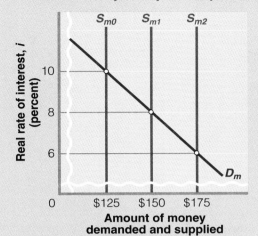

(a) The money market

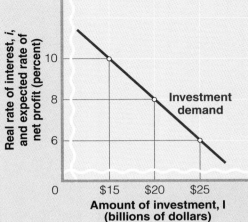

(b) Investment demand

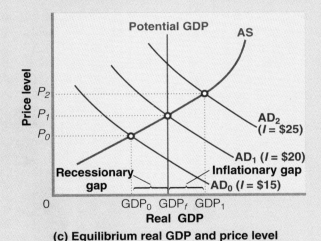

(c) Equilibrium real GDP and price level

An expansionary monetary policy will lower the interest rate, increase the investment component of aggregate demand, and increase the equilibrium level of GDP. Conversely, a contractionary monetary policy will raise the rate of interest, reduce the investment component of aggregate demand, and restrain demand-pull inflation.

Quick Quiz

recession

1. **The ultimate objective of an easy money policy is depicted by**
   a. a decrease in the money supply from S_{m2} to S_{m1}.
   b. a reduction of the interest rate from 8 percent to 6 percent.
   c. an increase in investment from $20 billion to $25 billion.
   d. an increase in real GDP from GDP_0 to GDP_f.

   inflation

2. **A successful tight money policy is shown as a shift in the money supply curve from**
   a. S_{m2} to S_{m1}, an increase in investment from $20 billion to $25 billion, and a decline in aggregate demand from AD_2 to AD_1.
   b. S_{m0} to S_{m1}, an increase in investment from $20 billion to $25 billion, and an increase in real GDP from GDP_0 to GDP_f.
   c. S_{m2} to S_{m1}, a decrease in investment from $25 billion to $20 billion, and a decline in the price level from P_2 to P_1.
   d. S_{m2} to S_{m1}, a decrease in investment from $25 billion to $20 billion, and an increase in aggregate demand from AD_1 to AD_2.

3. **The Bank of Canada could increase the money supply from S_{m0} to S_{m1} by**
   a. increasing the bank rate.
   b. reducing taxes.
   c. buying government securities in the open market.
   d. selling government securities in the open market.

4. **If the spending-income multiplier is 4 in the economy depicted, an increase in the money supply from $125 billion to $150 billion will**
   a. shift the aggregate demand curve rightward by $20 billion.
   b. increase real GDP by $25 billion.
   c. increase real GDP by $100 billion.
   d. shift the aggregate demand curve leftward by $5 billion.

ANSWERS: 1. d.; 2. c; 3. c; 4. a.

Changes in the interest rate mainly affect the investment component of total spending.

Changes in the interest rate mainly affect the investment component of total spending, although they also affect spending on durable consumers goods (such as autos and furniture) that are purchased on credit. The impact of changing interest rates on investment spending is great because of the large cost and long-term nature of capital purchases. Capital equipment, factory buildings, and warehouses are tremendously expensive. In absolute terms, interest charges on funds borrowed for these purchases are considerable.

Similarly, the interest cost on a house purchased on a long-term contract is very large: A one-half percentage point change in the interest rate could amount to a difference of thousands of dollars in the total cost of a home.

Also, changes in the interest rate may affect investment spending by changing the relative attractiveness of purchases of capital equipment versus purchases of bonds. In purchasing capital goods, the interest rate is the *cost* of borrowing the funds to make the investment. In purchasing bonds, the interest rate is the *return* on the financial investment. If the interest rate increases, the cost of buying capital goods increases while the return on bonds increases. Businesses are then more inclined to use business saving to buy securities than to buy equipment. Conversely, a drop in the interest rate makes purchases of capital goods relatively more attractive than bond ownership.

In brief, the impact of changing interest rates is mainly on investment (and, through that, on aggregate demand, output, employment, and price level). Moreover, as Figure 13-2b shows, investment spending varies inversely with the interest rate.

EQUILIBRIUM GDP

Figure 13-2c shows the impact of our three interest rates and corresponding levels of investment spending on aggregate demand. As noted, aggregate demand curve AD_0 is associated with the $15 billion level of investment, AD_1 with investment of $20 billion, and AD_2 with investment of $25 billion. That is, investment spending is one of the determinants of aggregate demand. Other things being equal, the greater this investment spending, the farther to the right lies the aggregate demand curve.

Suppose the money supply in Figure 13-2a is $125 billion ($S_{m0}$), producing an equilibrium interest rate of 10 percent. In Figure 13-2b we see this 10 percent interest rate will bring forth $15 billion of investment spending. This $15 billion of investment spending joins with consumption spending, net exports, and government spending to yield aggregate demand curve AD_0 in Figure 13-2c. The equilibrium levels of real output and prices are GDP_0 and P_0, as determined by the intersection of AD_0 and the aggregate supply curve AS.

To test your understanding of these relationships, you should explain why each of the other two levels of money supply in Figure 13-2a results in a different interest rate, level of investment, aggregate demand curve, and equilibrium real output and price level.

Effects of an Easy Money Policy

We have assumed the money supply is $125 billion ($S_m$) in Figure 13-2a. Because the resulting real output GDP_0 in Figure 13-2c is far below the full-employment output, GDP_f, the economy must be experiencing substantial unemployment, or a recessionary gap. The Bank of Canada therefore should institute an *expansionary monetary policy* (Column 1 of Table 13-2).

[handwritten: → B17 but in word]

TABLE 13-2	Monetary Policy: The Transmission Mechanism	
(1) Easy money policy	**(2) Tight money policy**	
Problem: Recessionary gap ↓	Problem: Inflationary gap ↓	
Bank of Canada buys bonds, switches government deposits into the chartered banks, or lowers the bank rate ↓	Bank of Canada sells bonds, switches government deposits out of the chartered banks, or raises the bank rate ↓	
Excess reserves increase ↓	Excess reserves decrease ↓	
Money supply rises ↓	Money supply falls ↓	
Interest rate falls ↓	Interest rate rises ↓	
Investment spending increases ↓	Investment spending decreases ↓	
Aggregate demand increases ↓	Aggregate demand decreases ↓	
Real GDP rises by a multiple of the increase in investment	Inflation declines	

[handwritten: P349 Fiscal Policy]

To increase the money supply the Bank of Canada will take one or both of the following actions: (1) buy government securities from chartered banks and the public in the open market; (2) switch government deposits to the chartered banks. The intended outcome will be an increase in excess reserves in the chartered banking system. Because excess reserves are the basis on which chartered banks can earn profit by lending and thereby expand the money supply, the nation's money supply likely will rise. An increase in the money supply will lower the interest rate, increasing investment, aggregate demand, and equilibrium GDP.

For example, an increase in the money supply from $125 to $150 billion ($S_{m0}$ to S_{m1}) will reduce the interest rate from 10 percent to 8 percent, as indicated in Figure 13-2a, and increase investment from $15 billion to $20 billion, as shown in Figure 13-2b. This $5 billion increase in investment spending will shift the aggregate demand curve rightward by more than the increase in investment because of the multiplier effect. If the open economy multiplier is 2, the $5 billion increase in investment will shift the AD curve rightward by $10 billion (= 2 × $5 billion) at each price level. Specifically, aggregate demand will shift from AD_0 to AD_1, as shown in Figure 13-2c. This rightward shift in the aggregate demand curve will increase from GDP_0 to the desired full-employment output at GDP_f, thereby closing the recessionary gap.

You should note that if the Bank of Canada chooses not to pursue an expansionary monetary policy to close a recessionary gap, the lower price level P_0, brought about by a drop in aggregate demand, will eventually lead to a fall in input prices (especially wages), causing the short-run aggregate supply curve to shift to the right until the gap has been closed (you should pencil in the new short-run aggregate supply curve). Recall that such a supply response could take years, needlessly prolonging a recession.

Column 1 of Table 13-2 summarizes the chain of events associated with an easy money policy.

Effects of a Tight Money Policy

Now let's assume the money supply and interest rate are $175 billion ($S_{m2}$) in Figure 13-2a. This results in an interest rate of 6 percent, investment spending of $25 billion, and aggregate demand of AD_2. As you can see in Figure 13-2c, we have depicted an inflationary gap. Aggregate demand AD_2 is excessive relative to the economy's full-employment level of real output GDP_f. To rein in spending, the Bank of Canada will institute a *contractionary monetary policy*.

The Bank of Canada will undertake one or both of the following actions: (1) sell government bonds to chartered banks and to the public in the open market; (2) switch government deposits out of the chartered banks. Banks then will discover their reserves are too low to meet possible cash withdrawals and therefore will need to reduce their demand deposits by refraining from issuing new loans as old loans are paid back. This will shrink the money supply and increase the interest rate. The higher interest rate will discourage investment, decreasing aggregate demand and closing the inflationary gap.

If the Bank of Canada reduces the money supply from \$175 billion to \$150 billion (S_{m2} to S_{m1} in Figure 13-2a), the interest rate will increase from 6 percent to 8 percent and investment will decline from \$25 billion to \$20 billion (Figure 13-2b). This \$5 billion decrease in investment, bolstered by the multiplier process, will shift the aggregate demand curve leftward from AD_2 to AD_1. For example, with an open economy multiplier of 2, the aggregate demand curve will shift leftward by \$10 billion (= 2 × \$5 billion of investment) at each price level. This leftward shift of the aggregate demand curve will eliminate the excessive spending and thus the inflationary gap.

If the Bank of Canada chooses not to embark on a contractionary policy to close the inflationary gap, the new price level P_2 will eventually lead the short-run aggregate supply curve to shift left until the economy is back to its natural rate of unemployment (you should pencil in the new short-run aggregate supply curve). As noted previously, such a supply response takes time, even if an inflationary gap will tend to resolve itself faster than a recessionary gap.

Column 2 of Table 13-2 summarizes the cause-effect chain of a tight money policy. *(Key Question 3)*

Monetary Policy in Action

Monetary policy has become the dominant component of Canadian national stabilization policy. It has two key advantages over fiscal policy:

- Speed and flexibility, and
- Isolation from political pressure

Compared with fiscal policy, monetary policy can be quickly altered. Recall that government deliberations can delay the application of fiscal policy. In contrast, the Bank of Canada can buy or sell securities from day to day and thus affect the money supply and interest rates almost immediately.

Also, because the Governor of the Bank of Canada is appointed and serves a 7-year term, the Bank of Canada is relatively isolated from lobbying and need not worry about being popular with voters. Thus, the Bank of Canada, more readily than the federal government, can engage in politically unpopular policies (higher interest rates) that may be necessary for the long-term health of the economy. For example, John Crow, the Governor of the Bank of Canada from 1987 to 1994, pursued what many vocal critics considered a much too restrictive monetary policy in the late 1980s and into the mid-1990s, even though many MPs in Parliament at the time disagreed strongly with his monetary policy stance. Although John Crow was not re-appointed at the end of his term, he was able to carry out the monetary policy he thought best for the Canadian economy without political pressure. Moreover, monetary policy is a subtler and more politically conservative measure than fiscal policy. Changes in government spending directly affect the allocation of resources, and changes in taxes can have extensive political ramifications. Because monetary policy works more subtly, it is more politically palatable.

Focus on the Overnight Lending Rate

Up to February 1996, the bank rate was set at one-quarter of a percentage point above the yield on the government three-month Treasury bill, set after a weekly auction. Since then the Bank of Canada has set the bank rate based on the upper limit of its operating band for the overnight lending rate. The operating band is set from time to time by the Bank of Canada, depending on the expected future performance of the Canadian economy. An increase in the upper limit of the operating band (for example, 4.5 percent to 5 percent) would signal "tighter" monetary policy is coming, but statements that it intends to reduce the upper limit of the operating band (for example, 3.0 percent to 2.5 percent) foretell an "easier" monetary policy. Such changes would be reflected in the bank rate, which in turn would affect interest rates in general. In Figure 13-3, observe that changes in the prime interest rate—the interest rate banks charge their most creditworthy customers—generally track changes in the bank rate.

The Bank of Canada does not set either the overnight lending rate or the prime rate; each is established by the interaction of lenders and borrowers. But because the Bank of Canada can change the supply of excess reserves in the banking system and then the money supply, it normally can obtain the short-term interest rate it desires. In Figure 13-3, note how closely the Bank of Canada's target overnight lending rate tracks the actual overnight lending rate. To increase the rate on overnight lending, the Bank of Canada can sell bonds in the open market or switch government deposits out of the banking system, lessening the excess reserves available for overnight lending in the overnight market. This decreased supply of excess reserves in the market increases the interest rate on overnight financing. In addition, reduced excess reserves decrease the amount of bank lending and hence the amount of deposit money. We know that declines in the supply of money lead to increases in interest rates in general, including the prime interest rate.

In contrast, if the Bank of Canada wants to reduce the interest rate on overnight loans, it can buy bonds from the chartered banks and the public. The supply of reserves in the overnight market increases and the overnight interest rate declines. The money supply rises because the increased supply of excess reserves leads to greater lending and creation of deposit money. As a result, interest rates in general fall, including the prime interest rate.

In recent years the overnight loans market has been the primary vehicle through which the Bank of Canada has implemented monetary policy. It can enter the overnight loans market through a *special purchase and resale agreement (SPRA)*, a transaction in which the Bank of Canada offers to purchase Government of Canada securities with an agreement to sell them back at a predetermined price the next business day. As you know by now, when the Bank of Canada buys bonds it puts downward pressure on short-term interest rates. Through SPRAs the Bank of Canada reinforces its target overnight rate.

when the r market is rising

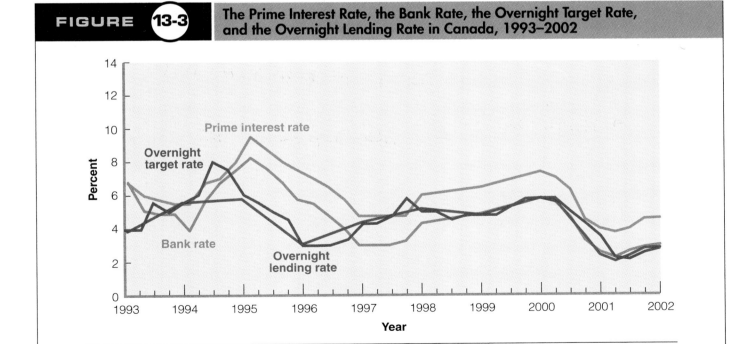

FIGURE 13-3

The Prime Interest Rate, the Bank Rate, the Overnight Target Rate, and the Overnight Lending Rate in Canada, 1993–2002

Source: Bank of Canada

The prime interest rate rises and falls with changes in the bank rate, the overnight target rate, and the overnight lending rate.

when market is going down ↓

Or the Bank of Canada enters a *sale and repurchase agreement (SRA)*, in which it offers to sell Government of Canada securities to designated counterparties with an agreement to buy them back at a predetermined price the next business day. Selling bonds puts upward pressure on interest rates. The Bank of Canada would enter into SRAs when it wants to see interest rates rise. Figure 13-3 shows that the bank rate and the prime interest rate mirror the Bank of Canada's overnight target rate and the overnight lending rate. *(Key Question 5)*

Recent Monetary Policy

Interest will high.

In the early 1990s, the restrictive monetary policy made the economic recovery after the recession of 1991–1992 relatively slow. But the continuing easing by the Bank of Canada after 1995 helped the Canadian economy grow at a healthy clip in the second half of the 1990s. By 2000 the Canadian unemployment rate had declined to 6.8 percent—the lowest rate in 25 years. To counter potential inflation during that strong expansion, the Bank of Canada began to reduce reserves in the banking system to raise the interest rate to keep inflation under control. The overnight rate was raised from a low of 3.0 percent in early 1997, to 5.75 percent in September 1998. The financial crisis in the

Interest ↓

Pacific Rim pressured the Bank of Canada to ease monetary policy late in 1998 and into mid 1999. But the vigorous Canadian economy and a stock market bubble in the making led the Bank of Canada to raise the overnight rate from 3.60 percent in May of 1999, to 5.75 percent by the end of 2000 to slow down the economy and ward off potential inflationary pressures.

Although inflation remained low in the late 1990s, in the last quarter of 2000 the economy began to slow. The Bank of Canada responded by cutting interest rates early in 2001. As it became evident that investment spending was dropping sharply, the Bank of Canada began cutting rates aggressively. The terrorist attack on September 11, 2001 gave the Bank of Canada more reasons to continue reducing interest rates. The overnight rate went from 5.75 percent in January 2001 to 2.0 percent by early 2002.

In 2002 the Canadian economy began to expand again and the Bank of Canada responded by increasing the overnight rate to 2.75 percent by the end of the year. Despite the increase in interest rates in 2002 the Canadian economy did very well, adding more than 500,000 jobs, and with GDP expanding at an annual rate of 3.4 percent.

Economists credit the Bank of Canada's adroit use of monetary policy as one of a number of factors that helped the Canadian economy achieve and maintain the rare combination of price stability and strong economic growth that occurred between 1996 and 2000. The Bank of Canada also deserves high marks for helping to keep the slowdown of 2001 relatively mild, particularly in view of the adverse economic impacts of the terrorists' attacks of September 11, 2001 in the United States, our largest trading partner, and the steep stock market drop in 2001–2002.

maybe multiple choice

13.4   Problems and Complications

Despite its recent successes in Canada, monetary policy has certain limitations and faces real-world complications.

Lags Monetary policy is hindered by a recognition lag and an operational lag (but not an administrative lag). Because of monthly variations in economic activity and changes in the price level, it may take the Bank of Canada some time to recognize that the economy is receding or the rate of inflation is rising. And once the Bank of Canada acts, it may take up to two years for interest rate changes to have their full impacts on investment, aggregate demand, real GDP, and the price level. These two lags complicate the timing of monetary policy.

velocity of money
The number of times per year the average dollar in the money supply is spent for final goods and services.

Changes in Velocity Total expenditures can be regarded as the money supply multiplied by the **velocity of money**—the number of times per year the average dollar is spent on goods and services. If the money supply is $150 billion and velocity is 4, total spending will be $600 billion (= $150 billion ×4). But if velocity is 3, total expenditures will be only $450 billion (= $150 billion × 3).

Velocity may move counter to changes in the money supply in some circumstances, frustrating monetary policy. During inflation, when the Bank of Canada restrains the money supply, velocity may increase. Conversely, during recession, when the Bank of Canada takes measures to increase the money supply, velocity may fall.

Velocity might behave this way because of the asset demand for money. An easy money policy, for example, means an increase in the supply of money relative to its demand and therefore a reduction in the interest rate [Figure 13-3(a)]. But the public will hold larger idle money balances when the interest rate (the opportunity cost of holding money as an asset) is lower. This means dollars will move from households to businesses and back again less rapidly. In short, the velocity of money will decline. A reverse sequence of events may cause a tight money policy to induce an increase in velocity. For monetary policy to work, the Bank of Canada may have to apply it quite vigorously in order to swamp these potentially offsetting changes in velocity.

Cyclical Asymmetry Monetary policy may be highly effective in slowing expansions and controlling inflation, but less reliable in pushing the economy from a severe recession. Economists say that monetary policy may suffer from *cyclical asymmetry*.

If pursued vigorously, a tight money policy could deplete chartered banking reserves to the point where banks were forced to reduce the volume of loans. That would mean a contraction of the money supply, higher interest rates, and reduced aggregate demand.

But, it cannot be certain of achieving its goal when it pursues an expansionary monetary policy. An expansionary monetary policy suffers from a "You can lead a horse to water, but you cannot make it drink" problem. The Bank of Canada can create excess reserves, but it cannot guarantee that

---

 Consider This

Asymmetry of Monetary Policy

In the late 1990s and early 2000s, the central bank of Japan used an easy money policy to reduce real interest rates to zero. Even with "interest-free" loans available most consumers and businesses did not borrow and spend more. Japan's severe recession continued, and the Japanese government turned to expansionary fiscal policy to stimulate spending. (The Japanese economy began to expand slowly in 1999 but stalled again in 2000.)

The Japanese circumstance illustrates the possible *asymmetry* of monetary policy, which economists have likened to "pulling versus pushing on a string." A string may be effective at pulling something back to a desirable spot, but it is ineffective at pushing it toward a desired location.

So it is with monetary policy, say some economists. Monetary policy can readily *pull* the aggregate demand curve to the left, reducing demand-pull inflation. There is no limit on how much a central bank can restrict a nation's money supply and hike interest rates. Eventually, a sufficiently tight money policy will reduce aggregate demand and inflation.

But during severe recession, participants in the economy may be highly pessimistic about the future. If so, an easy money policy may not be able to *push* the aggregate demand curve to the right, increasing real GDP. The central bank can produce excess reserves in the banking system by purchasing government securities and lowering the bank rate. But chartered banks may not be able to find willing borrowers for those excess reserves, no matter how low interest rates fall. Instead of borrowing and spending, consumers and businesses may be more intent on reducing debt and increasing saving in preparation for expected worse times ahead. If so, monetary policy will be ineffective. Using it under those circumstances will be much like pushing on a string.

Question: Visit the OECD website at http:// www.oecd.org/. Click "Statistical Portal", then go to the "Quarterly Growth Rate of GDP". Compare Japan's growth rate with Canada, the U.S., Germany, and France. Have the years of low interest rates in Japan finally stimulated growth, or is the central Bank of Japan still pushing on a string?

the chartered banks will actually make the added loans and thus increase the supply of money. If chartered banks seek liquidity and are unwilling to lend, the efforts of the Bank of Canada will be of little avail. Similarly, businesses and consumers can frustrate the intentions of the Bank of Canada by not borrowing excess reserves. And the public may use money paid to them through Bank of Canada sales of Canadian securities to pay off existing bank loans.

Furthermore, a severe recession may so undermine business confidence that the investment demand curve shifts to the left and frustrates an expansionary monetary policy. That is what happened in Japan in the 1990s and early 2000s. Although its central bank drove the real interest rate to zero percent, investment spending remained low and the Japanese economy stayed mired in recession. In fact, **deflation**—a fall in the price level—occurred. The Japanese experience reminds us that monetary policy is not an assured cure for the business cycle.

deflation
A decline in the economy's price level.

Inflation Targeting

inflation targeting
A Bank of Canada policy of maintaining the inflation rate within a specific range, currently 1–3 percent.

Some economists claim that the Bank of Canada's adoption of **inflation targeting**—the annual statement of a target range of inflation, currently 1–3 percent, for the economy is to be credited for its recent successes. The Bank of Canada now explains to the public how each monetary action fits within its overall strategy. If the Bank of Canada misses its target, it explains what went wrong. So inflation targeting has increased the "transparency" (openness) of monetary policy and increased the Bank of Canada's accountability. Proponents of inflation targeting say that, along with increasing transparency and accountability, it has focused the Canada's central bank on what should be its main mission: controlling inflation. They say that an explicit commitment to price-level stability has created more certainty for households and firms about future product and input prices and create greater output stability. The setting and meeting of an inflation target has also achieved its important subsidiary goals of full employment and economic growth. Several other countries have adopted inflation targeting, including New Zealand, Sweden, and the United Kingdom.

But many economists are unconvinced by the arguments for inflation targeting. They say that Canada's overall success with inflation targeting has come at a time in which inflationary pressures, in general, were weak. The truer test will occur under more severe economic conditions. Critics of inflation targeting say that it assigns too narrow a role for the Bank of Canada. They do not want to limit the Bank of Canada's discretion to adjust the money supply and interest rates to smooth the business cycle, independent of meeting a specific inflation target. Those who oppose inflation targeting point to the recent success of the central bank in the U.S., the Federal Reserve, which does not have specific inflation targets, but has followed sound principles of monetary policy, sometimes referred to as the Taylor Rule (the subject of this chapter's The Last Word).

QUICK REVIEW

- The Bank of Canada is engaging in an expansionary monetary policy when it increases the money supply to reduce interest rates and increase investment spending and real GDP; it is engaging in a contractionary monetary policy when it reduces the money supply to increase interest rates and reduce investment spending and inflation.

- The main strengths of monetary policy are (a) speed and flexibility and (b) political acceptability; its main weaknesses are (a) potential reduced effectiveness during recession and (b) the possibility that changes in velocity will offset it.

- The Bank of Canada communicates changes in monetary policy by announcing changes in the operating band for the overnight loans rate.

- In the past two decades, the Bank of Canada has quite successfully used alternate tight and easy money policies to stabilize the economy.

13.5　Monetary Policy and the International Economy

In Chapter 9 we noted that linkages among the economies of the world complicate domestic fiscal policy. These linkages extend to monetary policy as well.

Net Export Effect

As we saw in Chapter 9, an expansionary fiscal policy (financed by government borrowing) may increase the domestic interest rate because the government competes with the private sector in obtaining loans. The higher interest rate causes the Canadian dollar to appreciate in the foreign exchange market. So imports rise and exports fall and the resulting decline in net exports weakens the stimulus of the expansionary fiscal policy. This is the so-called *net export effect* of fiscal policy.

TABLE 13-3	**Monetary Policy and the Net Export Effect**
(1) **Easy money policy**	**(2)** **Tight money policy**
Problem: recession, slow growth ↓	Problem: inflation ↓
Easy money policy (lower interest rate) ↓	Tight money policy (higher interest rate) ↓
Decreased foreign demand for dollars ↓	Increased foreign demand for dollars ↓
Dollar depreciates ↓	Dollar appreciates ↓
Net exports increase (aggregate demand increases, strengthening the expansionary monetary policy)	Net exports decrease (aggregate demand decreases, strengthening the contractionary monetary policy)

Will an easy money policy have a similar effect? The answer is no. As outlined in column 1, Table 13-3, an easy money or expansionary monetary policy does indeed produce a net export effect, but its direction is opposite that of an expansionary fiscal policy. An easy money policy in, say, Canada, reduces the domestic interest rate. The lower interest rate discourages the inflow of financial capital to Canada. The demand for dollars in foreign exchange markets falls, causing the Canadian dollar to depreciate in value. It takes more dollars to buy, say, a Japanese yen or a euro. All foreign goods become more expensive to Canadian residents, and Canadian goods become cheaper to foreigners. Canadian imports thus fall, and Canadian exports rise; so Canada's net exports increase. As a result, aggregate expenditures and equilibrium GDP expand in Canada.

Conclusion: In contrast to an expansionary fiscal policy that reduces net exports, an expansionary monetary policy *increases* net exports and thus strengthens monetary policy. The depreciation of the Canadian dollar that results from the lower interest rate means that Canadian net exports rise along with domestic investment. Similarly, the net export effect strengthens a tight monetary policy. To see how this happens, follow through the analysis in column 2, Table 13-3.

Macroeconomic Stability and the Trade Balance

Assume that, in addition to domestic macroeconomic stability, a widely held economic goal is that Canada should balance its exports and imports on goods. That is, Canadian net exports should be zero. In simple terms, Canada wants to "pay its own way" in international trade by earning from its exports an amount of money sufficient to finance its imports.

Consider column 1 in Table 13-3 once again, but now suppose Canada initially has a very large balance-of-international-trade *deficit*, which means its imports exceed its exports and so it is *not* paying its way in world trade. By following through the cause-effect chain in column 1, we find that an expansionary monetary policy lowers the international value of the dollar and so that Canadian exports increase and Canadian imports decline. This increase in net exports works to correct the initial balance-of-trade deficit.

Conclusion: *The easy money policy that is appropriate for the alleviation of unemployment and sluggish growth is compatible with the goal of correcting a balance-of-trade deficit.* Similarly, if the initial problem was a Canadian trade surplus, a *tight* money policy would tend to resolve that surplus.

Now consider column 2 in Table 13-3 and assume again that Canada has a large balance-of-trade deficit. In using a tight money policy to restrain inflation, the Bank of Canada would cause net

Key Graph

FIGURE 13-4 The AD-AS Theory of the Price Level, Real Output, and Stabilization Policy

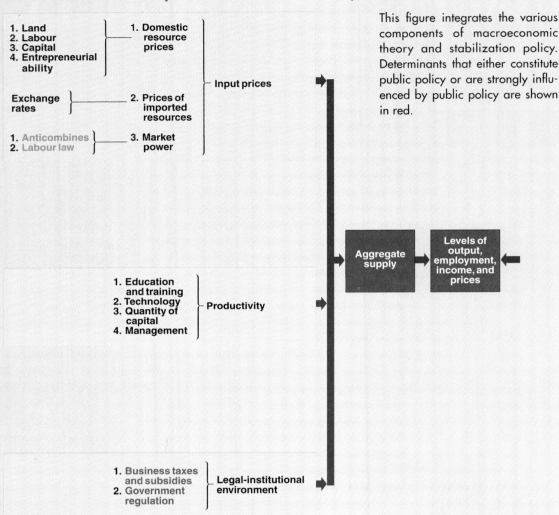

This figure integrates the various components of macroeconomic theory and stabilization policy. Determinants that either constitute public policy or are strongly influenced by public policy are shown in red.

Quick Quiz

1. All else equal, an increase in domestic resource availability will:
   a. increase input prices, reduce aggregate supply, and increase real output.
   b. raise labour productivity, reduce interest rates, and lower the international value of the dollar.
   c. increase net exports, increase investment, and reduce aggregate demand.
   d. reduce input prices, increase aggregate supply, and increase real output.

2. All else equal, an easy money policy during a recession will:
   a. lower the interest rate, increase investment, and reduce net exports.
   b. lower the interest rate, increase investment, and increase aggregate demand.
   c. increase the interest rate, increase investment, and reduce net exports.
   d. reduce productivity, aggregate supply, and real output.

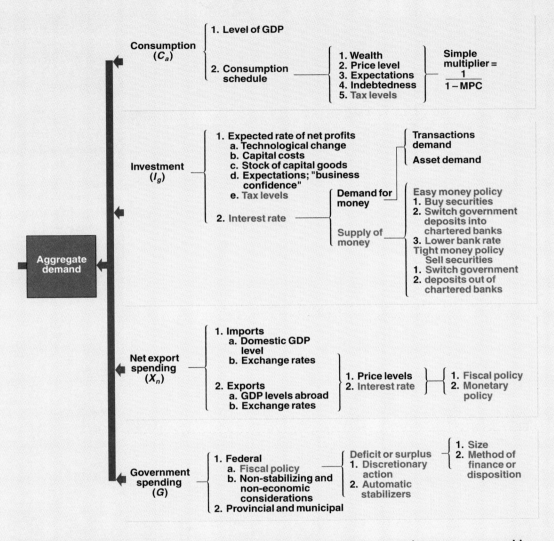

3. **A personal income tax cut, combined with a reduction in corporate income and excise taxes, would:**
   a. increase consumption, investment, aggregate demand, and aggregate supply.
   b. reduce productivity, raise input prices, and reduce aggregate supply.
   c. increase government spending, reduce net exports, and increase aggregate demand.
   d. increase the supply of money, reduce interest rates, increase investment, and expand real output.

4. **An appreciation of the dollar would:**
   a. reduce the price of imported resources, lower input prices, and increase aggregate supply.
   b. increase net exports and aggregate demand.
   c. increase aggregate supply and aggregate demand.
   d. reduce consumption, investment, net export spending, and government spending.

ANSWERS: 1. d; 2. b; 3. a; 4. a

exports to decrease—Canadian exports would fall and imports would rise. That would mean a larger trade deficit.

Conclusion: *A tight money policy used to alleviate inflation conflicts with the goal of correcting a balance-of-trade deficit.* However, if the initial problem were a trade surplus, a tight money policy would help to resolve it.

Overall we find that an easy money policy alleviates a trade deficit and aggravates a trade surplus; a tight money policy alleviates a trade surplus and aggravates a trade deficit. The point is that certain combinations of circumstances create conflicts or tradeoffs between the use of monetary policy to achieve domestic stability and the realization of a balance in the nation's international trade. *(Key Question 7)*

The "Big Picture"

Figure 13-6 (Key Graph) brings together the analytical and policy aspects of macroeconomics discussed in this and the eight preceding chapters. This "big picture" shows how the many concepts and principles discussed relate to one another and how they constitute a coherent theory of what determines the level of resource use in a market economy.

Study this diagram and you will see that the levels of output, employment, income, and prices all result from the interaction of aggregate supply and aggregate demand. In particular, note those items—shown in red—that constitute, or are strongly influenced by, public policy.

THE LASTword — The Taylor Rule: Could a Robot Replace the Bank of Canada?

Macroeconomist John Taylor of Stanford University calls for a new monetary rule that would institutionalize appropriate central bank policy responses to changes in real output and inflation.

There is an ongoing discussion among economists of "rules versus discretion" in implementing monetary policy. "Rules" are associated with a passive monetary policy, for example, a rule which requires a central bank to expand the money supply at a fixed annual rate regardless of the state of the economy, as was argued by the so-called monetarist, Milton Friedman. "Discretion," on the other hand, is associated with an active monetary policy in which the central bank changes interest rates in response to actual or anticipated changes in the economy.

Economist John Taylor has put a new twist on the "rules versus discretion" debate by suggesting a hybrid policy rule that dictates the precise active monetary actions a central bank should take when changes in the economy occur. This so-called Taylor rule combines passive monetary policy, and the view that active monetary policy is a useful tool for taming inflation and limiting recession. The Taylor rule holds that monetary policy should respond to changes in both real GDP and inflation, not simply inflation, as the Bank of Canada appears to be following. The key adjustment instrument is the interest rate, not the money supply.

The Taylor rule has three parts:

- If real GDP rises 1 percent above potential GDP, the Bank of Canada should raise the interest rate of overnight loans, relative to the current inflation rate, by 0.5 percent.

- If inflation rises by 1 percent above its target rate, then the Bank of Canada should raise the overnight rate by 0.5 percent relative to the inflation rate.

- When real GDP is equal to potential GDP and inflation is equal to its target rate of 2 percent, the overnight loans rate should remain at about 4 percent, which would imply a real interest rate of 2 percent.[1]

Taylor has neither suggested nor implied that a robot, programmed with the Taylor rule, should replace central banks. A central bank's discretion to override the rule (or "contingency plan for policy") would be retained, but it would have to explain why its policies diverged from the rule. So, the rule would remove the "mystery" associated with monetary policy and increase a central bank's accountability. Also, says Taylor, if used consistently the rule would enable market participants to predict central bank behaviour, which would increase credibility and reduce uncertainty.

Critics of the Taylor rule admit it is more in tune with countercyclical central bank policy than simple monetary rule. But they see no reason to limit central bank discretion in adjusting interest rates as it sees fit to achieve stabilization and growth. Monetary policy may be more art than science.

Since the early 1990s the Bank of Canada's main preoccupation has been, officially at least, to target only the rate of inflation at between 1 and 3 percent per year, which it claims indirectly promotes full employment and economic growth. Thus, it would appear that the Bank of Canada has pursued a kind of passive rule with only one main aim: price stability. But in reality, the Bank of Canada has used much more discretion than it would like to admit, in line with Taylor's rule. For example, during the course of 2001 it pursued an aggressive policy of lowering short term interest rates, even though the CPI during that year averaged 2.7 percent, very close to the upper ceiling of 3 percent that would ordinarily have triggered the Bank of Canada to increase its target overnight loans rate, not lower it. The Bank of Canada was concerned by the rapid slowdown of the American economy during 2001, which suffered a mild recession. Given that the U.S. is Canada's largest trading partner, a slowdown of its economy would mean that our exports to the U.S. would suffer, with negative consequences to Canada's employment and growth. It appears that the Bank of Canada has taken notice of John Taylor's rule, even if it does not officially say so.

[1] John Taylor, Inflation, Unemployment, and Monetary Policy (Cambridge, MA, MIT Press, 1998, pp. 33–37).

CHAPTER SUMMARY

13.1 FUNCTIONS OF THE BANK OF CANADA

- The major functions of the Bank of Canada are to (a) be a lender of last resort (banker's bank) to the chartered banks, (b) supply the economy with paper currency, (c) act as fiscal agent for the federal government, (d) supervise the operations of chartered banks (together with the Department of Finance), and (e) regulate the supply of money.

- The Bank of Canada's two major assets are government of Canada securities and advances to chartered banks. Its three major liabilities are chartered bank reserves, government of Canada deposits, and notes in circulation.

13.2 GOALS AND TOOLS OF MONETARY POLICY

- The goal of monetary policy is price stability. Full-employment and economic growth are secondary objectives that follow directly from price stability.

- As regards to monetary policy, the most important assets of the Bank of Canada are Government of Canada bonds and Treasury bills.

- The three instruments of monetary policy are (a) open-market operations, (b) switching of government deposits, and (c) the bank rate. Open-market operations is the instrument used most often.

13.3 MONETARY POLICY, REAL GDP, AND PRICE LEVEL

- Monetary policy operates through a complex cause-effect chain: (a) policy decisions affect chartered bank reserves; (b) changes in reserves affect the supply of money; (c) changes in the money supply alter the interest rate; (d) changes in the interest rate affect investment; (e) changes in investment affect aggregate demand; (f) changes in aggregate demand affect equilibrium real GDP and the price level. Table 13-3 draws together all the basic notions relevant to the use of monetary policy.

- The advantages of monetary policy include its flexibility and political acceptability. The Bank of Canada communicates its changes in monetary policy via announcements concerning its target for the overnight loans rate. When it deems necessary, the Bank of Canada uses open-market operations to change that rate, which is the interest rate banks charge one another on overnight loans of excess reserves. Interest rates in general, including the prime interest rate, rise and fall with the overnight loans rate. The prime interest rate is the benchmark rate that banks use as a reference rate for a wide range of interest rates on short-term loans to businesses and individuals.

- In the recent past, the Bank of Canada has adroitly used monetary policy to hold inflation in check as the economy boomed, avoided recession in the economic slowdown of 2001, and hastened economic recovery. The Bank of Canada's policy of *inflation targeting* appears to have been successful, although some critics believe it unnecessarily restricts the central bank's options in smoothing out economic fluctuations.

13.4 PROBLEMS AND COMPLICATIONS

- Monetary policy has some limitations and potential problems: (a) Recognition and operation lags complicate the timing of monetary policy. (b) Changes in the velocity of money may partially offset policy-instigated changes in the supply of money. (c) In a severe recession, the reluctance by firms to borrow and spend on capital goods may limit the effectiveness of an expansionary monetary policy.

13.5 MONETARY POLICY AND THE INTERNATIONAL ECONOMY

- The effect of an easy money policy on domestic GDP is strengthened by the increase in net exports that results from a lower domestic interest rate. Likewise, a tight money policy is strengthened by a decline in net exports. Depending on the situation, there may be a conflict or complementarity between the effect of monetary policy on domestic and international policy goals.

TERMS AND CONCEPTS

STUDY QUESTIONS

1. Use chartered bank and Bank of Canada balance sheets to demonstrate the impact of the following transactions on chartered bank reserves: (a) The Bank of Canada purchases securities from dealers. (b) The Bank of Canada makes an advance to a chartered bank.

2. **KEY QUESTION**   In the table below you will find simplified consolidated balance sheets for the chartered banking system and the Bank of Canada. Use columns 1 and 2 to indicate how the balance sheets would read after each transaction in (a) and (b) is completed. Do not accumulate your answers; analyze each transaction separately, starting in each case from the figures provided. All accounts are in billions of dollars. A decline in the bank rate prompts chartered banks to borrow an additional $1 billion from the Bank of Canada. Show the new balance-sheet figures in column 1 of each table.

   a. The Bank of Canada sells $3 billion in securities to the public, who pay for the bonds with cheques. Show the new balance sheet figures in column 2 of each table.

   b. The Bank of Canada buys $2 billion in securities from chartered banks. Show the new balance sheet figures in column 3 of each table.

   c. Now review both of these transactions, asking yourself these three questions: (1) What change, if any, took place in the money supply as a direct and immediate result of each transaction? (2) What increase or decrease in chartered banks' reserves took place in each transaction? (3) Assuming a desired reserve ratio of 20 percent, what change in the money-creating potential of the chartered banking system occurred as a result of each transaction?

3. **KEY QUESTION**   Suppose you are the governor of the Bank of Canada. The economy is experiencing a sharp and prolonged inflationary trend. What changes in (a) open-market operations and (b) switching government deposits would you consider? Explain in each case how the change you advocate would affect chartered bank cash reserves and influence the money supply.

4. What is *velocity* as it applies to money? Suppose the Bank of Canada decreases the money supply from $3 billion to $2 billion, but velocity rises from 3 to 5. By how much, if any, will total spending decline? What do economists mean when they say that monetary policy can exhibit *cyclical asymmetry*?

5. **KEY QUESTION**   Distinguish between the bank rate and the prime interest rate. In what way is the bank rate a measure of the tightness or looseness of monetary policy? In 2001 the Bank of Canada used open market operations to significantly reduce the bank rate. What was the logic of this action? What was the effect on the prime interest rate? What is the basic objective of monetary policy? State the cause-effect chain through which monetary policy is made effective. Discuss how (a) the shapes of the demand-for-money and investment-demand curves, and (b) the size of the MPS

CONSOLIDATED BALANCE SHEET: ALL CHARTERED BANKS (BILLIONS OF DOLLARS)

	(1)	(2)	(3)
Assets:			
Reserves $33	_____	_____	_____
Securities 60	_____	_____	_____
Loans 60	_____	_____	_____
Liabilities:			
Demand deposits . .$150	_____	_____	_____
Advances from Bank of Canada 3	_____	_____	_____

BALANCE SHEET: BANK OF CANADA (BILLIONS OF DOLLARS)

	(1)	(2)	(3)
Assets:			
Securities $60	_____	_____	_____
Advances to chartered banks 3	_____	_____	_____
Liabilities:			
Reserves of chartered banks $33	_____	_____	_____
Government of Canada deposits 3	_____	_____	_____
Notes in circulation . . 27	_____	_____	_____

and MPM influence the effectiveness of monetary policy. How do feedback effects influence the effectiveness of monetary policy?

6. What is inflation targeting? What are the main benefits of inflation targeting, according to its supporters? Why do some economists feel it is not needed, or even oppose it?

7. **KEY QUESTION**   Suppose the Bank of Canada decides to engage in a tight money policy as a way to close an inflationary gap. Use the aggregate demand-aggregate supply model to show what this policy is intended to accomplish in a closed economy. Now introduce the open economy and explain how changes in the international value of the dollar might affect the location of the aggregate demand curve.

8. **(The Last Word)** Compare and contrast the Taylor rule for monetary policy with the simpler inflation targets practiced by the Bank of Canada. Is the Bank of Canada's recent monetary policy consistent with Taylor's rule?

INTERNET APPLICATION QUESTIONS

1. **Monetary Policy Transmission Mechanism** Go to the McConnell-Brue-Barbiero Web site (Chapter 13) and access the Bank of Canada site which shows how monetary policy affects the economy. What factors affect the transmission mechanism?

2. **The Bank of Canada's Monetary Policy Report** Go to the McConnell-Brue-Barbiero Web site (Chapter 13) and access the Bank of Canada's Monetary Policy Report. It provides an overview of the performance of the Canadian economy, and the Bank of Canada's monetary policy goals given the economy's performance. What is (are) the current monetary policy goal(s)?

3. **Web-Based Question: The Stock Market Crash of 2000-02 and the Canadian Economy** Access the Bank of Montreal Financial Group research site through the McConnell-Brue-Barbiero home page (Chapter 13) to assess one researcher's analysis of the stock market crash of 2000–02 and its impact on the Canadian economy. (a) In what three ways does a decline in stock values reduce economic growth? (b) Have subsequent events in the stock market showed that the Canadian stock market was undervalued in mid 2002? Did the Canadian stock market rise from the levels of August 2002?

Part 4

The Long Run and Economic Growth

14

Chapter

Long-Run Macro-economic Adjustments

Economist John Maynard Keynes once remarked, "In the long run we are all dead." If the long run is a century or more, nobody can argue with Keynes' statement. But if the long run is just a few years or even a few decades, it becomes tremendously important to households, businesses, and the economy. For that reason, macroeconomists have recently focused much attention on long-run macroeconomic adjustments and outcomes. As we will see in this chapter and the next, that focus has produced significant insights relating to aggregate supply, economic growth, and government budgeting. We will also see that it has renewed debates over the causes of macro fluctuations and the effectiveness of stabilization policy.

Our goals in this chapter are to focus on the long-run aggregate supply, examine the inflation-unemployment relationship, and assess the effect of taxes on aggregate supply. The latter is a key concern of so-called *supply-side economics*.

14.1   Applying the Long-Run AD-AS Model

The long-run AD-AS model introduced in Chapter 8 helps us better understand the economy and the controversies occasionally swirling around macroeconomics. To get a handle on the long-run dynamics, we apply the long-run AD-AS model to three situations: demand-pull inflation, cost-push inflation, and recession.

Demand-Pull Inflation in the Long-Run AD-AS Model

Recall that *demand-pull inflation* occurs when an increase in aggregate demand pulls up the price level. With a long-run aggregate supply, however, an increase in the price level will eventually produce an increase in nominal wages and thus a leftward shift of the short-run aggregate supply curve. This is shown in Figure 14-1, where we initially suppose the price level is P_1 at the intersection of aggregate demand curve AD_1, short-run supply curve AS_1, and long-run aggregate supply curve AS_{LR}. Observe that the economy is achieving its full-employment real output GDP_f at point *a*.

Now consider the effects of an increase in aggregate demand as represented by the rightward shift from AD_1 to AD_2. This shift can result from any one of a number of factors, including an increase in investment spending and a rise in net exports. Whatever its cause, the increase in aggregate demand boosts the price level from P_1 to P_2 and expands real output from GDP_f to GDP_2 at point *b*.

So far, none of this is new to you. But now we want to emphasize the distinction between short-run and long-run aggregate supply. Once workers have realized that their real wages have declined, and when their existing contracts have expired, nominal wages will rise. As they do, the short-run aggregate supply curve will eventually shift leftward until it intersects long-run aggregate supply at point *c*.[1] There, the economy has re-established long-run equilibrium, with the price level and real

<table>
<tr>
<td>

FIGURE (14-1)

An increase in aggregate demand from AD_1 to AD_2 drives up the price level and increases real output in the short run. But in the long run, nominal wages rise and the short-run aggregate supply curve shifts leftward, as from AS_1 to AS_2. Real output then returns to its prior level, and the price level rises even more. In this scenario, the economy moves from *a* to *b* and then eventually to *c*.

</td>
<td>

Demand-Pull Inflation in the Long-Run AD-AS Model

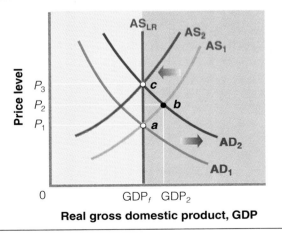

</td>
</tr>
</table>

[1] We say "eventually" because the initial leftward shift in short-run aggregate supply will intersect the long-run aggregate supply curve AS_{LR} at price level P_2. But the intersection of AD_2 and this new short-run aggregate supply curve (not shown) will produce a price level above P_2. (You may want to pencil this in to make sure that you understand this point.) Again nominal wages will rise, shifting the short-run aggregate supply curve farther leftward. The process will continue until the economy moves to point *c*, where the short-run aggregate supply curve is AS_2, the price level is P_3, and real output is GDP_f.

output now P_3 and GDP$_f$, respectively. Only at point c does the new aggregate demand curve AD$_2$ intersect both the short-run aggregate supply curve AS$_2$ and the long-run aggregate supply curve AS$_{LR}$.

In the short run, demand-pull inflation drives up the price level and increases real output; in the long run, only the price level rises. In the long run, the initial increase in aggregate demand has moved the economy *along* its vertical aggregate supply curve AS$_{LR}$. For a while, an economy can operate beyond its full-employment level of output. But the demand-pull inflation eventually causes adjustments of nominal wages that move the economy back to its full-employment output GDP$_f$.

Cost-Push Inflation in the Long-Run AD-AS Model

Cost-push inflation arises from factors that increase the cost of production at each price level—that is, factors that shift the aggregate supply curve leftward—and therefore increase the price level. But in our previous analysis we considered only short-run aggregate supply. We now want to examine cost-push inflation in its long-run context.

ANALYSIS

Consider Figure 14-2, in which we again assume the economy is initially operating at price level P_1 and output level GDP$_f$ (point a). Suppose that international oil producers get together and boost the price of oil by, say, 100 percent. As a result, the per-unit production cost of producing and transporting goods and services rises substantially in the economy, represented by Figure 14-2. The increase in per-unit production cost shifts the short-run aggregate supply curve to the left, as from AS$_1$ to AS$_2$, and the price level rises from P_1 to P_2 (as seen by comparing points a and b). In this case, the leftward shift of the aggregate supply curve is not a *response* to a price-level increase, as it was in our previous discussions of demand-pull inflation; it is the initiating *cause* of the price-level increase.

FIGURE 14-2   **Cost-Push Inflation in the Long-Run AD-AS Model**

Cost-push inflation occurs when the short-run aggregate supply curve shifts leftward, as from AS$_1$ to AS$_2$. If government counters the decline in real output by increasing aggregate demand to the broken line, the price level rises even more. That is, the economy moves in steps from a to b to c. In contrast, if government allows a recession to occur, nominal wages eventually fall and the aggregate supply curve shifts back rightward to its original location. The economy moves from a to b and then eventually back to a.

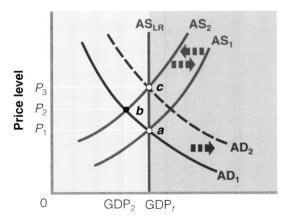

POLICY DILEMMA

Cost-push inflation creates a dilemma for policy-makers. Without expansionary stabilization policy, aggregate demand in Figure 14-2 remains at AD_1—the curve does not shift—and real output declines from GDP_f to GDP_2. Government can counter this recession and the attendant rise in unemployment by using fiscal policy and/or monetary policy to increase aggregate demand to AD_2. But there is a potential policy trap here: An increase in aggregate demand to AD_2 will further increase inflation by increasing the price level from P_2 to P_3 (a move from point b to c).

Suppose government recognizes this policy trap and decides *not* to increase aggregate demand from AD_1 to AD_2 (so you can now disregard the dashed AD_2 curve). Instead, it implicitly decides to allow a cost-push-created recession to run its course. How will that happen? Widespread layoffs, plant shutdowns, and business failures eventually occur. At some point the demands for oil, labour, and other inputs fall such that oil prices and nominal wages decline. When that happens, the initial leftward shift of the short-run aggregate supply curve is undone. In time the recession will shift the short-run aggregate supply curve rightward from AS_2 to AS_1. The price level will return to P_1, and the full-employment level of output will be restored at GDP_f (point a on the long-run aggregate supply curve AS_{LR}).

This analysis yields two generalizations:

- If government attempts to maintain full employment when there is cost-push inflation, an inflationary spiral may occur.

- If government takes a hands-off approach to cost-push inflation, a recession will occur. Although the recession eventually may undo the initial rise in per-unit production costs, the economy in the meantime will experience high unemployment and a loss of real output.

Recession and the Long-Run AD-AS Model

By far the most controversial application of the long-run AD-AS model is to recession (or depression). We look at this controversy in detail in Internet Chapter 1; here we simply want to present the model and identify the key point of contention.

Suppose in Figure 14-3 that aggregate demand initially is AD_1 and that short-run and long-run aggregate supply curves are AS_1 and AS_{LR}, respectively. Therefore, as shown by point a, the price

By far the most controversial application of the long-run AD-AS model is to recession.

| FIGURE 14-3 | Recession in the Long-Run AD-AS Model |

A recession occurs when aggregate demand shifts leftward, as from AD_1 to AD_2. If prices and wages are downwardly flexible, the price level falls from P_1 to P_2. This decline in the price level reduces nominal wages, which in turn eventually shift the aggregate supply curve from AS_1 to AS_2. The price level declines to P_3, and output increases back to GDP_f. The economy moves from a to b and then eventually to c.

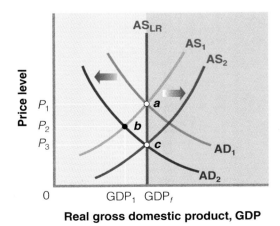

level is P_1 and output is GDP_f. Now suppose that investment spending dramatically declines, reducing aggregate demand to AD_2. Real output declines from GDP_f to GDP_1, meaning a recession has occurred. But if we make the assumption that prices and wages are flexible downward, the price level falls from P_1 to P_2. This lower price level increases *real* wages for people still working since each dollar of nominal wage has greater purchasing power. Eventually, nominal wages themselves fall to restore the previous real wage; when this happens, the short-run aggregate supply curve shifts rightward from AS_1 to AS_2. The recession ends—without expansionary fiscal or monetary policy—since real output expands from GDP_1 (point *b*) back to GDP_f (point *c*). The economy is again located on its long-run aggregate supply curve AS_{LR}, but now at lower price level P_3.

There is disagreement among economists about how long it would take in the real world for the necessary price and wage adjustments to occur to regain the full-employment level of output. Most economists believe that such adjustments are forthcoming, but will occur only after the economy has experienced a relatively long-lasting recession with its accompanying rise in unemployment and a loss of output. *(Key Question 1)*

QUICK REVIEW

- In the short run, demand-pull inflation raises both the price level and real output; in the long run, nominal wages rise, the short-run aggregate supply curve shifts to the left, and only the price level increases.

- Cost-push inflation creates a policy dilemma for the government: If it engages in an expansionary policy to increase output, an inflationary spiral may occur; if it does nothing, a recession will occur.

- In the short run, a decline in aggregate demand reduces real output (creates a recession); in the long run, prices and nominal wages fall, the short-run aggregate supply curve shifts to the right, and real output returns to its full-employment level.

14.2   The Inflation-Unemployment Relationship

Because both low inflation rates and low unemployment rates are major economic goals, economists are vitally interested in their relationship. Are low unemployment and low inflation compatible goals or conflicting goals? What explains situations in which high unemployment and high inflation coexist?

The long-run AD-AS model supports three significant generalizations relating to these questions:

- Under normal circumstances, there is a short-run tradeoff between the rate of inflation and the rate of unemployment.

- Aggregate supply shocks can cause both higher rates of inflation and higher rates of unemployment.

- There is no significant tradeoff between inflation and unemployment over long periods of time.

Let's examine each of these generalizations.

The Phillips Curve

Phillips curve
A curve showing the relationship between the unemployment rate and the annual rate of increase in the price level.

We can demonstrate the short-run tradeoff between the rate of inflation and the rate of unemployment through the **Phillips curve**, named after A. W. Phillips, who developed the idea in Great Britain. This curve, generalized later in Figure 14-5, suggests an inverse relationship between the rate of inflation and the rate of unemployment. Lower unemployment rates (measured as leftward movements on the horizontal axis) are associated with higher rates of inflation (measured as upward movements on the vertical axis).

FIGURE 14-4

The Effect of Changes in Aggregate Demand on Real Output and the Price Level

Comparing the effects of various possible increases in aggregate demand leads to the conclusion that the larger the increase in aggregate demand, the higher the rate of inflation and the greater the increase in real output. Because real output and the unemployment rate move in opposite directions, we can generalize that, given short-run aggregate supply, high rates of inflation should be accompanied by low rates of unemployment.

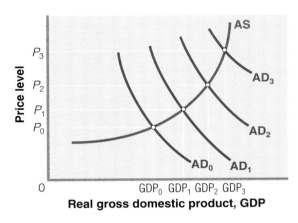

The underlying rationale of the Phillips curve becomes apparent when we view the short-run aggregate supply curve in Figure 14-4 and perform a simple mental experiment. Suppose that in some period aggregate demand expands from AD_0 to AD_2, either because firms decided to buy more capital goods or the government decided to increase its expenditures. Whatever the cause, in the short run the economy experiences inflationary pressures. The price level thus rises from P_0 to P_2 and real output rises from GDP_0 to GDP_2. A decline in the unemployment rate accompanies this increase in real output.

Now let's compare what would have happened if the increase in aggregate demand had been larger, say, from AD_0 to AD_3. The new equilibrium tells us that the price level and the growth of real output would both have been greater (and that the unemployment rate would have been lower). Similarly, suppose aggregate demand during the year had increased only modestly, from AD_0 to AD_1. Compared with our shift from AD_0 to AD_2, the amount of inflation and the growth of real output would have been smaller (and the unemployment rate higher).

The generalization we draw from this mental experiment is this: Assuming a constant short-run aggregate supply curve, high rates of inflation are accompanied by low rates of unemployment, and low rates of inflation are accompanied by high rates of unemployment. Figure 14-5a shows how the expected relationship should look, other things being equal.

Figure 14-5b reveals that for Canada the facts for the 1960s nicely fit the theory. On the basis of that evidence and evidence from other countries, most economists concluded there was a stable, predictable tradeoff between unemployment and inflation. Moreover, Canadian economic policy was built on that supposed tradeoff. According to this thinking, it was impossible to achieve "full employment without inflation:" Manipulation of aggregate demand through fiscal and monetary measures would simply move the economy along the Phillips curve. An expansionary fiscal and monetary policy that boosted aggregate demand and lowered the unemployment rate would simultaneously increase inflation. A restrictive fiscal and monetary policy would be used to reduce the rate of inflation, but only at the cost of a higher unemployment rate and more forgone production. Society had to choose between the incompatible goals of price stability and full employment; it had to decide where to locate on its Phillips curve.

For reasons we will soon see, economists now reject the idea of a stable, predictable long-run Phillips curve. Nevertheless, they agree there is a short-run tradeoff between unemployment and inflation. Given aggregate supply, increases in aggregate demand boost real output and reduce the unemployment rate. As the unemployment rate falls and dips below the natural rate, the excessive

FIGURE 14-5   The Phillips Curve: Concept and Canadian Empirical Data

(a) The Phillips curve relates annual rates of inflation and annual rates of unemployment for a series of years. Because this is an inverse relationship, there presumable is a tradeoff between unemployment and inflation. (b) Data points for the 1960s seemed to confirm the Phillips curve concept.

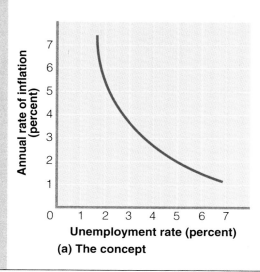

(a) The concept

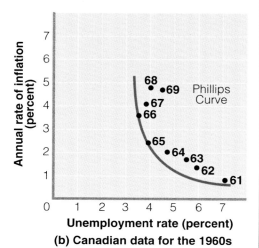

(b) Canadian data for the 1960s

spending produces demand-pull inflation. Conversely, when recessions set in and the unemployment rate increases, the weak aggregate demand that caused the recession also leads to lower inflation rates.

Periods of exceptionally low unemployment rates and inflation rates do occur, but only under special sets of economic circumstances. One such period was the late 1990s, when faster productivity growth increased aggregate supply and fully blunted the inflationary impact of rapidly rising aggregate demand.

Aggregate Supply Shocks and the Phillips Curve

The unemployment-inflation experience of the 1970s and early 1980s demolished the idea of an always-stable Phillips curve. In Figure 14-6 we show the Phillips curve for the 1960s in green and then add the data points for 1970 through 2002. Observe that in most of the years of the 1970s and early 1980s the economy experienced both higher inflation rates and higher unemployment rates than in the 1960s. In fact, inflation and unemployment rose simultaneously in some of those years. This latter condition is called **stagflation**—a term that combines the words "stagnation" and "inflation." If there still was any such thing as a Phillips curve, it had clearly shifted outward, perhaps as shown.

stagflation
Simultaneous increases in the price level and the unemployment rate.

aggregate supply shocks
Sudden, large changes in resource costs that shift an economy's aggregate supply curve.

ADVERSE AGGREGATE SUPPLY SHOCKS

The Phillips data points for the 1970s and early 1980s support our second generalization: *Aggregate supply shocks can cause both higher rates of inflation and higher rates of unemployment.* A series of adverse **aggregate supply shocks**—sudden, large increases in resource costs that jolt an economy's short-run aggregate supply curve leftward—hit the economy in the 1970s and early 1980s. The most significant of these shocks was a quadrupling of oil prices by the Organization of Petroleum Exporting Countries (OPEC). Consequently, the cost of producing and distributing virtually every product and service rose rapidly. (Other factors working to increase Canadian costs during this period included major agricultural shortfalls, a greatly depreciated dollar, wage hikes previously held down by wage-price controls, and declining productivity.)

These shocks shifted the aggregate supply curve to the left and distorted the usual inflation-unemployment relationship. Remember that we derived the inverse relationship between the rate

www.opec.com
OPEC

| FIGURE 14-6 | Inflation Rates and Unemployment Rates in Canada, 1961–2002 |

A series of aggregate supply shocks in the 1970s resulted in higher rates of inflation and higher rates of unemployment. So, data points for the 1970s and 1980s tended to be above and to the right of the Phillips curve for the 1960s. In the 1990s the inflation-unemployment data points slowly moved back toward the original Phillips curve. Points for the early 2000s are closer to those from the earlier era.

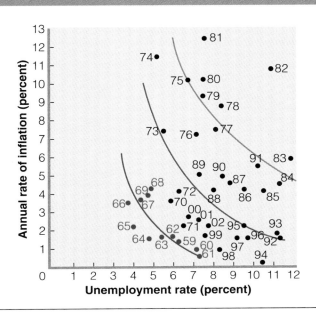

of inflation and the unemployment rate shown in Figure 14-5 by shifting the aggregate demand curve along a stable short-run aggregate supply curve (Figure 14-4). But the cost-push inflation model shown in Figure 14-1 tells us that a *leftward shift* of the short-run aggregate supply curve increases the price level and reduces real output (and increases the unemployment rate). This, say most economists, is what happened in two periods in the 1970s. The unemployment rate shot up from 5.6 percent in 1973 to 8.1 percent in 1977, contributing to a significant decline in real GDP. In the same period, the price level rose by 40 percent. The stagflation scenario recurred in 1978, when OPEC increased oil prices by more than 100 percent. The Canadian price level rose by 50 percent over the 1978–82 period, while unemployment increased from 9.4 to 11.0 percent.

STAGFLATION'S DEMISE

Another look at Figure 14-6 reveals a generally inward movement of the inflation-unemployment points between 1983 and 1989. By 1989 the lingering effects of the early period had subsided. One precursor to this favourable trend was the deep recession of 1981 to 1982, largely caused by a tight money policy aimed at reducing inflation. The recession increased the unemployment rate to 11.9 percent in 1983. With so many workers unemployed, those who were working accepted smaller increases in their nominal wages—or in some cases wage reductions—in order to preserve their jobs. Firms, in turn, restrained their price increases to try to retain their relative shares of a diminished market.

Other factors were at work. Foreign competition throughout this period held down wage and price hikes in several basic industries such as automobiles and steel. Deregulation of the airline and trucking industries also resulted in wage reductions or so-called wage givebacks. A significant decline in OPEC's monopoly power and a greatly reduced reliance on oil in the production process produced a stunning fall in the price of oil and its derivative products, such as gasoline.

All these factors combined to reduce per-unit production costs and to shift the short-run aggregate supply curve rightward (as from AS$_2$ to AS$_1$ in Figure 14-2). Employment and output expanded and the unemployment rate fell from 11 percent in 1983 to 7.5 percent in 1989. Figure 14-6 reveals

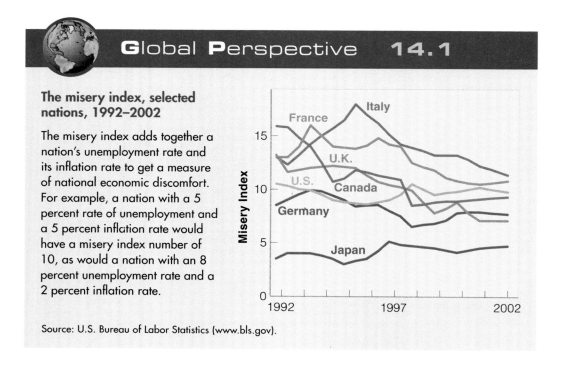

Global Perspective 14.1

The misery index, selected nations, 1992–2002

The misery index adds together a nation's unemployment rate and its inflation rate to get a measure of national economic discomfort. For example, a nation with a 5 percent rate of unemployment and a 5 percent inflation rate would have a misery index number of 10, as would a nation with an 8 percent unemployment rate and a 2 percent inflation rate.

Source: U.S. Bureau of Labor Statistics (www.bls.gov).

that the inflation-unemployment points for recent years are closer to the points associated with the Phillips curve of the 1960s than to the points in the late 1970s and early 1980s. The points for 1999–2002, in fact, are close to points on the 1960s curve. (The low inflation and relatively low unemployment rates in this later period produced an exceptionally low value of the so-called *misery index*, as shown in Global Perspective 14.1.)

14.3   The Long-Run Phillips Curve

The overall set of data points in Figure 14-6 points to our third generalization relating to the inflation-unemployment relationship: There is no apparent *long-run* tradeoff between inflation and unemployment. When decades as opposed to a few years are considered, any rate of inflation is consistent with the natural rate of unemployment prevailing at that time. We know from Chapter 6 that the natural rate of unemployment is the rate of unemployment that occurs when cyclical unemployment is zero; it is the rate of unemployment when the economy achieves its potential output.

How can there be a short-run inflation-unemployment tradeoff, but not a long-run tradeoff? Figure 14-7 provides the answer.

SHORT-RUN PHILLIPS CURVE

Consider Phillips curve PC_1 in Figure 14-7. Suppose the economy initially is experiencing a 3 percent rate of inflation and a 5 percent natural rate of unemployment. Such short-term curves as PC_1, PC_2 and PC_3 (drawn as straight lines for simplicity) exist because the actual rate of inflation is not always the same as the expected rate.

Establishing an additional point on Phillips curve PC_1 will clarify this. We begin at a_1, where we assume nominal wages are set on the assumption that the 3 percent rate of inflation will continue. But suppose that aggregate demand increases such that the rate of inflation rises to 6 percent. With a nominal wage rate set on the expectation that the 3 percent rate of inflation will continue, the higher product prices raise business profits. Firms respond to the higher profits by hiring more

The Long-Run Vertical Phillips Curve

Increases in aggregate demand beyond those consistent with full-employment output may temporarily boost profits, output, and employment (as from a_1 to b_1). But nominal wages eventually will catch up so as to sustain real wages. When they do, profits will fall, negating the previous short-run stimulus to production and employment (the economy now moves from b_1 to a_2). Consequently, there is no tradeoff between the rates of inflation and unemployment in the long run; that is, the long-run Phillips curve is roughly a vertical line at the economy's natural rate of unemployment.

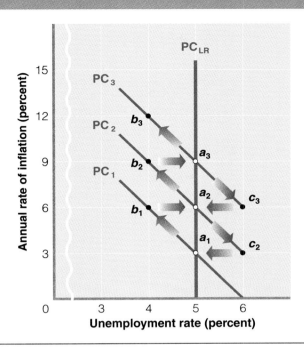

workers and increasing output. In the short run, the economy moves to b_1, which, in contrast to a_1, is at a lower rate of unemployment (4 percent) and a higher rate of inflation (6 percent). The movement from a_1 to b_1 is consistent both with an upward-sloping aggregate supply curve and with the inflation-unemployment tradeoff implied by the Phillips curve analysis. But this short-run Phillips curve simply is a manifestation of the following principle: *When the actual rate of inflation is higher than expected, profits temporarily rise and the unemployment rate temporarily falls.*

EXPECTATION AND THE LONG-RUN VERTICAL PHILLIPS CURVE

But point b_1 is not a stable equilibrium. Workers will recognize that their nominal wages have not increased as fast as inflation and will therefore try to obtain nominal wage increases to restore their lost purchasing power. But as nominal wages rise to restore the level of real wages that previously existed at a_1, business profits will fall to their prior level. The reduction in profits means that the original motivation to employ more workers and increase output has disappeared.

Unemployment then returns to its natural level at point a_2. Note, however, that the economy now faces a higher actual and expected rate of inflation—6 percent rather than 3 percent. The higher level of aggregate demand that originally moved the economy from a_1 to b_1 still exists, so the inflation it created persists.

In view of the higher 6 percent expected rate of inflation, the short-run Phillips curve shifts upward from PC_1 to PC_2 in Figure 14-7. An "along-the-Phillips-curve" kind of movement from a_1 to b_1 on PC_1 is merely a short-run occurrence. As expectation of inflation adjusts in the long run, nominal wages catch up with price-level increases, unemployment returns to its natural rate at a_2, and there is a new short-run Phillips curve PC_2 at the higher expected rate of inflation.

The scenario repeats if aggregate demand continues to increase. Prices rise momentarily ahead of nominal wages, profits expand, and employment and output increase (as implied by the move from a_2 to b_2). But, in time, the expected rate of inflation changes, and nominal wages increase so as to restore real wages. Profits then fall to their original level, pushing employment back to the normal rate at a_3. The economy's "reward" for lowering the unemployment rate below the natural rate is a still higher (9 percent) rate of inflation.

Movements along the short-run Phillips curve (a_1 to b_1 on PC_1) cause the curve to shift to a less favourable position (PC_2, then PC_3, and so on). A stable Phillips curve with the dependable series of unemployment rate-inflation rate tradeoffs simply does not exist in the long run.

The vertical line through a_1, a_2, and a_3 shows the long-run relationship between unemployment and inflation. Any rate of inflation is consistent with the 5 percent natural rate of unemployment.

REDUCTION IN THE INFLATION RATE

The distinction between the short-run and long-run Phillips curve also helps explain reductions in the inflation rate from year to year. Suppose that in Figure 14-7 the economy is at a_3, where the inflation rate is 9 percent. And suppose that a decline in aggregate demand (such as that occurring in the 1991–92 recession) reduces inflation below the 9 percent expected rate to, say, 6 percent. Business profits fall, because prices are rising less rapidly than wages. The nominal wage increases, remember, were set on the assumption that the 9 percent rate of inflation would continue. In response to the decline in profits, firms reduce their employment and consequently the unemployment rate rises. The economy temporarily slides downward from point a_3 to c_3 along the short-run Phillips curve PC_3. *When the actual rate of inflation is lower than the expected rate, profits temporarily fall and the unemployment rate temporarily rises.*

Firms and workers eventually adjust their expectations to the new 6 percent rate of inflation, and thus newly negotiated wage increases decline. Profits are restored, employment rises, and the

Consider This

The Bank of Canada and the Phillips Curve

In the spring of 2003 the Bank of Canada was concerned about the rate of inflation in Canada as it rose above its target rate, and subsequently raised the target overnight loans rate. The idea is that by increasing interest rates, the Canadian economy would slow and thus bring down the rate of inflation, and thereby also dampen the expectation of future inflation. The following is the Bank of Canada's highlights from its *Monetary Policy Report* of April 2003.

Highlights[2]

- Inflation has been well above the 2 percent inflation target, and inflation expectations have edged up.

- In view of the domestic inflation situation and the underlying momentum of domestic demand, the Bank has raised its target overnight rate to 3.25 percent.

- Global economic uncertainties will likely dampen near-term growth; however, the pace of activity should strengthen towards the end of this year and through 2004 as confidence levels improve.

- The Bank believes that further reductions in monetary stimulus over time will be necessary, but the timing and pace will depend on the evolution of inflation expectations and the strength of domestic and external demand.

[2]Bank of Canada, *Monetary Policy Report*, April 2003.

Question: The Bank of Canada hinted that it might have to raise interest rates again. The overnight loans rate stood at 3.25 percent in the spring of 2003. Go to http://www.bankofcanada.ca/en/mpr/mpr_previous.htm and click on the Monetary Policy Report summary for the end of 2003. Was the Bank of Canada right in predicting that growth would pick up in 2003? What occurred to the rate of inflation and the overnight loans during the course of 2003?

unemployment rate falls back to its natural rate of 6 percent at a_2. Because the expected rate of inflation is now 6 percent, the short-run Phillips curve PC_3 shifts leftward to PC_2.

If aggregate demand falls farther, the scenario will continue. Inflation declines from 6 percent to, say, 3 percent, moving the economy from a_2 to c_2 along PC_2. The lower-than-expected rate of inflation (lower prices) squeezes profits and reduces employment. But, in the long run, firms respond to the lower profits by reducing their nominal wage increases. Profits are restored and unemployment returns to its natural rate at a_1 as the short-run Phillips curve moves from PC_2 to PC_1. Once again, the long-run Phillips curve is vertical at the 5 percent natural rate of unemployment *(Key Question 3)*.

QUICK REVIEW

- As implied by the upward-sloping short-run aggregate supply curve, there may be a short-run tradeoff between the rate of inflation and the rate of unemployment. This tradeoff is reflected in the Phillips curve, which shows that lower rates of inflation are associated with higher rates of unemployment.

- Aggregate supply shocks that produce severe cost-push inflation can cause stagflation—simultaneous increases in the inflation rate and the unemployment rate.

Such stagflation occurred from 1973 to 1975 and recurred from 1978 to 1982, producing Phillips curve data points above and to the right of the Phillips curve for the 1960s.

- After all nominal wage adjustments to increases and decreases in the rate of inflation have occurred, the economy ends up back at its full-unemployment level of output and its natural rate of unemployment. The long-run Phillips curve therefore is vertical at the natural rate of unemployment.

14.4 Taxation and Aggregate Supply

supply-side economics
A view of macroeconomics that emphasizes the role of costs and aggregate supply in explaining inflation, unemployment, and economic growth.

A final topic in our discussion of aggregate supply is taxation. Government policies can either impede or promote rightward shifts of the short-run and long-run aggregate supply curve. One such policy is taxation. The effects of taxation on the supply curve is a key concern of **supply side economics**, which stresses the overriding importance of changes in aggregate supply in determining the levels of inflation, unemployment and economic growth.

A nation's tax system influences the incentive to work, save and invest. High tax rates impede productivity growth and hence the pace of expansion of long-run aggregate supply. By reducing the after-tax rewards of workers and producers, high tax rates reduce the financial attractiveness of work, saving, and investing. Particularly important is the marginal tax rates—the rates on extra dollars of income—because those rates affect the benefits from working, saving and investing more. In Canada the federal marginal tax rates vary from 17 percent to 29 percent. See this chapter's Consider This box for combined federal and provincial marginal tax rates across Canada.

TAXES AND INCENTIVES TO WORK

How long and how hard people work depends on the amount of additional after-tax earnings they derive from their efforts. Reductions in marginal tax rates on earned incomes induce more work, and therefore increase aggregate inputs of labour. Lower marginal tax rates make leisure relatively more expensive and thus work more attractive. The higher opportunity cost of leisure encourages people to substitute work for leisure. This increase in productive effort could be achieved in many ways: by increasing the number of hours worked per day or week, by encouraging workers to postpone retirement, by inducing more people to enter the labour force, by motivating people to work harder and giving people the incentive to avoid long periods of unemployment.

INCENTIVES TO SAVE AND INVEST

The rewards for saving and investing have also been reduced by high marginal tax rates. For example, suppose that Tony saves $10,000 at 8 percent, bringing him $800 of interest per year. If his marginal tax rate is 40 percent, his after-tax interest earnings will be $480, not $800, and his after-tax interest rate will fall to 4.8 percent. Although Tony might be willing to save (forgo current consumption) for an 8 percent return on his saving, he might prefer to consume when the return is only 4.8 percent.

Saving, remember, is the prerequisite of investment. Thus supply-side economists recommend lower marginal tax rates on interest earned from saving. They also call for lower taxes on income from capital to ensure that there are ready investment outlets for the economy's enhanced pool of saving. A critical determinant of investment spending is the expected after-tax return on that spending

To summarize: Lower marginal tax rates encourage saving and investing. Workers therefore find themselves equipped with more and technologically superior machinery and equipment. Labour productivity rises, and that expands aggregate supply, which in turn keeps unemployment rates and inflation low.

The Laffer Curve

In the supply-side view, reductions in marginal tax rates increase the nation's aggregate supply and can leave the nation's tax revenues unchanged, or even enlarge them. Thus, supply-side tax cuts need not result in federal budget deficits.

Laffer curve
A curve relating government tax rates and tax revenues.

This idea is based on the **Laffer curve**, named after Arthur Laffer, who developed it. As Figure 14-8 shows, the Laffer curve depicts the relationship between tax rates and tax revenues. As tax rates increase from zero to 100 percent, tax revenues increase from zero to some maximum level (at *m*) and then fall to zero. Tax revenues decline beyond some point because higher tax rates discourage economic activity, thereby shrinking the tax base. This is easiest to see at the extreme, where the tax rate is 100 percent. Tax revenues here are, in theory, reduced to zero because the 100 percent tax rate has halted production. A 100 percent tax rate applied to a tax base of zero yields no revenue.

In the early 1980s Laffer suggested that at a point such as *n* on the curve in Figure 14-8, tax rates are so high that production is discouraged to the extent that tax revenues are below the maximum at *m*. If the economy is at *n*, then lower tax rates can either increase tax revenues or leave them

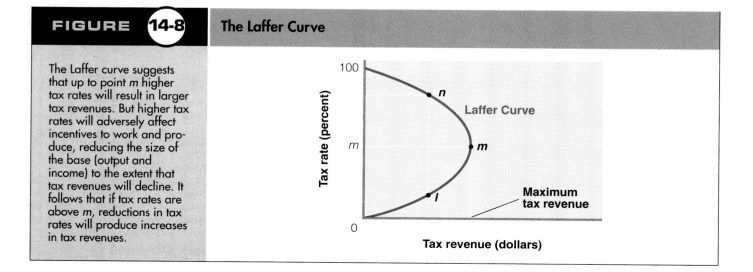

| **FIGURE** 14-8 | **The Laffer Curve** |

The Laffer curve suggests that up to point *m* higher tax rates will result in larger tax revenues. But higher tax rates will adversely affect incentives to work and produce, reducing the size of the base (output and income) to the extent that tax revenues will decline. It follows that if tax rates are above *m*, reductions in tax rates will produce increases in tax revenues.

unchanged. For example, lowering the tax rate point *n* to point *l* would bolster the economy such that the government would bring in the same total amount of tax revenue as before.

Laffer's reasoning was that lower tax rates stimulate incentives to work, save and invest, innovate, and accept business risks, thus triggering an expansion of real output and income. That enlarged tax base sustains tax revenues even though tax rates are lowered. Indeed, between *n* and *m* lower tax rates result in increased tax revenue.

Also, when tax rates are lowered, tax avoidance (which is legal) and tax evasion (which is not) decline. High marginal tax rates prompt taxpayers to avoid taxes through various tax shelters. High tax rates also encourage some taxpayers to conceal income from Canada Customs and Revenue Agency. Lower tax rates reduce the inclination to engage in either tax avoidance or tax evasion. *(Key Question 5)*

Criticisms of the Laffer Curve

The Laffer curve and its supply-side implications have been subject to severe criticism.

TAXES, INCENTIVES, AND TIME

A fundamental criticism relates to the degree to which economic incentives are sensitive to changes in tax rates. Skeptics say there is ample empirical evidence showing that the impact of a tax cut on incentives is small, of uncertain direction, and relatively slow to emerge. For example, with respect to work incentives, studies indicate that decreases in tax rates lead some people to work more but lead others to work less. Those who work more are enticed by the higher after-tax pay; they substitute work for leisure because the opportunity cost of leisure has increased. But other people work less because the higher after-tax pay enables them to "buy more leisure." With the tax cut, they can earn the same level of after-tax income as before with fewer work hours.

INFLATION

Most economists think that the demand-side effects of a tax cut exceed the supply-side effects. Thus, tax cuts undertaken when the economy is at or near its full-employment level of output may produce increases in aggregate demand that overwhelm any increase in aggregate supply. Demand-pull inflation is the likely result.

POSITION ON THE CURVE

Skeptics say that the Laffer curve is merely a logical proposition, and assert that there must be some level of tax rates between zero and 100 percent at which tax revenues will be at their maximum. Economists of all persuasions can agree with this. But the issue of where a particular economy is located on its Laffer curve is an empirical question. If we assume that we are at point *n* in Figure 14-8, then tax cuts will increase tax revenues. But critics say that the economy's location on the Laffer curve is undocumented and unknown. If the economy is at any point below *m* on the curve, then tax reductions will reduce tax revenues and create budget deficits. Most economists believe that Canada is operating in the range of the Laffer curve where tax rates and tax revenues move in the same, not the opposite, direction.

THE LASTword — Has the Impact of Oil Prices Diminished?

Significant changes in oil prices historically have had major impacts on the Canadian economy. Have the effects of such changes weakened?

As indicated in this chapter, Canada has experienced several aggregate supply shocks caused by significant changes in oil prices. In the mid-1970s the price of oil rose from $4 to $12 per barrel (all prices in U.S. dollars) and then again in the late 1970s it increased to $24 per barrel and eventually to $35. These oil price increases caused significant aggregate supply shocks, rising unemployment, and rapid inflation.

In the late 1980s and through most of the 1990s oil prices fell, sinking to a low of $11 per barrel in late 1998. This decline created a "reverse" aggregate supply shock beneficial to the Canadian economy. But in response to those low oil prices, in late 1999 OPEC teamed with Mexico, Norway, and Russia to restrict oil output to boost prices. That action, along with a rapidly growing international demand for oil, sent oil prices upward once again. By March of 2000 the price of a barrel of oil reached $34, before settling back to about $25–$28 in 2001 and 2002. The fear of a war with Iraq sent the spot price of a barrel of oil in early 2003 to over $35, a price not seen since the 1970s. (You can find the current daily basket price of oil at OPEC's website, www.opec.org.)

Some economists feared that the rising price of oil would increase energy prices by so much that the aggregate supply curve in Canada would shift to the left, creating cost-push inflation. But inflation in Canada remained modest. Why did changes in oil prices seemingly lose their inflationary punch? There are several reasons.

First, other aggregate supply determinants swamped the potential inflationary impacts of the oil price increases of early 2000. The overall trend of lower costs resulting from the rapid productivity advance associated with the New Economy (discussed in the next chapter) more than compensated for the rise in oil prices. So, aggregate supply did not decline as it had in earlier periods.

Second, oil prices are a less significant factor in the Canadian economy than in 1970s. Prior to 1980, changes in oil prices greatly affected *core inflation* (the inflation rate after changes in the prices of food and energy have been subtracted). Since 1980 changes in oil price have had little effect on core inflation in the G7 countries.[3] The amount of energy consumed in producing each dollar of GDP in North America has significantly declined. In 2000 about 7000 BTUs of energy were required to produce each dollar of real GDP compared to 14,000 BTUs in 1970. Part of this decline was fostered by new production techniques spawned by the high oil and energy prices. But also important has been the changing relative composition of the GDP from larger, heavier items (such as earth moving equipment) that are energy-intensive to make and transport toward smaller, lighter items (such as microchips and software). American experts on energy economics estimate that their economy is about 33 percent less sensitive to oil price fluctuations than in the early 1980s and 50 percent less sensitive than in the mid-1970s.[4] Given the similarities between the Canadian and U.S. economy, there is reason to believe that similar magnitudes also hold for the Canadian economy.

A final reason why changes in oil prices seem to have lost their inflationary punch is that the Bank of Canada has become more vigilant and adept at maintaining price stability through monetary policy. The Bank of Canada did not let the oil price increases of 1999–2000 become generalized as core inflation.

---

[3] Mark A. Hooker, "Are Oil Shocks Inflationary? Asymmetric and Nonlinear Specifications versus Changes in Regimes," *Journal of Money, Credit and Banking*, May 2002, pp. 540–561.

[4] Stephen P. A. Brown and Mine K. Yücel, "Oil Prices and the Economy," (Federal Reserve Bank of Dallas, July/August 2000), pp. 1–6.

CHAPTER SUMMARY

14.1 APPLYING THE LONG-RUN AD-AS MODEL

- In macroeconomics, the short run is a period in which nominal wages are fixed; they do not change in response to changes in the price level. In contrast, the long run is a period in which nominal wages are fully responsive to changes in the price level.

- The short-run aggregate supply curve is upward-sloping. Because nominal wages are fixed, increases in the price level (prices received by firms) increase profits and real output. Conversely, decreases in the price level reduce profits and real output. However, the long-run aggregate supply curve is vertical. With sufficient time for adjustment, nominal wages rise and fall with the price level, moving the economy along a vertical aggregate supply curve at the economy's full-employment output.

- In the short run, demand-pull inflation raises the price level and real output. Once nominal wages have increased, the temporary increase in real output is reversed.

14.2 THE INFLATION-UNEMPLOYMENT RELATIONSHIP

- Assuming a stable upward-sloping aggregate supply curve, rightward shifts of the aggregate demand curve of various sizes yield the generalization that high rates of inflation are associated with low rates of unemployment, and vice versa. This inverse relationship is known as the Phillips curve, and empirical data for the 1960s seem to be consistent with it.

- In the 1970s and early 1980s, the Phillips curve apparently shifted rightward, reflecting stagflation—simultaneously rising inflation rates and unemployment rates. The standard interpretation is that the stagflation mainly resulted from huge oil price increases that caused large leftward shifts in the short-run aggregate supply curve (so-called supply shocks). The Phillips curve shifted inward towards its original position in the 1980s. By 1989 stagflation had subsided.

14.3 THE LONG-RUN PHILLIPS CURVE

- Although there is a short-run tradeoff between inflation and unemployment, there is no such long-run tradeoff. Workers will adapt their expectations to new inflation realities, and when they do, and nominal wages adjust proportionally with the price level, the unemployment rate will return to the natural rate. The long-run Phillips curve is therefore vertical at the natural rate, meaning that higher rates of inflation do not "buy" the economy less unemployment.

14.4 TAXATION AND THE AGGREGATE SUPPLY

- Supply-side economists focus attention on government policies, such as high taxation, that impede the expansion of aggregate supply. The Laffer curve relates tax rates to levels of tax revenue and suggests that, under some circumstances, cuts in tax rates can expand the tax base (output and income) and increase tax revenues. Most economists, however, believe that Canada is operating in the range of the Laffer curve where tax rates and tax revenues move in the same, not the opposite, direction.

TERMS AND CONCEPTS

Phillips curve, p. 336
stagflation, p. 338

aggregate supply shocks, p. 338
supply-side economics, p. 343

Laffer curve, p. 344

STUDY QUESTIONS

1. **KEY QUESTION** Use graphical analysis to show how each of the following would affect the economy first in the short run and then in the long run. Assume that Canada is initially operating at its full-employment level of output, that prices and wages are eventually flexible both upward and downward, and that there is no counteracting fiscal or monetary policy.

   a. Because of a war abroad, the oil supply to Canada is disrupted, sending oil prices rocketing upward.

   b. Construction spending on new homes rises dramatically, greatly increasing total Canadian investment spending.

   c. Economic recession occurs abroad, significantly reducing foreign purchases of Canadian exports.

2. Assume that a particular short-run aggregate supply curve exists for an economy and that the curve is relevant for several years. Use the AD-AS analysis to show graphically why higher rates of inflation over this period would be associated with lower rates of unemployment, and vice versa. What is this inverse relationship called?

3. **KEY QUESTION** Suppose the government judges the natural rate of unemployment to be much lower than it actually is, and thus undertakes expansionary

fiscal and monetary policy to try to achieve the lower rate. Use the concept of the short-run Phillips curve to explain why these policies might at first succeed. Use the concept of the long-run Phillips curve to explain the long-run outcome of these policies.

4. What do the distinctions between short-run and long-run aggregate supply have in common with the distinction between the short-run and long-run Phillips curve? Explain.

5. **KEY QUESTION**   What is the Laffer curve and how does it relate to supply-side economics? Why is deter-

mining the location of the economy on the curve so important in assessing tax policy?

6. Why might one person work more, earn more, and pay more income tax when his or her tax rate is cut, while another person will work less, earn less, and pay less income tax under the same circumstance?

7. **(The Last Word)** Do oil prices play a smaller or a larger role in the Canadian economy today compared to the 1970s and 1980s? Explain.

INTERNET APPLICATION QUESTIONS

1. **The Phillips Curve—Do Real Data Confirm?** The Phillips curve purports to show a stable relationship between the rate of inflation and the unemployment rate. Plot the data points between inflation and unemployment over the past five years. For inflation data, use the Consumer Price Index (all items). Both the CPI and unemployment data for the latest period can be retrieved from the McConnell-Brue-Barbiero Web site (Chapter 14). Do any of your data point plots confirm the Phillips curve concept?

Σ-STAT

2. **Dynamic Tax Scoring—What is it and Who Wants it?**   Go to the McConnell-Brue-Barbiero Web site (Chapter 14) and search for information on "dynamic tax scoring." What is it? How does it relate to supply-side economics? Which political groups support this approach and why? Which groups oppose it and why?

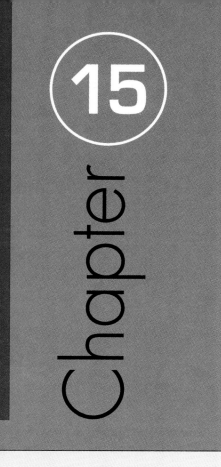

15
Chapter

Economic Growth

The world's market economies experienced impressive growth of real GDP and real GDP per capita during the last half of the twentieth century. In Canada, real GDP increased by over 600 percent between 1950 and 2002, and population increased by only 100 percent. In 2002 the value of goods and services available to the average Canadian resident was almost three times greater than that of fifty years earlier. Moreover, those goods and services in 2002 were generally of much higher quality than those of 1950. This increase and improvement of output—this *economic growth*—greatly improved material abundance and lifted the standard of living of most Canadians.

In Chapter 6 we explained how economic growth is measured and briefly looked at growth in Canada. In this chapter we explore economic growth in considerably more depth. Then, in optional Chapter 2W at our Web site, we extend the discussion of economic growth to the developing nations.

15.1   Ingredients of Growth

There are six main ingredients in economic growth. We can group them as supply, demand, and efficiency factors.

Supply Factors

Four of the ingredients of economic growth relate to the physical ability of the economy to expand. They are

- Increases in the quantity and quality of natural resources
- Increases in the quantity and quality of human resources
- Increases in the supply (or stock) of capital goods
- Improvements in technology

These **supply factors**—changes in the physical and technical agents of production—enable an economy to expand its potential GDP.

supply factor
An increase in the availability of a resource, an improvement in its quality, or an expansion of technological knowledge that makes it possible for an economy to produce a greater output of goods and services.

Demand Factor

The fifth ingredient of economic growth is the **demand factor**. To achieve the higher production potential created by the supply factors, households and businesses either domestically or abroad, must *purchase* the economy's expanding output of goods and services. Economic growth requires increases in total spending to realize the output gains made available by increased production capacity.

demand factor
The increase in the level of aggregate demand that brings about the economic growth made possible by an increase in the production potential of the economy.

Efficiency Factor

The sixth ingredient of economic growth is the **efficiency factor**. To reach its production potential, an economy must achieve economic efficiency as well as full employment. It must use its resources in the least costly way (productive efficiency) to produce the specific mix of goods and services that maximize people's well-being (allocative efficiency). The ability to expand production, together with the full use of available resources, is not sufficient for achieving maximum possible growth. Also required is the efficient use of those resources.

efficiency factor
The capacity of an economy to combine resources effectively to achieve growth of real output that the supply factors make possible.

The supply, demand, and efficiency factors in economic growth are interrelated. Unemployment caused by insufficient total spending (the demand factor) may lower the rate of new capital accumulation (a supply factor) and delay expenditures on research (also a supply factor). Conversely, low spending on investment (a supply factor) may cause insufficient spending (the demand factor) and unemployment. Widespread inefficiency in the use of resources (the efficiency factor) may translate into higher costs of goods and services and thus lower profits, which in turn may slow innovation and reduce the accumulation of capital (supply factors). Economic growth is a dynamic process in which the supply, demand, and efficiency factors all interact.

15.2   Production Possibilities Analysis

To put the six factors underlying economic growth in proper perspective, let's first use the production possibilities analysis introduced in Chapter 2.

Growth and Production Possibilities

Recall that a curve like *AB* in Figure 15-1 is a production possibilities curve. It indicates the various *maximum* combinations of products an economy can produce with its fixed quantity and quality of natural, human, and capital resources and its associated stock of technological knowledge. An improvement in any of the supply factors will push the production possibilities curve outward, as from *AB* to *CD*.

But the demand factor reminds us that an increase in total spending is needed to move the economy from point *a* on *AB* to a point on *CD*. And the efficiency factor reminds us that the location on CD must be optimal for the resources to make their maximum possible dollar contribution to total output. You will recall from Chapter 2 that this "best allocation" is determined by expanding production of each good until its marginal benefit equals its marginal cost. Here, we assume that this optimal combination of capital and consumer goods occurs at point *b*.

For example, the net increase in the size of the labour force in Canada in recent years has been 350,000 to 400,000 workers per year. That increment raises the economy's production capacity. But obtaining the extra output that these added workers could produce depends on their success in finding jobs. It also depends on whether or not the jobs are in firms and industries where the workers' talents are fully and optimally used. Society does not want new labour-force entrants to be unemployed. Nor does it want paediatricians working as plumbers or paediatricians producing services for which marginal costs exceed marginal benefits.

Normally, increases in total spending match increases in production capacity and the economy moves from a point on the previous production possibilities curve to a point on the expanded curve. Moreover, the competitive market system tends to drive the economy toward productive and allocative efficiency. But occasionally the curve may shift outward but leave the economy behind at some level of operation such as *c*. Because *c* is inside the new production possibilities curve *CD*, the economy has not realized its potential for economic growth. (*Key Question 1*)

Labour and Productivity

Although demand and efficiency factors are important, discussions of economic growth focus primarily on supply factors. Society can increase its real output and income in two fundamental ways: (1) by increasing its inputs of resources, and (2) by raising the productivity of those inputs. Figure

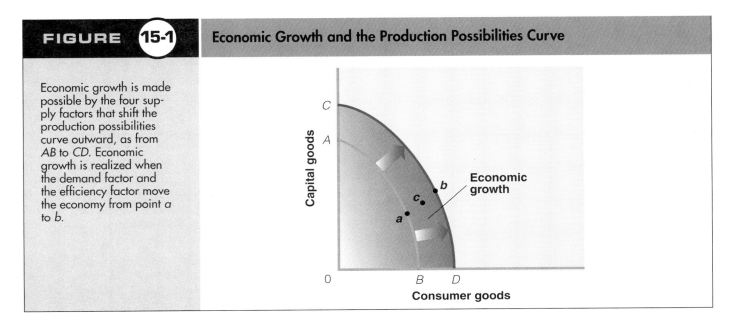

FIGURE 15-1

Economic Growth and the Production Possibilities Curve

Economic growth is made possible by the four supply factors that shift the production possibilities curve outward, as from *AB* to *CD*. Economic growth is realized when the demand factor and the efficiency factor move the economy from point *a* to *b*.

labour productivity
The average product of labour or output per worker per hour.

15-2 focusses on the input of *labour* and provides a useful framework for discussing the role of supply factors in growth. A nation's real GDP in any year depends on the input of labour (measured in worker-hours) multiplied by **labour productivity** (measured as real output per worker per hour).

Real GDP = worker-hours × labour productivity

Or expressed in terms of percentage change:

% change in GDP = % change in worker-hours + % change in productivity

So, thought of in this way, a nation's economic growth from one year to the next depends on its *increase* in labour inputs (if any) and its *increase* in labour productivity (if any).

Illustration: Suppose the hypothetical economy of Ziam has 10 workers in year 1, each working 2000 hours per year (50 weeks at 40 hours per week). The total input of labour therefore is 20,000 hours. If productivity (average real output per worker-hour) is $10 per hour, then real GDP in Ziam will be $200,000 (= 20,000 × $10) per year. If worker-hours rise to 20,200 and labour productivity rises to $10.40 per hour, Ziam's real GDP will increase to $210,080 in year 2. Ziam's rate of economic growth will be about 5 percent [= ($210,080 − $200,000)/$200,000)] for the year.

WORKER-HOURS

What determines the number of hours worked each year? As shown in Figure 15-2, the hours of labour input depend on the size of the employed labour force and the length of the average workweek. Not shown, labour-force size depends on the size of the working-age population and the **labour force participation rate**—the percentage of the working-age population actually in the labour force. The length of the average workweek is governed by legal and institutional considerations and by collective bargaining.

labour force participation rate
The percentage of the working-age population that is actually in the labour force.

LABOUR PRODUCTIVITY

Figure 15-2 tells us that labour productivity is determined by technological progress, the quantity of capital goods available to workers, the quality of the labour itself, and the efficiency with which inputs are allocated, combined, and managed. Productivity rises when the health, training, education, and motivation of workers improve; when workers have more and better machinery and natural resources with which to work; when production is better organized and managed; and when labour is reallocated from less efficient industries to more efficient industries.

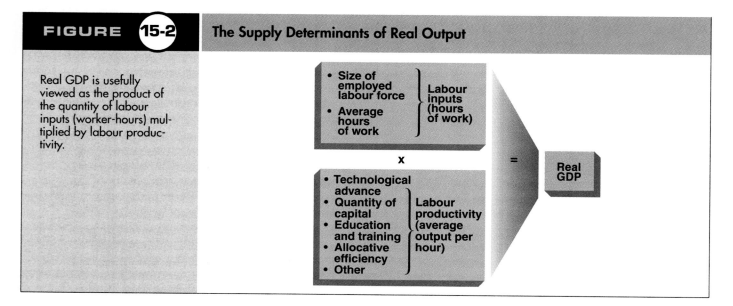

FIGURE 15-2 — **The Supply Determinants of Real Output**

Real GDP is usefully viewed as the product of the quantity of labour inputs (worker-hours) multiplied by labour productivity.

Consider This

Economic Growth Rates

When compounded over many decades, small differences in rates of economic growth add up to substantial differences in real GDP and standards of living. Consider three hypothetical countries—Alpha, Bravo, and Charlie. Suppose that in 2003 these countries have identical levels of real GDP ($1 trillion), population (30 million), and real/GDP capita ($33,000). Also, assume that annual real GDP growth is 2 percent in Alpha, 3 percent in Bravo, and 4 percent in Charlie.

How will these alternative growth rates affect real GDP and real GDP/capita over a long period, say, the 70-year life average life span of a Canadian? By 2073 the 2 percent, 3 percent, and 4 percent growth rates would boost real GDP from $1 trillion to approximately:

- $4 trillion in Alpha;
- $7.9 trillion in Bravo; and
- $15.6 trillion in Charlie.

For illustration, let's assume that each country experienced an average annual population growth of 1 percent over the 70 years. Then, in 2073 real GDP/capita would be about:

- $66,435 in Alpha,
- $131,519 in Bravo, and
- $258,652 in Charlie.

Economic growth rates matter!

Question: Go to the Central Intelligence Agency's World Fact Book Web site at http://www.cia.gov/cia/publications/factbook/geos/ca.html, select the following countries, one at a time, from the drop-down menu, and then click "Economy": Canada, the U.S., China, and Singapore. Which of these countries had the fastest growth rate?

Growth in the AD-AS Model

Let's now link the production possibilities analysis to long-run aggregate supply so that we can show the process of economic growth through the long-run aggregate demand–aggregate supply model developed in Chapter 8.

PRODUCTION POSSIBILITIES AND AGGREGATE SUPPLY

The supply factors that shift the economy's production possibilities curve outward also shift its long-run aggregate supply curve rightward. As shown in Figure 15-3, the outward shift of the production possibilities curve from AB to CD in graph (a) is equivalent to the rightward shift of the economy's long-run aggregate supply curve from AS_{LR1} to AS_{LR2} in graph (b). The long-run AS curves are vertical because an economy's potential output—its full-employment output—is determined by the supply and efficiency factors, not by its price level. Whatever the price level, the economy's potential output remains the same. Moreover, just as price level changes do not shift an economy's production possibilities curve, they do not shift an economy's long-run aggregate supply curve.

LONG-RUN AD-AS MODEL

In Figure 15-4 we use the long-run aggregate demand-aggregate supply model to depict the economic growth process. Suppose that an economy's aggregate demand curve, long-run aggregate supply curve, and short-run aggregate supply curve initially are AD_1, AS_{LR1}, and AS_1, as shown. The equilibrium price level and level of real output are P_1 and GDP_1. At price level P_1, the short-run aggregate supply is AS_1; it slopes upward because, in the short run, changes in the price level cause firms to adjust their output. In the long run, however, price-level changes do not affect the economy's real output, leaving the long-run aggregate supply curve vertical at the economy's potential level of output, here GDP_1. This potential level of output depends on the supply and efficiency factors previously discussed.

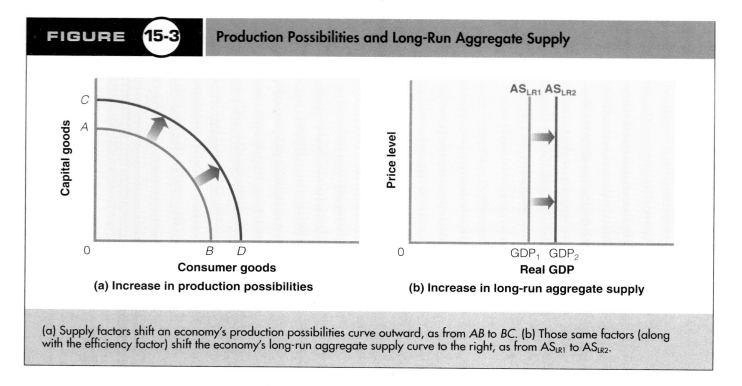

FIGURE 15-3   Production Possibilities and Long-Run Aggregate Supply

(a) Increase in production possibilities

(b) Increase in long-run aggregate supply

(a) Supply factors shift an economy's production possibilities curve outward, as from AB to BC. (b) Those same factors (along with the efficiency factor) shift the economy's long-run aggregate supply curve to the right, as from AS_{LR1} to AS_{LR2}.

Now let's assume that changes in the supply factors (quantity and quality of resources and technology) shift the long-run aggregate supply curve rightward from AS_{LR1} to AS_{LR2}. The economy's potential output has increased, as reflected in the shift of the long-run aggregate supply curve from AS_{LR1} to AS_{LR2}.

If prices and wages are inflexible downward, the economy can realize its greater production potential only through an increase in aggregate demand. Under usual circumstances, such an increase is forthcoming because the production of additional output results in additional income to households and businesses. In Figure 15-4, suppose that this additional income results in increases in consumption and investment spending such that the aggregate demand curve shifts from AD_1 to AD_2. Also suppose that the economy continues to use its resources efficiently.

The increases of aggregate supply and aggregate demand in Figure 15-4 have increased real output from GDP_1 to GDP_2 and have boosted the price level from P_1 to P_2. At the higher price level P_2, the economy confronts a new short-run aggregate supply curve AS_2. The result of the dynamics described in Figure 15-4 is economic growth, accompanied by mild inflation.

In brief, economic growth results from increases in aggregate supply and aggregate demand. Whether zero, mild, or rapid inflation accompanies economic growth depends on the extent to which aggregate demand increases relative to aggregate supply. *(Key Question 5)*

15.3   Canadian Economic Growth

Figure 15-5 shows the average annual growth rates of real GDP and real per capita GDP in Canada since 1950. Since 1950 real GDP grew by about 4 percent annually, whereas real GDP per capita grew by 2.1 percent annually. Economic growth was particularly strong in the 1960s, but declined during the 1970s and 1980s. Although the average annual growth rate for the early 1990s was also relatively slow, real GDP picked up in the closing years of the decade. Specifically, it grew by 3.9 percent in 1998, 5.1 percent in 1999, and 4.4 percent in 2000. Although the economy slowed down in

FIGURE 15-4 — Economic Growth in the Long-Run AD-AS Model

Long-run and short-run aggregate supply have increased over time, as from AS_{LR1} to AS_{LR2} and AS_1 to AS_2. Simultaneously, aggregate demand has shifted rightward, as from AD_1 to AD_2. The actual outcome of these combined shifts has been economic growth, shown as the increase in real output from GDP_1 to GDP_2, accompanied by inflation, shown as the rise in the price level from P_1 to P_2.

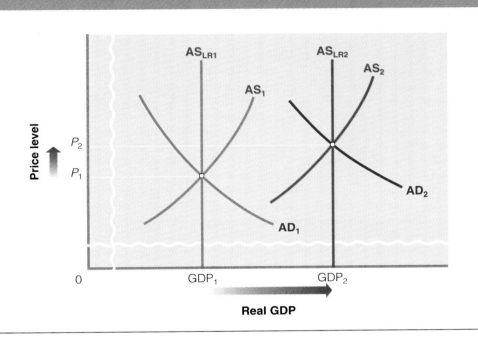

2001, GDP still advanced by 1.5 percent, and avoided the mild recession experienced in the U.S. In 2002, GDP grew by a respectable 3.4 percent. These recent rates not only were higher than previous rates, but higher than those in most other advanced industrial nations during this period. (We will defer discussion of this recent growth surge to later in this chapter.)

FIGURE 15-5 — Canadian Economic Growth, Annual Averages for Five Decades

Growth of real GDP has averaged about 4 percent annually in the last half century and annual growth of real GDP per capita averaged about 2.1 percent. Growth rates in the 1970s and 1980s were less than those in the 1960s, but the rates rebounded in the last half of the 1990s.

Source: Statistics Canada

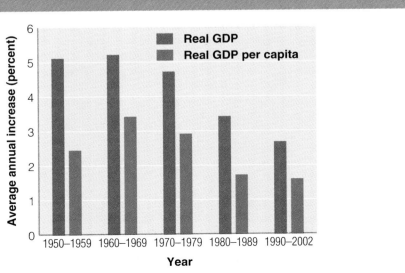

QUICK REVIEW

- The ingredients of economic growth include (a) four supply factors (increases in the quantity and quality of natural resources, increases in the quantity and quality of human resources, increases in the stock of capital goods, and improvements in technology); (b) a demand factor (increased total spending); and (c) an efficiency factor (achieving economic efficiency).

- Economic growth is shown as an outward shift of a nation's production possibilities curve (accompanied by movement from some point on the old curve to a point on the new curve), and combined rightward shifts of the long-run aggregate supply curve, the short-run aggregate supply curve, and the aggregate demand curve.

- Real GDP grew by an average of slightly more than 4 percent annually between 1950 and 2000; over that same period, real GDP per capita grew at an average annual rate of over 2 percent.

15.4 Accounting for Growth in Canada

Output growth in Canada has been considerably greater since 1950 than that which can be attributed solely to increases in the inputs of labour and capital. Two other factors are involved. The first is inter-industry shifts from lower to higher productivity occupations. The best-known example is the shift of workers out of relatively low-productivity farming to higher-productivity urban industry. The second factor is *multifactor productivity (MFP)*, the efficiency with which factors are used together in the production process. It includes technological progress, organizational structure, economies of scale, regulation, entrepreneurship and risk-taking, labour-management relations, capacity utilization, and the efficiency with which resources are allocated. MFP is output growth less input growth.

Table 15-1 shows the sources of the growth of real GDP in Canada from 1961 to 2000.

TABLE 15-1 — Sources of Growth of Real GDP, 1961–2000

Growth in	AVERAGE ANNUAL RATES OF REAL GROWTH (AS PERCENT)				CONTRIBUTION TO TOTAL REAL GROWTH (AS PERCENT)		
	1961-75	1975-82	1982-91	1961-2000	1961-75	1975-82	1961-2000
GDP	5.2	2.5	2.8	3.9			
Labour productivity[1]	3.3	1.5	1.3	2.0			
Capital/labour ratio	2.9	4.5	1.8	1.8			
Input of labour[2]	2.3	1.2	1.6	2.0	28.0	33.9	30.7
Input of capital	5.3	5.7	3.4	3.8	38.4	63.0	35.9
Multifactor Productivity (MFP)	1.7	−0.4	0.5	1.3	33.5	3.2	33.4

[1]Real GDP per person-hour.
[2]Measured in person-hours.
Source: Statistics Canada, Productivity Growth in Canada, Cat. no. 15-204-XPE.

Inputs versus Productivity

In Canada about two-thirds of our growth between 1961 and 2000 was due to the use of more inputs, and about one-third was the consequence of rising productivity—getting more output per unit of labour and capital input. These data emphasize that *productivity growth has been a significant force underlying the growth of our real GDP.* The rate of growth of productivity diminished from the mid-1970s to the early 1990s, but seems to have reversed in the last decade.

Quantity of Labour

The Canadian population and the size of the labour force have both expanded significantly. Between 1929 and 2002, total population grew from 10 million to 31.4 million, and the labour force increased from 4 million to almost 17 million workers. Reductions in the length of the workweek reduced the growth of labour inputs before World War II, but the workweek has remained relatively stable since then. Falling birth rates over the past 30 years have slowed the growth of the native population, but increased immigration has offset that slowdown. Of greatest significance has been the surge of women's participation in the labour force. Partly because of that increased participation, Canadian labour force growth has averaged about 250,000 workers per year during the past 25 years.

Technological Advance

Technological advance is a critical engine of productivity growth and has accounted for a significant percentage of the increase in real output.

Technological advance includes not only innovative production techniques, but also new managerial methods and new forms of business organization that improve the process of production. Generally, technological advance is generated by the discovery of new knowledge, which allows for resources to be combined in new ways that increase output. Once discovered and implemented, new knowledge soon becomes available to entrepreneurs and firms at relatively low cost. Technological advance therefore eventually spreads through the entire economy, boosting productivity and economic growth.

Technological advance and capital formation (investment) are closely related, since technological advance usually promotes investment in new machinery and equipment. In fact, technological advance is often *embodied* within new capital. For example, the purchase of new computers brings into industry speedier, more powerful computers that incorporate new technology.

Technological advance has been both rapid and profound. Gas and diesel engines, conveyor belts, and assembly lines were significant developments of the past. So, too, were fuel-efficient commercial aircraft, integrated microcircuits, personal computers, xerography, and containerized shipping. More recently, technological advance has exploded, particularly in the areas of information technology such as wireless communication and the Internet. Other fertile areas of recent innovation are medicine and biotechnology.

Quantity of Capital

Almost 36 percent of the annual growth of real output in Canada since 1961 is attributable to increases in the quantity of capital. A key determinant of labour productivity is the amount of capital goods available per worker. If both the aggregate stock of capital goods and the size of the labour force increase rapidly over a given period, the individual worker is not necessarily better equipped and productivity will not necessarily rise. But the quantity of capital equipment available per worker in Canada has increased greatly over time.

Public investment in Canada's **infrastructure** (highways and bridges, public transit systems, waste-water treatment facilities, water systems, airports, educational facilities, and so on) has also

infrastructure
The capital goods usually provided by the public sector for the use of its citizens and firms.

grown. This public capital (infrastructure) complements private capital. Investments in new highways promote private investment in new factories and retail stores along their routes. Industrial parks developed by local governments attract manufacturing and distribution firms.

Education and Training

Education and training contribute to a worker's stock of *human capital*—the knowledge and skill that make for a productive worker. Perhaps the simplest measure of labour quality is the level of educational attainment. Figure 15-6 reflects the educational gains in the past two decades. Just under 20 percent of those aged 18 to 24 years now attend university, as opposed to about 12 percent in the early 1970s; those attending community colleges have increased during the same period from 12 percent to almost 23 percent in the 1998–99 school year. It is clear from Figure 15-6 that education has become accessible to more people in Canada. Moreover, Canada ranks relatively highly on international standardized test scores (see Global Perspective 15-1).

Education and training contribute to a worker's stock of human capital.

Resource Allocation and Scale Economies

Labour productivity in Canada has increased in part because of economies of scale and improved resource allocation. Let's consider economies of scale first.

ECONOMIES OF SCALE

economies of scale
Reductions in the average total cost of producing a product as the firm expands the size of plant (its output) in the long run.

Reductions in per-unit cost that result from the increases in the size of markets and firms are called **economies of scale**. Markets have increased in size over time, allowing firms to achieve production advantages associated with greater size. As firms expand, they use more efficient plant, equipment, and methods of manufacturing and delivery that result in greater productivity. They also are better able to recoup substantial investments in developing new products and production

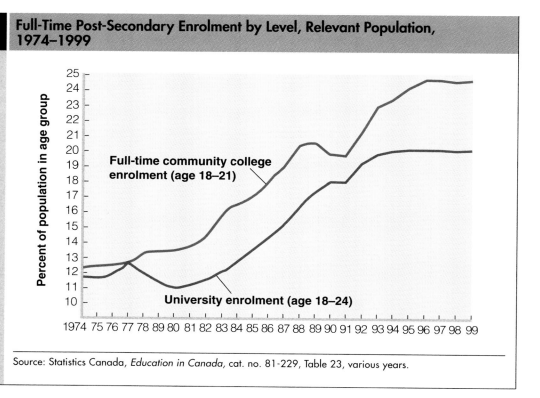

FIGURE 15-6

Full-Time Post-Secondary Enrolment by Level, Relevant Population, 1974–1999

The percentage of young Canadians attending colleges and universities has been rising in the last 25 years, although university enrolment has recently levelled off.

Source: Statistics Canada, *Education in Canada*, cat. no. 81-229, Table 23, various years.

Global Perspective 15.1

Average Test Scores of Eighth-Grade Students in Math and Science, Top 10 Countries, Canada, and the United States

The test performance of Canadian eighth-grade students ranked favourably with that of eighth-graders in several other nations in the Third International Math and Science Study (1999).

Mathematics		Science	
Rank	Score	Rank	Score
1. Singapore	604	1. Taiwan	569
2. South Korea	587	2. Singapore	568
3. Taiwan	585	3. Hungary	552
4. Hong Kong (China)	582	4. Japan	550
5. Japan	579	5. South Korea	549
6. Belgium	558	6. Netherlands	545
7. Netherlands	540	7. Australia	540
8. Slovak Republic	534	8. Czech Republic	539
9. Hungary	532	9. England	538
10. Canada	531	10. Finland	535
19. United States	502	14. Canada	533
		18. United States	515

methods. Examples: Large manufacturers of autos can use elaborate assembly lines with computerization and robotics, but smaller producers must settle for less advanced technologies using more labour inputs. Large pharmaceutical firms greatly reduce the average amount of labour (researchers, production workers) needed to produce each pill as they increase the number of pills produced. Accordingly, economies of scale enable greater real GDP and thus contribute to economic growth.

IMPROVED RESOURCE ALLOCATION

Improved resource allocation means that workers have moved over time from low-productivity employment to high-productivity employment. Historically, much labour has shifted from agriculture, where labour productivity is low, to manufacturing, where it is quite high. More recently, labour has shifted away from manufacturing industries to even higher-productivity industries such as computer software, business consulting, and pharmaceuticals. As a result of such shifts, the average productivity of Canadian workers has increased.

Also, discrimination in education and the labour market has historically deterred some women and minorities from entering high-productivity jobs. With the decline of such discrimination over time, many members of those groups have shifted from low-productivity jobs to higher-productivity jobs. The result has been higher overall labour productivity and real GDP.

Finally, tariffs, import quotas, and other barriers to international trade tend to relegate resources to relatively unproductive pursuits. The long-run movement toward liberalized international trade has improved the allocation of resources, increased labour productivity, and expanded real output, both here and abroad. *(Key Question 6)*

Other Factors

Several difficult-to-measure factors influence a nation's rate of economic growth. The overall social-cultural-political environment of Canada, for example, has fostered economic growth. The market system that has prevailed in Canada since its founding has fostered many personal and corporate incentives that promote growth. Canada has also had a stable political system characterized by democratic principles, international order, the right of property ownership, the legal status of enterprise, and the enforcement of contracts. Economic freedom and political freedom have been "growth-friendly."

Unlike some nations, there are virtually no social or moral taboos on production and material progress in Canada. The nation's social philosophy has embraced material advances as an attainable and desirable economic goal. The inventor, the innovator, and the businessperson are accorded high degrees of prestige and respect in Canadian society.

Moreover, Canadians have had positive attitudes toward work and risk-taking, resulting in an ample supply of willing workers and innovative entrepreneurs. A flow of determined immigrants has greatly augmented that supply.

> ## QUICK REVIEW
>
> - Improvements in labour productivity account for about a third of increases in Canadian real GDP.
>
> - Improved technology, more capital, greater education and training, economies of scale, and better resource allocation have been the main contributors to Cana-
>
> dian productivity growth and thus to Canadian economic growth.
>
> - Other factors that have been favourable to Canadian growth include reliance on the market system, a stable political system, a social philosophy that embraces material progress, and an abundant supply of willing workers and entrepreneurs.

15.5   The Productivity Speedup: A New Economy?

New Economy
The economy, developed since 1995, with the main characteristics of substantially faster productivity growth and economic growth, caused by rapid technological advance and the emergence of the global economy.

Table 15-2 shows the growth of labour productivity (as measured by changes in the index of labour productivity) in Canada from 1961 to 2000, along with separate trend lines for 1961–1975, 1975–1982, and 1982–1991. Labour productivity grew by an average of 2.0 percent per year over the entire 1961–2000 period, but only 1.3 percent yearly over the 1982–1991 period. But in the second half of the 1990s labour productivity growth averaged 2.0 percent, leading many economists to believe that this higher productivity growth resulted from a significant new wave of technological advance, coupled with global competition. Some economists say that Canada has achieved a **New Economy**—one with a higher projected trend-rate of productivity growth and therefore greater potential economic growth than in the 1975–1991 period.

This increase in productivity growth is important because real output, real income, and real wages are linked to labour productivity. To see why, suppose you are alone on an uninhabited island. The number of fish you can catch or coconuts you can pick per hour—your productivity—is your real wage (or real income) per hour. By *increasing* your productivity, you can improve your standard of living because greater output per hour means there are more fish and coconuts (goods) available to consume.

So it is for the economy as a whole: Over long periods, the economy's labour productivity determines its average real hourly wage. The economy's income per hour is equal to its output per hour. Productivity growth therefore is its main route for increasing its standard of living. It allows firms to pay higher wages without lowering their business profits. As we demonstrated in the Consider This box, even a seemingly small percentage change in productivity growth, if sustained over many years, can make a substantial difference to how fast a nation's standard of living rises. We know from the *rule of 70* (Chapter 6) that if a nation's productivity grows by 2.5 percent annually rather than 1.5 percent, its standard of living will double in about 28 years rather than 47 years.

Reasons for the Productivity Speedup

Why has productivity growth increased relative to earlier periods? What is "new" about the New Economy?

The Microchip and Information Technology   The core element of the productivity speedup is an explosion of entrepreneurship and innovation based on the microprocessor, or *microchip*, which bundles transistors on a piece of silicon. Advocates of the New Economy liken the invention of the microchip to that of electricity, the automobile, air travel, the telephone, and television in importance and scope.

The microchip has found its way into thousands of applications. It has helped create a wide array of new products and services and new ways of doing business. Its immediate result was the pocket calculator, the bar code scanner, the personal computer, the laptop computer, and more powerful business computers. But the miniaturization of electronic circuits also advanced the development of other products such as the cell phone and pager, computer-guided lasers, the deciphered genetic codes, global positioning equipment, energy conservation systems, Doppler radar, digital cameras, and many more.

Perhaps of greatest significance, the widespread availability of personal and notebook computers stimulated the desire to tie them together. That desire promoted rapid development of the Internet and all its many manifestations such as business-to-household and business-to-business electronic commerce (e-commerce). The combination of the computer, fibre optic cable, wireless technology, and the Internet constitute a spectacular advance in **information technology**, which has been used to connect all parts of the world.

information technology
New and more efficient methods of delivering and receiving information through use of computers, fax machines, wireless phones, and the Internet.

start-up firm
A new firm focussed on creating and introducing a particular new product or employing a specific new production or distribution method.

New Firms and Increasing Returns   Hundreds of new **start-up firms** advanced various aspects of the new information technology. Many of these firms created more "hype" than goods and services and quickly fell by the wayside. But a number of firms flourished, eventually to take their places among the nation's largest firms. Examples of those firms include Nortel Networks (Internet and wireless switching systems), Celestica (computer manufacturing), Rogers Communications (Cable Internet provider and wireless phone service), Intel (microchips); Apple and Dell (personal computers); Microsoft, Oracle, and Intuit (computer software); Cisco Systems (Internet switching systems); Yahoo and Google (Internet search engines); and Amazon.com (electronic commerce). There are scores more! Most of these firms were either "not on the radar" or "a small blip on the radar" twenty-five years ago. Today they each have large annual revenue and employ thousands of workers.

increasing returns
An increase in a firm's output by a larger percentage than the percentage increase in its inputs.

Successful new firms often experience **increasing returns**, which occur *when a firm's output increases by a larger percentage than the increase in its inputs (resources).* For example, suppose that Techco decides to double the size of its operations to meet the growing demand for its services. After doubling its plant and equipment and doubling its workforce, say, from 100 workers to 200 workers, it finds that its total output has tripled from 8000 units to 24,000 units. Techco has experienced increasing returns; its output has increased by 200 percent while its inputs have increased by only 100 percent. Consequently, its labour productivity has gone up from $80 (= 8000 units/100 workers) to $120 (24,000 units/200 workers). Increasing returns boost labour productivity, which, other things equal, lowers per-unit costs of production. These reductions in costs resulting from larger firm size are *economies of scale*.

There are a number of sources of increasing returns and economies of scale for newly emerging firms.

- *More specialized inputs*   Firms can use more specialized and thus more productive capital and workers as they expand their operations. A growing new e-commerce business, for example, can purchase highly specialized inventory management systems and hire specialized personnel, such as accountants, marketing managers, and system maintenance experts.

- *Spreading of development costs*   Firms can spread high product development costs over greater output. For example, suppose that a new software product cost $100,000 to develop and only $2 per unit to manufacture and sell. If the firm sells 1000 units of the software its per-unit cost will be $102 [= ($100,000 + $2000)/1000], but if it sells 500,000 units that cost will drop to only $2.20 [= $100,000 + $1 million)/500,000].

- *Simultaneous consumption*   Many of the products and services of the New Economy can satisfy many customers at the same time. Unlike a litre of gas that needs to be produced for each buyer, a software program needs to be produced only once. It then becomes available at very low expense to thousands or even millions of buyers. The same is true of entertainment delivered on CDs, movies distributed on DVDs, and information disseminated through the Internet.

- *Network effects*   Software and Internet services become more beneficial to a buyer the greater the number of households and businesses that also buy them. When others have Internet service you can send e-mail messages to them. When they also have software that allows display of documents and photos, you can attach those items to your e-mail messages. These systems advantages are called **network effects**, which are *increases in the value of the product to each user, including existing users, as the total number of users rise.* The domestic and global expansion of the Internet in particular has produced network effects, as have cell phones, pagers, handheld computers, and other aspects of wireless communication. Network effects magnify the value of output well beyond the costs of inputs.

network effects
Increases in the value of a product to each user, including existing users, as the total number of users rises.

learning-by-doing
Achieving greater productivity and lower average total cost through gains in knowledge and skill that accompany repetition of a task; a source of economies of scale.

- *Learning-by-doing*   Finally, firms that produce new products or pioneer new ways of doing business ultimately experience increasing returns through **learning-by-doing**. Tasks that initially may have taken them hours may take them only minutes, once the methods are perfected.

Whatever the particular source of increasing returns, the result is higher productivity, which tends to reduce the per-unit cost of producing and delivering products. Table 15-3 lists a number of specific U.S. examples of cost reduction from technology in the New Economy; the magnitude can be expected to be the same in Canada.

GLOBAL COMPETITION

The Canadian economy is now not only characterized by information technology and increasing returns, but also by heightened global competition. The collapse of the socialist economies in the late 1980s and early 1990s together with the success of market systems have led to a reawakening of

---

TABLE 15-2   Examples of Cost Reduction from Technology in the New Economy

- The cost of storing one megabyte of information—enough for a 320-page book—fell from $5257 in 1975 to 17¢ in 1999.
- Prototyping each part of a car once took Ford weeks and cost $20,000 on average. Using an advanced 3-D object printer, it cut the time to just hours and the cost to less than $20.
- Studies show that telecommuting saves businesses about $20,000 annually for a worker earning $44,000—a saving in lost work time and employee retention costs, plus gains in worker productivity.
- Using scanners and computers, Weyerhaeuser increased the lumber yield and value from each log by 30 percent.
- Amoco has used 3-D seismic exploration technology to cut the cost of finding oil from nearly $10 per barrel in 1991 to under $1 per barrel today.
- Wal-Mart reduced the operating cost of its delivery trucks by 20 percent through installing computers, global positioning gear, and cell phones in 4300 vehicles.
- Banking transactions on the Internet cost 1¢ each, compared with $1.14 for face-to-face and pen-and-paper communication.

Source: Compiled and directly quoted from W. Michael Cox and Richard Alm, "The New Paradigm." Federal Reserve Bank of Dallas Annual Report, May 2000, various pages.

Global Perspective 15.2

Growth Competitiveness Index

The World Economic Forum annually compiles a growth competitiveness index, which uses various factors (such as innovativeness, effective transfer of technology among sectors, efficiency of the financial system, rates of investment, and degree of integration with the rest of the world) to measure the ability of a country to achieve economic growth over time. Here is its latest top 10 list:

Country	Growth Competitiveness Ranking, 2001
United States	1
Finland	2
Taiwan	3
Singapore	4
Sweden	5
Switzerland	6
Australia	7
Canada	8
Norway	9
Denmark	10

Source: World Economic Forum, <www.weforum.org>.

www.europe.eu.int
European Union

capitalism throughout the world. The new information technologies have "shrunk the globe" and made it imperative for all firms to lower their costs and prices and to innovate in order to remain competitive. Free-trade zones such as NAFTA and the European Union (EU), along with trade liberalization through the World Trade Organization (WTO), have also heightened competition internationally by removing trade protection from domestic firms. The larger geographic markets, in turn, have enabled firms to expand beyond the borders of Canada. Global Perspective 15.2 shows the growth competitiveness index for 2002.

Macroeconomic Implications

Stronger productivity growth and heightened global competition have a number of important implications for the macro economy.

More rapid economic growth Of greatest importance, the productivity speedup allows the economy to achieve a higher rate of economic growth. A glance back at Figure 15-3 will help make this point. If the shifts of the curves reflect annual changes in the old economy, then the growth of the New Economy would be depicted by an outward shift of the production possibilities curve beyond CD in Figure 15-3a, and a shift of the long-run aggregate supply curve farther to the right than AS_{LR2} in Figure 15-3b. When coupled with economic efficiency and increased total spending, the economy's real GDP would rise by more than that shown. That is, the economy would achieve a higher rate of economic growth.

In this view, the New Economy has a higher "safe speed limit" than the old economy because production capacity rises more rapidly. The New Economy can grow by, say, 4 percent, rather than 2 or 3 percent each year without igniting demand-pull inflation. Increases in aggregate demand that in the past would have caused inflation, do not cause inflation because they are buffered by faster productivity growth. Even when nominal wage increases rise to match the productivity increases, as they usually do, per-unit production costs, and therefore prices, remain stable.

Global competition in the New Economy also contributes to price stability. Proponents of the New Economy say that increasing returns and global competition explain why inflation remained mild as real GDP rapidly increased between 1995 and 2000.

Low natural rate of unemployment   A falling natural rate of unemployment (NRU) such as that of 1995–2002 (down to about 7.5 percent) is also consistent with the New Economy. The new information technology reduces frictional unemployment by enabling workers and employers to quickly find each other.

Growing tax revenues   Finally, the faster economic growth enabled by the productivity speedup produces larger increases in personal income and, with given tax rates, larger increases in government tax revenues. The quick and unexpected elimination of the federal budget deficit during the last half of the 1990s resulted largely from the higher rates of growth of real GDP. In 1994 the federal government had a budget *deficit* of almost $40 billion; in 2002 it had a budget *surplus* of $8 billion.

A caution: Those who champion the idea of a New Economy emphasize that it does not mean that the business cycle is dead. Indeed, the economy slowed in 2001, but proceeded to expand by 3.4 percent in 2002. The New Economy is simply one for which the *trend lines* of productivity growth and economic growth are steeper than they were in the preceding two decades. Real output may periodically deviate below and above that trend line.

Skepticisms about the Permanence of the Productivity Speedup

Although most macroeconomists have revised their forecasts for long-term productivity growth upward, at least slightly, others are still skeptical and urge a "wait-and-see" approach. Skeptics acknowledge the economy has experienced a rapid advance of new technology, many new firms have experienced increasing returns, and global competition has increased. But they wonder if these factors are sufficiently profound to produce a 10–15 year period of substantially higher rates of productivity growth and real GDP growth.

The higher rates of productivity and real GDP growth between 1995 and 2001 *are* consistent with a long-lived New Economy. Unfortunately, they are also consistent with a rapid short-run economic expansion fuelled by an extraordinarily brisk rise in consumption and investment spending. Such *economic booms* raise productivity by increasing real output faster than employment (labour inputs), but they are unsustainable over longer periods. Skeptics point out that productivity surged between 1975 and 1978 and between 1983 and 1986, but in each case soon reverted to its lower long-run trend.

For a time, economic expansions need not create inflation, so long as wage growth does not exceed the growth of productivity. But economic booms eventually create shortages, which produce inflationary pressures. Even industries that once had decreasing or constant costs can begin to experience rising costs when the pool of available workers dries up. The excessive demand that is causing the boom eventually raises all prices, including the price of labour. Rising inflation or the threat of rising inflation prompt the Bank of Canada to increases in interest rates. For example, the Bank of Canada raised the overnight lending rate from 2.75 percent to 3.25 percent in a series of steps in 2002 and 2003.

By reducing investment spending, the higher interest rates dampen some of the inflationary pressure but may inadvertently slow the economy too much, causing recession. In any event, productivity and output growth stall. The higher trend line of productivity inferred from the short-run spurt of productivity proves to be an illusion. Only by looking backward over long periods can economists distinguish the start of a new long-term trend from a short-term boost in productivity related to the business cycle.

What Can We Conclude?

Given the different views on the New Economy, what should we conclude? Perhaps the safest conclusions are these:

- We should be pleased with the exceptional performance of the economy between 1995 and 2002, for its own sake, whether or not it represents a New Economy. These were remarkable times for the Canadian economy.

- The prospects for a long-lived productivity speedup are good (see Global Perspective 15.2). Studies indicate that productivity advance related to information technology has spread to a wide range of industries, including services.

- Time will tell. It will be several more years before economists can declare the recent productivity speedup a long-term reality. *(Key Question 9)*

QUICK REVIEW

- Over long time periods, labour productivity growth determines an economy's growth of real wages and its standard of living.

- Many economists believe that Canada has achieved a New Economy of faster productivity growth and higher rates of economic growth.

- The productivity speedup is based on rapid technological change in the form of the microchip and information technology, increasing returns and lower per-unit costs, and heightened global competition that helps hold down prices.

- Faster productivity growth means the economy has a higher "economic speed limit;" it can grow more rapidly than previously without producing inflation; the economy has a lower natural rate of unemployment; and it generates more rapid increases in tax revenues. Nonetheless, many economists caution that it is too early to determine whether the New Economy is a lasting long-run trend or a short-lived occurrence.

15.6   Is Growth Desirable and Sustainable?

Economists usually take for granted that economic growth is desirable and sustainable. But not everyone agrees.

The Antigrowth View

Critics of growth say industrialization and growth result in pollution, global warming, ozone depletion, and other environmental problems. These adverse spillover costs occur because inputs in the production process re-enter the environment as some form of waste. The more rapid our growth and the higher our standard of living, the more waste the environment must absorb—or attempt to absorb. In an already wealthy society, further growth usually means satisfying increasingly trivial wants at the cost of mounting threats to the ecological system.

Critics of growth also argue there is little compelling evidence that economic growth has solved sociological problems such as poverty, homelessness, and discrimination. Consider poverty. In the antigrowth view, Canadian poverty is a problem of distribution, not production. The solution to the problem requires commitment and political courage to redistribute wealth and income, not further increases in output.

Antigrowth sentiment also says that although growth may permit us to "make a better living," it does not give us "the good life." We may be producing more and enjoying it less. Growth means assembly-line jobs, worker burnout, and alienated employees who have little or no control over decisions affecting their lives. The changing technology at the core of growth poses new anxieties and new sources of insecurity for workers. Both high-level and low-level workers face the prospect of having their hard-earned skills and experience rendered obsolete by an onrushing technology. High-growth economies are high-stress economies, which may impair our physical and mental health.

Finally, critics of high rates of growth doubt that they are sustainable. The planet Earth has finite amounts of natural resources available, and they are being consumed at alarming rates. Higher rates of economic growth simply speed up the degradation and exhaustion of the earth's resources. In this view, slower economic growth that is sustainable is preferable to faster growth.

In Defence of Economic Growth

The primary defence of growth is that it is the path to the greater material abundance and higher living standards desired by the vast majority of people. Rising output and incomes allow people to buy more of the goods and services they want. Growth also enables society to improve the nation's infrastructure, improve the care of the sick and elderly, provide greater access for the disabled, and provide more police and fire protection. Economic growth may be the only realistic way to reduce poverty, since there is little political support for greater redistribution of income. The way to improve the economic position of the poor is to increase household incomes through higher productivity and economic growth. Also, a no-growth policy among industrial nations might severely limit growth in poor nations. Foreign investment and development assistance in those nations would fall, keeping the world's poor in poverty longer.

Economic growth has not made labour more unpleasant or hazardous, as critics suggest. New machinery is usually less taxing and less dangerous than the machinery it replaces. Air-conditioned workplaces are more pleasant than steamy workshops. Furthermore, why would an end to economic growth reduce materialism or alienation? The loudest protests against materialism are heard in those nations and groups who now enjoy the highest levels of material abundance! The high standard of living that growth provides has increased our leisure and given us more time for reflection and self-fulfillment.

Does growth threaten the environment? The connection between growth and environment is tenuous, say growth proponents. Increases in economic growth need not mean increases in pollution. Pollution is not so much a by-product of growth as it is a "problem of the commons." Much of the environment—streams, lakes, oceans, and the air—is treated as "common property," with no restrictions on its use. The commons have become our dumping grounds; we have overused and debased them. Environmental pollution is a case of spillover or external costs, and correcting this problem involves regulatory legislation or specific taxes ("effluent charges") to remedy misuse of the environment.

Those who support growth admit there are serious environmental problems. But they say that limiting growth is the wrong solution. Growth has allowed economies to reduce pollution, be more sensitive to environmental considerations, set aside wilderness, create national parks, and clean up hazardous waste, while still enabling rising household incomes.

Is growth sustainable? Yes, say the proponents of growth. If we were depleting natural resources faster than their discovery, we would see the prices of those resources rise. That has not been the case for most natural resources, and in fact, the prices of many of them have declined. And if one natural resource becomes too expensive, another resource will be substituted for it. Moreover, say economists, economic growth has more to do with the expansion and application of human knowledge and information, not on extractable natural resources. Economic growth is limited only by human imagination.

THE LASTword — The Kyoto Protocol and Economic Growth in Canada

Can economic growth be environmentally friendly?

At the end of 2002 the Canadian Parliament voted to support government plans to ratify the Kyoto Protocol, which commits Canada to cut greenhouse gases and emissions to 6 percent below their 1990 levels. The lead up to the vote generated much controversy in the Canadian media. Industry groups and some of the provinces, particularly energy rich Alberta, were against the ratification of the Kyoto Protocol on the grounds that it would hamper economic growth. The Canadian Trucking Alliance (CTA), a lobby group that may be potentially harmed, claimed that according to the governments own estimates, the Kyoto accord would result in a GDP loss of 1.9 percent per annum, or approximately $30 billion by 2010. The CTA noted that the federal government's proposal to adopt new smog-reducing standards for truck diesel fuel and truck engines would mean lower fuel efficiency, and thus increase costs for its members. If such costs could not be passed on to consumers it would result in lower profits and perhaps the elimination of trucking jobs.

Not everyone is critical of the federal government's ratification of the Kyoto Protocol. According to a study commissioned by the David Suzuki Foundation and the World Wild Life Fund, the Canadian economy will actually benefit from the target emission set out by the Kyoto Accord. Their study estimates that 52,000 net new jobs would be created in Canada by 2012, as consumers shift spending away from fossil fuels and electricity and towards other, presumably more environmentally friendly, goods and services. The study, released by Boston based Tellus Institute, also forecasts an actual increase of GDP of $2 billion per year above what it would have been without the reductions in emissions dictated by the Kyoto Accord.

In all likelihood, the Canadian economy is likely to grow at a slower pace to meet the Kyoto emission targets. But an economic assessment of reduced greenhouse emission gases in Canada must also include the expected benefits. The benefits include cleaner air and a slowing down of the global warming trend that appears to have started with the increase of gas emissions from the burning of fossil fuels in industrialized nations. Thus, while the implementation of the Kyoto Protocol may have costs, it will likely also have substantial benefits.

CHAPTER SUMMARY

15.1 INGREDIENTS OF GROWTH

- Economic growth—measured as either an increase in real output or an increase in real output per capita—increases material abundance and raises a nation's standard of living.
- The supply factors in economic growth are (a) the quantity and quality of a nation's natural resources, (b) the quantity and quality of its human resources, (c) its stock of capital facilities, and (d) its technology. Two other factors—a sufficient level of aggregate demand and economic efficiency—are necessary for the economy to realize its growth potential.

15.2 PRODUCTION POSSIBILITIES ANALYSIS

- The growth of production capacity is shown graphically as an outward shift of a nation's production possibilities curve or a rightward shift of its long-run aggregate supply curve. Growth is realized when total spending rises sufficiently to match the growth of production capacity.

15.3 CANADIAN ECONOMIC GROWTH

- Since 1950 the annual growth rate of real GDP for Canada has averaged slightly more than 4 percent; the annual growth rate of real GDP per capita has been over 2 percent.

15.4 ACCOUNTING FOR GROWTH IN CANADA

- Canada's real GDP has grown partly because of increased inputs of labour and primarily because of increases in the productivity of labour. The increases in productivity have resulted mainly from technological progress, increases in the quantity of capital per worker, improvements in the quality of labour, economies of scale, and an improved allocation of labour.

- Over long time periods, the growth of labour productivity underlies an economy's growth of real wages and its standard of living.

15.5 THE PRODUCTIVITY SPEEDUP: A NEW ECONOMY?

- The New Economy is based on (a) rapid technological change in the form of the microchip and information technology, (b) increasing returns and lower per-unit costs, and (c) heightened global competition that holds down prices.

- The main sources of increasing returns in the New Economy are (a) use of more specialized inputs as firms grow, (b) the spreading of development costs, (c) simultaneous consumption by consumers, (d) network effects, and (e) learning-by-doing. Increasing returns means higher productivity and lower per-unit production costs.

- Those who champion the New Economy say that it has a lower natural rate of unemployment than the old economy, can grow more rapidly without producing

inflation, and generates higher tax revenues because of faster growth of personal income.

- Skeptics of the New Economy urge a wait-and-see approach. They point out that surges in productivity and real GDP growth have previously occurred during vigorous economic expansions but do not necessarily represent long-lived trends.

15.6 IS GROWTH DESIRABLE AND SUSTAINABLE?

- Critics of rapid growth say that it adds to environmental degradation, increases human stress, and exhausts the earth's finite supply of natural resources. Defenders of rapid growth say that it is the primary path to the rising living standards nearly universally desired by people, that it need not debase the environment, and that there are no indications that we are running out of resources. Growth is based on the expansion and application of human knowledge, which is limited only by human imagination.

TERMS AND CONCEPTS

supply factor, p. 350
demand factor, p. 350
efficiency factor, p. 350
labour productivity, p. 352
labour force participation rate, p.352

infrastructure, p. 357
economies of scale, p. 358
New Economy, p. 360
information technology, p. 361
start-up firm, p. 361

increasing returns, p. 361
network effects, p. 362
learning-by-doing, p. 362

STUDY QUESTIONS

1. **KEY QUESTION**   What are the four supply factors of economic growth? What is the demand factor? What is the efficiency factor? Illustrate these factors in terms of the production possibilities curve.

2. Suppose that Alpha and Omega have identically sized working-aged populations, but that annual work hours are much greater in Alpha than in Omega. Provide two possible explanations.

3. Suppose that work hours in New Zombie are 200 in year 1 and productivity is $8 per hour. What is New Zombie's real GDP? If work hours increase to 210 in year 2 and productivity rises to $10 per hour, what is New Zombie's rate of economic growth?

4. What is the relationship between a nation's production possibilities curve and its long-run aggregate supply curve? How do each relate to the idea of a New Economy?

5. **KEY QUESTION**   Between 1990 and 1999 the Canadian price level rose by about 20 percent while its

real output increased by about 33 percent. Use the aggregate demand-aggregate supply model to illustrate these outcomes graphically.

6. **KEY QUESTION**   To what extent have increases in Canadian real GDP resulted from more labour inputs? From higher labour productivity?

7. True or false? If false, explain why.

   a. Technological advance, which to date has played a relatively small role in Canadian economic growth, is destined to play a more important role in the future.

   b. Many public capital goods are complementary to private capital goods.

   c. Immigration has slowed economic growth in Canada.

8. Explain why there is such a close relationship between changes in a nation's rate of productivity growth and changes in its average real hourly wage.

9. **KEY QUESTION** Relate each of the following to the New Economy:

   a. The rate of productivity growth

   b. Information technology

   c. Increasing returns

   d. Network effects

   e. Global competition

10. Provide three examples of products or services that can be simultaneously consumed by many people. Explain why labour productivity greatly rises as the firm sells more units of the product or service. Explain why the higher level of sales greatly reduces the per-unit cost of the product.

11. What is meant when economists say that the Canadian economy has "a higher safe speed limit" than previ-ously? If the New Economy has a higher safe speed limit, what explains the series of interest-rate hikes engineered by the Bank of Canada in 1999 and 2000?

12. Productivity often rises during economic expansions and falls during economic recessions. Can you think of reasons why? Briefly explain. (Hint: Remember that the level of productivity involves both levels of output and levels of labour input.)

13. Do you think economic growth is desirable and sus-tainable? Explain your position on this issue.

14. **(The Last Word)** Visit the Government of Canada Web site on climate change at http://www.climatechange.gc.ca/english/issues/how_will/fed_world.shtml. What diseases are likely to spread in Canada from other parts of the world as a result of global warming? Will spreading of such diseases have an economic impact?

INTERNET APPLICATION QUESTIONS

1. **Economic growth in Canada—what are the latest rates?** Visit the Statistics Canada Web site through the McConnell-Brue-Barbiero homepage (Chapter 15). What are the annual growth rates for the Cana-dian economy for the last five years? Is the average of those rates above or below the long-run Canadian annual growth rate of 3.5 percent?

2. **Web-Based Question: What's up with pro-ductivity?** Visit the Statistics Canada Web site through the McConnell-Brue-Barbiero homepage (Chapter 15), and compute the average annual labour productivity growth rate for the 1997–2000 period. Is the average of those rates higher or lower than the 1.3 percent average annual growth rate of productivity during the productiv-ity growth slowdown of the 1982–1991 period?

5 Part

International Economics and the World Economy

16

Chapter

International Trade

The WTO, trade deficits, dumping. Exchange rates, the EU, the G7 nations. The IMF, official reserves, currency interventions. Capital flight, special economic zones, the ruble. This is the language of international economics, the subject of Part Five. To understand the increasingly integrated world economy, we need to learn more about this language and the ideas that it conveys.

International trade and the global economy affect all of us daily, whether we are hiking in the wilderness, driving our cars, listening to music, or working at our jobs. We cannot "leave the world behind." We are enmeshed in a global web of economic relationships—trading of goods and services, multinational corporations, cooperative ventures among the world's firms, and ties among the world's financial markets. That web is so complex that it is difficult to determine just what is—or isn't—a Canadian product. A Finnish company owns Wilson sporting goods; a Swiss company owns Gerber baby food; and a British corporation owns Burger King. The Toyota Corolla sedan is manufactured in Canada. Many "Canadian" products are made with components from abroad, and, conversely, many "foreign" products contain numerous Canadian-produced parts.

In this chapter we build on Chapter 4 by providing both a deeper analysis of the benefits of international trade and a fuller appraisal of the arguments for protectionism. Then in Chapter 17 we examine exchange rates and the balance of payments. An Internet-only chapter looks at the special problems of developing economies, and another Internet-only chapter focusses on the transition economies of Russia and China.

read my own

16.1   Canada and International Linkages

www.oecd.org/eco/out/
eo.htm
OECD Economic Outlook

Several economic flows link the Canadian economy and the economies of other nations. As identified in Figure 16-1, these flows are:

- ***Goods and services flows*** or simply ***trade flows***   Canada exports goods and services to other nations and imports goods and services from them.

- ***Capital and labour flows*** or simply ***resource flows***   Canadian firms establish production facilities—new capital—in foreign countries and foreign firms establish production facilities in Canada. Labour also moves between nations. Each year many foreigners immigrate to Canada and some Canadians move to other nations.

- ***Information and technology flows***   Canada transmits information to other nations about Canadian products, price, interest rates, and investment opportunities and receives such information from abroad. Firms in other countries use technology created in Canada and Canadian businesses incorporate technology developed abroad.

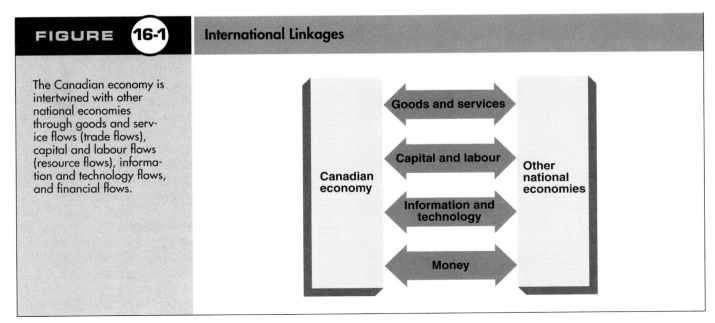

FIGURE 16-1   International Linkages

The Canadian economy is intertwined with other national economies through goods and service flows (trade flows), capital and labour flows (resource flows), information and technology flows, and financial flows.

- *Financial flows*   Money is transferred between Canada and other countries for several purposes; for example, paying for imports, buying foreign assets, paying interest on debt, and providing foreign aid. More will be said about financial flows in Chapter 17.

Canadian International Trade: Volume and Pattern

Global Perspective 16.1 suggests the importance of world trade for selected countries. Canada, with a limited domestic market, cannot efficiently produce the variety of goods its citizens want. So we must import goods from other nations. That, in turn, means that we must export, or sell abroad, some of our own products. For Canada, exports make up about 40 percent of our gross domestic output (GDP)—the market value of all goods and services produced in an economy. Other countries, the United States, for example, have a large internal market. Although the total volume of trade is huge in the United States, it constitutes a much smaller percentage of GDP than in a number of other nations.

VOLUME

For Canada and for the world as a whole the volume of international trade has been increasing both absolutely and relative to their GDPs. A comparison of the boxed data in Figure 16-2 reveals substantial growth in the dollar amount of Canadian exports and imports over the past several decades. The graph shows the growth of Canadian exports and imports of goods and services as percentages of GDP. Canadian exports and imports currently are approximately 40 percent of GDP, about double their percentages in 1971.

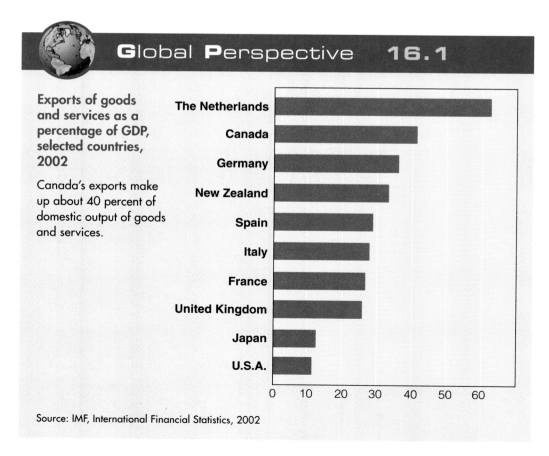

Global Perspective 16.1

Exports of goods and services as a percentage of GDP, selected countries, 2002

Canada's exports make up about 40 percent of domestic output of goods and services.

Source: IMF, International Financial Statistics, 2002

FIGURE 16-2 — Canadian Trade As Percentage of GDP

Canadian imports and exports of goods and services have increased in volume and have doubled as a percentage of GDP since 1971.

Source: Statistics Canada, CANSIM, series D15458 and D15471.

Visit www.mcgrawhill. ca/college/mcconnell for data update.

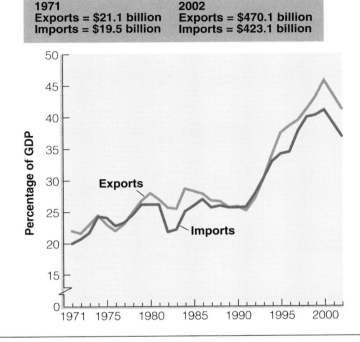

1971	2002
Exports = $21.1 billion	**Exports = $470.1 billion**
Imports = $19.5 billion	**Imports = $423.1 billion**

DEPENDENCE

Canada is almost entirely dependent on other countries for bananas, cocoa, coffee, spices, tea, raw silk, nickel, tin, natural rubber, and diamonds. Imported goods compete with Canadian goods in many of our domestic markets: Japanese cars, French and American wines, and Swiss and Austrian snow skis are a few examples.

Of course, world trade is a two-way street. Many Canadian industries rely on foreign markets. Almost all segments of Canadian agriculture rely on sales abroad; for example, exports of wheat, corn, and tobacco vary from one-fourth to more than one-half of the total output of those crops. The Canadian computer, chemical, aircraft, automobile, and machine tool industries, among many others, sell significant portions of their output in international markets. Table 16-1 shows some of the major Canadian exports and imports.

TRADE PATTERNS

The following facts will give you an overview of international trade:

- Canada had a *trade surplus* in goods in 2002. Canadian exports of goods exceeded Canadian imports of goods by $47 billion.

- Canada had a *trade deficit* in services (such as accounting services and financial services) in 2002. Canadian imports of services exceeded export of services by $7.2 billion.

- Canada imports some of the same categories of goods that it exports, specifically, automobiles products and machinery and equipment (see Table 16-2). This type of trade is called intra-industry trade.

TABLE 16-1 — Principal Canadian Exports and Imports of Goods, 2002

Exports	% of Total	Imports	% of Total
Machinery and equipment	24	Machinery and equipment	29
Automotive products	23	Automotive products	23
Industrial goods and materials	17	Industrial goods and materials	21
Forestry products	9	Consumer goods	13
Energy products	12	Agricultural and fishing products	6
Agricultural and fishing products	7	Energy products	5

Source: Statistics Canada.
Visit www.mcgrawhill.ca/college/mcconnell for data update.

Σ-STAT

- As Table 16-2 implies, Canada's export and import trade is mainly with other industrially advanced nations, not with developing countries. (Although data in this table are for *goods* only, the same general pattern applies to *services*).

- The United States is Canada's most important trading partner quantitatively. In 2002, 84 percent of Canadian exported goods were sold to Americans, who in turn provided 72 percent of Canada's imports of goods (see Table 16-2).

Rapid Trade Growth

Several factors have propelled the rapid growth of international trade since World War II.

TRANSPORTATION TECHNOLOGY

High transportation costs are a barrier to any type of trade, particularly among traders who are distant from one another. But improvements in transportation have shrunk the globe and have fostered world trade. Airplanes now transport low-weight, high-value items such as diamonds and semiconductors swiftly from one nation to another. We now routinely transport oil in massive tankers, significantly lowering the cost of transportation per barrel. Grain is loaded onto ocean-going ships at modern, efficient grain silos at Great Lakes and coastal ports. Natural gas flows through large-diameter pipelines from exporting to importing countries—for instance, from Russia to Germany and from Canada to the United States.

COMMUNICATIONS TECHNOLOGY

Dramatic improvements in communications technology have also advanced world trade. Computers, the Internet, telephones, and fax machines now directly link traders around the world, enabling exporters to assess overseas markets and to carry out trade deals. A distributor in Vancouver can get a price quote on 1000 woven baskets in Thailand as quickly as a quote on 1000 notebook computers in Ontario.

GENERAL DECLINE IN TARIFFS

Tariffs are excise taxes (duties) on imported products. They have had their ups and downs over the years, but

TABLE 16-2 — Canadian Exports and Imports of Goods by Area, 2002

Exports to	Percentage of total	Imports from	Percentage of total
United States	86	United States	74
European Union	5	European Union	9
Japan	3	Japan	3
Other countries	6	Other countries	14

Source: Statistics Canada.
Visit www.mcgrawhill.ca/college/mcconnell for data update.

Σ-STAT

since 1940 they have generally fallen. A glance ahead to Figure 16-9 shows that Canadian tariffs as a percentage of imports are now about 5 percent, down from over 40 percent in 1940. Many nations still maintain barriers to free trade, but, on average, tariffs have fallen significantly, thus increasing international trade.

Participants in International Trade

All the nations of the world participate to some extent in international trade.

NORTH AMERICA, JAPAN, AND WESTERN EUROPE

As Global Perspective 16.2 indicates, the top participants in world trade by total volume are the United States, Germany, and Japan. In 2002 those three nations had combined exports of $1.6 trillion. Along with Germany, other Western European nations such as France, Britain, and Italy are major exporters and importers. Canada is the world's sixth largest exporter. Canada, the United States, Japan, and the Western European nations also form the heart of the world's financial systems and provide headquarters for most of the world's largest **multinational corporations**—firms that have sizable production and distribution activities in other countries. Examples of such firms are Unilever (Netherlands), Nestlé (Switzerland), Coca-Cola (United States), Bayer Chemicals (Germany), Mitsubishi (Japan), and Nortel (Canada).

multinational corporation
A firm that owns production facilities in multiple countries and produces and sells its product abroad.

NEW PARTICIPANTS

Important new participants have arrived on the world trade scene. One group is made up of the newly industrializing Asian economies of Hong Kong (now part of China), Singapore, South Korea, and Taiwan. Although these Asian economies experienced economic difficulties in the 1990s, they have expanded their share of world exports from about 3 percent in 1972 to more than 10 percent

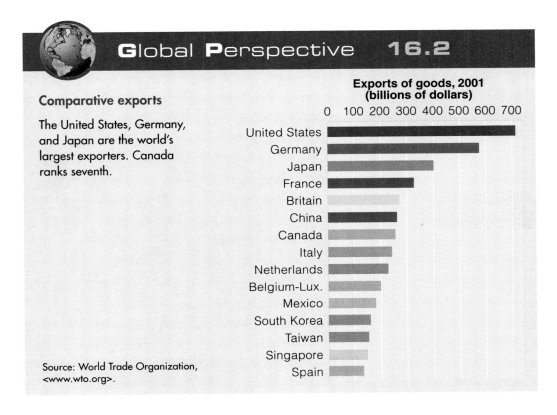

Global Perspective 16.2

Comparative exports

The United States, Germany, and Japan are the world's largest exporters. Canada ranks seventh.

Exports of goods, 2001 (billions of dollars)

United States
Germany
Japan
France
Britain
China
Canada
Italy
Netherlands
Belgium-Lux.
Mexico
South Korea
Taiwan
Singapore
Spain

Source: World Trade Organization, <www.wto.org>.

today. Together, they export about as much as either Germany or Japan and much more than France, Britain, or Italy. Other economies in southeast Asia, particularly Malaysia and Indonesia, also have expanded their international trade.

China, with its increasing reliance on the market system, is an emerging major trader. Since initiating market reforms in 1978, its annual growth of output has averaged 9 percent (compared with 2 to 3 percent annually over that period in Canada). At this remarkable rate, China's total output nearly doubles every eight years! An upsurge of exports and imports has accompanied that expansion of output. In 1989, Chinese exports and imports were each about $50 billion. In 2002, each topped $230 billion, with about a third of China's exports going to Canada and the United States.

The collapse of communism in Eastern Europe and the former Soviet Union in the early 1990s altered world trade patterns. Before that collapse, the Eastern European nations of Poland, Hungary, Czechoslovakia, and East Germany traded mainly with the Soviet Union and such political allies as North Korea and Cuba. Today, East Germany is reunited with West Germany, and Poland, Hungary, and the Czech Republic have established new trade relationships with Western Europe, Canada, and the United States.

Russia itself has initiated far-reaching market reforms, including widespread privatization of industry, and has major trade deals with firms around the globe. Although its transition to capitalism has been far from smooth, Russia may one day be a major trading nation. Other former Soviet republics—now independent nations—such as Estonia and Azerbaijan also have opened their economies to international trade and finance.

QUICK REVIEW

- There are four main categories of economic flows linking nations: goods and services flows, capital and labour flows, information and technology flows, and financial flows.

- World trade has increased globally and nationally. In terms of volume, Canada is the world's seventh largest international trader. With exports and imports of about 40 percent of GDP, Canada is more dependent on international trade than most other nations.

- Advances in transportation and communications technology and declines in tariffs have all helped expand world trade.

- North America, Japan, and the Western European nations dominate world trade. Recent new traders are the Asian economies of Singapore, South Korea, Taiwan, and China (including Hong Kong), the Eastern European nations, and the former Soviet states.

16.2　The Economic Basis for Trade

In Chapter 4 we found that international trade enables nations to specialize their production, improve their resource productivity, and acquire more goods and services. Nations, like individuals and the regions of a nation, can gain by specializing in those products they can produce with greatest relative efficiency and trading them for those goods they cannot produce as efficiently. A more complete answer to the question "Why do nations trade?" hinges on three facts:

- The distribution of natural, human, and capital resources among nations is uneven; nations differ in their endowments of economic resources.

- Efficient production of various goods requires different technologies or combinations of resources.

- Products are differentiated as to quality and other non-price attributes. Some people may prefer certain imported goods to similar goods made domestically.

To recognize the character and interaction of these three facts, think of Japan, for example, which has a large and well-educated labour force, and therefore relatively inexpensive skilled labour. As a

labour-intensive goods
Products that require a relatively large amount of labour to produce.

land-intensive goods
Products that require a relatively large amount of land to produce.

capital-intensive goods
Products that require a relatively large amount of capital to produce.

All nations, regardless of their labour, land, or capital intensity, can find special niches for products that are in demand worldwide.

result, Japan can produce efficiently (at low cost) a variety of **labour-intensive goods** such as cameras, portable CD players, video game players, and video recorders, the design and production of which require much skilled labour.

In contrast, Australia has vast amounts of land and can inexpensively produce such **land-intensive goods** as wheat, wool, and meat. Brazil has the soil, tropical climate, rainfall, and the ready supply of unskilled labour that are needed for the efficient, low-cost production of coffee.

Industrially advanced economies with relatively large amounts of capital can produce inexpensively those goods that require much capital to produce, including such **capital-intensive goods** as automobiles, agricultural equipment, machinery, and chemicals.

All nations, regardless of their labour, land, or capital intensity, can find special niches for individual products that are in demand worldwide because of their special qualities. Examples: fashions from Italy, luxury automobiles from Germany, software from the United States, watches from Switzerland, and ice wine from Canada.

As national economies evolve, the size and quality of their labour forces may change, the volume and composition of their capital stocks may shift, new technologies may develop, and even the quality of land and the quantity of natural resources may be altered. As such changes occur, the relative efficiency with which a nation can produce specific goods will also change. For example, in the past few decades South Korea has upgraded the quality of its labour force and has greatly expanded its stock of capital. Although South Korea was primarily an exporter of agricultural products and raw materials a half-century ago, it now exports large quantities of manufactured goods.

Specialization and Comparative Advantage

Let's now use the concept of comparative advantage to analyze the basis for international specialization and trade.

The Basic Principle

The central concept underlying comparative advantage can be illustrated by posing a problem. Consider the case of a chartered accountant (CA) who, we will assume, is also a skilled house painter. Suppose the CA can paint her house in less time than the professional painter she is thinking of hiring. Also suppose the CA can earn $50 per hour doing her accounting and must pay the painter $15 per hour. It will take the accountant 30 hours to paint her house; the painter, 40 hours. Finally, assume the CA receives no special pleasure from painting.

Should the CA take time off from her accounting to paint her own house or should she hire the painter? The CA should hire the painter. Her opportunity cost of painting her house is $1500 (= 30 hours × $50 per hour of sacrificed income). The cost of hiring the painter is only $600 (= 40 hours × $15 per hour paid to the painter). Although the CA is better at both accounting and painting, the CA's relative or comparative advantage lies in accounting. She will *lower her cost of getting her house painted* by specializing in accounting and using some of the proceeds to hire the house painter.

absolute advantage
When a region or nation can produce more of good Z and good Y with less resources compared to other regions or nations.

Note that the CA has an **absolute advantage** in both accounting and painting; she can do accounting and paint more efficiently than our hypothetical house painter. Despite this, the CA should hire the house painter to paint her house because of her "comparative advantage."

Similarly, the house painter can reduce his cost of obtaining accounting services by specializing in painting and using some of his income to hire the CA. Suppose it would take the painter 10 hours to prepare his income tax return, but the CA could handle this task in 2 hours. The house painter would sacrifice $150 of income (= 10 hours × $15 per hour of sacrificed time) to get a task done that he could hire out for $100 (= 2 hours × $50 per hour of the CA's time). By using the CA to prepare his tax return, the painter *lowers his cost of getting the tax return completed*.

What is true for our hypothetical CA and house painter is also true for two nations. Countries can reduce their cost of obtaining goods by specializing where they have comparative advantages.

With this simple example in mind, let's turn to an international trade model to acquire an understanding of the gains from international specialization and trade.

382

Two Isolated Nations

Suppose the world economy has just two nations, Canada and Brazil. Each can produce both steel and soybeans, but at differing levels of economic efficiency. Suppose Canadian and Brazilian domestic production possibilities curves for soybeans and steel are as shown in Figure 16-3a and b. Note especially two characteristics of these production possibilities curves:

- *Constant Costs* The "curves" are drawn as straight lines, in contrast to the concave-from-the-origin production possibilities frontiers introduced in Chapter 2. This means the law of increasing costs has been replaced with the assumption of constant costs. This substitution simplifies our discussion but does not change our analysis and conclusions. Later we will consider the effect of the more realistic increasing costs.

- *Different costs* The production possibilities curves of Canada and Brazil are different, reflecting different resource mixes and differing levels of technological progress. Specifically, they tell us that the opportunity costs of producing steel and soybeans differ between the two nations.

CANADA

cost ratio
An equality showing the number of units of two products that can be produced with the same resources.

In Figure 16-3a, with full employment, Canada will operate on its production possibilities curve. On that curve, it can increase its output of steel from 0 to 30 tonnes by forgoing an output of 30 tonnes of soybeans. This means the slope of the production possibilities curve is −1 (= −30 soybeans/+30 steel), implying that 1 tonne of steel can be obtained for every tonne of soybeans sacrificed. In Canada the domestic exchange ratio or **cost ratio** for the two products is 1 tonne of steel for 1 tonne of soybeans, or

$$1S_t = 1S_{oy}$$

Canada can internally "exchange" a tonne of steel for a tonne of soybeans. Our constant-cost assumption means this exchange or opportunity cost equation prevails for all possible moves from one point to another along Canada's production possibilities curve.

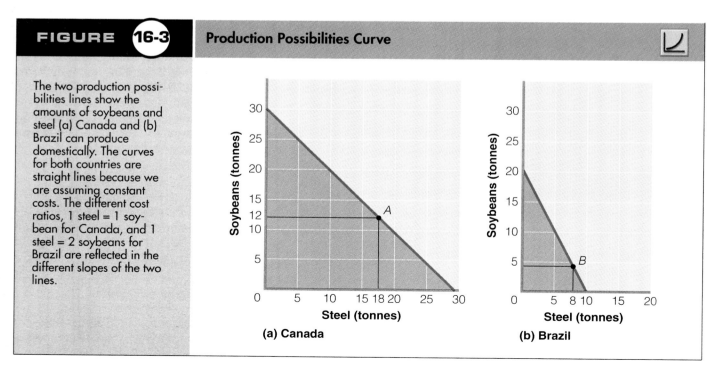

FIGURE 16-3

Production Possibilities Curve

The two production possibilities lines show the amounts of soybeans and steel (a) Canada and (b) Brazil can produce domestically. The curves for both countries are straight lines because we are assuming constant costs. The different cost ratios, 1 steel = 1 soybean for Canada, and 1 steel = 2 soybeans for Brazil are reflected in the different slopes of the two lines.

(a) Canada

(b) Brazil

BRAZIL

Brazil's production possibilities curve in Figure 16-3b represents a different opportunity cost ratio. In Brazil 20 tonnes of soybeans must be given up to get 10 tonnes of steel. The slope of the production possibilities curve is −2 (= −20 soybeans/+10 steel). This means that in Brazil the domestic cost ratio for the two goods is 1 tonne of steel for 2 tonnes of soybeans, or

$$1S_t = 2S_{oy}$$

SELF-SUFFICIENCY OUTPUT MIX

If Canada and Brazil were self-sufficient, each must choose some output mix on its production possibilities curve. Assume point *A* in Figure 16-3a is the optimal output mix in Canada. The choice of this combination of 18 tonnes of steel and 12 tonnes of soybeans equates the marginal benefit and marginal cost of both goods. Suppose Brazil's optimal product mix is 8 tonnes of steel and 4 tonnes of soybeans, indicated by point *B* in Figure 16-3b. These choices are reflected in column 1, Table 16-3.

Specialization Based on Comparative Advantage

comparative advantage
When a region or nation can produce a good at a lower domestic opportunity cost compared to a potential trading partner.

We can determine the product in which Canada and Brazil should specialize as follows: The principle of **comparative advantage** says that total output will be greatest when each good is produced by that nation that has the lowest domestic opportunity cost for that good. In our two-nation illustration, Canada's domestic opportunity cost is lower for steel. Canada need only forgo 1 tonne of soybeans to produce 1 tonne of steel, whereas Brazil must forgo 2 tonnes of soybeans for 1 tonne of steel. Canada has a comparative (cost) advantage in steel and should specialize in steel production. The "world" (that is, Canada and Brazil) is not economizing in the use of its resources if a high-cost producer (Brazil) produced a specific product (steel) when a low-cost producer (Canada) could have produced it. To have Brazil produce steel would mean that the world economy would have to give up more soybeans than is necessary to obtain a tonne of steel.

Brazil has the lower domestic opportunity cost for soybeans; it must sacrifice only ½ tonne of steel in producing 1 tonne of soybeans, whereas Canada must forgo 1 tonne of steel in producing a tonne of soybeans. Brazil has a comparative advantage in soybeans and should specialize in soybean production. Economizing requires that any particular good be produced by the nation with the lower domestic opportunity cost, or a comparative advantage. Canada should produce steel and Brazil soybeans. Note that this conclusion holds even though Canada has an absolute advantage in both steel and soybeans.

In column 2 of Table 16-3 we verify that specialization allows the world to get more output from fixed amounts of resources. By specializing completely in steel, Canada can produce 30 tonnes of steel and no soybeans; Brazil, by specializing completely in soybeans, produces 20 tonnes of soybeans and no steel. The world ends up with 4 more tonnes of steel (30 tonnes, compared with 26) *and* 4 more tonnes of soybeans (20 tonnes, compared with 16) than where there is self-sufficiency or unspecialized production.

TABLE 16-3	**International Specialization According to Comparative Advantage and the Gains from Trade (in Tonnes)**				
Country	(1) Outputs before specialization	(2) Outputs after specialization	(3) Amounts exported (−) and imported (+)	(4) Outputs available after trade	(5) Gains from specialization and trade (4) − (1)
Canada	18 steel 12 soybeans	30 steel 0 soybeans	−10 steel +15 soybeans	20 steel 15 soybeans	2 steel 3 soybeans
Brazil	8 steel 4 soybeans	0 steel 20 soybeans	+10 steel −15 soybeans	10 steel 5 soybeans	2 steel 1 soybeans
Total output	42	50		50	8

Terms of Trade

But consumers of each nation want *both* steel and soybeans. They can have both if the two nations trade or exchange the two products. But what will be the *terms of trade*? At what exchange ratio will Canada and Brazil trade steel and soybeans?

Because $1S_t = 1S_{oy}$ in Canada, Canada must get *more than* 1 tonne of soybeans for each tonne of steel exported or it will not benefit Canada to export steel in exchange for Brazilian soybeans. Canada must get a better "price" (more soybeans) for its steel in the world market than it can get domestically, or there is no gain from trade and it will not occur.

Similarly, because $1S_t = 2S_{oy}$ in Brazil, Brazil must get 1 tonne of steel by exporting some amount *less than* 2 tonnes of soybeans. Brazil must pay a lower "price" for steel in the world market than it must pay domestically, or it will not want to trade. The international exchange ratio or *terms of trade* must lie somewhere between

$$1S_t = 1S_{oy} \text{ (Canada's cost conditions)}$$

and

$$1S_t = 2S_{oy} \text{ (Brazil's cost conditions)}$$

But where between these limits will the world exchange ratio fall? Canada will prefer a ratio close to $1S_t = 2S_{oy}$, say, $1S_t = 1\frac{3}{4} S_{oy}$. Canada wants to get as much soybeans as possible for each tonne of steel it exports. Similarly, Brazil wants a rate near $1S_t = 1S_{oy}$, say $1S_t = 1\frac{1}{4} S_{oy}$. Brazil wants to export as little soybeans as possible for each tonne of steel it receives in exchange. The exchange ratio or terms of trade determines how the gains from international specialization and trade are divided between the two nations.

The actual exchange ratio depends primarily on world supply and demand for the two products, but also the relative competitiveness of world markets for soybeans and steel. If overall world demand for soybeans is weak relative to its supply and the demand for steel is strong relative to its supply, the price of soybeans will be lower and the price of steel higher. The exchange ratio will settle nearer the $1S_t = 2S_{oy}$ figure Canada prefers. If overall world demand for soybeans is great relative to its supply and if the demand for steel is weak relative to its supply, the ratio will settle nearer the $1S_t = 1S_{oy}$ level favourable to Brazil. (We will take up the topic of equilibrium world prices later in this chapter.)

Gains from Trade

trading possibilities line
A line that shows the different combinations of two products that an economy is able to obtain when it specializes in the production of one product and exports it to obtain the other product.

Suppose the international exchange ratio or terms of trade is $1S_t = 1\frac{1}{2} S_{oy}$. The possibility of trading on these terms permits each nation to supplement its domestic production possibilities line with a **trading possibilities line**. This can be seen in **Figure 16-4 (Key Graph)**. Just as a production possibilities line shows the amount of these products a full-employment economy can obtain by shifting resources from one to the other, a trading possibilities line shows the amounts of two products a nation can obtain by specializing in one product and trading for another. The trading possibilities lines in Figure 16-4 reflect the assumption that both nations specialize based on comparative advantage: Canada specializes completely in steel (point *W* in Figure 16-4a) and Brazil completely in soybeans (at point *c* in Figure 16-4b).

IMPROVED OPTIONS

Now Canada is not constrained by its domestic production possibilities line, which requires it to give up 1 tonne of steel for every tonne of soybeans it wants as it moves up its domestic production possibilities line, say, from point *W*. Instead, Canada, through trade with Brazil, can get $1\frac{1}{2}$ tonnes of soybeans for every tonne of steel it exports to Brazil, so long as Brazil has soybeans to export. Trading possibility line *WC′* thus represents the $1S_t = 1\frac{1}{2} S_{oy}$ trading ratio.

Similarly, Brazil, starting at, say, point c, no longer has to move down its domestic production possibilities curve, giving up 2 tonnes of soybeans for each tonne of steel it wants. It can now export

Key Graph

FIGURE 16-4 Trading Possibilities Lines and the Gains from Trade

As a result of international specialization and trade, Canada and Brazil both can have levels of output higher than those attainable on their domestic production possibilities curves. (a) Canada can move from point A on its domestic production possibilities curve to, say, A' on its trading possibilities line. (b) Brazil can move from B to B'.

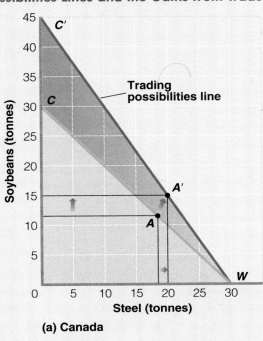

(a) Canada

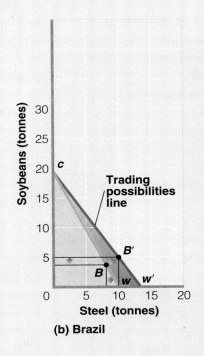

(b) Brazil

Quick Quiz

1. The production possibilities curves in graphs (a) and (b) imply:
   a. increasing domestic opportunity costs.
   b. decreasing domestic opportunity costs.
   c. constant domestic opportunity costs.
   d. first decreasing, then increasing, domestic opportunity costs.

2. Before specialization, the domestic opportunity cost of producing 1 unit of steel is:
   a. 1 unit of soybeans in both Canada and Brazil.
   b. 1 unit of soybeans in Canada and 2 units of soybeans in Brazil.
   c. 2 units of soybeans in Canada and 1 unit of soybeans in Brazil.
   d. 1 unit of soybeans in Canada and ½ unit of soybeans in Brazil.

3. After specialization and trade, the world output of steel and soybeans is:
   a. 20 tonnes of steel and 20 tonnes of soybeans.
   b. 45 tonnes of steel and 15 tonnes of soybeans.
   c. 30 tonnes of steel and 20 tonnes of soybeans.
   d. 10 tonnes of steel and 30 tonnes of soybeans.

4. After specialization and international trade:
   a. Canada can obtain units of soybeans at less cost than before trade.
   b. Brazil can obtain more than 20 tonnes of soybeans, if it so chooses.
   c. Canada no longer has a comparative advantage in producing steel.
   d. Brazil can benefit by prohibiting soybean imports from Canada.

ANSWERS: 1.c 2.b 3.c 4.a

just 1½ tonnes of soybeans for each tonne of steel it wants by moving down its trading possibilities line *cw'*.

Specialization and trade create a new exchange ratio between steel and soybeans, reflected in a nation's trading possibilities line. This exchange ratio is superior for both nations to the self-suffi-ciency exchange ratio embodied in the production possibilities line of each. By specializing in steel and trading for Brazil's soybeans, Canada can obtain more than 1 tonne of soybeans for 1 tonne of steel. By specializing in soybeans and trading for Canada's steel, Brazil can get 1 tonne of steel for less than 2 tonnes of soybeans. In both cases, self-sufficiency is undesirable.

ADDED OUTPUT

By specializing according to comparative advantage and trading for those goods produced in other nations with greater domestic efficiency, Canada and Brazil can realize combinations of steel and soybeans beyond their production possibilities boundaries. *Specialization according to comparative advantage results in a more efficient allocation of world resources, and larger outputs of both steel and soybeans are therefore available to both nations.*

Suppose that at the $1S_t = 1½ S_{oy}$ terms of trade, Canada exports 10 tonnes of steel to Brazil and in return Brazil exports 15 tonnes of soybeans to Canada. How do the new quantities of steel and soybeans available to the two nations compare with the optimal product mixes that existed before specialization and trade? Point *A* in Figure 16-4a reminds us that Canada chose 18 tonnes of steel and 12 tonnes of soybeans originally. But, by producing 30 tonnes of steel and no soybeans, and by trading 10 tonnes of steel for 15 tonnes of soybeans, Canada can obtain 20 tonnes of steel and 15 tonnes of soybeans. This new, superior combination of steel and soybeans is shown by point *A'* in Figure 16-4a. Compared with the non-trading figures of 18 tonnes of steel and 12 tonnes of soybeans, Canada's **gains from trade** are 2 tonnes of steel and 3 tonnes of soybeans.

Similarly, recall that Brazil's optimal product mix was 4 tonnes of soybeans and 8 tonnes of steel (point *B*) before specialization and trade. Now, by specializing in soybeans and trading—produc-ing 20 tonnes of soybeans and no steel and exporting 15 tonnes of its soybeans in exchange for 10 tonnes of Canadian steel—Brazil can have 5 tonnes of soybeans and 10 tonnes of steel. This new position is indicated by point *B'* in Figure 16-4b. Brazil's gains from trade are 1 tonne of soybeans and 2 tonnes of steel.

As a result of specialization and trade, both countries have more of both products. Table 16-3, which summarizes the transaction and outcomes, merits careful study.

The fact that points *A'* and *B'* are positions superior to *A* and *B* is enormously important. We know that a nation can expand its production possibilities boundary by (1) expanding the quan-tity and improving the quality of its resources or (2) realizing technological progress. We have now established that international trade can enable a nation to get around the output constraint imposed by its production possibilities curve. The effects of international specialization and trade are the equivalent of having more and better resources or discovering improved production techniques.

Trade with Increasing Costs

To explain the basic principles underlying international trade, we simplified our analysis in several ways. For example, we limited discussion to two products and two nations. But multiproduct/ multinational analysis yields the same conclusions. We also assumed constant opportunity costs (linear production possibilities curves), which is a more substantive simplification. Let's consider the effect of allowing increasing opportunity costs (concave-from-the-origin production possibil-ities curves) to enter the picture.

Suppose that Canada and Brazil are initially at positions on their concave production possibil-ities curves where their domestic cost ratios are $1S_t = 1S_{oy}$ and $1S_t = 2S_{oy}$, as they were in our con-stant-cost analysis. As before, comparative advantage indicates that Canada should specialize in steel and Brazil in soybeans. But now, as Canada begins to expand steel production, its $1S_t = 1S_{oy}$

Specialization according to compar-ative advantage results in more effi-cient allocation of world resources.

gains from trade
The extra output that trading partners obtain through special-ization of production and exchange of goods and serv-ices.

cost ratio will *fall;* it will have to sacrifice *more than* 1 tonne of soybeans to get 1 additional tonne of steel. Resources are no longer perfectly shiftable between alternative uses, as the constant-cost assumption implied. Resources less and less suited to steel production must be allocated to the Canadian steel industry in expanding steel output, and this means increasing costs—the sacrifice of larger and larger amounts of soybeans for each additional tonne of steel.

Similarly, Brazil, starting from its $1S_t = 2S_{oy}$ cost ratio position, expands soybean production. But as it does, it will find that its $1S_t = 2S_{oy}$ cost ratio begins to *rise.* Sacrificing a tonne of steel will free resources that can be used to produce something less than 2 tonnes of soybeans, because these transferred resources are less suitable to soybean production.

As the Canadian cost ratio falls from $1S_t = 1S_{oy}$ and Brazil's rises from $1S_t = 2S_{oy}$, a point will be reached at which the cost ratios are equal in the two nations, perhaps at $1S_t = 1\frac{3}{4} S_{oy}$. At this point, the underlying basis for further specialization and trade—differing cost ratios—has disappeared. Most importantly, this point of equal cost ratios may be reached where Canada is still producing *some* soybeans along with its steel and Brazil is producing some steel along with its soybeans. *The primary effect of increasing costs is to make specialization less than complete.* For this reason we often find domestically produced products competing directly against identical or similar imported products within a particular economy. *(Key Question 7)*

The Case for Free Trade Restated

The case for free trade reduces to one compelling argument. *Through free trade based on the principle of comparative advantage, the world economy can achieve a more efficient allocation of resources and a higher level of material well-being than without free trade.*

Since the resource mixes and technological knowledge of each country are somewhat different, each nation can produce particular commodities at different real costs. Each nation should produce goods for which its domestic opportunity costs are lower than the domestic opportunity costs of other nations, and exchange these specialties for products for which its domestic opportunity costs are high relative to those of other nations. If each nation does this, the world can realize the advantages of geographic and human specialization. The world and each free-trading nation can obtain a larger real income from the fixed supplies of resources available to it. Government trade barriers can reduce or eliminate gains from specialization. If nations cannot freely trade, they must shift resources from efficient (low-cost) to inefficient (high-cost) uses to satisfy their diverse wants.

One side benefit of free trade is that it promotes competition and deters monopoly. The increased competition from foreign firms forces domestic firms to adopt the lowest-cost production techniques. It also compels them to be innovative with respect to both product quality and production methods, thereby contributing to economic growth. And free trade provides consumers with a wider range of product choices. The reasons to favour free trade are the same reasons to endorse competition.

A second side-benefit of free trade is that it links national interest and breaks down national animosities. Confronted with political disagreements, trading partners tend to negotiate rather than make war.

QUICK REVIEW

- International trade has always been important to Canada, and it is becoming increasingly so.

- International trade enables nations to specialize, improve the productivity of their resources, and obtain a larger output.

- Comparative advantage means total world output will be greatest when each good is produced by that nation having the lowest domestic opportunity cost.

- Specialization is less than complete among nations because opportunity costs normally rise as any particular nation produces more of a particular good.

16.3   Supply and Demand Analysis of Exports and Imports

world price
The international market price of a good or service, determined by world demand and supply.

domestic price
The price of a good or service within a country, determined by domestic demand and supply.

Supply and demand analysis reveals how equilibrium prices and quantities of exports and imports are determined. The amount of a good or service that a nation will export or import depends on differences between equilibrium world and domestic prices. The interaction of *world* supply and demand determines **world price**, the price at which the quantities supplied and demanded are equal globally. *Domestic supply* and demand determine the equilibrium **domestic price**—the price that would prevail in a closed economy. It is a price at which domestic supply and demand are equal.

In the absence of trade, domestic prices in a closed economy may or may not equal world equilibrium prices. When economies are opened for international trade, differences between world and domestic prices motivate exports or imports. To see how, let's now look at the international effects of such price differences in a simple two-nation world consisting of Canada and the U.S., which are both producing aluminum. We assume there are no trade barriers, such as tariffs and quotas, and no international transportation costs.

Supply and Demand in Canada

Figure 16-5a shows the domestic supply curve S_d and domestic demand curve D_d for aluminum in Canada. The intersection of S_d and D_d determines the equilibrium domestic price of $1.25 per kilogram and the equilibrium domestic quantity is 100 million kilograms. Domestic suppliers produce

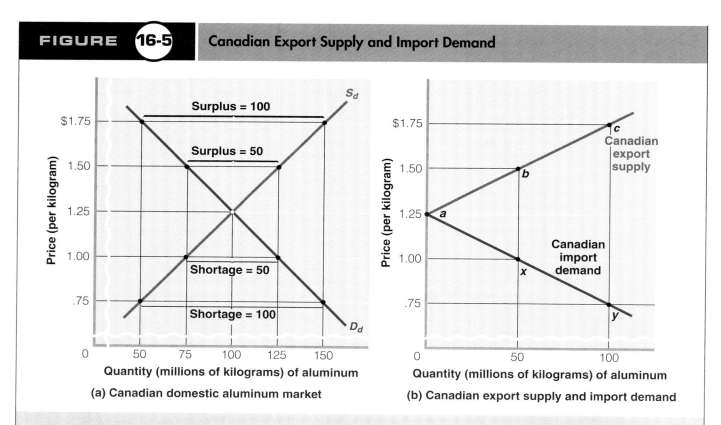

FIGURE 16-5   Canadian Export Supply and Import Demand

(a) Canadian domestic aluminum market

(b) Canadian export supply and import demand

In (a) world prices above the $1.25 domestic price create domestic surpluses of aluminum. As shown by the export supply curve in (b), these surpluses are exported. Domestic shortages occur when the world price is below $1.25 (a). These shortages are met by importing aluminum (b). The export supply curve shows the direct relationship between world prices and Canadian exports; the import supply curve portrays the inverse relationship between world prices and Canadian imports.

100 million kilograms and sell them at $1.25. So there are no domestic surpluses or shortages of aluminum.

But what if the Canadian economy is opened to world trade and the *world price* of aluminum is above or below this $1.25 domestic price?

CANADIAN EXPORT SUPPLY

If the world aluminum price exceeds $1.25, Canadian firms will produce more than 100 million kilograms and export the excess domestic output to the rest of the world (United States). First, consider a world price of $1.50. We see from the supply curve S_d that Canadian aluminum firms will produce 125 million kilograms of aluminum at that price. The demand curve D_d tells us that Canadians will purchase only 75 million kilograms at $1.50. The outcome is a domestic surplus of 50 million kilograms of aluminum. Canadian producers will export these 50 million kilograms at the $1.50 world price.

What if the world price is $1.75? The supply curve shows that Canadian firms will produce 150 million kilograms of aluminum, while the demand curve tells us that Canadian consumers will buy only 50 million kilograms. So Canadian producers will export the domestic surplus of 100 million kilograms.

Towards the top of Figure 16-5b we plot on the horizontal scale the domestic surpluses—the Canadian exports—occurring at world prices above the $1.25 domestic equilibrium price. When the world and domestic prices are equal (= $1.25), the quantity of exports supplied is zero (point *a*). There is no surplus of domestic output to export. But when the world price is $1.50, Canadian firms export 50 million kilograms of surplus aluminum (point *b*). At a $1.75 world price, the domestic surplus of 100 million kilograms is exported (point *c*).

The Canadian **export supply curve**, found by connecting points such as *a*, *b*, and *c*, shows the amount of aluminum that Canadian producers will export at each world price above $1.25. This curve *slopes upward*, revealing a direct or positive relationship between the world price and amount of Canadian exports. *As world prices increase relative to domestic prices, Canadian exports rise.*

CANADIAN IMPORT DEMAND

If the world price is below $1.25, Canada will end up importing aluminum. Consider a $1.00 world price. The supply curve in Figure 16-5a reveals that at that price Canadian firms will produce only 75 million kilograms of aluminum. But the demand curve shows that Canadians want to buy 125 million kilograms at that price. The result is a domestic shortage of 50 million kilograms. To satisfy that shortage, Canada will import 50 million kilograms of aluminum.

At an even lower $.75 world price, Canadian producers will supply only 50 million kilograms. Because Canadian consumers want to buy 150 million kilograms, there is a domestic shortage of 100 million kilograms. Imports will flow to Canada to make up the difference. That is, at a $.75 world price Canadian firms supply 50 million kilograms and 100 million kilograms will be imported.

In Figure 16-5b we plot the Canadian **import demand curve** from these data. This *downward-sloping curve* shows the amounts of aluminum that will be imported at world prices below the $1.25 Canadian domestic price. The relationship between world prices and imports is inverse or negative. At a world price of $1.25, domestic output will satisfy Canadian demand; imports will be zero (point *a*). But at $1.00 Canadians will import 50 million kilograms of aluminum (point *x*); at $.75, they will import 100 million kilograms (point *y*). Connecting points *a*, *x*, and *y* yields a *downward-sloping* Canadian import demand curve. *As world prices fall relative to domestic prices, Canadian imports increase.*

Supply and Demand in the United States

We repeat our analysis in Figure 16-6, this time for the United States. (We have converted U.S. dollar prices to Canadian dollar prices via an assumed exchange rate.) Note that the domestic supply curve S_d and demand curve D_d for aluminum in the United States yield a domestic price of $1.00, which is $.25 lower than the $1.25 Canadian domestic price.

export supply curve
An upward-sloping curve that shows the amount of a product domestic firms will export at each world price that is above the domestic price.

import demand curve
A downward-sloping curve that shows the amount of a product an economy will import at each world price below the domestic price.

FIGURE 16-6   **U.S. Export Supply and Import Demand**

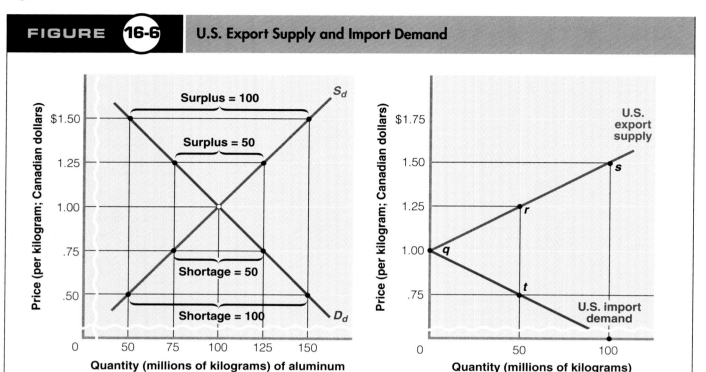

In (a) domestic production of aluminum in the United States exceeds domestic consumption at all world prices above the $1.00 domestic price. These domestic surpluses result in U.S. exports (b). When the domestic price falls below $1.00, domestic shortages occur (a) and imports flow to the United States (b). The U.S. export supply curve and import demand curve depict these relationships.

The analysis proceeds exactly as for Canada. If the world price is $1.00, Americans will neither export nor import aluminum (which gives us point *q* in Figure 16-6b). At world prices above $1.00, U.S. firms will produce more aluminum than U.S. consumers will buy. The surplus will be exported. At a $1.25 world price, Figure 16-6a tells us that the United States will export a domestic surplus of 50 million kilograms (yielding point *r*). At $1.50 it will export a domestic surplus of 100 million kilograms (point *s*). Connecting these points yields the upward-sloping U.S. export supply curve that reflects the domestic surpluses (and thus exports) occurring when the world price exceeds the $1.00 U.S. domestic price.

At world prices below $1.00 domestic shortages occur in the United States. At a $.75 world price, Figure 16-6a shows that U.S. consumers want to buy 125 million kilograms of aluminum but U.S. firms will produce only 75 million kilograms. The shortage will bring 50 million kilograms of imports to the U.S. (point *t* in Figure 16-6b). The U.S. import demand curve in that figure shows U.S. imports at world aluminum prices below the $1.00 U.S. domestic price.

equilibrium world price
A price determined by the inter-section of exporting nations' supply of a product and import-ing nations' demand for the same product.

Equilibrium World Price, Exports, and Imports

We now have the tools to determine the **equilibrium world price** of aluminum and the equilib-rium world levels of exports and imports. Figure 16-7 combines the Canadian export supply curve

FIGURE 16-7

Equilibrium World Price and Quantity of Exports and Imports

In a two-nation world, the equilibrium world price (= $1.12) is determined at the intersection of one nation's export supply curve and another nation's import demand curve. This intersection also decides the equilibrium volume of exports and imports. Here, the United States exports 25 million kilograms of aluminum to Canada.

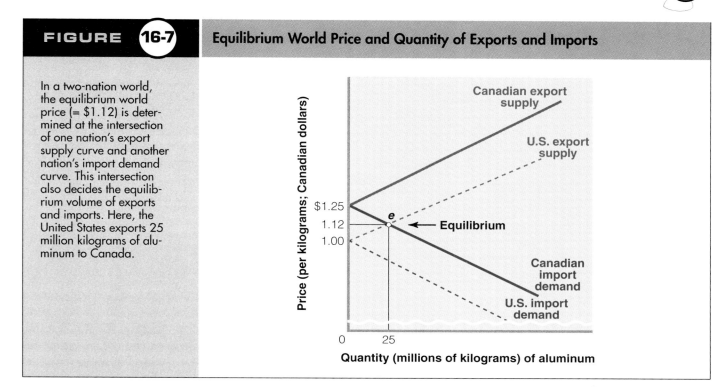

and import demand curve in Figure 16-5b and the U.S. export supply curve and import demand curve in Figure 16-6b. The two Canadian curves proceed rightward from the $1.25 domestic price; the two U.S. curves proceed rightward from the $1.00 U.S. domestic price.

International equilibrium occurs in this two-nation model where one nation's import demand curve intersects another nation's export supply curve. In this case Canada's import demand curve intersects America's export supply curve at e. There, the world price of aluminum is $1.12. The U.S. export supply curve indicates that the United States will export 25 million kilograms of aluminum at this price. Also at this price Canada will import 25 million kilograms from the United States, indicated by the Canadian import demand curve. The $1.12 world price equates the quantity of imports demanded and the quantity of exports supplied (= 25 million kilograms). Thus there will be world trade of 25 million kilograms of aluminum at $1.12 per kilogram.

Note that after trade, the single $1.12 world price will prevail in both Canada and the United States. Only one price for a standardized commodity can persist in a highly competitive market. With trade, all consumers can buy a kilogram of aluminum for $1.12 and all producers can sell it for that price. This world price means that Americans will pay more for aluminum with trade (= $1.12) than without it (= $1.00). The increased American output caused by trade raises U.S. production costs and therefore the price of aluminum in the United States. Canadians, however, pay less for aluminum with trade (= $1.12) than without it (= $1.25). The Canadian gain comes from America's comparative cost advantage in producing aluminum.

Why would the United States willingly send 50 million kilograms of its aluminum output to Canada for consumption? After all, producing this output uses up scarce U.S. resources and drives up the price of aluminum for Americans. Americans are willing to export aluminum to Canada because Americans can gain the means—the earnings of Canadian dollars—to import other goods, say telecommunications equipment, from Canada. U.S. exports enable Americans to acquire imports that have greater value to Americans than the exported aluminum. U.S. exports to Canada finance U.S. imports from Canada. (*Key Question 9*)

16.4   Trade Barriers

tariff
A tax imposed by a nation on an imported good.

revenue tariff
A tariff designed to produce income for the federal government.

protective tariff
A tariff designed to shield domestic producers of a good or service from the competition of foreign producers.

non-tariff barrier
All restrictions other than tariffs that nations erect to impede international trade.

import quota
A limit imposed by a nation on the quantity (or total value) of a good that may be imported during some period of time.

voluntary export restraint
Voluntary limitations by countries or firms of their exports to a particular foreign nation.

No matter how compelling the case for free trade, barriers to free trade *do* exist. Let's expand our discussion of trade barriers.

Excise taxes on imported goods are called **tariffs**; they may be imposed to raise government revenue or to protect domestic firms. A **revenue tariff** is usually applied to a product that is not being produced domestically, for example, tin, coffee, or bananas in the case of Canada. Rates on revenue tariffs are modest; their purpose is to provide the federal government with revenues. A **protective tariff** is designed to shield domestic producers from foreign competition. Although protective tariffs are usually not high enough to stop the importation of foreign goods, they put foreign producers at a competitive disadvantage in selling in domestic markets.

A **non-tariff barrier** (NTB) is a licencing requirement that specifies unreasonable standards pertaining to product quality and safety, or unnecessary bureaucratic red tape that is used to restrict imports. Japan and the European countries frequently require their domestic importers of foreign goods to obtain licences. By restricting the issuance of licences, imports can be restricted. Great Britain used this barrier in the past to bar the importation of coal.

An **import quota** specifies the maximum amount of a commodity that may be imported in any period. Import quotas can more effectively retard international commerce than tariffs. A product might be imported in large quantities despite high tariffs; low import quotas completely prohibit imports once quotas have been filled.

A **voluntary export restraint** (VER) is a trade barrier by which foreign firms "voluntarily" limit the amount of their exports to a particular country. VERs, which have the effect of import quotas, are agreed to by exporters in the hope of avoiding more stringent trade barriers. Japanese auto manufacturers agreed to a VER on exports to Canada under the threat of higher Canadian tariffs or the imposition of low import quotas.

Later in this chapter we will consider the arguments and appeals that are made to justify protection.

Economic Impact of Tariffs

Once again we use supply and demand analysis to examine the economic effects of protective tariffs. Curves D_d and S_d in **Figure 16-8 (Key Graph)** show domestic demand and supply for a product in which Canada has a comparative *dis*advantage, for example, digital versatile disc (DVD) players. (Disregard $S_d + Q$ for now.) Without world trade, the domestic price and output would be P_d and q respectively.

Assume now that the domestic economy is opened to world trade and that the Japanese, who have a comparative advantage in DVD players, begin to sell them in Canada. We assume that with free trade the domestic price cannot differ from the world price, which here is P_w. At P_w domestic consumption is d and domestic production is a. The horizontal distance between the domestic supply and demand curves at P_w represents imports of *ad*. Thus far, our analysis is similar to the analysis of world prices in Figure 16-5.

DIRECT EFFECTS

Suppose now that Canada imposes a tariff on each imported DVD player. This will raise the domestic price from P_w to P_t and has four effects.

- *Decline in consumption*   Consumption of DVD players in Canada will decline from d to c as the higher price moves buyers up and to the left along their demand curve. The tariff prompts consumers to buy fewer DVD players and to reallocate a portion of their expenditures to less-desired substitute products. Canadian consumers are injured by the tariff, since they pay P_wP_t more for each of the c units they now buy at price P_t.

- *Increased domestic production*   Canadian producers—who are *not* subject to the tariff—receive higher price P_t per unit. Because this new price is higher than the pre-tariff or world price

Key Graph

FIGURE 16-8 The Economic Effects of a Protective Tariff or an Import Quota

A tariff of $P_w P_t$ will reduce domestic consumption from d to c. Domestic producers will be able to sell more output (b rather than a) at a higher price (P_t rather than P_w). Foreign exporters are injured because they are able to sell less output (bc rather than ad) in Canada. The shaded area represents the amount of tariffs paid by Canadian consumers. An import quota of bc units will have the same effects as the tariff, with one exception: the shaded area will go to foreign producers rather than to the Canadian government.

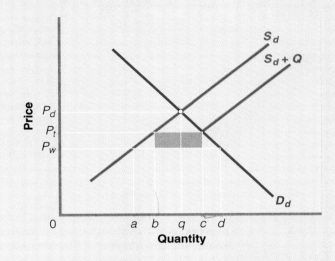

Quick Quiz

1. At world price P_w:
   a. domestic quantity demanded equals quantity supplied.
   b. domestic quantity demanded is less than quantity supplied.
   c. domestic quantity demanded is greater than quantity supplied.
   d. domestic quantity supplied is greater than quantity demanded.

2. At world prices above P_d Canada would:
   a. import.
   b. export.
   c. stop producing.
   d. None of the above.

3. A protective tariff:
   a. increases domestic production.
   b. decreases domestic production.
   c. does not affect domestic production.
   d. decreases government revenue.

4. A quota:
   a. decreases government revenue.
   b. increases government revenue.
   c. has no effect on government revenue.
   d. lowers domestic price.

ANSWERS: 1. c 2. b 3. a 4. c

of P_w, the domestic DVD player industry moves up and to the right along its supply curve S_d, increasing domestic output from a to b. Domestic producers thus enjoy both a higher price and expanded sales, which explains why domestic producers lobby for protective tariffs. But from a social point of view, the expanded domestic production of b instead of a means that the tariff permits domestic producers of DVD players to bid resources away from other, more efficient, Canadian industries.

- **Decline in imports**   Japanese producers are hurt. Although the sale price of DVD players is higher by $P_w P_t$, that amount accrues to the Canadian government, not to Japanese producers. The after-tariff world price, and thus the per-unit revenue to Japanese producers, remains at P_w, and the volume of Canadian imports (Japanese exports) falls from ad to bc.

- **Tariff revenue**   The shaded rectangle indicates the amount of revenue that the tariff yields. Total revenue from the tariff is determined by multiplying the tariff, $P_w P_t$ per unit, by the number of imported DVD players, bc. This tariff revenue is a transfer of income from consumers to government and does *not* represent any net change in the nation's economic well-being. The result is that government gains a portion of what consumers lose by paying more for DVD players.

INDIRECT EFFECTS

Tariffs have a subtle effect beyond what our supply and demand diagram can show. Because Japan sells fewer DVD players in Canada, Japan will earn fewer dollars with which to buy Canadian exports. Canadian export industries must then cut production and release resources. These are highly efficient industries, as evidenced by their comparative advantage and ability to sell goods in world markets.

Tariffs directly promote the expansion of inefficient industries that do not have a comparative advantage; they also indirectly cause contraction of relatively efficient industries that do have a comparative advantage. This means tariffs cause resources to be shifted in the wrong direction. We know that specialization and world trade lead to more efficient use of world resources and greater world output. But protective tariffs reduce world trade. Therefore, tariffs also reduce efficiency and the world's real output.

Economic Impact of Quotas

We noted earlier that an import quota is a legal limit placed on the amount of some product that can be imported each year. The economic impact of quotas is similar to that of a tariff with one salient difference: Although tariffs generate revenue for the Canadian government, a quota transfers that revenue to foreign producers.

Suppose in Figure 16-8 that, instead of imposing a tariff of $P_w P_t$ per unit, Canada prohibits any Japanese imports of DVD players in excess of bc units. In other words, an import quota of bc DVD players is imposed on Japan. We have deliberately chosen the size of this quota to be the same amount as imports would be under a $P_w P_t$ tariff so we are comparing "equivalent" situations. As a consequence of the quota, the supply of DVD players is $S_d + Q$ in Canada. This consists of the domestic supply plus the constant amount bc $(= Q)$, that importers will provide at each domestic price. The $S_d + Q$ supply curve does not exist below price P_w because Japanese producers would not export DVD players to Canada at any price *below* P_w; instead, they would sell them to other countries at the world market price of P_w.

Most of the economic results are the same as with a tariff. DVD player prices are higher (P_t instead of P_w) because imports have been reduced from ad to bc. Domestic consumption of DVD players is down from ad to bc. Canadian producers enjoy both a higher price (P_t rather than P_w) and increased sales (b rather than a).

The difference is that the price increase of $P_w P_t$ paid by Canadian consumers on imports of bc—the shaded area—no longer goes to Canada Custom and Revenue Agency as tariff (tax) revenue, but flows to those Japanese firms that have acquired the rights to sell DVD players in Canada. The economic effects of a tariff are better for Canadian taxpayers than are those of a quota, other things being the same. A tariff generates government revenue, which can be used to cut other taxes or to finance public goods and services that benefit Canadian citizens. In contrast, the higher price created by quotas results in additional revenue for foreign producers. *(Key Question 10)*

Net Costs of Tariffs and Quotas

Figure 16-8 shows that tariffs and quotas impose costs on domestic consumers but provide gains to domestic producers, and, in the case of tariffs, revenue to the federal government. The consumer costs of trade restrictions are calculated by determining the effect they have on consumer prices. Protection raises the price of a product in three ways: (1) The price of the imported product goes up, (2) the higher price of imports causes some consumers to shift their purchases to higher-priced domestically produced goods, and (3) the prices of domestically produced goods rise because import competition has declined.

Study after study finds that the costs to consumers substantially exceed gains to producers, workers and other suppliers of resources in the protected industry, and government. A sizable net cost or efficiency loss to society arises from trade protection. Furthermore, industries employ large amounts of economic resources to influence politicians to pass and retain protectionist laws. Because these rent-seeking efforts divert resources away from more socially desirable purposes, trade restrictions impose that cost on society.

Conclusion: The gains that Canadian trade barriers create for protected industries and their workers come at the expense of much greater losses for the entire economy. The result is economic inefficiency.

16.5   The Case for Protection: A Critical Review

Despite the compelling logic of specialization and trade, there are still protectionists in some union halls, corporate boardrooms, and the halls of Parliament. What arguments do protectionists make to justify trade barriers? How valid are these arguments?

Self-Sufficiency Argument

The argument here is not economic but political-military: Protective tariffs are needed to preserve or strengthen industries that produce the materials essential for national defence. In an uncertain world, the political-military objectives (self-sufficiency) sometimes must take precedence over economic goals (efficiency in the use of world resources).

Unfortunately, it is difficult to measure and compare the benefit of increased national security against the cost of economic inefficiency when protective tariffs are imposed. The economist can only point out that there are economic costs when a nation levies tariffs to increase military self-sufficiency.

The self-sufficiency argument is open to serious abuse. Nearly every industry can claim that it makes direct or indirect contributions to national security and hence deserves protection from imports.

Are there not better ways than tariffs to provide needed strength in strategic industries? When it is achieved through tariffs, this self-sufficiency increases the domestic prices of the products of the protected industry. Thus only those consumers who buy the industry's products shoulder the cost of greater military security. A direct subsidy to strategic industries, financed out of general tax revenues, would distribute these costs more equitably.

Increased Domestic Employment Argument

Arguing for a tariff to "save Canadian jobs" becomes fashionable as an economy encounters a recession. In an economy that engages in international trade, exports involve spending on domestic output and imports reflect spending to obtain part of another nation's output. So, in this argument, reducing imports will divert spending on another nation's output to spending on domestic output. Thus domestic output and employment will rise. But this argument has several shortcomings:

- **Job creation from imports**   While imports may eliminate some Canadian jobs, they create others. Imports may have eliminated the jobs of some Canadian steel and textile workers in recent years, but other workers have gained jobs unloading ships and selling imported cars and imported electronic equipment. Import restrictions alter the composition of employment, but they may have little or no effect on the volume of employment.

- **Fallacy of composition**   All nations cannot simultaneously succeed in restricting imports while maintaining their exports; what is true for one nation is not true for all nations. The exports of one nation must be the imports of another nation. To the extent that one country is able to expand its economy through an excess of exports over imports, the resulting excess of imports over exports worsens another economy's unemployment problem. It is no wonder that tariffs and import quotas meant to achieve domestic full employment are called "beggar my neighbour" policies: They achieve short-run domestic goals by making trading partners poorer.

- **Possibility of retaliation**   Nations adversely affected by tariffs and quotas are likely to retaliate, causing a "trade-barrier war" that will choke off trade and make all nations worse off.

- **Long-run feedbacks**   In the long run, forcing an excess of exports over imports cannot succeed in raising domestic employment. It is through Canadian imports that foreign nations earn dollars for buying Canadian exports. In the long run a nation must import to export. The long-run impact of tariffs is not to increase domestic employment but at best to reallocate workers away from export industries and to protected domestic industries. This shift implies a less efficient allocation of resources.

 Consider This

Shooting Yourself in the Foot

In the lore of the Wild West, a gunslinger on occasion would accidentally pull the trigger on his pistol while retrieving it from its holster, shooting himself in the foot. Since then, the phrase "shooting yourself in the foot" implies doing damage to yourself rather than the intended party.

That is precisely how economist Paul Krugman sees a trade war:

A trade war in which countries restrict each other's exports in pursuit of some illusory advantage is not much like a real war. On the one hand, nobody gets killed. On the other, unlike real wars, it is almost impossible for anyone to win, since the main losers when a country imposes barriers to trade are not foreign exporters but domestic residents. If effect, a trade war is a conflict in which each country uses most of its ammunition to shoot itself in the foot.[1]

The same analysis is applicable to trade boycotts between major trading partners. Such a boycott was encouraged by some American commentators against Canadian, French, and German imports because of these countries' opposition to the U.S. and British-led war in Iraq. But the decline of exports to the United States would leave the Canadians, French, and Germans with fewer U.S. dollars to buy American exports. So the unintended effect would be a decline in U.S. exports to these countries and reduced employment in U.S. export industries. Moreover, such a trade boycott, if effective, might lead Canadians, French, and German consumers to retaliate against American imports. As with a "tariff war," a "boycott war" typically harms oneself as much as the other party.

---

[1] Paul Krugman, *Peddling Prosperity* (New York: Norton, 1994), p. 287.

Question: During the Great Depression many nations increased tariffs in an attempt to export their unemployment problem. Why did it not work?

Diversification for Stability Argument

Highly specialized economies such as Saudi Arabia's (based on oil) and Cuba's (based on sugar) are very dependent on international markets for their incomes. In these economies, wars, international political developments, recessions abroad, and random fluctuations in world supply and demand for one or two particular goods can cause deep declines in export revenues and therefore in domestic income. Tariff and quota protection are allegedly needed in such nations to enable greater industrial diversification. That way, these economies will not be so dependent on exporting one or two products to obtain the other goods they need. Such goods will be available domestically, thereby providing greater domestic stability.

There is some truth in this diversification for stability argument. There are also two serious shortcomings:

- The argument has little or no relevance to Canada and other advanced economies.
- The economic costs of diversification may be great; for example, one-crop economies may be highly inefficient at manufacturing.

Infant-Industry Argument

The infant-industry argument says that protective tariffs are needed to allow new domestic industries to establish themselves. Temporarily shielding young domestic firms from the severe competition of more mature and more efficient foreign firms will give infant industries a chance to develop and become efficient producers.

This argument for protection rests on an alleged exception to the case for free trade. The exception is that young industries have not had, and if they face mature foreign competition will never have, the chance to make the long-run adjustments needed for larger scale and greater efficiency in production. In this view, tariff protection for such infant industries will correct a misallocation of world resources perpetuated by historically different levels of economic development between domestic and foreign industries.

COUNTER-ARGUMENTS

There are some logical problems with this infant industry argument:

- In the developing nations it is difficult to determine which industries are the infants that are capable of achieving economic maturity and therefore deserving protection.
- Protective tariffs may persist even after industrial maturity has been realized.
- Most economists believe that if infant industries are to be subsidized, there are better means than tariffs for doing it. Direct subsidies, for example, have the advantage of making explicit which industries are being aided and to what degree.

STRATEGIC TRADE POLICY

In recent years the infant-industry argument has taken a modified form in advanced economies. Now proponents contend that government should use trade barriers to reduce the risk of investing in product development by domestic firms, particularly where advanced technology is involved. Firms protected from foreign competition can grow more rapidly and achieve greater economies of scale than unprotected foreign competitors. The protected firms can eventually dominate world markets because of their lower costs. Supposedly, dominance of world markets will enable the domestic firms to return high profits to the home nation. These profits will exceed the domestic sacrifices caused by trade barriers. Also, advances in high-technology industries are considered to be beneficial because the advances achieved in one domestic industry often can be transferred to other domestic industries.

Japan and South Korea, in particular, have been accused of using this form of **strategic trade policy**. These two countries, according to critics, protect what they consider to be key sectors from

strategic trade policy
The use of trade barriers to reduce the risk inherent in product development by domestic firms, particularly that involving advanced technology.

foreign competition. The problem with this strategy, and therefore this argument for tariffs, is that the nations put at a disadvantage by strategic trade policies tend to retaliate with tariffs of their own. The outcome may be higher tariffs worldwide, reductions of world trade, and the loss of potential gains from technological advances.

Protection against Dumping Argument

This argument contends that tariffs are needed to protect domestic firms from "dumping" by foreign producers.

dumping
The sale in a foreign country of products below cost or below the prices charged at home.

Dumping is the selling of goods in a foreign market at a price below cost. Economists cite two possible reasons for this behaviour. First, firms may use dumping abroad to drive out domestic competitors there, thus obtaining monopoly power and monopoly prices and profits for the importing firm. The long-term economic profits resulting from this strategy may more than offset the earlier losses that accompany the below-cost sales. There is no evidence that such monopoly power has accrued in any Canadian industry through dumping.

Second, dumping may be a form of price discrimination, which is charging different prices to different customers even though costs are the same. The foreign seller may find it can maximize its profit by charging a high price in its monopolized domestic market while unloading its surplus output at a lower price in Canada. The surplus output may be needed so the firm can obtain the overall per-unit cost saving associated with large-scale production. The higher profit in the home market more than makes up for the losses incurred on sales abroad.

Canada prohibits dumping. Where dumping is shown to injure Canadian firms, the federal government imposes tariffs called "antidumping duties" on the specific goods. But there are relatively few documented cases of dumping each year, and those few cases do *not* justify widespread, permanent tariffs.

In fact, foreign producers argue that Canada uses dumping allegations and antidumping duties to restrict legitimate trade. Some foreign firms clearly can produce certain goods at substantially less per-unit cost than Canadian competitors. So, what may seem to be dumping actually is comparative advantage at work. If antidumping laws are abused, they can increase the price of imports and restrict competition in the Canadian market. This reduced competition can allow Canadian firms to raise prices at consumers' expense. And even where true dumping does occur, Canadian consumers gain from the lower-priced product, at least in the short run, much as they gain from a price war among Canadian producers.

Cheap Foreign Labour Argument

The cheap foreign labour argument says that domestic firms and workers must be shielded from the ruinous competition of countries where wages are low. If protection is not provided, cheap imports will flood Canadian markets and the prices of Canadian goods—along with the wages of Canadian workers—will be pulled down. That is, the domestic living standards in Canada will be reduced.

This argument can be rebutted at several levels. The logic of the argument suggests that it is *not* mutually beneficial for rich and poor persons to trade with one another. However, that is not the case. A low-income farm worker may pick lettuce or tomatoes for a rich landowner, and both may benefit from the transaction. And Canadian consumers gain when they buy a package of Taiwanese-made floppy disks for $6 as opposed to similar package of Canadian-made floppy disks selling for $10.

Also, recall that gains from trade are based on comparative advantage, not on absolute advantage. Looking back at Figure 16-1, suppose Canada and Brazil have labour forces of exactly the same size. Noting the positions of the production possibilities curves, we observe that Canadian labour can produce more of *either* good. Thus, it is more productive; it has an absolute advantage in the production of both goods. Because of this greater productivity, we can expect wages and living standards to be higher for Canadian labour. Brazil's less productive labour will receive lower wages.

The cheap foreign labour argument suggests that, to maintain our standard of living, Canada should not trade with low-wage Brazil. Suppose it does not. Will wages and living standards rise in Canada as a result? No. To obtain soybeans, Canada will have to reallocate a portion of its labour from its efficient steel industry to its less efficient soybean industry. As a result, the average productivity of Canadian labour will fall, as will real wages and living standards. The labour forces of *both* countries will have lower standards of living because without specialization and trade they will have less output available to them. Compare column 4 with column 1 in Table 16-2 or points *A'* and *B'* with *A* and *B* in Figure 16-4 to confirm this point.

A Summing Up

These many arguments for protection are not weighty. Under proper conditions, the infant-industry argument stands as a valid exception, justifiable on economic grounds. And on political-military grounds, the self-sufficiency argument can be used to validate some protection. But both arguments are open to severe overuse, and both neglect other ways of promoting industrial development and military self-sufficiency. Most other arguments are emotional appeals—half-truths and fallacies. These arguments see only the immediate and direct consequences of protective tariffs. They ignore the fact that in the long run a nation must import to export.

There is also compelling historical evidence suggesting that free trade has led to prosperity and growth and that protectionism has had the opposite effects. Here are several examples:

- The Canadian Constitution forbids individual provinces from levying tariffs, and that makes Canada a huge free-trade area. Economic historians cite this as a positive factor in the economic development of Canada.

- Great Britain's shift towards freer international trade in the mid-nineteenth century was instrumental in its industrialization and growth at that time.

- The creation of the Common Market in Europe after World War II eliminated tariffs among member nations. Economists agree that creation of this free-trade area, now the European Union, was a major ingredient in Western European prosperity.

- The trend towards tariff reduction since 1945 has stimulated expansion of the world economy.

- In general, developing countries that have relied on import restrictions to protect their domestic industries have had slow growth compared to those pursuing more open economic policies.

QUICK REVIEW

- A nation will export a particular product if the world price exceeds the domestic price; it will import the product if the world price is less than the domestic price.

- In a two-country model, equilibrium world prices and equilibrium quantities of exports and imports occur when one nation's export supply curve intersects the other nation's import demand curve.

- Trade barriers include tariffs, import quotas, non-tariff barriers, and voluntary export restrictions.

- A tariff on a product increases price, reduces consumption, increases domestic production, reduces imports, and generates tariff revenue for government; an import quota does the same, except a quota generates revenue for foreign producers rather than for the government imposing the quota.

- Most arguments for trade protection are special-interest pleas that, if followed, would create gains for protected industries and their workers at the expense of greater losses for the economy.

16.6   Multilateral Trade Agreements and Free-Trade Zones

When one nation enacts barriers against imports, the nations whose exports suffer may retaliate with trade barriers of their own. In such a *trade war,* escalating tariffs choke world trade and reduce everyone's economic well-being. Economic historians generally agree that high tariffs were a contributing cause of the Great Depression. Aware of that fact, nations have worked to lower tariffs worldwide. Their pursuit of free trade has been added by powerful domestic interest groups: Exporters of goods and services, importers of foreign components used in "domestic" products, and domestic sellers of imported products all strongly support lower tariffs.

Figure 16-9 makes clear that although Canada has been a high-tariff nation over much of its history, Canadian tariffs have declined substantially during the past half-century.

Reciprocal Trade Agreements

most-favoured-nation clause
An agreement by Canada to allow some other nation's exports into Canada at the lowest tariff levied by Canada.

The specific tariff reductions negotiated between Canada and any particular nation were generalized through **most-favoured-nation clauses**, which often accompany reciprocal trade agreements. These clauses stipulate that any subsequently reduced Canadian tariffs, resulting from negotiation with any other nation, would apply equally to any nation that signed the original agreement. So if Canada negotiates a reduction in tariffs on wristwatches with, say, France, the lower Canadian tariff on imported French watches also applies to the imports of the other nations having most-favoured-nation status, say, Japan and Switzerland. This way, the reductions in Canadian tariffs automatically applies to many nations.

General Agreement on Tariffs and Trade (GATT)

General Agreement on Tariffs and Trade (GATT)
The international agreement reached in 1947 in which 23 nations agreed to give equal and non-discriminatory treatment to one another, to reduce tariff rates by multinational negotiations, and to eliminate export quotas.

In 1947, 23 nations, including Canada, signed the **General Agreement on Tariffs and Trade (GATT)**. GATT was based on three principles: (1) equal, non-discriminatory trade treatment for all member nations; (2) the reduction of tariffs by multilateral negotiation; and (3) the elimination of import quotas. Basically, GATT provided a forum for the negotiation of reduced trade barriers on a multilateral basis among nations.

Since World War II, member nations have completed eight "rounds" of GATT negotiations to reduce trade barriers. The eighth and last "round" of negotiations began in Uruguay in 1986. After

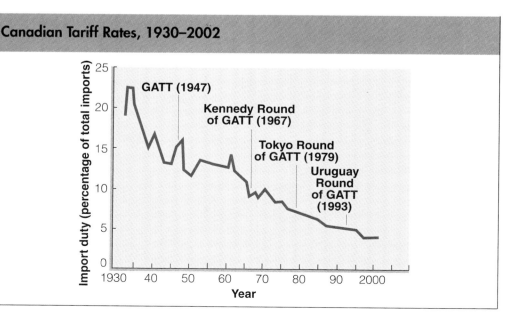

FIGURE 16-9   **Canadian Tariff Rates, 1930–2002**

Historically, Canadian tariff rates have fluctuated. But beginning with the mid-1930s, the trend has been downward.

GATT (1947)
Kennedy Round of GATT (1967)
Tokyo Round of GATT (1979)
Uruguay Round of GATT (1993)

(Vertical axis: Import duty (percentage of total imports), 0 to 25. Horizontal axis: Year, 1930 to 2000.)

seven years of wrangling, in 1993 the 128 member nations reached a new agreement. The *Uruguay Round* agreement took effect on January 1, 1995, and its provisions are to be phased in through 2005.

Under this agreement, tariffs on thousands of products have been eliminated or reduced, with overall tariffs eventually dropping by 33 percent. The agreement also liberalized government rules that in the past impeded the global market for such services as advertising, legal services, tourist services, and financial services. Quotas on imported textiles and apparel were phased out and replaced with tariffs. Other provisions reduced agricultural subsidies paid to farmers and protected intellectual property (patents, trademarks, copyrights) against piracy.

When fully implemented, the Uruguay Round agreement will boost the world's GDP by an estimated $6 trillion, or 8 percent. Consumers in Canada will save more than $3 billion annually.

World Trade Organization (WTO)

World Trade Organization (WTO)

An organization established of 145 nations (as of 2003) that oversees the provisions of the current world trade agreement, resolves trade disputes stemming from it, and holds forums for further rounds of trade negotiations.

The Uruguay Round agreement established the **World Trade Organization (WTO)** as GATT's successor. Some 145 nations belong to the WTO, with China being the latest entrant. The WTO oversees trade agreements reached by the member nations and rules on trade disputes among them. It also provides forums for further rounds of trade negotiations. The ninth and latest round of negotiations—the **Doha Round**—was launched in Doha, Qatar in late 2001. The Doha negotiations will take place in various locations around the world and are expected to last several years.

❋ Members of the WTO agreed to several trade liberalizations to be fully implemented by 2005. The liberalizations include (1) reductions in tariffs worldwide; (2) new rules to promote trade in services; (3) reductions in agricultural subsidies that have distorted the global pattern of trade in agricultural goods; (4) new protections for intellectual property (copyrights, patents, trademarks); and (5) the phasing out of quotas on textiles and apparel, replacing them with gradually declining tariffs. The WTO estimates that the world's GDP for 2005 will be $6 trillion greater (or 8 percent higher) because of the trade liberalizations.

GATT and the WTO have been positive forces in the trend toward liberalized world trade. The trade rules agreed upon by the member nations provide a strong and necessary bulwark against the protectionism called for by special-interest groups in various nations.

For that reason and others, the WTO is highly controversial. Critics are concerned that rules crafted to expand international trade and investment enable firms to circumvent national laws that protect workers and the environment. What good are minimum-wage laws, worker safety laws, collective bargaining rights, and environmental laws, if firms can easily shift their production to nations that have weaker laws or consumers can buy goods produced in those countries?

Proponents of the WTO respond that labour and environmental protections should be pursued directly in nations that have low standards and via international organizations other than the WTO. These issues should not be linked to the process of trade liberalization, which confers widespread economic benefits across nations. Moreover, say proponents of the WTO, many environmental and labour concerns are greatly overblown. Most world trade is among advanced industrial countries, not between them and countries that have lower environmental and labour standards. Moreover, the free flow of goods and resources raises output and income in the developing nations. Historically, such increases in living standards have engendered stronger, not weaker, protections for the environment and for workers.

www.wto.org
World Trade Organization

Trading Zones.

The European Union (EU)

European Union (EU)

An association of European nations that has eliminated tariffs among them, established common tariffs for goods imported from outside the member nations, and allowed the free movement of labour and capital among them.

Countries have also sought to reduce tariffs by creating regional *free-trade zones*—also called *trade blocs*. The most dramatic example is the **European Union (EU)**, formerly called the European Economic Community. Initiated in 1958 as the Common Market, in 2003 the EU comprised 15 European nations—France, Germany, United Kingdom, Italy, Belgium, the Netherlands, Luxembourg, Denmark, Ireland, Greece, Spain, Portugal, Austria, Finland, and Sweden. In 2004, the EU expanded by 10 additional European countries—Poland, Hungary, Czech Republic, Slovakia, Lithuania, Latvia, Estonia, Slovenia, Malta, and Cyprus.

THE EU TRADE BLOC

trade bloc
A group of nations that lower or abolish trade barriers among members. Examples include the European Union and the nations of the North American Free Trade Agreement.

The EU has abolished tariffs and import quotas on nearly all products traded among the participating nations and established a common system of tariffs applicable to all goods received from nations outside the EU. It has also liberalized the movement of capital and labour within the EU and has created common policies in other economic matters of joint concern, such as agriculture, transportation, and business practices. The EU is now a strong **trade bloc**: a group of countries having common identity, economic interests, and trade rules.

EU integration has achieved for Europe increased regional specialization, greater productivity, greater output, and faster economic growth. The free flow of goods and services has created large markets for EU industries. The resulting economies of large-scale production have enabled them to achieve much lower costs than they could have achieved in their small, single-nation markets.

The effects of EU success on non-member nations, such as Canada, have been mixed. A peaceful and increasingly prosperous EU makes its members better customers for Canadian exports. But Canadian firms and other non-member nations' firms have been faced with tariffs and other barriers that make it difficult for them to compete against firms within the EU trade bloc. For example, autos produced in Germany and sold in Spain or France face no tariffs, whereas North American and Japanese autos sold in those EU countries do. This puts non-EU firms at a serious disadvantage. Similarly, EU trade restrictions hamper Eastern European exports of metals, textiles, and farm products, goods that the Eastern Europeans produce in abundance.

By giving preferences to countries within their free-trade zone, trade blocs such as the EU tend to reduce their members' trade with non-bloc members. Thus, the world loses some of the benefits of a completely open global trading system. Eliminating that disadvantage has been one of the motivations for liberalizing global trade through the World Trade Organization.

euro
The common currency used by 12 European nations in the Euro zone, which includes all nations of the European Union except Great Britain, Denmark, and Sweden.

The Euro   One of the most significant accomplishments of the EU was the establishment of the so-called Euro Zone in the early 2000s. Today, 12 of the 15 members of the EU use the **euro** as a common currency. Great Britain, Denmark, and Sweden have opted out of the common currency, at least for now. But gone are French francs, German marks, Italian liras, and other national currencies within the Euro Zone.

Economists expect the euro to raise the standard of living of the Euro Zone members over time. By ending the inconvenience and expense of exchanging currencies, the euro will enhance the free flow of goods, services, and resources among the Euro Zone members. It will also enable consumers and businesses to comparison shop for outputs and inputs, and this will increase competition, reduce prices, and lower costs.

North American Free Trade Agreement

North American Free Trade Agreement (NAFTA)
A 1993 agreement establishing, over a 15-year period, a free trade zone composed of Canada, Mexico, and the United States.

In 1993, Canada, Mexico, and the United States formed a major trade bloc. **The North American Free Trade Agreement (NAFTA)** established a free-trade zone that has about the same combined output as the EU but encompasses a much larger geographical area. NAFTA has greatly reduced tariffs and other trade barriers between Canada, Mexico, and the United States and will eliminate them entirely by 2008.

Critics of NAFTA feared that it would cause a massive loss of Canadian jobs as firms moved to Mexico to take advantage of lower wages and weaker regulations on pollution and workplace safety. Also, there was concern that Japan and South Korea would build plants in Mexico and transport goods tariff-free to Canada, further hurting Canadian firms and workers.

In retrospect, the critics were much too pessimistic. In the seven year period 1993–2000, employment increased in Canada by almost 1.5 million workers and the unemployment rate fell from over 10 percent to under 7 percent. Increased trade between Canada, Mexico, and the United States has enhanced the standard of living in all three countries. *(Key Question 14)*

QUICK REVIEW

- Governments curtail imports and promote exports through protective tariffs, import quotas, non-tariff barriers, and export subsidies.

- The General Agreement on Tariffs and Trade (GATT) established multinational reductions in tariffs and import quotas. The Uruguay Round of GATT (1993) reduced tariffs worldwide, liberalized international trade in services, strengthened protections for intellectual property, and reduced agricultural subsidies.

- The World Trade Organization (WTO)—GATT's successor—rules on trade disputes and provides forums for negotiations on further rounds of trade liberalization. The current round is called the Doha round.

- The European Union (EU) and the North American Free Trade Agreement (NAFTA) have reduced internal trade barriers among their members by establishing large free-trade zones. Of the 25 EU members, 12 now have a common currency—the euro.

THE LASTword | Will the Softwood Lumber Dispute between Canada and the U.S. Ever End?

There has been an ongoing dispute between Canada and the U.S. over Canadian exports of softwood lumber to their market that goes back to the mid-1980s. In the latest turn of events, the U.S. Department of Commerce maintains that Canadian softwood lumber is subsidized, primarily through low provincial government levies for tree harvesting (stumpage fees). Thus in 2001 the U.S. imposed a combined tax and an antidumping duty averaging 27.2 percent on Canadian softwood lumber imports. An antidumping duty is imposed when it is believed an exporter is selling in export markets below its costs. The department of Commerce's claim of subsidy has been hotly disputed by the federal government, which initiated several challenges with the World Trade Organization (WTO) relating to the definition of "subsidy." The federal government also formally requested a panel review of the U.S. final subsidy and antidumping determination under Chapter 19 of the North America Free Trade Agreement. As of early 2003, no resolution was in sight, and negotiation between the two sides broke off.

Canada supplies about a third of the lumber used in the U.S. About half of this comes from the province of British Columbia. Softwood lumber trade between Canada and the U.S. amounts to about $10 billion a year. The B.C. government, which own 95 percent of the lands on which lumber harvesting takes place, has been heavily involved in the softwood lumber dispute because of the adverse economic impact of the duties on its lumber exporters. As of 2003 Canadian softwood lumbers producers had paid in excess of $1 billion in duties. The Canadian lumber producers hope that if a resolution of the dispute is reached, producers will be able get back at least some of the duty they paid. Major Canadian lumber companies affected include Abitibi, Canfor, Slocan, Tembec, West Fraser, and Weyerhaeuser.

It appears that behind the U.S. duties is a vocal interest group called the U.S. Coalition for Fair Lumber Imports, an alliance of sawmill and woodland owners and their employees, which claims that Canada is virtually giving away its forestlands to Canadian companies that export lumber to the U.S. Not everyone in the U.S. agrees with the U.S. Coalition for Fair Lumber Imports. Many commentators, including the influential *Washington Post*, have called the softwood lumber duty a tax on home ownership in the U.S. since such a large part of Canadian lumber goes to the home building industry. The conservative Cato Institute has also called the U.S. tariffs unjustified.

There is a strong case to be made that the benefits of the lower priced Canadian softwood lumber to U.S. consumers far outweigh the costs to American producers. It remains to be seen whether the U.S. Alliance for Fair Lumber Imports has enough political clout in Washington to continue to impose what amounts to a tax on American consumers of softwood lumber products.

CHAPTER SUMMARY

16.1 CANADA AND INTERNATIONAL LINKAGES

- Goods and services flows, capital and labour flows, information and technology flows, and financial flows link Canada and other countries.

- International trade is growing in importance globally and for Canada. World trade is significant to Canada in two respects: (a) Canadian imports and exports as a percentage of domestic output are significant; and (b) Canada is completely dependent on trade for certain commodities and materials that cannot be obtained domestically.

- Principal Canadian exports include automotive products, machinery and equipment, and grain; major Canadian imports are general machinery and equipment, automobiles, and industrial goods and machinery. Quantitatively, the United States is our most important trading partner.

- Global trade has been greatly facilitated by (a) improvements in transportation technology, (b) improvements in communications technology, and (c) general declines in tariffs. Although North America, Japan, and the Western European nations dominate the global economy, the total volume of trade has been lifted by the contributions of several new trade participants. They include the Asian economies of Singapore, South Korea, Taiwan, and China (including Hong Kong), the Eastern European countries (such as the Czech Republic, Hungary, and Poland), and the newly independent countries of the former Soviet Union (such as Estonia, Ukraine, and Azerbaijan).

16.2 THE ECONOMIC BASIS FOR TRADE

- World trade is based on two considerations: the uneven distribution of economic resources among nations, and the fact that efficient production of various goods requires particular techniques or combinations of resources.

- Mutually advantageous specialization and trade are possible between any two nations if they have different opportunity cost ratios for any two products. By specializing based on comparative advantage, nations can obtain larger real incomes with fixed amounts of resources. The terms of trade determine how this increase in world output is shared by the trading nations. Increasing (rather than constant) costs limits specialization and trade.

16.3 SUPPLY AND DEMAND ANALYSIS OF EXPORTS AND IMPORTS

- A nation's export supply curve shows the quantity of product it will export at world prices that exceed the domestic price—the price in a closed, no-international-trade economy. Its import demand curve reveals the quantity of a product it will import at world prices below the domestic price. In a two-nation model, the equilibrium world price and the equilibrium quantities of exports and imports occur where one nation's import supply curve intersects the other nation's export demand curve.

16.4 TRADE BARRIERS

- Trade barriers take the form of protective tariffs, quotas, non-tariff barriers, and "voluntary" export restraints. Supply and demand analysis reveals that protective tariffs and quotas increase the prices and reduce the quantities demanded of affected goods. Sales by foreign exporters diminish; domestic producers, however, enjoy higher prices and enlarged sales. Tariffs and quotas promote a less efficient allocation of domestic and world resources.

16.5 THE CASE FOR PROTECTION: A CRITICAL REVIEW

- The strongest arguments for protection are the infant-industry and military self-sufficiency arguments. Most of the other arguments for protection are half-truths, emotional appeals, or fallacies that emphasize the immediate effects of trade barriers while ignoring long-run consequences. Numerous historical examples suggest that free trade promotes economic growth; protectionism does not.

16.6 MULTILATERAL TRADE AGREEMENT AND FREE TRADE ZONES

- *Most-favoured-nation* status allows a nation to export goods into Canada at its lowest tariff level, then or at any later time.

- In 1947 the General Agreement on Tariffs and Trade (GATT) was formed to encourage non-discriminatory treatment for all member nations, to reduce tariffs, and to eliminate import quotas. The Uruguay Round of GATT negotiations (1993) reduced tariffs and quotas, liberalized trade in services, reduced agricultural subsidies, reduced pirating of intellectual property, and phased out quotas on textiles.

- GATT's successor, the World Trade Organization (WTO), had 145 member nations in 2003. The WTO oversees trade agreements among its members, resolves disputes over the rules, and periodically meets to discuss and negotiate further trade liberalization. In 2001 the WTO initiated a new round of trade negotiations in Doha, Qatar. The Doha Round (named after its place of initiation) will occur over the next several years.

- Free-trade zones (trade blocs) liberalize trade within regions but may at the same time impede trade with non-bloc members. Two examples of free-trade agreements are the fifteen-member European Union (EU) and the North American Free Trade Agreement (NAFTA), comprising Canada, Mexico, and the United States. Twelve of the EU nations have agreed to abandon their national currencies for a common currency called the euro.

TERMS AND CONCEPTS

multinational corporation, p. 377
labour-intensive goods, p. 379
land-intensive goods, p. 379
capital-intensive goods, p. 379
absolute advantage, p. 379
cost ratio, p. 380
comparative advantage, p. 381
trading possibilities line, p. 382
gains from trade, p. 384
world price, p. 386
domestic price, p. 386
export supply curve, p. 387

import demand curve, p. 387
equilibrium world price, p. 388
tariff, p. 390
revenue tariff, p. 390
protective tariff, p. 390
import quota, p. 390
non-tariff barrier, p. 390
voluntary export restraint (VER),
   p. 390
strategic trade policy, p. 395
dumping, p. 396

most-favoured-nation clause,
   p. 398
General Agreement on Tariffs and
   Trade (GATT), p. 398
World Trade Organization (WTO),
   p. 399
European Union (EU), p. 399
trade bloc, p. 400
euro, p. 400
North America Free Trade Agreement
   (NAFTA), p. 400

STUDY QUESTIONS

1. Describe the four major economic flows that link Canada with other nations. Provide a specific example to illustrate each flow. Explain the relationships between the top and bottom flows in Figure 16-1.

2. How important is international trade to the Canadian economy? Who is Canada's most important trade partner? How can persistent trade deficits be financed? "Trade deficits mean we get more merchandise from the rest of the world than we provide them in return. Therefore, trade deficits are economically desirable." Do you agree? Why or why not?

3. What factors account for the rapid growth of world trade since World War II? Who are the major players in international trade today? Who are the "Asian tigers" and how important are they in world trade?

4. Quantitatively, how important is international trade to Canada relative to other nations?

5. Distinguish among land-, labour- and capital-intensive commodities, citing an example of each. What role do these distinctions play in explaining international trade?

6. Suppose nation A can produce 80 units of X by using all its resources to produce X and 60 units of Y by devoting all its resources to Y. Comparative figures for nation B are 60 of X and 60 of Y. Assuming constant costs, in which product should each nation specialize? Why? What are the limits of the terms of trade?

7. **KEY QUESTION**   The following are hypothetical production possibilities tables for New Zealand and Spain.

NEW ZEALAND'S PRODUCTION POSSIBILITIES TABLE (MILLIONS OF BUSHELS)

Product	Production alternatives			
	A	B	C	D
Apples	0	20	40	60
Plums	15	10	5	0

SPAIN'S PRODUCTION POSSIBILITIES TABLE (MILLIONS OF BUSHELS)

Product	Production alternatives			
	R	S	T	U
Apples	0	20	40	60
Plums	60	40	20	0

Plot the production possibilities data for each of the two countries separately. Referring to your graphs, determine:

a. Each country's cost ratio of producing plums and apples.

b. Which nation should specialize in which product.

c. The trading possibilities lines for each nation if the actual terms of trade are 1 plum for 2 apples. (Plot these lines on your graph.)

d. Suppose the optimum product mixes before specialization and trade were B in New Zealand and S in Spain. What are the gains from specialization and trade?

8. "Canada can produce product X more efficiently than can Great Britain. Yet we import X from Great Britain." Explain.

9. **KEY QUESTION**   Refer to Figure 3-6. Assume the graph depicts Canada's domestic market for corn. How many bushels of corn, if any, will Canada export or import at a world price of $1, $2, $3, $4, and $5? Use this information to construct Canada's export supply curve and import demand curve for corn. Suppose the only other corn-producing nation is France, where the domestic price is $4. Why will the equilibrium world price be between $3 and $4? Who will export corn at this world price; who will import it?

10. **KEY QUESTION**   Draw a domestic supply and demand diagram for a product in which Canada does not have a comparative advantage. Indicate the impact of foreign imports on domestic price and quantity. Now

show a protective tariff that eliminates approximately one-half the assumed imports. Indicate the price-quantity effects of this tariff to (a) domestic consumers, (b) domestic producers, and (c) foreign exporters. How would the effects of a quota that creates the same amount of imports differ?

11. "The most valid arguments for tariff protection are also the most easily abused." What are these particular arguments? Why are they susceptible to abuse? Evaluate the use of artificial trade barriers, such as tariffs and import quotas, as a means of achieving and maintaining full employment.

12. Evaluate the following statements:

   a. "Protective tariffs limit both the imports and the exports of the nation levying tariffs."

   b. "The extensive application of protective tariffs destroys the ability of the international market system to allocate resources efficiently."

   c. "Unemployment can often be reduced through tariff protection, but by the same token inefficiency typically increases."

   d. "Foreign firms that 'dump' their products onto the Canadian market are in effect presenting the Canadian people with gifts."

   e. "In view of the rapidity with which technological advance is dispersed around the world, free trade will inevitably yield structural maladjustments, unemployment, and balance of payments problems for industrially advanced nations."

   f. "Free trade can improve the composition and efficiency of domestic output. Only the Volkswagen forced Detroit to make a compact car, and only for-

eign success with the oxygen process forced Canadian steel firms to modernize."

   g. "In the long run foreign trade is neutral with respect to total employment."

13. From 1981 to 1985 the Japanese agreed to a voluntary export restraint that reduced Canadian imports of Japanese automobiles by about 10 percent. What would you expect the short-run effects to have been on the Canadian and Japanese automobile industries? If this restriction were permanent, what would be its long-run effects in the two nations on (a) the allocation of resources, (b) the volume of employment, (c) the price level, and (d) the standard of living?

14. What is the Doha Round and why is it so-named? How does it relate to the WTO? How does it relate to the Uruguay Round?

15. **KEY QUESTION** Identify and state the significance of each of the following: (a) WTO; (b) EU; (c) euro; and (d) NAFTA. What commonality do they share?

16. Explain: "Free-trade zones such as the EU and NAFTA lead a double life: they can promote free trade among members, but they pose serious trade obstacles for non-members." Do you think the net effects of trade blocs are good or bad for world trade? Why? How do the efforts of the WTO relate to these trade blocs?

17. Speculate as to why some Canadian firms strongly support trade liberalization and other Canadian firms favour protectionism. Speculate as to why some Canadian labour unions strongly support trade liberalization and other Canadian labour unions strongly oppose it.

18. **(The Last Word)** What is the purpose of an antidumping duty? Why do you think the U.S. Coalition for Fair Lumber Imports has lobbied the U.S. government to impose duties on Canadian softwood lumber?

INTERNET APPLICATION QUESTIONS

1. **Trade Liberalization—The WTO** Access the World Trade Organization (WTO) Web site from the McConnell-Brue-Barbiero homepage (Chapter 16) and retrieve the latest news from the WTO. List and summarize three recent news items relating to the WTO. Search the sections on *Trade Topics and Resources* to find information on both international trade and the environment and international trade and poverty. Summarize the WTO's major conclusions on these two topics.

2. **Canada's Main Trading Partners** Statistics Canada lists Canada's main trading partners. Go to the McConnell-Brue-Barbiero Web site (Chapter 16). Which country is our largest trading partner? Now visit

www.statcan.ca/english/Pgdb/Economy/International/gblec04.htm to determine Canada's biggest export sector. What sector is a close second?

Σ-STAT

3. **Web-Based Question: The Doha Round—what is the current status?** Determine and briefly summarize the current status of the Doha Round of trade negotiations by accessing the World Trade Organization site through the McConnell-Brue-Barbiero Web site. Is the round still in progress or has it been concluded with an agreement? If the former, when and where was the latest ministerial meeting? If the latter, what are the main features of the agreement?

17

Chapter

Exchange Rates and the Balance of Payments

If you take a Canadian dollar to the bank and ask to exchange it for Canadian currency, you will get a puzzled look. If you persist, you may get a dollar's worth of change: One Canadian dollar can buy exactly one Canadian dollar. But in February 2003, for example, one Canadian dollar could buy 2.15 Argentine pesos, 1.10 Australian dollars, .43 British pounds, .67 American dollars, .62 European euros, 79 Japanese yen, or 7.5 Mexican pesos. What explains this seemingly haphazard array of exchange rates?

In Chapter 16 we examined comparative advantage as the underlying economic basis of world trade and discussed the effects of barriers to free trade. Now we introduce the monetary or financial aspects of international trade: How are currencies of different nations exchanged when import and export transactions occur? What is meant by a "favourable" or an "unfavourable" balance of payments? What is the difference between flexible exchange rates and fixed exchange rates?

17.1   Financing International Trade

Specialization and Trade

foreign exchange market
A market in which the money (currency) of one nation can be used to purchase (can be exchanged for) the money of another nation.

One factor that makes international trade different from domestic trade is the existence of different national currencies. When a Canadian firm exports goods to a Mexican firm, the Canadian exporter wants to be paid in Canadian dollars. But the Mexican importers use Mexican pesos. They must exchange pesos for dollars before the Canadian export transaction can occur.

This problem is resolved in **foreign exchange markets**, in which Canadian dollars can purchase Mexican pesos, European euros, South Korean won, British pounds, Japanese yen, or any other currency, and vice versa. Sponsored by major banks in Toronto, New York, London, Zurich, Tokyo, and elsewhere, foreign exchange markets facilitate exports and imports.

Canadian Export Transaction

Suppose a Canadian exporter agrees to sell $300,000 of telecommunications equipment to a British firm. Assume for simplicity that the rate of exchange—the rate at which pounds can be exchanged for, or converted into, dollars, and vice versa—is $2 for £1 (the actual exchange rate is about $2.50 = 1 pound). This means the British importer must pay the equivalent of £150,000 to the Canadian exporter to obtain the $300,000 worth of telecommunications equipment. Also assume that all buyers of pounds and dollars are in Canada and Great Britain. Let's follow the steps in the transaction:

Canadian exports create a foreign demand for dollars.

- To pay for the telecommunications equipment, the British buyer draws a cheque for £150,000 on its chequing account in a London bank and sends it to the Canadian exporter.

- But the Canadian exporting firm must pay its bills in dollars, not pounds. So the exporter sells the £150,000 cheque on the London bank to its bank in, say, Vancouver, which is a dealer in foreign exchange. The chartered bank adds $300,000 to the Canadian exporter's chequing account for the £150,000 cheque.

- The Vancouver bank deposits the £150,000 in a corresponding London bank for future sale to some Canadian buyer who needs pounds.

Note this important point: *Canadian exports create a foreign demand for dollars, and the fulfillment of that demand increases the supply of foreign currencies (pounds in this case) owned by Canadian banks and available to Canadian buyers.*

Canadian Import Transaction

Why would the Vancouver bank be willing to buy pounds for dollars? As just indicated, the Vancouver bank is a dealer in foreign exchange; it is in the business of buying (for a fee) and selling (also for a fee) one currency for another.

Let's now examine how the Vancouver bank would sell pounds for dollars to finance a Canadian import (British export) transaction. Suppose a Canadian retail firm wants to import £150,000 of compact discs produced in Britain by a hot new musical group. Again, let's track the steps in the transaction.

- A Canadian importer purchases £150,000 at the £1 = $2 exchange rate by writing a cheque for $300,000 on its Vancouver bank. Because the British exporting firm wants to be paid in pounds rather than dollars, the Canadian importer must exchange dollars for pounds, which it does by going to the Vancouver bank and purchasing £150,000 for $300,000. (Perhaps the Canadian importer purchases the same £150,000 that the Vancouver bank acquired from the Canadian exporter.)

- The Canadian importer sends its newly purchased cheque for £150,000 to the British firm, which deposits it in the London bank.

Here we see that *Canadian imports create a domestic demand for foreign currencies (pounds, in this case), and the fulfillment of that demand reduces the supplies of foreign currencies (again, pounds) held by Canadian banks and available to Canadian consumers.*

balance of payments
A summary of all the transactions that took place between the individuals, firms, and government units of one nation and those of all other nations during a year.

current account
The section in a nation's balance of payments that records its exports and imports of goods and services, its net investment income, and its net transfers.

The combined export and import transactions bring one more point into focus. Canadian exports (the telecommunications equipment) make available, or "earn," a supply of foreign currencies for Canadian banks, and Canadian imports (the compact discs) create a demand for those currencies. In a broad sense, any nation's exports finance or "pay for" its imports. Exports provide the foreign currencies needed to pay for imports.

Although our examples are confined to exporting and importing goods, demand for and supplies of pounds also arise from transactions involving services and the payment of interest and dividends on foreign investments. Canada demands pounds not only to buy imports but also to buy insurance and transportation services from the British, to vacation in London, to pay dividends and interest on British investments in Canada, and to make new financial and real investments in Britain. *(Key Question 2)*

17.2 The Balance of Payments

A nation's **balance of payments** is the sum of all transactions that take place between its residents and the residents of all foreign nations. Those transactions include merchandise exports and imports, imports of goods and services, tourist expenditures, interest and dividends received or paid abroad, and purchases and sales of financial or real assets abroad. *The balance of payments statement shows all the payments a nation receives from foreign countries and all the payments it makes to them.*

Table 17-1 is a simplified balance of payments statement for Canada in 2002. Let's take a close look at this accounting statement to see what it reveals about Canadian international trade and finance. To help our explanation, we divide the single balance of payments account into three components: the *current account*, the *capital account*, and the *official reserves account*.

Current Account

The top portion of Table 17-1 summarizes Canada's trade in currently produced goods and services and is called the **current account**. Items 1 and 2 show exports and imports of goods (merchandise) in 2002. Exports have a *plus* (+) sign because they are a credit; they earn and make available foreign exchange in Canada. As you saw in the previous section, any export-type transaction that obligates foreigners to make "inpayments" to Canada generates supplies of foreign currencies in the Canadian banks.

Imports have a *minus* (−) sign because they are a debit; they reduce the stock of foreign currencies in Canada. Our earlier discussion of trade financing indicated that Canadian imports obligate Canadians to make "outpayments" to the rest of the world that reduce available supplies of foreign currencies held by Canadian banks.

TABLE 17-1 Canada's Balance of Payments, 2002 (in Billions)

Current account:

(1) Merchandise exports	$+410.3	
(2) Merchandise imports	−356.1	
(3) *Balance of trade*		+54.2
(4) Exports of services	+58.2	
(5) Imports of services	−66.1	
(6) *Balance on goods and services*		+46.3
(7) Net investment income	−30.4	
(8) Net transfers	+1.4	
(9) **Current account balance**		**+17.3**

Capital account:

(10) Net change in foreign investment in Canada (capital inflow)	+69.1	
(11) Net change in Canadian investment abroad (capital outflow)	−75.7	
(12) **Capital account balance**		**−6.6**

Official settlements account:

(13) **Official international reserves**		−10.7
Balance of payments		0

Source: Statistics Canada.
Visit www.mcgrawhill.ca/college/mcconnell for data update. **Σ-STAT**

BALANCE ON GOODS

Items 1 and 2 in Table 17-1 reveal that in 2002 Canada's goods exports of $410.3 billion earned enough foreign currencies to more than finance Canada's goods imports of $356.1 billion. A country's *balance of trade on goods* is the difference between its exports and imports of goods. If exports exceed imports, the result is a trade surplus or "favourable balance of trade." If imports exceed exports, there is a trade deficit or "unfavourable balance of trade." We note in item 3 that in 2002 Canada had a trade surplus (of goods) of $54.2 billion. (Global Perspective 17.1 shows Canadian trade deficits and surpluses with selected nations or groups of nations.)

BALANCE ON SERVICES

Item 4 in Table 17-1 reveals that Canada not only exports goods, such as airplanes and computer software, but also services, such as insurance, consulting, travel, and brokerage services, to residents of foreign nations. These service "exports" totalled $58.2 billion in 2002 and are a credit (thus the + sign). Item 5 indicates that Canadians "import" similar services from foreigners; these service imports were $66.1 billion in 2002 and are a debit (thus the − sign).

balance on goods and services
The exports of goods and services of a nation less its imports of goods and services in a year.

trade surplus
The amount by which a nation's exports of goods (or goods and services) exceed its imports of goods (or goods and services).

trade deficit
The amount by which a nation's imports of goods (or goods and services) exceed its exports of goods (or goods and services).

The **balance on goods and services**, shown as item 6, is the difference between Canadian exports of goods and services (items 1 and 4) and Canadian imports of goods and services (items 2 and 5). In 2002, Canadian exports of goods and services exceeded Canadian imports of goods and services by $46.3 billion. So, a **trade surplus** occurred. In contrast, a **trade deficit** occurs when imports of goods and services exceed exports of goods and services.

BALANCE ON CURRENT ACCOUNT

Item 7, *net investment income*, represents the difference between interest and dividend payments people abroad have paid Canadians for the services of exported Canadian capital and what Canadians paid in interest and dividends for the use of foreign capital invested in Canada. It shows that in 2002 Canadian net investment income was $−30.4 billion; we paid more in interest and dividends to people abroad than they paid us.

Item 8 shows net transfers, both public and private, between Canada and the rest of the world. Included here are foreign aid, pensions paid to citizens living abroad, funds received from home by international students, and remittances by immigrants to relatives abroad. These $1.4 billion of transfers are net Canadian outpayments that decrease available supplies of foreign exchange. They are, in a sense, the exporting of good will and the importing of "thank-you notes."

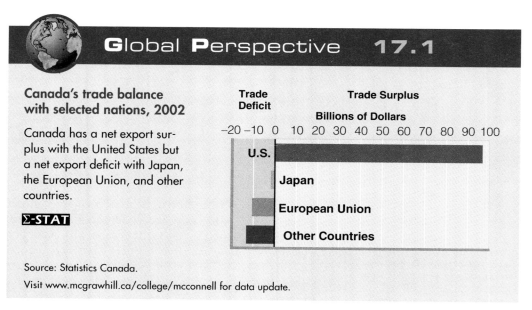

Global **P**erspective **17.1**

Canada's trade balance with selected nations, 2002

Canada has a net export surplus with the United States but a net export deficit with Japan, the European Union, and other countries.

Σ-STAT

Source: Statistics Canada.

Visit www.mcgrawhill.ca/college/mcconnell for data update.

By adding all transactions in the current account, we obtain the *current account balance* shown in item 9. In 2002 Canada had a current account surplus of $17.3 billion. This means that Canada's current account transactions (items 2, 5, and 8) created a greater inpayment of foreign currencies to Canada than an outpayment of foreign currencies from Canada.

Capital Account

capital account
The section of a nation's international balance of payments statement that records the foreign purchases of assets in Canada and Canadian purchases of assets abroad.

The second account within the overall balance of payment account is the **capital account**, which summarizes the flows of payments (money "capital") from the purchase or sale of real or financial assets. For example, a foreign firm may buy a *real* asset, say, an office tower in Canada, or a financial asset, for instance, a Canadian government bond. Both kinds of transactions involve the "export" of the ownership of Canadian assets from Canada in return for inpayments of foreign currency (money "capital" inflows). As indicated in line 10, these "exports" of ownership of assets are designated *net change in foreign investment in Canada*. It has a *plus* sign, since like exports of Canadian goods and services, it represents an inpayment of foreign currencies.

Conversely, a Canadian firm may buy, say, a hotel chain (real asset) in a foreign country or common stock (financial asset) of a foreign firm. Both transactions involve "imports" of the ownership of real or financial assets to Canada and are paid for by outpayments of Canadian currency (money "capital" outflows). These "imports" are designated Canadian *net change in Canadian investment abroad* and, as shown in line 11, has a minus sign; like Canadian imports of goods and services, it represents an outpayment of foreign currencies from Canada.

Items 10 and 11 combined yield a *capital account balance* of $–6.6 billion in 2002 (line 12). In 2002 Canada "exported" $69.1 billion of ownership of its real and financial assets and "imported" $75.7 billion. This capital account deficit depleted $6.6 billion of foreign currencies from Canada.

Official Settlement Account

official international reserves
Foreign currencies owned by the central bank of a nation.

The third account in the overall balance of payments is the official settlement account. The central banks of nations hold quantities of foreign currencies called **official international reserves**. These reserves can be drawn on to make up any net deficit in the combined current and capital accounts (much as you would draw on your savings to pay for a special purchase). In 2002 Canada had a $10.7 billion surplus in the combined current and capital accounts (line 9 plus line 12). Balance in the Canadian international payments led the Canadian government to increase its official international reserves of foreign currencies by $10.7 billion (item 13). The *negative* sign indicates that this increase of reserves is a debit—the inpayment to official international reserves needed to balance the overall balance of payments account.

In some years, the sum of the current and capital accounts balances may be negative, meaning that Canada earned less foreign currencies than it needed. The deficit would create an outpayment from the stock of official international reserves. As such, item 14 would have a positive sign since it is a credit.

The three components of the balance of payments—the current account, the capital account, and the official settlement reserves account—must together equal zero. Every unit of foreign exchange used (as reflected in a *minus* outpayment or debit transaction) must have a source (a *plus* inpayment or credit transaction).

Payments Deficits and Surpluses

balance of payments deficit
The amount by which the sum of the balance on current account and the balance on the capital account is negative in a year.

balance of payments surplus
The amount by which the sum of the balance on current account and the balance on the capital account is positive in a year.

Although the balance of payments *must always sum to zero*, economists and political officials speak of **balance of payments deficits and surpluses**; they are referring to imbalances between the current and capital accounts (line 9 minus line 12) which cause a drawing down or building up of foreign currencies. A drawing down of official international reserves (to create a positive official reserves entry in Table 17-1) measures a nation's balance of payments deficit; a building up of official international reserves (which is shown as a negative official international reserves entry) measures its balance of payments surplus.

FIGURE 17-1 **The Balance of Payments: 1975–2002**

Over the last three decades the current and capital accounts changed from surpluses to deficits several times.

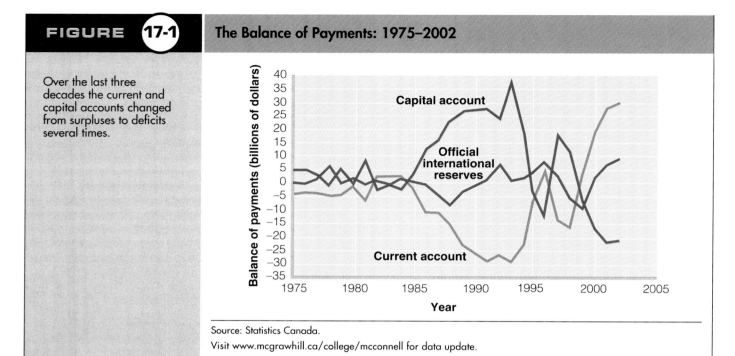

Source: Statistics Canada.

Visit www.mcgrawhill.ca/college/mcconnell for data update.

Figure 17-1 shows the trend in Canada's current, capital, and the official international reserves since 1975. What stands out is that for the period between 1985 and 1995 Canada's current account had a persistent deficit, while the capital account was in a surplus. The cause of the current account deficit during this period was the persistent deficit in services and investment income. The deficit in services and investment income still persists. But since 1995 the current account has actually swung to a surplus because of the large surplus in Canada's balance of trade, while the capital account surpluses of the 1985–95 period have turned into deficits.

A balance of payments deficit is not necessarily bad, nor is a balance of payments surplus necessarily good. Both simply are realities. However, any nation's official international reserves are limited. Persistent payments deficits, which must be financed by drawing down those reserves, would ultimately deplete the international reserves. That nation would have to make policies to correct its balance of payments. These policies might require painful macroeconomic adjustments, trade barriers and similar restrictions, or a major depreciation of its currency. For this reason, nations seek to achieve payments balance, at least over several-year periods. *(Key Question 3)*

QUICK REVIEW

• Canadian exports create a foreign demand for dollars, and fulfillment of that demand increases the domestic supply of foreign currencies; Canadian imports create a domestic demand for foreign currencies, and fulfillment of that demand reduces the supplies of foreign currency held by Canadian banks.

• The current account balance is a nation's exports of goods and services less its imports of goods and services plus its net investment income and net transfers.

• The capital account balance is a nation's sale of real and financial assets to people living abroad less its purchases of real and financial assets from foreigners.

• A balance of payments deficit occurs when the sum of the balances on current and capital accounts is negative; a balance of payments surplus arises when the sum of the balances on current and capital accounts is positive.

17.3   Foreign Exchange Markets: Flexible Exchange Rates

exchange rate
The rate at which the currency of one nation is exchanged for the currency of another nation.

We noted earlier that in a foreign exchange market, national currencies are exchanged for one another. The equilibrium prices in these markets are called **exchange rates**—*the rate at which the currency of one nation is exchanged for the currency of another nation.* (See Global Perspective 17.2.) Two points about the foreign exchange market are particularly noteworthy:

1. *A Competitive Market*   Real-world foreign exchange markets conform closely to the markets discussed in Chapter 3. They are competitive markets characterized by large numbers of buyers and sellers dealing in standardized products such as the Canadian dollar, the European euro, the British pound, the Swedish krona, and the Japanese yen.

2. *Linkages to all Domestic and Foreign Prices*   The market price or exchange rate of a nation's currency is an unusual price; it links all domestic (say, Canadian) prices with all foreign (say, Japanese or German) prices. Exchange rates enable consumers in one country to translate prices of foreign goods into units of their own currency: They need only multiply the foreign product price by the exchange rate. If the dollar-yen exchange rate is \$.01 (1 cent) per yen, a Sony television set priced at ¥20,000 will cost a Canadian \$200 (= 20,000 × \$.01). If the exchange rate is \$.02 (2 cents) per yen, it will cost a Canadian \$400 (= 20,000 × \$.02). Similarly, all other Japanese products would double in price to Canadian buyers. As you will see, a change in exchange rates has important implications for a nation's level of domestic production and employment.

Flexible Exchange Rates

flexible exchange rate
A rate of exchange determined by the international demand for and supply of a nation's currency.

fixed exchange rate
A rate of exchange that is prevented from rising or falling with changes in currency supply and demand.

Both the size and persistence of a nation's balance of payments deficits and surpluses and the adjustments it must make to correct these imbalances depend on the system of exchange rates being used. There are two "pure" types of exchange-rate systems:

- A **flexible** or **floating exchange-rate system** by which the rates that national currencies are exchanged for one another are determined by demand and supply. In such a system no government intervention occurs.

- A **fixed exchange-rate system** by which governments determine the rates at which currencies are exchanged and make necessary adjustments in their economies to ensure that these rates continue.

 We begin by looking at flexible exchange rates. Let's examine the rate, or price, at which Canadian dollars might be exchanged for British pounds. **Figure 17-2 (Key Graph)** shows demand D_1 and supply S_1 of pounds in the currency market.

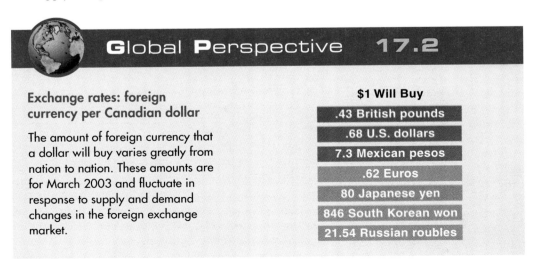

Global Perspective 17.2

Exchange rates: foreign currency per Canadian dollar

The amount of foreign currency that a dollar will buy varies greatly from nation to nation. These amounts are for March 2003 and fluctuate in response to supply and demand changes in the foreign exchange market.

$1 Will Buy

| .43 British pounds |
| .68 U.S. dollars |
| 7.3 Mexican pesos |
| .62 Euros |
| 80 Japanese yen |
| 846 South Korean won |
| 21.54 Russian roubles |

Key Graph

FIGURE 17-2 The Market for Foreign Currency (Pounds)

The intersection of the demand for pounds D_1 and the supply of pounds S_1 determines the equilibrium dollar price of pounds, here, $2. That means that the exchange rate is $2 = £1. The upward green arrow is a reminder that a higher dollar price of pounds (say, $3 = £1) means that the dollar has depreciated (pound has appreciated). The downward green arrow tells us that a lower dollar price of pounds (say, $1 = £1) means that the dollar has appreciated (pound has depreciated). Such changes in equilibrium exchange rates would result from shifts of the supply and demand curves.

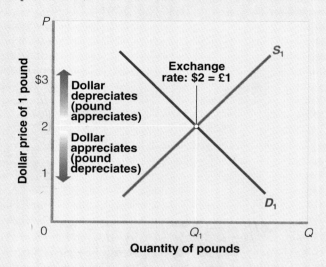

Quick Quiz

1. Which of the following is a true statement?
a. The quantity of pounds demanded falls when the dollar appreciates.
b. The quantity of pounds supplied declines as the dollar price of pounds rises.
c. At the equilibrium exchange rate, the pound price of $1 is ½ pound.
d. The dollar would appreciate if the demand for pounds increased.

2. At the price of $2 for £1 in this figure,
a. the dollar-pound exchange rate is unstable.
b. the quantity of pounds supplied equals the quantity demanded.
c. the dollar price of 1 pound equals the pound price of $1.
d. Canadian merchandise exports to Britain must equal Canadian merchandise imports from Britain.

3. All else equal, a leftward shift of the demand curve in this figure
a. would depreciate the dollar.
b. creates a shortage of pounds at the previous price of $2 for £1.
c. might be caused by a major recession in Canada.
d. might be caused by a significant rise of real interest rates in Britain.

4. All else equal, a rightward shift of the supply curve in this figure would
a. depreciate the dollar and might be caused by a significant rise of real interest rates in Britain.
b. depreciate the dollar and might be caused by a significant fall of real interest rates in Britain.
c. appreciate the dollar and might be caused by a significant rise of real interest rates in Canada.
d. appreciate the dollar and might be caused by a significant fall of interest rates in Canada.

ANSWERS: 1. c; 2. b; 3. c; 4. c.

The *demand for pounds curve* is downward sloping because, if pounds become less expensive to Canadians, then all British goods and services will be cheaper to Canadians. That is, at lower dollar prices for pounds, Canadians can get more pounds and therefore more British goods and services per dollar. To buy these cheaper British goods, Canadian consumers will increase the quantity of pounds they demand.

The *supply of pounds curve* is upward sloping because, as the dollar price of pounds rises (that is, the pound price of dollars falls), the British will purchase more Canadian goods. When the British buy more Canadian goods, they supply a greater quantity of pounds to the foreign exchange market. In other words, they must exchange pounds for dollars to purchase Canadian goods. So, when the price of pound rises, the quantity of pounds supplied goes up.

The intersection of the supply curve and demand curve will determine the dollar price of pounds. Here, that price (exchange rate) is $2 for £1.

Depreciation and Appreciation

An exchange rate determined by market forces can, and often does, change daily, just as do stock and bond prices. When the dollar price of pounds rises, for example, from $2 = £1 to $3 = £1, we say a **depreciation** of the dollar relative to the pound has occured. When a currency depreciates, more units of it (dollars) are needed to buy a single unit of some other foreign currency (a pound).

When the dollar price of pounds falls, for example, from $2 = £1 to $1 = £1, an **appreciation** of the dollar relative to the pound has occured. When a currency appreciates, fewer units of it (dollars) are needed to buy a single unit of some foreign currency (pounds).

In our Canada-Britain illustrations, depreciation of the dollar means an appreciation of the pound, and vice versa. When the dollar price of a pound jumps from $2 = £1 to $3 = £1 the pound has appreciated relative to the dollar because it takes more dollars to buy £1. But it now takes fewer pounds to buy $1. At $2 = £1, it took £½ to buy $1; at $3 = £1, it takes only £⅓ to buy $1.

Determinants of Exchange Rate Changes

What would cause a nation's currency to appreciate or depreciate in the market for foreign exchange? Here are three generalizations:

- If the demand for a nation's currency increases (all else equal), that currency will appreciate; if the demand declines, that currency will depreciate.

- If the supply of a nation's currency increases, that currency will depreciate; if the supply decreases, that currency will appreciate.

- If a nation's currency appreciates, some foreign currency depreciates relative to it.

With these generalizations in mind, let's examine the determinants of exchange rates, the factors that shift the demand or supply curve for a certain currency.

CHANGES IN TASTES

Any change in consumer tastes or preferences for the products of a foreign country may alter the demand for that nation's currency and change its exchange rate. If technological advances in lumber make it more attractive to British consumers and businesses, then the British will supply more pounds in the exchange market in order to purchase more Canadian lumber. The supply-of-pounds curve will shift rightward, the pound will depreciate, and the dollar will appreciate.

In contrast, if British woollen apparel becomes more fashionable in Canada, the Canadian demand for pounds will increase, the pound will appreciate, and the dollar will depreciate.

RELATIVE INCOME CHANGES

If the growth of a nation's income is more rapid than that of other countries, its currency is likely to depreciate. Here's why. A country's imports vary directly with its level of income. As total income

depreciation
A decrease in the value of the dollar relative to another currency, so a dollar buys a smaller amount of the foreign currency and therefore of foreign goods.

appreciation
An increase in the value of the dollar relative to the currency of another nation so that a dollar buys a larger amount of the foreign currency and thus of foreign goods.

Any change in consumer tastes or preferences for products of a foreign country may alter that nation's exchange rate.

rises in Canada, Canadians buy both more domestically produced goods *and* more foreign goods. If the Canadian economy is expanding rapidly and the British economy is stagnant, Canadian imports of British goods, and therefore Canadian demands for pounds, will increase. The dollar price of pounds will rise, so the Canadian dollar will depreciate.

RELATIVE PRICE-LEVEL CHANGES

Changes in the relative price levels of two nations can change the demand and supply of currencies and alter the exchange rate between the two nations' currencies.

The **purchasing power parity theory** holds that exchange rates equate the purchasing power of various currencies. That is, the exchange rates among national currencies adjust to match the ratios of the nations' price levels: If a certain market basket of goods costs $10,000 in Canada and £5000 in Great Britain, according to this theory the exchange rate will be $2 = £1. That way a dollar spent on goods sold in Britain, Japan, Turkey, and other nations will have equal purchasing power.

purchasing power parity theory
The idea that exchange rates between any two nations adjust to reflect the price level differences between the countries.

Consider This

Purchasing Power Parity: The Case of Hamburgers

The purchasing power parity (PPP) theory says that exchange rates will adjust such that a given market basket of goods and services will cost the same in all countries. If the market basket costs $1000 in Canada and 100,000 yen in Japan, then the exchange rate will be $1 = 100 yen (= 1000/100,000). If instead the exchange rate is $1 = 110 yen, we can expect the Canadian dollar to depreciate and the yen to appreciate such that the exchange rate moves to the purchasing power parity rate of $1=100 yen. Similarly, if the exchange rate is $1 = 90 yen, we can expect the Canadian dollar to appreciate and the yen to depreciate.

For the past 14 years, *The Economist* magazine has offered a light-hearted test of the purchasing power parity theory through its *Big Mac index*. It uses the exchange rates of 100 countries to convert the domestic currency price of Big Macs into U. S. dollar prices. If the converted U.S. dollar price in, say, Britain exceeds the dollar price in Canada, *The Economist* concludes (with a wink) that the pound is overvalued relative to the Canadian dollar. On the other hand, if the adjusted dollar price of the Big Mac in Britain is less than the dollar price in Canada, then the pound is undervalued relative to the Canadian dollar.

The Economist finds wide divergences in actual dollar prices across the globe and thus little support for the purchasing power parity theory. Yet it humorously trumpets any predictive success it can muster (or is that "mustard?").

Some readers find our Big Mac index hard to swallow. This year (1999), however, has been one to relish. When the euro was launched at the start of the year most forecasters expected it to rise. The Big Mac index, however,

suggested the euro was overvalued against the U.S. dollar—and indeed it has fallen [13 percent] ... Our correspondents have once again been munching their way around the globe ... [and] experience suggests that investors ignore burgernomics at their peril.[1]

Maybe so—bad puns and all. Economist Robert Cumby examined the Big Mac index for 14 countries for ten years.[2] Among his findings:

- A 10 percent undervaluation according to the Big Mac standard in one year is associated with a 3.5 percent appreciation of that currency over the following year.

- When the U.S. dollar price of Big Macs is high in a country, the relative local currency price of Big Macs in that country generally declines during the following year. Hmm. Not bad.

---

[1] "Big MacCurrencies," *The Economist*, April 3, 1999; "Mcparity," *The Economist*, December 11, 1999.

[2] Robert Cumby, "Forecasting Exchange Rates and Relative Prices with the Hamburger Standard: Is What You Want What You Get with Mcparity?" National Bureau of Economic Research, January 1997.

Question: Go to The Economist's Big Mac index Web site at http://www.economist. com/markets/Bigmac/index.cfm, click the Big Mac index for 2003. Which country has the most overvalued currency in 2003? Which has the most undervalued currency in 2003?

Although exchange rates depart from purchasing power parity, even over long periods, changes in relative price levels are a determinant of exchange rates. If, for example, the domestic price level rises rapidly in Canada and remains constant in Great Britain, Canadian consumers will seek out low-priced British goods, increasing the demand for pounds. The British will purchase fewer Canadian goods, reducing the supply of pounds. This combination of demand and supply changes will cause the pound to appreciate and the dollar to depreciate.

RELATIVE INTEREST RATES

Changes in relative interest rates between two countries can alter their exchange rate. Suppose that real interest rates rise in Canada but stay constant in Great Britain. British citizens will then find Canada an attractive place in which to make financial investments. To undertake these investments, they will have to supply pounds in the foreign-exchange market to obtain dollars. The increase in the supply of pounds results in depreciation of the pound and appreciation of the Canadian dollar.

SPECULATION

Currency speculators buy and sell currencies with an eye to reselling or repurchasing them at a profit. Suppose speculators expect the Canadian economy to (1) grow more rapidly than the British economy and (2) experience a more rapid rise in its price level than Britain. These expectations translate to an anticipation that the pound will appreciate and the Canadian dollar will depreciate. Speculators who are holding dollars will therefore try to convert them into pounds. This effort will increase the demand for pounds and cause the dollar price of pounds to rise (that is, the dollar to depreciate). A self-fulfilling prophecy occurs: The pound appreciates and the dollar depreciates because speculators act on the belief that these changes will in fact take place. In this way, speculation can cause changes in exchange rates. (We deal with currency speculation in more detail in this chapter's Last Word.)

Table 17-2 has more illustrations of the determinants of exchange rates; the table is worth careful study.

TABLE 17-2	**Determinants of Exchange Rate Changes: Factors that Change the Demand or the Supply of a Particular Currency and thus Alter the Exchange Rate**
Determinant	**Examples**
Changes in tastes	Japanese autos decline in popularity in Canada (Japanese yen depreciates, Canadian dollar appreciates)
	European tourists flock to Canada (Canadian dollar appreciates; European euro depreciates).
Changes in relative incomes	England encounters a recession, reducing its imports, while Canadian real output and real income surge, increasing Canadian imports (British pound appreciates, Canadian dollar depreciates).
Changes in relative prices	Switzerland experiences a 3% inflation rate compared to Canada's 10% rate (Swiss franc appreciates; Canadian dollar depreciates).
Changes in relative real interest rates	The Bank of Canada drives up interest rates in Canada while the Bank of England takes no such action (Canadian dollar appreciates; British pound depreciates).
Speculation	Currency traders believe South Korea will have much greater inflation than Taiwan (South Korean won depreciates; Taiwanese new dollar appreciates)
	Currency traders think Finland's interest rates will plummet relative to Denmark's rates (Finland's markka depreciates; Denmark's krone appreciates)

The Effectiveness of Markets

Advantages of Flexible Rates

Proponents say that flexible exchange rates have an important feature: They automatically adjust to eventually eliminate balance of payment deficits or surpluses. We can explain this concept with S_1 and D_1 in Figure 17-3, where they are the supply and demand curves for pounds from Figure 17-2.

The equilibrium exchange rate of $2 = £1 means there is no balance of payments deficit or surplus between Canada and Britain. At the $2 = £1 exchange rate, the quantity of pounds demanded by Canadian consumers to import British goods, buy British transportation and insurance services, and pay interest and dividends on British investments in Canada equals the amount of pounds supplied by the British in buying Canadian exports, purchasing services from the Canadians, and making interest and dividend payments on Canadian investments in Britain. Canada would have no need to either draw down or build up its official international reserves to balance its payments.

Suppose tastes change and Canadians buy more British automobiles, the Canadian price level increases relative to Britain's, or interest rates fall in Canada compared to those in Britain. Any or all of these changes will cause the Canadian demand for British pounds to increase from D_1 to, say, D_2 in Figure 17-3.

If the exchange rate remains at the initial $2 = £1, a Canadian balance of payments deficit will be created in the amount of ab. That is, at the $2 = £1 rate, Canadians consumers will demand the quantity of pounds represented by point b, but Britain will supply the amount represented by a; there will be a shortage of pounds. But this shortage will not last, because this is a competitive market. Instead, the dollar price of pounds will rise (the dollar depreciates) until the balance of payment deficit is eliminated. That occurs at the new equilibrium exchange rate of $3 = £1, where the quantity of pounds demanded and supplied are equal again.

To explain why this occurred, we need to re-emphasize that the exchange rate links all domestic (Canadian) prices with all foreign (British) prices. The dollar price of a foreign good is found by multiplying the foreign price by the exchange rate (in dollars per unit of the foreign currency). At an exchange rate of $2 = £1, a British automobile priced at £15,000 will cost a Canadian consumer $30,000 (= 15,000 × $2).

A change in the exchange rate alters the prices of all British goods to Canadian consumers and all Canadian goods to British buyers. The shift in the exchange rate (here from $2 = £1 to $3 = £1)

FIGURE 17-3

Adjustments under Flexible Exchange Rates and Fixed Exchange Rates

Under flexible exchange rates, a shift in the demand for pounds from D_1 to D_2, other things equal, would cause a Canadian balance of payments deficit ab; it would be corrected by a change in the exchange rate from $2 = £1 to $3 = £1. Under fixed exchange rates, Canada would cover the shortage of pounds ab by using international monetary reserves, restricting trade, implementing exchange controls, or enacting a contractionary stabilization policy.

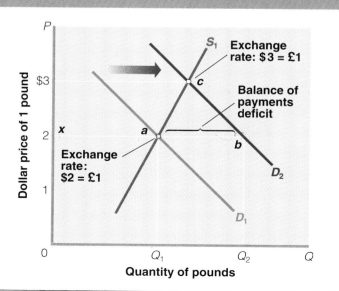

changes the relative attractiveness of Canadian imports and exports and restores equilibrium in the Canadian (and British) balance of payments. From the Canadian point of view, as the dollar price of pounds changes from $2 to $3, the British auto priced at £15,000, which formerly cost a Canadian consumer $30,000, now costs $45,000 (= 15,000 × $3). Other British goods will also cost Canadian consumers more, and Canadian imports of British goods will decline. A movement from point *b* towards point *c* in Figure 17-3 graphically illustrates this concept.

From Britain's standpoint, the exchange rate (the pound price of dollars) has fallen (from £½ to £⅓ for $1). The international value of the pound has appreciated. The British previously got only $2 for £1; now they get $3 for £1. Canadian goods are therefore cheaper to the British, and Canadian exports to Britain will rise. In Figure 17-3, this is shown by a movement from point *a* towards point *c*.

The two adjustments—a decrease in Canadian imports from Britain and an increase in Canadian exports to Britain—are just what are needed to correct the Canadian balance of payments deficit. These changes end when, at point *c*, the quantities of British pounds demanded and supplied are equal. (*Key Questions 6 and 9*)

Disadvantages of Flexible Exchange Rates

Even though flexible exchange rates automatically work to eliminate payment imbalances, some economists believe they may cause several significant problems. These problems include (a) reduced trade because of the risks and uncertainties associated with constantly changing exchange rates; (b) worsening of the terms of trade if there is a sizeable depreciation; (c) and the challenges to managing and designing domestic macroeconomic policies, particularly in economies heavily dependent on trade.

17.4   Fixed Exchange Rates

To avoid the disadvantages of flexible exchange rates, nations have at times fixed or "pegged" their exchange rates. For our analysis of fixed exchange rates, we assume Canada and Britain agree to maintain a $2 = £1 exchange rate.

The problem is that such a governmental agreement cannot keep the demand for and supply of pounds from changing. With the rate fixed, a shift in demand or supply will put pressure on the exchange rate system, and government must intervene if the exchange rate is to be maintained.

In Figure 17-3, suppose the Canadian demand for pounds increases from D_1 to D_2 and a Canadian payment deficit *ab* arises. This means that the Canadian government is committed to an exchange rate ($2 = £1) that is below the new equilibrium rate ($3 = £1). How can the Bank of Canada prevent the shortage of pounds from driving the exchange rate up to the new equilibrium level? The answer is to alter market demand and/or market supply so that they will intersect at the $2 = £1 rate of exchange. There are several ways to do this.

Use of Reserves

currency intervention
A government's buying and selling of its own or of foreign currencies to alter international exchange rates.

One way to maintain a pegged exchange rate is for the Bank of Canada to intervene in the market through the use of official international reserves. Such management is called **currency interventions**. By selling part of its reserves of pounds, the Bank of Canada can increase the supply of pounds, shifting supply curve S_1 to the right so that it intersects D_2 at *b* in Figure 17-3 and thereby maintains the exchange rate at $2 = £1.

How do official international reserves originate? Perhaps a balance of payment surplus occurred in the past. The Bank of Canada would have purchased that surplus. That is, at some earlier time the Bank of Canada may have spent dollars to buy surplus pounds that were threatening to reduce the exchange rate to below the $2 = £1 fixed rate. Those purchases would have built up the Canadian official reserves of pounds.

Nations have also used gold as "international money" to obtain official international reserves. In our example, the Bank of Canada could sell some of the gold it owns to Britain to obtain pounds. It could then sell pounds for dollars . That would shift the supply of pounds to the right and the $2 = £1 exchange rate could be maintained.

It is critical that the amount of international reserves and gold be enough to accomplish the required increase in the supply of pounds. This is not a problem if deficits and surpluses occur more or less randomly and are about the same size. Then, last year's balance of payments surplus with Britain will increase Canada's reserve of pounds, and that reserve can be used to "finance" this year's deficit. But if Canada encounters persistent and sizable deficits for an extended period, its international reserves can become depleted, forcing it to abandon fixed exchange rates. Or, if a nation with inadequate international reserves wishes to maintain fixed exchange rates, it must use less appealing options to maintain exchange rates. Let's consider some of those options.

Trade Policies

To maintain fixed exchange rates, a nation can try to control the flow of trade and finance directly. Canada could try to maintain the $2 = £1 exchange rate in the face of a shortage of pounds by discouraging imports (thereby reducing the demand for pounds) and encouraging exports (thus increasing the supply of pounds). Imports could be reduced with new tariffs or import quotas; special taxes could be levied on the interest and dividends Canadian financial investors receive from foreign investments. Also, the Canadian government could subsidize certain Canadian exports to increase the supply of pounds.

The fundamental problem is that these policies reduce the volume of world trade and change its makeup from what is economically desirable. When nations impose tariffs and quotas, they lose the economic benefits of a free flow of world trade. That loss should not be underestimated: Trade barriers by one nation lead to retaliatory responses from other nations, multiplying the loss.

Exchange Controls and Rationing

exchange control
The control a government may exercise over the quantity of foreign currency demanded by its citizens and firms and over the rates of exchange in order to limit its outpayments to its inpayments (to eliminate a payments deficit).

Another option is exchange controls and rationing. Under **exchange controls**, the Canadian government could handle the problem of a pound shortage by requiring that all pounds obtained by Canadian exporters be sold to the Bank of Canada. Then the government would allocate or ration this short supply of pounds (represented by xa in Figure 17-3) among various Canadian importers, who actually demand the quantity xb. The effect of this policy is to restrict the value of Canadian imports to the amount of foreign exchange earned by Canadian exports. Assuming balance in the capital account, there is then no balance of payments deficit. Canadian demand for British imports with the value ab would simply not be fulfilled.

There are major objections to exchange controls:

- **Distorted trade**   Like tariffs, quotas, and export subsidies (trade controls), exchange controls distort the pattern of international trade away from that suggested by comparative advantage.

- **Favouritism**   The process of rationing scarce foreign exchange can lead to government favouritism towards selected importers (big contributors to re-election campaigns, for example).

- **Restricted choice**   Controls limit freedom of consumer choice. The Canadian consumers who prefer Volkswagens may have to buy Chevrolets. The business opportunities for some Canadian importers may be impaired because government limits imports.

- **Black markets**   There are likely to be enforcement problems. Canadian importers might want foreign exchange badly enough to pay more than the $2 = £1 official rate, setting the stage for black-market dealings between importers and illegal sellers of foreign exchange.

Domestic Macroeconomic Adjustments

A final way to maintain a fixed exchange rate is to use domestic stabilization policies (monetary policy and fiscal policy) to eliminate the shortage of foreign currency. Tax hikes, reductions in government spending, and a high-interest-rate policy would reduce total spending in the Canadian economy and thus domestic income. Because imports vary directly with domestic income, demand for British goods, and therefore for pounds, would be restrained.

If these "contractionary" policies reduce the domestic price level relative to Britain's, Canadian buyers of consumer and capital goods would divert their demands from British goods to Canadian goods, also reducing the demand for pounds. Moreover, the high-interest-rate policy would lift Canadian interest rates relative to those in Britain.

Lower prices on Canadian goods and higher Canadian interest rates would increase British imports of Canadian goods and increase British financial investment in Canada. Both developments would increase the supply of pounds. The combination of a decrease in the demand for and an increase in the supply of pounds would reduce or eliminate the original Canadian balance of payments deficit. In Figure 17-3 the new supply and demand curves would intersect at some new equilibrium point on line ab, where the exchange rate remains at $2 = £1.

Maintaining fixed exchange rates is hardly appealing. The "price" of exchange-rate stability for Canada would be falling output, employment, and price levels—in other words, a recession. Eliminating a balance of payments deficit and realizing domestic stability are both important national economic goals, but to sacrifice stability for payments balance is to let the tail wag the dog.

QUICK REVIEW

- In a system in which exchange rates are flexible (meaning that they are free to float), the rates are determined by the demand for and supply of individual national currencies in the foreign exchange market.

- Determinants of flexible exchange rates—factors that shift currency supply and demand curves—include changes in (a) tastes, (b) relative national incomes, (c) relative price levels, (d) real interest rates, and (e) speculation.

- Under a system of fixed exchange rates, nations set their exchange rates and then maintain them by buying or selling reserves of currencies, establishing trade barriers, employing exchange controls, or incurring inflation or recession.

17.5 International Exchange-Rate Systems

In recent times the world's nations have used three different exchange-rate systems: a fixed rate system, a modified fixed rate system, and a modified flexible-rate system.

The Gold Standard: Fixed Exchange Rates

gold standard
A historical system of fixed exchange rates in which nations defined their currency in terms of gold.

Between 1879 and 1934 the major nations of the world adhered to a fixed-rate system called the **gold standard**. In this system, each nation must

- Define its currency in terms of a quantity of gold

- Maintain a fixed relationship between its stock of gold and its money supply

- Allow gold to be freely exported and imported

If each nation defines its currency in terms of gold, the various national currencies will have fixed relationships to one another. For example, if Canada defines $1 as worth 25 grains of gold, and Britain defines its pound as worth 50 grains of gold, then a British pound is worth 2 × 25 grains, or $2. This exchange rate would be fixed; it would not change in response to changes in currency demand and supply.

www.mcgrawhill.ca/college/mcconnell

GOLD FLOWS

If we ignore the costs of packing, insuring, and shipping gold between countries, under the gold standard the rate of exchange would not vary from this $2 = £1 rate. No one in Canada would pay more than $2 = £1 because 50 grains of gold could always be bought for $2 in Canada and sold for £1 in Britain. Nor would the British pay more than £1 for $2. Why should they when they could buy 50 grains of gold in Britain for £1 and sell it in Canada for $2?

Under the gold standard, the potential free flow of gold between nations resulted in fixed exchange rates.

DOMESTIC MACROECONOMIC ADJUSTMENTS

When the demand for, or supply of, currencies changes, the gold standard requires domestic macroeconomic adjustments for the fixed exchange rate to be maintained. To see why, suppose that Canadians' tastes change such that they want to buy more British goods. The demand for pounds increases such that there is a shortage of pounds in Canada (recall Figure 17-3), implying a Canadian balance of payments deficit.

What will happen? Remember that the rules of the gold standard prohibit the exchange rate from moving from the fixed $2 = £1 rate; the rate cannot move to, say, a new equilibrium at $3 = £1 to correct the imbalance. Instead, gold will flow from Canada to Britain to remove the payments imbalance.

But recall that the gold standard required participants to maintain a fixed relationship between their domestic money supplies and their quantities of gold. The flow of gold from Canada to Britain will require a reduction of the money supply in Canada. Other things equal, this will reduce total spending in Canada and thereby lower Canadian real domestic output, employment, income, and perhaps, prices. Also, the decline in the money supply will boost Canadian interest rates.

The opposite will occur in Britain. The inflow of gold will increase the money supply, which will increase total spending in Britain. Domestic output, employment, income, and perhaps prices will rise. The British interest rate will fall.

Declining Canadian incomes and prices will reduce Canadian demand for British goods and therefore reduce the Canadian demand for pounds. Lower interest rates in Britain will make it less attractive for Canadian investors to make financial investments there, also lessening the demand for pounds. For all these reasons, the demand for pounds in Canada will decline. In Britain, higher incomes, prices, and interest rates will make Canadian imports and Canadian financial investments more attractive. In buying these imports and making these financial investments, British citizens will supply more pounds in the exchange market.

In short, domestic macroeconomic adjustments in Canada and Britain, triggered by the international flow of gold, will produce new demand and supply conditions for pounds such that the $2 = £1 exchange rate is maintained. After all the adjustments are made, Canada will not have a payments deficit, and Britain will not have a payments surplus.

So the gold standard has the advantage of stable exchange rates and automatic correction of balance of payments deficits and surpluses. However, its critical drawback is that nations must accept domestic adjustments in such distasteful forms as unemployment and falling incomes, or inflation. Under the gold standard, a nation's money supply is altered by changes in supply and demand in currency markets and nations cannot set their own monetary policy in their own national interest. If Canada, for example, were to experience declining output and incomes, the loss of gold under the gold system would reduce the Canadian money supply. That would cause higher interest rates, lower borrowing and spending, and produce further declines in output and income.

COLLAPSE OF THE GOLD STANDARD

The gold standard collapsed under the weight of the worldwide depression in the 1930s. As domestic outputs and employment fell worldwide, the restoration of prosperity became the primary goal of afflicted nations. These nations enacted protectionist measures to reduce imports. The idea was to expand consumption of domestically produced goods and get their economies moving again. To make their exports less expensive abroad, many nations redefined their currencies at lower levels in terms of gold. For example, a country previously defining the value of its currency at 1 unit = 25 ounces of gold might redefine it as 1 unit = 10 ounces of gold. Such redefining is an example of **devaluation**—a deliberate action by government to reduce the international value of its currency. A series of such devaluations in the 1930s meant that exchange rates were no longer fixed; a major tenet of the gold standard was violated, and the system broke down.

The Bretton Woods System

The Great Depression and World War II left world trade and the world monetary system in shambles. To lay the groundwork for a new international monetary system, an international conference of nations was held at Bretton Woods, New Hampshire, in 1944. The conference produced a commitment to a modified fixed exchange-rate system called an *adjustable-peg system*, or, simply, the **Bretton Woods system**. The new system sought to capture the advantages of the old gold standard (fixed exchange rate) while avoiding its disadvantages (painful domestic macroeconomic adjustments).

Furthermore, the conference created the **International Monetary Fund (IMF)** to make the new exchange-rate system feasible and workable. The new international monetary system managed through the IMF prevailed with modifications until 1971. (The IMF still plays a basic role in international finance; in recent years it has performed a major role in providing loans to developing countries and to economies making transitions to a market system.)

IMF AND PEGGED EXCHANGE RATES

How did the adjustable-peg system of exchange rates work? First, as with the gold standard, each IMF member had to define its currency in terms of gold (or dollars), thus establishing rates of exchange between its currency and the currencies of all other members. In addition, each nation was obligated to keep its exchange rate stable with respect to every other currency. To do so, nations would have to use their official currency reserves to intervene in foreign exchange markets.

Assume again that the Canadian dollar and the British pound were "pegged" to each other at $2 = £1. Now again suppose that the demand for pounds temporarily increases so that a shortage of pounds occurs in Canada (Canada has a balance of payments deficit). How can Canada keep its pledge to maintain a $2 = £1 exchange rate when the new equilibrium rate is, say, $3 = £1? Canada can supply additional pounds to the exchange market, increasing the supply of pounds such that the equilibrium exchange rate falls back to $2 = £1.

Under the Bretton Woods system there were three main sources of the needed pounds:

- *Official international reserves* Canada might currently possess pounds in its official international reserves as the result of past actions against a payments surplus.

- *Gold sales* The Canadian government might sell some of its gold to Britain for pounds. The proceeds would then be offered in the exchange market to augment the supply of pounds.

- *IMF borrowing* The needed pounds might be borrowed from the IMF. Nations participating in the Bretton Woods system were required to make contributions to the IMF based on the size of their national income, population, and volume of trade. If necessary, Canada could borrow pounds on a short-term basis from the IMF by supplying its own currency as collateral.

FUNDAMENTAL IMBALANCES: ADJUSTING THE PEG

The Bretton Woods system recognized that from time to time a nation may be confronted with persistent and sizable balance of payments problems that cannot be corrected through the means listed above. In these cases, the nation would eventually run out of official reserves and be unable to maintain its fixed exchange-rate system. The Bretton Woods remedy was correction by devaluation, that is, by an "orderly" reduction of the nation's pegged exchange rate. Also, the IMF allowed each mem-

devaluation
A decrease in the governmentally defined value of a currency.

Bretton Woods system
The international monetary system developed after World War II in which adjustable pegs were employed, the International Monetary Fund helped to stabilize foreign exchange rates, and gold and the U.S. dollar were used as international monetary reserves.

International Monetary Fund (IMF)
The international association of nations formed after World War II to make loans of foreign monies to nations with temporary payments deficits and, until 1971, to administer the adjustable-peg system.

ber nation to alter the value of its currency by 10 percent, on its own, to correct a so-called fundamental (persistent and continuing) balance of payments deficit. Larger exchange-rate changes required the permission of the Fund's board of directors.

By requiring approval of significant rate changes, the Fund guarded against arbitrary and competitive currency devaluations by nations seeking only to boost output in their own countries at the expense of other countries. In our example, devaluation of the dollar would increase Canadian exports and lower Canadian imports, correcting its persistent payments deficit.

DEMISE OF THE BRETTON WOODS SYSTEM

Under this adjustable-peg system, gold and the dollar came to be accepted as international reserves. The acceptability of gold as an international medium of exchange derived from its earlier use under the gold standard. The U.S. dollar became accepted as international money because the United States had accumulated large quantities of gold and between 1934 and 1971 it maintained a policy of buying gold from, and selling gold to, foreign governments at a fixed price of $35 per ounce. The U.S. dollar was convertible into gold on demand; thus the dollar came to be regarded as a substitute for gold, or "as good as gold." And, since the discovery of new gold was limited, the growing volume of U.S. dollars helped provide a medium of exchange for the expanding world trade.

But a major problem arose. The United States experienced persistent payments deficits throughout the 1950s and 1960s. These deficits were financed in part by U.S. gold reserves, but mostly by payment of U.S. dollars. As the amount of dollars held by foreigners soared and the U.S. gold reserves dwindled, other nations began to question whether the dollar was really "as good as gold." The U.S. ability to continue to convert dollars into gold at $35 per ounce became increasingly doubtful, as did the role of U.S. dollars as international monetary reserves. Thus the dilemma was: To maintain the dollar as a reserve medium, the U.S. payment deficit had to be eliminated. But elimination of the payment deficit would remove the source of additional U.S. dollar reserves and thus limit the growth of international trade and finance.

The problem came to a head in 1971 when the United States ended its 37-year-old policy of exchanging gold for dollars at $35 per ounce. It severed the link between gold and the international value of the dollar, thereby "floating" the dollar and letting its value be determined by market forces. The floating of the dollar in effect withdrew U.S. support from the Bretton Woods system of fixed exchange rates and ended the system.

The Current System: The Managed Float

**managed floating
exchange rate**
An exchange rate that is allowed to change (float) as a result of changes in currency supply and demand but at times is altered (managed) by governments via their buying and selling of particular currencies.

The current international exchange-rate system (1971–present) is an "almost" flexible system called **managed floating exchange rates**. Exchange rates among major currencies are free to float to their equilibrium market levels, but nations occasionally intervene in the foreign exchange market to smooth out fluctuations.

Normally, the major trading nations allow their exchange rates to float up or down to equilibrium levels based on supply and demand in the foreign exchange market. They recognize that changing economic conditions among nations require continuing changes in equilibrium exchange rates to avoid persistent payments deficits or surpluses. They rely on freely operating foreign exchange markets to accomplish the necessary adjustments. The result has been considerably more volatile exchange rates than during the Bretton Woods era.

But nations also recognize that some trends in the movement of equilibrium exchange rates may be at odds with national or international objectives. On occasion, nations therefore intervene in the foreign exchange market by buying or selling large amounts of specific currencies. This way, they can "manage" or stabilize exchange rates by influencing currency demand and supply.

For example, in 1987 the Group of Seven industrial nations (G-7 nations)—Canada, the United States, Germany, Japan, Britain, France, and Italy—agreed to stabilize the value of the U.S. dollar. During the previous two years the U.S. dollar (as well as the Canadian dollar) had declined rapidly because of large U.S. trade deficits. Although the U.S. trade deficits remained sizable, the G-7

www.g7.utoronto.ca
Group of Seven

nations concluded that further dollar depreciation might disrupt economic growth in member nations (other than the United States). The G-7 nations therefore purchased large amounts of U.S. dollars to boost its value. Since 1987 the G-7 nations (now G-8 with the addition of Russia) have periodically intervened in foreign exchange markets to stabilize currency values.

In 2000 Canada, the United States, Japan, and European nations sold U.S. dollars and bought euros in an effort to stabilize the falling value of the euro relative to the U.S. dollar. In the previous year the euro had depreciated from €1 = U.S. $1.17 to €1 = U.S. $0.83. By mid-2003 the euro had climbed back to about €1 = U.S. $1.17.

The current exchange-rate system is thus an "almost" flexible exchange-rate system. The "almost" mainly refers to the periodic currency interventions by central banks. It also refers to the fact that the actual system is more complicated than described. While the major currencies—dollars, pounds, yen, and the like—fluctuate in response to changing supply and demand, some of the European nations have unified their currency into one, the euro. Also, many developing nations peg their currencies to the U.S. dollar and allow their currencies to fluctuate with it against other currencies. Finally, some nations peg the value of their currencies to a "basket" or group of other currencies.

How well has the managed float worked? It has both proponents and critics. Proponents argue that the managed float has functioned far better than anticipated. But skeptics say the managed float is basically a "nonsystem;" the guidelines of what a nation may or may not do are not specific enough to keep the system working in the long run.

So what are we to conclude? Flexible exchange rates have not worked perfectly, but neither have they failed miserably. Thus far they have survived, and no doubt eased, several major shocks to the international trading system. Meanwhile, the "managed" part of the float has given nations some sense of control over their collective economic destinies. On balance, most economists favour continuation of the present system of "almost" flexible exchange rates.

QUICK REVIEW

- Under the gold standard (1879–1934), nations fixed exchange rates by valuing their currencies in terms of gold, by tying their stocks of money to gold, and by allowing gold to flow between nations when balance of payments deficits and surpluses occurred.

- The Bretton Woods exchange-rate system (1944–71) fixed or pegged short-run exchange rates but permitted orderly long-run adjustments of the pegs.

- The managed floating system of exchange rates (1971–present) relies on foreign exchange markets to establish equilibrium exchange rates. The system also permits nations to buy and sell foreign currency to stabilize short-term changes in exchange rates or to correct exchange-rate imbalances that are negatively affecting the world economy.

THE LASTword — Speculation in Currency Markets

Contrary to popular belief, speculators often play a positive role in currency markets.

Most people buy foreign currency to facilitate the purchase of goods or services produced in another country. A Canadian importer buys Japanese yen to purchase Japanese-made automobiles. A British investor purchases euros to buy shares in the German stock market. But there is another group of participants in the currency market—speculators—who buy foreign currencies solely to resell for profit. A British pound bought for $2.00 earns a 10 percent return when it is sold for $2.20.

Speculators sometimes contribute to exchange-rate volatility. The expectation of currency appreciation or depreciation can be self-fulfilling. If speculators expect the Japanese yen to appreciate, they sell other currencies to buy yen. The sharp increase in demand for yen boosts its value, which may attract other speculators—people expecting the yen to rise further. Eventually, the yen's value may soar too high relative to economic realities such as tastes, real interest rates, price levels, and trade balances. The "speculative bubble" bursts and the yen plummets.

But speculative bubbles are not the norm in currency markets. Changed economic realities, not speculation, usually are the cause of changing currency values. Anticipating changes in currency values, speculators simply hasten the adjustment process. Most major adjustments in currency values persist long after the speculators have sold their currency and made their profits.

Speculation, in fact, has two positive effects in foreign exchange markets.

1. Lessening Rate Fluctuations

Speculation smooths out fluctuations in currency prices. When temporarily low demand or excess supply reduces a currency's value, speculators quickly buy it, adding to the demand and strengthening its value. When temporarily strong demand or weak supply increases a currency's value, speculators sell the currency. This selling increases the supply of the currency and reduces its value. In this way speculators smooth out supply and demand—and thus exchange rates—from period to period. And that exchange rate stability facilitates international trade.

2. Absorbing Risk

Speculators aid international trade in another way: *They absorb risk that others do not want to bear.* International transactions are riskier than domestic transactions because of potential adverse changes in exchange rates. Suppose AnyTime, a hypothetical Canadian retailer, signs a contract with a German manufacturer to buy 10,000 German clocks to be delivered in three months. The stipulated price is 75 euros per clock, which in Canadian dollars is $120 per clock at an exchange rate of $1 = .625 euro. AnyTime's total bill will be $1,200,000 (= 750,000 euros).

But if the euro were to appreciate, say, to $1 = .5 euro, the dollar price per clock would rise from $120 to $150 and AnyTime would owe $1,500,000 for the clocks (= 750,000 euros). AnyTime may reduce the risk of such an unfavourable exchange-rate fluctuation by hedging in the futures market. *Hedging is an action by a buyer or a seller to protect against a change in future prices. The futures market is a market where items are bought and sold at prices fixed now, for delivery at a specified date in the future.*

AnyTime can arrange now to purchase the needed 750,000 euros at the current $1 = .625 euro exchange rate, but with delivery in three months when the German clocks are delivered. And here is where speculators arrive on the scene. For a price determined in the futures market, they agree to deliver the 750,000 euros to AnyTime in three months at the $1 = .625 euro exchange rate, regardless of the exchange rate then. The speculators need not own euros at the time the agreement is made. If the euro *depreciates* to, say, $1 = 1 euro in this period, the speculators make a profit. They can buy the 750,000 euros stipulated in the contract for $750,000, pocketing the difference between that amount and the $1,200,000 AnyTime has agreed to pay for the 750,000 euros.

If the euro *appreciates*, the speculators—but not AnyTime—suffer a loss.

The amount AnyTime will have to pay for this futures contract will depend on how the market views the likelihood of the euro depreciating, appreciating, or staying constant over the three-month period. As in all highly competitive markets, supply and demand determine the price of the futures contract.

The futures market thus eliminates much of the exchange-rate risk associated with buying foreign goods for future delivery. Without it AnyTime might have decided against importing German clocks. But the futures market and currency speculators greatly increase the likelihood the transaction will occur. Operating through the futures market, speculation promotes international trade.

CHAPTER SUMMARY

17.1 FINANCING INTERNATIONAL TRADE

- Canadian exports create a foreign demand for dollars and make a supply of foreign exchange available to Canadians. Conversely, Canadian imports create a demand for foreign exchange and make a supply of dollars available to foreigners. Generally, a nation's exports earn the foreign currencies needed to pay for its imports.

17.2 THE BALANCE OF PAYMENTS

- The balance of payments records all international trade and financial transactions taking place between a given nation and the rest of the world. The trade balance compares exports and imports of goods. The balance on goods and services compares exports and imports of both goods and services. The current account balance includes not only goods and services transactions but also net investment income and net transfers.

- A deficit in the current account may be offset by a surplus in the capital account. Conversely, a surplus in the current account may be offset by a deficit in the capital account. A balance of payments deficit occurs when the sum of the current and capital accounts is negative. Such a deficit is financed with official international reserves. A balance of payments surplus occurs when the sum of the current and capital accounts is positive. A payments surplus results in an increase in official reserves. The desirability of a balance of payments deficit or surplus depends on its size and its persistence.

17.3 FOREIGN EXCHANGE MARKETS: FLEXIBLE EXCHANGE RATES

- Flexible or floating exchange rates between international currencies are determined by the demand for and supply of those currencies. Under floating rates a currency will depreciate or appreciate as a result of changes in tastes, relative income changes, relative price changes, relative changes in real interest rates, and speculation.

17.4 FIXED EXCHANGE RATES

- The maintenance of fixed exchange rates requires adequate international reserves to accommodate periodic payments deficits. If reserves are inadequate, nations must invoke protectionist trade policies, engage in exchange controls, or endure undesirable domestic macroeconomic adjustments.

17.5 INTERNATIONAL EXCHANGE-RATE SYSTEMS

- The gold standard, a fixed rate system, provided exchange-rate stability until its disintegration during the 1930s. Under this system, gold flows between nations precipitated sometimes painful changes in price, income, and employment levels in bringing about international equilibrium.

- Under the Bretton Woods system, exchange rates were pegged to one another and were stable. Participating nations were obligated to maintain these rates by using stabilization funds, gold, or loans from the IMF. Persistent or "fundamental" payments deficits could be resolved by IMF-sanctioned currency devaluations.

- Since 1971 the world's major nations have used a system of managed floating exchange rates. Rates are generally set by market forces, although governments intervene with varying frequency to alter their exchange rates.

TERMS AND CONCEPTS

foreign exchange market, p. 406
balance of payments, p. 407
current account, p. 407
balance on goods and services, p. 408
trade surplus, p. 408
trade deficit, p. 408
capital account, p. 409
official international reserves, p. 409
balance of payments deficit, p. 409

balance of payments surplus, p. 409
exchange rate, p. 411
flexible or floating exchange-rate system, p. 411
fixed exchange-rate system, p. 411
depreciation, p. 413
appreciation, p. 413
purchasing power parity theory, p. 414

currency intervention, p. 417
exchange control, p. 418
gold standard, p. 419
devaluation, p. 421
Bretton Woods system, p. 421
International Monetary Fund, p. 421
managed floating exchange rates, p. 422

STUDY QUESTIONS

1. Explain how a Canadian automobile importer might finance a shipment of Toyotas from Japan. Demonstrate how a Canadian export of machinery to Italy might be financed. Explain: "Canadian exports earn supplies of foreign currencies that Canadians can use to finance imports."

2. **KEY QUESTION** Indicate whether each of the following creates a demand for, or a supply of, European euros in foreign exchange markets:

   a. A Canadian importer purchases a shipload of Bordeaux wine.

   b. A Swedish automobile firm decides to build an assembly plant in Halifax.

   c. A Canadian university student decides to spend a year studying at the Sorbonne.

   d. A French manufacturer ships machinery from one French port to another on a Canadian freighter.

   e. Canada incurs a balance of payments deficit in its transactions with France.

   f. A Canadian government bond held by a French citizen matures and the loan amount is paid back to that person.

   g. It is widely believed that the international value of the euro will fall in the near future.

3. **KEY QUESTION** Alpha's balance of payments data for 1999 are shown below. All figures are in billions of dollars. What are (a) the balance of trade, (b) the balance on goods and services, (c) the balance on current account, and (d) the balance on capital account? Does Alpha have a balance of payments deficit or surplus? Explain.

Goods exports	+$40
Goods imports	− 30
Service exports	+ 15
Service imports	− 10
Net investment income	− 5
Net transfers	+$10
Foreign investment in Canada	+ 10
Foreign investment abroad	− 40
Official international reserves	+ 10

4. "A rise in the dollar price of yen necessarily means a fall in the yen price of dollars." Do you agree? Illustrate and elaborate: "The critical thing about exchange rates is that they provide a direct link between the prices of goods and services produced in all trading nations of the world." Explain the purchasing power parity theory of exchange rates.

5. Suppose that a Swiss watchmaker imports watch components from Sweden and exports watches to Canada. Also suppose the Canadian dollar depreciates, and the euro appreciates, relative to the Swiss franc. Speculate as to how each would hurt the Swiss watchmaker.

6. **KEY QUESTION** Explain why the Canadian demand for Mexican pesos is downward sloping and the supply of pesos to Canadians is upward sloping.

Assuming a system of flexible exchange rates between Mexico and Canada, indicate whether each of the following would cause the Mexican peso to appreciate or depreciate:

   a. Canada unilaterally reduces tariffs on Mexican products.

   b. Mexico encounters severe inflation.

   c. Deteriorating political relations reduce Canadian tourism in Mexico.

   d. The Canadian economy moves into a severe recession.

   e. Canada engages in a high-interest rate monetary policy.

   f. Mexican products become more fashionable to Canadians.

   g. The Mexican government encourages Canadian firms to invest in Mexican oil fields.

   h. The rate of productivity growth in Canada diminishes sharply.

7. Explain why you agree or disagree with the following statements:

   a. "A country that grows faster than its major trading partners can expect the international value of its currency to depreciate."

   b. "A nation with an interest rate that is rising more rapidly than in other nations can expect the international value of its currency to appreciate."

   c. "A country's currency will appreciate if its inflation rate is less than that of the rest of the world."

8. "Exports pay for imports. Yet in 1993 the rest of the world exported about $3.2 billion more worth of goods and services to Canada than were imported from Canada." Resolve the apparent inconsistency of these two statements.

9. **KEY QUESTION** Diagram a market in which the equilibrium dollar price of one unit of fictitious currency Zee is $5 (the exchange rate is $5 = Z1). Then show on your diagram a decline in the demand for Zee.

   a. Referring to your diagram, discuss the adjustment options Canada would have in maintaining the exchange rate at $5 = Z1 under a fixed exchange-rate system.

   b. How would the Canadian balance of payments surplus that is created (by the decline in demand) get resolved under a system of flexible exchange rates?

10. Compare and contrast the Bretton Woods system of exchange rates with that of the gold standard. What caused the demise of the gold standard? What caused the demise of the Bretton Woods system?

11. Describe what is meant by the term "managed float." Did the managed float system precede or follow the adjustable-peg system? Explain.

12. **(The Last Word)** Suppose Sportif de l'Hiver—a French retailer of snowboards—wants to order 5000 snowboards made in Canada. The price per board is $200, the present exchange rate is 1 euro = $1, and payment is due in dollars when the boards are delivered in 3 months. Use a numerical example to explain why exchange-rate risk might make the French retailer hesitant to place the order. How might speculators absorb some of Sportif de l'Hiver risk?

INTERNET APPLICATION QUESTIONS

1. **Canada's International Trade in Goods and Services** Go to the McConnell-Brue-Barbiero Web site (Chapter 17) to access data on Canada's merchandise trade balance for the last five years. Has Canada had a surplus or deficit on the merchandise trade balance in the last five years? With which country do we have a trade deficit? A trade surplus?

Σ-STAT

2. **Canada's Balance of International Payments** Go to the McConnell-Brue-Barbiero Web site (Chapter 17) to access the International Monetary Fund (IMF) data that sets out Canada's balance of international payments for the latest quarter for which data are available. What did Canada hold in international reserves in the latest quarter? What is the exchange rate between the Canadian and U.S. dollar for the latest period? Has the Canadian dollar appreciated or depreciated against the U.S. dollar in the last year?

Σ-STAT

Credits

Text Credits

Chapter 2

p. 38 From Organisation for Economic Co-operation and Development (OECD).

Chapter 4

p. 79 From The Heritage Foundation and *The Wall Street Journal*; p. 90 From Organisation for Economic Co-operation and Development (OECD); p. 93 From Kerney, A.T., *Foreign Policy*, www.foreignpolicy.com.

Chapter 5

p. 107 Adapted from the Statistics Canada web site, www.statcan.ca/english/Pgdb/econ04.htm; p. 111 Adapted from the Statistics Canada web site, www.statcan.ca/english/Pgdb/econ04.htm; p. 112 From World Bank, www.worldbank.org; p. 119 Adapted from the Statistics Canada web site, www.statcan.ca/english/Pgdb/econ04.htm; p. 121 From Friedrich Schneider and Dominic H. Enste, "Shadow Economies: Size, Causes, and Consequences," *Journal of Economic Literature* (March 2000), p. 104. The figure for Canada is from David E. A. Giles and Lindsay M. Tedds, *Taxes and the Canadian Underground Economy*, Toronto: Canadian Tax Foundation, 2002; p. 123 Adapted from the Statistics Canada web site, www.statcan.ca/english/freepub/15-547-XIE2001.pdf.

Chapter 6

p. 129 Adapted from the Statistics Canada web site, www.statcan.ca/english/freepub/11-516-XIE/sectiona/toc.htm and from the Statistics Canada CANSIM database, http://cansim2.statcan.ca, Table 380-0002; p. 130 From Organisation for Economic Co-operation and Development (OECD); p. 131 Adapted from the Statistics Canada web site, www.statcan.ca/english/freepub/11-516-XIE/sectiona/toc.htm and from the Statistics Canada CANSIM database, http://cansim2.statcan.ca, Table 380-0002; p. 132 Adapted from the Statistics Canada CANSIM database, http://cansim2.statcan.ca, Table 384-0002; p. 137 Adapted from the Statistics Canada CANSIM database, http://cansim2.statcan.ca, Series D15721 and Table 282-0002; p. 138

Adapted from the Statistics Canada CANSIM database, http://cansim2.statcan.ca, Table 282-0007; p. 139 Adapted from the Statistics Canada web site, www.statcan.ca/english/Pgdb/labor07c.htm; p. 139 From Organisation for Economic Co-operation and Development (OECD); p. 141 Adapted from the Statistics Canada web site, www.statcan.ca/english/Pgdb/econ46.htm; p. 142 From Organisation for Economic Co-operation and Development (OECD).

Chapter 7

p. 157 Adapted from the Statistics Canada publication, "National Income and Expenditure Accounts, Quarterly Estimates," Catalogue No. 13-001, various years; p. 161 From *Statistical Abstract of the United States*, 2002, p. 835, and author's calculations; p. 169 From World Bank, www.worldbank.com; p. 185 From World Trade Organization, www.wto.org.

Chapter 9

p. 244 Reproduced with the permission of the Minister of Public Works and Government Services Canada, Department of Finance, *Fiscal Reference Tables*, 2003; p. 244 From Organisation for Economic Co-operation and Development (OECD).

Chapter 10

p. 256 Adapted from the Statistics Canada CANSIM database, http://cansim2.statcan.ca, Series D469409, the Statistics Canada web site, www.statcan.ca/english/Pgdb/govt03.htm, and Bank of Canada; p. 257 Adapted from the Statistics Canada web sites, www.statcan.ca/english/Pgdb/govt38a.htm and www.statcan.ca/english/Pgdb/demo31a.htm; p. 258 From Organisation for Economic Co-operation and Development (OECD); p. 262 Adapted from the Statistics Canada CANSIM database, http://cansim2.statcan.ca, Table 385-0001.

Chapter 11

p. 272 From Bank of Canada, Weekly Financial Statistics, August 22, 2003; p. 274 From Canadian Bankers Association; p. 282 From The Banker; p. 283 From Bank of Canada, Weekly Financial Statistics, August

22, 2003; p. 284 From Canadian Bankers Association; p. 286 From Bank of Canada, www.bankofcanada.ca/en/banknotes/general/index.htm.

Chapter 13

p. 308 From Bank of Canada, Weekly Financial Statistics, February 14, 2003, www.bankofcanada.ca/en/wfsgen.htm.

Chapter 14

p. 342 From U.S. Bureau of Labor Statistics, www.bls.gov; p. 344 From Bank of Canada, *Monetary Policy Report*, April 2003.

Chapter 15

p. 358 Adapted from the Statistics Canada publication, "Productivity Growth in Canada," Catalogue No. 15-204-XPE, December 2002; p. 360 Adapted from the Statistics Canada publication, "Education in Canada, 2000," Catalogue No. 81-229, Table 23, May 2001; p. 364 Compiled and directly quoted from W. Michael Cox and Richard Alm, "The New Paradigm," Federal Reserve Bank of Dallas Annual Report, May 2000, various pages; p. 365 From World Economic Forum, www.weforum.org.

Chapter 16

p. 376 From IMF, International Financial Statistics, 2000; p. 377 Adapted from the Statistics Canada CANSIM database, Series D15458 and D15471; p. 378 Adapted from the Statistics Canada web site, www.statcan.ca/english/Pgdb/gblec05.htm; p. 378, Adapted from the Statistics Canada web site, www.statcan.ca/english/Pgdb/gblec02.htm; p. 379, World Trade Organization, www.wto.org.

Chapter 17

p. 409 Adapted from the Statistics Canada web site, www.statcan.ca/english/Pgdb/econ01a.htm; p. 410 Adapted from the Statistics Canada web site, www.statcan.ca/english/Pgdb/gblec02a.htm; p. 412 Adapted from the Statistics Canada web site, www.statcan.ca/english/Pgdb/econ01b.htm and from the Statistics Canada CANSIM database, http://cansim2.statcan.ca, Tables 376-0001 and 376-0002.

Photographs

Chapter 1
p. 3, Photodisc

Chapter 2
p. 35, Photodisc

Chapter 3
p. 49, Photodisc; p. 65, Photodisc;
p. 67, Photodisc

Chapter 4
p. 88, Canapress; p. 92, Photodisc

Chapter 5
p. 108, EyeWire

Chapter 6
p. 128, Photodisc

Chapter 7
p. 163, Photodisc; p. 168, Photodisc

Chapter 8
p. 212, Photodisc; p. 220, Photodisc

Chapter 9
p. 237, EyeWire

Chapter 10
p. 255, Photodisc

Chapter 11
p. 271, Photodisc

Chapter 12
p. 290, Photodisc

Chapter 13
p. 318, EyeWire

Chapter 14
p. 337, EyeWire

Chapter 15
p. 360, Photodisc

Chapter 16
p. 381, EyeWire; p. 386, Photodisc

Chapter 17
p. 408, Photodisc; p. 415, EyeWire

Glossary

A

Absolute advantage When a region or nation can produce more of good Z and good Y with less resources compared to other regions or nations.

Actual investment The amount that *firms* do invest; equal to *planned investment* plus *unplanned investment*.

Actual reserves The funds that a bank has as vault cash plus any deposit it may have with the Bank of Canada.

Adjustable pegs The device used in the *Bretton Woods system* to alter *exchange rates* in an orderly way to eliminate persistent payments deficits and surpluses. Each nation defined its monetary unit in terms of (pegged it to) gold or the dollar, kept the *rate of exchange* for its money stable in the short run, and adjusted its rate in the long run when faced with international payments disequilibrium.

Aggregate A collection of specific economic units treated as if they were one unit.

Aggregate demand A schedule or curve that shows the total quantity of goods and services demanded (purchased) at different *price levels*.

Aggregate demand–aggregate supply model The macroeconomic model that uses *aggregate demand* and *aggregate supply* to explain *price level* and *real domestic output*.

Aggregate expenditures The total amount spent for final goods and services in an economy.

Aggregate expenditures schedule A schedule or curve that shows the total amount spent for final goods and services at different levels of GDP.

Aggregate expenditures-domestic output approach Determination of the *equilibrium gross domestic product* by finding the real GDP at which

aggregate expenditures equal *domestic output.*

Aggregate supply A schedule or curve that shows the total quantity of goods and services supplied (produced) at different *price levels.*

Aggregate supply shocks Sudden, large changes in resource costs that shift an economy's aggregate supply curve.

Aggregation Combining individual units or data into one unit or number. For example, all prices of individual goods and services are combined into a price level, or all units of output are aggregated into real gross domestic product.

Allocative efficiency The distribution of resources among firms and industries to produce the goods most wanted by society.

Annually balanced budget A budget in which government expenditures and tax collections are equal each year.

Anticipated inflation Increases in the price level that occur at the expected rate.

Applied economics (See *Policy economics.*)

Appreciation (of the dollar) An increase in the value of the dollar relative to the currency of another nation so that a dollar buys a larger amount of the foreign currency and thus of foreign goods.

Asset Anything of monetary value owned by a firm or individual.

Asset demand for money The amount of *money* people want to hold as a *store of value*; this amount varies inversely with the *rate of interest.*

Average propensity to consume Fraction (or percentage) of *disposable income* that households plan to spend for consumer goods and services.

Average propensity to save Fraction (or percentage) of disposable income that households save.

Average tax rate Total tax paid divided by total (taxable) income, as a percentage.

B

Balanced-budget multiplier The extent to which an equal change in government spending and taxes changes equilibrium gross domestic product; always has a value of 1, since it is equal to the amount of the equal changes in G and T.

Balance of payments A summary of all the transactions that took place between the individuals, firms, and government units of one nation and those in all other nations during a year.

Balance of payments deficit The amount by which the net sum of the *balance on current account* and the *balance on the capital account* is negative in a year.

Balance of payments surplus The amount by which the net sum of the *balance on current account* and the *balance on the capital account* is positive in a year.

Balance on current account The exports of goods and services of a nation less its imports of goods and services plus its *net investment income* and *net transfers* in a year.

Balance on goods and services The exports of goods and services of a nation less its imports of goods and services in a year.

Balance on the capital account The foreign purchases of assets in a nation less its purchases of assets abroad in a year.

Balance sheet A statement of the *assets, liabilities,* and *net worth* of a firm or individual at a certain time.

Bank deposits The deposits that individuals or firms have at financial institutions or that banks have at the *central bank*.

Bank of Canada notes Paper money issued by the Bank of Canada.

Bank rate The interest rate that the Bank of Canada charges on advances made to the chartered banks.

Bankers' bank A bank that accepts the deposits of and makes loans to *chartered banks*; in Canada, the Bank of Canada.

Barter The exchange of one good or service for another good or service.

Base year The year with which other years are compared when an index is constructed; for example, the base year for a *price index*.

Bond A financial device through which a borrower (a firm or government) is obligated to pay the principle and interest on a loan at a specific date in the future.

Brain drain The emigration of highly educated, highly skilled workers from a country.

Break-even income The level of disposable income at which households plan to consume all their income and to save none of it.

Bretton Wood system The international monetary system developed after World War II in which adjustable pegs were employed, the International Monetary Fund helped to stabilize foreign exchange rates, and gold and the U.S.dollar were used as international monetary reserves.

Budget deficit The amount by which the expenditures of the federal government exceed its revenues in any year.

Budget surplus The amount by which the revenues of the federal government exceed its expenditures in any year.

Built-in stabilizer A mechanism that increases government's budget deficit (or reduces its surplus) during a recession and increases government's budget surplus (or reduces its deficit)

during inflation without any action by policymakers.

Business cycle Recurring increases and decreases in the level of economic activity over periods of years. Consists of peak, recession, trough, and recovery phases.

Business firm (See *Firm*.)

C

Capital Human-made resources (buildings, machinery, and equipment) used to produce goods and services.

Capital account The section of a nation's *international balance of payments* statement that records the foreign purchases of assets in Canada and Canadian purchases of assets abroad.

Capital account deficit A negative *balance on the capital account*.

Capital account surplus A positive *balance on the capital-account*.

Capital consumption allowance Estimate of the amount of capital worn out or used up (consumed) in producing the *gross domestic product; depreciation*.

Capital flight The transfer of savings from developing countries to industrially advanced countries to avoid government expropriation, taxation, and high rates of inflation or to realize better investment opportunities.

Capital gain The gain realized when securities or properties are sold for a price greater than the price paid for them.

Capital goods Goods that do not directly satisfy human wants.

Capital-intensive goods Products that require a relatively large amount of *capital* to produce.

Capitalism An economic system in which property resources are privately owned and markets and prices are used to direct and coordinate economic activities.

Capital-saving technology *Technology* that permits a greater quantity of a product to be produced with a specific

amount of *capital* (or permits the same amount of the product to be produced with a smaller amount of capital).

Capital stock The total available *capital* in a nation.

Capital-using technology *Technology* that requires the use of a greater amount of *capital* to produce a specific quantity of a product.

Cartel A formal agreement among firms (or countries) in an industry to set the price of a product and establish the outputs of the individual firms (or countries) or to divide the market for the product geographically.

Central bank A bank whose chief function is the control of the nation's money supply; in Canada, the Bank of Canada.

Central economic planning Government determination of the objectives of the economy and how resources will be directed to attain those goals.

Ceteris paribus **assumption** (See "*Other things equal*" assumption.)

Change in demand A change in the quantity demanded of a good or service at every price.

Change in quantity demanded A movement from one point to another on a *demand curve*.

Change in quantity supplied A movement from one point to another on a fixed *supply curve*.

Change in supply A change in the quantity supplied of a good or service at every price; a shift of the supply curve to the left or right.

Chartered bank One of the multi-branched, privately owned, commercial, financial intermediaries that have received charters by Act of Parliament and that may call themselves "banks."

Chequable deposit Any deposit in a financial institution against which a cheque may be written and which deposit, if it is in a bank, is thus part of the M1 money supply.

Chequing account A *demand deposit* in a financial institution.

Circular flow model The flow of resources from households to firms and of products from firms to households. These flows are accompanied by reverse flows of money from firms to households and from households to firms.

Classical economics The macroeconomic generalizations accepted by most economists before the 1930s that led to the conclusion that a capitalistic economy was self-regulating and therefore would usually employ its resources fully.

Closed economy An economy that neither exports nor imports goods and services.

COLA (See *Cost-of-living adjustment*.)

Command system An economic system in which most property resources are owned by the government and economic decisions are made by a central government body.

Commercial bank (See *Chartered bank*.)

Communism (See *Command economy*.)

Comparative advantage When a region or nation can produce a good at a lower domestic opportunity cost compared to a potential trading partner.

Competing goods (See *Substitute goods*.)

Competition The presence in a market of a large number of independent buyers and sellers competing with one another and the freedom of buyers and sellers to enter and leave the market.

Complementary goods Products and services that are used together.

Complex multiplier The multiplier that exists when changes in the gross domestic product change net taxes and imports, as well as saving.

Conglomerates Firms that produce goods and services in two or more separate industries.

Consumer goods Products and services that satisfy human wants directly.

Consumer price index (CPI) An index that measures the prices of a fixed "market basket" of goods and services bought by a "typical" consumer.

Consumer sovereignty Determination by consumers of the types and quantities of goods and services that will be produced with the scarce resources of the economy.

Consumption of fixed capital Estimate of the amount of *capital* worn out or used up (consumed) in producing the *gross domestic product*; also called depreciation.

Consumption schedule A schedule showing the amounts *households* plan to spend for *consumer goods* at different levels of *disposable income*.

Contractionary fiscal policy A decrease in government spending, an increase in net taxes, or some combination of the two, for the purpose of decreasing *aggregate demand* and thus controlling inflation.

Contractionary monetary policy Coordination failure A situation in which people do not reach a mutually beneficial outcome because they lack some way to jointly coordinate their actions; a possible cause of macroeconomic instability.

Corporate income tax A tax levied on the net income (profit) of corporations.

Corporation A legal entity ("person") chartered by a province or the federal government that is distinct and separate from the individuals who own it.

Correlation A systematic and dependable association between two sets of data (two kinds of events); does not necessarily indicate causation.

Cost-of-living adjustment (COLA) An automatic increase in the incomes (wages) of workers when inflation occurs.

Cost-push inflation Increases in the price level resulting from an increase in resource costs and hence in *per-unit production costs*.

Cost ratio An equality showing the number of units of two products that can be produced with the same resources.

Creative destruction The hypothesis that the creation of new products and production methods simultaneously destroys the market power of existing monopolies.

Credit An accounting item that increases the value of an asset (such as the foreign money owned by the residents of a nation).

Credit union An association of persons who have a common tie (such as being employees of the same firm or members of the same labour union) that sells shares to (accepts deposits from) its members and makes loans to them.

Crowding-out effect A rise in interest rates and a resulting decrease in *planned investment* caused by the federal government's increased borrowing in the money market.

Currency Coins and paper money.

Currency appreciation (See *Exchange rate appreciation*.)

Currency depreciation (See *Exchange rate depreciation*.)

Currency intervention A government's buying and selling of its own or of foreign currencies to alter international exchange rates.

Current account The section in a nation's *international balance of payments* that records its exports and imports of goods and services, its net investment income, and its net transfers.

Cyclical deficit A federal *budget deficit* that is caused by a recession and the consequent decline in tax revenues.

Cyclically adjusted budget What the budget balance would be for the total government sector if the economy were operating at full employment.

Cyclically balanced budget The equality of government expenditures and *net tax collections* over the course of a *business cycle*.

Cyclical unemployment *Unemployment* caused by a decline in total spending (or by insufficient *aggregate demand*).

D

Debit An accounting item that decreases the value of an asset (such as the foreign money owned by the residents of a nation).

Deflating Finding the *real gross domestic product* by decreasing the dollar value of the GDP for a year in which prices were higher than in the *base year*.

Deflation A decline in the economy's price level.

Demand A schedule or curve that shows the various amounts of a product that consumers are willing and able to purchase at each of a series of possible prices during a specified period of time.

Demand curve A curve illustrating the inverse (negative) relationship between the quantity demanded of a good or service and its price, other things equal.

Demand deposit A deposit in a *chartered bank* against which cheques may be written.

Demand-deposit multiplier (See *Monetary multiplier*.)

Demand factor The increase in the level of *aggregate demand* that brings about the *economic growth* made possible by an increase in the production potential of the economy.

Demand management The use of *fiscal policy* and *monetary policy* to increase or decrease *aggregate demand*.

Demand-pull inflation Increases in the price level caused by an excess of total spending beyond the economy's capacity to produce.

Dependent variable A variable that changes as a consequence of a change in some other (independent) variable; the "effect" or outcome.

Depreciation (See *Capital consumption allowance*.)

Depreciation (of the dollar) A decrease in the value of the dollar relative to another currency so that a dollar buys a smaller amount of the foreign currency and therefore of foreign goods.

Derived demand The demand for a factor of production that depends on the demand for the products it can be used to produce.

Desired reserve ratio The specified percentage of deposit liabilities a chartered bank chooses to keep as vault cash.

Desired reserves The amount of vault cash each *chartered bank* chooses to keep on hand for daily transactions, plus its deposits at the Bank of Canada.

Determinants of aggregate demand Factors (such as consumption spending, *investment*, government spending, and *net exports*) that, shift the *aggregate demand curve*.

Determinants of aggregate supply Factors such as input prices, *productivity*, and the legal-institutional environment that shift the *aggregate supply curve*.

Determinants of demand Factors other than its price that determine the quantities demanded of a good or service.

Determinants of supply Factors other than its price that determine the quantities supplied of a good or service.

Devaluation A decrease in the governmentally defined value of a currency.

Developing countries Many countries of Africa, Asia, and Latin America that are characterized by a lack of capital goods, use of non-advanced technologies, low literacy rates, high unemployment, rapid population growth, and labour forces heavily committed to agriculture.

Direct foreign investment The building of new factories (or the purchase of existing capital) in a particular nation by corporations of other nations.

Direct relationship The relationship between two variables that change in the same direction, for example, product price and quantity supplied.

Discouraged workers People who have left the labour force because they have not been able to find employment.

Discretionary fiscal policy Deliberate changes in taxes (tax rates) and government spending by Parliament to promote full-employment, price stability, and economic growth.

Discrimination According individuals or groups different treatment in hiring, occupational access, education and training, promotion, wage rates, or working conditions, even though they have the same abilities, education and skills, and work experience as other workers.

Disposable income *Personal income* less personal taxes.

Dissaving Spending for consumer goods and services in excess of *disposable income*; the amount by which *personal consumption expenditures* exceed disposable income.

Dividends Payments by a corporation of all or part of its profit to its shareholders (the corporate owners).

Division of labour Dividing the work required to produce a product into a number of different tasks that are performed by different workers.

Dollar votes The "votes" that consumers and entrepreneurs cast for the production of consumer and capital goods, respectively, when they purchase them in product and resource markets.

Domestic capital formation Addition to a nation's stock of *capital* by saving and investing part of its own domestic output.

Domestic price The price of a good or service within a country, determined by domestic demand and supply.

Double taxation The taxation of both corporate net income (profits) and the *dividends* paid from this net income when they become the personal income of households.

Dumping The sale in a foreign country of products below the prices charged at home.

Durable good A consumer good with an expected life (use) of three or more years.

E

Earnings The money income received by a worker; equal to the *wage* (rate) multiplied by the amount of time worked.

Easy money policy Bank of Canada actions that increase the money supply to lower interest rates and expand real GDP.

Economic analysis Deriving *economic principles* from relevant economic facts.

Economic cost A payment that must be made to obtain and retain the services of a *resource*; the income a firm must provide to a resource supplier to attract the resource away from an alternative use; equal to the quantity of other products that cannot be produced when resources are instead used to make a particular product.

Economic efficiency Obtaining the socially optimal amounts of goods and services using minimum necessary resources; entails both *productive efficiency* and *allocative efficiency*.

Economic growth (1) An outward shift in the *production possibilities curve* that results from an increase in factor supplies or quality or an improvement in technology; (2) an increase either in real output (*gross domestic product*) or in real output per capita.

Economic law An *economic principle* that has been tested and retested and has stood the test of time.

Economic perspective A viewpoint that envisions individuals and institutions making rational decisions by com-

paring the marginal benefits and marginal costs associated with their actions.

Economic policy A course of action intended to correct or avoid a problem.

Economic principle A widely accepted generalization about the economic behaviour of individuals and institutions.

Economic problem Choices are necessary because society's material wants for goods and services are unlimited but the resources available to satisfy these wants are limited (scarce).

Economic profit The *total revenue* of a firm less its *economic costs* (which includes both *explicit costs* and *implicit costs*); also called "pure profit" and "above normal profit."

Economic resources The *land, labour, capital,* and *entrepreneurial ability* that are used in the production of goods and services.

Economics The social science concerned with the efficient use of scarce resources to obtain the maximum satisfaction of society's unlimited wants.

Economic system A particular set of institutional arrangements and a coordinating mechanism for producing goods and services.

Economic theory Deriving economic principles from relevant economic facts; an economic principle.

Economies of scale Reductions in the average total cost of producing a product as the firm expands the size of plant (its output) in the long run.

Economizing problem The choices necessitated because society's material wants for goods and services are unlimited but the *resources* available to satisfy these wants are limited (scarce).

Efficiency factor The capacity of an economy to combine resources effectively to achieve growth of real output that the *supply factors* make possible.

Efficiency wages Wages that elicit maximum work effort and thus minimize labour cost per unit of output.

Efficient allocation of resources That allocation of an economy's resources among the production of different products that leads to the maximum satisfaction of consumers' wants; producing the socially optimal mix of output with society's scarce resources.

Electronic Transactions Transactions that are made using an electronic medium.

Employment rate The percentage of the civilian *labour force* employed at any time.

Entrepreneurial ability The human talents that combine the other resources to produce a product, make non-routine decisions, innovate, and bear risks.

Equation of exchange $MV = PQ$, in which M is the supply of money, V is the velocity of money, P is the price level, and Q is the physical volume of *final goods and services* produced.

Equilibrium GDP The level at which the total quantity of goods produced (GDP) equals the total quantity of goods purchased.

Equilibrium price The *price* in a competitive market at which the *quantity demanded* and the *quantity supplied* are equal.

Equilibrium price level The price level at which the *aggregate demand curve* intersects the *aggregate supply curve*.

Equilibrium quantity The quantity demanded and supplied at the equilibrium price in a competitive market.

Equilibrium real domestic output The real domestic output at which the *aggregate demand curve* intersects the *aggregate supply curve*.

Equilibrium World Price A price determined by the intersection of exporting nations' supply of a product and importing nations' demand for the same product.

Euro The common currency used by 12 European nations in the Euro zone, which includes all nations of the *European Union* except Great Britain, Denmark, and Sweden.

European Union (EU) An association of European nations that has eliminated tariffs among them, established common tariffs for goods imported from outside the member nations, and allowed the free movement of labour and capital among them.

Excess reserves The amount by which a *chartered bank's actual reserves* exceed its *desired reserves*.

Exchange control (See *Foreign exchange control*.)

Exchange rate The rate at which the currency of one nation is exchanged for the currency of another nation.

Exchange rate appreciation An increase in the value of a nation's currency in foreign exchange markets; an increase in the rate of exchange for foreign currencies.

Exchange rate depreciation A decrease in the value of a nation's currency in foreign exchange markets; a decrease in the rate of exchange for foreign currencies.

Excise tax A tax levied on the production of a specific product or on the quantity of the product purchased.

Exclusion principle The ability to exclude those who do not pay for a product from receiving its benefits.

Expansionary fiscal policy An increase in government spending, a decrease in *net taxes*, or some combination of the two, for the purpose of increasing *aggregate demand* and expanding real output.

Expansionary monetary policy Expectations The anticipations of consumers, firms, and others about future economic conditions.

Expected rate of return The increase in profit a firm anticipates it will obtain by purchasing capital.

Expenditures approach The method that adds all expenditures made for final goods and services to measure the gross domestic product.

Export controls The limitation or prohibition of the export of certain products on the basis of foreign policy or national security objectives.

Exports Goods and services produced in a nation and sold to customers in other nations.

Export subsidies Government payments to domestic producers to enable them to reduce the *price* of a good or service to foreign buyers.

Export supply curve An upward-sloping curve that shows the amount of a product domestic firms will export at each world price above the domestic price.

External cost (See *Spillover cost*.)

External debt Private or public debt owed to foreign citizens, firms, and institutions.

External public debt Public debt owed to foreign citizens, firms, and institutions.

Externality (See *Spillover*.)

F

Face value The dollar or cents value stamped on a coin.

Factor market A market in which households sell and firms buy factors of production.

Factors of production *Economic resources*: land, capital, labour, and entrepreneurial ability.

Fallacy of composition Incorrectly reasoning that what is true for the individual (or part) is necessarily true for the group (or whole).

Fallacy of limited decisions The false notion that there are a limited number of economic decisions to be made so that, if government makes more decisions, there will be fewer private decisions to render.

Fiat money Anything that is money because government has decreed it to be money.

Final goods Goods and services that have been purchased for final use and not for resale or further processing or manufacturing.

Financial intermediary A *chartered bank* or other financial institution that uses the funds deposited with it to make loans.

Firm An organization that employs resources to produce a good or service for profit.

Fiscal policy Changes in government spending and tax collections designed to achieve a full-employment and noninflationary domestic output.

Fixed cost Any cost which in total does not change when the firm changes its output; the cost of fixed resources.

Fixed exchange rate A *rate of exchange* that is prevented from rising or falling with changes in currency supply and demand.

Flexible exchange rate A rate of exchange determined by the international demand for and supply of a nation's currency.

Floating exchange rate (See *Flexible exchange rate*.)

Foreign exchange control The control a government may exercise over the quantity of foreign currency demanded by its citizens and firms and over the *rates of exchange* in order to limit its *outpayments* to its *inpayments* (to eliminate a *payments* deficit).

Foreign exchange market A market in which the money (currency) of one nation can be used to purchase (can be exchanged for) the money of another nation.

Foreign exchange rate (See *Rate of exchange*.)

Foreign trade effect The inverse relationship between the *net exports* of an economy and its price level relative to price levels in the economies of trading partners.

45° (degree) line A reference line that bisects the 90° angle formed by the two axes, and along which consumption equals disposable income.

Four fundamental economic questions The four questions that every economy must answer: what to produce, how to produce it, how to divide the total output, and how to ensure economic flexibility.

Fractional reserve A *reserve ratio* that is less than 100 percent of the deposit liabilities of a *chartered bank*.

Freedom of choice The freedom of owners of property resources to employ or dispose of them as they see fit, and of consumers to spend their incomes in a manner that they think is appropriate.

Freedom of enterprise The freedom of *firms* to obtain economic resources, to use these resources to produce products of the firm's own choosing, and to sell their products in markets of their choice.

Free-rider problem The inability of potential providers of an economically desirable but indivisible good or service to obtain payment from those who benefit.

Free trade The absence of artificial (government-imposed) barriers to trade among individuals and firms in different nations.

Frictional unemployment A type of unemployment caused by workers voluntarily changing jobs and by temporary layoffs; unemployed workers between jobs.

Full employment Use of all available resources to produce want-satisfying goods and services.

Full-employment unemployment rate The *unemployment rate* at which there is no *cyclical unemployment* of the *labour force*; equal to about 7.5 percent in Canada because some *frictional* and *structural unemployment* is unavoidable.

Full production Employment of available resources so that the maximum amount of goods and services is produced.

Functional finance The use of *fiscal policy* to achieve a non-inflationary full-employment *gross domestic product* without regard to the effect on the *public debt*.

G

G-7 Nations A group of seven major industrial nations (the United States, Japan, Germany, United Kingdom, France, Italy, and Canada) whose leaders meet regularly to discuss common economic problems and try to coordinate economic policies. (Recently has also include Russia, making it unofficially the G-8.)

Gains from trade The extra output that trading partners obtain through specialization of production and exchange of goods and services.

GDP (See *Gross domestic product.*)

GDP deflator An implicit price index calculated by dividing nominal GDP by real GDP and multiplying by 100.

GDP gap The amount by which actual *gross domestic product* falls below potential *gross domestic product.*

General Agreement on Tariffs and Trade (GATT) The international agreement reached in 1947 in which 23 nations agreed to give equal and nondiscriminatory treatment to the other nations, to reduce tariff rates by multinational negotiations, and to eliminate import quotas.

Generalization Statement of the nature of the relation between two or more sets of facts.

Gold standard A historical system of fixed exchange rates in which nations defined their currency in terms of gold.

Government deposit switching Action of the Bank of Canada to increase (decrease) backingfor money supply by switching government deposits from (to) itself to (from) the chartered banks.

Government purchases The expenditures of all governments in the economy for final goods and services.

Government transfer payment The disbursement of money (or goods and services) by government for which government receives no currently produced good or service in return.

Gross domestic product (GDP) The total market value of all *final goods and services* produced annually within the boundaries of Canada.

Gross investment Expenditures for newly produced capital goods (such as machinery, equipment, tools, and buildings) and for additions to inventories.

Gross private domestic investment Expenditures for newly produced capital goods (such as machinery, equipment, tools, and buildings) and for additions to inventories.

Guiding function of prices The ability of price changes to bring about changes in the quantities of products and resources demanded and supplied.

H

Horizontal axis The "left-right" or "west-east" axis on a graph or grid.

Household An economic unit (of one or more persons) that provides the economy with resources and uses the income received to purchase goods and services that satisfy material wants.

Human capital The accumulation of prior investments in education, training, health, and other factors that increase productivity.

Human-capital investment Any expenditure undertaken to improve the education, skills, health, or mobility of workers, with an expectation of greater productivity and thus a positive return on the investment.

Hyperinflation A very rapid rise in the price level.

Hypothesis A tentative, untested economic principle.

I

IMF (See *International Monetary Fund.*)

Import competition The competition that domestic firms encounter from the products and services of foreign producers.

Import demand curve A downward-sloping curve that shows the amount of a product that an economy will import at each world price below the domestic price.

Import quota A limit imposed by a nation on the quantity (or total value) of a good that may be imported during some period of time.

Imports Spending by individuals, firms, and governments for goods and services produced in foreign nations.

Income approach The method that adds all the income generated by the production of *final goods and services* to measure the *gross domestic product*.

Income effect A change in the price of a product changes a consumer's real income (purchasing power) and thus the quantity of the product purchased.

Increase in demand An increase in the *quantity demanded* of a good or service at every price; a shift of the *demand curve* to the right.

Increase in supply An increase in the *quantity supplied* of a good or service at every price; a shift in the *supply curve* to the right.

Increasing returns An increase in a firm's output by a larger percentage than the percentage increase in its inputs.

Independent goods Products or services for which there is no relationship between the price of one and the demand for the other; when the price of one rises or falls, the demand for the other remains constant.

Independent variable The variable causing a change in some other (dependent) variable.

Indirect taxes Such taxes as sales, business property taxes, and custom duties that firms treat as costs of producing a product.

Industrially advanced countries High-income countries such as Canada, the United States, Japan, and the nations of Western Europe that have highly developed market economies

based on large stocks of technologically advanced capital goods and skilled labour forces.

Industry A group of (one or more) firms that produce identical or similar products.

Inferior good A good or service whose consumption declines as income rises (and conversely), price remaining constant.

Inflating Determining real *gross domestic product* by increasing the dollar value of the nominal *gross domestic product* produced in a year in which prices are lower than in a base year.

Inflation A rise in the general level of prices in an economy.

Inflation premium The component of the *nominal interest rate* that reflects anticipated inflation.

Inflation targeting A Bank of Canada policy of maintaining the inflation rate within a specific range, currently 1–3 percent.

Inflationary expectations The belief of workers, firms, and consumers that substantial inflation will occur in the future.

Inflationary gap The amount by which the equilibrium GDP exceeds full-employment GDP.

Information technology New and more efficient methods of delivering and receiving information through use of computers, fax machines, wireless phones, and the Internet.

Infrastructure The capital goods usually provided by the *public sector* for the use of its citizens and firms (for example, highways, bridges, transit systems, wastewater treatment facilities, municipal water systems, and airports).

Injection An addition of spending to the income-expenditure stream.

Innovation The first commercially successful introduction of a new product, the use of a new method of production, or the creation of a new form of business organization.

Inpayments The receipts of its own or foreign money that individuals, firms, and governments of one nation obtain from the sale of goods and services abroad, or as investment income, remittances, and capitals inflows from abroad.

Insider-outsider theory The hypothesis that nominal wages are inflexible downward because firms are aware that workers ("insiders") who retain employment during recession may refuse to work cooperatively with previously unemployed workers ("outsiders") who offer to work for less than the current wage.

Interest The payment made for the use of money (of borrowed funds).

Interest income Payments of income to those who supply the economy with capital.

Interest rate The annual rate at which interest is paid; a percentage of the borrowed amount.

Interest-rate effect The direct relationship between price level and the demand for money, which affects interest rates, and, as a result, total spending in the economy.

Intermediate goods Products that are purchased for resale or further processing or manufacturing.

Internally held public debt *Public debt* owed to citizens, firms, and institutions of the same nation issuing the debt.

International balance of payments (See *Balance of payments*.)

International balance of payments deficit (See *Balance of payments deficit*.)

International balance of payments surplus (See *Balance of payments surplus*.)

International gold standard (See *Gold standard*.)

International Monetary Fund (IMF) The international association of nations formed after World War II to make loans of foreign monies to nations with temporary *payments deficits* and, until 1971, to administer the adjustable peg system.

International monetary reserves The foreign currencies and such assets as gold a nation may use to settle a payments deficit.

International value of the dollar The price that must be paid in foreign currency (money) to obtain one Canadian dollar.

Intrinsic value The market value of the metal within a coin.

Inventories Goods that have been produced but are still unsold.

Inverse relationship The relationship between two variables that change in opposite directions, for example, product price and quantity demanded.

Investment Spending for the production and accumulation of *capital* and additions to inventories.

Investment demand curve A curve that shows the amount of *investment* demanded by an economy at a series of *real interest rates*.

Investment goods Same as *capital.*

Investment schedule A curve or schedule that shows the amounts firms plan to invest at various possible values of *real gross domestic product.*

Investment in human capital (See *Human-capital investment.*)

Invisible hand The tendency of firms and resource suppliers seeking to further their own self-interests in competitive markets to also promote the interest of society as a whole.

K

Keynesian economics The macroeconomic generalizations that lead to the conclusion that a capitalistic economy is characterized by macroeconomic instability and that *fiscal policy* and *monetary policy* can be used to promote *full employment, price-level stability,* and *economic growth.*

Keynesianism The philosophical, ideological, and analytical views pertaining to *Keynesian economics.*

L

Labour The physical and mental talents and efforts of people that are used to produce goods and services.

Labour force Persons 15 years of age and older who are not in institutions and who are employed or are unemployed and seeking work.

Labour-force participation rate The percentage of the working-age population that is actually in the labour force.

Labour-intensive goods Products that require a relatively large amount of labour to produce.

Labour productivity The average product of labour or output per worker per hour.

Labour theory of value The Marxian idea that the economic value of any commodity is determined solely by the amount of labour required to produce it.

Labour union A group of workers organized to advance the interests of the group (to increase wages, shorten the hours worked, improve working conditions, and so on).

Laffer curve A curve relating government tax rates and tax revenues.

Laissez faire capitalism (See *Pure capitalism.*)

Land Natural resources ("free gifts of nature") used to produce goods and services.

Land-intensive goods Products that require a relatively large amount of land to produce.

Law of demand All else equal, as price falls, the quantity demanded rises, and vice versa.

Law of increasing opportunity costs As the production of a good increases, the *opportunity cost* of producing an additional unit rises.

Law of supply The principle that, other things equal, an increase in the price of a product will increase the quantity of it supplied; and conversely for a price decrease.

Leakage (1) A withdrawal of potential spending from the income-expenditures stream via *saving,* tax payments, or *imports.* (2) A withdrawal that reduces the lending potential of the banking system.

Learning-by-doing Achieving greater *productivity* and lower *average total cost* through gains in knowledge and skill that accompany repetition of a task; a source of *economies of scale.*

Legal tender Anything that government says must be accepted in payment of a debt.

Lending potential of an individual chartered bank The amount by which a single bank can safely increase the *money supply* by making new loans to (or buying securities from) the public; equal to the bank's excess reserves.

Lending potential of the banking system The amount by which the banking system can increase the *money supply* by making new loans to (or buying securities from) the public; equal to the excess reserves of the banking system multiplied by the monetary multiplier.

Liability A debt with a monetary value; an amount owed by a firm or an individual.

Limited liability Restriction of the maximum loss to a predetermined amount for the owners (stockholders) of a corporation, the maximum loss is the amount they paid for their shares of stock.

Limited-liability company An unincorporated business whose owners are protected by limited liability.

Liquidity The ease with which an asset can be converted into cash with little or no loss of purchasing power.

Long run (1) In *microeconomics,* a period of time long enough to enable producers of a product to change the quantities of all the resources they employ; period in which all resources and costs are variable and no resources or costs are fixed. (2) In *macroeconomics*, a period sufficiently long for nominal wages and other input prices to change in response to a change in the nation's price level.

Long-run aggregate supply curve The *aggregate supply curve* associated with a time period in which input prices (especially nominal wages) are fully responsive to changes in the price level.

Lump-sum tax A tax that yields the same amount of tax revenue at all levels of GDP.

M

M1 *Currency* (coins and paper money) and *demand deposits* in *chartered banks*.

M2 A broad definition of money that includes M1 plus personal and business savings deposits requiring notice before withdrawal.

M2+ A very broad definition of money that includes M2, plus deposits at non-bank deposit-taking institutions, money market mutual funds, and individual annuities at life insurance companies.

Macroeconomics The part of economics concerned with the economy as a whole.

Managed floating exchange rate An *exchange rate* that is allowed to change (float) as a result of changes in currency supply and demand but at times is altered (managed) by governments via their buying and selling of particular currencies.

Marginal analysis The comparison of marginal ("extra" or "additional") benefits and marginal costs, usually for decision making.

Marginal benefit The extra (additional) benefit of consuming one more unit of some good or service; the change in total benefit when one more unit is consumed.

Marginal cost The extra (additional) cost of producing one more unit of output; equal to the change in *total cost* divided by the change in output (and in the short run to the change in total *variable cost* divided by the change in output).

Marginal propensity to consume The fraction (or percentage) of any change in disposable income spent for consumer goods.

Marginal propensity to import The fraction (or percentage) of any change in GDP spent for imported goods and services.

Marginal propensity to save The fraction (or percentage) of any change in disposable income that households save.

Marginal tax rate The tax rate paid on each additional dollar of income.

Marginal utility The extra *utility* a consumer obtains from the consumption of one additional unit of a good or service.

Market Any institution or mechanism that brings together buyers and sellers of particular goods, services, or resources for the purpose of exchange.

Market demand (See *Total demand*.)

Market failure The inability of markets to bring about the allocation of resources that best satisfies the wants of society.

Market system An economic system in which property resources are privately owned and markets and prices are used to direct and coordinate economic activities.

Medium of exchange Items sellers generally accept and buyers generally use to pay for a good or service.

Menu costs Costs associated with changing the prices of goods and services.

Microeconomics The part of economics concerned with such individual units as industries, firms, and households.

Minimum wage The lowest wage employers may legally pay for an hour of work.

Monetarism The macroeconomic view that the main cause of changes in aggregate output and the price level are fluctuations in the money supply; advocates a monetary rule.

Monetary multiplier The multiple of its *excess reserves* by which the banking system can expand *demand deposits* and thus the *money supply* by making new loans.

Monetary policy A central bank's changing of the money supply to influence interest rates and assist the economy in achieving a full-employment, non-inflationary level of total output.

Monetary rule The rule suggested by *monetarism*; as traditionally formulated, the rule says that the *money supply* should be expanded each year at the same annual rate as the potential rate of growth of the *real gross domestic product*; the supply of money should be increased steadily between 3 to 5 percent per year.

Money Any item that is generally acceptable to sellers in exchange for goods and services.

Money capital Money available to purchase capital.

Money income (See *Nominal income*.)

Money market The market in which the demand for and the supply of money determine the *interest rate* in the economy.

Money supply Narrowly defined, M1; more broadly defined, M2 and M2+.

Monopoly A market structure in which the number of sellers is so small that each seller is able to influence the total supply and the price of the good or service. (Also see *Pure monopoly*.)

Most-favoured-nation clause An agreement by Canada to allow some other nation's *exports* into Canada at the lowest tariff level levied by Canada.

Multinational corporation A firm that owns production facilities in other countries and produces and sells its product abroad.

Multiple counting Wrongly including the value of *intermediate goods* in the *gross domestic product*; counting the same good or service more than once.

Multiplier The ratio of a change in the *equilibrium GDP* to the change in *investment* or in any other component of *aggregate expenditures*.

Multiplier effect The effect on equilibrium GDP of a change in *aggregate expenditures* or *aggregate demand* (caused by a change in the consumption schedule, investment, government expenditures, or net exports).

Mutually exclusive goals Two or more goals that conflict and cannot be achieved simultaneously.

N

National income Total income earned by resource suppliers for their contributions to *gross national product*; equal to the gross domestic product minus *non-income charges*, minus *net foreign factor income*.

National income accounting The techniques used to measure the overall production of the economy and other related variables for the nation as a whole.

Natural monopoly An industry in which economies of scale are so great the product can be produced by one firm at a lower average total cost than if the product were produced by more than one firm.

Natural rate of unemployment The unemployment rate that occurs when there is no cyclical unemployment and the economy is achieving its potential output.

Near-monies Financial assets, such as saving and term deposits in banks and savings institutions, that are not a medium of exchange but can be readily converted into money.

Negative relationship (See *Inverse relationship*.)

Net domestic income All the income earned by Canadian-supplied resources.

Net domestic product (NDP) *Gross domestic product* less the part of the year's output needed to replace the *capital goods* worn out in producing the output.

Net export effect The idea that the impact of a change in *monetary policy* or *fiscal policy* will be strengthened or weakened by the consequent change in net exports.

Net exports *Exports* minus *imports*.

Net foreign factor income Payments by a nation of resource income to the rest of the world minus receipts of resource income from the rest of the world.

Net investment Gross investment less consumption of fixed capital.

Net investment income The interest and dividend income received by the residents of a nation from residents of other nations less the interest and dividend payments made by the residents of that nation to the residents of other nations.

Net National Income (NNI) Total income earned by resource suppliers for their contribution to GDP.

Net taxes The taxes collected by government less government transfer payments.

Net transfers The personal and government transfer payments made by one nation to residents of foreign nations, less the personal and government transfer payments received from residents of foreign nations.

Network effects Increases in the value of a product to each user, including existing users, as the total number of users rises.

Net worth The total *assets* less the total *liabilities* of a firm or an individual; the claims of the owners of a firm against its total assets.

New classical economics The theory that, although unanticipated price level changes may create macroeconomic instability in the short run, the economy is stable at the full-employment level of domestic output in the long run because prices and wages adjust automatically to correct movements away from the full-employment, non-inflationary output.

New Economy The economy, developed since 1995, with the main characteristics of substantially faster productivity growth and economic growth, caused by rapid technological advance and the emergence of the global economy.

Nominal gross domestic product The GDP measured in terms of the price level at the time of measurement (unadjusted for inflation).

Nominal income The number of current dollars received as wages, rent, interest, or profits.

Nominal interest rate The interest rate expressed in terms of annual amounts currently charged for interest and not adjusted for inflation.

Nominal wage The amount of money received by a worker per unit of time (hour, day, etc.); money wage.

Non-discretionary fiscal policy (See *Built-in stabilizer*.)

Non-durable good A consumer good with an expected life (use) of less than three years.

Non-exhaustive expenditure An expenditure by government that does not result directly in the employment of economic resources or the production of goods and service; see *Government transfer payment*.

Non-financial investment An investment that does not require households to save a part of their money incomes, but which uses surplus (unproductive) labour to build capital goods.

Non-income charges *Consumption of fixed capital* and *indirect business taxes*; amounts subtracted from GDP (along with *net foreign factor income*) in determining national income.

Non-income determinants of consumption and saving All influences on *consumption* and *saving* other than the level of *GDP*.

Non-interest determinants of investment All influences on the level of investment spending other than the *interest rate*.

Non-investment transaction An expenditure for stocks, bonds, or second-hand capital goods.

Non-market transactions The production of goods and services excluded in the measurement of the gross domestic product because they are not bought and sold.

Non-production transaction The purchase and sale of any item that is not a currently produced good or service.

Non-tariff barrier All restrictions other than tariffs that nations erect to impede international trade.

Normal good A good or service whose consumption rises when income increases and falls when income decreases, price remaining constant.

Normal profit The payment made by a firm to obtain and retain entrepreneurial ability; the minimum income entrepreneurial ability must receive to induce it to perform entrepreneurial functions for a firm.

Normative economics The part of economics involving value judgments about what the economy should be like.

North American Free Trade Agreement (NAFTA) A 1993 agreement establishing, over a 15-year period, a free trade zone composed of Canada, Mexico, and the United States.

O

Official international reserves (See *Official reserves*.)

Official reserves Foreign currencies owned by the central bank of a nation.

Okun's Law The generalization that any one percentage point rise in the *unemployment rate* above the *natural rate of unemployment* will increase the GDP gap by 2 percent of the *potential output* (GDP) of the economy.

Old Age Security Act The 1951 federal act, as subsequently amended, by which a pension is payable to every person aged 65 and older provided the person has resided in Canada for ten years immediately preceding the approval of an application for pension; in addition a Guaranteed Income Supplement may be paid; the pension is payable in addition to the Canada Pension.

OPEC (See *Organization of Petroleum Exporting Countries*.)

Open economy An economy that exports and imports goods and services.

Open-market operations The buying and selling of Canadian government bonds by the Bank of Canada to carry out monetary policy.

Operating band The Bank of Canada's 50-basis-point range (one-half of one percentage point) for the overnight lending rate.

Opportunity cost The amount of other products that must be forgone or sacrificed to produce a unit of a product.

Organization of Petroleum Exporting Nations (OPEC) The cartel formed in 1970 by 13 oil-producing countries to control the price and quantity of crude oil exported by its members, and that accounts for a large proportion of the world's export of oil.

Other-things-equal assumption The assumption that factors other than those being considered are held constant.

Outpayments The expenditures of its own or foreign currency that the individuals, firms, and governments of one nation make to purchase goods and services, for remittances, as investment income, and capital outflows abroad.

Overnight lending rate The interest rate at which major participants in the money market borrow and lend one-day funds to each other.

Overnight loans rate The interest rate banks charge to borrow and lend one-day funds to each other.

P

Paper money Pieces of paper used as a *medium of exchange*; in Canada, Bank of Canada notes.

Partnership An unincorporated firm owned and operated by two or more persons.

Patent An exclusive right to inventors to produce and sell a new product or machine for a set period of time.

Payments deficit (See *Balance of payments deficit*.)

Payments surplus (See *Balance of payments surplus*.)

Peak A phase in the business cycle during which the economy is at full employment and the level of real output is at or very close to the economy's capacity.

Per-capita GDP *Gross domestic product* (GDP) per person; the average GDP of a population.

Per-capita income A nation's total income per person; the average income of a population.

Personal consumption expenditures The expenditures of households for *durable* and *non-durable consumer goods* and services.

Personal distribution of income The manner in which the economy's *personal* or *disposable income* is divided among different income classes or different households.

Personal income The earned and unearned income available to resource suppliers and others before the payment of *personal income taxes*.

Personal income tax A tax levied on the taxable income of individuals, households, and unincorporated firms.

Personal saving The *personal income* of households less *personal taxes* and *personal consumption expenditures*;

disposable income not spent for consumer goods.

Per-unit production cost The average production cost of a particular level of output; total input cost divided by units of output.

Phillips Curve A curve showing the relationship between the unemployment rate and the annual rate of increase in the price level.

Planned investment The amount that firms plan or intend to invest.

Plant A physical establishment that performs one or more functions in the production, fabrication, and distribution of goods and services.

Policy economics The formulation of courses of action to bring about desired economic outcomes or to prevent undesired occurrences.

Political business cycle The alleged tendency of government to destabilize the economy by reducing taxes and increasing government expenditures before elections and to raise taxes and lower expenditures after elections.

Positive economics The analysis of facts or data to establish scientific generalizations about economic behaviour.

Positive relationship Direct relationship between two variables.

Post hoc, ergo propter hoc **fallacy** Incorrectly reasoning that when one event precedes another the first event must have caused the second event.

Potential GDP The real output (*GDP*) an economy can produce when it fully employs its available resources.

Premature inflation A type of inflation that sometimes occurs before the economy has reached *full employment*.

Price The amount of money needed to buy a particular good, service, or resource.

Price ceiling A legally established maximum price for a good or service.

Price floor Legally determined prices above equilibrium prices.

Price index An index number that shows how the weighted average price of a "market basket" of goods changes through time.

Price level The weighted average of the prices of all the final goods and services produced in an economy.

Price-level surprises Unanticipated changes in the price level.

Price-level stability A steadiness of the price-level from one period to the next; zero or low annual inflation; also called "price stability."

Price-wage flexibility Changes in the prices of products and in the wages paid to workers; the ability of prices and wages to rise or fall.

Price war Successive and continued decreases in the prices charged by the firms in an oligopolistic industry; each firm lowers its price below rivals' prices, hoping to increase it sales and revenues at its rivals' expense.

Prime rate The *interest rate* banks charge their most creditworthy borrowers.

Principal-agent problem A conflict of interest that occurs when agents (workers or managers) pursue their own objectives to the detriment of the principal's (stockholders) goals.

Principles Statements about economic behaviour that enable prediction of the probable effects of certain actions.

Private good A good or service subject to the *exclusion principle* and that is provided by privately owned firms to consumers who are willing to pay for it.

Private property The right of private persons and firms to obtain, own, control, employ, dispose of, and bequeath land, capital, and other property.

Private sector The *households* and business *firms* of the economy.

Production possibilities curve A curve showing the different combinations of goods or services that can be produced in a full-employment, full-production economy where the available

supplies of resources and technology are fixed.

Production possibilities table A table showing the different combinations of two products that can be produced with a specific set of resources in a full-employment, full-production economy.

Productive efficiency The production of a good in the least costly way.

Productivity A measure of average output or real output per unit of input.

Productivity growth The percentage change in *productivity* from one period to another.

Product market A market in which products are sold by *firms* and bought by *households*.

Profit The return to the resource entrepreneurial ability (see *Normal profit*); total revenue minus total cost (see *Economic profit*).

Progressive tax A tax with an average tax rate that increases as the taxpayer's income increases and decreases as the taxpayer's income decreases.

Property tax A tax on the value of property (*capital, land*, stocks and bonds, and other *assets*) owned by *firms* and *households*.

Proportional tax A tax with an average tax rate that remains constant as the taxpayer's income increases or decreases.

Protective tariff A *tariff* designed to shield domestic producers of a good or service from the competition of foreign producers.

Public debt The total amount owed by the federal government to the owners of government securities.

Public good A good or service that can be simultaneously consumed by everyone, and from which no one can be excluded, even if they don't pay for it.

Public Investments Government expenditures on public capital (such as roads and highways) and on *human capital* (such as education and health).

Public sector The part of the economy that contains all government entities; government.

Purchasing power The amount of goods and services that a monetary unit of income can buy.

Purchasing power parity theory The idea that exchange rates between any two nations adjust to reflect the price level differences between the countries.

Pure rate of interest An essentially risk-free, long-term interest rate that is free of the influence of market imperfections.

Q

Quantity demanded The amount of a good or service buyers (or a buyer) desire to purchase at a particular price during some period.

Quantity supplied The amount of a good or service producers (or a producer) offer to sell at a particular price during some period.

Quasi-public good A good or service to which the *exclusion principle* could apply, but that has such a large *spillover benefit* that government sponsors its production to prevent an under-allocation of resources.

R

R&D Research and development activities undertaken to bring about technological advance.

Rate of exchange The price paid in one's own money to acquire one unit of a foreign currency; the rate at which the money of one nation is exchanged for the money of another nation.

Rate of return The gain in net revenue divided by the cost of an investment or an R&D expenditure; expressed as a percentage.

Rational expectations theory The hypothesis that firms and households expect monetary and fiscal policies to

have certain effects on the economy and (in pursuit of their own self-interests) take actions that make these policies ineffective.

Rationing function of prices The ability of market forces in a competitive market to equalize quantity demanded and quantity supplied and to eliminate shortages and surpluses via changes in prices.

Real-balances effect The inverse relationship between the price level and the real value (or purchasing power) of financial assets with fixed money value.

Real-business-cycle theory The theory that *business cycles* result from changes in technology and resource availability, which affect *productivity* and thus increase or decrease *long-run aggregate supply*.

Real capital (See *Capital*.)

Real GDP per capita The real GDP per person, found by dividing real GDP by a country's population.

Real gross domestic product (GDP) *Nominal gross domestic product* adjusted for inflation.

Real GDP (See *Real gross domestic product*.)

Real income The amount of goods and services that *nominal income* can buy.

Real interest rate The interest rate expressed in dollars of constant value (adjusted for *inflation*).

Real wage The amount of goods and services a worker can purchase with his or her nominal wage; the purchasing power of the nominal wage.

Recession A period of declining real GDP, accompanied by lower real income and higher unemployment.

Recessionary gap The amount by which equilibrium GDP falls short of full-employment GDP.

Recovery The expansion phase of the business cycle, during which output and employment rise toward full employment.

Refinancing the public debt Paying owners of maturing government securities with money obtained by selling new securities or with new securities.

Regressive tax A tax with an average tax rate that decreases as the taxpayer's income increases and increases as the taxpayer's income decreases.

Resource market A market in which *households* sell and *firms* buy resources or the services of resources.

Retiring the public debt Reducing the size of the *public debt* by paying money to owners of maturing Government of Canada securities.

Revaluation An increase in the governmentally defined value of its currency relative to other nations' currencies.

Revenue tariff A *tariff* designed to produce income for the federal government.

Roundabout production The construction and use of capital to aid in the production of consumer goods.

Rule of 70 A method for determining the number of years it will take for some measure to double, given its annual percentage increase by dividing that percentage increase into 70.

S

Sales tax A tax levied on the cost (at retail) of a broad group of products.

Saving Disposable income not spent for consumer goods; equal to disposable income minus personal consumption expenditures.

Savings deposit A deposit that is interest-bearing and that can normally be withdrawn by the depositor at any time.

Saving schedule A schedule that shows the amounts *households* plan to save at different levels of *disposable income*.

Say's law The largely discredited macroeconomic generalization that the production of goods and services (supply) creates an equal *demand* for these goods and service.

Scarce resources The limited quantities of land, capital, labour, and entrepreneurial ability that are never sufficient to satisfy the virtually unlimited material wants of humans.

Scientific Method The systematic pursuit of knowledge through the formulation of a problem, collection of data, and the formulation and testing of hypotheses to obtain theories, principles, and laws.

Seasonal variations Increases and decreases in the level of economic activity within a single year, caused by a change in the season.

Secular trend Long-term tendency; change in some variable over a very long period of years.

Self-interest That which each firm, property owner, worker, and consumer believes is best for itself.

Separation of ownership and control The fact that different groups of people own a *corporation* (the shareholders) and manage it (the directors and officers).

Service An (intangible) act or use for which a consumer, firm, or government is willing to pay.

Shirking Actions by workers to increase their utility or well-being by neglecting or evading work.

Shortage The amount by which the *quantity demanded* of a product exceeds the *quantity supplied* at a particular (below-equilibrium) price.

Short run (1) In *macroeconomics*, a period in which nominal wages and other input prices to not change in response to a change in the price level. (2) In *microeconomics*, a period of time in which producers are able to change the quantity of some but not all of the resources they employ; a period in which some resources (usually plant) are fixed and some are variable.

Short-run aggregate supply A schedule or curve that shows the level of real domestic output that will be produced at each price level.

Simple multiplier The *multiplier* in an economy in which government collects no *net taxes*, there are no *imports*, and *investment* is independent of the level of income; equal to one divided by the *marginal propensity to save*.

Slope of a line The ratio of the vertical change (the rise or fall) to the horizontal change (the run) between any two points on a line. The slope of an upward sloping line is positive, reflecting a direct relationship between two variables; the slope of a downward sloping line is negative, reflecting an inverse relationship between two variables.

Sole proprietorship An unincorporated *firm* owned and operated by one person.

Special economic zones Regions of China open to foreign investment, private ownership, and relatively free international trade.

Specialization The use of the resources of an individual, a firm, a region, or a nation to produce one or a few goods and services.

Speculation The activity of buying or selling with the motive of later reselling or rebuying for profit.

Spillover A benefit or cost from production or consumption, accruing without compensation to non-buyers and non-sellers of the product (see *Spillover benefit* and *Spillover cost*).

Spillover benefit A benefit obtained without compensation by third parties from the production or consumption of sellers or buyers.

Spillover costs A cost imposed without compensation on third parties by the production or consumption of sellers or buyers.

Stagflation Simultaneous increases in the price level and the unemployment rate.

Start-up firm A new firm focussed on creating and introducing a particular new product or employing a specific new production or distribution method.

State-owned enterprises Businesses that are owned by government; the major types of enterprises in Russia and China before their transitions to the market system.

Stock (corporate) An ownership share in a corporation.

Store of value An *asset* set aside for future use.

Strategic trade policy The use of trade barriers to reduce the risk inherent in product development by domestic firms, particularly that involving advanced technology.

Structural unemployment Unemployment of workers whose skills are not demanded by employers, who lack sufficient skill to obtain employment, or who cannot easily move to locations where jobs are available.

Subsidy A payment of funds (or goods and services) by a government, firm, or household for which it receives no good or service in return; when made by a government, it is a *government transfer payment*.

Substitute goods Products or services that can be used in place of each other.

Substitution effect (1) A change in the price of a *consumer good* changes the relative expensiveness of that good and hence changes the consumer's willingness to buy it rather than other goods. (2) The effect of a change in the price of a *resource* on the quantity of the resource employed by a firm, assuming no change in its output.

Superior good (See *Normal good*.)

Supply A schedule or curve that shows the amounts of a product that producers are willing and able to make available for sale at each of a series of possible prices during a specific period.

Supply curve A curve illustrating the positive (direct) relationship between the quantity supplied of a good or service and its price, other things equal.

Supply factor An increase in the availability of a resource, an improvement in its quality, or an expansion of technological knowledge that makes it possible for an economy to produce a greater output of goods and services.

Supply-side economics A view of macroeconomics that emphasizes the role of costs and aggregate supply in explaining inflation, unemployment, and economic growth.

Surplus The amount by which the *quantity supplied* of a product exceeds the *quantity demanded* at a specific (above-equilibrium) price.

Surplus value A Marxian term; the amount by which the value of a worker's daily output exceeds his or her daily wage; the output of workers appropriated by capitalists as profit.

T

Tariff A tax imposed by a nation on an imported good.

Tax An involuntary payment of money (or goods and services) to a government by a *household* or *firm* for which the household or firm receives no good or service directly in return.

Tax incidence The person or group who ends up paying a tax.

Technology The body of knowledge and techniques that can be used to produce goods and services from economic resources.

Technological advance New and better goods and services and new and better ways of producing or distributing them.

Terms of trade The amount of one good or service that must be given up to obtain one unit of another good or service.

Theoretical Economics The process of deriving and applying economic theories and principles.

Tight money policy Bank of Canada actions that contract, or restrict, the growth of the nation's money supply for

the purpose of reducing or eliminating inflation.

Till money (See *Vault cash*.)

Token money Coins that have a face value greater than their intrinsic value.

Total cost The sum of *fixed cost* and *variable cost*.

Total demand The demand schedule or the *demand curve* of all buyers of a good or service; also called market demand.

Total demand for money The sum of the *transactions demand for money* and the *asset demand for money*.

Total spending The total amount buyers of goods and services spend or plan to spend; also called aggregate expenditures.

Total supply The supply schedule or the supply curve of all sellers of a good or service; also called market supply.

Township and village enterprises Privately owned rural manufacturing firms in China.

Trade balance The export of goods (or goods and services) of a nation less its imports of goods (or goods and services).

Trade bloc A group of nations that lower or abolish trade barriers among members. Examples include the *European Union* and the nations of the *North American Free Trade Agreement*.

Trade controls *Tariffs, export subsidies, import quotas*, and other means a nation may employ to reduce imports and expand exports.

Trade deficit The amount by which a nation's *imports* of goods (or goods and services) exceed its *exports* of goods (or goods and services).

Tradeoffs The sacrifice of some or all of one economic goal, good, or service to achieve some other goal, good, or service.

Trade surplus The amount by which a nation's exports of goods (or goods and services) exceed its imports of goods (or goods and services).

Trading possibilities line A line that shows the different combinations of two products an economy is able to obtain when it specializes in the production of one product and exports it to obtain the other product.

Transactions demand for money The amount of money people want to hold for use as a *medium of exchange*, and which varies directly with the *nominal GDP*.

Transfer payment A payment of *money* (or goods and services) by a government to a *household* or *firm* for which the payer receives no good or service directly in return.

Trough A *recession* or *depression*, when output and employment reach their lowest levels.

U

Unanticipated inflation Increases in the price level that occur at a rate greater than expected.

Underemployment (1) Failure to produce the maximum amount of goods and services that can be produced from the resources employed; failure to achieve *full production*. (2) A situation in which workers are employed in positions requiring less than the amount of education and skill than they have.

Undistributed corporate profits After-tax corporate profits not distributed as dividends to shareholders; corporate or business saving; also called retained earnings.

Unemployment Failure to use all available economic resources to produce goods and services; failure of the economy to fully employ its labour force.

Unemployment rate The percentage of the *labour force* unemployed at any time.

Unit labour cost Labour costs per unit of output; total labour cost divided by total output; also equal to the *nominal wage rate* divided by the average product of labour.

Unit of account A standard unit in which prices can be stated and the value of goods and services can be compared.

Unlimited liability Absence of any limits on the maximum amount that an individual (usually a business owner) may become legally required to pay.

Unlimited wants The insatiable desire of consumers for goods and services that will give them satisfaction or utility.

Unplanned changes in inventories Changes in inventories that firms did not anticipate.

Unplanned investment Actual investment less planned investment; increases or decreases in the inventories of firms resulting from production greater than sales.

Urban collectives Chinese enterprises jointly owned by their managers and their workforces, located in urban areas.

Uruguay Round The eighth and most recent round of trade negotiations under *GATT* (now the *World Trade Organization*).

Utility The satisfaction a person gets from consuming a good or service.

V

Value added The value of the product sold by a firm, less the value of the products purchased and used by the firm to produce the product.

Value judgment Opinion of what is desirable or undesirable; belief regarding what ought or ought not to be (regarding what is right or just and wrong or unjust).

Value of money The quantity of goods and services for which a unit of money (a dollar) can be exchanged; the purchasing power of a unit of money; the reciprocal of the price level.

Variable cost A cost that in total increases when the firm increases its output and decreases when it reduces its output.

Vault cash The *currency* a bank has in its vault and cash drawers.

Velocity of money The number of times per year the average dollar in the *money supply* is spent for *final goods and services.*

Vertical axis The "up-down" or "north-south" axis on a graph or grid.

Vertical combination A group of *plants* engaged in different stages of the production of a final product and owned by a single *firm.*

Vertical intercept The point at which a line meets the vertical axis of a graph.

Vicious circle of poverty A problem common in some developing countries in which their low per-capita incomes are an obstacle to realizing the levels of saving and investment requisite to acceptable rates of economic growth.

Voluntary export restraint Voluntary limitations by countries or firms of their exports to a particular foreign nation.

W

Wage The price paid for the use or services of *labour* per unit of time (per hour, per day, and so on).

Wage rate (See *Wage.*)

Wealth effect A downward shift of the saving schedule and an upward shift of the consumption schedule due to higher asset wealth.

World Trade Organization (WTO) An organization established of 145 nations (as of 2003) that oversees the provisions of the current world trade agreement, resolves trade disputes stemming from it, and holds forums for further rounds of trade negotiations.

"Will to develop" Wanting economic growth strongly enough to change from old to new ways of doing things.

World Bank A bank that lends (and guarantees loans) to developing nations to assist them in increasing their capital stock and thus to achieve economic growth; formally, the International Bank for Reconstruction and Development.

World price The international market price of a good or service, determined by world demand and supply.

Index

National Income and Related Statistics for 1926–2002 (in billions of dollars)

	1926	1927	1928	1929	1930	1931	1932
Expenditure approach							
Personal consumption expenditure	3.508	3.868	4.272	4.583	4.336	3.759	3.182
Investment	1.088	1.267	1.366	1.364	1.189	0.580	0.245
Government expenditure	0.390	0.404	0.412	0.469	0.502	0.515	0.472
Exports	1.633	1.602	1.757	1.617	1.272	0.951	0.793
Imports	− 1.473	− 1.580	− 1.757	− 1.894	− 1.579	− 1.112	− 0.878
Gross domestic product	5.146	5.561	6.050	6.139	5.720	4.693	3.814
Income approach							
Wages, salaries, and supplementary labour income	2.366	2.506	2.715	2.940	2.786	2.408	1.975
Interest and investment income	0.094	0.109	0.143	0.160	0.135	0.088	0.077
Profits of corporations and government enterprises	0.420	0.474	0.548	0.554	0.321	0.163	0.032
Income of farm and unincorporated businesses	0.641	0.691	0.746	0.770	0.688	0.548	0.422
Net domestic product at factor cost	4.086	4.310	4.678	4.652	4.343	3.331	2.597
Indirect taxes less subsidies	0.627	0.653	0.707	0.711	0.619	0.578	0.552
Capital consumption	0.572	0.618	0.676	0.726	0.719	0.649	0.578
Gross domestic product	5.146	5.561	6.050	6.139	5.720	4.693	3.814
Real GDP (billions of 1997 dollars)	59.149	64.663	71.176	71.384	68.095	59.405	53.718
Real GDP growth rate (percent per year)	—	8.5	9.2	0.3	− 4.8	− 14.6	− 10.6
Related data							
Population (thousands)	9,451	9,637	9,835	10,029	10,208	10,377	10,510
Labour force (thousands)	3,663	3,762	3,866	3,969	4,066	4,156	4,216
Employment (thousands)	3,555	3,695	3,801	3,853	3,695	3,675	3,475
Unemployment (thousands)	108	67	65	116	371	481	741
Unemployment rate (percent of labour force)	2.9	1.8	1.7	2.9	9.1	11.6	17.6
Labour force participation (percent)	57.8	57.9	58	58.1	58.2	58.3	58.2
Real GDP per capita (1997 dollars)	6,258	6,710	7,237	7,118	6,671	5,725	5,111
Growth rate of real GDP per capita (percent)	—	7.2	7.9	− 1.6	− 6.3	− 14.2	− 10.7
Money supply (M2+, billions of dollars)*	2.01	2.24	2.32	2.27	2.16	2.04	1.97
GDP deflator (1997 = 100)	8.7	8.6	8.5	8.6	8.4	7.9	7.1
Consumer Price Index (1992 = 100)	10.9	10.8	10.8	11	10.9	9.8	8.9
CPI inflation rate (percent per year)	1.6	− 0.9	0	1.9	− 0.9	− 10.1	− 9.2
Short term interest rate (3 month Treasury bill yield)	—	—	—	—	—	—	—
Federal government gross debt (billions)	2.8	2.8	2.7	2.7	2.6	2.7	2.9
Foreign exchange rate (Canadian dollar per U.S. dollar)	1.00	1.00	1.00	1.00	1.00	1.04	1.14

	1933	1934	1935	1936	1937	1938	1939	1940	1941	1942	1943	1944
	2.974	3.174	3.331	3.542	3.878	3.884	3.972	4.464	5.089	5.466	5.783	6.260
	0.123	0.303	0.399	0.394	0.705	0.744	0.951	1.015	1.130	1.136	0.654	0.680
	0.392	0.418	0.442	0.450	0.471	0.534	0.566	1.048	1.576	3.622	4.093	4.929
	0.813	1.004	1.129	1.413	1.575	1.343	1.437	1.795	2.456	2.347	3.429	3.541
	−0.810	−0.930	−1.000	−1.165	−1.388	−1.233	−1.305	−1.609	−1.969	−2.306	−2.906	−3.562
	3.492	3.969	4.301	4.634	5.241	5.272	5.621	6.713	8.282	10.265	11.053	11.848
	1.788	1.939	2.079	2.241	2.538	2.515	2.601	2.959	3.608	4.282	4.812	4.998
	0.055	0.074	0.094	0.085	0.094	0.068	0.080	0.115	0.148	0.185	0.227	0.220
	0.171	0.295	0.357	0.475	0.598	0.509	0.698	0.849	1.119	1.305	1.281	1.234
	0.360	0.392	0.434	0.502	0.564	0.596	0.632	0.699	0.815	0.939	0.980	1.065
	2.328	2.732	3.051	3.314	3.830	3.942	4.172	4.985	6.206	7.977	8.678	9.453
	0.547	0.591	0.601	0.680	0.727	0.661	0.759	0.859	1.090	1.133	1.170	1.167
	0.532	0.536	0.550	0.575	0.624	0.639	0.671	0.786	0.934	1.091	1.099	1.077
	3.492	3.969	4.301	4.634	5.241	5.272	5.621	6.713	8.282	10.265	11.053	11.848
	49.886	55.901	60.577	62.622	68.961	69.368	74.947	84.975	97.435	115.337	120.141	126.043
	−7.7	10.8	7.7	3.3	9.2	0.6	7.4	11.8	12.8	15.5	4.0	4.7
	10,633	10,741	10,845	10,950	11,045	11,152	11,267	11,381	11,507	11,654	11,795	11,946
	4,280	4,343	4,407	4,472	4,532	4,595	4,658	4,714	4,762	4,961	5,283	5,327
	3,454	3,712	3,782	3,901	4,121	4,073	4,129	4,291	4,567	4,826	5,207	5,264
	826	631	625	571	411	522	529	423	195	135	76	63
	19.3	14.5	14.2	12.8	9.1	11.4	11.4	9.0	4.1	2.7	1.4	1.2
	58.0	57.9	57.8	57.6	57.5	57.4	57.2	56.6	55.4	56.5	58.0	57.4
	4,692	5,204	5,586	5,719	6,244	6,220	6,652	7,466	8,467	9897	10186	10551
	−8.2	10.9	7.3	2.4	9.2	−0.4	6.9	12.2	13.4	16.9	2.9	3.6
	1.99	2.10	2.27	2.39	2.48	2.60	2.90	2.99	3.33	3.76	4.36	5.19
	7.0	7.1	7.1	7.4	7.6	7.6	7.5	7.9	8.5	8.9	9.2	9.4
	8.5	8.6	8.7	8.8	9.1	9.2	9.2	9.5	10.1	10.5	10.7	10.8
	−4.5	1.2	1.2	1.1	3.4	1.1	0.0	3.3	6.3	4.0	1.9	0.1
	2.5	2.5	1.5	0.8	0.7	0.6	0.7	0.7	0.6	0.5	0.5	0.4
	3.1	3.2	3.5	3.5	3.6	3.6	3.7	4.0	5.0	6.6	8.8	11.8
	1.09	0.99	1.01	1.00	1.00	1.01	1.04	1.11	1.11	1.11	1.11	1.11

National Income and Related Statistics for 1926–2002 (in billions of dollars), *continued*

	1945	1946	1947	1948	1949	1950	1951
Expenditure approach							
Personal consumption expenditure	6.972	8.012	9.362	10.370	11.365	12.482	13.857
Investment	0.660	1.798	2.708	3.260	3.562	4.415	5.500
Government expenditure	3.576	1.655	1.343	1.454	1.722	1.928	2.811
Exports	3.561	3.281	3.661	4.055	4.004	4.158	5.052
Imports	− 2.906	− 2.861	− 3.601	− 3.630	− 3.853	− 4.492	− 5.580
Gross domestic product	11.863	11.885	13.473	15.509	16.800	18.491	21.640
Income approach							
Wages, salaries, and supplementary labour income	5.037	5.487	6.662	7.754	8.349	8.998	10.538
Interest and investment income	0.227	0.170	0.194	0.243	0.291	0.396	0.463
Profits of corporations and government enterprises	1.244	1.474	1.854	2.041	2.009	2.608	3.144
Income of farm and unincorporated businesses	1.166	1.320	1.506	1.604	1.773	1.882	1.976
Net domestic product at factor cost	9.506	9.363	10.582	12.334	13.323	14.553	17.199
Indirect taxes less subsidies	1.084	1.371	1.678	1.832	1.878	2.065	2.548
Capital consumption	1.042	1.071	1.227	1.449	1.644	1.876	2.098
Gross domestic product	11.863	11.885	13.473	15.509	16.800	18.491	21.640
Real GDP (billions of 1997 dollars)	122.299	118.850	124.75	127.123	132.283	142.238	149.241
Real GDP growth rate (percent per year)	− 3.1	− 2.9	4.7	1.9	3.9	7.0	4.7
Related data							
Population (thousands)	12,072	12,292	12,551	12,823	13,447	13,712	14,009
Labour force (thousands)	5,256	5,075	4,991	5,070	5,134	5,245	5,304
Employment (thousands)	5,183	4,951	4,899	4,989	5,033	5,103	5,223
Unemployment (thousands)	73	124	92	81	101	142	81
Unemployment rate (percent of labour force)	1.4	2.4	1.8	1.6	2.0	2.7	1.5
Labour force participation (percent)	56.2	55	54.9	54.6	54.5	53.7	53.7
Real GDP per capita (1997 dollars)	10,131	9,669	9,939	9,914	9,837	10,373	10,653
Growth rate of real GDP per capita (percent)	− 4.0	− 4.6	2.8	− 0.3	− 0.8	5.4	2.7
Money supply (M2+, billions of dollars)*	5.88	6.76	7.02	7.66	8.05	8.51	8.67
GDP deflator (1997 = 100)	9.7	10.0	10.8	12.2	12.7	13.0	14.5
Consumer Price Index (1992 = 100)	10.9	11.2	12.3	14.0	14.5	14.9	16.4
CPI inflation rate (percent per year)	0.9	2.8	9.8	13.8	3.6	2.8	10.1
Short term interest rate (3 month Treasury bill yield)	0.4	0.4	0.4	0.4	0.4	0.5	0.7
Federal government gross debt (billions)	14.9	17.9	17.7	17.2	16.9	16.7	16.7
Foreign exchange rate (Canadian dollar per U.S. dollar)	1.11	1.0	1.0	1.0	1.03	1.09	1.05

	1952	1953	1954	1955	1956	1957	1958	1959	1960	1961	1962	1963
	15.162	16.181	16.934	18.388	20.090	21.492	22.845	24.390	25.479	25.954	27.681	29.480
	5.607	− 5.358	5.565	6.745	8.856	8.836	8.070	8.834	8.687	8.882	10.041	10.645
	3.620	3.824	3.825	4.036	4.426	4.573	4.854	4.976	5.281	6.624	7.130	7.593
	5.568	5.380	5.137	5.749	6.350	6.379	6.329	6.674	7.004	7.310	7.951	8.730
	− 5.369	5.806	− 5.543	− 6.390	− 7.664	− 7.767	− 7.321	− 8.028	− 8.092	− 7.517	− 8.048	− 8.389
	24.588	25.833	25.918	28.528	32.058	33.513	34.777	36.846	38.359	41.253	44.755	48.059
	11.768	12.714	13.043	13.930	15.696	16.988	17.435	18.596	19.582	21.184	22.785	24.318
	0.523	0.583	0.628	0.764	0.869	0.977	1.063	1.062	1.129	1.286	1.390	1.489
	3.071	2.985	2.755	3.485	3.928	3.554	3.669	3.966	3.870	4.185	4.639	5.164
	2.155	2.359	2.498	2.748	2.827	2.962	3.133	3.207	3.192	0.839	1.379	1.558
	19.468	20.125	19.998	21.908	24.383	25.356	26.436	27.757	28.837	33.275	36.129	38.847
	2.799	2.994	3.042	3.321	3.731	3.975	4.036	4.401	4.587	2.964	3.261	3.495
	2.333	2.634	2.930	3.337	3.814	4.159	4.135	4.461	4.739	5.014	5.365	5.717
	24.588	25.833	25.918	28.528	32.058	33.513	34.777	36.846	38.359	41.253	44.755	48.059
	162.834	171.079	169.399	185.247	200.363	205.601	209.500	218.024	224.322	237.900	254.150	267.126
	8.3	4.8	− 1.0	8.6	7.5	2.5	1.9	3.9	2.8	5.7	6.4	4.9
	14,459	14,845	15,287	15,698	16,081	16,610	17,080	17,483	17,870	18,238	18,583	18,931
	5,439	5,490	5,589	5,703	5,855	6,087	6,239	6,306	6,511	6,642	6,741	6,871
	5,334	5,375	5,368	5,489	5,689	5,891	5,869	5,972	6,112	6,176	6,351	6,497
	105	115	221	214	166	196	370	334	399	466	390	374
	1.9	2.1	4.0	3.8	2.8	3.2	5.9	5.3	6.1	7.0	5.8	5.4%
	53.5	53.1	52.9	52.9	53.5	54.0	53.9	53.8	54.2	54.1	53.9	53.8
	11,262	11,524	11,081	11,801	12,460	12,378	12,266	12,471	12,553	13,044	13,676	14,111
	5.7	2.3	− 3.8	6.5	5.6	− 0.7	− 0.9	1.7	0.7	3.9	4.8	3.2%
	9.26	9.32	10.14	10.88	11.19	11.50	12.93	12.79	13.40	14.37	14.91	15.87
	15.1	15.1	15.3	15.4	16.0	16.3	16.6	16.9	17.1	17.3	17.6	18.0
	16.9	16.7	16.8	16.8	17.1	17.6	18.0	18.2	18.5	18.7	18.9	19.2
	3.0	− 1.2	0.6	0.0	1.8	2.9	2.3	1.7	1.1	1.1	1.1	1.6
	1.1	1.7	1.5	1.6	2.9	3.8	2.3	4.8	3.3	2.8	4.1	3.6
	16.8	17.4	17.6	17.6	18.7	18.0	18.0	19.7	20.4	20.9	22.8	24.5
	0.98	0.98	0.97	0.99	0.98	0.96	0.97	0.96	0.97	1.01	1.07	1.08

National Income and Related Statistics for 1926–2002 (in billions of dollars), *continued*

	1964	1965	1966	1967	1968	1969	1970
Expenditure approach							
Personal consumption expenditure	31.606	34.229	37.349	40.351	44.024	47.989	50.607
Investment	12.154	14.811	16.905	16.374	17.257	19.968	18.925
Government expenditure	8.278	9.078	10.669	12.399	14.078	15.963	18.542
Exports	10.137	10.772	12.574	14.161	16.161	17.818	20.124
Imports	− 9.522	− 10.840	− 12.554	− 13.451	− 15.235	− 17.732	− 17.831
Gross domestic product	52.653	58.050	64.943	69.834	76.285	84.006	90.367
Income approach							
Wages, salaries, and supplementary labour income	26.580	29.630	33.508	37.067	40.297	45.065	48.851
Interest and investment income	1.699	1.917	2.130	2.360	2.796	3.158	3.493
Profits of corporations and government enterprises	5.985	6.543	7.031	7.211	8.079	8.579	8.089
Income of farm and unincorporated businesses	1.329	1.450	2.000	1.272	1.367	1.503	1.342
Net domestic product at factor cost	42.376	46.580	52.172	56.044	61.494	68.062	72.604
Indirect taxes less subsidies	4.099	4.735	5.345	5.714	6.112	6.459	7.428
Capital consumption	6.178	6.735	7.426	8.076	8.679	9.485	10.335
Gross domestic product	52.653	58.050	64.943	69.834	76.285	84.006	90.367
Real GDP (billions of 1997 dollars)	284.612	303.008	322.874	332.517	350.302	368.963	378.623
Real GDP growth rate (percent per year)	6.1	6.1	6.2	2.9	5.1	5.1	2.6
Related data							
Population (thousands)	19,291	19,644	20,015	20,378	20,701	21,001	21,297
Labour force (thousands)	7,052	7,253	7,526	7,800	8,019	8,259	8,466
Employment (thousands)	6,728	6,973	7,259	7,485	7,637	7,877	7,971
Unemployment (thousands)	324	280	267	315	382	382	495
Unemployment rate (percent of labour force)	4.6	3.9	3.5	4.0	4.8	4.6	5.8
Labour force participation (percent)	54.1	54.4	55.1	55.5	55.5	55.8	55.8
Real GDP per capita (1997 dollars)	14,754	15,425	16,132	16,317	16,922	17,569	17,778
Growth rate of real GDP per capita (percent)	4.6	4.5	4.6	1.1	3.7	3.8	1.2
Money supply (M2+, billions of dollars)*	17.03	19.08	20.31	23.59	26.72	27.72	34.60
GDP deflator (1997 = 100)	18.5	19.2	20.1	21.0	21.8	22.8	23.9
Consumer Price Index (1992 = 100)	19.6	20.0	20.8	21.5	22.4	23.4	24.2
CPI inflation rate (percent per year)	2.1	2.0	4.0	3.4	4.2	4.5	3.4
Short term interest rate (3 month Treasury bill yield)	3.7	3.9	5.0	4.6	6.2	7.1	6.1
Federal government gross debt	26.2	26.8	27.7	29.8	32.0	34.4	35.8
Foreign exchange rate (Canadian dollar per U.S. dollar)	1.08	1.08	1.08	1.08	1.08	1.08	1.01

	1971	1972	1973	1974	1975	1976	1977	1978	1979	1980	1981	1982
	55.072	61.621	70.496	82.189	95.022	108.120	120.570	134.772	150.598	169.127	190.430	204.121
	21.476	24.804	31.148	40.639	44.012	50.107	51.823	56.104	68.873	73.002	90.979	74.004
	20.462	22.703	25.735	31.246	37.903	43.499	49.349	53.738	59.270	67.290	76.448	86.939
	21.110	23.820	29.892	37.760	38.950	44.293	51.229	61.336	75.153	88.288	97.027	97.586
	− 19.490	− 22.824	− 28.075	− 37.544	− 41.994	− 45.723	− 51.613	− 60.424	− 73.585	− 82.462	− 94.413	− 82.791
	98.630	110.124	129.196	154.290	173.893	200.296	221.358	245.526	280.309	315.245	360.471	379.859
	53.555	60.109	69.243	82.571	96.306	111.412	123.390	134.216	150.946	170.642	196.716	210.085
	3.959	4.700	5.845	8.594	10.407	12.961	15.489	18.877	23.185	27.256	33.277	37.991
	9.092	11.237	15.939	20.738	20.220	21.009	21.922	26.409	34.927	38.382	35.831	26.697
	1.442	1.349	2.828	3.593	3.731	3.111	2.420	3.015	3.103	3.167	2.823	2.191
	79.140	89.121	105.228	126.240	144.734	166.181	182.308	203.656	233.573	264.294	297.047	311.279
	8.249	8.796	9.765	10.868	9.483	11.653	14.145	14.062	14.663	13.739	20.412	21.863
	11.241	12.207	14.203	17.182	19.676	22.462	24.905	27.808	32.073	37.212	43.012	46.717
	98.630	110.124	129.196	154.290	173.893	200.296	221.358	245.526	280.309	315.245	360.471	379.859
	399.550	420.929	451.197	469.894	480.304	506.675	524.205	545.592	568.529	576.398	594.082	576.744
	5.2	5.1	6.7	4.0	2.2	5.2	3.3	3.9	4.0	1.4	3.0	− 3.0
	21,568	21,802	22,043	22,364	22,697	22,993	23,258	23,964	24,202	24,516	24,820	25,117
	8,719	8,975	9,361	9,743	10,095	10,514	10,774	11,138	11,521	11,860	12,222	12,295
	8,167	8,413	8,841	9,229	9,405	9,776	9,915	10,212	10,658	10,970	11,297	10,947
	552	562	520	514	690	738	859	926	863	890	925	1,348
	6.3	6.3	5.6	5.3	6.8	7.0	8.0	8.3	7.5	7.5	7.6	11.0
	56.1	56.5	57.5	58.3	58.8	61.5	61.8	62.6	63.6	64.2	65.0	64.4
	18,525	19,307	20,469	21,011	21,162	22,036	22,539	22,767	23,491	23,511	23,936	22,962
	4.2	4.2	6.0	2.6	0.7	4.1	2.3	1.0	3.2	0.1	1.8	− 4.1
	37.72	42.31	52.68	64.09	73.66	88.57	101.04	118.87	141.99	162.13	181.5	181.28
	24.7	26.2	28.6	32.8	36.2	39.5	42.2	45.0	49.3	54.7	60.7	65.9
	24.9	26.1	28.1	31.1	34.5	37.1	40.0	43.6	47.6	52.4	58.9	65.3
	2.9	4.8	7.7	10.7	10.9	7.5	7.8	9.0	9.2	10.1	12.4	10.9
	3.6	3.5	5.3	7.8	7.4	8.9	7.3	8.6	11.6	12.7	17.8	13.8
	39.9	43.8	46.2	49.1	55.1	61.9	69.7	82.4	100.5	110.6	127.7	144.5
	1.01	0.99	1.0	0.98	1.01	0.99	1.06	1.14	1.17	1.17	1.19	1.23

	1983	1984	1985	1986	1987	1988	1989
Expenditure approach							
Personal consumption expenditure	224.100	244.218	266.683	288.591	312.325	338.518	365.520
Investment	80.473	91.433	101.664	107.563	122.159	141.939	153.534
Government expenditure	93.417	98.085	106.065	111.411	117.868	127.912	138.461
Exports	104.735	128.759	137.379	142.758	149.913	163.842	168.936
Imports	− 91.339	− 112.913	− 126.077	− 137.782	− 143.316	− 159.117	− 168.723
Gross domestic product	411.386	449.582	485.714	512.541	558.949	613.094	657.728
Income approach							
Wages, salaries, and supplementary labour income	220.282	237.248	255.826	272.755	296.442	325.248	350.743
Interest and investment income	37.062	39.618	40.763	39.481	38.841	42.188	48.013
Profits of corporations and government enterprises	36.730	45.686	49.728	45.217	57.888	64.891	59.661
Income of farm and unincorporated businesses	1.827	2.099	2.839	3.825	1.985	3.283	1.986
Net domestic product at factor cost	338.448	371.211	400.200	416.327	453.342	500.203	532.119
Indirect taxes less subsidies	23.290	25.055	27.149	33.574	39.354	42.414	49.669
Capital consumption	49.648	53.316	58.365	62.640	66.253	70.477	75.940
Gross domestic product	411.386	449.582	485.714	512.541	558.949	613.094	657.728
Real GDP (billions of 1997 dollars)	592.684	626.378	660.318	667.802	705.701	740.592	759.820
Real GDP growth rate (percent per year)	2.7	5.4	5.1	1.1	5.4	4.7	2.5
Related data							
Population (thousands)	25,367	25,608	25,843	26,101	26,450	26,798	27,286
Labour force (thousands)	12,523	12,739	13,002	13,257	13,512	13,778	14,047
Employment (thousands)	11,027	11,300	11,617	11,979	12,321	12,710	12,986
Unemployment (thousands)	1,496	1,439	1,385	1,278	1,191	1,068	1,061
Unemployment rate (percent of labour force)	11.9	11.3	10.7	9.6	8.8	7.8	7.6
Labour force participation (percent)	64.7	65.0	65.5	66.0	66.4	66.8	67.2
Real GDP per capita (1997 dollars)	23,364	24,460	25,551	25,585	26,681	27,636	27,847
Growth rate of real GDP per capita (percent)	1.8	4.7	4.5	0.1	4.3	3.6	0.8
Money supply (M2+, billions of dollars)*	178.77	191.03	200.97	218.83	233.637	257.899	291.315
GDP deflator (1997 = 100)	69.4	71.8	73.6	76.8	79.2	82.8	86.6
Consumer Price Index (1992 = 100)	69.1	72.1	75.0	78.1	81.5	84.8	89.0
CPI inflation rate (percent per year)	5.8	4.3	4.0	4.1	4.4	4.0	5.0
Short term interest rate (3 month Treasury bill yield)	9.3	11.1	9.5	9.0	8.2	9.4	12.0
Federal government gross debt	173.1	209.3	250.5	284.0	318.3	349.9	380.0
Foreign exchange rate (Canadian dollar per U.S. dollar)	1.23	1.29	1.36	1.39	1.33	1.23	1.18